Locations of Key Supreme Court Decisions Involving Students' Constitutional Rights

REC'D

D0394783

Wisconsin

Michigan

New York

Providence

Rhode Island

New Glarus

Detroit

Hyde Park

New

Levittown

Iowa

Waterloo

Cleveland

Pennsylvania

Minersville

Piscataway Township

Des Moines

Garfield Heights

Abington Township

New Jersey

Omaha

Ohio

Philadelphia

Columbus

Wilmington

Delaware

Kansas City

West Virginia

New Kent County

Washington, D.C.

Missouri

Louisville

Charleston

Virginia

Gloucester County

Topeka

St. Louis

Frankfort

Prince Edward County

Kentucky

Chapel Hill

North Carolina

Charlotte

Arkansas

Little Rock

DeKalb County

South Carolina

Clarendon County

ATLANTIC OCEAN

Bolivar County

Augusta

Alabama

Georgia

Mississippi

Tyler

Mobile County

Louisiana

New Orleans

Florida

Santa Fe

Miami

N

Gulf of Mexico

0	200	400 Miles
0	200	400 Kilometers

The Schoolhouse Gate

THE SCHOOLHOUSE GATE

*Public Education, the Supreme Court,
and the Battle for the American Mind*

Justin Driver

PANTHEON BOOKS, NEW YORK

Library of Congress Cataloging-in-Publication Data
Name: Driver, Justin, author
Title: The schoolhouse gate : public education, the Supreme Court,
and the battle for the American mind / Justin Driver.
Description: New York : Pantheon, 2018. Includes index.
Identifiers: LCCN 2017058167. ISBN 9781101871652 (hardcover).
ISBN 9781101871669 (ebook).
Subjects: LCSH: Students—Civil rights—United States. Educational law and
legislation—United States. Constitutional law—Social aspect—United States.
BISAC: EDUCATION/Educational Policy & Reform/General.
LAW/Constitutional. LAW/Civil Rights.
Classification: LCC KF4150 .D75 2018 | DDC 344.73/0793—dc23 |
LC record available at lccn.loc.gov/2017058167

www.pantheonbooks.com

Jacket design by Jenny Carrow
Endpaper maps by Mapping Specialists

Printed in the United States of America

First Edition
2 4 6 8 9 7 5 3 1

For Rebecca Callen Driver and Terrell Glenn Driver,
my first and most formative educators

Contents

The Schoolhouse Gate

Introduction

On June 5, 1940, hours before Katharine Meyer would marry Philip Graham at her family's sprawling, lavish estate in Mount Kisco, New York, the happy couple joined an intimate collection of friends for what was meant to be a celebratory luncheon. It would have been difficult to envision a more stately location for the gathering, as the property called Seven Springs Farm contained one thousand acres of land and a nearly thirty-thousand-square-foot Georgian mansion, boasting some fourteen bedrooms, three swimming pools, two servants' quarters, and its own elevator. Despite this grand setting, the pre-wedding luncheon proved anything but festive. Instead, what began as an engaging discussion rapidly descended into a ferocious dispute, with several members of the wedding party—including both bride and groom—excoriating Justice Felix Frankfurter for an opinion that he issued on behalf of the U.S. Supreme Court only two days earlier. Frankfurter—who prior to joining the Court had been a legendary professor at Harvard Law School, where he was also Philip Graham's beloved mentor—usually relished nothing more than vigorous, even combative intellectual exchange. Indeed, *The New York Times* would remember Frankfurter as "the greatest talker of his time" and noted, "He loved to argue, his head darting here and there, his hand suddenly gripping the listener's elbow as he made a point."[1]

In Mount Kisco, however, the silver-tongued Frankfurter received more than he could handle. Even close to six decades after the incident, the ugly scene at Seven Springs remained with Katharine Graham, as she recalled in her memoir, *Personal History:* "Felix loved and encouraged loud and violent arguments, which everyone usually enjoyed, but this time the argument went over the edge into bitter passion." Those in attendance reviled Frankfurter's opinion as "deeply disturb[ing]" and "shock[ing]," she noted. The debate grew so intense, so strained that the groom's best man dissolved into emotion as he emitted not merely discreet sniffles, but full-fledged waterworks—shedding "great large tears" that he permitted to stream down his crimson cheeks.[2] Frankfurter gamely sought to defend his view, but the onslaught provoked the justice to lose his composure, exclaiming that he would never again discuss judicial business in social settings. Katharine Graham recollected that "[t]he argument went on and on," persisting so long, in fact, that they inadvertently kept the Lutheran minister waiting to perform the ceremony for more than an hour.[3] The row did not finally dissipate, she noted, until Frankfurter "grabb[ed] [her] arm with his always iron hand and [said], 'Come along, Kay. We will go for a walk in the woods and calm down.'"[4]

What legal decision elicited this acrimony on such an improbable occasion? The underlying dispute dated back five years, to a community located roughly two hundred miles southwest of Seven Springs but whose reality stood much further removed still from the heights of Mount Kisco's rarefied air—in the valleys of Pennsylvania's coal country. On October 22, 1935, in a small town suitably, if unimaginatively, called Minersville, a ten-year-old public school student named William Gobitis refused to recite the Pledge of Allegiance along with his fifth-grade classmates. When Gobitis's teacher noticed that he had not joined the others in saluting the American flag, she marched right over and tried to force his arm into the proper position. But Gobitis managed to resist her entreaties, locking his arm into place, with his right hand clutching his pocket. In response, Minersville's notoriously austere school superintendent, Charles Roudabush, contacted state education officials to ensure that he possessed the authority to expel Gobitis for this brazen act of insubordination. It made no difference to Roudabush that Gobitis attributed his unwillingness to recite the pledge to his faith as a Jehovah's Witness. As Gobitis subsequently explained in a letter to the school board, he—and many other Witnesses, including his older sister Lillian—interpreted Exodus's prohibition on worshipping graven images to preclude participation in the ritual.

"I do not salute the flag not because I do not love my country," he explained, "but [because] I love God more and I must obey His commandments."[5] Despite the claim that the pledge requirement interfered with the Witnesses' right to free exercise of religion protected by the Constitution's First Amendment, Roudabush nevertheless expelled the Gobitises, ordering them not to return until they were prepared to salute Old Glory.

Although two lower federal courts vindicated the family's claim, Justice Frankfurter's opinion for the Court in *Minersville School District v. Gobitis* maintained that expelling Jehovah's Witnesses for refusing to recite the pledge did not violate the First Amendment. Portions of Justice Frankfurter's opinion, in the 8–1 decision, extolled the unifying potential of requiring students around the nation to honor the American flag. "We are dealing with an interest inferior to none in the hierarchy of legal values," Frankfurter proclaimed. "National unity is the basis of national security. . . . The flag is the symbol of our national unity, transcending all internal differences, however large, within the framework of the Constitution."[6] Ultimately, however, Frankfurter's reasoning in *Gobitis* hinged not on the appeal of patriotism but on the overarching principle that it would be improper for the judiciary to reach into public schools, overturning educators' independent decisions. "The wisdom of training children in patriotic impulses by . . . compulsions which necessarily pervade so much of the educational process is not for our independent judgment," Frankfurter warned in a critical passage. "[T]he courtroom is not the arena for debating issues of educational policy. . . . So to hold would in effect make us the school board for the country."[7] The negative consequences of vindicating the Gobitises' constitutional challenge in this instance ought not be overlooked, Frankfurter insisted, for invalidating Minersville's expulsions would undermine "the authorities in a thousand counties and school districts of this country," amounting to the imposition of "pedagogical and psychological dogma in a field where courts possess no marked and certainly no controlling competence."[8] *Gobitis* concluded, in sum, that judges should mind their own business, and leave educators to the business of molding American minds.

In Minersville, news of the Supreme Court's decision stunned the Gobitises. After hearing a radio broadcaster announce the adverse outcome, Lillian and her mother sat speechless in their kitchen for several minutes, paralyzed in disbelief. Their refusal to pledge had long ago transformed the Gobitis children into town pariahs, with peers flinging stones in their direction and sometimes shouting, "Here comes Jehovah!"[9] The family's successive victories in lower courts caused them to dismiss any concern that the Supreme Court would not also redeem their sacrifices. "It never really occurred to us that the Court's decision would be anything but favorable," Lillian recalled.[10] Yet the Court's rejection hardly signaled the end of their ordeal. Shortly after the decision, a close friend called to warn the Gobitises that vigilantes planned to destroy their family-owned grocery store if they persisted in refusing to salute the flag. Fearing violence, the Gobitis parents hastily arranged for their children to relocate to a safe house, and contacted law enforcement to protect the family's modest business. Although a state police cruiser parked outside the store evidently deterred the plot for physical destruction, Minersville's anti-Gobitis contingent soon alighted upon an alternate strategy of damaging the business: a boycott. This economic approach gained enough adherents to inflict serious financial distress on the Gobitises, who were forced to borrow money from relatives simply to pay their mortgage.

The Gobitises were far from the only members of their faith to suffer in the aftermath of Frankfurter's opinion, as many contemporaneous observers connected a surge of anti-Witness violence to the Court's legitimation of student salute requirements. The opinion arrived at an especially fraught political moment in American history as patriotic fervor reached a crescendo due to widespread fears that the nation would soon enter World War II. One day before *Gobitis* appeared, a Gallup poll revealed that 65 percent of Americans anticipated that Germany would attack the United States imminently. American flags sold so briskly during the month of the decision that leading outlets in New York City could not keep the item stocked. Given this frenzied environment, it should hardly be surprising that post-*Gobitis* the practice of expelling Jehovah's Witness students for refusing to salute spread dramatically throughout the country. When the Court issued *Gobitis*, students in fifteen states either had been or were in the process of being expelled due to the saluting controversy. Just three years later, schools had expelled students in every one of the nation's forty-eight states, totaling approximately two thousand students, virtually all of whom were Witnesses. Some jurisdictions, moreover, followed up on the expulsions by prosecuting Witness parents for contributing to the delinquency of minors, asserting that their children violated compulsory school attendance laws.[11]

While *Gobitis* enjoyed approval in much of the country, the media overwhelmingly reviled the opinion, as more than 170 newspapers condemned the opinion, and only a handful of publications praised it.* For present purposes, however, the most remarkable aspect of that reaction was that no single passage in *Gobitis* drew more ire than Frankfurter's assertion that had the Court invalidated Minersville's salute requirement, it would have succeeded in transforming the Supreme Court into a national school board. This dismissive sentiment especially rankled periodicals concerned with religious autonomy. Thus, *The Christian Science Monitor* seized upon Frankfurter's line to suggest that *Gobitis* "has . . . taken a step toward abdicating [the Court's] position as a constitutional guarantor of freedom of worship."[12] Similarly, in an editorial titled "The Court Abdicates," *The Christian Century* insisted that "a question of educational policy may also be a question of fundamental rights," and noted that "[c]ourts that will not protect even Jehovah's Witnesses will not long protect anybody."[13] Paul Blakely—writing in the Jesuit magazine *America*—also contended that *Gobitis*'s avowed withdrawal from the educational domain succeeded in making school boards all-powerful. "What further restrictions upon the right of parents to direct the education of their children will the States impose?," Blakely lamented. "We do not know; all we know is that these are hysterical days, and that objectors will find no protection in the Supreme Court."[14]

* * *

This book examines the intersection of two distinctively American institutions: the public school and the Supreme Court. The United States has long exhibited an uncommonly strong belief in the importance of public education and its centrality to national identity. As Adlai Stevenson once remarked, "The free common school system is the most American thing about America."[15] But many other

---

* In a curious twist, *The Washington Post*—owned by Katharine Meyer's father—offered one of the few flattering assessments of *Gobitis*, calling it "skillful []" and even contending that the opinion "detracts nothing" from the Court's "reputation as a bulwark of civil rights." "Rights and Privileges," *Washington Post*, June 4, 1940, 6. See also "Supreme Court Trends," *Washington Post*, June 5, 1940, 10.

observers have suggested that the nation's faith in public education may be rivaled only by the faith it places in the judiciary to resolve critical disputes. In the 1830s, Alexis de Tocqueville's *Democracy in America* offered what remains the most famous formulation of this idea. "There is hardly a political question in the United States which does not sooner or later turn into a judicial one," Tocqueville contended.[16] Since this statement appeared, the federal judiciary—with the Supreme Court at its apex—has assumed only a more expansive role in American society.

For a long season, however, many observers believed, with Justice Frankfurter in *Gobitis*, that these two institutions should have nothing to do with each other. Elementary and secondary public schools, the thinking ran, were singularly local endeavors that educators should be free to administer without needing to worry about anything so grand as the Supreme Court's decisions interpreting the Constitution. Yet, as matters would turn out, *Gobitis* can be understood as the fulcrum of modern American education law, as the Supreme Court soon began to abandon its traditional non-interventionist approach to public schools. Three years after *Gobitis*, the Court dramatically reversed course in *West Virginia State Board of Education v. Barnette*, declaring it unconstitutional for public schools to expel students for refusing to salute the American flag. Directly rejecting Frankfurter's effort to erect a barrier between schools and courts, *Barnette* insisted that the Constitution "protects the citizen against the State itself and all of its creatures—Boards of Education not excepted. These have, of course, important, delicate, and highly discretionary functions, but none that they may not perform within the limits of the Bill of Rights."[17] Ultimately, *Barnette* marked merely the Court's first meaningful step on the path toward establishing that students retained a wide array of constitutional rights within public schools. Even if those rights do not assume precisely the same contours that minors enjoy outside the public school context, the Court has consistently held that educators cannot disregard the Constitution's central protections. By 1969, less than three decades after *Gobitis*, the Supreme Court broadly announced that the era of separate spheres for law and education had ended: "It can hardly be argued that . . . students . . . shed their constitutional rights . . . at the schoolhouse gate."[18]

Although education and constitutional law were once viewed as fundamentally distinct entities, a panoramic view of this area now establishes that, without exploring the extensive interaction of the public school and the Supreme Court, it is impossible to grasp the full meaning of either quintessentially American institution. One cannot plausibly claim to understand public education in the United States today, that is, without appreciating how the Supreme Court's decisions involving students' constitutional rights shape the everyday realities of schools across the country. Conversely, one cannot plausibly hope to comprehend the role of the Supreme Court in American society without appreciating how its opinions involving public education reveal the judiciary's underappreciated capacity for both spurring and forestalling major social change.

At its core, this book argues that the public school has served as the single most significant site of constitutional interpretation within the nation's history. No other arena of constitutional decisionmaking—not churches, not hotels, not hospitals, not restaurants, not police stations, not military bases, not automobiles, not even homes—comes close to matching the cultural import of the Supreme Court's jurisprudence governing public schools. Houses of public education, though seldom viewed as legal entities by the general public, claim this mantle due to four closely related reasons.

The first reason that schools should be deemed our most significant theaters of constitutional conflict is owed to the sheer magnitude of public elementary and secondary education. Today, more than fifty million students attend public schools in the United States, and in order to function they require a few million adults to serve as teachers, administrators, and support staff. Those figures mean that on any given weekday, during school hours, at least one-sixth of the U.S. population can be found in a public school—making it easily the single largest governmental entity that Americans encounter for sustained periods on a near-daily basis. Those ubiquitous interactions are, of course, governed by the constitutional parameters that the Supreme Court and lower courts have articulated for public education. Yet even this large fraction dramatically underestimates the constitutional footprint of public schools; not only does it fail to account for the parents of those students who currently attend public schools, but it also overlooks that the vast majority of adults in the United States are themselves products of those schools. Given that—as the Supreme Court has recognized— the attitudes students develop during their first sustained exposure to governmental authority do not simply vanish on graduation day, moreover, it seems eminently reasonable to hold that everyone in the country has a vested interest in the form that constitutional meaning assumes in public schools.[19]

Second, the school's great significance in our constitutional order stems from the fact that cases arising in this setting offer an excellent prism for examining the preceding one hundred years of American history, as the cultural anxieties that pervade the larger society often flash where law and education converge. The legal history of the Court's educational encounters thus illuminates both the hopes and the fears that have captivated the American people during the last century.

Consider only a few examples of this phenomenon. In the wake of World War I—when the nation wrestled with how to assimilate its swelling immigrant population—the Court confronted laws that prohibited schools from teaching young pupils in languages other than English and that mandated attendance at public schools (because speaking the mother tongue and attending parochial schools were both thought to shield minorities from "Americanization"). During World War II, the Court contemplated patriotism by weighing whether schools could expel students for refusing to salute the American flag. In the aftermath of World War II, the Court in the 1950s considered anew whether the nation that had so recently toppled Aryan supremacy abroad could allow schools to separate children by race at home. During the 1960s, the Court weighed whether students who opposed the Vietnam War could express their views without facing reprisals from educators. Within that same decade, the Court accelerated its lengthy and ongoing examination of how, in a nation characterized by increasing religious diversity, various religious groups might peacefully coexist within public schools. When the Silent Majority of the 1970s feared that American youth culture had spiraled dangerously out of control, the Court contemplated what limits, if any, should exist on schools that attempt to impose discipline on students through suspensions or corporal punishment. In the late 1970s, as the nation debated the Equal Rights Amendment, the Court weighed whether single-sex public schools could be reconciled with gender equality. During the 1980s, when prominent political figures expressed deep concern about the effects of exposing youngsters to explicit content, the Court entertained cases asking whether a school could punish a student for delivering a speech laced with sexual innuendo and whether a school newspaper could be forced to publish student-written articles addressing teen sexuality. One year after First Lady Nancy Reagan launched her "Just Say No" campaign, the Supreme Court for the first time contemplated what tolls the war on drugs may exact upon students' privacy rights. The Court has repeatedly visited this same terrain during the twenty-first century, as it has addressed whether exigencies created by the war on drugs can justify subjecting students both to suspicionless drug tests and to strip searches, and limiting their free speech rights.[20] In no other sphere of constitutional meaning do the Supreme Court's major interventions so closely reflect the nation's larger social concerns.

Third, as the previous paragraph intimated, cases arising from the schooling context involve many of the most doctrinally consequential, hotly contested constitutional questions that the Supreme Court has ever addressed—including lawsuits related to sex, race, crime, safety, liberty, equality, religion, and patriotism. That thumbnail sketch, moreover, omits the Court's momentous cases addressing the permissibility of massive funding disparities between school districts in the same metropolitan area and efforts to exclude unauthorized immigrants from public schools—among many other contentious lawsuits. Outside the schooling context, cases implicating these various issues contain ample capability of rousing strong emotions. But bringing these matters into the educational arena elevates the temperature higher still, both because the cases tend to involve minors and because of the central place that public schools occupy in the nation's cultural imagination. The recent legal controversy that exploded over transgender students' access to restrooms offers but the latest illustration of public schools' penchant for hosting the most incendiary legal debates that divide American society.

Katharine Graham's characterization of the clash at Mount Kisco as "bitter" accurately conveys the intense emotions that have constantly engulfed decisions involving students' rights. Two well-known figures, writing more than four decades apart, independently invoked this same word when they identified the definitive characteristic of legal disputes in schools. In 1928, the noted intellectual Walter Lippmann—remarking upon the controversies in state courts then raging over teaching evolution—observed that "the struggles for the control of the schools are among the bitterest political struggles," and claimed further, "It is inevitable that it should be so. Wherever two or more groups within a state differ in religion, or in language and in nationality, the immediate concern of each group is to use the schools to preserve its own faith and tradition."[21] In 1973, Hillary Rodham—then a recent graduate of Yale Law School, affiliated with the Children's Defense Fund—wrote an article in the *Harvard Educational Review* that echoed Lippmann's assessment. "From the first confrontations between parents and the state," Rodham noted, "education has been the subject of continuous and often bitter struggles, primarily over the proper social role of education and the proper treatment of children within the schools."[22] The last four decades have, if anything, only deepened this statement's accuracy, as the Court's subsequent student rights decisions have continued to reveal an unusually powerful capacity for eliciting fervent sentiments in American society. What is true of society generally, moreover, also holds within the Supreme Court's marble walls. An unusually large percentage of these cases witness justices adopting seldom-used techniques to signal their profound disagreement with the majority—either by reading their opinions from the bench or by omitting the standard claim that they dissent from the majority "respectfully." It is hardly mysterious why disputes in this arena spark such passion: when we disagree over what the Constitution means in public schools, we engage in an argument that is fundamentally about what sort of nation we want the United States to be.[23]

The final reason that the public school should be viewed as the preeminent site of constitutional interpretation is that the Supreme Court itself has repeatedly, and convincingly, highlighted the importance of that venue for shaping attitudes toward the nation's governing document. Beginning in the 1940s, the Court made several high-profile declarations that public schools had a special responsibility to honor constitutional rights; otherwise students would incorrectly conclude that governmental authority had no limits. No one expressed this proposition better than Justice Robert Jackson, when he wrote the Court's opinion overturning *Gobitis* in 1943: "That [public schools] are educating the young for citizenship is reason for scrupulous protection of Constitutional freedoms of the individual, if we are not to strangle the free mind at its source and teach youth to discount important principles of our government as mere platitudes."[24] In *Brown v. Board of Education*, moreover, Chief Justice Earl Warren in 1954 testified to "the importance of education to our democratic society," before he concluded that permitting racial segregation in schools could harm black students' "hearts and minds in a way unlikely ever to be undone."[25]*Six years later, Justice Potter Stewart wrote an opinion for the Court that explicitly identified the public school as a constitutional setting of paramount import: "The vigilant protection of constitutional freedoms is nowhere more vital than in the community of American schools."[26]

In recent decades, however, such sentiments appear more often in the Court's dissenting opinions than in its majority opinions. Justice John Paul Stevens, for example, advanced this idea in 1985 when he dissented in part from an opinion offering an anemic conception of the Fourth Amendment's protection against unreasonable governmental searches in the context of public schools. "The schoolroom is the first opportunity most citizens have to experience the power of government," Stevens wrote. "Through it passes every citizen and public official, from schoolteachers to policemen and prison guards. The values they learn there, they take with them in life. One of our most cherished ideals is the one contained in the Fourth Amendment: that the government may not intrude on the personal privacy of its citizens without a warrant or compelling circumstance. The Court's decision today is a curious moral for the Nation's youth."[27] Transforming public schools into Constitution-free zones, Justice Stevens sagely warned, was dangerous because when today's students become tomorrow's adults, they may well retain their anemic understanding of constitutional protections. That risk, if realized, would harm the nation as a whole by distorting the relationship between citizens and their government. The Fourth Amendment, alas, represents only one of many constitutional areas where the Court has in recent decades taught student-citizens regrettable lessons about our constitutional protections.

Given the vast significance of judicial opinions regarding students' constitutional rights, one might suspect this body of decisions has been explored ad nauseam. Yet this volume is the first effort to present this narrative in its full range—providing portraits

---

* During an oral argument in the set of cases known as *Brown v. Board of Education*, John W. Davis sought to defend racial segregation in South Carolina's public schools by echoing Frankfurter's contested line from *Gobitis*. Davis asserted, "Your honors do not sit, and cannot sit, as a glorified board of education for the state of South Carolina or any other state." Richard Kluger, *Simple Justice: The History of* Brown v. Board of Education *and Black America's Struggle for Equality* 675 (2004 ed.) (1975).

of the students and their families who have challenged school policies in the most important disputes, distilling the decisions in a manner accessible to a general audience, placing those decisions in their relevant historical context, and evaluating critically how existing legal doctrine should change in the future.*

The absence of such a book is lamentable because many citizens harbor deep interests in constitutional law and public education but lack a firm grasp of how the one informs the other. Various subcommunities have certainly scrutinized discrete aspects of the material canvassed in the pages that follow. But those fragmented approaches by definition cannot yield work that adequately wrestles with the mass of cases involving students' constitutional rights. Instead of viewing this body of law as a coherent whole, a wide array of groups—including educators, judges, lawyers, legislators, pundits, and scholars—have fractured that body into its component parts. Decisions arising from the school context involving free speech, due process, criminal procedure, racial equality, sex equality, and religion—to name only a few areas—have all been hauled off and placed into their own intellectual silos. Within their various silos, moreover, school cases are often relegated to the margins of some larger animating concern, or are not primarily understood as cases involving students' rights. Sometimes, school cases do not even make it into the relevant silo at all. This book aims to move beyond these isolated approaches by reconceptualizing students' constitutional rights as forming a cohesive whole, and in so doing seeks to reinvigorate education law as a field of intellectual inquiry. To be sure, some authors have produced insightful work on important parts of schooling law in recent years; indeed, this book draws upon those scholars' work where relevant. But no one other than a partisan would seriously maintain that the field of education law consistently claims the attention of many prominent scholars in legal academia. Notably, at several of the nation's leading law

---

* In order to provide relevant historical context, I extensively chronicle the reactions that major Supreme Court opinions generated in a variety of circles, including among educators, elected officials, lawyers, law professors, parents, students, and—most extensively—journalists. By highlighting the media's assorted reactions to momentous decisions, I heed the counsel of Professor Louis H. Pollak, who long ago suggested that mainstream periodicals offer underappreciated sources of legal understanding. *Life* magazine, Pollak observed, was "America's most widely read law review." Louis H. Pollak, "The Supreme Court Under Fire," 6 *Journal of Public Law* 428, 436 (1957). Pollak later served as dean of Yale Law School before ultimately becoming a revered federal judge.

schools, not a single member of the academic faculty regularly offers a class focused on the law of schools.[28]

If we examine the Supreme Court's decisions weighing students' constitutional rights in a holistic fashion, several patterns and themes emerge that elude detection when these issues are viewed in isolation. First, this body of decisions reveals that students and their families who contest school practices must often exhibit deep reservoirs of courage when the Supreme Court addresses their disputes. In most instances, these lawsuits witness genuinely brave families who resist not only the wishes of local educators but also the norms of their surrounding communities. Members of these communities, in response, frequently announce their displeasure with litigants by showering them with an assortment of insults, hate mail, intimidating telephone calls, and even death threats. Thus, even if one disagrees with the underlying constitutional claims, it is often difficult not to admire the students and their families for being willing to stand up for their understandings of the Constitution. Accordingly, in the pages that follow, I endeavor where possible to chronicle the personal ordeals that have habitually accompanied the judicial recognition of students' constitutional rights. Although analysis of constitutional law often veers toward the arid and the abstract, detailing these concrete personal sacrifices underscores that many otherwise ordinary citizens have exhibited extraordinary valor to make enduring contributions to our constitutional order.*

* By foregrounding my analysis of these constitutional disputes with the students and their families, I aim—in some small measure—to keep alive the tradition that attained its highest form in Richard Kluger's *Simple Justice*. As Professor Randall Kennedy has appositely noted,

> Kluger's detailed descriptions of the plaintiffs in the school desegregation cases—their backgrounds, their ties to their communities, their aspirations, their sacrifices—are his most valuable contribution to the *Brown* literature. The plaintiffs in *Brown* are often either rendered invisible by commentators or depicted as mere "extras" in a drama starring Earl Warren and, to a lesser extent, Thurgood Marshall. Kluger rightly begins his book by placing the plaintiffs at center stage. By doing so, he underlines the fact that the school desegregation cases emerged not only from the labors of lawyers and Supreme Court justices but also from the efforts of regular folk, many of whom were poor, vulnerable, and unlettered, but all of whom were determined to better their children's prospects. *Brown* was not simply a legal declaration from on high. It was also a response to a moral demand from below.

Randall Kennedy, "Schoolings in Equality," *New Republic*, July 5 and 12, 2004, 29, 34.

Appreciating the toll that litigation exacts on the families of students who contest school policies is critical because members of the Supreme Court themselves have on occasion appeared to lose sight of this essential lesson. In 2004, the Court heard oral argument in a case from Northern California, where Michael Newdow, an atheist, contended that having his daughter's class recite "under God" as part of the Pledge of Allegiance violated the First Amendment's Establishment Clause. The Court dubiously invoked a legal technicality to avoid reaching a decision on the merits in the case, and in so doing suggested that Newdow had behaved imprudently by filing a lawsuit that thrust his daughter into the fiercely contested issue. According to the Supreme Court, the "most important" considerations leading it to sidestep the case's underlying question included that the lawsuit "implicates the interests of a young child who finds herself at the center of a highly public debate over . . . the propriety of a widespread national ritual, and the meaning of our Constitution."[29]

Yet the logic of this argument sweeps much too broadly. After all, many of the Court's important decisions involving schools have similarly placed minors in the middle of an intense national dispute over the meaning of constitutional rights. To take the foremost example, Oliver Brown thrust his seven-year-old daughter, Linda, into the teeth of a raging debate over racial equality when he agreed to challenge the constitutionality of segregated schools in Topeka, Kansas, during the 1950s. The same criticisms, moreover, could easily have been leveled at both the Barnette family for challenging the flag-salute mandate during the height of World War II, and the Tinker family for refusing to accept educators' efforts to censor student speech protesting the Vietnam War in Des Moines, Iowa, during the 1960s. However one assesses the merits of Newdow's basic legal claim, it seems bizarre to construe the controversial nature of his lawsuit as somehow rendering his actions verboten; it comes closer to the mark to view Newdow as participating in an honored American tradition.

Second, surveying the full scale of this jurisprudence highlights the futility of the many reflexive objections that have resisted the Supreme Court's involvement in ensuring that public schools comply with constitutional requirements. Such objections have arisen on virtually every occasion that the Court has vindicated students' constitutional rights, and typically assume one of three primary variants: the Constitution does not expressly mention "education," therefore the student's claim must fail; public schools are quintessentially local endeavors, therefore the federal government should not interfere with this domain; and the judiciary lacks the requisite knowledge to monitor public schools, a task that properly belongs in the hands of principals, school boards, or elected officials.

Each of these three broad objections is, however, vulnerable to targeted counterarguments. Regarding the Constitution's omission of the word "education," this feeble effort to construe constitutional meaning—what might be termed the "Control+F" theory of constitutional interpretation—cannot possibly justify transforming schools into places where the nation's foundational document goes unrecognized. In reaction to southerners' protests during the 1950s asserting that *Brown* lacked legitimacy because the Constitution lacked the magic word, Professor Alexander Bickel offered perhaps the pithiest response: "Of course the Constitution does not mention education. Nor does it mention an Air Force, but the President's title to the commander-in-chief in the air as well as on land is not consequently the less."[30] This epigram suggests that *Brown*'s invalidation of racially segregated schools was lawful because the Constitution proscribes governmental action and public schools are plainly covered subunits of larger governmental entities.

Regarding the invocation of federalism, whatever authority this argument once wielded, the notion that Washington, D.C., plays no role in educational matters has long since been abandoned. Dating back to at least the 1980s, presidents of both parties have sought (often successfully) to influence aspects of elementary and secondary education policy. Going back even further still, Congress has appropriated significant sums to public schools in order to shape educational approaches at the local level. If the judiciary suddenly announced a total retreat from the educational sphere, it would become the only branch of the federal government to vacate the field. Joel Klein, the former chancellor of New York City's Department of Education, recently dispatched the federalism claim with notable vigor: "The historically quaint notion that communities should control their kids' education—long a hobby horse of conservatives who fear anything originating from the federal government—has led neither to active citizen involvement nor to real experimentation at the local level."[31]*

Regarding judges' alleged incompetence to adjudicate school litigation, it seems worth observing that members of the Supreme Court—as a result of having once been students themselves—possess much richer experiences with schools than they do with many contexts that consistently appear on their docket. Justices do not, for instance, usually spend much time walking police beats before ascending to the bench; yet the Court cannot, of course, permit that inexperience to prevent it from interpreting the Constitution to regulate the conduct of law enforcement officers. Justice Jackson in *Barnette* memorably defeated this expertise-based objection by noting that at least sometimes the Constitution compels the judiciary to enter schools: "We cannot, because of modest estimates of our competence in such specialties as public education, withhold the judgment that history authenticates as the function of this Court when liberty is infringed."[32]†

Yet perhaps the most powerful response to these habitual complaints assumes the general form, rather than the particular: the Supreme Court's extensive jurisprudence vindicating students' constitutional rights—ranging over a period of several decades and touching on a multitude of constitutional provisions—establishes that generic objections to its involvement in this arena simply have not carried the day. As a descriptive matter, then, the broad non-interventionist position toward public schools would constitute a demand for radically reassessing a major area of constitutional law. When courts entertain students' constitutional challenges in the future, they should do so fully aware that the judiciary's long-standing and deep-seated involvement in this sphere complicates

---

* It may be surprising to learn Klein began his legal career by serving as a law clerk to Justice Lewis F. Powell Jr., who can justifiably be deemed the patron saint of local control within the field of education law. At Klein's press conference announcing his taking the helm of New York City's schools, his evidently strong aversion to federalism arguments did not prevent him from identifying Justice Powell as one of his heroes. See Joel Klein, *Lessons of Hope: How to Fix Our Schools* 27 (2014).

† Even if one were to limit the inquiry to whether members of the Supreme Court were once students at public schools, the conclusion here would not change. As it turns out, at least a majority of the current Supreme Court justices—including Samuel Alito, Stephen Breyer, Ruth Bader Ginsburg, Elena Kagan, and Anthony Kennedy—attended public school as minors.

the instinctual protests holding that judges should avoid engaging with schools.

This claim should not, of course, be mistaken to contend that the Constitution resolves *every* dispute that arises within public schools. That view is nothing less than absurd. Take only two of the many potential schoolhouse quarrels where the Constitution plays no role: students who dislike their grades have no cognizable right under the Fourteenth Amendment's Due Process Clause to challenge their marks; nor do students assigned to write a paper about the American Revolution—who would prefer to tackle the Cuban Revolution—have a legitimate claim to their preferred topic under the First Amendment's right to free expression. While many excellent reasons exist for refusing to recognize these matters—and many others besides—as posing live constitutional questions, modern judges should not automatically retreat to prefabricated claims of nonengagement with schools. Had their predecessors invoked such canned reasoning, our nation's public schools would look very different—and far worse. It may well be, as two scholars recently asserted, "that the courtroom is rarely the optimal venue for education policymaking."[33] The real question, however, is not whether the courtroom offers the *ideal* forum for school reform, but whether it has been the *necessary* forum. Judge J. Skelly Wright pressed this point ably in an opinion involving students' constitutional rights in 1967. "It would be far better . . . for these great social and political problems to be resolved in the political arena by other branches of government," Wright noted. "But these are social and political problems which seem at times to defy such resolution. In such situations, under our system, the judiciary must bear a hand and accept its responsibility to assist in the solution where constitutional rights hang in the balance."[34]

The third theme that emerges from assessing the judiciary's school jurisprudence through a wide lens is the vast importance of the overall contributions to American society that the Supreme Court has made in the course of protecting students' constitutional rights. This claim would once have been wholly unremarkable, simply applying to the discrete field of education law what constitutional scholars assumed was accurate as a general proposition. During an earlier era, legal academics frequently asserted—without marshaling any real evidence—that the Court had transformed the nation on a wide array of topics by extending constitutional protection to disfavored groups and causes. More recently, however, several distinguished scholars have succeeded in revising that assessment, contending that the Court was hardly the mighty institution that older professors held as an article of faith. Upon examination, these revisionist scholars insisted, the Court's salient decisions almost invariably ratified (rather than resisted) public opinion, and should be viewed as the reflection of national consensus or the anticipation of an emerging national consensus. This revisionist band of scholars observed that the Court's decisions invalidating measures often did not challenge the legislative landscape across the country, as the prior generation had believed, but instead typically tackled practices found in a handful of states—which they labeled "outliers." While this revisionism might have begun as a relatively small intellectual movement, its views have now become dominant within legal academia, and gained purchase in popular circles as well.[35]

Scrutinizing the broad jurisprudence involving students' constitutional rights succeeds in complicating this revisionist school's unduly frail conception of the Supreme Court's capacity for shaping American society. Indeed, if constitutional professors from earlier times were wrong to believe that the institution could achieve almost anything, today's revisionist legal scholars are incorrect to suggest that it can accomplish virtually nothing. Consider some of the Court's many momentous interventions in this area that offer meaningful complications to the prevailing conception. In some instances, the available polling data and other contemporaneous indicators reveal that the Court's opinions vindicating those interests ran counter to the preferences of national majorities. This dynamic occurred when the Court upheld students' free speech rights in the 1960s and afforded students due process rights before they could be suspended or expelled from school during the 1970s. Relatedly, in other instances, the Court's decisions invalidated practices found throughout the country, not merely those concentrated in isolated pockets. This dynamic transpired when the Court rejected statutes that prohibited teaching in languages other than English during the 1920s and school requirements to salute the American flag in the 1940s. Thus, far from imposing the consensus values of the American people and invalidating outliers, it often seems more accurate to view the Court's decisions vindicating students' constitutional rights as overcoming popular sentiment.

Even if the Court strikes down practices found in only a small number of states, moreover, it is severely mistaken to construe those judicial invalidations as representing insignificant acts in shaping our constitutional order. Thus, for example, when the Court invalidated Oregon's measure requiring all students to attend public school in the 1920s, or when it struck down Kentucky's requirement that classrooms display the Ten Commandments during the 1980s, or when it nullified Texas's measure excluding unauthorized immigrants from attending public school in that same decade, those statutes were the only ones of their kind in the nation. Yet contemporaneous evidence in all three instances suggests that the Court's actions extinguished those flickering statutory sparks before they could become a genuine blaze, as—if left unchecked—other states would have sought to enact similar policies, potentially causing substantial harm to the nation's constitutional values.

Two of the Supreme Court's most prominent interventions in history—its invalidation of racially segregated schools and its invalidation of teacher-led prayers—also succeed in complicating the revisionists' general conception. Contrary to those accounts, *Brown v. Board of Education* cannot convincingly be construed primarily as either the ratification of an emerging national consensus on racial equality or the invalidation of outlier legislation. Instead, the best available evidence indicates that racial attitudes—even in the supposedly enlightened North—were a good deal more ambivalent and conflicted than revisionist scholars typically allow. If the North were nearly as committed to racial egalitarianism as revisionist scholars suggest, one would have expected that integrationist project to bear a good deal more fruit than it did before the Court banned race-conscious student assignment plans in 2007. In addition, while some revisionists correctly concede that the Court's opinions banning teacher-led prayers in public schools encountered major opposition during the 1960s, they then quickly proceed to alternate ground, noting that those decisions were routinely flouted, most often in the South. Yet fixating on the Court's failure to achieve universal and immediate adherence to those decisions has succeeded in obscuring the extent to which they earned widespread adherence immediately, and nearly universal implementation over time. In a testament to the revisionist mindset's gravitational pull within the legal community today, one scholar has recently emerged to contend that even the Court's early decisions from the 1960s on teacher-led prayer

should not actually be understood as resisting majoritarian preferences.[36] As I demonstrate in these pages, however, this latest effort
to demonstrate the revisionist account's absolute supremacy ultimately proves unavailing.

In order to avoid misunderstanding, allow me to emphasize that
I in no way seek to restore the older conception of an almighty
Supreme Court. To the contrary, revisionists made a valuable contribution by critiquing and dislodging that flawed conception of the
Court as colossus. But the revisionist effort has yielded an over-
correction in the opposite direction. Whereas scholars previously
erred by portraying the judiciary as omnipotent, revisionists today
err by depicting it as impotent. In contrast, this book, attempting
to locate the capacious middle ground between these polar conceptions, contends that the Court is neither omnipotent nor impotent,
but, simply, unambiguously potent. Thus, although this book trains
its focus principally on students' constitutional rights, my examination of this particular field aims to supplant, inform, and reframe
broader conceptions of the Supreme Court's role in American
society.

Lest readers mistake my portrayal of the Supreme Court's work
in this sphere as embracing a Panglossian vision, I should hasten to
add that this book advances many pointed, far-reaching critiques of
the prevailing legal order. In recent decades, the Court has often
foundered badly in its commitment to vindicating constitutional
rights in schools. Since the 1970s, its decisions have frequently
risked "teach[ing] youth to discount important principles of our government as mere platitudes," as *Barnette* long ago warned, by issuing opinions finding that the following actions taken by educators
pass constitutional muster: inflicting severe corporal punishment
on students, without providing any procedural protections; searching students and their possessions, without probable cause, in bids
to uncover violations of mere school rules; engaging in drug testing of students who are not suspected of any wrongdoing; and suppressing student speech solely for the viewpoint that it espouses.[37]
The Supreme Court has also stumbled by refusing to review many
wrongheaded decisions from lower courts, including opinions that
have in recent years upheld repressive restrictions on off-campus
speech during the internet age; misguided "zero tolerance" disciplinary policies; degrading student strip searches; permissive search
regulations geared toward educators, even though uniformed police

officers have now become a common sight in public schools; and the quiet resurgence of single-sex public schools, but only in inner-city communities. Such decisions should, in my view, alarm not only schoolchildren and their parents, but the entire nation because—as the Supreme Court once recognized—it is impossible to disregard the constitutional rights of students without ultimately damaging the republic to which students pledge allegiance.

I harbor no illusions that everyone—or perhaps even any single person—will agree with all of the particular arguments regarding students' constitutional rights contained in this book. More common ground on these issues may exist, however, than initially seems apparent, as many of the positions I endorse could appeal to a broad coalition that bridges liberalism with the libertarian-inflected vision of limited government now ascendant in some right-leaning circles. Nevertheless, I welcome disagreement with my suggestions, for that will reflect a substantive exchange on how public schools should be reformed to reflect our nation's foremost constitutional commitments. And serious discourse on these topics has in the recent past been notable primarily for its absence.

While this book addresses an expansive range of constitutional provisions and controversies, its scope is not limitless. My focus on providing a thorough examination of judicial opinions interpreting students' constitutional rights within elementary and secondary public schools necessarily means that some peripheral issues will not receive full treatment in these pages. First, the emphasis on *students'* constitutional rights indicates that the particular constitutional rights courts have afforded *teachers* in their capacity as public employees, without direct bearing on their educational responsibilities, claim virtually no attention. Second, the emphasis on *constitutional* law indicates that student rights arising under various federal *statutory* laws—including the Bilingual Education Act, the Individuals with Disabilities Education Act (IDEA), and Title IX of the Education Amendments Act of 1972—receive limited analysis. Third, the emphasis on *elementary and secondary education* indicates that constitutional opinions regulating *higher education* merit addressing only to the extent that those interpretations are required to understand decisions at the inquiry's forefront. The minimal treatment of these matters should not be misconstrued as asserting that they are unimportant. To the contrary, each of these issues deserves—and in some instances has already received—a book-length examination of its own. But these matters rest beyond the reach of this project, which even in their absence includes an abundance of thorny matters that require addressing.[38]*

A brief word on the book's organization, which—as a general proposition—arranges the material thematically and then within those theme-based chapters examines judicial opinions and trends in rough chronological order. Chapter 1 sets the stage by examining the Supreme Court's earliest constitutional encounters with schools, charting its increased willingness to invalidate state and local educational decisions prior to the close of World War II. The second chapter explores free expression, where students during the 1960s scored a momentous victory in securing their right to speak on contentious topics but have since suffered a series of prominent defeats. Chapter 3 analyzes school discipline, focusing upon procedural safeguards for suspensions and the stubborn persistence of corporal punishment in modern America. In chapter 4, I examine criminal procedure, including when educators may search students' belongings, conduct strip searches, and impose urinalysis drug testing. The fifth chapter investigates the shifting meaning of equal protection in the context of race, explaining how *Brown v. Board of Education*—once thought the summit of the nation's integrationist ideals—now prohibits educators from considering the race of individual students to combat segregated schools. Continuing the examination of equal protection, chapter 6 surveys school-funding

---

* I focus on *public* schools, of course, because the Constitution overwhelmingly imposes limits on actions taken by governmental entities, rather than on actions taken by private actors. Therefore, private schools need not adhere to the Court's opinions vindicating students' constitutional rights. Approximately two million students now attend charter schools, which might be viewed as straddling the public-private divide. Charter schools are publicly funded entities that operate independently of the standard requirements of local public school systems. Although few judicial bodies have considered whether charter schools must afford their students constitutional rights to date, the Constitution is best understood to govern their actions. After all, the Constitution cannot convincingly be construed as merely some piece of bureaucratic red tape. Moreover, the negative consequences that would flow from permitting schools to disregard students' constitutional rights by delegating their authority are nothing less than breathtaking. See Gillian E. Metzger, "Privatization as Delegation," 103 *Columbia Law Review* 1367, 1495–96 (2003); Martha Minow, "Public and Private Partnerships: Accounting for the New Religion," 116 *Harvard Law Review* 1229, 1267–68 (2003); and Maren Hulden, "Charting a Course to State Action: Charter Schools and § 1983," 111 *Columbia Law Review* 1244, 1248 (2011). For a provocative argument holding that charter schools themselves may, under certain circumstances, be unconstitutional, see Wendy Parker, "The Color of Choice: Race and Charter Schools," 75 *Tulane Law Review* 563 (2001).

disparities, single-sex education, transgender students' right to access bathrooms congruent with their gender identities, and unauthorized immigrants' right to access public education at all. Finally, chapter 7 addresses religion, an issue that for many years stood as the most controversial constitutional terrain involving schools but has for a variety of reasons now quietly become an area of relative tranquillity. A brief conclusion follows, identifying the Supreme Court's significant accomplishments in the schooling domain and the significant obstacles that still remain.*

* * *

On occasions when I have presented my ideas about education law at various venues, audience members have—at some point— invariably asked what prompted me to undertake this project. Although the claim may initially sound overstated, it is no exaggeration to maintain that I have been actively contemplating this subject matter for most of my life, dating back to my days as a public school student in Washington, D.C. My earliest explorations of these ideas were not, of course, undertaken with the benefit of a law degree, but the absence of legal training does not render my early, untutored thoughts irrelevant. I grew up in a nearly all-black neighborhood within the city's Southeast quadrant, east of the Anacostia River—an area that travel guidebooks routinely warned tourists to avoid, citing its penchant for drugs and violence. Although neither

---

* Throughout this book, I adhere to the lawyers' convention of using the name of individual litigants, or other private entities, when shortening the name of cases in which the opposing party is a government entity or official. See, for example, *The Bluebook: A Uniform System of Citation* Rule 10.9(a)(i), 116 (20th ed. 2015) ("When using only one party's name in a short form citation, avoid using the name of a geographical or governmental unit, a governmental official, or another common litigant"). Thus, following this method, *Tinker v. Des Moines Independent Community School District* is shortened to *Tinker,* not, say, *Des Moines Independent Community School District,* or even simply *Des Moines.* For whatever reason, though, the field of education law often honors this rule in the breach. To take only one example, *Hazelwood School District v. Kuhlmeier* is commonly, though not invariably, reduced to *Hazelwood.* Compare *Morse v. Frederick,* 551 U.S. 393, 405 (2007) (using *Kuhlmeier* as the short form), with William G. Buss, "School Newspapers, Public Forum, and the First Amendment," 74 *Iowa Law Review* 505, 507 (1989) (using *Hazelwood* as the short form). Adhering to the standard convention of case names is advisable, in my view, not only because it may help to decrease the risk of confusion when education law specialists converse with constitutional scholars, but also because it advances my goal of highlighting the students and their families who have challenged the constitutional administration of public schools.

of my parents graduated from college, they constantly extolled the importance of education and believed that I would never realize my full academic potential if I attended the local schools. Accordingly, beginning in the fifth grade, my parents received permission for me to attend a public school in upper Northwest Washington, where the educational outcomes were much brighter and the student bodies, not incidentally, were much whiter. Attending school on the opposite side of Washington—about as far away as one could get from my neighborhood, both literally and figuratively—required a lengthy commute that called for a city bus, two different subway lines, and a walk that lasted nearly a mile. This daily journey into Washington's most privileged segment of society afforded me plenty of time to reflect upon the racial and socioeconomic inequities that exist within even relatively small geographic areas, and to observe how the disparate schools that serve different communities foster those inequities. As an elementary school student in the mid-1980s, moreover, I can distinctly remember learning that the Supreme Court had formally outlawed racial segregation in public schools back in 1954. But I also vividly recall thinking that many schools in my hometown—some located within shouting distance of the Supreme Court's marble palace—still contained entirely black student populations more than three decades after *Brown v. Board of Education.* Even to my ten-year-old self, the upshot of this early legal lesson seemed unmistakable: law on the books does not always resemble life in the streets.

No single recollection from my public school years, however, is clearer than the day in ninth grade when I was summoned to the principal's office at my junior high school—also located in far upper Northwest—to receive a three-day suspension. A few weeks earlier, some friends and I managed to access a liquor cabinet on an overnight field trip and proceeded to get rip-roaring drunk. Although our severe intoxication and its many unkind effects somehow escaped detection during the trip, talk of our exploits gradually spread among our classmates, until word finally reached school administrators. On the fateful Friday afternoon, the intercom repeatedly interrupted classes to beckon first one, then another, and then yet another of my co-conspirators to the principal's office. I can remember the sinking feeling in my stomach as I waited for the intercom, inevitably, to squawk my name. When I made the long walk to the principal's office and was instructed not to return to school for three full days, I unsuccessfully attempted to blink away the tears that had quickly formed in my eyes. Although I then styled myself something of a tough young man, the shock of being banished from my school—even for a short while—packed an unexpectedly forceful punch. The white-hot feeling of shame I experienced upon being suspended felt like anything but "a welcome holiday," which Supreme Court justices have contended characterizes a typical student's view of suspension. However mortifying my suspension was at the time, though, I now consider myself incredibly fortunate that my schoolboy indiscretion occurred in the late 1980s rather than, say, ten or fifteen years later. In the era of "zero tolerance" policies that swept the nation's schools during the 1990s, my rash decision to consume alcohol on a school-related excursion would almost certainly have resulted in my expulsion for the remainder of the school year. Had I been expelled, it seems safe to conclude, my life would have been untracked, perhaps irrevocably. The price for adolescents making regrettable, but classically adolescent, mistakes should not amount to their entire future prospects. Yet that is precisely the ill-conceived, pathologically punitive disciplinary system that "zero tolerance" has established in many schools around the nation.

One year after my suspension, my parents enrolled me in an all-boys Catholic high school to begin the tenth grade. Neither one of my parents practiced Catholicism—or any other religion, for that matter—and the high school's religious component played virtually no role in their determination. Instead, the schooling decision was driven by their firm belief that the environment would provide me with the sturdy academic foundation needed to thrive amid stiff competition in college, a destination they held out less as an ambition than as a presumption. Seven years later, as I neared graduation from Brown University, I felt both immense gratitude for the many outstanding teachers I encountered in public schools and a deep desire to help others achieve uplift through education. These dual sentiments led me to plan on becoming a public school teacher. With this goal in mind, I enrolled in a one-year teacher certification program at Duke University that allowed me, under the supervision of a lead instructor, to acquire experience teaching students at a local public high school. I taught civics to ninth graders and American history to eleventh graders, and found the work enjoyable and rewarding. Indeed, I would have been delighted to teach

in public schools for a long time to come. During that year, however, I received a Marshall Scholarship that offered me two years of
all-expense-paid study at Oxford University, enabling me to leave
North America for the very first time; the opportunity seemed
simply too enticing to let pass. I dedicated my time at Oxford to
exploring the history of challenges to school-financing disparities
by focusing on a Supreme Court decision that weighed the issue
in 1973. My desire to comprehend the constitutional underpinnings of that opinion ultimately led to law school and to my career
as a constitutional law professor. This project thus simultaneously
returns me to my origins and propels me forward, combining as it
does my long-standing interest and experience in education with
my expertise in constitutional law.

I include these brief autobiographical snapshots here in an
effort to address curiosity about the book's genesis. I do not claim,
of course, that my educational experiences should endow the views
advanced in this work with increased authority or entitle my arguments to increased deference. This book is not a memoir but something very close to its opposite. My various schooling experiences
are pertinent, if at all, only because of what they triggered: a desire
both to cast a critical eye upon the momentous body of constitutional law that now shapes the nation's public schools and to reflect
upon how it might be improved. My fondest hope for this volume
is that its existence will inspire others to do the same.

Early Encounters with Race, Culture, Religion, and Patriotism

Prior to the end of World War II in 1945, the Supreme Court seldom issued constitutional opinions involving schools. But what decisions in that domain might have lacked in volume, they more than compensated for in significance. In its earliest decisions exploring the Constitution's relationship to schools, the Supreme Court addressed crucial topics that would, in various guises, become perennial features of its docket: the desire to maintain racially segregated schools; anxiety regarding the school's role in fostering cultural assimilation; and the ability of schools to mandate that students conform their behavior to educators' expectations.

These momentous early opinions can usefully be divided into three distinct categories that unfolded in rough chronological order. The first set of cases involved two different race-based claims that are most naturally understood as arising under the Fourteenth Amendment's Equal Protection Clause. In 1899, the Supreme Court in *Cumming v. Richmond County Board of Education* refused to find that a southern school district's decision to discontinue its high school for black students violated the Constitution—even though the district continued offering white students access to high school. Twenty-eight years later, the Court in *Lum v. Rice* refused to find that Mississippi constitutionally erred by assigning a student of Chinese descent to the town's black school, rather than to its white school. The second set is a trilogy of cases, all decided during the 1920s, where the Court relied upon due process considerations to strike down legislative attempts to assimilate various minorities by regulating nonpublic schools. In 1923, the Court in *Meyer v. Nebraska* invalidated a state law that prohibited all schools, including private and parochial institutions, from teaching students in languages other than English prior to high school. Two years later, the Court in *Pierce v. Society of Sisters* determined that Oregon could not, consistent with the Constitution, eliminate private and parochial schools to ensure that assorted minority groups would encounter nonminorities in public school settings. Another two years after affirming the legitimacy of nonpublic schools, the Court in *Farrington v. Tokushige* invalidated Hawaii's effort to impose onerous regulations on private language academies in an effort to purge them. The final set of opinions applied the First Amendment to a pair of cases challenging the expulsions of Jehovah's Witness students for refusing to recite the Pledge of Allegiance. In 1940, the Court upheld measures requiring that all students recite the pledge against a challenge under the First Amendment's guarantee of free exercise of religion in *Minersville School District v. Gobitis*, which prompted the Mount Kisco eruption. Three years later, however, the Court reversed course on this question, determining in *West Virginia State Board of Education v. Barnette* that the compulsory recitation measures violated students' First Amendment right to free speech.

While each of these opinions merits attention in its own right, the broader arc of the Supreme Court's early involvement with schools also deserves notice. These decisions evinced an increased willingness of the Court over time to interpret the Constitution in a manner that prevented states and educators from exercising unfettered authority over schools and students. In the first set of opinions, the Court demonstrated no willingness to interfere with the race-based assignments of public schools, as the Court expressly contended that education was an inappropriate sphere for regulation by federal officials. In the second set of opinions, however, the Court's traditional aversion to invalidating educational arrangements began to break down, as the Court repeatedly held that legislators overstepped their bounds by exercising undue control over private and parochial schools in the name of promoting cultural assimilation. Finally, in the third set of opinions, the Court embraced its responsibility to vindicate the constitutional rights of students within the nation's public schools by recognizing that expelling students for refusing to participate in patriotic rituals cannot be squared with the nation's commitment to free expression. These three phases should not, of course, be understood too mechanically, as this historical development occurred in tentative fits and starts, not in a seamless procession. Some of the transformation, moreover, is a product of historical happenstance; to take the most glaring example, it would be foolhardy to believe that the Court would have eliminated segregated public schooling if the issue had arisen in the early 1940s. Despite these caveats, the broad trend lines are both discernible and consequential, as the Court's rising constitutional involvement with schools during this period nicely anticipated the intricate relationship between the federal judicial system and the nation's educational system that has emerged in more recent decades.

CUMMING V. RICHMOND COUNTY BOARD OF EDUCATION: RACIAL INEQUALITY IN THE ERA OF SEPARATE BUT EQUAL

During the summer of 1897, the local school board in Augusta, Georgia, decided to eliminate the area's lone public high school for black students. The school board justified discontinuing Ware High School, which annually served about sixty pupils, by noting that the building was not to be shuttered, but instead would be repurposed to serve three hundred black elementary school students who would otherwise be unable to receive an education at public expense. Leading members of Augusta's black community— including Joseph Cumming and John Ladeveze—almost immediately resolved to challenge the school board's dissolution of Ware. Cumming and Ladeveze shared at least three notable characteristics. Both men enrolled their children as students at Ware. Both men led lives of relative economic privilege. And both men had skin so fair that they could, at least among strangers, elect to cross the color line by passing for white. Despite their intimate familiarity with the vagaries of racial realities, the lawsuit did not initially mount a frontal assault on racial segregation in schools. Indeed, the seemingly fundamental issue of separated educational institutions went ignored in their written legal filings, and arose only during oral argument at the Supreme Court level—a time when advancing novel legal claims is traditionally disfavored. The lawsuit instead contended that the school board's decision to eliminate secondary education for black students violated the Fourteenth Amendment because the school board continued offering secondary education to white students.[1]

Before the Supreme Court addressed the dispute, *The Augusta Chronicle*'s reactions to the lawsuit revealed considerable ambivalence. In December 1897, the *Chronicle* saluted the school board's utilitarian-inflected justification for eliminating Ware by offering an unusually vivid metaphor: "When several hundred people are hungry it would be wiser, it seems, to spend the money for bread and meat that all can enjoy than to put it in pati de foie gras that only a few can eat." In that same editorial, however, the *Chronicle* suggested that legal considerations, if not practical ones, supported the black plaintiffs' position: "If the negroes demand the high school, it seems to be their right under the law to have it, and no doubt the board of education, while disagreeing with their judgment . . . will cheerfully comply with their wishes."[2] But when the Georgia Supreme Court rejected this legal claim three months later, the *Chronicle* shifted its assessment of the underlying merits. "While [opponents] of the board of education were, no doubt, impelled by a desire to maintain the interests of their race as they saw them," the *Chronicle* claimed, "they will in the end see that the board has acted wisely in the matter, and has done what is really for the best."[3]

In 1899, Justice John Marshall Harlan wrote an opinion on behalf of a unanimous Supreme Court in *Cumming v. Richmond County Board of Education* finding that the school board's actions did not violate the Constitution. Justice Harlan's opinion rigidly construed the lawsuit's requested relief as seeking not the reopening of Ware for black students, but instead the closing of Augusta's high schools for white students. "[I]f that were done," Harlan cautioned, "the result would only be to take from white children educational privileges enjoyed by them, without giving to colored children additional opportunities for the education furnished in high schools." The board's decision, according to Harlan, reasonably advanced "the interest of the greater number of colored children," as he observed that black families who wished to send their children to high school could avail themselves of private academic options.[4] In *Cumming*'s most significant passage, Harlan made clear that the federal judiciary should—in the absence of extraordinary circumstances—avoid interfering with local decisions involving schools. "[T]he education of the people in schools maintained by state taxation is a matter belonging to the respective states," Harlan announced, "and any interference on the part of Federal authority with the management of such schools cannot be justified except in the case of a clear and unmistakable disregard of rights secured by the supreme law of the land. We have here no such case to be determined."[5]

Although *Cumming*'s validation of blatant racial inequality singes modern sensibilities, the decision failed to generate much reaction, let alone outrage, among contemporaneous observers—at least among mainstream audiences. *The Augusta Chronicle*, *The Macon Telegraph*, and *The Washington Post*—along with a handful of other newspapers—published articles drawn from a wire service that simply recounted the Court's decision without offering any editorial criticisms. Nor did *Cumming* perceptibly raise eyebrows within legal academia. The few law review publications that mentioned *Cumming* also typically refrained from assessing the opinion. While a comment in *The Yale Law Journal* ventured a brief normative evaluation of *Cumming*, that esteemed periodical did so not to censure the Court's reasoning but to endorse it. One of the very few publications that denounced *Cumming* was *The Cleveland Gazette*, a newspaper geared toward black Ohioans.[6]

Some of the black Augusta litigants who failed in their legal challenge ultimately opted to flee not only the region but also the race. The defeat in *Cumming* evidently left John Ladeveze so crestfallen that one year later he decided to exchange the South for Southern California, where he shed his black identity, assumed a white one, and enjoyed a lucrative career in real estate and insurance. Roughly fifteen years later, Joseph Cumming followed Ladeveze's lead, as he moved to Philadelphia, Pennsylvania, crossed the color line, and also entered the real estate business. Following the Supreme Court's decision in 1899, Augusta would not again establish a four-year high school for black students until 1945.[7]

The extreme rarity of high school education at the time of *Cumming* may help to explain—though not excuse—the Court's decision. Augusta's Ware High School was the only public school that offered secondary education to black students in Georgia, and one of only four such institutions in the eleven states of the former Confederacy. In 1890, less than one-half of 1 percent of black adolescents in the South attended high school. Throughout the country, moreover, high school graduates of any race were extremely uncommon in 1900, as only about 6 percent of adolescents obtained a diploma at that time. (Six decades later, by way of contrast, 70 percent of students graduated from high school.) These stark figures suggest why the Court in 1899 might have construed a high school education as something akin to a luxury good—an item that localities provided at their own discretion and that therefore could not properly be subjected to litigation protesting its absence. On this account, it might have seemed unwise to require localities to dispense such a rarefied item on a racially equal basis because the effect of doing so could have plausibly curtailed educational opportunities throughout the nation for white citizens—and ultimately black citizens, too. *Cumming* can thus be viewed as seeking to avoid placing a cap on schooling options that arrived at the lowest common denominator among the black and white populations in any given community. The relatively small percentage of black parents who were privileged enough to send their offspring to high school explains why *Cumming* appeared simply to assume that Ware's former students would be able to afford tuition at a private school. While it may be possible to understand *Cumming* as in effect blessing the school board's decision to accommodate larger numbers of the black unwashed in elementary school at the expense of a high school for the black elite, nothing explains why the board spared Augusta's white community from confronting a similar trade-off.[8]

Some readers will doubtless wonder how *Cumming* can possibly be reconciled with the Court's opinion from three years earlier in *Plessy v. Ferguson*. In that notorious case, the Supreme Court in a 7–1 decision found that Louisiana's measure requiring separate but equal railcars for black and white passengers did not violate the Fourteenth Amendment's Equal Protection Clause. Although the opinion did not formally involve schools, *Plessy* nevertheless held up segregated education as an instance of racial separation that—in its estimation—plainly satisfied the Equal Protection Clause's requirements. In *Cumming*, though, the decision to discontinue Ware High School could plausibly be viewed as running afoul of even *Plessy*, as the asymmetric educational options extended to black and white students represented an approach that has memorably been labeled "separate and *un*equal."[9] On this understanding, a straightforward application of *Plessy* should have triggered the invalidation of the school board's decision to introduce undeniable racial inequality into Augusta's secondary school system.

Yet this well-intentioned effort to convert *Plessy* into a weapon for equality misfires because it inaccurately conflates the language in Louisiana's statute, which the Supreme Court validated, with the legal test that the Court itself enunciated. Louisiana's Separate Car Act of 1890 mandated " 'equal but separate accommodations' " for black and white passengers.[10] While Justice Henry Brown's opinion for the Court in *Plessy* upheld this measure as satisfying the Equal Protection Clause, his opinion did not impose that standard as a generalized requirement. Rather than mandating equality as a universal approach, *Plessy* announced that racial arrangements would pass constitutional muster provided that they were merely reasonable.[11] For at least two decades following *Plessy*, the legal community understood that decision to bar only racial regulations that could not satisfy its extraordinarily deferential reasonableness standard. This understanding of *Plessy*'s standard thus helps to explain why the Court displayed no compunction about upholding the school board's actions in *Cumming*, even though its elimination of Ware yielded racially unequal educational opportunities.[12]

Cumming's final, potentially confounding point surrounds the opinion's author: Why did Justice John Marshall Harlan—who alone voted in *Plessy* to invalidate railcar segregation—seemingly make an about-face on racial equality by upholding the school board's actions in *Cumming*? Justice Harlan's evident defection in *Cumming* is particularly striking because some of the enduring language he wrote in *Plessy* established his reputation as a prophet of racial equality. In 2007, for example, one of the nation's most distinguished legal historians commended Harlan for his "messianic commitment to black rights."[13] Similarly, many prominent jurists have hailed Harlan's *Plessy* dissent as an early beacon of modern racial enlightenment. How could the Court's racial hero in *Plessy* become the Court's racial villain in *Cumming* only three short years later? Several scholars have offered a variety of theories endeavoring to explain how Harlan's position in *Cumming* ought not be viewed as merely excusing state-backed racism, and therefore should not be construed as sullying the racial conviction he displayed in *Plessy*.[14]

In a limited sense, these scholars are correct: Justice Harlan did not experience a sudden turnaround on race in the late 1890s. That statement is true, however, not because Harlan's vote in *Cumming* was free from untoward racial sentiment but because his *Plessy* dissent *also* evinced untoward racial sentiment. Although Harlan's dissent in *Plessy* certainly reached the correct outcome in voting to invalidate Louisiana's statute, the deeply flawed, repugnant reasoning contained in that opinion renders it the single most overrated opinion ever written by a Supreme Court justice and—not incidentally—the most misunderstood.

Harlan's *Plessy* dissent claims so many fervent admirers in the modern era largely because people cite an isolated fragment from the opinion. Read in its entirety, though, Harlan's dissent espouses unabashedly white supremacist and anti-Asian attitudes. In one breathtaking passage, Harlan defended his position by maintaining that, even if railcars were racially integrated, such a development would in no way jeopardize the superior status of whites. "The white race deems itself to be the dominant race in this country," Harlan instructed. "And so it is, in prestige, in achievements, in education, in wealth, and in power. So, I doubt not, it will continue to be for all time, if it remains true to its great heritage, and holds fast to the principles of constitutional liberty."[15] Harlan challenged Louisiana's statute by highlighting what he regarded as its fundamental absurdity: excluding black passengers from white railcars when "a Chinaman can ride in the same passenger coach with white citizens," even though members of "the Chinese race" are "so different from our own that we do not permit those belonging to it to become citizens of the United States."[16]

Even the much-celebrated portion of Harlan's *Plessy* dissent is not the embodiment of racially egalitarian attitudes that its admirers hold it out to be. "Our constitution is color-blind, and neither knows nor tolerates classes among citizens," Harlan famously wrote. "In respect of civil rights, all citizens are equal before the law. The humblest is the peer of the most powerful. The law regards man as man, and takes no account . . . of his color when his civil rights as guaranteed by the supreme law of the land are involved."[17] Readers today generally understand Harlan's invocation of equal "civil rights" as a broad, all-encompassing formulation. But that is not the sentiment that Harlan actually conveyed, as contemporaneous readers would have understood that term in a far more constrained sense. The widespread confusion about this venerated passage's meaning stems from the fractured conception of equality that prevailed during the nineteenth century, which viewed "civil rights" as conceptually distinct from "social rights." Where "civil rights" typically connoted the ability to enter valid contracts and similar concepts, "social rights" connoted interracial sex and all other forms of interracial interactions that might lead to such contact—including integrated schools.[18]*All nine justices in both *Plessy* and *Cumming* agreed that the Equal Protection Clause afforded black people civil equality and denied them social equality. But Justice Harlan dissented in *Plessy* because he—idiosyncratically—viewed riding in integrated railcars as involving merely civil rights, not social rights. And the most persuasive explanation for Justice Harlan's unwillingness to write an opinion declaring that segregated schools violated the Constitution in *Cumming* is not because the claim had been raised delinquently but because Harlan viewed education as involving social rights, and therefore not subject to the Equal Protection Clause.[19]

Recovering the largely forgotten case of *Cumming* contains significant implications because it suggests that today's legal conservatives, who habitually invoke Harlan's ballyhooed language from *Plessy*, misapprehend him as a paragon of modern racial attitudes. While Justice Harlan held *relatively* enlightened views on racial equality for a Supreme Court justice of his day, those views— properly grasped—have now become retrograde. Understanding Harlan's racial attitudes with greater nuance, which grappling with his generally overlooked opinion in *Cumming* invites, should prompt legal conservatives to reevaluate their reverence for the patron saint of colorblind constitutionalism. Even if they opt to retain their basic jurisprudential commitments, they should acknowledge that Harlan is woefully miscast in the role of racial prophet.

---

* Booker T. Washington's speech at the Atlanta Exposition in 1895—delivered one year before the Court decided *Plessy v. Ferguson*—employed this distinctive meaning of the "social" sphere. In this address—generally referred to as the "Atlanta Compromise" for the racially accommodationist tone that it adopted—Washington stated to his white audience, "In all things that are purely social we can be as separate as the fingers, yet one as the hand in all things essential to mutual progress." Booker T. Washington, *Up from Slavery* 221–22 (1907).

LUM V. RICE: PRESERVING WHITE SCHOOLS IN MISSISSIPPI

During the first half of the twentieth century, the Supreme Court decided only a single case arising from the context of segregated elementary or secondary schools. The curious events leading to that dispute began in 1924, when a nine-year-old girl named Martha Lum arrived for her first day of school in Bolivar County, Mississippi. Lum, a U.S.-born citizen of Chinese descent, was one of a small number of Asian Americans living in the Mississippi Delta, many of whom owned and operated grocery stores. Over time, the Delta's modest Asian American population attained the precarious status of what might be termed "honorary whiteness," whereby Martha Lum not only played with white children but also attended a white church. It must have seemed only natural to the Lums, then, that Martha would also attend a white school. Although this prospect did not seem to vex Bolivar County's white population, the State of Mississippi deemed it intolerable. Accordingly, the principal called Lum into his office during the recess hour and apologetically informed her that students with Chinese backgrounds had been rendered ineligible to learn alongside white students. "We're sorry," the principal stated, "but you have to leave school."[20]

The Lums secured one of the area's leading law firms to contest Martha's exclusion from the white school. Their legal argument did not, however, contest the legitimacy of racially designated schools outright. Instead, their argument objected merely to assigning students of Asian descent to attend school with black students. The brief ultimately filed on Lum's behalf in the Supreme Court not only trafficked in nakedly antiblack tropes; it was predicated on them. The brief began with the proposition that communities separated black and white students because "the purity of each [race] is jeopardized by the mingling of the children in the school room[, and] that such association among children means social intercourse and social equality."[21] Whites wished to avoid such "repulsive" interracial contact, the brief maintained, "to preserve the integrity of the Caucasian race," and due to the history that "the negroes were once slaves and, as a race, had to begin as children," for these conditions had endowed them with "racial peculiarities, physical as well as moral."[22] With this foundation established, the brief proceeded to contend that it should be impermissible for whites to require

Chinese Americans to expose their children in school to the potential of black racial contaminant: "If there is danger in the association it is a danger from which one race is entitled to protection just the same as another. The White race may not legally expose the Yellow race to a danger that the dominant race recognizes and, by the same laws, guards itself against."[23] The State of Mississippi's brief defended the assignment of Chinese Americans to black schools by also construing the case in terms of its implications for social equality among the races. Although Mississippi law expressly prohibited people of Asian descent from marrying Caucasians, the brief noted, no law prevented "intermarriage between members of the Chinese and negro races. Is it not better to confine [Martha Lum's] association, so far as is possible, to those with whom she may associate on more intimate terms in the future years?"[24]

In 1927, Chief Justice William Howard Taft wrote an opinion for a unanimous Supreme Court in *Lum v. Rice* refusing to interfere with Mississippi's race-based method of assigning students to schools. Early in the opinion, Chief Justice Taft invoked *Cumming*—which he expressly noted had been written by Justice Harlan—for a broad notion of judicial noninterference with public schools: "The right and power of the state to regulate the method of providing for the education of its youth at public expense is clear."[25] With that underpinning in place, it did not take long to dispose of the case. Taft largely conceived of Martha Lum as attacking racial segregation in schools itself—rather than her place within the system—and he observed that numerous state courts, including in the North, had previously rejected such claims. "Most of the [precedents] arose, it is true, over the establishment of separate schools as between white pupils and black pupils," Taft conceded, "but we cannot think that the question is any different, . . . where the issue is as between white pupils and the pupils of the yellow races."[26] Returning to what will become the familiar theme of judicial deference to state educational decisions, Taft concluded that "[Lum's assignment] decision is within the discretion of the state in regulating its public schools, and does not conflict with the Fourteenth Amendment," as such matters fall "within the constitutional power of the state Legislature to settle, without intervention of the federal courts under the federal Constitution."[27]

In 1965, nearly four decades after *Lum*, Professor Arthur

Sutherland criticized the opinion in the *Harvard Law Review* as "far out of the spirit of its time."[28]* Although Sutherland, who was in his sixties when the article appeared, plainly felt that Taft's opinion collided with the racial sentiments of the United States in 1927 as he recollected that era, his assessment is difficult to square with the historical record. Recall that *Lum* did not draw a single dissent, at a time when the Court's composition included Justice Harlan Fiske Stone and Justice Louis Brandeis, both of whom might have been expected to cast a skeptical eye on Mississippi's race-based student assignment plans.† Combined with the earlier unanimous decision in *Cumming*, the two race-based challenges to schooling decisions had by 1927 been defeated in the Supreme Court by a combined tally of 18–0. As with *Cumming*, moreover, newspapers responded to *Lum* more with placidity than ire. The *Chicago Tribune, The New York Times,* and *The Washington Post* all published articles noting *Lum*, but in no way indicating disapproval. For its part, the *Los Angeles Times* loudly applauded *Lum*. "That race segregation in cities is desirable and necessary has long been felt by the thinking men of all the races represented," the *Los Angeles Times* explained. "Segregation plans are not predicated upon the assumption that any races are either superior or inferior, but upon their irreconcilable differences, making them as impracticable of mixture as oil and water."[29] Within the world of law reviews, *Lum* largely elicited the shrugged shoulders that often accompany expected decisions. Revealingly, the opinion drew nearly identical reactions from legal publications based in locations as disparate as New Haven, Connecticut, and Oxford, Mississippi. Where *The Yale Law Journal* commented, "The instant case is in line with authority on the question of separation of races in schools," the *Mississippi Law Journal* noted, "The decision announced is in line with the weight of authority of other states."[30]

    Lum did, however, attract some contemporaneous criticism. Not

---

* Sutherland—as if to place an exclamation mark on this critique—invoked Bob Dylan's hit song to contend that Chief Justice Taft's opinion in *Lum* embodied a "failure to recognize that, welcome or not, . . . '[T]he times they are a-changin'.'" Arthur E. Sutherland, "Book Review," 79 *Harvard Law Review* 222, 226 (1965) (quoting Bob Dylan, "The Times They Are A-changin'," *The Times They Are A-changin'* [Columbia 1964]).

† Justice Oliver Wendell Holmes also joined the Court's opinion in *Lum v. Rice.* But, as will soon become clear, Holmes adhered to the doctrine of judicial restraint, and therefore would have been unlikely to override a determination involving a student's placement. For a skeptical assessment of Holmes's generally revered judicial career, see Albert W. Alschuler, *Law Without Values: The Life, Work, and Legacy of Justice Holmes* (2000).

surprisingly, black newspapers led the attack. *The Chicago Defender's* appraisal of the decision warrants particular attention. That newspaper's editorial board, while leaving no doubt that it reviled *Lum*, nevertheless expressed hope that permitting the assignment of nonblack students to black schools signaled that racial segregation's days were numbered, as it would soon collapse under its increased weight. As the *Defender* noted,

> [H]eretofore other races have been immune to the [ ] humiliations [of Jim Crow schools]. Chinese, Japanese, Hindus, Greeks, Italians, Turks—all have received full welcome in Mississippi and the rest of the South—heretofore. Now that great state has started operations on the first named of these groups. The others will follow in their order—and the result will be that all of these Jim Crow schools will be abolished.[31]*

A few legal publications also critiqued *Lum*, occasionally even using severe terms. In response to the decision, the *California Law Review* deemed racial segregation in schools "questionable," and the *St. John's Law Review* went even further, calling *Lum* "deplorable."[32]

Nevertheless, such isolated criticisms hardly serve to confirm Professor Sutherland's retrospective assertion that *Lum* contravened predominant sentiment throughout the nation in 1927. It seems far more accurate to contend that Americans at that time generally backed *Lum*, rather than bucked it. *Cumming* and *Lum*, viewed in tandem, thus indicated that the Court would not disturb segregation in elementary and secondary schools—a conclusion that stood at least until *Brown v. Board of Education* in 1954.

---

* In perhaps the most dispiriting response to *Lum* that appeared in any publication, *The Brooklyn Eagle*—a black newspaper—condemned the decision not so much because it left racial segregation undisturbed but because it required people of Chinese descent to rub shoulders with African Americans. With no trace of sarcasm evident, the *Eagle* commented,

> The Chinese have a background of the oldest culture on earth. They were living under established law and order and doing much with the arts when our own ancestors were barbarians. The Negroes, remarkable as has been their progress since emancipation, can claim no culture not absorbed from the whites in the past three hundred years.

"Expressed by Our Contemporaries: Negro Schools and the Chinese," *New York Amsterdam News*, Oct. 26, 1927, 20 (reprinting article from *The Brooklyn Eagle*).

MEYER V. NEBRASKA: PROHIBITIONS ON TEACHING
IN LANGUAGES OTHER THAN ENGLISH

On May 25, 1920, a schoolteacher named Robert Meyer at Zion Parochial School in rural Hamilton County, Nebraska, looked up from his desk to discover that a strange man had, without knocking, entered his classroom full of fifth-grade students. Although Meyer had never met the uninvited guest, the teacher harbored no doubts about his purpose. One year earlier, Nebraska enacted a law that prohibited teachers in all schools—public, private, and parochial— from instructing students in languages other than English before they reached the ninth grade. Meyer quickly realized that his guest had entered the classroom to observe whether he was honoring the new language ban. One student, even seventy years later, could still recall the tense scene that unfolded as a hush descended over the room: "We were wondering what was going on. We could tell by the look on Teacher Meyer's face that something pretty serious was happening." At this pivotal moment, Meyer—who had in fact been leading the students in German prior to the inspection— confronted a choice. "I knew that, if I changed into the English language, he would say nothing," Meyer subsequently recalled. "If I went on in German, he would . . . arrest me. I told myself that I must not flinch. And I did not flinch. I went on in German." Meyer violated the law because he felt that it was his personal responsibility to instruct students in the mother tongue for at least thirty minutes every day so that the German language as spoken would not vanish within the United States. Many members of the community volunteered to pay the twenty-five-dollar fine that Meyer received for his transgression. Meyer, a forty-two-year-old father of six children, steadfastly refused the offers, even though the sum equaled one month's salary. Instead, he resolved to wage a legal battle against what he deemed an unjust law: "I shall not pay the fine. It is not a matter of money. This is a question of principle. If I go to jail for doing what I know to be right, I go to jail. I shall not compromise with what I know is . . . right."[33]

Although Nebraska's prohibition on teaching foreign languages seems imprudent and intemperate today, such bans enjoyed widespread support during World War I and its aftermath. In July 1918, four months before Germany and the Allies reached armistice, *The New York Times* noted, "Our growing antipathy to things German apparently knows no limit this side of extirpation."[34] Anti-German sentiment grew so intense that, in an effort to cleanse the English language of words with Germanic origins, some communities re-designated sauerkraut as "liberty cabbage" and abandoned the term "kindergarten."[35] In one notorious incident, students in Pittsburgh, Pennsylvania, had their German textbooks not only confiscated but burned en masse. After Nebraska enacted its statute, more-over, several newspaper editorials cheered the measure for its rela-tive restraint and even extolled it as a model for the entire country. While *The Washington Post* commended the statute for not applying the language ban to high schools (whose students presumably al-ready grasped English), it nevertheless bemoaned that immigrants "have made us a polyglot nation" and advised, "It would be a great help in the process of Americanization . . . if a similar law were generally adopted."[36] In an item titled "Nebraska Germans Re-main Unchanged," *The Boston Globe* condemned efforts to resist the language statute and asserted that it must not be "forgotten what a menace [Germans] have been to Americanization in the United States."[37]

Support for language prohibitions in schools could also be found in the most rarefied strata of American society. The histo-rian Robert McNutt McElroy of Princeton spearheaded the lan-guage ban movement in his capacity as educational director of the National Security League, a newly formed nativist organization. "Those who urge 'business as usual' when speaking of the teaching of German are simply oiling the wheels for the German war char-iot called 'kultur,'" McElroy inveighed.[38] Elihu Root—who served in President Theodore Roosevelt's cabinet before being elected U.S. senator from New York—also advanced the cause in strident terms. "Our country is engaged in a life and death struggle with the great German-speaking powers of the world," Root commented in 1918, "and we have suddenly come to realize that vast numbers of our population receive their ideas, both as to facts and opinions, exclusively or chiefly through the language of our enemies. To be a strong and united nation we must be a one-language people."[39] One year later, TR himself echoed this broad sentiment. "We have room for but one language here, and that is the English language," Roosevelt commented. "For we intend to see that the crucible turns our people out as Americans, of American nationality, and not as dwellers of a polyglot boardinghouse."[40]

The nation's preeminent education scholar, Ellwood P. Cubberley of Stanford University, emphatically endorsed Roosevelt's concerns. In 1919, Cubberley's masterwork—*Public Education in the United States*—identified the assimilation of immigrants as a dominant schooling challenge of the time, and further identified ethnic enclaves as posing an existential threat to American identity. "The problem which has faced and still faces the United States is that of assimilating these thousands of foreigners into our national life and citizenship," Cubberley wrote. "We must do this or lose our national character."[41]* Cubberley deemed "Germans . . . trying to preserve their language and racial habits and *Kultur*" as presenting one of the nation's chief obstacles to achieving assimilation.[42]† Enthusiasm for language bans became so pervasive that when the Supreme Court resolved the issue in 1923, at least thirty-three states had enacted legislation similar to Nebraska's.[43]

---

* The shifting ethnic character of immigration to the United States during this era appears to have left Cubberley stupefied. In 1919, Cubberley displayed unease and astonishment at the nation's increased ethnic diversity by noting,

> We buy our groceries of Knudsen and Larsen, our meats of Klieber and Engelmeier, our bread of Rudolf Krause, Petar Petarovich delivers our milk, Guiseppe Battali removes our garbage, Swen Swensen delivers our ice, Takahira Matsui is our cook, and Nicholas Androvsky has recently taken the place of Pancho Garcia as our gardener. We occasionally take dinner at a café managed by Schiavetti and Montagnini, we buy our haberdashery of Moses Ickelheimer, Isaac Rosenstein is our tailor, Azniv Arakelian sells us our cigars, and Thirmutis Poulis supplies our wants in ice cream and candies.

Ellwood P. Cubberley, *Public Education in the United States* 340 (1919). After detailing a few more occupations in this fashion, Cubberley noted that "Emil Frankfurter" works as a bank cashier. Ibid. In a similar vein, he noted that the U.S. casualties from World War I included "such representative American citizens as Rudolph Kochensparger, Robert Emmet O'Hanlon, Ralph McGregor, John Jones, Rastus Brown, Pietro Sturla, Rafael Gonzales, Dominico Sebatino, Ignace Olzanski, Diego Lemos, and Manthos Zakis." Ibid., 340–41.

† Predictably, educators' anxieties about cultural assimilation crept into the U.S. history textbooks that immigrants encountered in public schools. A textbook published in 1921, for example, asserted that most immigrants in the last five decades "have been from the lower classes . . . and they give much trouble. They are for the most part very ignorant, and having been downtrodden in their old homes, they have no respect for law or government. In fact, many of them would like to see the government of the United States destroyed. How to deal with this undesirable class of immigrants is one of the most serious problems that we have to-day." Waddy Thompson, *The First Book in United States History* 294 (1921). See also David Tyack, *Seeking Common Ground: Public Schools in a Diverse Society* (2003).

In *Meyer v. Nebraska*, Justice James McReynolds's opinion for the Court invalidated the school-based language prohibitions found in states around the country. McReynolds began by carefully delineating particular questions of state authority that the case did not call into question—including compulsory education requirements for minors, power over public schools' curricula, and even the ability to require all schools to provide at least some instruction in English. With those parameters established, McReynolds nevertheless insisted that states did not possess total control over schools within their jurisdictions, and declared instead that the judiciary played an essential role in reviewing state legislation. "Determination by the Legislature of what constitutes proper exercise of [its legal authority] is not final or conclusive but is subject to supervision by the courts," McReynolds wrote.[44]

While *Meyer* expressed some sympathy for the assimilative aims of Nebraska's legislation, it also noted that the state's reach cannot exceed its constitutional grasp. "The protection of the Constitution extends to all, to those who speak other languages as well to those born with English on the tongue," McReynolds observed. "Perhaps it would be highly advantageous if all had ready understanding of our ordinary speech, but this cannot be coerced by methods which conflict with the Constitution—a desirable end cannot be promoted by prohibited means."[45] Although Sparta plucked its males from their homes and raised them in barracks starting at age seven "[i]n order to submerge the individual and develop ideal citizens," McReynolds contended that such methods contravened American ideals. And Nebraska's legislation—aiming as it did to "foster a homogeneous people"—bore a striking resemblance to Sparta's tactics, according to McReynolds.[46] *Meyer* can thus be understood to declare as follows: in its zeal to assimilate the foreign element within its borders, Nebraska erred by implementing a practice that was itself foreign to the nation's constitutional order.

Regarding the particular constitutional provision the language ban violated, *Meyer* identified the Fourteenth Amendment's protection for liberty located in its Due Process Clause. The paean to a robust conception of constitutional liberty that McReynolds penned in *Meyer* rests among the most resonant passages that the Supreme Court has issued throughout its history:

> While this court has not attempted to define with exactness the liberty thus guaranteed, [without] doubt, it denotes not merely freedom from bodily restraint but also the right of the individual to contract, to engage in any of the common occupations of life, to acquire useful knowledge, to marry, establish a home and bring up children, to worship God according to the dictates of his own conscience, and generally to enjoy those privileges long recognized at common law as essential to the orderly pursuit of happiness by free men.[47]

With this capacious understanding of liberty in mind, McReynolds determined that Nebraska's legislation impinged the constitutional rights of two distinct sets of actors: "[Meyer's] right . . . to teach and the right of parents to engage him so to instruct their children."[48]

Justice Oliver Wendell Holmes, joined by Justice George Sutherland, dissented from the majority's outcome in *Meyer*. It is possible to attribute Holmes's dissent to his position as the Court's foremost practitioner of judicial restraint—the doctrine that counsels judges strongly, though not absolutely, against invalidating democratically enacted legislation. Proponents of judicial restraint often pride themselves on refusing to invalidate measures that they vehemently dislike, insisting that an unwise statute need not be an unconstitutional one. But in *Meyer* it was far from clear that Holmes disliked Nebraska's statute, vehemently or otherwise. To the contrary, Holmes appeared to assert that the legislation prudently advanced the goal of ensuring citizens speak a common language: "I cannot bring my mind to believe that in some circumstances, and circumstances existing it is said in Nebraska, the statute might not be regarded as a reasonable *or even necessary* method of reaching [this] desired result." The Nebraska measure, in Holmes's estimation, embodied a sensible effort to counteract the effects of various ethnic enclaves, "where a child would hear only Polish or French or German spoken at home," by guaranteeing "that in his early years he shall hear and speak only English at school." Holmes concluded the dissent by suggesting that—whatever one's view on the wisdom of language bans—it was mistaken to assert the nation's foundational document resolved the question one way or another: "I think I appreciate the objection to the law but it appears to me to present a question upon which men reasonably might differ and therefore I am unable to say that the Constitution of the United States prevents the experiment being tried."[49]*

Newspaper editorial boards broadly approved *Meyer,* even as many took pains to acknowledge what they regarded as legitimate concerns about the immigrant assimilation patterns that motivated the statutes. *The New York Times,* for example, found the legislators' motives "honorable" but maintained, "To foster 'Americanization' by shutting off school children, at the very age when foreign language can be thoroughly acquired, from the rich intellectual content of those languages . . . is decidedly queer."[50] Somewhat surprisingly, even newspapers that unambiguously applauded Nebraska's adoption of the language ban in 1919 now cheered the Court's invalidation of that ban four years later. *The Washington Post,* while acknowledging how passions created by the war could understandably lead to language bans, insisted that *Meyer* "will be hailed by every right-thinking person as another vindication of that liberty which the Constitution and the amendments thereto guarantee."[51] *The Boston Globe* offered *Meyer* ardent support, as it condemned "the repressive laws" and congratulated the Court for "render[ing] one of its rare services to culture in America."[52]

---

* As a formal matter, Justice Holmes's dissent on language bans appears in a companion case to *Meyer* originating in Waterloo, Iowa: *Bartels v. Iowa,* 262 U.S. 404 (1923) (Holmes, J., dissenting). This factor may at least partially explain why—though every major casebook in the fields of constitutional law and education law continues to excerpt *Meyer*—several leading casebooks now omit Justice Holmes's dissent altogether. Holmes is perhaps the most widely admired American jurist who lived during the twentieth century. His dissent on this high-profile issue should reenter the constitutional canon because it casts illuminating light on his jurisprudence of judicial restraint.
    While Justice Holmes voted to uphold the language prohibitions enacted by both Iowa and Nebraska, he was not, as mentioned above, a judicial restraint absolutist. Hence, Justice Holmes concurred with the Court's decision to invalidate Ohio's language ban. Where Iowa and Nebraska framed their foreign-language bans in broadly applicable terms, the text of Ohio's statute expressly singled out the German language as forbidden. That facial hostility sufficed to render the Ohio measure constitutionally infirm, even in the eyes of Justice Holmes. See ibid., at 413 (Holmes, J., dissenting) ("I agree with the Court as to the special proviso against the German language contained in the statute dealt with in *Bohning v. Ohio*"). This line separating constitutional statutes from unconstitutional statutes will strike many readers as artificial because the distinction, in effect, could be understood to hinge on whether legislators are savvy enough to draft statutes that conceal their actual hostilities. Perhaps somewhat surprisingly, then, this broad methodology—which focuses on identifying impermissible motives, rather than impermissible effects—forms the predominant basis for evaluating claims of racial discrimination under the Equal Protection Clause. See chapter 5.

The nation's leading education scholars disparaged *Meyer*. In 1923, Dean Cubberley of Stanford continued to view assimilating immigrants as the single most pressing issue confronting the nation's schools, and he accordingly deemed *Meyer* "almost incomprehensible," complaining further, "How the Court could conclude that such an important nationalizing requirement interfered with the guaranteed individual and family freedom . . . passes my understanding." *Meyer* arrived at an inopportune moment for the assimilative project, Cubberley insisted, because "[o]ur national digestive organs broke down."[53] Where *Meyer* portrayed Nebraska's statute as overreaching, the University of Chicago professor I. N. Edwards countered that the Supreme Court's decision itself exceeded proper authority. Edwards asserted that educational decisions "are essentially local in their character," and *Meyer* intruded into that local terrain by "revers[ing] an important educational policy of . . . the states," thereby exhibiting the remarkable "power which the Supreme Court may exercise in controlling educational policy." Edwards found the opinion sufficiently wrongheaded that he seriously entertained the possibility of a constitutional amendment designed to restore balance between the state and the federal governments, a dynamic that had—in his estimation—drifted ever closer toward centralization in recent years.[54]

The legal community showered *Meyer* with a mixture of roughly equal parts consternation and celebration. Some commentators—echoing the dismay of education scholars—criticized *Meyer* for interfering in school affairs. Voicing this critique with notable indignation, the *Virginia Law Register* called *Meyer* "the most far-reaching [decision] against the rights of the States we have ever seen," and further contended, "If there is anything on the face of the earth that the State should have the right to control it is its system of education."[55] The opinion portended disaster, according to the *Register*, as it represented "a dangerous entering wedge and we may expect to see the time when the United States Government under this decision will allow the Federal courts to take charge of the education in any State in the Union."[56]*

---

* Relatedly, some distinguished legal liberals criticized *Meyer* not because they approved of language bans but because the decision's reliance on the Due Process Clause recalled the Court's penchant for using that provision to invalidate legislation treasured by progressives. See, for example, *Lochner v. New York*, 198 U.S. 45 (1905). What the Court gives to liberal causes today, this critique ran, it could take from liberal causes tomorrow.

Other legal authorities, however, applauded *Meyer* for dispatching the language bans as flagrant incursions on constitutional liberty. In an address to the American Bar Association titled "Liberty and Law," the former Secretary of State Charles Evans Hughes critiqued Nebraska's measure as "interfer[ing] with instruction in our schools, not to promote the acquisition of knowledge, but to obstruct it." Hughes, who would become chief justice of the United States in 1930, found the measure so brazen that it effectively demanded judicial intervention: "Even the Court, with its necessarily-limited judicial vision, could see what lay behind [Nebraska's] enactment and condemned it as an unwarranted interference with the constitutional guarantee of liberty."[57]

With *Meyer*, the Supreme Court crossed a major threshold, as the opinion marked the first time in the institution's history it announced that a state had infringed an individual's civil liberties in a case involving schools. This decision thus had the effect of signaling that states could not unilaterally control elementary and secondary education within their jurisdictions, free from any concern that their determinations could run afoul of the U.S. Constitution. The Court, moreover, did not as might be expected select some trivial dispute—involving legislation found in only a handful of states, and of negligible interest—to declare its willingness to intervene in educational affairs. To the contrary, *Meyer* invalidated language bans that were found in the overwhelming majority of states, and those measures aroused passionate, enthusiastic support from a broad cross section of American society. Accordingly, it would be sorely mistaken to dismiss *Meyer*'s invalidation of these statutes as a foreordained conclusion, a notion that is further underscored by recalling that Justices Holmes and Sutherland both found that Nebraska's

---

Professor Felix Frankfurter of Harvard advanced precisely this view of *Meyer* in a private letter to Judge Learned Hand:

> Of course, I regard such know-nothing legislation as uncivilized, but for the life of me I can't see how it meets the condemnation of want of "due process" unless we frankly recognize that the Supreme Court . . . is the revisory legislative body. . . . The more I think about this whole "due process" business, the less I think of lodging that power in those nine gents at Washington.

In reply, Judge Hand colorfully affirmed his correspondent's assessment: "I can see no reason why, if a state legislature wishes to make a jackass of itself by that form of Americanization, it should not have the responsibility for [remedying the issue] rather than the Supreme Court." See Gerald Gunther, *Learned Hand: The Man and the Judge* 322 (2d ed. 2011).

statute passed constitutional muster. Instead, the Supreme Court should be saluted for ridding the nation of this xenophobic legislation that, had it successfully taken root, could conceivably still be in existence today. Even if anti-German animus no longer enjoys widespread currency within the United States, *Meyer* should nevertheless also be saluted for effectively interring attempts to target the native languages of other marginalized groups in recent years.[58]

While *Meyer* represented a critical breakthrough, it is also essential to understand that it did not in one fell swoop inaugurate the judiciary's modern approach to education law. Recall that a few years later in *Lum* the Court would reaffirm its extreme deference to state educational decisions. Nothing in *Meyer*, moreover, can be cited to indicate that the Constitution regulates a state's influence over its public schools, as compared with its nonpublic schools. In addition, *Meyer* conceived the rights that were infringed by a language ban as belonging to the parent rather than the student. Whatever the opinion's limitations, though, *Meyer* represents the Court's first consequential step in its path toward vindicating the rights of public school students.

PIERCE V. SOCIETY OF SISTERS:
STATE EFFORTS TO OUTLAW NONPUBLIC SCHOOLS

In the second installment of its three opinions limiting states' ability to force assimilation during the 1920s, the Supreme Court in *Pierce v. Society of Sisters* nullified a statewide referendum enacted by Oregon voters that effectively abolished private and parochial schools, and thus required children between the ages of eight and sixteen to attend public school. According to the measure, which was the first of its kind to be enacted in the nation, parents who failed to heed the public schooling requirement would have received a fine and a jail term of at least two days for each day of noncompliance. The newly revived Ku Klux Klan sponsored the referendum because it believed that nonpublic educational environments—particularly Catholic schools—sheltered their pupils from encountering students whose ancestors had lived on these shores for generations, and prevented them from absorbing the nation's fundamental values. Although the initial incarnation of the KKK accepted white men from a wide variety of backgrounds, the reformulated Klan narrowed its ranks of membership (admitting only native-born white Protestants) and broadened its portfolio of adversaries (adding immigrants, Catholics, and Jews to its core anti-Negro ideology). One Klansman's statement vividly captured the almost primal fear that gripped nativists during this era, as they felt that the nation's identity was under assault: "Somehow these mongrel hordes must be Americanized; failing that, deportation is the only remedy."* Shortly before Oregon voters cast their ballots on the public school measure in 1922, *The Portland Telegram* made a potent nativist pitch backing the referendum: "We, the majority, have decided what is necessary. . . . The public schools please us. Why not make them please the other fellow? Why not march him up to the school of our choice and say to him in effect: 'There, take that, it's good for you.'" It would be difficult to overstate this referendum's salience to Oregon voters, as *The New York Times* called it "the outstanding issue of the [gubernatorial] campaign." Many observers attributed the Republican Ben Olcott's opposition to the measure as enabling his surprising loss to the Democrat Walter Pierce, occurring as it did in a state where registered Republicans outnumbered registered Democrats by a ratio of more than 2.5 to 1.[59]

If a novelist were tasked with conjuring a sympathetic school to mount the strongest possible challenge to Oregon's law, it would

---

* On Thanksgiving Eve 1915—not long after seeing D. W. Griffith's incendiary film, *The Birth of a Nation*—William J. Simmons initiated the Klan's revival with a small group of men by burning a cross atop Stone Mountain in Georgia and designating himself Imperial Wizard. Seven years later, this second KKK claimed thousands of members spread across at least forty-five different states. Although the Scottish Free Masons also backed the Oregon school measure, the issue was most readily identified with, and most integrally supported by, the KKK. See John Higham, *Strangers in the Land: Patterns of American Nativism, 1860–1925* 286–91, 296 (1955); William G. Ross, *Forging New Freedoms: Nativism, Education, and the Constitution, 1917–1927* 149 (1994); and "The Various Shady Lives of the Ku Klux Klan," *Time*, April 9, 1965, 85. For contemporaneous news coverage identifying the Klan with the measure, see, for example, "Kuklux School Bill Is Approved in Oregon," *Washington Post*, Nov. 10, 1922, 1; and "The Oregon School Law," *New York Times*, Aug. 5, 1923, E4.

The Klan's support for compulsory public schooling may confound readers today. If the KKK believed in the superiority of Anglo-Saxon Protestants, after all, one might think that Klansmen would view the prospect of having Catholics and immigrants educated in their own, isolated institutions as optimal. The Klan's internal ideological tensions on this front seem insoluble. As one volume has insightfully put the point, the Klan's support for the Oregon measure was animated by "a peculiar mix of fear, paranoia, nostalgia, and hope," as "conflicting assumptions about heredity and environment sat side by side in mute antagonism." David Tyack, Thomas James, and Aaron Benavot, *Law and the Shaping of Public Education, 1785–1954* 177 (1987).

strain the imagination to improve upon the actual party at the center of the case. The Society of the Sisters of the Holy Names of Jesus and Mary had been educating children—including many orphans—in Portland, Oregon, dating back to 1859, the year that the territory obtained statehood. The Catholic institution's inaugural class was composed of three Catholics, two Jews, and one Episcopalian, and the nuns who administered its various schools within the state continued to pride themselves on their student body's diverse religious affiliations and their refusal to encroach upon their students' religious scruples. The Society of Sisters was also fondly remembered for demonstrating unusual bravery in the course of combating a smallpox epidemic that plagued Oregon during the nineteenth century.[60]

In 1925, Justice McReynolds wrote a succinct opinion for a unanimous Court in *Pierce v. Society of Sisters* that depicted the invalidation of Oregon's measure as following virtually a fortiori from *Meyer v. Nebraska*—decided only two years prior. McReynolds, as he had in *Meyer*, identified particular issues of state authority involving education that the lawsuit did not even purport to dispute in this case, including the "reasonabl[e] regulat[ion of] all schools, . . . that certain studies plainly essential to good citizenship . . . be taught, and that nothing be taught which is manifestly inimical to the public welfare."[61] Yet, McReynolds continued, states' authority over educational matters should not be mistaken for unbridled discretion. Oregon exceeded the bounds of its discretionary authority, according to McReynolds, because the law amounted to "unreasonabl[e] interfere[nce] with the liberty of parents and guardians to direct the upbringing and education of children under their control."[62] McReynolds contended that the Fourteenth Amendment's Due Process Clause ensures that states do not possess "any general power . . . to standardize [their] children by forcing them to accept instruction from public teachers only." *Society of Sisters* then distilled this constitutional principle into a brilliant epigram, one that has, in subsequent decades, been repeated an untold number of times in widely varying contexts. "The child," McReynolds wrote, "is not the mere creature of the state."[63]

In contrast to the generally ambivalent reception that newspapers accorded *Meyer*, journalists overwhelmingly praised *Society of Sisters*. The *Los Angeles Times* observed the measure "was based on hatred" and crowed that "[f]riends of justice rejoice that a body blow has been struck by the United States Supreme Court against the outrageously intolerant Oregon school law."[64] *The New York Times* viewed the decision through a similar prism, calling the law "one of the most hateful by-products of the Ku Klux movement," and contending "it was plainly directed most intolerantly at a single class."[65] Yet perhaps the most remarkable aspect of the rapturous response was how McReynolds's newly coined ten-word aphorism shaped, and even dominated, editorial coverage of the opinion. *The Boston Globe*, in an editorial titled "Child Is Not the Mere Creature of the State," quoted the line in its opening sentence and hailed it as an "outstanding declaration."[66] The *Chicago Tribune*'s editorial also quoted the line approvingly and condemned Oregon's measure as "a throwback to the age of religious intolerance, an age in which religious zealots seized the powers of government to impose their creeds upon their fellow men."[67] Even when popular periodicals did not directly quote McReynolds's pithy language, moreover, its shadow often loomed large and appeared to influence the coverage.[68]*

Within legal academia, contemporaneous scholarship generally approved of the Court's outcome in *Society of Sisters*, as commentators noted—echoing both Justice McReynolds and journalists— that Oregon's measure represented an unprecedented, unjustified intrusion into the child-parent relationship. But the opinion's academic detractors, while comparatively small in number, offered observations far more noteworthy than its more numerous supporters. An article appearing in the *Virginia Law Register* lambasted the Court's decision as improperly treading on educational terrain— a place where the views of Washington, D.C., should be wholly irrelevant. Framing this critique in language that reads almost as self-satirical, the *Register* protested that the opinion would have severely displeased the Sage of Monticello: "[W]e wonder . . . whether the soul of Thomas Jefferson would not have wept aloud if it could see the interference of the Federal government through its courts with his pet school system."[69]

---

* *The Washington Post* also commented that the thinking behind Oregon's law left "only the logical further step of putting all children in uniform garb and giving each a number by which to be known instead of a family name." "The Blight of Standardization," *Washington Post*, June 7, 1925, E1. Although schools within the United States have not yet attempted to substitute numbers for family names, school uniform policies are now rampant. For background and a criticism of these policies, see chapter 2.

Professor Felix Frankfurter, however, offered the most search-ing and durable critique of the decision, advancing his views in an unsigned editorial for *The New Republic* titled "Can the Supreme Court Guarantee Toleration?" Ultimately, Frankfurter would answer the question posed in this headline with a resounding no. But the route that he took to reach this destination was a rather winding one. Tracking Frankfurter's path in some detail here is nec-essary because, even after becoming an associate justice, he would retrace his steps in a high-profile judicial opinion involving schools. Frankfurter began by noting that "[t]he Oregon decision, like its Nebraska forerunner, . . . gives just cause for rejoicing" because the Court performed "immediate service on behalf of the essen-tial spirit of liberalism."[70] Nevertheless, Frankfurter insisted, this pair of recent opinions ought not be considered in isolation: "In rejoicing over the Nebraska and the Oregon cases, we must not forget that a heavy price has to be paid for these occasional services to liberalism."[71] Frankfurter noted that the Court had in recent decades repeatedly harmed the cause of liberalism by invalidating legislation designed to help laborers, including requirements for both minimum wages and maximum hours. Frankfurter contended that the Court's finding in those notorious cases that such legisla-tion violated the Due Process Clause's protection of "liberty"—the very same constitutional provision at issue in its two recent school opinions—should cause liberals to understand all too well how such indeterminate language can be used to nullify beneficial measures, as well as benighted ones.

Frankfurter then advanced what, at least in retrospect, can be understood as his judicial restraint apologia—not in the sense of offering regret, but instead as providing a grand explanation for his worldview. When assessing the "promotion of the liberal spirit by the Supreme Court's invalidation of illiberal legislation," Frank-furter ventured,

> [i]t must never be forgotten that our constant preoccupation with the constitutionality of legislation rather than its wisdom tends to preoccupation of the American mind with a false value. . . . [T]he tendency of focusing attention on constitutionality is to make constitutionality synonymous with propriety; to regard a law as all right so long as it is "constitutional." Such an attitude is a great enemy of liberalism. Particularly in legislation affecting

freedom of thought and freedom of speech much that is highly illiberal would be clearly constitutional. Reliance for the most precious interests of civilization, therefore, must be found outside of their vindication under the guarantees of the Constitution— particularly as those guarantees are likely to be construed in the future as they have been in the past.[72]

In Frankfurter's holistic appraisal, the liabilities imposed by the Supreme Court's invalidation of legislation exceeded any advantages it conferred. The same ends, Frankfurter hastened to add, could also be obtained through democratic means. "[T]he hysteria and chauvinism that forbade the teaching of German in Nebraska schools may subside, and with its subsidence bring repeal of the silly measure," Frankfurter noted, and Oregonians similarly may well overturn by referendum their abolition of nonpublic schools "with invigorated effort on the part of the liberal forces."[73] Frankfurter concluded his essay with a rhetorical flourish. "[H]ere is ample warning to the liberal forces that the real battles of liberalism are not won in the Supreme Court," Frankfurter wrote. "To a large extent the Supreme Court . . . is the reflector of . . . the general drift of public opinion. Only a persistent, positive translation of the liberal faith into the thoughts and acts of the community is the real reliance against the unabated temptation to straightjacket the human mind."[74] When Frankfurter exchanged the professor's tweed jacket for the judge's black robe fourteen years after writing these words, he would not jettison these philosophical commitments concerning the proper judicial function.

At first blush, *Society of Sisters* might be interpreted as a case of marginal consequence to the nation. After all, unlike the language bans in *Meyer* that were prevalent throughout the country, Oregon was the only state that had ever enacted a measure mandating attendance at public schools when the Court declared such legislation unconstitutional. Indeed, distinguished constitutional theorists have advanced this view minimizing the decision's importance. But it would be severely mistaken to believe that simply because Oregon was the first state to abolish nonpublic schools, it would necessarily have been the last. Catholic leaders, for example, expressed fears that Oregon's measure represented only an early skirmish in a forthcoming war on Catholic education across the country. Nor is it possible to reject this concern as irrational. On the heels of the

Oregon referendum, the *Los Angeles Times* reported in 1922 that "[m]any regard the measure as the first step in a campaign to close all private elementary schools over the entire country. Thus they invest the movement with a national significance."[75] One year later, *The New York Times* noted that Oregon's campaign had inspired similar nativist movements to abolish nonpublic schools in California and Washington and that they awaited only judicial resolution of the matter before seeking to implement their plans. One reliable source has suggested that at least ten additional states had active plans to eradicate private and parochial schools when the Court issued *Society of Sisters*, and another has remarked that the opinion held "momentous significance to all the country."[76]

Rather than viewing the Court's decision in *Society of Sisters* as restricting an isolated statute, then, it seems far more accurate to understand the opinion as a nationally significant judicial intervention that defended minority rights, protected parental authority, and imposed a meaningful limitation on the states' ability to control education. It also seems mere wishful thinking to believe, with Professor Frankfurter, that the Oregon statute would have disappeared through nonjudicial means. At the time, several observers credited the Supreme Court with performing a valuable service for constitutional democracy that they believed would otherwise have gone unfulfilled. The *New York Times* editorial board commented, "The need of having some Federal tribunal to maintain the rights of the citizen when they are invaded by local legislation has never been more evident than in the case of this Oregon School law."[77] The *Chicago Tribune* viewed *Society of Sisters* in much the same light, as it identified Oregon's statute along with Nebraska's language ban as instances that illustrate "[t]he vital importance of retaining in the courts the power to protect the rights of the individual. . . . Both cases are good examples, not merely of what may happen, but of what most certainly will happen, if there is no independent and judicially trained agency to insist upon constitutional rights."[78]

Since *Meyer v. Nebraska* and *Pierce v. Society of Sisters* were decided more than nine decades ago, the legacies of these two opinions have remained closely linked. Writing in *American Constitutional Law* in 1978, Professor Laurence Tribe commented that the two decisions were "nearly always cited in tandem" and further noted that they retained their vitality as founts of constitutional doctrine: "The cardinal principle animating the Court's decisions . . .

was that the state had no power to 'standardize its children' [*Pierce*] or 'foster a homogeneous people' [*Meyer*] by completely foreclosing the opportunity of individuals and groups to heed the music of different drummers."[79] It is a testament to how widely accepted these two decisions are that—even though their reliance on substantive due process marks them as part of a notorious era at the Supreme Court—legal thinkers as varied as Judge Robert Bork, Justice William O. Douglas, and Justice Anthony Kennedy have all at various times sought not to dismantle the precedents but instead to place the opinions on sturdier textual foundations. Rather than relying upon the notion of "liberty" contained in the Fourteenth Amendment's Due Process Clause, each of these jurists has suggested the school-related opinions could have been justified under the First Amendment's freedom of speech, or perhaps even the First Amendment's free exercise of religion (at least as applied to the Society of Sisters organization).[80]* Whatever their precise doctrinal foundations, though, the pair of opinions continues to command esteem in the nation's constitutional discourse. When the Supreme Court recognized a constitutional right to same-sex marriage in 2015, for example, Justice Kennedy's opinion for the Court prominently cited both *Meyer* and *Society of Sisters* as supporting that proposition. Although four justices dissented from that decision, not one of them questioned the legitimacy of either *Meyer* or *Society of Sisters*. Today, rejecting the outcomes in those foundational school opinions, which have become pillars of our modern legal framework, places one well outside the constitutional mainstream.[81]

FARRINGTON V. TOKUSHIGE:
THE BIRTH OF CONSTITUTIONAL RIGHTS FOR STUDENTS

In the final installment of its trio of cases evaluating assimilative efforts during the 1920s, the Supreme Court in *Farrington v. Tokushige* invalidated a Hawaiian measure that extensively regulated the territory's foreign-language schools. Unlike its two companion decisions, *Tokushige* has now receded into obscurity in the field of

---

* The primary reason that the original opinions in *Meyer* and *Society of Sisters* would not have relied upon the First Amendment stemmed from the fact that it was not then clear that the Bill of Rights' protections applied to actions taken by state governments, as compared with the federal government.

constitutional law. Its arcane status is regrettable for many reasons, not least because the opinion represented the first time that the Court vindicated a claim in a school case and expressly acknowledged that the constitutional rights at stake belonged to students themselves, rather than flowing only from their parents and teachers. Even if this acknowledgment was fleeting, *Tokushige* nevertheless marked a noteworthy development, as the decision heralded the shape of things to come in education law.

The dispute in *Tokushige* arose from the procedures that Hawaii introduced during the early 1920s to combat what it regarded as the excessive influence of the more than 160 foreign-language schools that existed within the territory. Hawaiian students of Asian descent overwhelmingly attended traditional public schools, where classroom instruction occurred in English. But many of these students supplemented that education outside typical school hours with study in private language academies, where they learned to speak Chinese, Korean, or—most commonly—Japanese. The new regulations invaded almost every aspect of the foreign-language schools' administration, as—among other initiatives—Hawaii aimed to exercise curricular control, collect annual fees on a per-pupil basis, prohibit students from taking any lessons until after second grade, restrict students' attendance to no more than one hour per day, and require teachers to obtain a government permit indicating they satisfactorily knew "American history and institutions" and were "possessed of the ideals of democracy." Hawaii sought to distinguish the Court's recent ruling in *Meyer* by contending that it imposed mere *regulations* upon the foreign-language schools, whereas Nebraska had enacted outright *prohibitions* on teaching foreign languages. But as the measure's more candid supporters conceded, it sought less to adjust the language schools than to eliminate them. As one unguarded backer of the procedures contended, "A condition of things had developed in Hawaii which could no longer be tolerated—two antagonistic systems of education in the same country teaching the same children!" It was particularly urgent to assimilate the children of Hawaii's largest ethnic subgroup, this proponent continued, because many residents hailed from "the most backward sections of the Japanese empire; sheltered nooks where the customs and ideas of old Japan still lingered."[82]

In 1927, Justice McReynolds (yet again) wrote a concise opinion for the Court in *Tokushige* that rejected Hawaii's efforts to differentiate its measure from Nebraska's legislation in *Meyer*. In practical terms, McReynolds emphasized, no meaningful distance separated the two scenarios, as enforcement of Hawaii's regulations would "destroy most, if not all, of [the foreign-language schools]."[83] McReynolds acknowledged "the grave problems incident to the large alien population of the Hawaiian Islands," and suggested that those problems "should be given due weight," but he insisted that "the limitations of the Constitution must not be transcended."[84] Just as McReynolds had previously construed Nebraska's law as driven by anti-German sentiment in *Meyer*, moreover, he construed Hawaii's measure as motivated by hostility toward Japan in *Tokushige*: "The Japanese parent has the right to direct the education of his own child without unreasonable restrictions; the Constitution protects him as well as those who speak another tongue."[85] While that statement retained the traditional lens of parents' authority over their offspring, elsewhere in the opinion McReynolds portrayed *Meyer* and *Society of Sisters* as having instructed that students themselves also possessed at least some constitutional rights in the educational sphere. Referring to those recent precedents, *Tokushige* provided that "[t]he general doctrine touching rights guaranteed by the Fourteenth Amendment to owners, parents *and children* in respect of attendance upon schools has been announced in recent opinions."[86]* *Tokushige* did not tarry on the point for long, but its brief summary of the most relevant precedents also succeeded in subtly extending them.

Many commentators condemned *Tokushige*. The *New York Times*, for example, asserted the opinion will "make more difficult the task of the Hawaiian Government in dealing with the complex racial problems of the islands," and feared that teaching foreign "languages . . . in accordance with the traditions of other lands, [would] . . . accentuate rather than weaken racial barriers."[87] A few months later, moreover, the *Times* editorial board revisited Hawaii's foreign-language schools and contended "the real question seems to be whether the Hawaiian Islands . . . are to become Oriental or Occidental."[88] *The Honolulu Advertiser* largely assessed *Tokushige*

* Hawaii's status as a federal territory—not a state—technically meant that *Tokushige* invoked the Fifth Amendment's Due Process Clause, rather than the Fourteenth Amendment's Due Process Clause, which binds the states. But the different source of controlling constitutional authority in *Tokushige* does not otherwise alter the underlying legal analysis.

through this same framework, as it deemed the schools "alien and oriental in a community which is becoming more occidental," and further proclaimed that "[u]nited popular sentiment in Hawaii still holds that the double educational system is not good for the children."[89]* But feelings on the islands toward the schools were, of course, a good deal more complicated than this tidy account suggested. The *Hawaii Herehi*, a Japanese-language newspaper, celebrated *Tokushige* as a miraculous judicial intervention that spared precious cultural institutions: "Suddenly out of a clear sky came the news of great victory of Japanese-language schools. . . . We worship the Supreme Court of the United States as God who protects the Constitution."[90]

Tokushige richly illustrates how a judicial defense of constitutional rights can sometimes inspire subordinated members of society to assert their own constitutional claims. After Hawaii introduced its new procedures, foreign-language schools generally accepted the regulations as a fait accompli. The Supreme Court's invalidation of the language statute in *Meyer*, however, provided a beam of hope that the judiciary might also set aside Hawaii's regulations and motivated more than half of the Japanese-language schools to litigate the issue during the summer of 1923.[91] This broad assertion of rights, in turn, enabled the Court to reaffirm *Meyer* and provided an opportunity to build upon it. *Tokushige* thus advanced the burgeoning notion that governmental entities do not exercise unfettered discretion over educational matters, and solidified the foundation for bringing the Constitution to bear within the corridors of the nation's public schools.

One final issue requires addressing here: Justice McReynolds wrote each of these three decisions rejecting school-related efforts to mandate assimilation during the 1920s, and his close association with this set of opinions has—in more recent decades—elicited a mixture of anxiety and embarrassment within constitutional law circles. Some portion of this discomfort stems from the fact that Justice McReynolds was, even as assessed by the standards of his

---

* Some indication of the intensity of anti-Japanese attitudes within the United States during the 1920s can be found in a front-page *Washington Post* article that commended imposing regulations on foreign-language schools: "The Japanese are not naturally assimilable. . . . American-born Japanese are American citizens, but anti-American at heart." Arthur Sears Henning, "Future of Hawaii Overshadowed by Tokyo's Influence," *Washington Post*, May 20, 1925, 1.

own time, a deeply unpleasant bigot. Professor Michael Klarman of Harvard has, along with many others, called McReynolds a "notorious racist and anti-Semite."[92] A particularly graphic manifestation of McReynolds's racism occurred in 1938, when he swiveled his chair to turn his back on an eminent black lawyer who appeared before the justices to present oral argument. McReynolds's anti-Semitism prevented the Supreme Court from having an official photograph taken to commemorate one term because he refused to pose for the portrait seated next to a Jewish colleague, as the Court's internal protocol would have dictated. If anything, though, Professor Klarman's indictment of McReynolds—damning though it is—leaves significant conduct uncharged. It omits, for example, that McReynolds also exhibited shameless misogyny. On a rare occasion when a woman argued before the Court during this era, McReynolds immediately exited the courtroom, muttering, "I see that the female is here."[93] McReynolds's position as an associate justice was also evidently owed to his nasty temperament, as President Woodrow Wilson reportedly placed the former attorney general on the Court largely to remove McReynolds from his cabinet.

An additional portion of this discomfort, however, stems more overtly from McReynolds's jurisprudential views. McReynolds's career was marked by a commitment to laissez-faire economics and a concomitant disapproval of legislative regulation of the economy, which resulted in his voting to invalidate progressive state laws and New Deal legislation. Given that many lawyers today view these positions as reactionary, some observers take McReynolds's authorship of *Meyer, Society of Sisters,* and *Tokushige* as unmistakable proof that they are in effect the fruits of a poisonous tree.[94]

While apprehension surrounding McReynolds's association with these three opinions is certainly understandable, it also seems time to lay it to rest. American history is littered with figures who, though in many ways admirable, also articulated some odious views; it seems only fitting that there should be at least a few figures who, while generally odious, were capable of admirable utterances. Even if McReynolds's resonant language does not fully counterbalance his serious personal and judicial failings, moreover, it seems churlish to remove that language from his ledger altogether. Justice McReynolds could certainly have written the opinions in these three cases solely to vindicate the economic interests of private and parochial schools. While the opinions contain some language striking that theme, McReynolds nevertheless decided to frame these opinions far more broadly, making it clear that the Constitution's protections extend to noneconomic interests. It seems deeply misguided to treat McReynolds's lasting language in these opinions as the product of a sort of unwitting judicial accident, rather than as the knowing articulation of deeply held constitutional principles that many people continue to extol today. Just because an unsavory character voices an idea does not render the idea itself unsavory. McReynolds's unwarranted skepticism of state economic regulations should not be permitted to cast a pall over his quite warranted refusal to rubber-stamp state educational regulations.[95]

WEST VIRGINIA STATE BOARD OF EDUCATION V. BARNETTE: THE FLAG SALUTE REVISITED

In January 1942, a teacher at Slip Hill Grade School, located just outside Charleston, West Virginia, apologetically informed Marie and Gathie Barnette that they were no longer welcome at the school. The Barnette sisters—the only two Jehovah's Witness students at Slip Hill—had committed "insubordination" by refusing to recite the Pledge of Allegiance on account of their religious faith. Although the teacher volunteered that she disagreed with these expulsions, the call was not hers to make. Earlier that month, the West Virginia Board of Education enacted a compulsory flag-salute measure that barred students from school unless they joined their classmates in reciting the pledge. The ordinance's language consisted largely of quotations drawn from Justice Frankfurter's opinion in *Gobitis*, where the Supreme Court upheld, but did not mandate, flag-salute requirements in schools. Apart from barring noncompliant students from public education, West Virginia's statute threatened additional, devastating consequences for students and their families. Expelled students would be deemed "unlawfully absent" from school, a marker that permitted the state to initiate juvenile delinquency proceedings, which in turn could result in the children being sent to live in reformatories. Their parents, meanwhile, could be prosecuted for child neglect and upon conviction faced a jail term of thirty days and a fifty-dollar fine. That last penalty, even standing alone, would have posed a major threat to the Barnettes, who eked out an unsteady subsistence based on the father's job as an assistant pipe fitter at the local DuPont plant. Despite having powerful incentives to cave in to the state's pressure and simply recite the pledge, the Barnettes adhered to their religious convictions and joined a lawsuit challenging the West Virginia statute.[96]

Some evidence indicated that the Barnettes' legal challenge would fail. The Supreme Court had, of course, rejected a virtually identical lawsuit to the Barnettes' only two years earlier, and such rapid about-faces have been extraordinarily rare events throughout the Court's history. Following *Gobitis*, moreover, compulsory flag-salute requirements became increasingly prevalent across the country, as schools in only scattered states expelled Jehovah's Witnesses for the offense prior to the opinion, but schools in every state expelled students afterward. The marked popularity of the compulsory flag-salute practice—at least among many citizens in small communities—could quite plausibly be understood to undermine the likelihood that the Court would agree to reject the measure.*

Nevertheless, these matters were more than offset by the countervailing considerations suggesting that the Barnettes would prevail. The media's reaction to *Gobitis* evinced overwhelming contempt. The *St. Louis Post-Dispatch* offered a particularly barbed, but not substantively peculiar, critique:

> We think this decision . . . is dead wrong. We think [it] is a violation of American principle. We think it is a surrender to popular hysteria. If patriotism depends on such things as this—on violation of the fundamental right of religious freedom, then it becomes not a noble emotion of love for country, but something to be rammed down our throats by the law.[97]

Legal audiences also roundly condemned *Gobitis*. Professor Fred Rodell of Yale called *Gobitis* "the Court's most anti-liberal decision

---

* Support for the notion that *Barnette* would have been unpopular among most Americans can be found in contemporaneous newspaper coverage. Arthur Krock commented that while the Court "has often justified Mr. Dooley's statement that it follows the election returns," *Barnette* should not be viewed as ratifying popular opinion. "Today was one of those when the Supreme Court rose to its full height as champion of the lowly," he contended. Arthur Krock, "The Supreme Court at Its Peak," *New York Times*, June 15, 1943, 20.

in years," as, "in effect, [Frankfurter's opinion had] ordered the children to 'Heil.' "[98]* Professor Edward Corwin of Princeton called *Gobitis* "distasteful" and ridiculed "Frankfurter's smug assumption that the Court [possessed] a patent formula which enables it . . . to dispense with exercising its own judgment."[99] In addition, post-*Gobitis*, vigilantes inflicted violence against Jehovah's Witnesses in a wave of ugly incidents that occurred across the country—from Kennebunk, Maine, to Jackson, Mississippi. In one searing incident, the sheriff of a southern hamlet watched without objection as a mob used menacing tactics to drive a small group of families on a forced march toward the outskirts of town. When a reporter inquired what provoked the strife, the sheriff responded, "Jehovah's Witnesses. . . . They're traitors—the Supreme Court says so. Ain't you heard?"[100] Many observers, including the U.S. Department of Justice, drew a direct causal link between *Gobitis* and the surging violence against Jehovah's Witnesses. Finally, and most important, some individual justices made public statements that left little doubt that the pledge requirements would be invalidated if the issue returned to the Court. In one case that had nothing to do with the pledge, three Supreme Court justices who joined the Court's opinion in *Gobitis* went out of their way to repudiate their prior votes, expressly calling the precedent "wrongly decided."[101] Shortly before his appointment to the Court, moreover, Attorney General Robert Jackson published a book that derided *Gobitis*. These four seemingly assured votes against the pledge requirements—combined with the vote of Chief Justice Harlan Fiske Stone, who had dissented in *Gobitis*—provided the Barnettes with a firm basis for hoping that at least a five-justice majority supported their position when the Court heard oral argument in March 1943.

A little more than three months later, Justice Robert Jackson vindicated those hopes by writing an opinion for the Court in *West Virginia State Board of Education v. Barnette*, declaring it unconsti-

---

* Professor Rodell was not the only commentator who likened Minersville's stance on the Pledge of Allegiance to the practices of Nazi Germany. Even before the Court's decision in *Gobitis*, the *New York Herald Tribune* observed, "To compel school children to salute the flag is a step in the 'Heil Hitler' direction." "The Flag-Salute Issue," *New York Herald Tribune*, April 29, 1940, 14. Similarly, in one of its many editorial comments on the case, *The New Republic* observed, "[W]e are sure that the majority members of our Court who concurred in the Frankfurter decision would be embarrassed to know that their attitude was in substance the same as that of the German tribunal." "Unser Gott and Jehovah's Witnesses," *New Republic*, Aug. 5, 1940, 174.

tutional to expel public school students for refusing to recite the Pledge of Allegiance. In timing that seems too perfect to be sheer coincidence, the decision arrived on June 14, 1943: Flag Day. No less an authority than Judge Richard Posner has contended that Justice Jackson's work in *Barnette* "may be the most eloquent majority opinion in the history of the Supreme Court."[102]* The only objectionable portion of Posner's assessment is his qualification: Justice Jackson was the single finest writer in the Court's history, and *Barnette* finds him at the apex of his authorial powers. Indeed, whatever Supreme Court majority opinion might claim the runner-up spot in eloquence lags so far behind *Barnette* as to render the event no contest at all.

Even apart from the opinion's fine prose, however, *Barnette* stands out for making three primary substantive innovations that appear at the intersection of constitutional law and education law. First, as a matter of constitutional doctrine, Justice Jackson dramatically reconceptualized the pledge requirement as raising a question not about the First Amendment's freedom of religion but about the First Amendment's freedom of speech. The positive right to speak, Jackson reasoned, necessarily also entailed a negative right—the right not to speak, a constitutional doctrine that has exerted great influence beyond the schooling context.† By reframing the debate in these terms, Jackson made the question not whether the religious beliefs of Jehovah's Witnesses ought to permit them—and them alone—to avoid the pledge but instead whether people of all backgrounds have an interest in avoiding government-compelled speech. Elaborating upon this free speech framework, Jackson suggested that tolerating nonconformity, and even dissidence, was essential to enabling this unusually diverse nation to function: "We can have intellectual individualism and the rich cultural diversities that we owe to exceptional minds only at the price of occasional

---

* As might be expected, the majestic quality of Justice Jackson's prose in *Barnette* made an immediate impression. *Time*, for example, reprinted a few striking lines from what it called *Barnette*'s "ringing polysyllables." "Blot Removed," *Time*, June 21, 1943, 16. Relatedly, *The Christian Century* proclaimed that portions of *Barnette* "should become part of the 'American Scriptures,' to be memorized and taken to heart by every patriot." "Court Upholds Freedom of Conscience," *Christian Century*, June 23, 1943, 731.

† For a high-profile instance of *Barnette*'s influence beyond the educational realm, see *Wooley v. Maynard*, 430 U.S. 705 (1977) (invalidating New Hampshire's effort to require cars to display its "Live Free or Die" motto on license plates when drivers objected).

eccentricity and abnormal attitudes."[103] For Jackson, it was precisely because the American flag embodied freedom that requiring
students to recite the pledge would represent a subversion of that
freedom and the imposition of an ideological orthodoxy that was
in some meaningful sense un-American. In a particularly inspired
passage, Jackson delivered this point by drawing upon the iconog-
raphy of the American flag itself to suggest that genuine patriots
would support the Court's outcome in *Barnette:* "If there is any fixed
star in our constitutional constellation, it is that no official, high or
petty, can prescribe what shall be orthodox in politics, nationalism,
religion, or other matters of opinion or force citizens to confess by
word or act their faith therein."[104]

Second, in terms of the judicial duty, Jackson's opinion in *Barnette* innovated by insisting that courts play an indispensable constitutional role in monitoring public schools, and by observing,
conversely, that granting local authorities overly broad control over
educational matters could present a recipe for ruin. *Barnette* directly
repudiated the notion *Gobitis* advanced three years earlier suggesting that judges should construe schoolhouse affairs as beyond their
comprehension: "[W]e act in these [schoolhouse] matters not by
authority of our competence but by force of our commissions."[105]
Instead of portraying the federal government's involvement with
schools as an unwarranted affront to the natural order of things,
Jackson upended the traditional idea that local authority over education was, from a constitutional perspective, necessarily a virtue.
"Such Boards [of Education] are numerous and their territorial jurisdiction often small," Jackson wrote. "But small and local authority
may feel less sense of responsibility to the Constitution. . . . There
are village tyrants as well as village Hampdens, but none who acts
under color of law is beyond reach of the Constitution."[106]*

---

* *Barnette*'s usage of the term "village Hampdens" alludes to Thomas Gray's indelible
poem, which runs in relevant part:

> Some village-Hampden, that with dauntless breast
> The little tyrant of his fields withstood;
> Some mute inglorious Milton here may rest,
> Some Cromwell guiltless of his country's blood.

Thomas Gray, *Elegy Written in a Country Churchyard* (1751). But, for many readers
today, the next question becomes, who was Hampden? In the seventeenth century, John
Hampden was an English politician who won fame for refusing to pay a tax assessed by
King Charles I, the "little tyrant" of Gray's poem. The "village tyrants," in Justice Jack-

Third, and closely related to the previous point, Justice Jackson in *Barnette* fundamentally reconceived the constitutional relationship between the school and the citizen. For Justice Frankfurter in *Gobitis*, schools could demand obedience from students toward the pledge in order to foster unity in a nation made up of disparate groups: "A society which is dedicated to the preservation of these ultimate values of civilization may in self-protection utilize the educational process for inculcating those almost unconscious feelings which bind men together in a comprehending loyalty, whatever may be their lesser differences and difficulties."[107] In *Barnette*, however, Justice Jackson emphasized quite distinct priorities. Even as educators enjoy considerable discretion in carrying out their functions, Jackson contended, it was essential that schools honor the constitutional rights of their students. If schools were to trample the constitutional rights of their young citizens, the long-term societal consequences would be disastrous. As Jackson expressed this notion memorably, ignoring the Constitution's protections in public schools would "strangle the free mind at its source and teach youth to discount important principles of our government as mere platitudes."[108]

In response to *Barnette*, Justice Frankfurter filed an intensely personal, highly acerbic dissent. It requires neither extraordinary powers of perception nor psychological acuity to appreciate that *Barnette*'s reversal of his three-year-old opinion in *Gobitis* deeply wounded Frankfurter. In his opening lines, Frankfurter alluded not only to his Jewish background but also to his history as a founder of the American Civil Liberties Union (ACLU). "One who belongs to the most vilified and persecuted minority in history is not likely to be insensible to the freedoms guaranteed by our Constitution," Frankfurter began. "Were my purely personal attitude relevant I should whole-heartedly associate myself with the general libertarian views in the Court's opinion, representing as they do the thought and action of a lifetime. But as judges we are neither Jew nor Gentile, neither Catholic nor agnostic."[109] With these declarations, Frankfurter effectively stated: I am a Jew, I am a civil libertarian, and I am a judge, and it is only the last of these three identities that guides my

---

son's phrase, thus suggests that autocratic overreach can occur at various governmental levels, including the local. For an exegesis of Hampden's life, see Winston Churchill, "A History of the English Speaking Peoples," *Life*, Nov. 12, 1956, 179, 184.

decision here. Frankfurter's personalization of the case (particularly with respect to his religious background) rankled his colleagues at the moment and has preoccupied scholars ever since.

Regrettably, however, this fixation on Frankfurter's opening has eclipsed some of the intriguing material that subsequently appeared in his dissent. For example, Justice Frankfurter's dissent in *Barnette* contained two notable echoes from prior writing. Seeking to align his position with an esteemed, earlier proponent of judicial restraint, Frankfurter used strikingly similar syntax to a passage that appeared in Justice Holmes's dissent on the language bans twenty years earlier. In his homage to Holmes, whom Frankfurter knew and revered, he noted, "I think I appreciate fully the objections to the law before us. But to deny that it presents a question upon which men might reasonably differ appears to me to be intolerance."[110] Even more significantly, though, Frankfurter's dissent in *Barnette* also borrowed extensively—and without acknowledgment—language from his *New Republic* article in 1925, where he warned against the Court's invalidating the statutes at issue in *Meyer v. Nebraska* and *Pierce v. Society of Sisters*. The following quotation appears in Frankfurter's dissent, and the italicized portions previously appeared in his magazine article:

> Of course patriotism cannot be enforced by the flag salute. But neither can *the liberal spirit* be enforced *by* judicial *invalidation of illiberal legislation. Our constant preoccupation with the constitutionality of legislation rather than with its wisdom tends to preoccupation of the American mind with a false value. The tendency of focusing attention on constitutionality is to make constitutionality synonymous with* wisdom, *to regard a law as all right if it is constitutional. Such an attitude is a great enemy of liberalism. Particularly in legislation affecting freedom of thought and freedom of speech much* which should offend a free-spirited society is *constitutional. Reliance for the most precious interests of civilization, therefore, must be found outside of their vindication* in courts of law. *Only a persistent positive translation of the faith* of a free society *into the* convictions and habits *and* actions *of* a *community is the* ultimate *reliance against unabated temptations to* fetter *the human* spirit.[111]

Frankfurter's broad appropriation of identical language that he wrote before ascending to the bench is highly anomalous; indeed,

I am aware of no other instance where a Supreme Court justice has ever included such sustained pre-published material in a judicial opinion. It seems unlikely, though, that Frankfurter was much concerned about his replication becoming detected because, while his initial article appeared nearly two decades before *Barnette*, the piece also appeared in a collection of Frankfurter's pre-judicial writings that was published shortly after his confirmation to the Court in 1939.[112]

Journalists nearly across the board praised *Barnette*. Understandably, much of the editorial coverage portrayed the opinion as an act of atonement for the Court's judicial sin from 1940. In this vein, an article in *Time*—evocatively headlined "Blot Removed"—contended that *Barnette* "reaffirmed [the Court's] faith in the Bill of Rights—which, in 1940, it had come perilously close to outlawing."[113] Similarly, *America* construed *Barnette* as tantamount to a restoration, and even an extension, of the nation's central commitments: "By reversing the *Gobitis* decision of three years ago the Supreme Court has added new glory to Old Glory."[114] Several observers found it remarkable and commendable that the Supreme Court issued the decision, even though it meant protecting a widely disparaged group in American society. "The principles of Jehovah's Witnesses can be pretty annoying to the majority of citizens," *The Saturday Evening Post* wrote. "They insist on propagating their beliefs at the most inconvenient times and places, and they make no concessions to the sensibilities of the majority. To our way of thinking, this makes all the more impressive the action of the court."[115]

The Supreme Court's willingness to issue *Barnette* in the midst of the nation's involvement in World War II struck many observers as adding to the decision's luster. According to *The Wall Street Journal*, *Barnette* arrived "at the time when it is, perhaps, most needed," as "[w]e are in a war for our very life," and it was never more imperative to reject the view that minority rights are "privileges or acts of grace by an omnipotent state which can be withdrawn at any time when the majority which happens to exercise the State's power chooses to do so."[116] A columnist for *The New York Times* brought *Barnette*'s wartime implications into more dramatic focus still: "At home, the decision was a warning to professional patriots and ardent flag wavers to control their emotions. Abroad, it was a clear contradiction of the Hitler method—that every child, indeed every grown-up, must learn to click his heels, salute and shout 'Heil Hitler.'"[117]

Law professors also generally applauded *Barnette*, as favorable commentary outstripped critical commentary by a ratio of more than four to one. Among *Barnette* enthusiasts, the response offered by Professor Thomas Reed Powell of Harvard was particularly notable. Justice Frankfurter's dissent severely erred, according to Powell, by contending that judicial restraint was equally imperative in cases involving civil liberties as in cases involving economic regulations. In addition, unlike most other academic observers, Powell astutely grasped that Justice Jackson's opinion offered protection to both religious and nonreligious objectors who wished to remain silent: "The freedom of silence and the freedom of abstention extend to those who have other than religious objections to compulsion of public avowals."[118] In contrast, Professor Madaline Kinter Remmlein exhibited considerable misapprehension on precisely this point, as she read *Barnette* as a religion-based decision that foretold chaos. "Like the camel which got its head into the tent," Remmlein wrote, "religious minorities may be expected to press upon the courts enlarged immunities based upon the new freedom accorded them."[119] But Remmlein's more fundamental objection to *Barnette* stemmed from her view that it improperly encroached on schools' authority. "Educators may well fear that the Supreme Court has indeed made itself the 'school board for the country,'" she contended.[120] If the Pledge of Allegiance should be made noncompulsory, Remmlein maintained, that determination properly belonged to educators or legislators, not federal judges.

The legacy of Justice Jackson's opinion in *Barnette* is among the most meaningful in the field of education law and beyond. *Barnette* marked the first significant decision where the Supreme Court declared that the Constitution protects students within the corridors of the nation's public schools. By authorizing students to avoid participating in a pervasive ritual that begins school days across the country, the Court selected a highly salient moment to indicate that educators did not possess absolute command over their pupils. While as a formal matter *Barnette* merely conferred upon students a right to remain mute, the opinion nevertheless spoke volumes. In addition, *Barnette* provided a deep testament to the Court's ability to fundamentally alter the everyday realities of American schools. The Court took what had been a widespread practice—expelling students for refusing to recite the pledge—and issued an opinion invalidating that practice. Consequently, schools around the nation overwhelmingly, and virtually overnight, discarded that practice. Even in the relatively few areas where schools did not immediately act in accordance with *Barnette*, however, the decision nonetheless materially transformed matters, providing students who wished not to recite the pledge with a license of protection that either educational officials or, if necessary, lower courts would redeem. In *Barnette*, then, Jackson's language not only soared but also settled a new, more tolerant constitutional order.[121]

In the wake of *Barnette*, as his opinion received widespread adulation, Justice Jackson took a moment in his personal correspondence for reflection. "I had anticipated a good deal more criticism of [*Barnette*] than has taken place," Jackson wrote. "Perhaps the American people have a stronger appreciation of what liberty is and of its value than we sometimes think."[122] Perhaps. What is beyond dispute, however, is that the capacity of this appreciation has been repeatedly tested in the Supreme Court since the summer of 1943. And in no arena has the American appreciation for liberty witnessed more significant disputes during the last seven decades than the Supreme Court's many and varied decisions interpreting how the Constitution protects the nation's public school students.

2

Freedom of Expression
from Black Armbands to BONG HiTS 4 JESUS

In the late 1960s, the Supreme Court began contemplating how the First Amendment's commitment to "the freedom of speech" should protect the right of students to introduce their own ideas into the schoolhouse. This constitutional question extended well beyond the matter addressed in *Barnette*, because that opinion—momentous though it was in 1943—held simply that students could refuse to recite the Pledge of Allegiance. But *Barnette* did not establish that students possessed an affirmative right to advance their own opinions, on topics of their own selection, much less in the face of school officials' objections. The right to sit out, in other words, did not necessarily confer the right to speak out. Of course, no serious person asserted that honoring the First Amendment in schools meant students could—unsolicited, and in the middle of class—announce their views on presidential power, lead their classmates in a sing-along, or recite a Walt Whitman verse. Such actions would disturb classroom proceedings, and offending students would in no way be permitted to escape school sanctions by blithely invoking free speech. Yet, as advocates of students' First Amendment rights noted, teacher-led instruction did not account for all communication that occurs on school grounds. Students express themselves in many different locations throughout the school day and in different forms—as student expression assumes both vocal and nonvocal variants. Assuredly, free speech advocates contended, at least some of that student expression enjoys the First Amendment's protection.

With *Tinker v. Des Moines Independent Community School District*, the Court in 1969 heartily embraced the principle that students retain affirmative free speech rights in school. Of even greater significance, though, *Tinker* reconceptualized the roles of both the student and the school in American society. *Tinker* asserted that students must not be viewed as mere empty vessels that teachers—and teachers alone—fill with knowledge on discrete topics. That conception offered an impoverished understanding of education. Instead, *Tinker* insisted, students must be permitted to exchange independent ideas with one another—on an extensive array of topics—because those exchanges constitute an essential part of the educational process itself. Relatedly, *Tinker* further asserted that schools must not squelch speech on contentious subjects in a misguided effort to manufacture civility. *Tinker* maintained that public schools should foster an atmosphere of candid debate, as befitting a nation that prides itself on clamorous civic engagement. As if to exemplify this point about the fractious nature of life within the United States, *Tinker* itself drew a belligerent dissent that claimed extending free speech rights to students was a profound mistake—one that would inflict catastrophic damage on schools and on society. Although this dissent could not carry the day in 1969, some observers have insisted that it would be mistaken to view it as the last gasp of a dying regime.

Since *Tinker*, the Court has issued three major opinions considering students' First Amendment rights. In each of those three decisions, the Court has validated a school's effort to silence student speech. Those subsequent decisions, according to some sophisticated commentators, have succeeded in corroding *Tinker*. Critics now contend that the judiciary has either left *Tinker* on life support or perhaps even left it for dead. In order to assess the accuracy of this claim, it is necessary first to appreciate *Tinker*'s contributions and its complications.

TINKER V. DES MOINES INDEPENDENT COMMUNITY SCHOOL DISTRICT: STANDING UP FOR STUDENT SPEECH

In early December 1965, a small group of students in Des Moines, Iowa—including Christopher Eckhardt (sixteen years old), John

Tinker (fifteen years old), and Mary Beth Tinker (thirteen years old)—formed a plan to protest the Vietnam War by wearing black armbands to their various schools. They hoped that the armbands would spark conversations about their views and help in some modest way to mobilize antiwar sentiment. When plans of the impending protest leaked, however, Des Moines school officials hastily arranged a meeting to create a policy announcing that pupils wearing armbands in school would be suspended until they agreed to remove the offending pieces of cloth. This policy was necessary, the officials maintained, in order to avoid disruptions they believed would result from the protest. In addition to learning that some students intended to wear nonblack armbands as a sort of counterprotest, the officials noted that a former Des Moines student had been killed in Vietnam and expressed concern that his friends who remained in school would create a volatile, hot-tempered environment.

The antiwar students, undeterred, proceeded with their plans. When Christopher Eckhardt arrived at school wearing the forbidden item, he made his way directly to the principal's office so that he could be suspended for violating the newly adopted rule. One school official sought to coax Eckhardt into removing his armband by observing that he might need to find a new school as a result of his protest; "colleges [don't] accept demonstrators"; and—above all—he "was too young and immature to have too many views." For his part, John Tinker managed to wear his armband at school through lunchtime, before a teacher finally instructed him to report to the principal's office for discipline. During his half day at school, several different groups of students alternately ridiculed him for wearing the armband and beseeched him to remove it. Like her brother, Mary Beth Tinker wore her armband for much of the school day—until she attracted the notice of her mathematics teacher, who had dedicated the entire previous day of class to condemning student demonstrators and to announcing that he would eject anyone wearing an armband from his classroom. Throughout the day, her classmates repeatedly encouraged her to discard the armband before she got into trouble—including at least twice during classes. Despite the suspensions, all three students remained steadfast in their convictions and did not return to school until January, when their scheduled period of protest had concluded. The student protesters filed a lawsuit contending that their suspensions violated the First Amendment right of free expression, and thus set in motion what would eventually culminate in the Supreme Court's most consequential student rights opinion in its entire history.[1]

In *Tinker v. Des Moines Independent Community School District*, the Supreme Court, by a 7–2 margin, vindicated the right of students to express their views in school. Justice Abe Fortas issued the majority's opinion in February 1969, less than three months before financial improprieties would force him to resign from the Court and well after the clouds of scandal had begun to form. Fortas opened the opinion by asserting that the Supreme Court had held for nearly five decades that students retained First Amendment rights in school—a claim that he bolstered by citing *Meyer v. Nebraska*, *Pierce v. Society of Sisters*, and *West Virginia State Board of Education v. Barnette*. Fortas advanced this proposition in stirring language, using a turn of phrase that not only became a staple of judicial opinions but even entered the larger national culture: "It can hardly be argued that . . . students . . . shed their constitutional rights to freedom of speech or expression at the schoolhouse gate."[2] If *Tinker* were memorable only for containing that sentence, the opinion would nevertheless rank high on the list of the Court's momentous defenses of students' constitutional rights, as that language established the fundamental terms of debate for subsequent cases. But *Tinker* also held great significance beyond that lone sentence.

Two additional, closely related points in *Tinker*'s conceptualization of student rights demand attention. First, Fortas made clear that the state—through its public schools—could not prevent students from expressing particular ideas simply because their message may run contrary to the state's own preferred message. That the Des Moines school district sought to prohibit students from expressing an antiwar viewpoint—when it otherwise permitted students to express their viewpoints on a whole range of issues—rendered the policy constitutionally dubious, according to Fortas. "In our system, state-operated schools may not be enclaves of totalitarianism," he wrote. "School officials do not possess absolute authority over their students. . . . In our system, students may not be regarded as closed-circuit recipients of only that which the State chooses to communicate."[3] Second, linking the opinion to a broad notion of citizenship, Fortas emphasized that it would be particularly unwise for a society that values uninhibited public debate to permit schools to suppress views, as today's students will soon assume responsibility for maintaining tomorrow's civic discourse. "The classroom is peculiarly the 'marketplace of ideas,'" Fortas noted. "The Nation's future depends upon leaders trained through wide exposure to that robust exchange of ideas which discovers truth out of a multitude of tongues, [rather] than through any kind of authoritative selection."[4] Some of the most essential learning that occurs in schools happens not only during teacher-led classroom instruction, but during "personal intercommunication among the students," interactions that Fortas affirmed as embodying "an inevitable . . . [and] an important part of the educational process."[5]

Tinker did not suggest, of course, that schools invariably violated the First Amendment if they placed limitations on student speech. Fortas's opinion pointedly observed that the speech at issue in *Tinker* did not involve "the length of skirts or the type of clothing, . . . hair style, or deportment"—matters that had already begun to roil schools and courts during the 1960s.[6] While Fortas's opinion did not go so far as to hold that schools could sanction students with impunity in those areas, *Tinker* did make clear that it regarded those issues as distinct from the matter at hand.

In what instances did the Supreme Court affirmatively authorize schools to prohibit student speech? Here, *Tinker* contained considerable ambiguity, as the opinion can be understood to contain no fewer than three different, competing approaches for regulating student speech. While the Court left no doubt that it believed that the Des Moines school officials overstepped their bounds as measured by any of these three potential tests, *Tinker*'s ambiguity as to what measure actually governed student speech would beset educators and judges alike in subsequent years.

On *Tinker*'s most speech-restrictive reading, school officials may prohibit student expression if they can articulate reasonable grounds for predicting that the speech will meaningfully hinder school operations. In Fortas's language, "[T]he record does not demonstrate any facts which might reasonably have led school authorities to forecast substantial disruption of or material interference with school activities."[7] This interpretation has clearly been the most influential in lower courts.

On *Tinker*'s more demanding intermediate interpretation, however, school officials could not censor speech on merely the reasonable *prediction* of disruption; instead, the relevant inquiry would center on whether the controverted speech actually interfered with school activities. "When he is in the cafeteria, or on the playing field, or on the campus during the authorized hours," Fortas wrote, "he may express his opinions, even on controversial subjects like the conflict in Vietnam, if he does so without 'materially and substantially interfer[ing] with the requirements of appropriate discipline in the operation of the school' and without colliding with the rights of others."[8] Fortas, assessing *Tinker*'s facts through this prism, conceded that some students directed unkind remarks toward the armband wearers outside class. But he noted that the school witnessed no threats of violence—let alone violent acts—and that schoolwork had not been compromised. The virtually nonexistent record of actual disruption could hardly justify the schools' decision to silence student speech.

Finally, on *Tinker*'s least speech-restrictive reading, school officials could not justify prohibiting student expression based on their classmates' disruptive reactions to the speech but instead must look to whether the speakers themselves disrupted school activities. While students who espouse "unpopular viewpoint[s]" may create "discomfort and unpleasantness," *Tinker* maintained, educators may not censor expression out of a desire to avoid those sensations.[9] To the contrary, protecting dissident speech was, in Fortas's telling, intimately connected to the very core of American identity:

> Any variation from the majority's opinion may inspire fear. Any word spoken, in class, in the lunchroom, or on the campus, that deviates from the views of another person may start an argument or cause a disturbance. But our Constitution says we must take this risk, and our history says that it is this sort of hazardous freedom—this kind of openness—that is the basis of our national strength and of the independence and vigor of Americans who grow up and live in this relatively permissive, often disputatious, society.[10]

Although Justice Hugo Black's vehement dissent did not distinguish among *Tinker*'s various tests, he left no doubt that he assigned the majority opinion a flunking mark. Only days shy of celebrating his eighty-third birthday, Black excoriated his colleagues by reading aloud a version of his written dissent from the bench for some twenty minutes—a judicial performance seldom rivaled not only in its length but also in its vitriol. In the grand courtroom that invites solemnity, Justice Black used sarcastic tones to quote from a disfavored precedent and concluded his jeremiad with the following declaration: "I want it thoroughly known that I disclaim any sentence, any word, any part of what the Court does today."[11]

The published version of Black's dissent made little effort to conceal his deep displeasure. Justice Black ardently supported free speech rights in most contexts, but he asserted that the principle had no business in schools. "It may be that the Nation has outworn the old-fashioned slogan that 'children are to be seen not heard,' but one may, I hope, be permitted to harbor the thought that taxpayers send children to school on the premise that at their age they need to learn, not teach," he wrote.[12] For Justice Black, *Tinker* represented a profound mistake because it "usher[ed] in . . . an entirely new era in which the power to control pupils . . . in the United States is in ultimate effect transferred to the Supreme Court," and—if that were not bad enough—also marked "the beginning of a new revolutionary era of permissiveness in this country."[13] This new permissiveness, in Black's view, could not have arrived at a worse moment, as the 1960s had already witnessed "groups of students all over the land . . . running loose, conducting break-ins, sit-ins, lie-ins, and smash-ins." Black further contended that those inclined to protest were the public schools' "loudest-mouthed, but maybe not their brightest, students."[14] In Black's estimation, *Tinker* thus did not merely permit the inmates to run the asylum but thrust the least equipped inmates among them into the warden's role.

Justice Black did implicitly locate one area of overlap with the Court's opinion in *Tinker*, as he agreed that the case implicated the importance of citizenship. But where the majority entertained a broad conception of citizenship—commanding that schools in a disputatious society should not wantonly squelch dissenting viewpoints—Justice Black floated a comparatively thin conception of citizenship. Instead of focusing on larger societal considerations, Justice Black's conception of citizenship resembled the subject found on some elementary students' report cards, which extols respect, deference, and obedience toward school officials. "School discipline, like parental discipline, is an integral and important part of training our children to be good citizens—to be better citizens," Black contended.[15] In the dissent's final paragraph, he ominously observed, "One does not need to be a prophet or the son of a prophet to know that after the Court's holding today some students in Iowa schools and indeed in all schools will be ready, able, and willing to defy their teachers on practically all orders."[16] While he surely agreed with the *Tinker* majority that adult American society thrives on dissent, Black insisted that students should mind their p's and q's before they worried about expressing their own views.

Tinker immediately garnered extensive acclaim for reining in overzealous educators who had trampled upon students' First Amendment rights. Back in Iowa, *The Des Moines Register* called *Tinker* "an admonition to school officials that panic is no substitute for calm judgment and common sense when free speech is at stake."[17] *The Boston Globe* portrayed the decision in much the same terms, contending *Tinker* "struck a ringing blow for liberty and common sense."[18] *The New York Times* celebrated *Tinker* even more expansively, viewing the opinion, with a clear debt to Fortas's framing, in almost patriotic terms. "Freedom of expression—in an open manner by those holding minority or unpopular views—is part of the vigor and strength of our schools and society," the *Times* editorial argued. "So long as it does not obstruct the right of others in the classroom or on campus, it must be allowed in this country. If dissent ever has to go underground, America will be in real trouble."[19] A columnist for the *Times* contended that a contrary outcome in *Tinker* was virtually unfathomable: "The only real alternative . . . was to say that students have no free speech rights, and the law had almost developed too far to take that position now."[20] Law professors, even those leaning right, generally echoed that assessment. Professor Charles Alan Wright, a lifelong Republican who would join President Richard Nixon's Watergate legal team, termed the *Tinker* decision "an easy one" to rebuff a "clearly invalid" school policy: "Constitution or no, it is hardly thinkable that we could deny to today's generation of students freedom of expression or procedural fairness."[21]

Much of the early *Tinker* commentary also conspicuously condemned Justice Black's dissent. *The Washington Post* deemed it "strange" that *Tinker* drew any dissent at all, let alone Black's "harsh" opinion, which it predicted "students of our judicial history [would find] puzzl[ing]."[22] Seeking to allay concerns among educators that Black's alarmist opinion might have raised, *The Des Moines Register* cautioned, "[T]here is nothing in the ruling that gives sanction to disorderly or obstructive behavior. The ruling does not tie the hands of school authorities in the face of breaches of discipline or conduct likely to cause trouble in the schools."[23] Relatedly, *The Boston Globe* challenged Black's contention that both *Tinker* and the armband demonstration stemmed from excessively indulgent attitudes toward modern youth. "There is nothing 'permissive' in according students (or anyone else) rights which the Constitution guarantees them," the *Globe* reasoned. "And it is not 'permissiveness' which stimulates students to make such protests as the one in Des Moines. It is the earnest belief . . . that their elders have botched the job of bringing peace to the world they are going to inherit."[24]

Justice Black's dissent was not, of course, rejected in all quarters. In an editorial titled "Revolt Invited in the Romper Set," the *Chicago Tribune* endorsed Black's position as it assailed the Supreme Court, "which is always ready to meddle in local affairs," and *Tinker* for rendering it more difficult to "maintain[ ] discipline and order in the nation's schools."[25]* While the *Tribune* was one of the few major newspapers that criticized *Tinker,* the dissent found many admirers in the public who sent letters to Justice Black commending him on the opinion. It is hardly surprising that Black's opinion won the admiration of school officials, in positions ranging from superintendent to cafeteria manager. But the appeal of Black's position reached beyond its natural constituency. A physician based in Springfield, Illinois, for example, congratulated Black for resisting "this [nation's] new sweeping plague of permissiveness," a term that could quite easily have appeared in the dissent itself. "[Y]ou speak eloquently my feelings and those of so many of my countrymen," the physician noted. "I'm sick and intolerant of permissive parents, permissive teachers, permissive law enforcement agencies, permissive legislators, and permissive courts."[26]

Justice Black's vehement dissent in *Tinker* certainly made a deep impression on his colleagues, leading Chief Justice Earl Warren to remark, "Old Hugo really got hung up in his jock strap on that one."[27] What inspired Black's stridency in this case? According to one assessment, a searing episode from Black's familial life spurred

---

* The *Chicago Tribune* editorial board demonstrated foresight in detecting the First Amendment issues involving students that appeared on the judicial horizon, even if it inaccurately predicted the ultimate outcomes of those disputes: "Will it be possible for a principal to censor a school paper which uses profane or obscene language? We doubt it." "Revolt Invited in the Romper Set," *Chicago Tribune,* Feb. 26, 1969, 20.

him to adopt this hard line against student speech.[28] Proponents
of this interpretation note that—after the oral argument in *Tinker*,
but before the Court issued its decision—Black's grandson was suspended for his role in producing an underground newspaper that
used intemperate language to criticize school administrators. When
Black learned of his grandson's suspension and that the family was
contemplating a lawsuit against the school, the justice penned a letter to his daughter-in-law condemning the idea in pointed terms.
"[P]ersonally I think the school has done exactly the right thing,"
he wrote. "The time has come in this country when it must be
known that children cannot run the school which they attend at
government expense."[29] This anecdote contains irresistible appeal,
as Black's frosty private letter about his grandson seems to fore-
shadow the public posture he would adopt in *Tinker*.

Upon deeper reflection, however, it seems mistaken to invest
much stock in this episode's explanatory power for Justice Black's
position on student speech. Some of the reason for caution on
this front surrounds the sequence of events. Years before *Tinker*
arrived at the Court, for instance, Black demonstrated a willingness to retreat from his traditionally staunch defense of free speech
rights when he confronted cases involving the civil rights movement's direct action phase, which can be seen as a forerunner of
the antiwar movement. Similarly, at oral argument in *Tinker*, Black
appeared deeply skeptical of First Amendment rights for students,
something noted in contemporaneous media accounts. With a tinge
of irritation piercing his Alabama drawl, Black asked the protesting students' attorney the following question: "Which do you think
has the most control in the school . . . the pupils or the authorities
that are running the school?"[30] Furthermore, on the heels of oral
argument, when the Court's members shared their views of the case
in Conference, Black contended that the school board's position
should be broadly affirmed, and he did so in the same distraught
tones that would ultimately appear in his dissent. "The schools are
in great trouble," Black informed his colleagues. "Children need
discipline—the country is going to ruin because of it. This is no
First Amendment problem."[31] Black almost certainly voiced these
concerns before his grandson's suspension, so it seems improbable
that this event accounted for much, if any, of his apocalyptic tenor.

More important, though, it is misguided to construe Justice
Black's dissent in *Tinker* primarily as a cranky grandfather's fit of

pique because that interpretation obscures the prevalence of such views among Americans during the late 1960s. Instead of viewing Black's dissent as the ranting of an elderly codger whose mischievous grandson caused him to become unhinged, it seems far more accurate to view him as tapping into a deep wellspring of cultural anxiety that engulfed the Court's efforts to extend constitutional rights to students. Moreover, although some readers may intuit that Black's sentiments from *Tinker* have disappeared in the nearly five decades since the decision, that intuition misses the mark; Black's views continue to claim admirers within society, the legal academy, and even on the Supreme Court.

While some observers perceived *Tinker*'s outcome as inevitable, when assessed from the viewpoint of the 1960s, it seemed quite plausible that the Supreme Court could have reached precisely the opposite outcome. To appreciate how *Tinker* could have resulted in a defeat for students' First Amendment rights, contemplate that no less a personage than the author of the Court's opinion himself viewed the matter as thorny. When *Tinker* initially arrived at the Court, Fortas wrote, "this is a tough case" on a law clerk memorandum outlining the students' petition for certiorari.[32] Fortas eventually voted to deny the students' petition, a stance that (if not overcome by his colleagues) would have permitted the school officials' suppression of student speech to remain intact from their victory at the circuit court level. Even at oral argument, Fortas's comments to the students' lawyer revealed at least some unease at the prospect of finding that the Des Moines educators' actions violated the Constitution: "This gets the Supreme Court of the United States pretty deep in the trenches of ordinary day to day [school] discipline."[33]

The notion that *Tinker* was far from an assured triumph for student rights finds further support when one contemplates the events swirling outside the Court in the late 1960s. The Court heard oral arguments in *Tinker* on November 12, 1968—only ten weeks after the Democratic National Convention in Chicago was overshadowed by demonstrations and violence, and exactly one week after Richard Nixon defeated Hubert Humphrey for the presidency. Prior to the election, Nixon's campaign condemned the Supreme Court for its supposedly indulgent treatment of the criminal element and promised to restore "law and order," a protean term that encompassed criminal defendants and antiwar protesters alike.

Against these groups, President Nixon would purport to speak on behalf of "the forgotten Americans," an assemblage that was chiefly defined by its not assembling—in order to protest the Vietnam War, or anything else for that matter. In a nod toward Nixon's forgotten Americans, *Time* designated "The Middle Americans" its "Man and Woman of the Year" for 1969, and placed an image of a school on its cover to represent a chief concern for these ordinary folks. In the accompanying article, the Middle Americans were depicted as flaunting an obsessive, flag-bearing patriotism and as "fear[ing] they were beginning to lose their grip on the country," as "[o]thers seemed to be taking over—the liberals, the radicals, the defiant young."[34]* *Time* quoted a resident of Pittsfield, Massachusetts, who groused, "Dissent is disgusting. If you have a complaint, write your Congressman or the President. School is to get an education."[35]† This statement bears an uncanny resemblance to the view offered by the Des Moines school officials in *Tinker* who contended that "schools are no place for demonstrations," and asserted if students "didn't like the way our elected officials were handling things, it should be handled with the ballot box and not in the halls of our public schools."[36] Such views were hardly confined to the middle and working classes, as *Time* noted that the University of Chicago's Daniel J. Boorstin, one of the nation's foremost intellectuals, shared these concerns. In 1969, Boorstin published *The Decline of Radicalism*, where he contended, "Dissent is the great problem of America today. It overshadows all others. It is a symptom, an expression, a consequence, and a cause of all others."[37]

During the late 1960s, polling data suggests that more Americans would have embraced Justice Black's dissent than Justice For-

---

* On the patriotic nature of Middle Americans, *Time* observed, "Everywhere, they flew the colors of assertive patriotism. Their car windows were plastered with American-flag decals, their ideological totems. In the bumper-sticker dialogue of the freeways, they answered MAKE LOVE NOT WAR with HONOR AMERICA or SPIRO IS MY HERO." "Man and Woman of the Year: The Middle Americans," *Time*, Jan. 5, 1970, 10.

† In a related vein, *Time* quoted a leader of the National Confederation of American Ethnic Groups, which purported to represent 18 million first- and second-generation immigrants, as saying, "Our families don't have long-haired brats—they'd tear the hair off them. Our boys don't smoke pot or raise hell or seek deferments. Our people are too busy making a living and trying to be good Americans." Ibid.

These sentiments almost eerily managed to channel Merle Haggard's indelible country music anthem, "Okie from Muskogee," which offered a paean to conservative values and ridiculed the counterculture in September 1969. Merle Haggard, "Okie from Muskogee," *Okie from Muskogee: If I Had Left It Up to You* (Capitol Records 1969).

tas's majority opinion. In a Harris poll taken only one month after *Tinker*, 52 percent of respondents opposed granting rights to student protesters, and only 38 percent of respondents supported granting such rights.[38] If anything, these figures may well overstate the actual support for affording free speech rights to pupils in elementary and secondary schools; the Harris question asked about "student[ ] . . . protests" generally, and many respondents could have interpreted the question to apply to the college level, where demonstrations had received widespread media attention.* When Gallup conducted its first comprehensive poll gauging attitudes toward education in February 1969, moreover, respondents identified a lack of student discipline as the foremost problem confronting the nation's schools.[39] Many respondents would doubtless have identified the behavior at issue in Des Moines, with students disobeying direct orders from their principals, as a cardinal example of the breakdown in student discipline that must be corrected.

In short, *Tinker* represented a momentous innovation in the recognition of students' constitutional rights. For the first time, the Supreme Court recognized that students retain the essential power to communicate their ideas to one another; such communication is not extraneous to the educational process but instead forms an integral part of that process; and public schools have an acute responsibility to tolerate dissident speech, so both the marketplace of ideas functions properly and citizens will be prepared to participate in the freewheeling debate that characterizes the United States. *Tinker's* constitutional contributions to our society would deserve to be honored if they arrived at any time. But that *Tinker* resisted, rather than ratified, the era's prevailing attitudes on student dissent makes those contributions all the more remarkable.

For all of *Tinker's* laudable qualities, however, the opinion also contained major frailties. The most significant of these shortcomings was its milquetoast depiction of the potential for student speech opposing the Vietnam War to inflame students who supported the

---

* Perhaps the most notorious protest on a college campus occurred in April 1968, when Students for a Democratic Society took over Columbia University. Mark Rudd—leader of the student protests and devotee of Che Guevara—addressed an open letter to the university's president that confrontationally concluded with a quotation from a LeRoi Jones poem: "Up against the wall, motherfucker, this is a stick-up." James T. Patterson, *Grand Expectations: The United States, 1945–1974* 686 (1996). Jones subsequently adopted the name Amiri Baraka. See *The Norton Anthology of African American Literature* 1877 (Henry Louis Gates Jr. and Nellie Y. McKay eds., 1997).

effort and to create a volatile situation in school—particularly in December 1965, when the students displayed their armbands. Although opposition to the Vietnam War is remembered today as an extremely widespread phenomenon—and it had become so by 1969, when the Supreme Court issued *Tinker*—that state of affairs had yet to emerge by the end of 1965. At the time of the protest in Des Moines, the United States had committed relatively few troops to Vietnam and sustained relatively few casualties, and polling data indicated that Americans supported President Johnson's handling of the war by a ratio of more than two to one.

The actual events prompted by the armband displays—rather than the sanitized version recounted in *Tinker*—bolster this notion that the antiwar protest carried the potential to create a volatile situation in Des Moines schools and, indeed, can even be viewed as having realized that potential. Consider that long before the lawsuit in *Tinker* had ever been filed, media coverage related to the armbands appeared in not only *The Des Moines Register* but also *The New York Times*. Students contended that Donald Prior, a gym teacher and football coach at Roosevelt High School, expressed his disdain for the protest by altering the calisthenics chant from the usual "BEAT EAST HIGH" to the newfangled "BEAT THE VIET-CONG."[40] Coach Prior denied orchestrating the event to the *Register*, suggesting instead that the students had improvised the new slogan of their own accord. But Prior's denial left little doubt that his sympathies ran decidedly against the protesters. "I didn't see any reason to stop [the chanters]," Prior explained. "They are proving their Americanism. They are on the side of President Johnson."[41] One witness informed the *Times* that Prior accused students who refused to use the new chant of being "pinkos or Communists."[42] With such accusations flying, it should hardly be surprising that fists and feet followed suit, as both the *Register* and the *Times* reported that some students wearing armbands had been punched and kicked by classmates prior to the suspensions. When the Des Moines School Board held a public meeting to contemplate reinstating the suspended students, the Reverend Robert Keck gestured toward these various issues, even as he urged his fellow board members to override the suspensions. "Controversy is at the heart of education, and the disturbance of set thinking is the catalyst," Keck reasoned. "We have been intimidated by the threat of violence, and have thus let the ruffian element dictate educational policies."[43]

Beyond such news coverage, the armbands stood at the center of several other intense events in Des Moines. One day before the protest was scheduled to begin, a group of male students warned Eckhardt, "If you [wear the armbands] . . . you'll find our fists in your face and our foot up your ass."[44] Furthermore, both the Eckhardt and the Tinker family homes were turned into steady targets for anonymous hatred. Consider only one of the many hectoring postcards addressed to Eckhardt's parents: "It seems that someone needs to psychoanaly[ze] you two parents for what you are putting your children thru . . . because it looks like you are going to have a Lee Harvey Oswald on your hands. . . . We think the community would be a better place for all concerned if people like you would move out."[45] For their part, the Tinkers received numerous death threats and had red paint splattered on their front door—the apparent message being that only a communist would oppose the Vietnam War.[46]

Given this turbulent series of events, why did Justice Fortas neglect to mention them in his opinion, and—even more to the point—why did Justice Black disregard them in his scalding dissent? The answer is that none of the facts in the preceding two paragraphs appeared in the case's official record, which the parties developed in the district court. The student protesters had a clear incentive for minimizing, or even ignoring, the hostile reaction to their armbands, as acknowledging the rancor would increase the likelihood that judges would find the schools' silencing of their speech permissible. From the school district's perspective, while detailing the acrimonious reception to the armbands might have increased its likelihood of prevailing, it appears that professional pride in overseeing schools where conditions are under control overcame any inclination to disclose the actual state of affairs. In this vein, the school district's brief filed in the Supreme Court seemed almost to boast that, while John Tinker's classmates directed some unfriendly remarks toward him when he wore the armband, "[t]here were no threats to hit him."[47] To the extent that the Des Moines officials contemplated this case setting an important legal precedent, moreover, it is at least plausible that they wanted to establish educators' authority to regulate student speech without their needing to demonstrate that school conditions had deteriorated to the point of physical altercations. If such strategic considerations in fact motivated the school district's legal analysis, that thinking was hardly deranged; even based on a thinly supported record for fearing school disturbances, the educators prevailed in both the district court and the circuit court.

While Justice Fortas's refusal to reach beyond the official record in *Tinker* is certainly understandable, he nevertheless erred by writing the opinion in a manner that failed to paint even a remotely accurate portrait of the genuine dynamics that surrounded the antiwar armbands. It seems unmistakable that Fortas's opinion sought to sanitize the scene that actually unfolded in the Des Moines schools because it neglected to mention one of the very few facts in the record that provided a glimpse into the tense environment. Although Fortas referred in the abstract to the impermissibility of school officials enacting policies seeking merely to "avoid the controversy which might result from the expression [of antiwar sentiment]," he did not disclose that several of John Tinker's classmates called him a "commie"—a term that contained serious venom at the height of the Cold War.[48] In addition, Justice Fortas need not have relied on newspaper coverage or other non-record sources to observe that the student protesters in Des Moines sought to express themselves on an incendiary issue and that they sought to advance a viewpoint that many of their classmates would have deemed less antiwar than anti-American. One needed only to be an inhabitant of the United States during the mid-1960s to realize displaying antiwar armbands created a potentially combustible situation.

With these contextual complications forefront in mind, it is worth revisiting the various legal tests that *Tinker* can be understood as propounding. First, can it genuinely be maintained that the Des Moines school officials were, before the demonstrations, *unreasonable* to anticipate the armbands leading to a substantial disruption occurring on school grounds? Really? As discussed above, this reasonable-forecast-of-substantial-disruption test has emerged as the dominant approach from *Tinker* for assessing student speech cases today. It is a bitter irony, indeed, that the Supreme Court's most iconic defense of student speech rights was—at least as assessed by applying the test that it spawned to the dispute's actual (rather than the manicured) facts—decided incorrectly. *Tinker,* in other words, failed its own rule. Proceeding to the second test, it seems clear that the armbands could be viewed as having sparked an actual disruption in the Des Moines schools. If the demonstrators were being physically assaulted and even, on John Tinker's own testimony, being addressed with inflammatory terms like "commie," such disturbances could readily qualify as having disturbed the school day. Viewed through the prism of this second test, then, the Des Moines educators also should have been permitted to prohibit the armbands.

It is viewed only through *Tinker's* third potential test—which looks to whether the student speakers themselves created any disturbance, or instead whether disturbances came from reactions to the speech—that the Court seems justified in upholding the ability of students to wear their armbands. On this account, which offers the strongest protection to student speech, the school should not have been permitted to silence opposition to the Vietnam War simply because such speech was likely to, or did in fact, encounter negative reactions from other students. Instead of silencing the speaker, that is, the school should sanction the students who issue threats of violence or engage in violent acts. This test can be viewed as ensuring that students' First Amendment rights are not vulnerable to the phenomenon that Professor Harry Kalven in 1965 dubbed the heckler's veto. "If the [state] can silence the speaker," Kalven explained, "the law in effect acknowledges a veto power in hecklers who can, by being hostile enough, get the law to silence any speaker of whom they do not approve."[49] Only one year after Kalven coined the term, the Supreme Court used that terminology to affirm that the First Amendment generally forbids the practice of allowing hypersensitive listeners to shut down speech by reacting violently.[50] *Tinker* undoubtedly contains elements of prohibiting heckler's vetoes in the student speech context, and a few subsequent federal appellate courts have so interpreted the opinion. But astute commentators even at the time of *Tinker* expressed concern that Fortas's opinion—with its repeated emphasis on the lack of disruption that supposedly greeted the armbands in Des Moines—virtually invited courts to permit hecklers, and the mere possibility of hecklers, to suppress students' First Amendment rights.[51]

THE PATH NOT TAKEN IN STUDENT SPEECH

Even if the Supreme Court were not prepared in 1969 to announce unequivocally that the general prohibition on heckler's vetoes applied to student speech, *Tinker* nevertheless could have quite plausibly adopted a rule that afforded greater protection to students' First Amendment rights than did the reasonable-forecast-of-substantial-disruption test. In a pair of cases involving public schools in Mississippi during the civil rights movement, the U.S. Court of Appeals for the Fifth Circuit in 1966 enunciated a rule that required educators to determine that student speech created an actual disruption—rather than merely having a reasonable basis for predicting such a disruption—before prohibiting its expression. The Fifth Circuit's approach to student speech merits examination not only because it arose from an unusually gripping chapter in the nation's history but also because it represents a significant path not taken within the domain of student speech.

In September 1964, the dispute resting at the center of *Burnside v. Byars* began when Montgomery Moore—principal of an all-black high school in Philadelphia, Mississippi—discovered that some students were wearing "freedom buttons" adorned with the phrase "One Man One Vote" and the acronym "SNCC," which stood for the Student Nonviolent Coordinating Committee, a leading civil rights organization. Principal Moore promptly announced a new policy prohibiting the buttons because, he contended, the items "didn't have any bearing on their education" and would interrupt school activities.[52] Although Moore's explanation for banning the "freedom buttons" made no mention of the larger historical events that recently consumed Philadelphia, Mississippi, September 1964 was an extraordinarily fraught period for that community. In August, the bodies of three slain civil rights activists who had been working to register black voters—James Chaney, Andrew Goodman, and Michael Schwerner—were unearthed in Philadelphia, after white supremacists had abducted, killed, and buried the trio earlier that summer.[53] In the wake of these events, a small group of students, over their principal's objection, decided to continue wearing the forbidden buttons to school. Principal Moore dismissed the students, sending them home with the following note: "Dear Parent: This is to inform you that your child has been suspended from school until you can come and have a talk with me. *It is against school policy for anything to be brought into the school that is not educational.*"[54] In *Burnside*, the Fifth Circuit in July 1966 invalidated Moore's prohibition of the buttons because it found no evidence that the items caused a commotion or hampered the schooling enterprise in any way; indeed, Moore's own explanation for the suspensions cited

no disturbances but instead merely the violation of school regulations. While *Burnside* protected the Philadelphia students' free
speech rights, the Fifth Circuit made it clear that if the buttons
had in fact created a different, more combustible atmosphere, then
a different outcome would be required: "If the decorum had been
so disturbed by the presence of the 'freedom buttons,' the principal would have been acting within his authority and the regulation
forbidding the presence of buttons on school grounds would have
been reasonable."[55]

The Fifth Circuit had no need to concoct some hypothetical scenario in an effort to illustrate when a decision to ban freedom buttons would be permissible. On the very same day that the
Fifth Circuit issued *Burnside*, it simultaneously issued an opinion
in *Blackwell v. Issaquena County Board of Education*, a case that also
involved a ban on freedom buttons at another all-black high school
in Mississippi—this one in a town called Rolling Fork. At that point,
however, the striking factual similarities between the two cases
ended. The juxtaposition of the two schooling environments in
response to the freedom buttons could not have been starker, as the
Fifth Circuit explained: "In [*Blackwell*], as distinguished from the
facts in *Burnside*, there was more than a mild curiosity on the part
of those who were wearing, distributing, discussing and promoting
the . . . buttons. There was an unusual degree of commotion, boisterous conduct, a collision with the rights of others, an undermining
of authority, and a lack of order, discipline and decorum."[56] In this
vein, the record in *Blackwell* revealed that some students who wore
freedom buttons tossed the buttons through the school's open windows, interrupted classes in which they were not enrolled seeking to
enlist support, and even attempted to pin buttons on those who had
not requested them (prompting at least one student to cry). In *Blackwell*, the Fifth Circuit concluded that this tumultuous environment
legitimated the school ban on freedom buttons in Rolling Fork, as
it termed the protesters' actions "reprehensible" in demonstrating
"complete disregard for the rights of their fellow students."[57]

Neither *Burnside* nor *Blackwell* should be regarded as beyond
criticism. In *Burnside*, for instance, the Fifth Circuit's actual disruption standard seemed to endow hecklers (or others who respond
energetically to a message) with the ability to silence particular
speech.[58] In *Blackwell*, moreover, rather than permitting school

officials to bar freedom buttons altogether, effectively holding the entire group responsible for the actions of a few, it would have been better to permit school officials to discipline only the individual students responsible for creating the disturbances.[59] Whatever the tender spots of the Fifth Circuit's approach, however, the actual disruption standard would have afforded student speakers considerably more protection than *Tinker* actually ended up providing. Perhaps surprisingly, the Supreme Court in *Tinker* did favorably cite the Fifth Circuit's resolution of *Burnside* and *Blackwell*, even intermittently appearing to embrace an actual disruption standard. Yet *Tinker*'s less demanding language—requiring educators only to have a reasonable basis for anticipating a substantial disruption—dwarfed those occasional passages and emerged as the dominant test for student speech.

In recent decades, it has become almost clichéd to remark that *Tinker* established "the high-water mark" for students' free speech rights in the Supreme Court.[60] The comment capitalizes on the knowledge that—following an initial victory in *Tinker*—the Court has subsequently handed pupils a series of First Amendment defeats. Far too seldom appreciated, though, is that the water from that early opinion should have crested much higher still.

BETHEL SCHOOL DISTRICT V. FRASER AND CRUDE STUDENT SPEECH

On April 26, 1983—just six weeks shy of his graduation from Bethel High School, in Spanaway, Washington—Matthew Fraser approached the podium before the assembled student body to deliver a speech nominating Jeff Kuhlman to serve on the next year's student government. Fraser enjoyed an excellent reputation for public speaking, having been selected the top high school debater in the entire state of Washington during both his junior and his senior years. As Fraser strode toward the lectern, some enthusiastic audience members yelled with anticipation for an address they hoped would be memorable. Along that dimension, at least, Fraser's remarks did not disappoint. The full text follows of what is the most renowned—if not exactly the most celebrated—speech ever delivered at a high school assembly:

> I know a man who is firm. He's firm in his pants; he's firm in his shirt; his character is firm. But most of all, his belief in you, the students of Bethel, is firm. Jeff Kuhlman is a man who takes his point and pounds it in. If necessary, he'll take an issue and nail it to the wall. He doesn't attack things in spurts. He drives hard, pushing and pushing until finally he succeeds. Jeff is a man who will go to the very end, even the climax, for each and every one of you. So vote for Jeff for [student government] Vice President. He'll never come between you and the best our high school can be.

It took Fraser approximately one minute to deliver the speech, but the legal controversy it sparked proved considerably more enduring. One day after the assembly, a school administrator informed Fraser that his speech violated Bethel's "disruptive conduct" policy, which the Court's language in *Tinker* appeared to have partly inspired: "Conduct which materially and substantially interferes with the educational process is prohibited, including the use of obscene, profane language or gestures." The administrator further informed Fraser that, as punishment for the speech, he would receive a three-day suspension and that his name would be stricken from the ballot for selecting graduation speakers.[61]

In response, Fraser filed a lawsuit contending that the sanctions violated his constitutional right to free expression. Fraser entertained no delusions that his nominating speech advanced some particularly noble idea. In his public commentary, he freely conceded that the address in no way resembled "a great piece of literature," and even acknowledged that it was "sophomoric."[62] Yet Fraser also insisted that he selected his words carefully to accomplish the discrete task at hand: securing Kuhlman's election with a speech that would appeal to Bethel's adolescent electorate. "The reason I used the allusion was very simple: I was representing a candidate, and it was my job . . . to establish a rapport with the audience," Fraser explained. "To meet the expectations and desires of students continually exposed to prime-time television shows like Three's Company, with their heavy use of sexual humor, I chose sexual innuendo as my most telling rhetorical option."* For Fraser,

---

* After school nearly every weekday afternoon during the mid-1980s, I watched *Three's Company* in syndicated reruns. Some of my favorite childhood memories of television

Kuhlman's winning the vice presidency with some 90 percent of the vote indicated that his controversial speech was electorally effective, but he also maintained that it was legally protected: "I won't deny that it seemed possible to me at the time that school officials might be displeased with my speech. But I also strongly believed that my First Amendment rights were of far greater importance than what school officials wanted to hear."[63]

Going further, Fraser contended the lawsuit carried important implications not just for students' rights but also for American society as a whole. "I think it's really important that the First Amendment actually be in existence in high school," he said. "You can't expect students to learn about [free speech] if they're not able to exercise it."[64] In Fraser's view, even if his initial, admittedly juvenile campaign advocacy seemed of modest import, his decision to resist the school's punishment for his speech presented a matter of considerable consequence. The district court appeared broadly sympathetic to this assessment, as it found that the school's disciplinary measures violated the Constitution—a decision that enabled Fraser to deliver the graduation speech (which he did without incident), after he won the honor via write-in vote. While the federal appellate court affirmed that Fraser's suspension violated his First Amendment rights, the Supreme Court granted certiorari to answer that question definitively.[65]

In July 1986, Chief Justice Warren Burger wrote an opinion for the Court in *Bethel School District v. Fraser* concluding that the suspension did not violate the freedom of speech. Burger's opinion emphasized that the contested speech—which it characterized variously as "lewd," "vulgar," "indecent," "offensive," and "sexually explicit"—stood a great distance from the political speech that *Tinker* involved.[66] At times, though, Burger's opinion seemed to edge toward employing a *Tinker*-inflected analysis, as it contemplated how Fraser's speech struck various audiences (both actual and conjectural). The oration, Burger noted, generated a range of responses among the six hundred students in attendance—as many joyously shouted their approval, some seemed bewildered, and two

---

involve Jack Tripper, Janet Wood, Chrissy Snow, and the show's overlooked major character: the Regal Beagle. This painstaking, exhaustive field research enables me to affirm that a large percentage of *Three's Company* humor featured sexual themes, and further that an inordinate number of episodes hinged on (wholly implausible) misapprehensions arising from the sort of sexual double entendre that Fraser deployed in his speech.

even gyrated their hips to mime sexual intercourse. Burger's opinion identified two overlapping groups of audience members that he supposed Fraser's speech may especially affront: "By glorifying male sexuality . . . the speech was acutely insulting to teenage girl students. The speech could [also] be seriously damaging to its less mature audience, many of whom were only 14 years old and on the threshold of awareness of human sexuality."[67] But Burger stopped shy of concluding that Fraser's speech substantially disrupted or materially interfered with school activities, evidently because—even according to the testimony of Bethel's educators—raucous speeches and boisterous conduct were hardly unknown at Bethel's student assemblies. While one teacher dedicated ten minutes of class to inviting discussion of Fraser's speech, that scant evidence hardly seemed to suggest that Bethel teetered on the brink of bedlam.

Rather than applying *Tinker*'s disruption analysis, the Court's opinion in *Fraser* created a First Amendment exception for student speech of a sexual nature. Burger conspicuously identified Justice Black's dissent in *Tinker*—not the majority opinion—as providing *Fraser*'s lodestar, citing it for the idea that the Constitution in no way compels parents and educators to relinquish control of the American school system to students. Implicitly, moreover, *Fraser* appeared to implement Justice Black's thinner conception of citizenship, as it extolled schools' responsibility for both "inculcat[ing] the habits and manners of civility" and "teaching students the boundaries of socially appropriate behavior."[68] *Fraser* was careful to acknowledge that students retained the right to advance unpopular ideas. But it stressed that in so doing, they "must also take into account consideration of the sensibilities of . . . [their] fellow students."[69] Whereas *Tinker* identified our "relatively permissive, often disputatious, society" as a source of national vitality—and further highlighted the need for schools to tolerate even speech that creates "discomfort and unpleasantness"—*Fraser* turned a blind eye to such values in favor of decorum, etiquette, and politesse: "[S]chools must teach by example the shared values of a civilized social order. . . . The schools, as instruments of the state, may determine that the essential lessons of civil, mature conduct cannot be conveyed in a school that tolerates [the speech] indulged in by this confused boy."[70] With this guiding framework established, *Fraser* held that the First Amendment presented no obstacle for Bethel's assessment that permitting Fraser's speech "would undermine the school's basic educational mission" because "[a] high school assembly or classroom is no place for a sexually explicit monologue. . . . Accordingly, it was perfectly appropriate for the school to disassociate itself to make the point to the pupils that vulgar speech and lewd conduct is wholly inconsistent with the 'fundamental values' of public school education."[71]

Fraser drew two separate dissenting opinions. In sharp contrast to the majority's depiction of Matthew Fraser as a "confused boy," Justice John Paul Stevens's dissent labeled him "an outstanding young man"—one who possessed "a fine academic record."[72] In finding that his suspension exceeded the school's authority, Stevens's dissent scrutinized the language of Bethel's disruptive conduct policy and found that Fraser's nominating speech employed neither "profane" nor "obscene" language. Although the speech's absence of profanity is clear, Stevens's construing the address as lacking obscenity may require slightly more explanation. Evidently, Stevens understood the policy prohibiting obscene language as invoking a First Amendment term of art, in effect incorporating the legal standard for evaluating pornographic materials. Whatever the sins of Fraser's speech, Stevens seemed to reason, it was designed to amuse, not to arouse. While acknowledging that Fraser's "sexual metaphor . . . may unquestionably be offensive to some listeners in some settings," Stevens found that Bethel's policy failed to alert Fraser that his usage of mere sexual innuendo could result in suspension.[73] Even if the school's policy was ambiguous, moreover, Stevens maintained that such ambiguity should be resolved in favor of the speaker and against the censor. Justice Thurgood Marshall also wrote a brief dissent, concluding simply that Fraser's suspension violated *Tinker* because Bethel had not demonstrated that his speech disrupted school activities.[74]

Newspaper editorial boards expressed widespread approval of the Court's opinion, as even the liberal outlets generally depicted Fraser as a wisenheimer who got precisely what he deserved. While *The Washington Post* noted Fraser "probably thought of himself as a creative campaign manager, a rousing speaker and a subtle wit," the editors found the speech unamusing, and deemed the Court's resolution eminently "sens[ibl]e."[75] *The New York Times* concurred in that assessment, calling it "common sense" that *Fraser* gave "school authorities broad discretion to discipline students for ill-mannered speech," as "[n]o school can function without such authority."[76] Both newspapers did caution educators against reading *Fraser* too broadly, noting that Burger's opinion indicated that it left student speech of a "political" nature undisturbed.[77] From the vantage point of the more conservative *Chicago Tribune*, however, the smart aleck should count himself fortunate: "After all, it wasn't as if the principal washed out young Master Fraser's mouth with soap."[78]

Among the intelligentsia, *Fraser* received a considerably cooler reception. The literary critic Diana Trilling argued the speech contained "no sentiment to raise a blush to any cheek," and further avowed, "We are indeed in trouble in this country when a student's decent acceptance of male sexuality as an aspect of male strength is punishable by suspension. This carries censorship into a new era of authoritarianism."[79] Professor Alan Dershowitz admitted disliking Fraser's remarks, but he also insisted that the school's punishment was distasteful in a nation committed to free expression. "A high-school education is supposed to prepare young men and women to participate in an adult democratic society that is diverse in its tastes," Dershowitz noted. "We tolerate a wider variety of free expression than any other society in history. The process of tolerance must begin in school. Students should be taught to discuss controversial ideas, formulations and lifestyles, rather than to try to close down disagreeable stalls in the marketplace of ideas."[80] Although Dershowitz's academic work specialized in criminal law, most First Amendment scholars adopted roughly this same line.[81]

Some of the opinion's detractors viewed the opinion as owing more to political considerations than legal ones. When word of the decision reached Fraser at the University of California, Berkeley—where he had recently completed his junior year and had become a standout intercollegiate debater on one of the nation's finest teams—he responded, "I'm not really surprised. The court has become mindlessly conservative lately. The rationale used in this case is nothing less than idiotic."[82] Some of that harsh assessment may well be attributed to a competitor's raw feelings after suffering a high-profile defeat. But Fraser was far from alone in viewing the opinion through the lens of politics and in perceiving that the Court as composed during the *Tinker* era might have issued a very different decision. As one prominent observer of the education field put it at the time, "Fraser was hit by the swing of the political pendulum," and "only 15 years ago, [his] words would not likely have raised any judicial eyebrows."[83]

From the perspective of conservatives within the political arena, *Fraser* represented an overdue restoration of authority to education officials. In December 1983, President Ronald Reagan delivered a major address on schools where he identified the "need to restore good old-fashioned discipline" as the top priority. "We need to write stricter discipline codes, then support our teachers when they enforce those codes," Reagan advised. "Back at the turn of the century, one education handbook told teachers that enforcing discipline—and I quote—'You have the law back of you. You have intelligent public sentiment back of you.' We must make both those statements true once again."[84] Aligned with this vision, Reagan's solicitor general Charles Fried filed an important amicus brief supporting Bethel's authority to punish Fraser. Fried's brief evidently supplied critical information for Burger, as it quoted an obscure passage from a U.S. history textbook that contended schools "must inculcate the habits and manners of civility," and that language would, of course, figure prominently in *Fraser*'s analysis.[85] In the opinion's wake, moreover, a raft of officials from Reagan's Department of Education stepped forth to trumpet *Fraser* as providing an essential lesson in morality. Secretary of Education William Bennett stated that the opinion "reminds us that schools must possess the moral authority to prepare our young people for citizenship."[86] Similarly, Wendell L. Willkie II, the department's general counsel, praised *Fraser* for acknowledging "a school, at least within its own walls, must have clear moral authority in governing the lives of students," and further construed the opinion as an effort to atone for prior societal excesses: "As we have seen too often in the last generation, when misconduct goes unpunished, students learn that rules need not be obeyed."[87]*

---

* It is probably mistaken to understand *Fraser*'s appeal as confined to the right, as left-leaning political figures also voiced concerns about youngsters being exposed to sexualized content during the mid-1980s. The Court decided *Fraser* less than one year after Tipper Gore, spouse of Senator Al Gore of Tennessee, testified on Capitol Hill, encouraging the music industry to adopt "parental guidance" warnings. Gore was spurred into action after buying her eleven-year-old daughter a copy of Prince's *Purple Rain* and being shocked and embarrassed to hear masturbation mentioned in the song "Darling Nikki." It seems likely that Gore, and the many people who supported her ultimately successful mission, would applaud the Court's decision in *Fraser*. See "Tipper Gore Widens War on Rock," *New York Times*, Jan. 4, 1988, C18; Bryan Reesman, "25 Years After Tipper

Assessing whether the Supreme Court was correct to hold that Fraser's speech lacked First Amendment protection is, in my view, one of the closest, most vexing calls within the entire canon of constitutional opinions involving students. The difficulty of this task is not made any easier by Chief Justice Burger's majority opinion, which is suffused with slipshod reasoning. Consider only two of the more glaring examples. First, in categorizing the speech, Burger confoundingly deemed Fraser's address not "political" for purposes of the First Amendment, and therefore not entitled to the highest standard of protection. But Fraser's remarks were delivered within the context of a student government election, and many people would regard advocacy for candidates as the very heart of political speech.[88] Second, in describing the speech itself, Burger oddly termed Fraser's speech "sexually explicit" and even "graphic." But Fraser instead deliberately confined himself to metaphor and double entendre, generally viewed as falling much closer to implicit (which is not necessarily to say subtle) language.

These and related criticisms so permeate Burger's opinion that even those inclined to cast *Fraser* in the most flattering possible light have expressed frustration with its lack of analytical clarity. Thus, even Professor James Ryan's sympathetic effort to reconstruct the Supreme Court's school jurisprudence conceded that *Fraser* was "a difficult decision to characterize, primarily because the Court took a scattershot approach to reach its holding," and further noted it "failed to articulate a standard for assessing the school officials' actions and instead offered several justifications for it."[89] More tellingly still, Chief Justice John Roberts in 2007, in a majority opinion for the Court that like *Fraser* cut back on student speech, candidly allowed, "The mode of analysis employed in *Fraser* is not entirely clear."[90] Given that majority opinions are traditionally loath to criticize the conceptual acuity on display in recent precedents—especially when they point in the direction the majority is marching—Roberts's rebuke, which would seem mild in many contexts, is best understood as evincing real exasperation.

Noting the limitations of Burger's opinion, however, should not be viewed as suggesting that the outcome in *Fraser* lacks solid

---

Gore's PMRC Hearings, the Opposing Sides Aren't So Far Apart," Vulture.com, Sept. 20, 2010; and Scott A. Moss, "The Overhyped Path from *Tinker* to *Morse*: How the Student Speech Cases Show the Limits of Supreme Court Decisions—for the Law and for the Litigants," 63 *Florida Law Review* 1407, 1407 (2011).

points in its favor. Supporters of *Fraser*'s outcome might emphasize that the speech's setting—delivered as it was not just in school or to a group of classmates but before an audience that included administrators—makes the address seem almost designed to flout school authority. Indeed, had Bethel not suspended Fraser, some supporters might argue, it could have seemed as though the school effectively endorsed, or at least tacitly approved, the nominating speech. Bolstering this claim, Fraser—like many teenagers both before and after him—knowingly tested the outer limits of permissibility. By Fraser's own admission, he showed the speech to a few Bethel teachers ahead of time to gauge their reactions, and they predicted it would go over poorly—even if they stopped short of warning him that it might result in suspension. On this account, then, Fraser (a skilled orator) understood very well that he was playing with rhetorical fire, and he should not have been surprised when administrators found its content inflammatory.

Related to this point, supporters of the outcome in *Fraser* could well note that an opinion granting even this speech constitutional protection would only delay the announcement of precisely what succeeds in crossing the line. Would *any* nondisruptive speech that steered clear of profanity also receive constitutional protection? The line separating protected speech from unprotected speech must be drawn somewhere, and *Fraser*'s line effectively—if inartfully—warns students not to get too clever with sexual references, or else they can be punished.

Finally, an additional factor supporting *Fraser*'s bottom line requires contemplating how school administrators could conceivably respond to a Supreme Court opinion reaching the opposite conclusion. If *Fraser* determined that the suspension violated the First Amendment, that is, schools might well react by simply forbidding students to address assemblies, or perhaps even eliminating student government (and its attendant elections) altogether. For some readers, then, permitting Fraser's suspension—even if not ideal as a first-order solution—presents a more attractive universe than the alternate universes that could have emerged in the wake of Fraser prevailing at the Supreme Court.

While these arguments for *Fraser*'s outcome contain some force, the more compelling view, in my assessment, maintains that the Supreme Court erred by holding that Fraser's speech lacked First Amendment protection. Given its surrounding context, it seems clear that Fraser's speech must be viewed as political in nature, and therefore entitled to a high level of protection. It is undoubtedly true that Bethel sought to punish Fraser not for the viewpoint he espoused but for the language he selected. The reason we know that Fraser was not punished for his viewpoint is that the fundamental idea he advanced was supporting Jeff Kuhlman's run for student government, and it seems safe to conclude that the school was agnostic on the question. Yet acknowledging Bethel's neutrality in this contest undermines the idea that any genuine danger existed of students attributing Fraser's juvenile speech to the school and that the school needed to punish him in order to establish that it did not endorse his sexual innuendo.

To the extent that Bethel truly sought to disassociate the school from Fraser's speech, moreover, it should have selected a more effective way than simply suspending him. As a general matter, the First Amendment supposes that the most powerful response to disfavored speech is not censorship but more speech.[91] This principle could surely have figured into this schooling context. Bethel's leadership could have, for example, encouraged teachers during a particular course to dedicate some time to explaining why they found Fraser's language objectionable and then opened up the matter for a brief discussion. One teacher on her own initiative adopted precisely that approach, and it seems appropriate in a nation committed to free speech, seeking as it does to use the remarks as an opportunity for "a teachable moment" rather than as an opportunity to drop the hammer. Some of the most enduring lessons in classrooms occur when teachers, at least on occasion, veer from the conventional material. Admittedly, opportunities for discussions in some classrooms would no doubt be greeted with silence, nervous laughter, and perhaps even vociferous defenses of Fraser's speech. In my estimation, however, each of those responses represents a result that is far more attractive and, indeed, more educational than simply declaring the address verboten and removing the speaker.

As to the language that Matthew Fraser actually used, the strongest available evidence indicates that while his remarks might well have toed the line of speech permissibly punishable by schools, he did not actually cross it. Fraser steered clear of vulgarity, limiting himself to sexual innuendo in the course of contending that Jeff Kuhlman was steadfast, driven, persistent, and—above all—committed to Bethel. The notion that Fraser's speech was "acutely insulting" to female students and "seriously damaging" to students completing the ninth grade, as the Court posited, betrayed an old-fashioned paternalism whose adherents deemed it improper to expose young "ladies" to coarse talk and revealed a tenuous grasp of the discourse that students actually encounter. Many high school students on a daily basis hear considerably more intense language in school (from their classmates) and in popular culture (including in films rated PG-13, a category that was introduced two years before *Fraser*).[92]*

Yet perhaps the strongest indication that Fraser's sexual innu-endo did not actually transgress the borders of the relevant com-munity standards involves how journalists treated the speech. Not only did several national newspapers publish Fraser's speech in its entirety; others, including the famously prudish *New York Times*, reprinted the most salacious parts of the speech without emenda-tion. Closer to home, Bethel's own school newspaper reprinted Fraser's speech in full after the legal controversy made its way to the Court.[93] If Fraser's speech were actually so outré as to merit a suspension, it seems difficult to believe that the school newspa-per would have deemed the material fit to print. While it is true that newspaper readers can always move to a different article if they find an article's content too racy, it is also true that students were permitted to report to a study hall if they disliked the assembly's content. Thus, Fraser's speech was not delivered to a "captive audi-ence," and that factor cannot explain why the school newspaper's publication of the speech should be viewed as conceptually distinct.

It is far from clear that—even from the perspective of an edu-cator who disliked Fraser's speech and wanted its reverberations minimized—Bethel's decision to sanction represented a sound

---

* For some pop cultural context, consider that *Ferris Bueller's Day Off* received a PG-13 rating from the Motion Picture Association of America and was released one month before the Supreme Court issued *Fraser*. This film, among other choice moments, includes about twenty-five uses of "ass" or "asshole," roughly twenty-two uses of "shit" and variants, ten uses each of "hell," "bastard," and "son of a bitch," two uses of "dick-head," and at least one clearly audible "fuck." In addition, the movie contains discus-sion of drug use; teenagers nude in front of each other (though offscreen); mention of "lay[ing]" a "chick"; and a voluptuous, cleavage-baring, shimmying Nurse-O-Gram, who sings, "I've come to restore your pluck / 'cause I'm the nurse who likes to f——," as the door shuts. See "Ferris Bueller's Day Off: Parents Guide," IMDb.com. Nor should *Ferris Bueller's Day Off* be regarded as pressing the upper limit of the PG-13 category. The IMDb Parents Guide rated the film a "*Mild* PG-13" and assigned it 21 out of a potential 50 rating for maturity.

choice in school management. As is often the case for punishing speakers (perhaps especially so for student speakers), imposing sanctions here might well have backfired, as they succeeded mainly in transforming Fraser into a martyr and making elements of the speech a rallying point for his classmates. After imposition of the sanctions, several students created placards to voice support for Fraser (and opposition to the administration) in the form of sexual innuendo inspired by the speech—with signs reading "Stand Firm[,] Matt," and "Don't Be Hard on Matt."[94] Intriguingly, though, Bethel opted against disciplining any of the students who supported Fraser with these slogans.

This defense of Fraser's constitutional right to free speech should not, of course, be misconstrued as support for the underlying manner in which he expressed himself. Fraser called his own speech "sophomoric," and even that assessment seems rather too gentle. At its very best, the speech seems severely ill-advised. Disliking Fraser's puerile speech, though, hardly means that it should be found to have exceeded the bounds of First Amendment protection. The First Amendment, even in school, must not be taken to protect only elevated discourse. As James Madison—widely deemed the father of the Constitution—wrote in early commentary on the First Amendment: "Some degree of abuse is inseparable from the proper use of everything."[95] And Fraser's verbal abuse, such as it was, did not deviate sufficiently from the proper use of free speech in school to merit punishment.

HAZELWOOD SCHOOL DISTRICT V. KUHLMEIER: REGULATING SCHOOL NEWSPAPERS

In May 1983, at Hazelwood East High School in St. Louis, Missouri, when the latest edition of the school newspaper became available for purchase, the small group of student editors found the issue distressingly thin. Rather than containing the entire six pages of articles that they had laid out, this issue of *Spectrum* contained only four. The two missing pages, it would soon become clear, had not been inadvertently omitted. A few days earlier, Hazelwood East's journalism teacher brought the page proofs to Principal Robert Eugene Reynolds for his final review—a standard step in *Spec-*

trum's pre-publication process. On this unusual occasion, though, Reynolds quickly decided that two of the scheduled articles were inappropriate for publication in *Spectrum*. "I knew darn well those articles weren't going to fly—I didn't have to look at them twice," Reynolds subsequently explained to one reporter. "The board and administration, even though they're good law-abiding citizens, want things run in their district the way they want them to run. They hire people who can do that, and when they can't do it any longer, they get rid of them." The first article that Reynolds deemed unacceptable addressed how students cope with parental divorces. Although the divorce piece included numerous quotations from anonymous students, it also quoted one ninth grader by name as stating, "My dad wasn't spending enough time with my mom, my sister and [me]. He was always out of town on business or out late playing cards with the guys. My parents always argued about everything." Reynolds contended that this student's parents should have been contacted for responses, allowing them to provide their own accounts of what triggered the divorce. The second article that Reynolds found objectionable provided extensive excerpts from interviews with three Hazelwood East students who had become pregnant. The piece noted at the outset, "All names have been changed to keep the identity of these girls a secret." But Reynolds contended that the article's accompanying details would allow some readers to identify the students, and claimed further that the article's references to sexual activity and birth control were unsuitable for Hazelwood East's younger students.[96]

With time running short before the scheduled press run, Reynolds feared that a significant delay in publication would prevent the issue from appearing before the school year concluded. He determined that the best available course of action demanded eliminating the two pages with the offending articles from the planned six-page issue. Although this approach also necessitated cutting a few additional articles that Reynolds considered unobjectionable, he believed that the circumstances in effect dictated a choice between publishing the reduced, four-page *Spectrum* and publishing nothing at all.

Cathy Kuhlmeier, *Spectrum*'s layout editor, found Principal Reynolds's shearing of *Spectrum* devastating. "I was so mad because we had worked so hard on those articles," she recalled.[97] In addition to feeling as though she had labored for naught, though, Kuhlmeier detested the excisions because the articles on divorce and teen pregnancy represented an important shift away from the dreary, uninspired topics that school newspapers perennially covered and toward a more socially conscious style of journalism. "We were trying to make a change with the school paper and not just write about school proms, football games and piddling stuff," Kuhlmeier said. "I don't think the administration wanted anyone to know that there were problems in the school or allow us to tackle issues that had some relevance to the students."[98] In addition, Kuhlmeier might have found the article on divorce particularly relevant to her own life, as it quoted her on the dissolution of her own parents' union. Eventually, Kuhlmeier—along with two fellow *Spectrum* editors— filed a lawsuit contending Reynolds's deletion of the contested articles contravened their free speech rights.

In *Hazelwood School District v. Kuhlmeier*, the Supreme Court in 1988 found that Reynolds's actions did not violate the student editors' freedom of speech. Justice Byron White's opinion for the Court made clear that the circumstances under which students produced *Spectrum*'s articles placed that speech in a different First Amendment category from the speech at issue in *Tinker*. *Spectrum* was not an independent outlet, where students could express themselves in any way they deemed fit, White reasoned. To the contrary, *Spectrum* was intimately interwoven with Hazelwood East's educational mission: not only did the students produce the newspaper as part of Journalism II, a graded academic class held during regular school hours, but educators oversaw the entire endeavor, exercising ultimate editorial authority. Thus, where *Tinker* addressed "educators' ability to silence students' personal expression . . . on the school premises," *Kuhlmeier* addressed "educators' authority over school-sponsored publications [and other activities that observers] might reasonably perceive to bear the imprimatur of the school."[99] In cases involving school-sponsored speech, *Kuhlmeier* announced, educators need not meet *Tinker*'s burden of demonstrating that they barred speech because they feared it would cause a substantial disruption. Instead, they needed to satisfy the far less demanding test of demonstrating that their actions bore a reasonable relationship to legitimate educational concerns. This lenient standard was appropriate, White suggested, because "the education of the Nation's youth is primarily the responsibility of parents, teachers, and state and local school officials, and not of federal judges."[100] Applying this new test to Principal Reynolds's actions, *Kuhlmeier* concluded that his decision to discard two pages of *Spectrum* constituted reasonable conduct under the conditions, as he understood them. Justifying Reynolds's concerns about the pregnancy article, the Court reasoned that "[i]t was not unreasonable for the principal to have concluded that such frank talk was inappropriate in a school-sponsored publication distributed to 14-year-old freshmen and presumably taken home to be read by students' even younger brothers and sisters."[101]

Justice William Brennan wrote a scathing dissent—joined by Justices Harry Blackmun and Thurgood Marshall—that depicted the Court as shirking its traditional responsibility for vindicating students' constitutional rights and preparing them for citizenship. The dissent opened ominously: "When the young men and women of Hazelwood East High School registered for Journalism II, they expected a civics lesson."[102] Brennan then proceeded to light into Principal Reynolds for his displays of "brutal censorship" and "unthinking contempt for individual rights."[103] While such actions would be "intolerable from any state official," Brennan continued, "[i]t is particularly insidious from [a principal,] one to whom the public entrusts the task of inculcating in its youth an appreciation for the cherished democratic liberties that our Constitution guarantees."[104] Brennan closed the dissent with a powerful flourish, bringing readers full circle: "The young men and women of Hazelwood East expected a civics lesson, but not the one the Court teaches them today."[105]

Among journalists, *Kuhlmeier* was widely portrayed as undermining both constitutional principles and Supreme Court precedent. Emphasizing the first theme, a *Chicago Tribune* columnist contended *Kuhlmeier* "tugs at an elemental thread in the nation's constitutional fabric: the grand notion of a free press."[106] An opinion piece in *The Christian Science Monitor* similarly termed *Kuhlmeier* an "erosion of the Constitution" that incorrectly elevated "[o]bedience and orthodoxy" above "learning."[107] Emphasizing the second theme, a *Los Angeles Times* editorial, titled "Censorship as a Lesson," contended *Kuhlmeier* "brushed aside perfectly good law" regulating student speech in order to "trash[ ] what young writers and editors produce."[108] The front-page articles on *Kuhlmeier* that appeared in *The New York Times* and *The Washington Post* agreed that

Reynolds's actions amounted to "censorship" and that the opinion signaled a clear retreat from *Tinker*.[109]*

Predictably, the intimate world of student journalism assailed the opinion with even greater ferocity. *Kuhlmeier* was "frightening," according to the Student Press Law Center's director, because "[s]chool newspapers are often the only avenue young people have for expressing their views, and this opinion says school officials can cut off that avenue whenever they disagree with what students are saying."[110] Student journalists themselves, fittingly, published op-eds in major newspapers denouncing the decision. "Censorship! Can you believe it? This is the United States of America in the 1980's," fumed one editor in chief of a school newspaper in New York.[111] Her counterpart at a school newspaper in New Jersey also pronounced herself "enraged" by *Kuhlmeier* and suggested that members of the majority "should have their eyes checked, since they seem to see 'for adults only' at the end of the First Amendment."[112] Back in Missouri, Cathy Kuhlmeier found the opinion bearing her name "extremely disappoint[ing]" and expressed fear that "this decision will turn kids off to journalism."[113] One of Kuhlmeier's fellow litigants, interviewed one month after the Court's decision, conceded that the outcome led her to doubt their entire legal endeavor: "I thought I was entitled to freedom of expression, freedom of speech and freedom of the press. I don't think I'd do it again. It has limited expression for all students."[114]

It was far from clear, however, that *Kuhlmeier* actually changed the status quo, either in schools or in newsrooms. In the decision's wake, various school officials, school district lawyers, and nation-

---

* Many law professors viewed *Kuhlmeier* in a similarly critical light. At the Supreme Court, Professor Martha Minow of Harvard filed an insightful amicus brief supporting the student editors' First Amendment claim in *Kuhlmeier*. See Brief for the NOW Legal Defense and Education Fund et al. supporting Respondents, *Kuhlmeier*, 484 U.S. 260, 1987 S. Ct. Briefs LEXIS 1134. After the Court's decision, Professor William Buss dismissed the Court's opinion as "unpersuasive." William G. Buss, "School Newspapers, Public Forum, and the First Amendment," 74 *Iowa Law Review* 505, 507 (1989). Over time, this broadly negative academic view of *Kuhlmeier* has not diminished. For example, Professor Catherine Ross's recent comprehensive examination of the First Amendment in public schools contended *Kuhlmeier* was a "frontal attack on the *Tinker* regime." Catherine J. Ross, *Lessons in Censorship: How Schools and Courts Subvert Students' First Amendment Rights* 45 (2015). See also James B. Raskin, "No Enclaves of Totalitarianism: The Triumph and Unrealized Promise of the *Tinker* Decision," 58 *American University Law Review* 1193, 1202 (2009) ("[H]eavy frontal damage was inflicted on *Tinker* in the *Hazelwood* decision").

wide educational organizations indicated that *Kuhlmeier* simply affirmed the broad authority that educators already exerted over school newspapers. For example, counsel for the National Association of Secondary School Principals contended that even before *Kuhlmeier* educators in effect served as editors in chief of school newspapers because "[t]hey are responsible for what" ultimately appears in print, and noted further, "No reporter has an unfettered right to publish whatever he wants in the paper."[115] That analogy also appeared to resonate with at least two newspaper columnists, located at polar ends of the political spectrum. In assessing the claim advanced by *Spectrum*'s editors, the nationally syndicated conservative columnist James J. Kilpatrick issued the following decree: "Horsefeathers! . . . In a real, grown-up world an editor is subject to a publisher, and if the publisher says 'Kill the piece,' that's it, the piece is killed. The right of a free press attaches to the guy who owns one. Students do not own a school paper."[116] Writing at *The Washington Post*, the liberal columnist Judy Mann agreed that the Court taught Hazelwood East's students "a lesson in reality"; as she elaborated, "Unfortunately for high school newspapers, most of them exist at the mercy of the school boards that fund them just as most grown-up newspapers exist at the mercy of the publishers who own them. First Amendment or not, we all live with somebody looking over our shoulders."[117]

It is difficult to overstate Principal Reynolds's astoundingly poor judgment and flagrantly illogical decisionmaking. As an initial matter, the articles that Reynolds identified as motivating the pre-publication purge addressed two topics—divorce and teenage pregnancy—that hold profound implications for high school students. Reading the drafted articles in their entirety, moreover, demonstrates that the students did not handle these important topics in a slapdash, immature manner. To the contrary, the articles contained material that not only would have been acceptable for high school students to encounter but would have been vital for that audience along dimensions both emotional and educational. The article on divorce, to take one example, quoted a student who poignantly revealed, "In the beginning I thought I caused the problem, but now I realize it wasn't me."[118] It seems quite probable that many Hazelwood East students would have derived comfort from these simple words—perhaps especially so during the early 1980s as the nation's divorce rate surged. Similarly, all three profiles regarding teen pregnancy contained first-person accounts suggesting that their pregnancies stunned them. The opening line of one profile ran, "I didn't think it could happen to me," and another began, "At first I was shocked. You always think, 'It won't happen to me.'"[119] Again, such information would be invaluable for the (presumably, many) additional Hazelwood East students who assume as an article of faith that their own sexual activity will, magically, not result in pregnancy. To the extent that Reynolds's stated objections actually drove him, furthermore, those concerns could have quite easily been redressed by other means. Omitting the student's name with the allegedly card-playing father from the divorce article, and altering the particulars of some details in the pregnancy article (and updating the disclaimer accordingly) should have remedied Reynolds's concerns. Finally, even accepting that these minor modifications presented logistical impossibilities, Reynolds should have both exhibited greater effort to salvage the unobjectionable articles and informed *Spectrum* editors of his actions instead of allowing them to discover the excisions in the published edition.* All told, then, Reynolds's management of *Spectrum* amounted to a parade of spectacular ineptitude.

Despite my antipathy for how Principal Reynolds handled the contested issue of *Spectrum*, I nevertheless contend that the Supreme Court reached the correct constitutional outcome in *Kuhlmeier* by finding that no free speech violation occurred in the case. The most persuasive basis for affirming the result in *Kuhlmeier*, however, departs in significant ways from the reasoning offered by Justice White's opinion for the Court. White's opinion was, in my estimation, unnecessarily convoluted, nowhere more so than in its severely strained efforts to deem Reynolds's actions reasonable. Instead, building upon the intuition shared by Kilpatrick and Mann, *Kuhlmeier* should have declared simply that the content of Hazelwood East's *Spectrum* belonged in a First Amendment category called "government speech," which permits the government to say what it wishes. One virtue of that approach is that it would

* One year after the Court's decision, Principal Reynolds—to his credit—expressed some remorse, at least for how he handled this last issue. If he were to handle the situation anew, Reynolds indicated that "he would call in the students involved and discuss his decision, rather than let them find out about it when they saw the paper." Virginia Hick, "Hazelwood Journalism Case Spreads Ripples a Year Later," *St. Louis Post-Dispatch*, Jan. 13, 1989, C1.

not require legal inquiry into the reasonableness of a public school's determination over what is said in its own name.

Admittedly, while adumbrations of the "government speech" doctrine appeared back in the 1970s, the Supreme Court did not formally announce the doctrine until three years after *Kuhlmeier.* Even at the time of *Kuhlmeier,* however, some astute legal commentators sought to conceptualize the case as in effect involving the nascent government speech category. Professor Mark Yudof—who wrote a book titled *When Government Speaks* in 1983 and would go on to head three major state university systems—insisted immediately after *Kuhlmeier* that the widespread teeth gnashing over the opinion was unwarranted. "The mass media and the public need to understand a simple truth: There is a difference between government controlling its own communications and its censorship of private speech," Yudof explained.[120] Headlines asserting that *Kuhlmeier* authorized principals to "censor" school newspapers, in Yudof's view, should hold all the shock value of a headline proclaiming Katharine Graham determined what appeared in *The Washington Post.* Extending the analogy, if Bob Woodward and Carl Bernstein could not have persuaded Graham and Ben Bradlee to publish their articles probing the Watergate scandal, no one would believe that their free speech rights had been violated because *The Washington Post* is a private entity and not covered by the freedom of speech. Some support for the government speech approach to school newspapers can be found on the current Supreme Court. In 2007, Justice Samuel Alito wrote a brief concurring opinion, joined by Justice Anthony Kennedy, that in passing wisely sought to reconceive *Kuhlmeier* as "allow[ing] a school to regulate what is in essence the school's own speech, that is, articles that appear in a publication that is an official school organ."[121]

Importing typical free speech principles into the school newspaper context could, if taken seriously, succeed in transforming even routine journalistic practices into constitutional violations. Recall that as a matter of standard procedure Principal Reynolds received for his review page proofs of *Spectrum* before publication. Yet it is black-letter law that the First Amendment generally forbids government officials to review expression before it is articulated or disseminated—an idea known in free speech circles as the prohibition on "prior restraint."[122] The very act of anticipating governmental review, the thinking runs, would invite people to censor themselves. Yet can it seriously be maintained that when Reynolds reviewed the proofs—or even when the teacher offered editorial guidance to students enrolled in Journalism II—a constitutional violation occurred? That view seems extraordinarily difficult to credit. Consider further the standard First Amendment requirement that the government may not suppress speech based on the viewpoint it advances. But if *Spectrum* can run an editorial encouraging the football team to beat its crosstown rival, could it also really be required to print an editorial—otherwise meeting its criteria for publication—urging Hazelwood East's defeat? That position seems downright bizarre.

Supporting the outcome in *Kuhlmeier* should not be taken as supporting the notion that public schools can control media coverage of those institutions as a general proposition. The school newspaper is a constitutionally distinct entity from the underground, or independent, student-run newspaper. The government, through the public school, may say what it wishes through its official house organ. But that does not mean that the government can unilaterally prevent others from criticizing the institution and the officials who run it. While the rise of the internet may mean that the underground newspaper has gone the way of the lava lamp, the larger principle remains: students should express themselves about their schools through unofficial venues. If student editors feel that the school newspaper imprudently refuses to publish an article because of its message, moreover, they ought to find another, unofficial outlet for that message. Eventually, that very dynamic unfolded in the factual dispute that produced *Kuhlmeier.* A little less than two years after Principal Reynolds deleted two pages from *Spectrum*, the *St. Louis Globe-Democrat*, in a multipage spread called "Too Hot for Hazelwood," published all of the excised articles. Nor is this instance unique, as the *Chicago Tribune* has also published an article originating at a suburban high school newspaper, which detailed some educators' questionable reimbursement submissions.[123] (It seems safe to assume that both stories would have received considerably less circulation had they appeared in their intended venues.) If citizens wish to provide student journalists writing for school newspapers with greater levels of protection than *Kuhlmeier* affords, moreover, they can do so by supporting legislation at the state level. This suggestion is hardly a pipe dream, as post-*Kuhlmeier* no fewer than ten states have passed such legislation. Finally, endorsing the outcome in *Kuhlmeier* should in no way be understood to endorse some of the egregious lower court decisions, where judges have stretched the notion of school-sponsored speech beyond recognition.[124]*

CONTEMPLATING *KUHLMEIER*
IN LIGHT OF PROHIBITIONS ON BOOK BANNING

Nor should support for *Kuhlmeier*'s outcome be regarded as incompatible with the Supreme Court's opinion in *Island Trees Union Free School District v. Pico*, which in 1982 acknowledged some limitations on the ability of public school libraries to ban books. This point merits analysis because Justice Brennan's dissenting opinion in *Kuhlmeier* suggested that the two factual scenarios were legally indistinguishable. "Just as a school board may not purge its state-funded library of all books that offen[d] [its] social, political and moral tastes," Brennan wrote, "school officials may not, out of like motivation, discriminatorily excise objectionable ideas from a student publication."[125] Brennan's analogy is not obviously erroneous. But in order to apprehend why the comparison ultimately falls short, it is helpful first to grasp the circumstances that culminated in *Pico*.

In autumn 1975, in Levittown, New York, a school board official (and retired police officer) named Frank Martin headed to the local high school one evening and persuaded a janitor to give him access to the library. Martin had recently received a list of "objectionable" books commonly found in libraries, and he sought to determine whether the school in his community contained any of the offending volumes. All told, Martin located nine of the listed books, including Alice Childress's *A Hero Ain't Nothin' but a Sandwich*, Eldridge Cleaver's *Soul on Ice*, Bernard Malamud's *The Fixer*, Kurt Vonnegut's *Slaughterhouse-Five*, and Richard Wright's *Black Boy*. Although

---

* Nothing here should be taken as suggesting that the government speech doctrine is invariably easy to apply. To the contrary, identifying where government speech begins and where private speech ends sometimes presents nettlesome questions. Nevertheless, as Professor Douglas Laycock long ago suggested, "[The government speech] line is *conceptually* clear, even if in some *applications* its location is murky." Douglas Laycock, "Equal Access and Moments of Silence: The Equal Status of Religious Speech by Private Speakers," 81 *Northwestern University Law Review* 1, 30 (1986) (emphasis added). *Kuhlmeier* does not, however, present a particularly difficult application of the government speech doctrine.

each of these volumes had acquired widespread acclaim and some of them garnered major prizes, Martin nevertheless successfully led his fellow board members to demand their removal from the school library. This action drew a firestorm of criticism. In an effort to quell the outcry and to explain their actions, the school board issued a press release, calling the removed books "anti-American, anti-Christian, anti-Sem[i]tic, and just plain filthy," and concluding that "[i]t is our duty, our moral obligation, to protect the children in our schools from this moral danger as surely as from physical and medical dangers." Martin subsequently testified that he objected to Childress's book because it mentioned that George Washington owned slaves: "I believe it is anti-American to present one of the nation's heroes, the first President, . . . in such a negative and obviously one-sided light."* One of Martin's colleagues on the school board offered testimony that cast the book-removal issue in a broader light: "I am basically a conservative in my general philosophy and feel that the community I represent as a school board member shares that philosophy. . . . I feel that it is my duty to apply my conservative principles to the decision making process in which I am involved as a board member."[126]

Following the controversy, several students agreed to challenge the school board's removal of books. Student Council President Steven Pico suggested that the school board's actions, though well intentioned, were deeply misguided. Pico cited a line from Malamud's *The Fixer* as animating his opposition to the board: "There are no wrong books . . . ; what's wrong is the fear of them."[127] One of Pico's classmates and fellow litigants contended that it was hardly accidental that those particular books—which offered accounts of

---

* The frustrations that Martin experienced as a school board member appear to have frequently had a racial dimension. Consider, for example, the explanation he offered to one reporter for rejecting a textbook that mentioned one of the twentieth century's preeminent musicians, in jazz or any other form. "Hey, I like Louie Armstrong's music, but dammit, it doesn't belong in a social studies textbook," Martin groused, "especially when they're taking space away from the Second World War or American history." Charles R. Babcock, "Book Banning Spreads," *Washington Post*, May 10, 1982, A1. It is not surprising that Eldridge Cleaver's *Soul on Ice* appeared on Martin's list of forbidden books. Many years earlier, *Time*'s issue recognizing the Middle American observed, "Perhaps the most authentic individual villains to Middle America are the Black Panther leaders, Eldridge Cleaver and Bobby Seale." "Man and Woman of the Year: The Middle Americans," 10. The Middle Americans' cultural heroes, by way of contrast, included Governor Ronald Reagan of California for his "hard line on dissent" among college students. Ibid., 11.

anti-Semitism and racial oppression, among other themes—had been targeted in her hometown. "Levittown," she said, "is a community where we don't get to see too much of what is in those books."[128]

Located about forty-five minutes outside Manhattan on what had been potato fields prior to World War II, Levittown was a planned community featuring scores of modest, indistinguishable ranch houses. Levittown made the American Dream of homeownership a reality for many white working-class families and had also long practiced racial exclusion. Before the Supreme Court's decision, several media outlets suggested that Levittown's demographic homogeneity might have been partly responsible for the drive toward banning books. Whatever the accuracy of that assessment, Kurt Vonnegut insisted that book banning—while it boosted his sales—had no place within the United States. "As an American," Vonnegut stated, "I am distressed that this sort of thing can happen in my country."[129]

Pico divided the Supreme Court 5–4, but even that figure probably understates the degree of its division, as the nine justices produced six different opinions, and no opinion claimed a majority. Justice Brennan, in a plurality opinion for himself and two colleagues, relied upon *Barnette* in reasoning that the school board's book removal violated students' First Amendment rights. Making it clear that the opinion addressed only book excision and not book acquisition, Brennan wrote, "[W]e hold that local school boards may not remove books from school library shelves simply because they dislike the ideas contained in those books and seek by their removal to 'prescribe what shall be orthodox in politics, nationalism, religion, or other matters of opinion.'"[130] Justice Blackmun wrote a concurring opinion that, for reasons only faintly distinct from the plurality's, also found the school board's actions violated the First Amendment. While Justice White, the critical fifth vote, refused to find a First Amendment violation, he did issue a terse opinion that had the effect of sending the matter back to the trial court to determine in the first instance whether impermissible motives animated the school board's book removal. The upshot of these three opinions in *Pico* has meant that public school libraries cannot banish volumes for overtly ideological reasons. Despite the absence of a clean First Amendment holding, *Pico*'s bottom line has enjoyed considerable vitality in lower courts that have subsequently addressed the issue—with successful battles being waged over the expulsion of titles ranging from *Annie on My Mind* to the Harry Potter series.*

While reconciling *Kuhlmeier* with *Pico* may raise some tension, that tension is not insoluble. Recall that Justice Brennan in *Kuhlmeier* likened what he referred to as a school newspaper's "excis[ing]" of an article to a school board's "purg[ing]" of a library book. But, upon close inspection, that comparison does not quite hold. The analytical difficulty arises from Justice Brennan's mischaracterization of the contested publishing decisions at issue in *Kuhlmeier.* School newspapers do not excise articles; they refuse to publish them. Properly understood, then, requiring the school newspaper to publish an article in *Kuhlmeier* would be tantamount not to the library's desire to expunge a book in *Pico* but to requiring the school library to purchase a particular volume. Even on Justice Brennan's own account in *Pico*, though, students cannot successfully claim that their First Amendment rights have been violated if a librarian refuses to purchase any particular title—no matter how deserving. The newspaper's refusal to publish, thus, peacefully coexists with the library's refusal to purchase. After a school library has already purchased particular books, however, the constitutional dynamics shift materially. While one can certainly trouble the dis-

---

* In *Case v. Unified School District*, a federal district court in Kansas found that a school board violated the First Amendment by requiring its schools to purge copies of Nancy Garden's *Annie on My Mind*—a young adult novel published by Farrar, Straus and Giroux in 1982 that chronicled a romantic relationship between two seventeen-year-old girls in New York City. In finding that the decision violated the First Amendment, the district court quoted extensively from the blatantly homophobic testimony school board members offered in support of their decision. For instance, one board member objected to the book's alleged "glorification of the gay lifestyle" and further stated, "I do not believe that homosexuality is a normal way of life." Another board member testified that it was unacceptable to be gay "[b]ecause engaging in a gay lifestyle can lead to death, destruction, disease, emotional problems." *Case v. Unified School District*, 908 F. Supp. 864, 870, 871 (D. Kan. 1995).

In *Counts v. Cedarville School District*, a federal district court in Arkansas invalidated a principal's plan—enacted at the school board's behest—to restrict access to J. K. Rowling's Harry Potter books after some community members objected that the series taught "witchcraft" and "the occult." Although the principal permitted students to access the books with signed permission from their parents, the district court nevertheless reasoned that this arrangement did not remedy the board's First Amendment violation. *Counts v. Cedarville School District*, 295 F. Supp. 2d 996, 1001, 1002 (W.D. Ark. 2003).

Professor Richard Peltz has observed that *Pico*'s plurality opinion "had substantial impact in the lower courts." Richard J. Peltz, "Pieces of *Pico*: Saving Intellectual Freedom in the Public School Library," 2005 *BYU Education and Law Journal* 103, 136.

tinction between expelling a book and failing to acquire it in the first instance, the distinction does have an identifiable logic. Libraries opt not to obtain books for many legitimate reasons, the thinking runs here, but secreting a book away (for reasons unrelated to shelf capacity) raises hackles and suspicions. The distinction, moreover, has proven workable within the lower courts. And so conceived, embracing *Kuhlmeier* does not require spurning *Pico*.

MORSE V. FREDERICK: PERMITTING VIEWPOINT RESTRICTIONS ON PRO-DRUG SPEECH

On January 24, 2002, Principal Deborah Morse of Juneau-Douglas High School in Juneau, Alaska, excused students from their usual morning classes, enabling them to attend a parade in front of the building to observe the Olympic torch pass through town en route to the winter games. Even by the standards of Juneau, it was an uncommonly cold January day. As students awaited the torch's arrival in the freezing temperatures, some students jostled classmates, throwing the occasional snowball and empty plastic bottle at one another to pass the time. Joseph Frederick, an eighteen-year-old senior, arrived late on the scene, having missed his first-period class. He had driven himself from home, parked on a public street a few blocks away, and—without first entering the school building—joined some classmates across the street from the school to watch the festivities. As the parade finally approached the school, Frederick (with assistance from a few compatriots) unfurled a homemade banner, measuring fourteen feet long, emblazoned with the following phrase: "BONG HiTS 4 JESUS." Principal Morse immediately crossed Glacier Avenue to confront the group and directed them to lower the banner. Frederick refused, asserting that the First Amendment protected this off-campus speech. Morse begged to differ, however, and confiscated Frederick's sign. Later that day, Morse suspended him for ten days, contending that the banner's message violated the school's rule against promoting illegal drug use. Although a "bong hit" is a slang term for a method of smoking marijuana, Frederick insisted the banner was meant to comment on neither drugs nor religion. Instead, Frederick claimed that the banner was intended to proclaim his First Amendment rights: "What the banner says is, 'I have the right to free speech, and I'm asserting it.'" Frederick also maintained that he created the banner in the hopes that it would attract the attention of television cameras covering the event. Although the record does not establish whether Frederick's banner ever appeared on Alaska's airwaves in 2002, it is unmistakably clear that the dispute on Glacier Avenue would garner the sustained focus of the Supreme Court five years later.[131]

In 2007, Chief Justice John Roberts wrote the Court's majority opinion in *Morse v. Frederick* finding that the First Amendment did not protect the "BONG HiTS 4 JESUS" banner. Roberts made short work of Frederick's contention that because he displayed the banner off campus, it should be treated as falling outside the student speech framework. In dispatching this claim, Roberts noted that the parade occurred during typical school hours, Morse had authorized students' attendance, school officials supervised the proceedings, and the high school band even performed—all of which made the event the equivalent of a field trip. While some speech scenarios may raise close calls, Roberts reasoned, *Frederick* did not fall anywhere near this line. Roberts then conceded that the banner's message was cryptic, but noted that not even Frederick himself contended that the sign contained a political message. Determining the sign's precise meaning was unnecessary, though, because Morse's reading it to promote illegal drug use was clearly a reasonable interpretation. With that foundation established, Roberts produced an incredibly narrow opinion that nevertheless carved out yet another exception to *Tinker*'s approach: "[W]e hold that schools may take steps to safeguard those entrusted to their care from speech that can reasonably be regarded as encouraging illegal drug use."[132] Roberts took pains to emphasize that *Frederick* should not be construed as authorizing schools to punish students for speech that could not rationally be viewed as pro-drug. This specialized approach was appropriate for this category, Roberts contended, because "[d]rug abuse can cause severe and permanent damage to the health and well-being of young people."[133]

Justice Clarence Thomas's concurring opinion in *Frederick* is genuinely startling. True to his reputation for being the justice most willing to upend seemingly settled areas of constitutional law, Thomas asserted *Frederick* had not gone nearly far enough in drawing back on student speech. *Tinker* was incorrectly decided in the first instance and ought to be overturned, Thomas maintained, because—under the original meaning of the Constitution—

students held no free speech rights whatsoever: "Historically, courts reasoned that only local school districts were entitled to make [disciplinary] calls. The *Tinker* Court usurped that traditional authority for the judiciary."[134] Waxing nostalgic for the days of yore, when "teachers managed classrooms with an iron hand," Thomas wrote, "[I]n the earliest public schools, teachers taught, and students listened. Teachers commanded, and students obeyed. Teachers did not rely solely on the power of ideas to persuade; they relied on discipline to maintain order."[135] For Thomas, the passage of time had sadly borne out Justice Black's prophecy of doom in *Tinker.* "Justice Black may not have been 'a prophet or the son of a prophet,' but his dissent in *Tinker* proved prophetic," Thomas lamented. "In the name of the First Amendment, *Tinker* has undermined the traditional authority of teachers to maintain order in public schools."[136] Thomas's opinion spoke only for himself, as even his fellow originalist Justice Antonin Scalia seemed to view *Tinker* as a precedent not worth fighting.*

Justice Stevens, joined by two other justices, wrote a passionate dissenting opinion that denounced *Frederick*'s blessing of a viewpoint-based restriction on speech. The First Amendment traditionally disfavors such restrictions, Stevens noted, because they prevent the marketplace of ideas from functioning properly. Stevens criticized

---

* Justice Alito, joined by Justice Kennedy, wrote a brief concurring opinion that sought to underscore that the opinion was limited to pro-drug speech. See *Morse v. Frederick*, 551 U.S. 393, 422 (2007) (Alito, J., concurring). Justice Stephen Breyer wrote an opinion that did not resolve the First Amendment question, and would have instead limited the decision to granting Principal Morse qualified immunity because her actions did not violate clearly established constitutional law. Justice Breyer cautioned against the wisdom of having the federal judiciary become further involved in school disputes:

> Students will test the limits of acceptable behavior in myriad ways better known to schoolteachers than to judges; school officials need a degree of flexible authority to respond to disciplinary challenges; and the law has always considered the relationship between teachers and students special. Under these circumstances, the more detailed the Court's supervision becomes, the more likely its law will engender further disputes among teachers and students. Consequently, larger numbers of those disputes will likely make their way from the schoolhouse to the courthouse. Yet no one wishes to substitute courts for school boards, or to turn the judge's chambers into the principal's office.

Ibid., 425, 428 (Breyer, J., concurring in the judgment in part and dissenting in part). This passage inspired the title of an edited collection of essays on law and education published by Brookings. See *From Schoolhouse to Courthouse: The Judiciary's Role in American Education* (Joshua M. Dunn and Martin R. West eds., 2009).

the Court for failing to note that the legalization of marijuana had generated considerable debate in Alaska, and observed that Morse's interpretation of the banner meant that Frederick could be viewed as seeking—"however inarticulately"—to participate in that discussion.[137] "In the national debate about a serious issue, it is the expression of the minority's viewpoint that most demands the protection of the First Amendment," Stevens wrote. "Whatever the better policy may be, a full and frank discussion of the costs and benefits of the attempt to prohibit the use of marijuana is far wiser than suppression of speech because it is unpopular."[138] Drawing upon recollections from his youth, the octogenarian Stevens cautioned that the nation's disastrous experience with alcohol during the Prohibition era should make the Supreme Court particularly reluctant to uphold restrictions on speech that can be viewed as condemning extant drug laws. In language that grows more prescient with each passing year, Stevens commented,

> [T]he current dominant opinion supporting the war on drugs in general, and our antimarijuana laws in particular, is reminiscent of the opinion that supported the nationwide ban on alcohol consumption when I was a student. While alcoholic beverages are now regarded as ordinary articles of commerce, their use was then condemned with the same moral fervor that now supports the war on drugs. . . . [J]ust as prohibition in the 1920's and early 1930's was secretly questioned by thousands of otherwise law-abiding patrons of bootleggers and speakeasies, today the actions of literally millions of otherwise law-abiding users of marijuana . . . lead me to wonder whether the fear of disapproval by those in the majority is silencing opponents of the war on drugs.[139]

Frederick is the rare Supreme Court decision that pleased just about no one. That liberal audiences disparaged the opinion's crackdown on student speech should hardly surprise. Even before *Frederick* landed, the *New York Times* and the *Washington Post* editorial boards advised the Court against further eroding free speech in schools. For these broadsheets, examining Chief Justice Roberts's treatment of the issue did not prompt a reassessment. "[Frederick's] oblique reference to drugs hardly justifies such mangling of sound precedent and the First Amendment," the *Times* chided.[140] The *Post*, in an editorial cleverly titled "A Less-than-Banner Ruling," went even further: "Issues of drug use and drug policy are matters of serious contention. High school students must be able to debate them frankly—and that might even involve students taking the position that bong hits are not that bad."[141]

While many decorated liberal legal scholars—including Ronald Dworkin, Martha Nussbaum, and Laurence Tribe—criticized *Frederick*, perhaps the most devastating academic critique came from a left-leaning professor who espoused no view on the Court's bottom line. Writing in *The Supreme Court Review*, Professor Frederick Schauer instead used the opinion as an occasion to underscore how deeply idiosyncratic the Court's intervention must appear from the perspective of both educators and judges who wrestle with student speech disputes. "Faced with an opportunity to say something helpful to and for those in the trenches," Schauer commented, "the Court not only selected a highly unrepresentative case for its first foray into the area in [many] years, but it also decided the case on narrow grounds, [focusing] on those dimensions of the case least likely to be found in the conflicts that bedevil school administrators and lower courts."[142] For Schauer, then, *Frederick* seemed less incorrect than irrelevant.

Many right-leaning legal commentators also branded *Frederick* a deeply disappointing, misconceived opinion, though for different reasons. Some of these observers flatly contended the Court should have declared the banner protected by the First Amendment. David French, writing in *National Review*, found *Frederick*'s effort to distinguish pro-drug speech from all other types of student speech intellectually unsatisfying, and further suggested that this weak analytical foundation portended additional restrictions on student speech—restrictions that many conservatives would dislike. "All of the justifications that Justice Roberts applied to limiting speech regarding drug use could be used by school administrators to silence dissent on controversial issues regarding, for example, homosexual behavior, religion, and gender politics," French noted.[143] Writing for a publication affiliated with the Cato Institute, Hans Bader panned *Frederick* for its willingness to police speech occurring off school grounds and attributed the Court's opinion to "its zeal to give the government a win in the 'War on Drugs.'"[144] The former Whitewater independent counsel, Kenneth Starr, who argued in the Supreme Court on behalf of Morse and the school district, technically won the case. But his post-decision analysis of the opinion sounded nothing less than despondent. Starr's Supreme Court brief proposed a much broader legal rule than *Frederick* actually adopted, one that would have permitted schools to suppress any student speech that interfered with the school's educational mission. Not only did the Court reject this approach, however, but Starr detected in *Frederick* a retreat from the notion that schools are responsible for inculcating community values. "*Fraser*'s normative vision is dead," Starr wrote. "Individual liberty reigns supreme. Justice Fortas and the *Tinker* Court would be very pleased indeed."[145]

Even conservatives who did not express open hostility to *Frederick* found very little to applaud in the opinion, as they struck the refrain holding that federal judges had no business resolving schoolhouse disputes in the first instance. Robert Bork, the former judge and rejected Supreme Court nominee, was the most prominent member of this camp. "Deploying the federal judicial system in full regalia for the Morse-Frederick squabble is like hunting field mice with an elephant gun," Bork stated. "My own view is that Frederick's complaint should have been dismissed out of hand. The speech clause took a wrong turn some time back, and, in cases like this, it very likely does more harm than good to both law and education."[146]

In my assessment, the Supreme Court in *Frederick* unwisely betrayed the traditional First Amendment principle permitting restrictions on speech only if they are neutral with respect to viewpoint. Chief Justice Roberts's effort to cast speech promoting illegal drug use as somehow uniquely harmful to teenagers—deserving a specialized approach, applicable on that one issue, to that one position—is wholly unpersuasive. *Frederick* retreats from the central idea in *Tinker*, as the Court's foremost opinion involving student speech made it a point of national pride that public schools should host a vigorous exchange of ideas on even controversial topics. The school not only can, but should, promote its antidrug agenda through a variety of different mechanisms—including posters, student assemblies, and health courses. But it is another matter entirely to prevent students from advancing their own views on topics *because* of the opinion they wish to advance, and when they do so in a way that cannot remotely be understood as disrupting school activities. While it would have been permissible for the school to punish Frederick had he in the middle of calculus class unfurled a fourteen-foot banner (promoting marijuana or anything else), he waited for a perfectly appropriate school setting to communicate his idea.[147]

Some readers may doubt whether prior to *Frederick* any school officials actually believed that *Tinker* required them to permit students to espouse pro-drug speech. On this account, Principal Morse did what any sensible educator would have done during the last five decades. *Frederick*, thus viewed, should be understood as codifying, rather than upending, school law as it has played out on the ground. Yet considerable evidence undermines this intuition. In 1970, a federal appellate court invalidated disciplinary actions taken against two students who distributed at school an underground publication they made titled *Grass High*. (Get it?) Tellingly, educators did not even attempt to cite the publication's title (which could reasonably be viewed as promoting illegal drug use) to justify the students' punishment. Instead, they (unsuccessfully) aimed to hang their hat on statements that criticized the school administration and, unrelatedly, that extolled oral sex. A few years later, an attorney for a school district expressly warned against seeking to discipline students for wearing T-shirts with the word "Marijuana" stenciled across the front. Finally, by the mid-1980s, this view was sufficiently widespread that Professor Lawrence Friedman of Stanford Law School could write that "*of course*, students can . . . distribute pro-pot or anti-pot literature. . . . This is . . . the message of modern law."[148] Accordingly, *Frederick* cannot be dismissed as an opinion that simply legitimated the status quo.

As commentators predicted when *Frederick* was decided, moreover, some lower courts have interpreted the opinion's reasoning to encompass student speech that has nothing to do with drugs. Thus, a few federal appellate courts have relied upon *Frederick*'s concern about the effects of drugs on student health to extrapolate a broader principle that permits schools to punish students for speech— sometimes in the form of creative writing—that can be understood as advocating harm to the safety of students or educators in the school context. While no rational person in the current era would gainsay educators' concerns about violence in school, it is extremely doubtful that judges should resort to distorting *Frederick* in order to permit schools to address such speech. Other jurisprudential avenues, including current understandings of *Tinker* itself, should permit schools to take the steps necessary to address such speech.

More troublingly, though, Judge Richard Posner—one of the

nation's most distinguished federal judges in recent decades—wrote an opinion in 2008 contending that *Frederick*'s concern about drugs' effects on adolescent minds permits schools to quash student speech that may be thought to hurt a classmate's psyche. Reading *Frederick* to authorize school censorship of student speech because of its negative "psychological effects," as Posner insists, stretches that supposedly narrow precedent in truly dangerous ways.[149] Indeed, taken seriously, this logic may even suggest that *Tinker* itself was decided incorrectly because, after all, the Des Moines School District contended that friends of a student who was killed in Vietnam would become anguished if they were confronted with antiwar armbands. The broad, almost limitless nature of Judge Posner's gloss on *Frederick* can be glimpsed when, immediately after musing upon the "psychological effects" of student speech, he cites the Court's precedent to support the following proposition: "[W]e infer that if there is reason to think that a particular type of student speech will lead to a decline in students' test scores, *an upsurge in truancy, or other symptoms of a sick school* . . . the school can forbid the speech."[150] Can it really be accurate that students who encourage one-day school boycotts to protest political injustice—speech that could be regarded as increasing truancy—would not enjoy First Amendment protections? Judge Posner's language—particularly the incredibly expansive "other symptoms of a sick school"—veritably invites educators to punish students for disfavored speech, and then to support their decisions by creating flimsy school-based rationales that would not suffice under *Tinker*. Hopefully, educators will decline this invitation, and other federal courts will eschew the "psychological effects" standard that Judge Posner indecorously grafted onto *Frederick*.

Students who wish to express themselves can derive an important lesson from a strategic error that Frederick made in framing his First Amendment argument. Rather than contending that his banner was meant to convey either a nonsensically humorous phrase or a bare assertion of his free speech rights, Frederick should have suggested that he intended the banner to advance his views about political issues, including the war on drugs. By draining his banner of political meaning, Frederick made it considerably easier for the Supreme Court to dismiss its significance and uphold the school's suspension. When educators (and judges) ask students why they made a particular statement, students who wish to have their First Amendment rights observed should avoid offering an answer that can be reduced to the classic teenager response: "Just 'cause." Setting aside whether it is just to impose an additional hurdle on student speech in school, there can be no doubt that this hurdle exists and that it has tripped up students since shortly after the dawn of the judiciary's involvement in this area. In 1970, for example, a school in El Paso, Texas, refused to permit a student to enroll for his junior year because his hair was longer than school rules permitted for male pupils. The student could have considered contending he wore his hair long to convey an antiwar message, to communicate his rejection of social conformity, or even to express solidarity with the founding fathers.* Instead of those more viable explanations, however, the student explained he wore long hair "because I like my hair long."[151]† Grounding students' statements and conduct in political ideology certainly does not guarantee that courts will vindicate their First Amendment claims. But it does ensure that courts will view their arguments through the most favorable prism.

One final piece of advice merits offering: even students who are interested in expressing antidrug views should not necessarily believe they are automatically permitted to express such sentiments in any fashion. In 1992, Kimberly Broussard, a seventh-grade student in Norfolk, Virginia, received a one-day suspension for wearing a T-shirt to school that read, "Drugs Suck!" To justify

---

* In *Massie v. Henry*, in the course of invalidating a hair-length restriction, a federal appellate court reasoned that long hair on males "is no more than a harkening back to the fashion of earlier years. For example, many of the founding fathers . . . wore their hair (either real or false) in a style comparable to that adopted by [student] plaintiffs." 455 F.2d 799, 780 (4th Cir. 1972). *Massie*'s rationale can also be understood to contain a religious justification for long hair: "Although there exists no depiction of Jesus Christ, either reputedly or historically accurate, He has always been shown with hair at least the length of that of plaintiffs." Ibid.

† Despite the poor quality of the student's argument in this case, Judge John Minor Wisdom wrote a powerful dissenting opinion, gesturing toward *Barnette*'s prohibition on compelled speech, which would have vindicated the student's right to wear long hair:

> Like other elements of costume, hair is a symbol: of elegance, of efficiency, of affinity and association, of non-conformity and rejection of traditional values. A person shorn of the freedom to vary the length and style of his hair is forced against his will to hold himself out symbolically as a person holding ideas contrary, perhaps, to ideas he holds most dear. Forced dress, including forced hair style, humiliates the unwilling complier, forces him to submerge his individuality in the "undistracting" mass, and in general, smacks of the exaltation of organization over member, unit over component, and state over individual. I always thought this country does not condone such repression.

Karr v. Schmidt, 460 F.2d 609, 621 (5th Cir. 1972) (Wisdom, J., dissenting).

the suspension, school officials did not suggest that she wore the garment ironically—a stoner's effort to mock the school's antidrug mission as square. Instead, the school suggested that the presence of the word "Suck" rendered the shirt inappropriate school attire. Surprisingly, the federal district court found that Broussard's suspension did not violate the First Amendment, because "a reasonable middle school administrator could find that the word 'suck,' even as used on the shirt, may be interpreted to have a sexual connotation."[152] In support of its decision, the court relied overwhelmingly upon the Supreme Court's opinion in *Fraser*.

ASSESSING FREE SPEECH TODAY: *TINKER*'S CONTINUING VITALITY

Following *Tinker*'s defense of student speech in 1969, the Supreme Court has handed students a series of high-profile defeats in this area—events that have provoked many observers over time to express grave doubts whether the First Amendment retains vitality in schools. In 2000, Professor Erwin Chemerinsky articulated this idea most prominently in an article subtitled "What's Left of *Tinker*?" His assessment registered somewhere between not much and nothing at all. Chemerinsky contended that the Supreme Court "views schools as authoritarian institutions," to which it all-too-readily deferred: "[T]he *Tinker* majority's approach to student speech is no longer followed; the subsequent cases are much closer to Justice Black's dissent than to Justice Fortas's majority opinion."[153] *Frederick*, of course, did nothing to tamp down such dire evaluations. In 2009, the *Journal of Law and Education* contained an article asserting that *Fraser, Kuhlmeier,* and *Frederick* had collectively "deflected the import of the *Tinker* opinion to the point of practically reversing or, at least, effectively compartmentalizing it," and a law review article likewise contended that the trio has "render[ed] *Tinker* negligible to a large extent."[154]

Each step along the way has, however, elicited fresh spasms of concern that the judiciary has jettisoned *Tinker*. Thus, in 1988, the *Duke Law Journal* contained a piece contending "*Kuhlmeier* eviscerates . . . *Tinker*," only two years after *Phi Delta Kappan* asked post-*Fraser*: "Is *Tinker* Dead?"[155] As early as 1970, *The Georgetown Law Journal*, in an article subtitled "*Tinker* Distinguished," could already be heard lamenting that the Court had effectively interred its one-year-old precedent: "[S]ince *Tinker*, the Supreme Court has declined to review several controversial federal court of appeals decisions dealing with student conduct and discipline."[156]

Reports of *Tinker*'s demise have, however, been greatly exaggerated. While the Court's post-*Tinker* opinions should not be dismissed as inconsequential, neither should they be viewed as draining student speech of all vitality. The Supreme Court in *Fraser*, *Kuhlmeier*, and *Frederick* did not purport to undercut *Tinker*'s core contribution: students, typically speaking, continue to possess the right to express themselves in schools, even if educators do not support their messages. The Court's subsequent opinions can plausibly be viewed as retreating in particular areas—involving speech that is lewd, school-sponsored, or pro-drug. But it is implausible to contend that those decisions indicate that *Tinker* has been hollowed out entirely, so that only its edifice remains. To the contrary, today's students enjoy far greater First Amendment protections than did their counterparts in the pre-*Tinker* era.[157]

Lower courts often issue decisions permitting students to express themselves, even over the objections of school administrators. In recent years, for example, the federal judiciary has issued opinions vindicating students' First Amendment rights to oppose President George W. Bush by wearing a T-shirt that refers to him as an "International Terrorist"; advance gay equality by wearing items that read, "Gay? Fine by Me," "I Support Gays," and "Pro-Gay Marriage"; and support a national breast cancer awareness campaign by wearing a bracelet that reads "I ♥ boobies!"[158]

After *Tinker*, moreover, some lower courts have even held that student hecklers must not be permitted to silence student speech. In 2004, for example, a federal appellate court upheld a student's right to thrust his fist in the air as his classmates recited the Pledge of Allegiance, even though the school contended that other students would react with hostility to his silent protest. In doing so, the Eleventh Circuit expressly rejected the notion that *Tinker* must permit hecklers to veto student speech:

> If certain bullies are likely to act violently when a student wears long hair, it is unquestionably easy for a principal to preclude the outburst by preventing the student from wearing long hair. To do so, however, is to sacrifice freedom upon the alt[a]r of order, and

allow the scope of our liberty to be dictated by the inclinations of the unlawful mob. . . . The fact that other students might take such a hairstyle as an incitement to violence is an indictment of those other students, not long hair. . . . While the same constitutional standards do not always apply in public schools as on public streets, we cannot afford students less constitutional protection simply because their peers might illegally express disagreement through violence instead of reason.[159]

One particularly notable anti-heckler's-veto decision occurred in 1980 when a high school senior in Rhode Island named Aaron Fricke wished to bring another young man to the prom as his date. School administrators responded that Fricke could not do so because they could not guarantee his safety against attacks from his classmates—an assertion that had at least some factual basis because the school recently witnessed physical altercations over sexual orientation. Nevertheless, the district court invalidated the school's response as impermissibly infringing upon Fricke's First Amendment expressive rights. To rule otherwise, the court explained, would endorse "mob rule" and "completely subvert free speech in the schools by granting other students a 'heckler's veto,' allowing them to decide through prohibited and violent methods what speech will be heard."[160] In 2000, a Massachusetts Superior Court relied upon that decision to invalidate a school's effort to prohibit a transgendered student from wearing clothing to school that corresponded to her gender identity.[161]

Perhaps even more revealing of *Tinker*'s legacy than these judicial opinions, though, are the many instances in recent years where educators have initially sought to suppress student speech only to realize that their stance cannot be squared with the Constitution. Following this pattern, school districts have retreated from efforts to prohibit students from weighing in on the Middle East conflict by displaying a pin featuring the Palestinian flag; expressing pro-life views by wearing a T-shirt that reads, "Abortion Kills Kids"; and expressing solidarity with the Black Lives Matter movement by wearing "I Can't Breathe" T-shirts in honor of the dying words that Eric Garner wheezed as a police officer choked him.[162] If *Tinker* were truly as feeble as some observers maintain, educators in these instances—and many others besides—would have squelched these student statements with impunity.

While *Tinker* is best construed as retaining vitality, that position should not be mistaken for complacency, contending that all is well with the First Amendment in schools. Today, three primary areas stand out as demanding significant interventions. First, although some judges have wisely rejected hecklers' efforts to veto speech, such opinions are sporadic rather than universal. Lower courts still too frequently indulge that practice and rely upon related techniques in order to uphold schools' efforts to silence student speech on contentious issues. Second, school policies regarding dress codes and school uniforms ought to draw far closer judicial scrutiny than they currently receive. Finally, lower courts have permitted school officials to exert excessive authority over student speech that is articulated off campus.

Lower courts often permit schools to stifle student expression of views on divisive topics, including on major questions of national significance. Consider a few examples. In 2007, a federal district court in Southern Texas upheld a school's decision to prohibit students from wearing T-shirts that read "Border Patrol" and "We Are Not Criminals" as methods of expressing competing positions on unauthorized immigration. In 2014, the U.S. Court of Appeals for the Ninth Circuit upheld a Northern California school's decision to prohibit students from wearing clothes featuring images of the American flag on the day celebrating Cinco de Mayo. The courts in those two cases found that the schools' actions were justified because the contested speech had generated angry reactions and even threats from classmates—classic instances of the heckler's veto at work. Even when schools cannot persuasively claim that student speech caused any tempers to flare or disruption of school activities, however, courts have nonetheless sometimes upheld bans on expression about divisive topics. In 2006, for example, the Ninth Circuit upheld a Southern California school's decision to prohibit a student from wearing a T-shirt, in protest of a school-sanctioned Day of Silence, that read, "Be Ashamed, Our School Embraced What God Has Condemned" and "Homosexuality Is Shameful 'Romans 1:27.'"* In 2010, moreover, the U.S. Court of Appeals for

* According to the Gay, Lesbian, and Straight Education Network (GLSEN), which sponsors the Day of Silence, the event is an "effort in which participants take a vow of silence to peacefully protest the discrimination and harassment faced by lesbian, gay, bisexual and transgender (LGBT) youth in schools." Press Release, "A New Record for the Day of Silence," GLSEN, April 14, 2004.

the Sixth Circuit upheld a Tennessee school's ban of clothes featuring the Confederate flag when a student wore a T-shirt with the controversial emblem and text reading, "If you have a problem with this flag you need a history lesson."[163]

The desire of schools to curtail speech on these acrimonious topics is certainly understandable. Few topics have demonstrated the ability to stir passions more intensely in recent years than unauthorized immigration, cultural assimilation among Mexican Americans, the quest for gay equality, and the Confederate flag's relationship to racial subordination. Nevertheless, the courts, in my view, erred by permitting these speech prohibitions in all four of these instances. That view is influenced in no small part, of course, by the knowledge that the Iowa students who expressed opposition to the Vietnam War in 1965 also stirred intense passions. Students in the above cases who disagreed with the messages they believed their classmates were conveying should have either informed them of their disagreement or—if they could not manage to do so in a composed fashion—simply ignored them. In the marketplace of ideas, boycotts too can sometimes be an effective instrument for change.

Contemplate each of the four cases in turn. While there can be no doubt that the topic of immigration reform generates strong feelings and that some students on both sides of the debate may well feel affronted by those T-shirts, schools should not take it upon themselves to ban this sort of communication on this vital topic. If either students threaten their classmates or an outbreak of violence occurs, the students who are responsible for actually causing those disruptions should be disciplined, not the speaker. That same analysis pertains to the students who threatened violence against classmates who displayed the American flag on Cinco de Mayo. I maintain that view even though I well understand that some celebrants may genuinely feel aggrieved by classmates who display Old Glory on the lone day during the entire school year set aside to honor Mexican heritage. In both instances, however, rewarding angry hecklers by silencing speakers incentivizes students in precisely the wrong manner.

The remaining two cases present closer calls. The student who opposed the Day of Silence sought to express his religious-based opposition to the school's embrace of gay equality; he expressed that position without resorting to epithets, and it is difficult to know how he could have expressed his particular view (which is distinct from expressing pride in heterosexuality) in a way that educators would have deemed permissible. Although I vehemently disagree with the T-shirt's stance and regard it as animated by antigay sentiment, I also believe that a school should not make it virtually impossible to express a particular viewpoint—especially when that opinion opposes the school's own position. Finally, the Confederate flag case presents, in my estimation, the most vexing case of all. I associate that flag primarily with an expression of racial hostility and for that reason detest it. Nevertheless, I do not believe that it usually connotes a threat of violence, as is true with burning crosses.* Ultimately, my assessment that this school's ban on the Confederate flag should not have been permitted to stand is due in no small part to the accompanying action it took to make that ban viable. To comply with the requirement for viewpoint neutrality, the school also barred paraphernalia promoting Malcolm X. While it is far from clear that the opposite view of the Confederate flag is actually communicated by a Malcolm X hat—rather than, say, the American flag—it does seem clear that public schools are spectacularly ill suited to making that determination.

Consider a few more broadly applicable reasons why upholding these bans on student speech might have been unwise in these four

---

* CNN conducted a nationwide poll on the Confederate flag in June 2015, shortly after the racially motivated murders of nine black parishioners at a church in Charleston, South Carolina, and the emergence of photographs that depicted the gunman displaying the divisive banner. The poll revealed that 57 percent of Americans viewed the Confederate flag more as a symbol of "southern pride" than of "racism," and only one in three Americans thought that it indicated more "racism" than "southern pride." Predictably, black respondents generally viewed the flag as symbolizing more "racism" than "southern pride," and white respondents generally adopted the opposite view. A poll taken in 2000 revealed roughly the same assessment as the 2015 poll, as 59 percent of Americans then viewed the Confederate flag as indicating more "southern pride" than "racism." Question 23, CNN/ORC Poll, June 26–28, 2015. See also Frances Robles, "Roof's Photos Appear on Site with Manifesto," *New York Times*, June 21, 2015, A1.

Displays of the Confederate flag cannot credibly be understood as *always* racist. In 2013, Kanye West explained his appropriation of the Confederate flag during his *Yeezus* tour thusly: "The Confederate flag represented slavery in a way. That's my abstract take on what I know about it, right? . . . So I took the Confederate flag and made it my flag. It's *my* flag now. Now what are you going to do?" Stereo Williams, "Why Rappers Rock the Confederate Flag," *Daily Beast*, June 30, 2015. West's effort to transform the meaning of a symbol of oppression into a symbol of liberation has important precursors. Most notably, the gay liberation movement beginning in the 1970s claimed the pink triangle—which Nazis affixed to gay prisoners' uniforms during the Holocaust—as a symbol of resistance.

cases. First, validating these bans sends the message that particular groups of students may be more psychologically fragile and lacking in self-control than actually seems warranted. Second, because the bans apply only within school, it seems important to remember that these groups of students may well encounter versions of this speech outside school and that they may be less adept at navigating those situations because the experience is unfamiliar. Third, the bans seem unlikely to rid the school of the disfavored message because clever students can locate alternate phrasing or symbols to serve as a substitute for the prohibited speech. (Contemplate, for example, how the Confederate flag could be swapped for iconic images of Robert E. Lee.) Fourth, the bans themselves may even prove counterproductive because they render particular expression taboo, which will for some subset of students elevate its status and make it more attractive, precisely because it is forbidden in school.

To argue that courts have exhibited excessive deference when schools forbid student speech on divisive topics is hardly to argue that courts should treat schools as equivalent to public parks for First Amendment purposes. If students in school, for example, express themselves using a derogatory epithet that attacks students on the grounds of sex, race, religion, nationality, or sexual orientation, then schools should be permitted to discipline those students—even though the First Amendment would protect students who used exactly the same language in a public park. No student should be required to sit behind someone in class with a T-shirt that reads on its back, "Deport Wetbacks" or "Faggots Stink." Schools should permit students to express their views on unauthorized immigration and gay equality, but that does not mean students must be permitted to do so in any language they desire. The most compelling legal justification for prohibiting such statements would announce that the threshold for being deemed "fighting words" is lower in schools than in public parks. Fighting words—like true threats—are traditionally understood as falling completely outside the First Amendment's protection, because their bare utterance tends to incite a breach of the peace. While the Supreme Court has narrowed the fighting-words doctrine since it debuted in 1942, the Court also has repeatedly (and recently) insisted that the doctrine remains good law. The school context presents a particularly appropriate venue for the doctrine's application because—unlike in a public park, where listeners can walk away from speakers peddling inflammatory language—students are captive audiences for one another's speech because their presence is required. The invocation of the fighting-words doctrine should not, moreover, be understood as simply permitting a heckler's veto by another name. The notion of the heckler's veto occurs when particularly sensitive audiences become outraged and threaten a speaker whose speech would not typically provoke listeners. In contrast, the invocation of the fighting-words doctrine—when properly applied—hinges not on an audience's subjective reaction but on whether the speaker's language itself passed an objective threshold.[164]*

At this point, some readers may believe that the most attractive solution to these issues would grant schools broad authority to impose dress codes or uniforms on students as they deem appropriate. Authorizing schools to prohibit students from wearing clothing that communicates any point of view on a wholesale basis would have the virtue of removing educators from the delicate business of enforcing vaguely worded clothing policies on a retail basis. When a school prohibits articles of clothing through individualized assessments, opportunities for arbitrary discrimination present themselves. In tiny Van Wert, Ohio, for example, high school educators prohibited one student from wearing a T-shirt promoting the rock band Marilyn Manson because they contended the item violated the school's policy on "offensive" clothing. According to school officials, the T-shirt was "offensive because the band promotes destructive conduct and demoralizing values contrary to the educational mission of the school."[165] The school bolstered its case by citing disliked lyrics from particular songs (that did not appear in any form on the student's shirt) and by citing media reports that portrayed the group's eponymous front man as possessing "a pro-drug persona." In 2000, a federal appellate court—relying upon a combination of *Fraser* and *Kuhlmeier*—upheld the school's actions, reasoning that schools need not tolerate clothes that "promote values that are so patently contrary to the school's educational mis-

---

* It seems essential here to appreciate just how unvarnished and free-ranging statements within the public sphere can become without being deemed "fighting words." In 2011, the Supreme Court, by an 8–1 margin, found that the First Amendment protected Westboro Baptist Church's protest of a military funeral with placards reading—among other phrases—"Fag troops," "Semper fi fags," "Thank God for dead soldiers," and "You're going to hell." *Snyder v. Phelps*, 562 U.S. 443, 443, 455 (2011). Justice Alito was the sole dissenter who would have deemed the speech unprotected by the First Amendment.

sion."[166] Although the panel's decision drew a powerful dissent arguing that the majority incorrectly interpreted *Fraser* and *Kuhlmeier* as overruling *Tinker*, the Supreme Court denied the petition for certiorari without comment.

While singling out Marilyn Manson apparel for special treatment seems clearly unconstitutional, courts should also demonstrate greater skepticism in cases contesting generally applicable student dress codes and uniforms. Lower courts that have entertained legal challenges to these policies almost reflexively uphold them, even when doing so requires considerable contortions. In 2005, for example, a federal appellate court upheld a school dress code that—among other ills—contained extraordinarily vague restrictions, giving its enforcers overwhelming discretion. The policy, for example, prohibited trousers that were either "baggy" or "form-fitting" and shirts that were not "of an appropriate size and fit."[167]* The policy also forbade students to wear T-shirts with writing—a measure that effectively prohibited students from using one of the most efficient methods available of expressing themselves on matters political and cultural. If students cannot even wear a T-shirt to school promoting a particular candidate for president, that policy should be presumed to exceed educators' constitutional authority. School uniforms—even more so than dress codes, which typically allow for greater sartorial variance—recall, however faintly, Sparta's efforts to submerge individuality in an effort to mold the ideal citizen. The Supreme Court in *Meyer v. Nebraska* wisely rejected the enforcement of homogeneity as contradicting constitutional principles. It is one thing for parents voluntarily to

---

* The student who contested this dress code, Amanda Blau, made the all-too-familiar tactical blunder of suggesting that her opposition stemmed from her desire to wear clothes that she "feel[s] good in" and that "look[ ] nice on [her]." *Blau v. Fort Thomas Public School District*, 401 F.3d 381, 386 (6th Cir. 2005). She would have been well advised to omit such statements from the record and focus instead on the specific statements that she wished to advance through her clothing. Perhaps predictably, a large number of the school's restrictions can be understood as communicating anxiety about clothing that is thought to display young women's sexuality. In addition to prohibiting tops with "low, scoop, plunging or revealing necklines," the policy banned skirts that do not "reach mid-thigh or longer" and "clothing that is too tight [or] revealing . . . as well as tops and bottoms that do not overlap." Ibid., 385, 386 (internal quotation marks omitted). The policy's gendered elements could have conceivably rendered it vulnerable to a challenge under the Fourteenth Amendment's Equal Protection Clause. For analysis of clothing and its connections to sex, see Anne Hollander, *Sex and Suits: The Evolution of Modern Dress* (1994); and Jo B. Paoletti, *Sex and Unisex: Fashion, Feminism, and the Sexual Revolution* (2015).

send their children to a private school that enforces dress regulations; it is quite another when the government requires adolescents to don particular attire simply because they attend the local school. Proponents of these regulations frequently contend that they have the ability to foster unity, diminish socioeconomic differences, and maintain attention on schoolwork. Doubt might easily be cast on each of these alleged virtues. Whatever their actual benefit, though, these regulations impinge upon students' right to liberty in a fundamental way that modern courts simply refuse to recognize.

Admittedly, *Tinker* expressly noted that its logic did not necessarily undermine school dress codes, a passage that led *The New York Times* to run an editorial headlined "Armbands Yes, Miniskirts No."[168] But that logic itself demands revisiting, particularly because many more public schools today have adopted highly restrictive clothing regulations than had them in the late 1960s. School uniforms became dramatically more widespread after President Bill Clinton advocated that schools adopt the policies as he prepared for his reelection bid in 1996. It would be fanatical to assert that such measures *always* violate the Constitution. Such policies may pass muster in schools that have particular histories, including where clothing has been used to disclose affiliations with violent gangs. Courts should refrain, however, from automatically presuming the constitutional legitimacy of broad fashion restrictions. Beyond the military and incarceration contexts, only in extreme circumstances should the government ever be able to tell citizens, even young ones, what clothing they are and are not permitted to place on their bodies. Yet modern courts have mistakenly transformed what should be the exceptional into the routine.[169]*

* Some First Amendment specialists may object that school uniforms and dress codes are content-neutral regulations because they do not target particular subjects or viewpoints but instead regulate merely the time, place, and manner of expression. First Amendment doctrine holds that such content-neutral restrictions are subjected to lower levels of judicial scrutiny than content-based restrictions. See Geoffrey R. Stone, "Content-Neutral Restrictions," 54 *University of Chicago Law Review* 46 (1987). At least three responses address this objection. First, as a factual matter, school policies do in fact sometimes regulate student dress based on content. See, for example, *Blau*, 401 F.3d at 391 (adjudicating a school policy that prohibited all large logos on clothing, except those promoting school spirit). Second, even conceding that the contested policy is content neutral, that concession does not mean it automatically satisfies the First Amendment. Typically, content-neutral regulations fail if they "burden substantially more speech than is necessary to further the government's legitimate interests." *Ward v. Rock Against Racism*, 491 U.S. 781, 799 (1989). Dress codes prohibiting students from wearing

Finally, an urgent free speech question involves the ability of educators to sanction students for comments made off campus but online whose effects may eventually be felt within the school—an issue of ever increasing significance during the internet era. To date, the Supreme Court has studiously evaded this question, despite being presented with numerous viable opportunities to consider it.* The Court's continued reticence on this front seems regrettable, because ample evidence suggests that lower courts have generally taken an unduly deferential approach to articulating legal standards for school regulations regarding off-campus speech.

The downside of the judiciary's lax approach to protecting students' off-campus speech is seldom more apparent than when students use harsh language to criticize school officials. In one particularly egregious example, the U.S. Court of Appeals for the Second Circuit in 2011 found that a Connecticut high school did not violate Avery Doninger's clearly established First Amendment rights when it punished the eleventh grader in her capacity as junior

---

T-shirts bearing all text—no matter how anodyne—may well run afoul of such require-ments. For a case employing such reasoning, see *Wallace v. Ford*, 346 F. Supp. 156, 165 (E.D. Ark. 1972) (striking a dress restriction because "[i]t has the effect of excluding other legitimate forms of expression" and emphasizing that such "restriction[s] must not exceed that which is . . . necessary to carry out . . . legitimate objectives"). Third, even conceding dress policies do not violate the First Amendment, that concession does not necessarily mean those policies pass constitutional muster. Courts periodically rely upon the Fourteenth Amendment's Due Process Clause to render those policies uncon-stitutional. See ibid., 161–63 (emphasizing due process considerations). It hardly seems outlandish to believe that deciding what clothing goes on one's body should be informed by the Fourteenth Amendment's protection of liberty. Again, none of the foregoing is to argue that school dress provisions are *invariably* unconstitutional, only that judges should refuse to approve them reflexively.

* The most recent, prominent case involving off-campus speech that the Supreme Court declined to hear arose from a dispute in Fulton, Mississippi. Taylor Bell, a high school senior, recorded a hip-hop song at an off-campus studio that criticized certain school officials for their alleged sexual harassment of female students. In expressing those criticisms, the aspiring rapper boasted in vulgar terms about the bodily harm he would inflict upon the officials—part of the hip-hop genre's standard artistic conven-tions, not serious threats. But because Bell posted the song online, school officials sus-pended him for the lyrics—a decision that a divided court of appeals found did not violate the First Amendment. See *Bell v. Itawamba County School Board*, 799 F.3d 379 (5th Cir. 2015). Celebrated rappers—including Big Boi, Pharoahe Monch, T.I., and Killer Mike—elevated the case's profile when they filed an amicus brief in the Supreme Court supporting Bell and urging the justices to reverse the decision below. See Adam Liptak, "Hip-Hop Stars Stand Up for First Amendment Rights of a Student," *New York Times*, Dec. 21, 2015, A18. Nevertheless, the Supreme Court denied Bell's petition without comment in February 2016.

class secretary for calling school administrators "douchebags" in a blog post written from her home during nonschool hours. The dispute arose when an administrator informed students that Jamfest, an annual battle-of-the-bands concert, could not be held in the school's new auditorium on the upcoming weekend as previously planned. That evening, Doninger took to her personal blog—unaffiliated with the high school's website—and encouraged readers to contact school administrators (whom she termed "the douchebags in central office") to register their displeasure with the changed plans for Jamfest. Doninger's post, along with an email campaign that she coordinated, succeeded in motivating many people to call the school; the unusually high volume of phone calls, in turn, caused some tumult within the central office. After the school learned of the blog, it punished Doninger by prohibiting her from running for election as senior class secretary as she had intended. Even had the Second Circuit felt tempted to uphold the school's punishment by citing *Fraser*—on the theory that the term "douchebag," while not sexual, is simply inappropriate—that option appeared unavailable, as *Frederick* stated that Fraser's speech would have been protected in a nonschool setting. Nevertheless, the federal appellate court refused to find that the school's sanctioning of Doninger violated her First Amendment rights, reasoning that "it was objectively reasonable for school officials to conclude that Doninger's behavior was potentially disruptive of student government functions (such as the organization of Jamfest) and that Doninger was not free to engage in such behavior while serving as a class representative."[170]*

Fortunately, federal appellate courts have not universally rubber-stamped schools' efforts to sanction students for off-campus speech that criticizes educators. In 2011, the U.S. Court of Appeals for the Third Circuit found a free speech violation when a Pennsylvania school suspended an eighth-grade student—identified by the courts as J.S.—for creating a vulgar, absurd Myspace profile of

---

* The Second Circuit's opinion in *Doninger v. Niehoff* contained an additional highly dubious First Amendment holding. When Doninger's classmates learned of her punishment, several of them brought T-Shirts to school that read "Team Avery" on the front, and "Support . . . Freedom of Speech" on the back. When school officials learned of the apparel, however, they prohibited students from wearing the T-shirts during that day's assembly for student government elections. Although the school officials' actions clearly seem to contravene *Tinker,* the Second Circuit found that the students' First Amendment right to don the T-shirts had not been clearly established. See *Doninger v. Niehoff,* 642 F.3d 334, 354–56 (2d Cir. 2011).

a fictitious middle-school principal in Alabama that featured a photograph of her actual principal. The online profile for the Alabama
principal whom J.S. dubbed "M-Hoe"—which she created from
her home computer and made accessible only to approved users—
contained the following greeting:

> HELLO CHILDREN[.] yes. It's your oh so wonderful, hairy,
> expressionless, sex addict, fagass, put on this world with a small
> dick PRINCIPAL[.] I have come to myspace so i can pervert
> the minds of other principal[ ]s to be just like me. I know, I
> know, you're all thrilled[.] Another reason I came to myspace is
> because—I am keeping an eye on you students (who[m] I care for
> so much)[.] For those who want to be my friend, and aren't in my
> school[,] I love children, sex (any kind), dogs, long walks on the
> beach, tv, being a dick head, and last but not least my darling wife
> who looks like a man.[171]

In the section listing M-Hoe's general interests, J.S. included
the following: "detention, being a tight ass, riding the fraintrain,
spending time with my child (who looks like a gorilla), baseball,
my golden pen, fucking in my office, hitting on students and their
parents."[172] Despite the precautions J.S. took limiting access to the
profile, and the absence of evidence that it significantly disturbed
school proceedings, her principal nevertheless suspended J.S. for
ten days after he learned of its existence. The Third Circuit, however, invalidated the suspension, reasoning, "The profile was so
outrageous that no one could have taken it seriously, and no one
did. Thus, it was not reasonably foreseeable that J.S.'s speech would
create a substantial disruption or material interference in school."[173]
As the Third Circuit further explained in a companion case released
the same day, "It would be an unseemly and dangerous precedent
to allow the state, in the guise of school authorities, to reach into
a child's home and control his/her actions there to the same extent
that it can control when he/she participates in school sponsored
activities."[174]

The finding of a First Amendment violation here seems plainly
appropriate with respect to J.S.'s suspension. As the Third Circuit
suggested, schools should not rely upon the existence of the internet to render actionable students' off-campus disparagement of
educators—particularly when the critiques are clearly satirical.

At the same time, though, if forced to select only Doninger's post or J.S.'s profile as meriting First Amendment protection, it seems difficult to escape the conclusion that the First Amendment should be understood as more readily protecting Doninger than J.S. On first impression, Doninger's protest over Jamfest may seem to involve a frivolous issue; the Constitution does not recognize a fundamental right to rock out. But Doninger's protest should not be dismissed, because it can also be viewed as raising important questions of democratic representation and the importance of government accountability. Recall that Doninger's speech involved an issue that directly criticized the governance of her school, and encouraged her classmates and fellow citizens in effect to petition the government about a grievance, a right that receives independent protection under the First Amendment. Moreover, although the Second Circuit appeared to regard Doninger's punishment of being banned from serving in the student government as lighter than a suspension, it seems plausible that this particular sanction may actually be graver in this context. The school is in effect sanctioning Doninger for daring to speak out against the local government by stripping her of the ability to occupy a formal leadership position, and also prohibiting her classmates from voting for her. Finally, regarding the language itself, Doninger's usage of "douchebag," while pejorative, commonly appeared on network television shows, and by the time that she used the term, it had largely been severed from a connection to anything literal. In contrast to Doninger's speech, J.S.'s mock profile was by her own testimony designed to amuse because it was "outrageous," not to communicate any serious idea, and used shocking language to achieve its intended effect. It seems downright bizarre to think that Avery Doninger might well have had better luck prevailing on her First Amendment claim if, in addition to calling school officials "douchebags," she remarked upon their genitalia, suggested they were pedophiles, and insulted their relatives' physical appearances.[175]

During the internet age, lower courts have also sometimes exhibited unduly broad deference to schools' decisions to punish students for off-campus speech that criticizes not educators but their fellow students. In approaching these cases, courts ought to demonstrate a stronger understanding that students uttered extremely harsh comments both about and toward one another long before the internet existed. While the internet may now make educators aware of critical comments that previously went undetected by school officials, that fact alone should not inspire educators to ignore the traditional boundary separating off- and on-campus speech.

This suggestion should not be mistaken as suggesting that educators should simply turn a blind eye to social media. (Cyberbullying is a real phenomenon, even if media reports may exaggerate its prevalence.) This suggestion does mean, however, that educators have focused too much energy on suspending students for statements made on social media and too little energy on proactive efforts, including informing students and their parents how abuses of social media can be harmful. Instead of using suspensions as the mechanism of first resort, moreover, schools should use other, more profitable interventions to address troubling instances of off-campus speech. Lower courts have generally demonstrated insufficient attentiveness to the adverse consequences that would flow from treating any student comment that is typed at home as potentially falling within the purview of school disciplinarians—provided it can be portrayed as potentially disrupting school.

Applying the restrictive rules of *Tinker* to students in their online lives twenty-four hours per day, 365 days per year promises to inhibit free expression in ways that would damage the exchange of ideas. While an all-*Tinker*-all-the-time standard would undeniably succeed in silencing some adolescent speech that most people would agree possesses little or no value, focusing only on that point provides a severely distorted assessment of its constitutional consequences. That standard should be resisted because it would also indisputably succeed in suppressing some adolescent speech that many people would agree possesses enormous value. If students do not surrender their constitutional rights upon entering the schoolhouse gate, it should be intolerable that students would forfeit them when they stand outside that gate.[176]

Given the sometimes ugly content of student speech today, some readers may now have greater sympathy for the notion that Justice Black voiced long ago in *Tinker*—and that Justice Thomas exuberantly endorsed in *Frederick*—contending students do not know enough to express views that enjoy First Amendment protection in schools. Judge Posner offered a somewhat softened version of this claim in 2008, when he wrote an opinion for the Seventh Circuit that voiced deep hesitation about the wisdom of having the federal judiciary review free speech determinations made by educators, even as he sided with the student in the immediate case. "A heavy federal constitutional hand on the regulation of student speech by school authorities would make little sense," Judge Posner posited, because "[t]he contribution that kids can make to the marketplace in ideas and opinions is modest."177*

This effort to diminish the importance of conferring First Amendment rights on students, however, elicited a powerful, rousing response from Judge Ilana Rovner:

> Youth are often the vanguard of social change. Anyone who thinks otherwise has not been paying attention to the civil rights movement, the women's rights movement, the anti-war protests for Vietnam and Iraq, and the [2008] presidential primaries where the youth voice and the youth vote are having a substantial impact. . . . The young adults to whom the majority refers as "kids" and "children" are either already eligible, or a few short years away from being eligible to vote, to contract, to marry, to serve in the military, and to be tried as adults in criminal prosecutions. To treat them as children in need of protection from controversy . . . is contrary to the values of the First Amendment.179

Students, as Judge Rovner attests, have made valuable contributions to the nation's marketplace of ideas, and the school itself has often been an important site for exchanging ideas on the topic of the day. The student-led protests supporting gun control legislation in response to the mass shooting at Marjory Stoneman Douglas High School in Parkland, Florida, in February 2018 are but the latest, high-profile examples of this longstanding trend. As the preceding material establishes, moreover, the judiciary played a critical role in ensuring that students retain the ability to speak out on these issues—even if educators themselves have initially dismissed their statements as incoherent, incorrect, or irrelevant. When schools have sought to prevent students from wearing black armbands to protest the Vietnam War or freedom buttons to support the quest

---

* Evidently, Judge Posner believes that *Tinker* was wrongly decided, as he has cited the student speech jurisprudence as one of the few major blemishes on the modern First Amendment. In 2014, he stated in an interview, "[T]he basic structure of American free speech law seems okay. Some of it strikes me as silly, notably granting rights of free speech to school kids." Ronald K. L. Collins, "On Free Expression and the First Amendment," *Concurring Opinions*, Dec. 10, 2014.

for equal voting rights—when educators have tried to stop students from revealing their sexual orientation through their prom dates or their gender identity through their clothing choices—it seems clear that majoritarian sentiment within those communities would have supported the schools. While many observers now view those student messages as presenting valued input to our schools and our polity, they were not always so considered at the outset. Yet courts in all four of those instances have prohibited educators from banning those contested student messages. The First Amendment provides space to disfavored ideas today in the event that they may, over time, flourish and perhaps eventually become the dominant view.

Make no mistake, though: students will not *invariably* avail themselves of the space created by the First Amendment to articulate ideas that ultimately become the wave of the future. Instead, much of what students say will no doubt seem puerile, spiteful, ill-conceived, and wrongheaded—initial impressions that the passage of time will only cement. On this score, though, it is essential to appreciate that speech from students has no small amount in common with speech from adults.

3

Suspensions, Corporal Punishment, and Intolerable "Zero Tolerance" Policies

During the 1970s, slightly more than two years apart, the Supreme Court issued two momentous decisions probing constitutional limitations on the ability of public schools to sanction students. Both cases were decided by the narrowest possible margin, 5–4, and while the Court's composition remained unaltered during the relevant twenty-seven-month interval, the pair of decisions nonetheless pulled in sharply contrasting directions. First, in January 1975, the Court in *Goss v. Lopez* delivered a victory to student rights, when it provided that schools could not remove pupils—in the form of either suspensions or expulsions—without affording them some modest procedural protections. Then, in April 1977, the Court in *Ingraham v. Wright* beat a marked retreat, when it provided not only that schools could inflict corporal punishment upon pupils by striking them with foreign objects but that they could do so without even affording them the same basic protections that it had so recently required in the removal context. The seeming tension between these two decisions—issued in rapid succession—presents one of education law's great constitutional enigmas.

Apart from posing an intriguing historical puzzle, though, both *Lopez* and *Ingraham* continue to reverberate in the modern era. School suspensions and expulsions have escalated dramatically in recent years, and have assumed a severe form that would have been difficult to envision as recently as the early 1990s, let alone when the Court first addressed the issue more than four decades ago. Contrary to popular perception, moreover, public schools within the United States continue to impose corporal punishment on students. In perhaps no arena of education law is there greater need for renewed attention than in assessing how schools sanction wayward students, even though the precise justifications vary in the two contexts. With suspensions and expulsions, the need is great due to the staggering number of students annually removed from school and the ruinous consequences that often accompany such actions. In comparison with their peers, students who are removed from school are more likely to experience not only academic difficulties but also long-range adverse outcomes, including criminal involvement and incarceration as adults.[1] With corporal punishment, that need is great not due to the sheer number of students who receive corporal punishment, which is infinitesimal when compared with the total number of students attending public schools. Instead, the need for intervention here is great because no governmental practice today more violently contravenes core American ideals than permitting educators to beat their students.

GOSS V. LOPEZ: PROCEDURAL PROTECTIONS FOR SUSPENSIONS

On the morning of February 26, 1971, officials at Central High School in Columbus, Ohio, suspended an extraordinarily large number of students—estimates ranged from a minimum of 75 to as many as 150—for participating in a protest that spiraled out of control. Although Central's principal, Calvin Park, described the events as beginning with a "well organized and pre-planned refusal of many students to attend class," the demonstration ultimately spilled into the school cafeteria, where some protesters overturned lunch tables and broke windows.[2] The disturbance grew sufficiently chaotic that, while no teachers or students suffered injuries, Principal Park felt compelled to cancel the day's remaining classes. These tumultuous events represented the culmination of racial tensions that had engulfed Central in recent weeks, dating back to its cancellation of an assembly scheduled to honor Black History Week. Several other schools in Columbus also suspended students during this period for protesting what they regarded as inadequate attention accorded to black history. Widespread parental unrest over these suspensions led Columbus's chapter of the National Association for the Advancement of Colored People to challenge the unilateral authority of these public schools to suspend their pupils.

Many Columbus students asserted that they had been suspended unjustly because they played no role in creating the disturbances. At Central, for example, the twelfth grader Dwight Lopez insisted that he was an innocent bystander to the cafeteria fracas, present for the trouble only because he had a free study period— guilty, in other words, of nothing more than being in the wrong place at the wrong time. Lopez did not avail himself of the opportunity to notify school administrators of his innocence because he was denied such an opportunity. Instead, Central officials simply informed Lopez—and dozens of his fellow classmates—that he was suspended but provided no justification for this disciplinary action, let alone an opportunity to rebut the charges.[3] In earlier eras, assertions that a school violated a student's constitutional rights by the manner in which it suspended him would have seemed laughable. By the dawn of the 1970s, however, such thinking was no longer radical; if anything, it had become downright conventional.

In 1957, some fourteen years before the Columbus conflagration, Professor Warren Seavey wrote an article in the *Harvard Law Review* that spanned a not-so-grand total of four pages but nevertheless signaled the wave of the future in student discipline. Seavey, in arguing that administrators should grant pupils at least minimal procedural protections before issuing suspensions or expulsions, opened with a cri de coeur: "It is shocking that the officials of a state educational institution . . . should not understand the elementary principles of fair play. It is equally shocking to find that a court supports them in denying to a student the protection given to a pickpocket."[4]

It did not take long for lower federal courts to heed this wake-up call. In 1961, the U.S. Court of Appeals for the Fifth Circuit cited Seavey's verbal jolt in an opinion reversing the summary expulsion of students from Alabama State College for their participation in a sit-in demonstration. The Fourteenth Amendment's Due Process Clause, the Fifth Circuit reasoned, "requires notice and some opportunity for hearing before a student at a tax-supported college is expelled for misconduct."[5] Over time, every circuit court throughout the country adopted the Fifth Circuit's—and thus

Seavey's—general due process approach to expulsions and lengthy suspensions, and many federal courts extended these protections to students in primary and secondary public schools.[6] As Professor Charles Alan Wright subsequently observed, "The [Fifth Circuit's] opinion . . . had the force of an idea whose time had come and it has swept the field."[7]

In January 1975, the Supreme Court endorsed this principle when it vindicated Dwight Lopez's challenge to his suspension from Central, but it also took pains to avoid issuing an opinion that would be misconstrued as sweeping. Writing for the Court in *Goss v. Lopez*, Justice Byron White—building upon judicial precedents not involving schools—identified the Columbus suspensions as raising two distinct interests under the Due Process Clause, which forbids the government to deprive people "of life, liberty, or property, without due process of law."[8] First, because the Ohio Constitution provides a right to education, the suspensions involved a "property" interest in learning. Second, because the sanctions could adversely affect the students' future educational and occupational opportunities, the suspensions involved a "liberty" interest in reputation. With that framework established, Justice White found that the Columbus schools failed to accord suspended students the necessary procedural protections. In order to discharge their constitutional obligations, *Lopez* held, schools must give "the student . . . oral or written notice of the charges against him and, if he denies them, an explanation of the evidence the authorities have and an opportunity to present his side of the story."[9] No passage of time must transpire between notification of the charge and the student's opportunity to explain why the suspension is unmerited. The Court explained that in most instances the "informal give-and-take between student and disciplinarian" must occur prior to the suspension, but it acknowledged that in some situations extenuating circumstances might justify holding the hearing after the suspension begins.[10]

Justice White stressed that *Lopez* in no way imposed staggering procedural burdens on school administrators. The "rudimentary precautions" were designed to expose "unfair or mistaken findings of misconduct," White explained, establishing procedures that were, "if anything, less than a fair-minded school principal would impose upon himself in order to avoid unfair suspensions."[11] In support of this characterization, White noted that—even during the student protests in Columbus—one high school voluntarily adopted (though did not always follow) procedures strongly resembling the approach now required by *Lopez,* and after the protest the city's public school system voluntarily enacted rules for suspensions that would have satisfied the opinion had they existed in 1971. At the same time, though, *Lopez* identified certain procedures that it declined to require. For example, schools need not permit students to call their own witnesses, cross-examine witnesses, or acquire legal representation as part of the hearing process. While *Lopez* entertained the possibility that expulsions and suspensions lasting longer than ten days may demand more extensive procedures, the Court expressly refrained from resolving that question.

Justice Lewis F. Powell Jr., on behalf of four justices, wrote a vehement dissent in *Lopez.* Powell found the decision so execrable that he took the unusual step of delivering his dissenting opinion orally from the bench, the first time he felt moved to do so in more than three years on the Court. According to then-Professor J. Harvie Wilkinson III—who not only served as a law clerk to Powell but also knew him as a close family friend—the depth of Powell's feelings about *Lopez* may partially be attributable to his own biography.[12] Before ascending to the Supreme Court in 1972, Powell successfully dedicated his life to realizing the twin goals of becoming a leading lawyer and a leading citizen of his beloved hometown, Richmond, Virginia. As a pillar of the local establishment, Powell served as chairman of the Richmond School Board for nine years and subsequently served on the state Board of Education for eight years. Powell came to believe that schools work best when school officials possess the authority to make decisions for students in their communities without meddling from the federal courts. In Powell's view, *Lopez* defiled this core belief. "Few rulings would interfere more extensively in the daily functioning of schools than subjecting routine discipline to the formalities and judicial oversight of due process," Powell inveighed.[13] *Lopez* was deeply mistaken, Powell argued, because it validated the notion "for the first time that the federal courts, rather than educational officials and state legislatures, have the authority to determine the rules applicable to routine classroom discipline of children and teenagers in the public schools."[14]

Powell further contended that with *Lopez* the judiciary illegitimately intruded into the special, almost sacred bond linking teachers with students. "The role of the teacher in our society historically has been an honored and respected one," Powell wrote, "rooted in the experience of decades that has left for most of us warm memories of our teachers, especially those of the formative years of primary and secondary education."[15] Throughout his dissent, Powell returned to this ode to teachers: "There is an ongoing relationship, one in which the teacher must occupy many roles—educator, adviser, friend, and, at times, parent-substitute. It is rarely adversary in nature except with respect to the chronically disruptive or insubordinate pupil whom the teacher must be free to discipline without frustrating formalities."[16] According to Powell, the Court inflicted *Lopez* on school officials at a particularly inopportune moment. "In an age when the home and church play a diminishing role in shaping the character and value judgments of the young," he warned, "a heavier responsibility falls upon the schools."[17] A suspension, Powell concluded, was not a catastrophic event in the life of typical students, hardly an action requiring constitutional protections: "For average, normal children—the vast majority—suspension for a few days is simply *not* a detriment . . . it leaves no scars; affects no reputations; indeed, it often may be viewed by the young as a badge of some distinction and a welcome holiday."[18]

Despite Justice Powell's apocalyptic warnings, the Court's decision in *Lopez* elicited largely shrugged shoulders and stifled yawns from many school officials across the nation because it essentially required what was already standard operating procedure. The National School Boards Association—an organization not exactly known for its measured responses to the Supreme Court's education decisions—issued a press release noting that *Lopez* would require little reform given that "most schools already follow this course."[19] The reaction of Columbus's director of school personnel, Norval Goss, the lawsuit's named defendant, encapsulates how little *Lopez* fazed education officials. "Technically, we're supposed to have lost, but personally I am satisfied," Goss told *The New York Times*. Even in school districts that did not typically afford students pre-suspension hearings, the reaction was mild.[20]

While school officials—the technical losers in *Lopez*—seemed content with the opinion, *Lopez*'s purported winners reacted with ambivalence. Peter Roos, the attorney from Harvard's Center for Law and Education who represented the Columbus students, expressed hope that *Lopez* "will have a substantial impact on the way schools treat kids," but also conceded, "We would have been more pleased if proceedings outlined for short-term suspensions had been more stringent." A representative from the Children's Defense Fund, which filed an amicus brief in *Lopez*, echoed Roos's assessment that the opinion was a valuable first step but insisted that "more substantial due process proceedings should be used," including a right to appeal and a right to written notice of the basis for suspension.[21] In *Lopez*'s wake, reformers increasingly viewed the opinion as a missed opportunity to curtail school suspensions. In September 1975, eight months after the Court decided *Lopez*, the Children's Defense Fund issued a comprehensive 237-page report that encouraged schools to reduce school suspensions drastically. According to the report, the overwhelming majority of the more than one million school suspensions that occur annually are issued for nonviolent student behavior, including roughly 250,000 for mere tardiness and truancy. "Suspensions are not necessary, except in a small minority of cases, to maintain order," the report noted. The Children's Defense Fund's director, Marian Wright Edelman, elaborated upon this idea at a press conference trumpeting the report's release. "We're not saying that seriously disruptive youngsters shouldn't be removed from class," Edelman stated. "But rather than suspending them, get counseling and other resources. Schools haven't begun to explore the kinds of resources they have."[22]

Commentators condemned Justice Powell's dissenting opinion for its sanguine conception of the educational enterprise, criticizing what they variously labeled its "romantic notion" of the teacher-student relationship and its "euphoric view" of the school as an institution where interests do not collide.[23] These criticisms are sound, as far as they go. Powell seems to have encountered genuine difficulty comprehending that many students—rather than only a few bad apples—do not view their schooling experiences through his rose-tinted spectacles. Regardless of whether a particular student generally views educators as attempting to help pupils realize their academic potential, this general conception quickly dissipates in the face of a potential suspension. The moment that an educator seeks to remove a student from the educational setting, it seems awfully difficult to construe that relationship primarily as harmonious rather than adversarial.

Criticisms along these lines can helpfully be pressed further still, as Powell's opinion—even accepted on its own terms—betrays deep internal incoherence. On the one hand, Powell insisted that *most* students hold their teachers in high esteem, construing them as revered cultural figures that not only provide education but also dispense advice, friendship, and—on occasion—parenting; educators, Powell averred, have been left to fill the void created by the declining significance of family and religion in modern America. On the other hand, Powell insisted that the *vast majority* of students view being suspended from school as simply no big deal; students frequently perceive suspensions, Powell suggested, less as a significant rebuke from a respected authority within the national ethos and more as an opportunity to beat the crowd to the shopping mall.

The insoluble tension between Justice Powell's two educational precepts should by now be plain: If teachers are generally ennobled figures and the schoolhouse has become a substitute for home and church, then most students cannot dismiss their ejection from this quasi-sacred institution as a rejuvenating mini-vacation. The more exalted the role of teachers and schools in our society, the more serious and grave the decision to suspend students becomes. Justice Powell can thus maintain one of his cultural conceits or the other, but he cannot simultaneously maintain both.

DUE PROCESS AND ITS DETRACTORS

Few Supreme Court opinions are more fundamentally misunderstood than *Lopez*, with many commentators falsely contending that the opinion required schools to offer suspended students elaborate procedural protections. Only a few months after *Lopez* appeared, the sociologist Nathan Glazer of Harvard contended in a widely circulated *Public Interest* article that the Supreme Court had become "an imperial judiciary" and assailed *Lopez*'s supposedly broad holding as providing a prime example of judicial overreach. "In [*Lopez*, the Court] spread the awesome limitations of 'due process' to the public schools, which now could not restrict the constitutional rights of students by suspending or expelling them without at least something resembling a criminal trial," Glazer complained.[24] Twenty-five years later, George Will similarly asserted that *Lopez* pulled "lawyers and judges . . . into school discipline procedures, presiding over—at a minimum—elaborate hearings with witnesses."[25] In 2004, *National Review* published an article announcing that *Lopez* ordered schools to afford expelled students extensive due process protections, including "the right to a formal hearing, the right to legal counsel, and the right to call witnesses."[26]

Each of these contentions severely overstates *Lopez*'s modest holding. In reality, the opinion required schools only to notify students why they were being suspended and provide them with an informal opportunity to rebut the justification. While *Lopez* suggested that more extensive procedures could be appropriate for lengthy suspensions and expulsions, it expressly refrained from mandating that schools provide those procedures. Such mangled understandings of *Lopez* have obtained enough currency that influential commentators suggest in effect that Professor Seavey's pickpocket, in a wild turnabout, now envies the procedural protections afforded students. The lawyer Philip K. Howard can be understood as enunciating a version of this idea in *The Death of Common Sense*, a best-selling jeremiad that denounced what he viewed as law's stultifying effects on American society. "Criminals probably wish they had some of the procedural protections of students," Howard wrote.[27]

Admittedly, suspended or expelled students today frequently do receive more extensive protections at disciplinary hearings than those that *Lopez* sketched. A major study conducted by the National Center for Education Statistics, taken only ten years after *Lopez*, indicated that the overwhelming majority of school districts provided for at least some questioning of witnesses and an ability to appeal suspensions.[28] By 2009, moreover, nearly two-thirds of states had enacted statutes or regulations that far exceeded the basic procedural rights that *Lopez* initially provided.[29] These figures suggest that disciplinary hearings, once marked by informality, have become more formalized in most jurisdictions, including in some places allowing counsel.

The Court's decision in *Lopez*, however, cannot be held responsible for formalizing school disciplinary hearings. To the contrary, the formalization of disciplinary hearings is not primarily attributable to *Lopez* or any other judicial decisions handed down from the Supreme Court or elsewhere. *Lopez* merely established a constitutional floor for disciplinary procedures, below which localities could not fall. Officials in states and localities serving on school boards and in legislatures could, however, choose to elevate the baseline in their particular jurisdictions by providing students with additional protections, and that is precisely what transpired. Although Justice Powell in dissent bemoaned *Lopez*'s incursion on the local control of education—a critique that many observers have voiced over the years—modern opponents of formalized disciplinary procedures direct their enmity at the wrong target.[30] The elevated procedures that suspended students receive today were produced not by some out-of-control Supreme Court but by government actors at the local and state levels.[31]

Perhaps in part because its holding is so roundly distorted, *Lopez* has, somewhat improbably, become a bête noire within the conservative legal community in recent years. Conservative intellectuals deride *Lopez* for what they assert are its deleterious consequences on school discipline. Richard Arum's book *Judging School Discipline* provides the most influential articulation of the idea that the *Lopez* decision ultimately damaged school administration. *Lopez* and other legal decisions "overturning school discipline," Arum contended, "had a significant role in contributing to the decline in moral authority and the erosion of effective disciplinary practices in American public schools."[32] Although Arum is a sociologist, not a lawyer, his formulation of the *Lopez* critique shaped discussion in legal circles, including among right-leaning law professors. Thus, Professor Anne Proffitt Dupre echoed Arum's analysis in contending "the legitimacy and the moral authority of the public school as the institution that had the trust and the capacity to socialize the young for a constructive role in society was seriously undermined."[33] Likewise, Professor Lino Graglia asserted, "The Court's intervention in the running of the nation's public schools, the effect of which has been to seriously impair school discipline and the ability of teachers to teach, . . . illustrate[s] the danger of giving the Court the final word on matters about which it can know very little."[34]

Such anti-*Lopez* sentiments are in no sense confined to the halls of academia. Indeed, two of the most distinguished conservative jurists of the post–World War II era have also contended that *Lopez* harmed school discipline. The former judge Robert Bork, in *Slouching Towards Gomorrah*, lamented that "the American judiciary [arguably] is the single most powerful force shaping our culture," as the

Supreme Court "decide[s] hot button questions of culture and politics that are, strictly speaking, none of its business."[35] *Lopez* made an appearance on Bork's bill of particulars, as he contended that the decision wrought havoc in "public schools, where the power to discipline has been severely circumscribed and the power to expel virtually amputated."[36] Justice Antonin Scalia, in a speech delivered at Georgetown University, also cast aspersions on *Lopez*, remarking, "Swift and effective punishment of even a non-physical sort, has been all but banished from today's public school classrooms."[37]

Major newspapers and high-profile authors have also disparaged *Lopez*. In a *Wall Street Journal* piece titled "Unsafe at Any Grade," Heather Mac Donald opened by recounting a litany of sensational events to suggest that American schools were dens of mayhem and then stated, "How did things get so bad? Blame one of the most ill-conceived chapters of . . . legal activism: the student-rights revolution." Mac Donald raised the specter of a student "suspended for rampaging in the hallways" who would "sue his school for not first giving him a trial filled with procedural rights," and asserted, "The intrusion of lawyers into what for centuries had been regarded as the schools' essential prerogative—the correction of unruly students—had predictable results [with teachers required to] follow[ ] the latest byzantine procedures dictated by the courts."[38] Howard, in a follow-up to *The Death of Common Sense*, cited Arum's work: "[I]t's not hard to identify why [school] authority collapsed. The decline of order . . . is directly tied to the rise of 'due process.' . . . Due process, our constitutional protection against being sent to jail arbitrarily, now applied before a student could be sent home [from school]."[39]

Despite the prominence of anti-*Lopez* sentiment among conservatives, the precise explanation for how the opinion has diminished school discipline is generally left nebulous. Arum has provided the most systematic account. Many educators are uncertain about what *Lopez* actually requires, Arum maintains, and this cloud of uncertainty hovers over them throughout the day, forcing educators to second-guess themselves during encounters with misbehaving students whom they would have instantly chastened in the pre-*Lopez* world. Today's students sense that uncertainty, Arum further claims, and exploit it, rendering it difficult for educators to maintain order over the institutions that they are charged with leading.[40]

The charge that *Lopez* played a primary role in ruining discipline in the nation's public schools is a serious one, but there are many reasons to doubt that the opinion must shoulder the blame that its numerous critics seek to assign it. The first major cause for skepticism centers on broad questions about timing. For one thing, deep dissatisfaction with discipline in schools long precedes the Court's due process decision in *Lopez*—indeed, such concerns seem to be perennial, as they predate the lower courts' involvement with school-based due process as well. For another thing, the Court's decision in *Lopez* did not initiate conflict between students and educators. As the facts of *Lopez* themselves reveal, conflict between Columbus's students and teachers was well under way by the time the Supreme Court weighed in on the matter. It seems more profitable to view *Lopez*—with Professor Martha Minow—as *translating* conflict rather than *initiating* it.[41] For still another, the trend of schools affording students due process rights was already well under way pre-*Lopez*, and the trend of schools affording students greater due process rights has continued post-*Lopez*. Schools featuring robust procedural protections would likely have, even in the absence of *Lopez*, enacted substantially similar mechanisms due to larger, nonjudicial developments in American society.

The second major cause for skepticism centers on the claim that modern educators are reluctant to issue suspensions and expulsions because of the obstacles imposed by *Lopez*. In a major survey undertaken by the National Center for Education Statistics in 1985 that asked about *Lopez*'s hearing requirement, only 3 percent of respondents indicated that the event imposed a significant burden on schools.[42] Claims that educators feel inhibited about suspending and expelling students, moreover, are difficult to square with the modern empirical realities. The nation has witnessed a dramatic increase in school suspensions and expulsions, which have doubled during the last two decades alone.[43] If more than 3.5 million different students are annually suspended when educators feel inhibited, one struggles to comprehend the state of affairs that would exist if educators felt unbridled.

The third major cause for skepticism, closely related to the second, stems from the claim that educators do not know the governing disciplinary rules. As a preliminary matter, some evidence suggests that educators possess a much firmer grasp of many constitutional decisions affecting school administrators, including *Lopez*, than the alarmist reports that frequently appear in education circles would lead one to believe.[44] Yet, even assuming that many educators actually do not know the relevant requirements for suspensions and expulsions, that hardly means *Lopez* introduced the uncertainty. Whatever *Lopez*'s flaws, complexity is not among them. There is nothing mysterious about a decision that holds in effect, "Talk with students when you are thinking about suspending or expelling them." To the extent that a lack of educator knowledge stems from the more elaborate procedures that have supplemented *Lopez*, moreover, either those procedures should be simplified so that they are more easily comprehended, or educators should receive training in the material—or a combination of the two approaches should occur. Teacher confusion surrounding rules today does not mean that *Lopez*'s modest grant of rights created that confusion.

LOPEZ'S UNDERAPPRECIATED SIGNIFICANCE

Even if it is difficult to understand the Court's decision in *Lopez* as ruining discipline in public schools, should it nevertheless be viewed as an insignificant opinion? Justice White's opinion for the Court in *Lopez* characterized the required procedures—notice and a brief, informal hearing—as "rudimentary."[45] Contemporaneous observers from a wide variety of perspectives have intimated that even White's sober characterization actually exaggerated matters, as they contend that the due process protections *Lopez* afforded to students were so slight as to be virtually nonexistent. Professor David Kirp predicted that school administrators could turn *Lopez*'s procedures into "hollow formalisms" and "prepunishment ceremonies."[46] The Due Process Clause, according to Kirp, was simply too crude an instrument to transform schools into the educational atmosphere reformers sought. Similarly, Wilkinson—who went on to become an eminent federal judge after leaving the legal academy—suggested that hearings prior to suspensions could become "a charade which authorities play as quickly as possible in order to reach the predetermined result. If, as the Court says, the fair-minded school principal would quickly impose such rudimentary requirements himself, the unfair principal will hardly be led by the slight protections . . . to a more elevated frame of mind."[47] Even some commentators who applauded *Lopez*'s general willingness to regulate school officials nevertheless adopted a jaundiced attitude toward the particulars. "[*Lopez*] is surely much ado about very little," Professor Leon Letwin wrote. "Given the miniscule opportunities it provides for a student's defense . . . , [*Lopez*] is remarkable not for its innovation but for the fact that it was so long in coming, so vigorously contested en route, so narrowly affirmed when it finally came, and so parsimonious in the rights it recognized upon arrival."[48]

Claims that *Lopez* was an insignificant decision should be rejected for three primary reasons. The first reason stems from the opinion's effects within schoolhouses located throughout the nation. Even if most school districts already implemented some variant of the due process procedures that *Lopez* mandated, some school districts still had no such procedures. The Supreme Court's decision elevated the salience of school disciplinary procedures, requiring the lagging districts to adopt a minimal level of process and encouraging other districts to afford stronger protections. In at least some percentage of potential school suspensions, the procedural protections that flowed from *Lopez* proved decisive, permitting students who had been marked for suspension to avert that unwelcome outcome.

More important than the (presumably small) percentage of dramatic cases where students succeed in convincing disciplinarians that suspension was not warranted, though, is the expressive function of schools affording students even basic due process rights. In *Lopez*'s immediate wake, Professor Laurence Tribe of Harvard understood that due process mattered, even if the student's hearing did not ultimately alter the outcome: "The student's opportunity to confront the disciplinarian . . . not only is a minimum safeguard to assure factual accuracy, but is part of the process of education itself."[49] Tribe's observation complemented an argument that Professor William Buss advanced in an exceptionally perceptive law review article published in 1971, when he managed to anticipate and defend the Court's school removal doctrine a full four years before its emergence in *Lopez*. Buss warned against dismissing school discipline procedures as "peripheral or even frivolous" because such procedures may "be vitally important insofar as they project an image of a fair society to school children." Buss understood that observing students' due process protections mattered not only to students facing suspension. "[F]air procedures in disciplinary proceedings represent a virtue with immediate impact—on students in trouble and on those who merely watch," Buss wrote. "To insist upon fair treatment before passing judgment against a student accused of wrongdoing is to demonstrate that society has high principles and the conviction to honor them."[50]

Such nuanced appreciation of *Lopez*'s meaning in schools was hardly confined to law's ivory tower. A *Chicago Tribune* editorial, titled "Fair Play at the Schoolhouse," commended *Lopez* in language that echoed Buss's assessment: "[W]here is a better place than at school for young citizens to learn to expect justice and to practice holding up their own end in pursuing it in matters involving them?"[51] This point can also be tweaked: Students are invariably going to derive *some* lessons about justice (and injustice) from the treatment they and their classmates receive within the corridors of our nation's public schools. The only real question is what the content of those lessons will be.*

The second reason that *Lopez* should not be deemed trivial is that its application of the Fourteenth Amendment's Due Process Clause to school suspensions signaled that the Supreme Court recognized that students retained the Constitution's protections in a setting that historically had not recognized the document. From today's vantage point, it is easy to entertain the notion that the Court had no realistic choice other than to apply various constitutional provisions in at least some form to the school setting. That belief is unfounded. The Court's jurisprudence protecting student rights demonstrates far more contingency and uncertainty than this foreordained account allows.

In 1975, when the Court issued *Lopez*, the most celebrated precedent vindicating students' individual constitutional rights was *Tinker*'s protection of free expression in 1969. Six years after *Tinker*,

---

* Critics of *Lopez* might latch onto the opinion's expressive effects to contend that it had negative consequences. On this account, *Lopez* raised the salience of students' rights, causing schools to offer ever more elaborate procedural protections that exceeded the foundational opinion's requirements. Before accepting this contention, however, readers should recall that the broad trend of schools affording students greater procedural protections actually preceded *Lopez*. Accordingly, it seems doubtful that *Lopez* should be deemed solely—or even largely—responsible for the bulk of schools that demonstrated greater awareness of students' procedural safeguards. But, even conceding the nub of this critique, should it really be deemed a deleterious consequence? If *Lopez* made some educators, parents, and students more conscious that pupils accused of wrongdoing should not be railroaded, it seems possible to construe that development as—on the whole—salutary.

it was not just possible but distinctly plausible that the Court could have confined *Tinker's* holding to the First Amendment and that the movement for students' constitutional rights would have thus been extinguished in its infancy. Between *Tinker* and *Lopez*, four new justices joined the Supreme Court as the Warren Court yielded both literally and figuratively to the Burger Court.[52] President Richard Nixon appointed all four of the new justices, and those four voted as a bloc against the importation of due process into public schools, a fact that journalists at the time noted.[53] Had they been able to peel off only one of their colleagues from the majority, the future of students' constitutional rights could have assumed a far bleaker path. Indeed, *Tinker's* most famous sentence readily admits a limited construction of students' rights. Today, judges often elide that sentence so that it reads, "It can hardly be argued that . . . students . . . shed their constitutional rights . . . at the schoolhouse gate." But it actually reads in full: "It can hardly be argued that either students or teachers shed their constitutional rights *to freedom of speech or expression* at the schoolhouse gate."[54] The standard elision became possible because of subsequent decisions applying the Constitution to students beyond free expression, and *Lopez* represented a critical step in that doctrinal development.[55]

Considering public attitudes toward student discipline at the time of *Lopez* furthers the understanding that the Court could have plausibly ruled that constitutional notions of due process had no place in schools. Although no contemporaneous polling data exists squarely gauging reactions to *Lopez*, the most relevant data available from that era hardly suggests American citizens were eager to witness the Court afford procedural protections to students on the verge of being suspended. In 1975, in Gallup's annual poll of attitudes toward education, respondents identified "lack of discipline" as the single most pressing problem confronting public schools.[56] The disciplinary concern also ranked first in Gallup's education poll in each of the preceding five years, topping other serious concerns such as "use of drugs," "lack of proper financial support," and even "integration/segregation problems."[57] *Lopez's* vindication of students' due process rights in the face of deep concerns over school discipline should give pause to modern legal scholars who contend that Supreme Court opinions almost ineluctably reflect the consensus attitudes of American citizens.[58]

The final reason *Lopez* should not be mistaken for an insignificant opinion stems from its connection to the march toward racial equality. Justice White's opinion for the Court in *Lopez* did not overtly address the racial tensions that ultimately resulted in the Columbus suspensions. Instead, the opinion obliquely noted that the suspensions "arose out of a period of widespread student unrest" without endeavoring to explain the source of that unrest.[59] But Justice White's efforts to sanitize *Lopez* of its racial dimensions did not prevent observers from linking the case to race. The NAACP Legal Defense and Educational Fund and the Southern Christian Leadership Conference jointly filed an amicus brief in *Lopez* highlighting the disproportionately high rates at which schools suspended black students, and other briefs also addressed the issue.[60] *The New York Times*'s coverage of *Lopez* referred to this tension: "Underlying the Columbus lawsuit were charges by civil rights organizations that white school officials across the nation had been increasingly relying on unjustified suspensions as a discriminatory weapon against black pupils in the city districts where their relative numbers had been on the increase."[61]

Although Professor Wilkinson ultimately opposed the outcome of *Lopez*, he nevertheless offered an incisive portrayal of how the opinion could be construed as an analogue to *Brown v. Board of Education*:

> If in *Brown* the racial question was very much on the surface, in *Goss* it lay not very far below. In the years since *Brown*, the problem of race has moved from the perpetuation of segregation to one involving the implementation of integration. . . . School discipline remains perhaps the foremost source of aggravation [for black students in integrated schools]. Many in the black community view the suspension of minority students as the rearguard attempt of school officials to perpetuate dual school systems, a problem calling for the exercise of judicial remedial powers just as surely as the breakup of de jure segregation mandated by *Brown*.[62]

Lopez, of course, in no way resolved concerns about racial disproportionality in the administration of school discipline. Yet disappointment on the part of some observers that *Lopez* did not go far enough should not be mistaken for believing that the relief it granted was altogether meaningless. And had the Court in *Lopez* flatly held that the Constitution did not even afford suspended students the right to a basic colloquy, that snub to the cause of racial justice would have been conspicuous. *Lopez* is thus an important decision, even if it is not an all-important decision.

JESSE JACKSON, DECATUR, ILLINOIS, AND THE MISGUIDED SHOWDOWN OVER ZERO TOLERANCE

In the autumn of 1999, the eyes of the nation focused intensely, if fleetingly, on a school discipline controversy in Decatur, Illinois, a small, blue-collar city in the central part of the state. Seven black freshmen received two-year expulsions for participating in a fight that erupted in the bleachers at a high school football game. The issue created a local stir that divided Decatur largely along racial lines, with many in the black community—including a councilwoman—viewing the punishments as excessive, and many in the white community viewing the punishments as justice served. The simmering local dispute suddenly attracted the national media spotlight when the Reverend Jesse Jackson traveled to Decatur in order to assail the usage of zero-tolerance disciplinary policies, which penalize a disproportionately large percentage of black students. "The so-called zero-tolerance policy is without mercy and without sensitivity," Jackson declared.[63]

The rise of zero-tolerance policies dates back to the mid-1990s. As part of the Gun-Free Schools Act of 1994, the federal government conditioned the receipt of aid on states adopting policies requiring schools to expel for a minimum of one year all students who possess firearms on school grounds. All fifty states soon thereafter enacted those policies, and many jurisdictions went further by proclaiming "zero tolerance" not only for knives and other items that could be used as weapons but also for other sorts of banned substances. In 1999, only five years after Congress approved the measure, 94 percent of the nation's schools had adopted zero-tolerance policies for weapons, 87 percent had such policies for alcohol, and 79 percent had such policies for tobacco.[64] And many school districts also adopted zero-tolerance policies for fistfights and even verbal abuse; some particularly harsh school districts permitted yearlong suspensions under the guise of zero tolerance for

students who exhibit willful disobedience.[65] Zero-tolerance policies, like the excessively punitive criminal laws that also flourished
during the 1990s, quickly had catastrophic consequences around
the nation. In the span of their first three years of zero tolerance,
expulsions in Chicago increased by more than tenfold, and Massachusetts witnessed a sixteen-fold increase.[66]*

For opponents of zero-tolerance policies, Reverend Jackson's
selection of the Decatur dispute as a place to take a stand proved
endlessly frustrating because, as details surfaced, it would have
been difficult to select a less sympathetic poster child for that cause
if one affirmatively set out to do so. In the classical phase of the
civil rights movement, leaders demonstrated great care in sifting
through individuals' backgrounds to ensure that the people that
they chose to embody the struggle against Jim Crow would reflect
admirably upon the black community.[67] It seems safe to conclude
that the young men Jackson sought to transform into the Decatur
Seven would not have made the cut. Three of the young men were
described as "third-year freshmen," and the seven students collectively managed to amass 350 high school absences.

Apart from the students' dismal collective record, moreover,
the motivating event that prompted the suspensions was no minor
school-yard scuffle but a full-fledged donnybrook. After Jackson
gathered the media, a video of the fight—recorded by a parent who
attended the football game—emerged. According to *The New York
Times*'s description, "It showed a melee that swept through one end
of the grandstands, with kicking and punching, as some of the fight-
ers tumbled over the rails." A high school principal who attended
the game recounted, "You had people pushed through bars, people
covering little children so they wouldn't get hurt. It was violent."[68]
The violence captured by the video spurred the councilwoman who
initially requested leniency for the young men to withdraw her
appeal. "This was a horrendous brawl," she said, after viewing the
images. "This was scary."[69]

Even in terms of timing, the Decatur events arose at an inopportune moment to mount a challenge to zero-tolerance policies,
particularly with respect to violent acts. Eric Harris and Dylan Kle-

* The Gun-Free Schools Act of 1994 ought not be confused with the Gun-Free School
Zones Act of 1990. The Supreme Court invalidated the 1990 measure in 1995, finding
that Congress exceeded its authority under the Commerce Clause. See *United States v.
Lopez*, 514 U.S. 549 (1995).

bold perpetrated the Columbine High School massacre in Colorado only six months prior to Jackson's efforts in Decatur. "A fistfight is different from a knife fight is different from a gunfight," Jackson said.[70] Fair enough. But the recent, highly salient events in Colorado almost certainly diminished the public's appetite for parsing those distinctions for purposes of school discipline.

Regrettably, Jackson's efforts to spur a broad conversation about zero-tolerance policies never gained much traction; instead, the ensuing discourse descended into a simple referendum on the appropriate punishment for seven Decatur students with a taste for pugilism and truancy. Waged on that rocky terrain, opponents of zero-tolerance policies had little chance of achieving reform. Nearly twenty years have now elapsed since Jackson sought to initiate a reassessment of zero-tolerance policies; the passage of time has made the need for that reassessment only more urgent.

To appreciate the increased severity of modern school disciplinary regimes, contemplate the comparatively lenient sanctions that existed as recently as the 1980s. During that era, Principal Joe Clark became something of a national folk hero for the stern method of school discipline that he championed at Paterson, New Jersey's Eastside High School, where he was known for stalking the hallways, toting a bullhorn and a baseball bat, and periodically bellowing, "I am the Constitution."[71] Clark's no-nonsense, take-no-prisoners approach to disciplining students—including mass expulsions that failed to comply with the requirements of due process—won him the praise of President Reagan and various administration officials. According to Secretary of Education William Bennett, "Sometimes, you need Mr. Chips, and sometimes you need Dirty Harry."[72] In 1988, a photograph of Clark wearing a three-piece suit and a scowl, clutching his signature Willie Mays baseball bat, appeared on the cover of *Time*, and one year later Morgan Freeman portrayed him in a major motion picture.[73]

Yet, as the notoriously severe Clark revealed in his memoir, *Laying Down the Law*, the new list of sanctions he devised for Eastside in the early 1980s included default suspensions of only ten days for using drugs or alcohol, selling drugs or alcohol, and possessing knives or guns.[74] Although Clark reserved the authority to increase suspension lengths for any infraction as he saw fit, it is far more notable that his baseline sentences for even serious matters were so lenient—at least as assessed by the modern preoccupation with what might be called "education law and order."[75] In the span of three decades, fueled by the rise and rise of zero tolerance, the disciplinary code of yesterday's Dirty Harry has been transformed into that of today's Mr. Chips.*

The good news is that widespread agreement now exists that zero-tolerance policies are themselves intolerable. It may arrive as no great shock that liberal media outlets, including *The New York Times* and *The Washington Post*, have dedicated considerable attention over the years to criticizing the excesses of zero-tolerance policies. Those newspapers have, for example, published dueling articles noting the absurdity of school officials who mindlessly apply prohibitions on weapons to a student caught in possession of a spork. As one might imagine, such articles are the stuff of headline writers' dreams. *The New York Times* offered "It's a Fork, It's a Spoon, It's a . . . Weapon?" in response to *The Washington Post*'s earlier "Drop That Spork! 'Zero Tolerance' Goes to Richmond."[76]

It may be somewhat more surprising to learn, however, that many right-leaning commentators agree that zero-tolerance policies are unduly harsh when applied to a wide range of conduct. Intriguingly, many of the same conservative voices who have criticized the Court's decision in *Lopez*—including Richard Arum, Philip

---

* In the last five decades, no development in the world of American education appears more bizarre, at least when viewed in retrospect, than the outpouring of national affection heaped upon Principal Joe Clark. Consider only a few of the many sobriquets that Clark had for Eastside students. Clark referred to expelled pupils variously as "parasites," "leeches," "hoodlums," "thugs," and "pathological deviants." In the presence of a reporter, Clark said to one female student that her new hairdo made her "look[ ] like a stone fox," and his memoir identified a group of students as "whorey looking girls." If Clark made even the slightest efforts to check his extraordinary ego, it was not in evidence near reporters. To wit, "I'm the star, there can be only one star. If you want to be the star, get your own school," and "In this building, everything emanates and ultimates from me." In one unusually revealing statement to *The New York Times*, it seemed unmistakably clear that Clark valued his own reputation as a miracle worker above the students of Eastside. "When I leave this school," Clark said, "if it didn't plummet to the depths of despair, if it didn't become violence-ridden, if drugs and stabbings, all the things that I inherited did not reappear, I would be chagrined." Nearly thirty years later, it is hard to believe that these words came from the man whom some media members treated as an educational savior and whom a presidential administration fawned over, going so far as to offer him a position in the White House as a policy adviser. Not everyone, of course, was enamored of his tactics. As one principal stated to *Time*, "If [Eastside's] students were not poor black children, Joe Clark would not be tolerated." For some of the contemporaneous media coverage of Clark, see Sara Rimer, "Paterson Principal: A Man of Extremes," *New York Times*, Jan. 14, 1988, B1; and Ezra Bowen, "Getting Tough," *Time*, Feb. 1, 1988, 52–53. For Clark's self-rebutting memoir, see Joe Clark (with Joe Picard), *Laying Down the Law* 9 (1989).

Howard, and George Will—have also chastised school officials for exhibiting zero tolerance by expelling students for merely technical violations.[77] Criticism of zero-tolerance policies can also be found within the most conservative chambers of the Supreme Court. In 2009, Justice Clarence Thomas, in a case involving a criminal search of a student, wrote an opinion that offered lengthy, pointed criticism of the excessive application of zero-tolerance policies. Justice Thomas peppered his opinion with instances drawn from newspaper coverage, where the application of zero tolerance would be humorous were the examples not so outrageous. *The Atlanta Journal-Constitution*, per Justice Thomas, noted the uproar surrounding "'an 11-year old [being] arrested, handcuffed, and taken to jail for bringing a plastic butter knife to school.'"[78]

Justice Thomas, along with his fellow conservatives, believes that any reform of zero-tolerance policies should occur not through the judiciary but through school boards and the legislature.[79] Adherence to this notion regarding the appropriate route for reform explains how some conservatives manage to be simultaneously anti-*Lopez* and anti–zero tolerance. If the necessary political will can be mustered to dial back zero tolerance in sensible ways that achieve meaningful reform, that development would be salutary. Any such available deals should be pursued. It must be stated, however, that some of the legislative victories that are marshaled in support of pursuing relief through nonjudicial means are so meek as to invite discouragement that the reform measures must be enacted at all. Justice Thomas's opinion criticizing zero-tolerance policies, for instance, quoted a *Washington Times* article from 2009 that recounted, "'[A] few states have moved to relax their laws. Utah now allows students to bring asthma inhalers to school without violating the zero-tolerance policy on drugs.'"[80] These achievements, such as they are, may not exactly send reformers rushing to chill the champagne. After the issue of permitting asthma inhalers in schools gains more steam, perhaps the political appetite for addressing the daunting matter of legalizing spork possession may finally materialize.

The conviction that the judiciary has virtually no role to play in reviewing school disciplinary measures—including zero-tolerance policies—claims a distressingly large group of supporters, including judges themselves. Seldom has this conviction been more acutely displayed within the judiciary than in 2001, when the U.S. Court of Appeals for the Fourth Circuit flatly rejected a claim from the middle-school student Benjamin Ratner. After a friend of Ratner's who had previously attempted suicide on multiple occasions informed him that she brought a knife to school with her and revealed that she contemplated slitting her wrists, Ratner removed the knife from her possession and placed it in his locker. A school official who learned of these events shortly thereafter found that "Ratner acted in what he saw as the girl's best interest and that at no time did Ratner pose a threat to anyone with the knife."[81] Rather than presenting Ratner with a medal at a school-wide assembly, the school gave him a ten-day suspension—a penalty that the school board ultimately increased to expulsion for the remaining four months of the school year. In a terse opinion, a panel of Fourth Circuit judges deemed themselves powerless to counter this miscarriage of justice. "However harsh the result in this case, the federal courts are not properly called upon to judge the wisdom of a zero tolerance policy . . . or of its application to Ratner," the opinion stated. "Instead, our inquiry here is limited to whether Ratner's complaint alleges sufficient facts which if proved would show that the implementation of the school's policy in this case failed to comport with the United States Constitution."[82] One judge on the panel wrote an anguished concurring opinion, deriding Ratner's expulsion as "calculated overkill" and "not justifiable" before ultimately reaching the same conclusion: "But alas . . . this is not a federal constitutional problem."[83]

The fundamental notion that the Constitution of the United States is somehow too rarefied a document to have any real bearing on petty disputes about school discipline is not a new concept. Justice Powell's dissent in *Lopez* expressed a version of this idea when he contended that any "arguable infringement [of student rights] is too speculative, transitory, and insubstantial to justify imposition of a *constitutional* rule."[84] The emphasis appears in Justice Powell's opinion from 1975, but many observers continue to endorse that notion emphatically. In 2005, on *Lopez*'s thirtieth anniversary, the counsel for the National School Boards Association reflected, "By making student discipline a constitutional issue, by elevating it to a 'federal issue,' the court has left educators fumbling away through their daily disciplinary dealings with students wondering and working at their peril. Every day in every school we have teachers and administrators making decisions of constitutional import all across the nation."[85]

The Court in *Lopez*, of course, rejected this idea that students contesting disciplinary actions were too trifling to merit the Constitution's consideration. To the contrary, *Lopez* provided, "[E]ducation is perhaps the most important function of state and local governments, and the total exclusion from the educational process . . . is a serious event in the life of the suspended child."[86] The express, overarching purpose of *Lopez*'s requiring school officials to provide students with hearings was to prevent "unfair or mistaken" suspensions and to offer "a meaningful hedge against erroneous action."[87] Turning a completely blind eye to the mindset of students who commit merely technical violations of school policies undermines *Lopez* and the most elemental notions of due process.[88]

Happily, some lower court opinions have refused to rubber-stamp the implementation of zero-tolerance policies when school districts make no effort to discern students' mental states, including whether they had knowledge that contraband items were in their possession. One memorable case involved a student who contended he had no knowledge of a knife that had been placed in the glove compartment of a vehicle he parked in the school's lot. The U.S. Court of Appeals for the Sixth Circuit in 2000 rebuked the school district for refusing even to consider whether the student had knowledge of the knife's presence. The court reasoned,

> [T]he Board may not absolve itself of its obligation, legal and moral, to determine whether students intentionally committed the acts for which their expulsions are sought by hiding behind a Zero Tolerance Policy that purports to make the students' knowledge a non-issue. We are also not impressed by the Board's argument that if it did not apply its Zero Tolerance Policy ruthlessly, and without regard for whether students accused of possessing a forbidden object knowingly possessed the object, this would send an inconsistent message to its students. Consistency is not a substitute for rationality.[89]

This opinion correctly concludes that students who truly lack the factual basis for knowing that their actions constitute prohibited conduct should not be sanctioned. Holding otherwise would mean that students at a school dance who consumed punch that, without their knowledge, had been (imperceptibly) spiked could be expelled for the consumption of alcohol on school grounds.[90] A rule that countenances such a result cannot be sound. Regrettably, though, the Sixth Circuit's skeptical approach toward the implementation of zero-tolerance policies remains unusual within the judiciary. Courts would be well advised to follow the lead of this important opinion and expand upon it in an effort to combat one of the most spectacular policy failures within any realm during the modern era.[91]

INGRAHAM V. WRIGHT:
THE PERSISTENT PROBLEM OF CORPORAL PUNISHMENT

On October 6, 1970, an eighth-grade student in Miami, Florida, named James Ingraham endured an episode of corporal punishment so severe that its aftermath led him to acquire an unwelcome new moniker: Rain Bummy. The trouble began when a teacher identified Ingraham as one of several students who, when instructed to depart the auditorium's stage, responded with insufficient urgency. While students leaving the stage at a leisurely pace would not qualify as a noteworthy event at most schools, Charles R. Drew Junior High School stood little chance of being confused with most schools.

At Drew, this typical adolescent behavior amounted to flagrant insubordination and earned the group a visit to the principal's office. Principal Willie J. Wright informed the wayward students that he would deliver five blows—or "licks," in the parlance—to their backsides with a wooden paddle measuring two feet in length. When Ingraham's turn to be paddled arose, however, he protested his innocence and refused to assume the position. Principal Wright then summoned assistance from two colleagues, who restrained Ingraham's extremities and bent his body at the waist so that he lay facedown over a table. With Ingraham now prone before him, Wright proceeded to strike him more than twenty times, the extra licks evidently due to the eighth grader's initial resistance. The force of these accumulated blows left Ingraham's face in tears and his backside in agony. Indeed, the pain was so excruciating that he required medical attention at the local hospital. The examining physician diagnosed Ingraham as suffering from a hematoma (an abnormal buildup of blood in human tissue), directed Ingraham to recover at home for at least a week, and prescribed a battery of pain-killers, laxatives, cold compresses, and sleeping pills. Three days after the paddling, Ingraham returned to the hospital, where a doctor described his injuries as including "a hematoma approximately six inches in diameter which was swollen, tender and purplish in color," and—in a detail that formed the basis for his regrettable nickname—noted "fluid oozing from the hematoma." Eight full days after the paddling occurred, Ingraham sought further medical attention, and his condition remained debilitating enough that a physician suggested convalescing at home for three additional days. Ingraham eventually returned to school after missing nearly two weeks, but another week would pass before he could sit in a chair without experiencing discomfort.[92]

Rather than suffering in shame and in silence, Ingraham elected to cast a spotlight on the brutal treatment that he and many other students experienced at Drew. He did so by initiating a federal lawsuit challenging the infliction of corporal punishment in public schools. When the Supreme Court agreed to review the matter in May 1976, Ingraham's lawsuit succeeded in bringing the issue of corporal punishment to the national fore.

American educators, influenced by religious considerations, had administered corporal punishment dating back to the colonial era. Within the Bible, Proverbs alone contains no fewer than six different verses extolling the virtues of parents physically disciplining their children. Consider only two of the more familiar instances, taken from the King James Version: "He that spareth the rod hateth his son; he that loveth him chasteneth him betimes"; and "Foolishness is bound in the heart of a child; but the rod of correction shall drive it far from him."[93] Bible-based corporal punishment sentiment made its way into the nation's first public schools in virtually unadulterated form. Thus, in 1645, the town records of Dorchester, Massachusetts, authorized the local schoolmaster to wield "the Rodd of Correction" to keep his "schollers" in line.[94] Whipping posts were common sights near early elementary and secondary schools and were sometimes located within the classrooms themselves.[95]*

---

* In seventeenth-century America, students did not escape corporal punishment even when they embarked upon higher education. Harvard College's rules of 1660 provided, "It is hereby ordered that the president and fellows of Harvard College have the power to punish all misdeeds of the young men in their college." This power, at least occa-

Despite corporal punishment's lengthy history, opponents of the practice greeted the Supreme Court's decision to grant certiorari in *Ingraham* with enthusiasm. *The New York Times*'s editorial page hailed it as "a sign of some progress in the assessment of children's rights," and expressed hope that the "case . . . will make it difficult to condone the practice as a benign application of old-fashioned pedagogy."[96] A leading psychologist and critic of corporal punishment similarly exulted: "People who once boasted about and laughed about [paddling] now are getting self-conscious and covering it up. The tide is turning."[97] Those assessments did not represent the cockeyed optimism of true believers.

Even clear-eyed appraisals provided ample reason for optimism that *Ingraham*'s arguments would prevail in the Supreme Court of the 1970s. Judicial decisions had recently eliminated the use of corporal punishment in prisons, and contemporaneous observers deemed it unfathomable that the constitutional safeguards afforded to convicted criminals would not also be afforded to public school students.* When Ingraham filed the lawsuit early in 1971, commentators from the worlds of both academia and journalism were already suggesting that corporal punishment in schools clashed with modern sensibilities. "[A] doctrine supporting the right to beat a child is unquestionably inconsistent with current values," Professor Buss confidently asserted in February 1971.[98] Later that year, *Newsweek* ran an article amplifying that view: "At a time when students'

---

sionally, was exercised; in 1674, one Harvard student received a public whipping in the library, under the president's supervision, for blasphemy. See Ellwood P. Cubberley, *Public Education in the United States* 57, 57n1 (rev. ed. 1934).

* In 1968, then-Judge Harry Blackmun wrote the opinion for the U.S. Court of Appeals for the Eighth Circuit that vanquished the usage of corporal punishment in American prisons. Many of the arguments against using "the strap" on inmates that Blackmun articulated also militate against using the paddle on students. Blackmun's opinion, for example, observed, "Corporal punishment is easily subject to abuse in the hands of the sadistic and the unscrupulous." In addition, Blackmun contended, "Corporal punishment generates hate toward the keepers who punish and toward the system which permits it. It is degrading to the punisher and to the punished alike." *Jackson v. Bishop*, 404 F.2d 571, 579–80 (8th Cir. 1968). Despite his powerful condemnation of corporal punishment in prisons, when Judge Blackmun became Justice Blackmun, he joined the Supreme Court's 5–4 opinion upholding corporal punishment in schools. Blackmun would eventually become one of the most liberal justices of his era. But, as his vote in *Ingraham* suggests, that development took time to emerge. For an incisive treatment of Blackmun's life and times, but one that does not, alas, analyze how his vote in *Ingraham* clashes with his most important opinion from his days as a circuit court judge, see Linda Greenhouse, *Becoming Justice Blackmun: Harry Blackmun's Supreme Court Journey* (2006).

rights have become a national issue . . . the reality of life in numerous classrooms around the country is still rooted in nineteenth-century notions of discipline."[99] By the mid-1970s, moreover, the overwhelming majority of psychological authorities rejected corporal punishment, frequently arguing that its infliction had detrimental effects on the mental health of educators and students alike. One of the very few authorities who was willing to support corporal punishment in the period leading up to *Ingraham* stopped well short of condoning the draconian regime that ruled Drew: "I don't believe in any brutality—in school or out—but sometimes a little pat on the behind is necessary."[100]

These social developments can be understood to contain constitutional import. The Eighth Amendment prohibits the government from inflicting "cruel and unusual punishment[ ]."[101] In 1958, the Supreme Court interpreted that provision to reflect "the evolving standards of decency that mark the progress of a maturing society."[102] Subsequently, moreover, the Court has ascertained those "evolving standards" by consulting numerous sources, including "the views . . . expressed by respected professional organizations."[103]

Corporal punishment's opponents could also draw solace from the Supreme Court's recent sensitivity to the constitutional claims of students. The Court's decision in *Tinker*, vindicating the free speech rights of student protesters, and—of even greater relevance—its decision in *Lopez*, affording suspended students procedural rights, combined to suggest that corporal punishment would soon be tamed. Even if the Court stopped short of eliminating all corporal punishment—under either the Eighth Amendment's prohibition on cruel and unusual punishment or the Fourteenth Amendment's protection of fundamental rights—it seemed eminently reasonable to anticipate the Court would afford procedural protections to students before imposing corporal punishment. If due process required that students who were suspended for even brief intervals receive notice and an opportunity to be heard, logic suggested that those protections should also be extended to students who were going to be struck with foreign objects. After all, the students' interest in avoiding bodily harm would seem to be at least as compelling as the students' interest in avoiding a few days away from school.

The final reason that opponents of corporal punishment could have anticipated a favorable decision was also the most straightforward: it would have been difficult to dream up a scenario that offered a ghastlier portrayal of corporal punishment than the underlying record established in *Ingraham*. Even setting aside the lead plaintiff's searing account, the trial court heard testimony from a steady procession of students who also experienced intense corporal punishment at the hands of Drew officials for petty infractions, including tardiness, having an untucked shirttail, not having gym shorts, and sitting in the wrong seat. Perhaps more disturbingly still, Drew students sometimes received corporal punishment when school officials did not allege that they had misbehaved in even a trivial sense. If a teacher declared that a few students in a class had somehow fallen out of line, then the entire class could receive corporal punishment in the form of a "mass paddling." Although the Supreme Court brief filed by the Dade County School Board attempted to place Drew's disciplinary regime in a larger context, the resulting effort awkwardly ended up making the egregious record look even worse. The brief noted that, in stark contrast to Drew, some schools in Dade County refrained from using corporal punishment altogether: "The principal of Miami Beach Senior High School cast light upon this, testifying that he found it philosophically unacceptable, but also unnecessary in his school, which serves a predominantly Jewish population with a culture of oral persuasion and strong family response."[104] The brief thus none too subtly suggested that where the misbehaving students in Miami Beach understood reason, the very different population at schools like Drew—which had an entirely black student body—responded only to brute force.[105] In sum, *Ingraham v. Wright* appeared to call out for the Supreme Court's intervention against corporal punishment.

In a 5–4 decision, however, the Supreme Court in April 1977 issued an opinion resisting that call. Justice Powell wrote the opinion for the five-justice majority. Two years after suffering the stinging defeat in *Lopez*, Powell must have relished the opportunity to speak again from the bench in a prominent school case, announcing his views this time not in the form of an anguished dissent but instead as the law of the land.

Justice Powell quickly dispatched Ingraham's first claim for relief, which suggested that, while mild forms of corporal punishment may be permissible, extreme forms violated the Eighth Amendment's protection against cruel and unusual punishment. Given that only two states (Massachusetts and New Jersey) then prohibited corporal punishment, Powell explained that he could discern no legislative trend toward abolition. Justice Powell then asserted that, when educators dispense corporal punishment, those actions do not even constitute "punishment" at all—at least for purposes of the Eighth Amendment. In order to fall within the Eighth Amendment's scope, *Ingraham* reasoned, the punishment in question must stem from some connection to a criminal conviction. Acknowledging that this construction meant students could receive treatment that even prison inmates are spared, Justice Powell sought to alleviate this apparent tension by focusing on what he deemed an essential distinguishing feature of public schools. "The schoolchild has little need for the protection of the Eighth Amendment," Justice Powell wrote. "Though attendance may not always be voluntary, the public school remains an open institution." Powell observed that students, unlike inmates, return home at the end of the day, and then offered an idyllic conception of the school that seemed discordant amid the grim realities of Drew: "Even while at school, the child brings with him the support of family and friends and is rarely apart from teachers and other pupils who may witness and protest any instances of mistreatment."[106]

Ingraham's second constitutional claim asserted that the absence of procedural protections afforded students before they were paddled violated the Fourteenth Amendment's Due Process Clause. Justice Powell, consistent with his approach in *Lopez*, rejected the notion that due process required any type of even informal hearing to occur before school authorities imposed corporal punishment. In Powell's view, requiring such hearings could harm the ability of teachers to maintain order in the nation's classrooms by delaying the period between student misbehavior and punishment. Powell argued that such delays could, counterintuitively, make matters even worse from the student's perspective because an extended period awaiting punishment would serve only to heighten anxiety.

More fundamentally, *Ingraham* construed the due process claim as attempting to drag the Supreme Court into arenas of local school governance, a place where it simply did not belong. "Elimination or curtailment of corporal punishment would be welcomed by many as a societal advance," Powell wrote. "But when such a policy choice may result from this Court's determination of an asserted right to due process, rather than from the normal processes of community debate and legislative action, the societal costs cannot be dismissed as insubstantial."[107] Striking the local-control theme with even greater force, Powell claimed that vindicating Ingraham's lawsuit would be "revolutionary," as "it departs from the ancient faith based on the premise that experience in making local laws by local people themselves is by far the safest guide for a nation like ours to follow."[108] According to *Ingraham*, students who received truly excessive corporal punishment should seek relief not by invoking constitutional law in the federal court system but by invoking tort law, which governs personal injuries, in the state court system.

Justice Byron White, joined by three other justices, wrote a dissenting opinion in *Ingraham* that parted company with the majority on both constitutional claims. As to the Eighth Amendment argument, Justice White contended that the majority in effect improperly inserted the word "criminal" into the relevant constitutional text so that it prohibited only "cruel and unusual *criminal* punishment"—a limitation that the Constitution's framers had declined to make. "If the Eighth Amendment does not bar moderate spanking in public schools," White wrote, "it is because moderate spanking is not 'cruel and unusual,' not because it is not 'punishment' as the majority suggests."[109] Justice White made clear that he did not believe paddling invariably violated the Constitution, but instead wrote to reject "the extreme view of the majority that corporal punishment in public schools, no matter how barbaric, inhumane, or severe, is never limited by the Eighth Amendment."[110] For White, viewing that constitutional provision as applying to punishment only if it is inflicted for committing a crime violated even recently decided Court precedent. One year earlier, after all, the Court held that prison officials who deliberately ignored the medical needs of inmates violated the Eighth Amendment, even though no one believed those actions constituted punishment for committing a crime.[111] As to the due process claim, Justice White skewered the majority opinion for requiring a student who had already been paddled to seek redress only after the fact: "The infliction of physical pain is final and irreparable; it cannot be undone in a subsequent proceeding."[112] In other words, just as an egg cannot be unscrambled, a backside cannot be unpaddled.[113]

Legal scholars almost universally excoriated *Ingraham*. Powell's opinion for the Court, critics repeatedly charged, offered a parsimonious conception of the Eighth Amendment, one that was in no way compelled by precedent. In assessing *Ingraham*'s due process reasoning, Professor Tribe memorably repaired to the ranks of children's literature to contend that the Court's "rationale pushes uncomfortably close to that of the Queen in Alice's Wonderland, who extolled the virtues of punishing the King's Messenger before trial, and holding the trial before the crime."[114] In an article appearing in the *Columbia Law Review*, evocatively subtitled "The Supreme Court's Whipping Boy," Professor Irene Rosenberg identified the Court's decision in *Ingraham* as one part of a larger conservative legal effort to close the federal courts to civil rights plaintiffs. "[T]he Court has evinced a marked concern for husbanding the resources of the federal judiciary—somewhat like librarians who suffer great anxiety when books are removed from the shelves," Rosenberg wrote. "Many of these decisions rest ultimately either on the view that . . . courts are not the appropriate forums for resolution of a large variety of disputes . . . or on the view that . . . state courts are the appropriate tribunals for vindication of claims against state and municipal officials."[115] Another legal commentator attributed *Ingraham*'s missteps to a more elemental fear—a fear that engulfed the judiciary's decisions involving education dating back to at least the 1920s—of the Supreme Court becoming the "school superintendent for the nation."[116]

The editorial pages of prominent newspapers also roundly vilified the Court's decision in *Ingraham*. The *Chicago Tribune* complained that it "makes no ethical, legal, or common sense to tolerate corporal punishment against children when it is not permitted against any other group of people in our society."[117] Echoing that assessment, the *Los Angeles Times* further suggested that paddling in schools could intensify the very sorts of behavioral problems that the practice sought to alleviate: "Corporal punishment is not only the infliction of physical pain, it is a demeaning assault on the feelings and the dignity of the child, and it tends to provoke more rebellious attitudes and actions leading to more behavior problems than it prevents."[118] But *The New York Times* featured perhaps the harshest assessment of *Ingraham*, as it condemned the opinion's "tortuous bit of reasoning," and concluded, "Each member of the majority deserves at least five whacks."[119]

One of the more telling reactions to *Ingraham* was that numerous observers expressed disbelief, not only that the Supreme Court propped up corporal punishment, but that the practice continued to exist in the nation's public schools at all. As *Newsweek* reported after *Ingraham*, "Many parents were astonished and angry to hear that pupils are still paddled in public schools. 'If any teacher hit my daughter,' said a Connecticut father, 'I'd be down at school the next day to suggest that the teacher get some discipline, too.'"[120] Even months after the Court's decision, *The New York Times* published an article that drastically understated the prevalence of corporal punishment: "Although the Supreme Court's decision may well encourage some teachers and principals to dust off their canes and rulers, most parents and students have little to fear; corporal punishment has been generally abandoned and is currently outlawed in all but a few states."[121] The Gray Lady reported matters almost exactly backward here; in reality, only two states had banned the practice as it continued to flourish in areas across the nation. This difficulty grasping the actual landscape of corporal punishment almost certainly stemmed from the fact that the nation's most cosmopolitan cities—including Chicago, Los Angeles, New York City, San Francisco, and Washington, D.C.—had all abolished corporal punishment prior to *Ingraham*.[122] From the metropolis, corporal punishment inflicted in the provinces simply went unseen.

Ingraham did not, of course, find a hostile reception in all quarters. A newspaper published in Martinsburg, West Virginia, applauded the decision as it described children being "born into this world as wild and unruly little animals who have to be trained in order to fit into a civilized society."[123] James J. Kilpatrick, a nationally syndicated columnist, pronounced *Ingraham* "plainly right" and complained, "To listen to the howls of liberal critics, you might suppose the five-man majority had studied law at the feet of Torquemada."[124] Many educators also expressed relief that corporal punishment remained a viable disciplinary approach in public schools. A spokesman for the American Federation of Teachers, which filed an amicus brief in supporting Principal Wright, commented after the Court's decision, "I shudder that people will say that we are Nazis who want to beat up kids. That's not it: teachers want to maintain a healthy atmosphere and they need options."[125] And in Miami, Florida, Pat Torillo, head of the local teachers' union, heartily endorsed that notion: "What's involved here is the teacher's right to lay hands on students—with as much force as necessary."[126]*

---

* After *Ingraham*, several commentators contended that the treatment Drew students endured was too savage to be captured by the relatively benign term "corporal punish-

The outcome of the Supreme Court opinion that bore his name reached James Ingraham, then twenty-one years old, in a Florida jail cell, where he was serving a one-year sentence for resisting arrest. Not surprisingly, Ingraham declared the decision "a big let-down."[127] Professor Irene Rosenberg speculated that Ingraham's legal difficulties may have some connection, however tenuous, to the epic paddling that he received at Drew: "James Ingraham's subsequent conviction for resisting arrest may not be unrelated to the brutal beating he received as a result of his failure to respond with sufficient swiftness to his teacher's order."[128] Perhaps.

It seems at least as plausible to maintain, however, that Ingraham's receipt of corporal punishment in 1970—even if it played no causal role in his jail stint—signaled his membership among society's marginalized citizens who account for an overwhelming portion of the nation's incarcerated population. The tradition of American schools deploying corporal punishment to manage social outsiders stretches back more than a century. In 1889, a member of the Boston School Committee sought to justify the use of corporal punishment on students who attend schools located within immigrant wards by contending, "[M]any of these children come from homes of vice and crime. In their blood are generations of iniquity. . . . They hate restraint or obedience to law. They know nothing of the feelings which are inherited by those who were born on our shores."[129] During the 1970s, a teacher in Wisconsin suggested that corporal punishment could more readily be imposed on students from downtrodden backgrounds than on students from affluent backgrounds: "It all depends on who you grab. Grab the dumb ones—they don't know what the hell to do. Don't grab a lawyer's kid."[130] In the wake of *Ingraham*, the school superintendent in

---

ment." Robert Chanin, the National Education Association's general counsel, noted, "The facts here are outrageous; this was by anybody's terms a beating." Gene I. Maeroff, "Spanking Rule Found an Aid to Discipline," *New York Times*, April 25, 1977, 24. See also Richard Cohen, "A License to Beat Children in School," *Washington Post*, April 21, 1977, B1 ("[T]he Supreme Court has ruled that corporal punishment, which is a nice way of saying the hitting of children, is permissible in the schools"); Ellen Goodman, "Judgment on Violence," *Boston Globe*, April 29, 1977, 16 ("Last week the Supreme Court upheld child abuse. Oh, they didn't call it that. . . . The justices wrote in measured tone about 'corporal punishment.' "); and William Raspberry, "The Schoolkids Catch It on Their Bottoms," *Los Angeles Times*, May 13, 1977, D7 (calling the treatment "child-beating").

Alexandria, Virginia, made a similar point, but for the purpose of condemning the practice. "In my measure, the punishment is ineffective because it's selective," he said. "I've never seen the mayor's kid get a paddling, I've never seen the school superintendent's get a paddling."[131]

Today, critics of corporal punishment frequently make their case against the practice by observing that the percentage of black students who receive the paddle is dramatically higher than their percentage of the overall public school population.[132] According to the most recent set of statistics compiled by the Department of Education in 2012, black students make up about 16 percent of the nation's public school students but receive about 35 percent of the nation's corporal punishment.[133] The thrust of such assertions is unmistakable: black students receive more than twice the amount of corporal punishment that one would expect them to receive if—assuming equal rates of misbehavior—the practice were distributed in a manner uninfected by racial bias.

Some loathsome evidence supports the idea that black students have been singled out for corporal punishment solely because of their race. In May 1971, a *Newsweek* article recounted the following events that unfolded in Dallas, Texas, as that city finally began to meet its long-delayed date with school desegregation:

> As he edged hesitantly into his new sixth-grade classroom . . . in Dallas earlier this year, 11-year-old Terry Collins was visibly nervous—and, as events quickly proved, with good reason. For no sooner had class begun than teacher Aaron Day summoned the fidgeting black transfer student to the front of the room. "Here comes fresh meat," Day chortled. And with that, he proceeded to strike Terry Collins on the backside with a wooden paddle. Since then, young Terry has been repeatedly whipped for a variety of transgressions, ranging from misspelling words and tardiness to "inattentiveness."[134]

One year later, Carole Duncan, leader of a national organization opposed to corporal punishment, suggested that Collins's experience was not an isolated one. "It is a tragic admission of racial misunderstanding to acknowledge that integration of blacks into white schools has served to bring about increased physical assaults on black school children," she said. "Statistics indicate that when black children attended black schools in black communities with black personnel they were not subjected to excessive punishments."[135]

While racial disparities in the administration of corporal punishment are important, scholars should demonstrate greater care when analyzing this issue than simply invoking *nationwide* statistical disparities involving race. This is so because, unlike the issue of suspensions and expulsions (which are spread throughout the nation in a relatively uniform fashion), the infliction of corporal punishment today varies greatly by region. According to the federal figures from 2012, five states located in the South—Alabama, Arkansas, Georgia, Mississippi, and Texas—accounted for more than 70 percent of the nation's corporal punishment. With the exception of Texas (13 percent), those states all contain significantly higher percentages of black students than the national average: Alabama (34 percent); Arkansas (21 percent); Georgia (37 percent); and Mississippi (50 percent).[136] In other words, some of the black overrepresentation among corporal punishment recipients may stem from the higher percentages of black students attending schools in states where corporal punishment is dispensed most frequently. Nonetheless, within four of these five southern states, black students receive a disproportionately large share of corporal punishment. (Alabama is the lone exception.) Moreover, these states at least possibly continue to use corporal punishment at unusually high rates precisely *because* they contain high percentages of black students.* Thus, while leav-

---

* It bears noting, though, that—in contrast to the experience of young Terry Collins at his new school—black students often receive corporal punishment not from white educators but from black educators. Indeed, Sarah Carr recently observed that in Mississippi, which claims the nation's highest per capita rate of corporal punishment, the most enthusiastic "wielders of the paddle and its most vocal defenders" are overwhelmingly black educators. Proponents of paddling who are black often seek to sustain the practice by contending that its abolition would illegitimately impinge upon the black community's right to autonomy. As Carr explained, "It's one of the ironies of the debate that defenders speak of corporal punishment in terms of black self-sufficiency—emphasizing a community's right to determine how it educates its children—while critics speak of it in terms of black subjugation." Observing that black educators often inflict corporal punishment upon black students does not, of course, render the practice unobjectionable. As one Mississippian opposed to paddling argued to Carr, "During slavery, we were whipped on the back, beat on the back and dehumanized. The sad part is that we are doing it . . . to ourselves now." See Sarah Carr, "Why Are Black Students Being Paddled More in the Public Schools?," *The Hechinger Report*, April 14, 2014. This argument is not a new one. In 1974, the celebrated psychologist Kenneth Clark expressed opposition to black educators paddling black students through similar means: "I do not believe that

ing the analysis at the national level may somewhat amplify the degree of racial disparity, it is unmistakable—even accounting for regional variations—that black students receive inordinate amounts of corporal punishment.

If corporal punishment's connection to race receives abundant attention, one of the most underutilized objections to corporal punishment stems from the practice's relationship to sex. By this statement, I do not mean to object to the fact that male students receive nearly four in five instances of corporal punishment.[137] Instead, I intend to draw attention to the fact that male educators often paddle female students in manners that seem highly objectionable. Consider the following description of corporal punishment offered by Tamara May Torbert, a fifteen-year-old high school student in Mesquite, Texas, during the late 1970s: "They make you spread your legs, bend over and put your hands on the desk. Then they rub the paddle lightly on your rear and bring it back as far as they can and hit you. It hurts real bad."[138]* One critic of corporal punishment called such practices "an exercise in pornographic amusement for the perpetrators."[139] Alvin Burstein, a professor of psychology at the University of Texas, appeared to share this view, even if he did not believe that it typically operated on a conscious level: "We all have unconscious sexual fantasies, and the problem becomes more acute as the child victim grows older."[140]

---

the fact that these charges involved black deans and a black principal make the matter any less grave. And the fact that some parents have supported the use of brutal corporal punishment of their children can be viewed merely as another example of the extent to which past victimization leads to the acceptance and perpetuation of cruelty." Justine Wise Polier et al., "Corporal Punishment and School Suspensions: A Case Study," in *Corporal Punishment in American Education: Readings in History, Practice, and Alternatives* 237, 240 (Irwin A. Hyman and James H. Wise eds., 1979).

* Tamara May Torbert's connection to corporal punishment briefly became a cause célèbre in 1977, when her parents' refusal to permit school officials to paddle their daughter yet again prompted a confrontation. The Torberts threatened to keep their daughter home from school for as long as corporal punishment awaited her upon return. The standoff attracted media attention not just from the *Mesquite Daily News* but also from the *New York Post* and the *London Evening Standard*. Torbert's parents explained that some of their objections arose from the fact that a man was to wield the paddle. The stalemate ended when Torbert's mother agreed to strike her daughter with a belt in the principal's office. Accounts varied as to the vigor with which she undertook the task. Where Torbert's mother contended that she delivered three "real soft" whacks, an assistant principal claimed, "Tammy would have been better off taking the paddle swats from us: her Mom really sizzled her behind with that strap." See "School Lets Mom Spank Daughter," *New York Post*, Sept. 13, 1977, 9; and "The Girl Who Took a Spanking," *London Evening Standard*, Sept. 15, 1977.

With Burstein's comment in mind, consider a recent, high-profile invitation to reevaluate corporal punishment in schools that the Supreme Court rejected, and also contemplate how the underlying facts resemble those at the heart of *Ingraham*. In June 2004, Jessica Serafin arrived on campus for one of her final days as a high school student in San Antonio, Texas. Serafin walked across the street to purchase a breakfast taco and then arrived for her first-period class on time. The school's interim principal, a man in his early thirties, soon thereafter called Serafin to his office and informed her that the taco excursion violated the closed-campus rule. He then instructed the eighteen-year-old young woman to bend over a chair with her buttocks raised in order to receive punishment from Ole Thunder, the nickname bestowed upon the school's four-foot-long wooden paddle. Serafin refused to comply and insisted that she would rather withdraw from the school than submit to the paddling. Two other school officials then restrained Serafin. The ensuing encounter with Ole Thunder left Serafin with her eyes crying, her buttocks bleeding, and even her hand swelling (as a result of blocking the paddle, after she briefly managed to wriggle free). Serafin's mother picked her up from school and took her directly to the hospital for emergency treatment. Thus, like James Ingraham some thirty-four years earlier, Jessica Serafin committed a modest infraction, refused to surrender to corporal punishment, was restrained by school officials, and suffered physical injuries requiring a hospital visit. Although Serafin's petition received considerable media attention and many advocates expressed hope that the justices would finally seize the opportunity to eliminate corporal punishment from public schools once and for all, the Supreme Court simply refused to hear the case without comment in June 2008.[141]

RECONCILING *LOPEZ* WITH *INGRAHAM*

The Supreme Court's decisions in *Lopez* and *Ingraham*, decided less than three years apart, unmistakably pull in competing directions regarding constitutional limitations on schools' ability to sanction students. Where the Court vindicated students' rights in *Lopez*, the Court abandoned students' rights in *Ingraham*, a case that if anything appeared to pose a more blatant infringement than the procedural question presented in *Lopez*. More jarring than *Ingra-ham*'s refusal to use the Eighth Amendment to abolish corporal punishment was its unwillingness to extend the sorts of procedural protections to corporal punishment that the Court had applied to suspensions in *Lopez*. Why did the Supreme Court issue this discordant pair of decisions in rapid succession? Although addressing this question necessarily enters the realm of speculation, it seems essential to analyze potential explanations for the disparate outcomes. At the outset, though, it is important to realize that framing the question as to why *the Supreme Court* reversed course provides a misleading portrait of the judicial dynamic at work.[142] Both *Lopez* and *Ingraham* were decided by 5–4 margins, indicating that each individual justice did not careen between the two opinions, even if the institution did. Only one member of the Supreme Court, Justice Potter Stewart, voted with the majority in both decisions. Regrettably, Justice Stewart did not write an opinion explaining his reasoning in either of the two cases.

James E. Ryan, who was a distinguished legal scholar at the University of Virginia before becoming dean of Harvard's Graduate School of Education, has offered one of the relatively few sustained efforts to reconcile the Court's decisions in *Lopez* and *Ingraham*. In an important law review article published in 2000, Ryan generally argued that the Supreme Court tends to defer to educational authorities in cases where schools act in their academic (rather than their social) function, and then imported that framework to analyze the Court's decisions involving student sanctions:

> Requiring rudimentary protections [for suspensions] is not likely to disrupt seriously the academic function of schools, if only because the student can presumably be immediately removed from the classroom. . . . Allowing the immediate infliction of corporal punishment, by contrast, is at least arguably justified by the need of teachers to respond quickly to disruptions that occur within the classroom. Thus, *Ingraham* can be reconciled with [*Lopez*] by positing that the need to react swiftly to maintain order in the classroom justifies granting school teachers authority to impose punishment unilaterally.[143]

In recent decades, no legal scholar has written more first-rate work in the field of education law than Ryan, but his argument here fails to persuade. As a preliminary matter, Ryan's argument over-looked the many students who receive corporal punishment for alleged misdeeds committed outside the classroom setting, includ-ing James Ingraham and several of his Drew classmates. More important, though, Ryan's argument disregarded the fact that stu-dents who disrupt class, in a jurisdiction where corporal punish-ment exists, may also be instantly removed from the classroom (by, say, ordering the disruptor to the principal's office) so that class-work may resume. Indeed, if a student who disrupts class is going to receive corporal punishment, being ordered to the principal's office may be akin to standard practice because—contrary to the scenario Ryan sketched—individual teachers are often prohibited from pad-dling students. Regulations typically require central administrators to apply corporal punishment, often in the presence of another edu-cator and outside the sight of fellow students. That state of affairs was already common at the time of *Ingraham* and became more common still when Ryan assessed matters twenty-three years later. Teachers thus frequently lack "unilateral[ ]" authority to paddle, and corporal punishment is not dispensed nearly as "swiftly," as Ryan's account presupposed. Even assuming the scenario that Ryan out-lined more accurately resembled reality, however, it seems far from obvious that having educators take a break from teaching to pad-dle errant pupils would actually "maintain order in the classroom" rather than merely introduce a new type of disorder. The academic utility of the paddling-on-demand system that Ryan warrants seems at best highly speculative. Finally, Ryan's argument seems strained because had *Ingraham* held that students were entitled to *Lopez*-style precautions before they received corporal punishment, it seems difficult to believe that the supposed academic benefits of paddling would vanish. An informal exchange that lasts for a short period before paddling would not look so terribly different from the regime that Ryan envisions.

Several commentators have attempted to explain the shift from *Lopez* to *Ingraham* by noting that concerns about violence within the nation's public schools seem to have stood at a fevered pitch in the period preceding *Ingraham*.[144] Some evidence can certainly be mar-shaled that appears to bolster this analysis, including the existence of disquieting media coverage and U.S. Senate reports that chronicled school violence during the interval between *Lopez* and *Ingraham*.[145] One should be wary about placing too much stock in the violence-driven explanation for *Ingraham*, however, because alarming depictions of school violence in the media and political realms were hardly a development of the post-*Lopez* era. In November 1969, for example, *Time* declared, "A new wave of violence is sweeping U.S. classrooms. Much of it is centered in junior high schools, which have long coped with the most combustible years of adolescence. Yet the incidence of burglary, larceny, assault, and even murder is rising in all public schools, reports the Senate Subcommittee on Juvenile Delinquency."[146] By 1971, a law review article drew upon such reports in both the media and the Senate to observe, "Crime and violence . . . are becoming problems of frightening proportions in many school systems."[147] When the Supreme Court decided both *Lopez* and *Ingraham*, the justices likely perceived those reports as if not quite background noise, then at least an awfully familiar tune.

One potentially more fruitful way of reconciling *Lopez* and *Ingraham* is to view the Supreme Court in both opinions as ratifying the dominant approach that schools across the nation adopted regarding the respective sanctions. To recall: in *Lopez*, most schools (particularly those in big cities) had instituted the type of minimal due process precautions the decision required; in *Ingraham*, forty-eight states permitted corporal punishment. In this way, the Court's two opinions served to reinforce the status quo and conversely— perhaps even more important—avoided demanding any actions that would require a sea change in how schools already tended to order their affairs.

A second plausible explanation for the turnabout from *Lopez* to *Ingraham* hinges on the increased concern over what mainstream commentators regarded as the federal courts' outsized role in American society and, relatedly, the explosion of litigation engulfing American schools and courts. Between *Lopez* in January 1975 and *Ingraham* in April 1977, consider only three of the many articles in mainstream publications exploring these themes: *The Public Interest* warned of an overreaching "Imperial Judiciary"; *The New York Times Magazine* chronicled "Legal Pollution"; and *Newsweek* asked whether there was "Too Much Law?"[148] To elaborate the point through the last article, *Newsweek*'s treatment of the topic began by noting, "A number of legal authorities, by no means all of them conservative, worry that reliance on the courts is damaging to the American system of government—and to the courts themselves." *Newsweek* further identified student litigation as an area of particular judicial overreach ("Does a child have the right to wear long hair in school?") and also observed that "[t]he deluge of lawsuits is swamping the courts."[149] This trend of mainstream articles addressing the growth of litigation did not exist when the Court decided *Lopez*.

Arguments in this vein would have had particular purchase in the context of the dispute about corporal punishment in schools, given the terms of debate that existed at that time. Recall that neither Justice White's dissent nor Ingraham's own attorney contended that corporal punishment invariably violated the Eighth Amendment. Instead, they argued more modestly that severe inflictions of corporal punishment crossed the constitutional line. That argument necessarily raises thorny questions regarding precisely how much punishment falls on either side of that line. As the attorney for Dade County vividly expressed to the media following oral argument in *Ingraham*, a decision against his client would place "federal courts into the business of second-guessing school authorities over whether two licks or swats are appropriate."[150] Justice Powell's opinion expressly entertained the possibility that deciding the case the other way would trigger an avalanche of line-drawing litigation: "[T]he logic of the dissent would make the judgment of which disciplinary punishments are reasonable and which are excessive a matter of constitutional principle in every case, to be decided ultimately by this Court."[151]

The Court's grant of relief in *Lopez*, by way of contrast, did not inherently involve similar line-drawing difficulties. The procedural obligations *Lopez* imposed were so scant that school districts could easily discharge those commitments and confront no ambiguity as to whether they had met their obligations. Although Justice Powell's dissent in *Lopez* raised the potential menace of due process creeping into other scholastic domains—students suing schools over being cut from varsity sports teams or not being placed in accelerated courses—the removal of students from school altogether is logically discrete and thus could be understood to sidestep that type of line-drawing question as well.[152]

Today, these line-drawing arguments militating against the judiciary's engagement with corporal punishment in schools are irrelevant because the time for an incremental challenge—one that attacks only severe inflictions—has long since disappeared. In 1977, when the Court decided *Ingraham*, Justice Powell could plausibly assert that he detected no trend toward the abolition of school paddling. Four decades later, however, that claim would seem absurd. Where national polling data during the 1970s revealed that a majority of respondents supported corporal punishment, a nationwide study from 2006 revealed that less than one in four respondents support the practice.[153] Where only two states (both in the Northeast) had abolished corporal punishment in 1977, thirty-one states now prohibit the practice. The Supreme Court routinely consults shifts in the state statutory landscape in the course of determining that "evolving standards of decency" require a punishment to be abolished under the Eighth Amendment.[154] While nineteen states have not abolished corporal punishment, that figure suggests that paddling remains far more widespread than the underlying statistics actually bear out; a large majority of the nation's corporal punishment occurs in just a handful of southern states.[155] Even within those southern states, moreover, corporal punishment is administered unevenly, as schools in rural areas implement the practice at higher rates than schools in urban areas. Recently, in finding an Eighth Amendment violation, the Supreme Court expressly noted with skepticism that a small number of states accounted for an inordinately large percentage of a particular type of punishment.[156] Beyond the nation's borders, moreover, the trend toward abolishing corporal punishment in schools becomes even more striking. At the beginning of this decade, more than one hundred countries—including nearly every nation the United States traditionally regards as a peer—had abolished the practice.[157] Again, the Court has often canvassed other nations' punishment practices as part of its Eighth Amendment inquiry, viewing with hostility America's retention of unusual punishment practices.[158]

It may be comforting to believe that the Supreme Court's engagement with corporal punishment is unnecessary because the practice is dwindling through nonjudicial means. On this account, the days of educators laying hands on students is a rapidly disappearing phenomenon—a scourge that, like the new math before it, will soon be safely consigned to our educational past. While the two most recent sets of data collected by the federal government certainly reveal a decrease in corporal punishment, they do not support the blithe assumption that educators must be on the verge of voluntarily relinquishing their paddles. In 2006, more than 223,000 students received corporal punishment in public schools during the preceding school year. In 2012, nearly 167,000 students still received corporal punishment in schools. Importantly, during that six-year period, some of the states where the paddle is wielded most frequently experienced only negligible declines. Arkansas, for example, went from slightly more than 22,000 instances of corporal punishment in 2006 to slightly more than 20,000 such instances in 2012.[159]

That students in American public schools continue to be paddled today is an atrocity. Future generations will regard our unwillingness to eradicate this act of barbarism in the year 2018 as a source of shame and embarrassment. No legal issue sits higher atop the long list of needed educational reforms than eliminating corporal punishment against students—the sole remaining group that governmental actors are permitted to strike with impunity. This notion that corporal punishment in schools conflicts with enlightened sentiment is hardly a novel observation. In 1853, a member of the Indiana Supreme Court noted,

> The public seems to cling to the despotism in the government of schools which has been discarded everywhere else. . . . The husband can no longer moderately chastise his wife; nor . . . the master his servant or his apprentice. Even the degrading cruelties of the naval service have been arrested. Why the person of the schoolboy . . . should be less sacred in the eyes of the law than that of the apprentice or the sailor, is not easily explained.[160]

The intervening sixteen decades have succeeded in rendering that explanation impossible.

4

Policing Student Investigations:
Searching Students' Bodies, Suspicionless
Drug Testing, and *Miranda* Warnings

In recent decades, two broad ideological camps have vehemently
disputed whether the Constitution should be understood as impos
ing significant limitations on the ability of public school educators
and police officers to search students and to question them about
criminal investigations. The first camp expresses grave doubts that
constitutional criminal procedure properly belongs within the
schoolhouse at all. This camp stresses that the dual imperatives of
maintaining order in schools and keeping them free from drugs
and weapons require furnishing government officials with virtually whatever discretion they desire to ensure the education and
safety of students in their charge. Although the existence of this
camp dates back many decades, three relatively recent events now
figure prominently in the minds of its adherents: the mass school
shootings that occurred in 1999 in Columbine, Colorado, in 2012
in Newtown, Connecticut, and in 2018 in Parkland, Florida. For
this camp, policies and judicial opinions that may inhibit educators
and police officers from taking the steps necessary to prevent school
disorder, let alone school carnage, are anathema.

The second camp contends that largely untrammeled government authority to search and interrogate students in public schools
jeopardizes core constitutional guarantees—primarily, the Fourth
Amendment's prohibition on unreasonable searches and the Fifth

Amendment's protection against self-incrimination. This camp emphasizes that students suffer irrevocable harm when they are subjected to invasive searches by governmental officials on the basis of little more than a hunch—or perhaps even under no suspicion at all. In 2015, this camp's supporters rallied against images from a South Carolina classroom where a white police officer arrested a black student, after violently dislodging her from her desk, because she would not vacate the classroom. For this camp, that scene encapsulated several interrelated afflictions that beset the intersection of crime and education. The increased presence of police officers in schools has led to excessive numbers of arrested students, too many of whom are racial minorities, for often negligible infractions—a set of issues that has combined to produce what critics label "the school-to-prison pipeline."

Taking the measure of the Supreme Court's five opinions involving criminal procedure in schools, some observers may perceive the institution as beginning in the first camp but more recently making its way into the second camp. On this account, its earliest three opinions in this arena—all of which arose from student searches involving drugs—evinced great aversion to interpreting the Fourth Amendment in a manner that meaningfully constrained educators' discretion. First, in 1985, the Supreme Court in *New Jersey v. T.L.O.* held that school officials required merely reasonable suspicion, not probable cause, that students violated either the law or school regulations in order to search students and their belongings. Ten years later, the Court authorized schools to conduct suspicionless drug tests for student athletes in *Vernonia School District v. Acton*, and in 2002 extended that decision to cover students engaged in extracurricular activities in *Board of Education v. Earls*. In its two latest opinions, however, the Court can be viewed as turning in the opposite direction, as it issued opinions defending students' constitutional rights in the face of overreaching government officials. Thus, the Court in 2009 found that educators violated the Fourth Amendment by strip-searching a pupil for prescription-strength pain relievers in *Safford Unified School District v. Redding*, and then two years later strongly suggested that extensive police questioning of a seventh grader about criminal activity—without first informing him of his rights—violated the Fifth Amendment in *J.D.B. v. North Carolina*. That the Court issued these opinions so recently— and that they are its latest involving students' constitutional rights in any realm—may prompt some observers to believe that the Court is on the verge of embracing the second camp's liberty-based commitments.

However alluring, the notion that the Supreme Court has over time experienced a dramatic transformation in this domain is severely misguided. While *Redding* and *J.D.B.* undoubtedly represent welcome steps toward limiting how educators and police officers may handle students within schools, it is important to recognize that the decisions constitute mere baby steps—tentative, awkward, and stumbling. Both cases involved truly flagrant facts, making it eminently plausible that the Court would have reached similar bottom lines, even had they been decided during an earlier era. In addition, the transformational account obscures the relative significance of the Court's five criminal procedure opinions involving public schools. In fact, *T.L.O.*—the Court's first foray in this area, which established the overarching framework for student searches—dwarfs the subsequent four cases in terms of their import for the everyday reality of students across the country. In this area, what the Supreme Court has done lately matters much less than what it did more than three decades ago.

NEW JERSEY V. T.L.O.:

THE FOURTH AMENDMENT AND REASONABLE SUSPICION

In March 1980, a math teacher at New Jersey's Piscataway High School walked into a restroom and discovered two ninth-grade girls smoking cigarettes. Although the school still permitted students to smoke in designated areas, the lavatory was not among them. Accordingly, the teacher escorted the students to Assistant Vice Principal Theodore Choplick's office and informed him that they violated school rules by smoking in a nonsmoking area.* One of the

---

* Antismoking sentiment has become sufficiently pervasive that it now seems difficult to believe that a high school in New Jersey as recently as 1980 permitted students to smoke on campus. Yet, even in 1987, a national publication directed toward education officials aimed to reassure them that the scarcity of litigation contesting no-smoking policies "appear[s] to indicate school boards have notable legal latitude in this area." Perry A. Zirkel, "Banning Smoking in Your Schools," 18 *Updating School Board Policies* 3, 3–4 (1987). Scarcity of litigation, of course, is not the same thing as its total absence. The publication recounted a lawsuit in North Carolina, where a tenth-grade student whose parents permitted her to smoke contested the suspension she received for repeat-

girls immediately conceded the infraction, and Choplick ordered her to attend a smoking clinic for three days as punishment. But the other girl—subsequently labeled "T.L.O." by courts to preserve her anonymity—denied that she had been smoking in the bathroom and further contended that she did not smoke cigarettes at all. Choplick then seized T.L.O.'s purse and opened it to discover a package of Marlboro cigarettes resting on top. When he reached into the bag to remove the Marlboros, moreover, Choplick noticed a set of rolling papers—a product he associated with marijuana usage. The presence of rolling papers prompted Choplick to search T.L.O.'s purse in its entirety. Among other assorted items, her purse contained a metal pipe, empty plastic bags, a small amount of marijuana, and—in a separate, zippered compartment—an index card listing names of "people who owe me money," along with two letters that implicated T.L.O. in selling marijuana. Choplick then called T.L.O.'s mother and turned over the evidence to the police. Consistent with the comparatively lenient approach to school discipline policies of the 1980s, T.L.O. received a three-day suspension for smoking in a non-designated area and an additional seven-day suspension for possessing marijuana. Far more significantly, however, the State of New Jersey brought delinquency charges in juvenile court against T.L.O. for possession of marijuana with intent to distribute. In response, T.L.O. sought to suppress the evidence from her purse, asserting that Choplick violated her Fourth Amendment right to be free from unreasonable searches. Although lower state courts rejected T.L.O.'s claim, the New Jersey Supreme Court vindicated her argument. The U.S. Supreme Court accepted New Jersey's petition to review the case, and in so doing agreed for the first time to weigh how the Constitution's criminal procedure protections applied to students within the nation's public schools.[1]

President Ronald Reagan and his administration were no doubt delighted with the Court's decision to review *New Jersey v. T.L.O.* because they had been spoiling for an event to highlight their views on the state of public schooling. In January 1984, the White House

---

edly violating the school's new policy prohibiting tobacco usage on campus. The student asserted, "If the parents say you can and the school says you can't I think the parents have the word over the school." Not surprisingly, the North Carolina trial court disagreed, summarily rejecting her lawsuit that asserted various constitutional violations, and the appellate court affirmed. See ibid.; and *Craig v. Buncombe County Board of Education*, 343 S.E.2d 222 (N.C. Ct. App. 1986).

issued a report titled "Chaos in the Classroom: Enemy of American Education," which identified the twin evils of crime and violence as plaguing the nation's public schools. As part of the report's promotion, Deputy Undersecretary of Education Gary Bauer and other Reagan administration officials indicated that the Solicitor General's Office should look to file amicus briefs in cases supporting school administrators, with one White House lawyer claiming that such briefs would make "an enormous difference."[2] President Reagan himself highlighted the report in his weekly radio address: "The sad truth is many classrooms across the country are not temples of learning, teaching the lessons of good will, civility and wisdom important to the whole fabric of American life."[3] The amicus brief that the solicitor general ultimately filed in *T.L.O.* would (without attribution) include that quotation nearly verbatim, with the largest alteration being the brief's substitution of "central" for Reagan's "important."[4] In addition, the brief contended that school disorder had become a "national problem," as "many schools are in such a state of disorder that not only is the educational atmosphere polluted, but the very safety of students and teachers is imperiled."[5] This lamentable state of affairs, according to the solicitor general's brief, made it essential for the Supreme Court to provide educators with sufficient latitude to conduct student searches without fear of violating the Constitution. The brief's filing in late July, just as the Reagan reelection campaign shifted into high gear, garnered extensive media coverage, portraying it as the opening salvo in the administration's broader effort to combat crime and violence in schools.[6*]

On January 15, 1985—less than one week before President Reagan's second inauguration—Justice Byron White wrote an opinion for the Supreme Court in *New Jersey v. T.L.O.* supporting the administration's permissive approach to student searches. Before we explore that approach, though, it is important to understand that the Court rebuffed a more permissive proposal still. That

* In an inversion of the standard dynamic, some members of the civil rights community blanched at the idea of the federal government potentially assuming a larger role in the educational arena. As Althea Simmons of the NAACP stated, "I'm extremely skeptical of the Federal Government stepping in on school discipline. That's a state and local issue." Robert Pear, "Reagan Expected to Present Plan to Fight Crime in Public Schools," *New York Times*, Jan. 1, 1984, 1. In the realm of education law, of course, local-control arguments are typically advanced by conservatives seeking to forestall liberal reforms.

proposal—one advocated by New Jersey in *T.L.O.*, which some lower courts adopted—held school officials could *never* violate the Fourth Amendment because of the in loco parentis doctrine, which construes educators as standing in place of the students' parents, not as state officials. On this view, just as the Fourth Amendment does not prevent parents from searching their child's room at home, neither does it prevent educators from searching a student's belongings at school. Justice White concluded, however, that such reasoning conflicted with compulsory schooling laws (which effectively require most parents to enroll their children in public schools) and the Supreme Court's own precedents—*Tinker v. Des Moines Independent Community School District* and *Goss v. Lopez*—depicting educators as state officials who are capable of infringing students' constitutional rights.

While *T.L.O.* thus affirmed that the Fourth Amendment affords students some protections within schools, it also held that educators need not satisfy the usual *probable cause* standard when conducting a search for evidence of either unlawful behavior or even violations of school rules. In lieu of probable cause, *T.L.O.* announced, student searches would be governed by the less demanding standard of *reasonable suspicion*. "By focusing attention on the question of reasonableness," Justice White explained, "the standard will spare teachers and school administrators the necessity of schooling themselves in the niceties of probable cause and permit them to regulate their conduct according to the dictates of reason and common sense."[7] *T.L.O.* articulated a two-part test to guide lower courts and educators in assessing whether student searches comported with this reasonable suspicion requirement. First, a student search must be "justified at its inception"—an obligation that would be met if "reasonable grounds [existed] for suspecting that the search will turn up evidence that the student has violated or is violating either the law or the rules of the school." Second, the scope of a student search must be "reasonably related to the objectives of the search and not excessively intrusive in light of the age and sex of the student and the nature of the infraction."[8]

Applying its newly articulated test, the Court determined that Choplick's conduct did not violate the Constitution along either dimension. In deeming Choplick's conduct justified at its inception, the Court segmented the overall examination of T.L.O.'s purse into distinct, smaller searches: the initial search for cigarettes was justified by the teacher's accusation, and the discovery of rolling papers—following removal of the Marlboros—justified the subsequent search for marijuana. In deeming the search's scope not excessively intrusive, the Court reasoned that the incriminating evidence of marijuana usage located in the purse's main compartment supported Choplick's decision to access the zippered section containing the index card and two letters; the index card's suspicious title, likewise, justified Choplick's decision to peruse T.L.O.'s letters for further evidence of drug distribution.

Justices Lewis F. Powell Jr. and Harry Blackmun filed significant concurring opinions, both of which seemed more dedicated to reflecting nostalgically on the authors' own school days from more than five decades earlier than to grappling with comtemporary educational realities. Justice Powell—returning to themes he voiced one decade earlier, first dissenting in *Lopez* and then for the Court in *Ingraham v. Wright*—extolled "[t]he special relationship between teacher and student," one that is quite distinct from the oppositional relationship between law enforcement and criminal suspects.[9] "Rarely does this type of adversarial relationship exist between school authorities and pupils," Justice Powell contended. "Instead, there is a commonality of interests between teachers and their pupils. The attitude of the typical teacher is one of personal responsibility for the student's welfare as well as for his education."[10] For his part, Justice Blackmun even more directly invoked his own schoolboy memories—which he projected as the universal schooling experience—in seeking to underscore the difficult task teachers confront in maintaining order: "Every adult remembers from his own schooldays the havoc a water pistol or peashooter can wreak until it is taken away."[11] Justice Blackmun further contended that the "special needs" of the school environment, going "beyond the normal need for law enforcement," rendered it impractical to apply an unadulterated Fourth Amendment in schools.[12]

Three of the Court's most reliably liberal members—Justices William Brennan, Thurgood Marshall, and John Paul Stevens—vigorously dissented in *T.L.O.* Justice Brennan, writing for himself and Justice Marshall, contended that the Court should not deviate from the probable cause standard in schools. In support of this claim, Justice Brennan noted that a leading criminal law treatise found that most student search cases that reached appellate courts contained sufficiently detailed underlying facts and suspicions to cross the probable cause threshold. In sharp contrast to the quaint depictions of the student-educator relationship offered by his colleagues in the majority, Justice Brennan emphasized that Choplick provided the evidence obtained from T.L.O.'s purse to the police, and the state in turn introduced that evidence against her in a delinquency proceeding.[13] Justice Stevens's dissent focused upon the harms that would flow from applying the diluted reasonable suspicion requirement to violations of not just the law but even school rules and regulations. By the logic of the Court's opinion, Stevens noted, "a search for curlers and sunglasses in order to enforce the school dress code is apparently just as important as a search for evidence of heroin addiction or violent gang activity."[14] Upholding Choplick's search for the "trivial . . . no-smoking rule violated by T.L.O.," Stevens warned, yielded a decision articulating a legal principle "so open-ended that it may make the Fourth Amendment virtually meaningless in the school context."[15]

Despite their varied focal points, both dissents highlighted the heavy toll that *T.L.O.* would exact on students' burgeoning notions of citizenship. Justice Stevens's dissent in *T.L.O.* featured the single most stirring opinion linking the form that students' constitutional rights assume in school to the nation's overall conception of citizenship since Justice Robert Jackson's magisterial opinion in *West Virginia State Board of Education v. Barnette* more than four decades earlier. "Schools are places where we inculcate the values essential to the meaningful exercise of rights and responsibilities by a self-governing citizenry," Justice Stevens explained. "If the Nation's students can be convicted through the use of arbitrary methods destructive of personal liberty, they cannot help but feel that they have been dealt with unfairly."[16] Justice Stevens continued,

> The schoolroom is the first opportunity most citizens have to experience the power of government. Through it passes every citizen and public official, from schoolteachers to policemen and prison guards. The values they learn there, they take with them in life. One of our most cherished ideals is the one contained in the Fourth Amendment: that the government may not intrude on the personal privacy of its citizens without a warrant or compelling circumstance. The Court's decision today is a curious moral for the Nation's youth.[17]

Similarly, Justice Brennan's dissent contended that having educators honor the Fourth Amendment was vital because students "learn as much by example as exposition" and that "[i]t would be incongruous and futile to charge teachers with the task of [i]mbuing their students with an understanding of our system of constitutional democracy, while at the same time immunizing those same teachers from the need to respect constitutional protections."[18]

Predictably, education officials enthusiastically welcomed *T.L.O.* Piscataway High School's principal called the decision not only "fantastic" but "one of the greatest decisions in education in the last decade" because it would bring "an element of safety and stability back into public schools."[19] Albert Shanker, president of the American Federation of Teachers, likewise rejoiced that *T.L.O.* "sends a message to students that school buildings are . . . off [limits] to troublemakers."[20]

More surprisingly, though, the American Civil Liberties Union, which filed a brief in support of T.L.O., viewed the opinion more as a bullet dodged than an opportunity missed. After the decision, one ACLU official acknowledged having feared "a serious chance the court would say the Fourth Amendment didn't apply in schools at all."[21] Similarly, the ACLU's legal director, Burt Neuborne, pronounced himself "quite relieved" with the outcome: "The truth is you can't always play 'Chicken Little.' This ruling is not going to change very much. The point is that the special circumstances of the school setting require some tailoring of the Fourth Amendment to students."[22] Neuborne's colleague Carl Loewenson appeared to agree that any visions that the ACLU entertained of the Supreme Court imposing a probable cause standard on student searches were chimerical. "We had hoped the court would give students the same protection that all citizens have," Loewenson said, "but the Supreme Court seemed to be looking at how things operate in the real world. School administrators don't walk around with copies of the Constitution and the latest court decisions in their hip pockets. If they think a student was violating a rule, they'll search him."[23]

Newspaper editorial boards largely expressed cautious approval of *T.L.O.* The *Los Angeles Times* contended the decision conferred "a broad grant" to educators, but cautioned them to exercise "common-sense restraint" in conducting student searches because "[w]hether they retain that authority, or should retain it, will depend . . . on the prudence with which they use it."[24] Echoing this assessment, *The New York Times* allowed that "the [schools'] new authority is welcome" but also noted the "powerful tool [must] be used with care" and that "[t]he surest way to lose it will be to abuse it."[25] The *Chicago Tribune*, for its part, offered unequivocal praise for the decision: "[I]t would have been absurd to say that the Constitution must apply in the classroom precisely the way it does in a public park. . . . If Johnny can't make a federal case out of a teacher's looking in his locker for drugs, maybe Johnny will be more likely to read by the time he graduates."[26] Among the very few newspapers that criticized the decision, *The Boston Globe* stood out for its sharp tone—depicting *T.L.O.* as the product of an "increasingly conservative court" that revealed "a disturbing tendency . . . to exclude young people from the . . . guarantees of the Constitution."[27]

Such editorial rebukes were mild, however, compared with academia's withering attacks. Yale Kamisar, a prominent criminal law professor at the University of Michigan, derided *T.L.O.*'s reasonable suspicion standard as "extraordinarily spongy and unhelpful." In Kamisar's estimation, "The Court is telling school authorities 'We're sympathetic with your problems; take the ball and run with it,' and it's unclear how far they really can run." Extending Kamisar's critique, one legal expert on juvenile rights called *T.L.O.* "wrong and disappointing" because the reasonable suspicion standard effectively amounted to no standard at all: "What it really means is that school officials have a license to do as they wish."[28] Professor Austin Sarat asserted *T.L.O.* must "be regretted and deplored" for its "departure from the Court's own efforts to accord maximum protection for the rights of students and is yet another clear indicator of the Burger Court's understanding, or misunderstanding, of the Bill of Rights."[29] Professor Geoffrey Stone—endorsing the position of Justice Brennan, for whom he had served as a law clerk more than ten years earlier—expressly advocated that the Supreme Court should have applied the probable cause standard in *T.L.O.* because it failed to demonstrate that the school setting required diminished criminal procedure protections. "[T]here must be specific, concrete justification for concluding that the school environment makes it necessary to restrict constitutional rights," Stone contended. "It is not enough to proclaim that 'students have fewer rights.' And nothing in the special characteristics of the school setting justifies dilution of the traditional probable cause standards."[30]

One need not believe, however, that student searches should be held to the probable cause standard in order to deem the search of T.L.O.'s purse highly questionable under the Fourth Amendment. Even under the reasonable suspicion standard, a genuine application of that measure could well deem the search invalid. In order to grasp this position, reconsider in turn each part of *T.L.O.*'s two-step test for assessing student searches.

T.L.O.'s first step requires educators who are on the cusp of searching a student to reasonably suspect that the search will uncover—at a minimum—a violation of school rules. From the outset, however, the search that Choplick engaged in could not have succeeded in demonstrating that T.L.O. had been smoking in the restroom. Instead, the material that Choplick hoped to discover as he prepared to delve into her purse would demonstrate that T.L.O. possessed cigarettes, and thus undermine (though certainly not refute) her claim that she did not smoke at all. Given that Piscataway High School did not prohibit students from *possessing* cigarettes, it seems eminently reasonable to construe Choplick's search for cigarettes as a mere fishing expedition. This conclusion is strengthened given that nothing, evidently, turned on the outcome of Choplick's search. Suppose, in other words, that Choplick's search yielded no contraband. In that case, is it really credible that T.L.O. would have been permitted to escape sanction altogether? Letting T.L.O. off the hook because her purse contained no cigarettes would have allowed an accused student's denial to overcome a teacher's eyewitness report, and that result, in these particular circumstances, strains credulity. After all, it hardly seems extravagant to presume school administrators would generally conclude that, even if T.L.O.'s purse did not contain cigarettes, some other explanation for the teacher's account must obtain: perhaps she received a cigarette from her classmate, or perhaps the teacher apprehended T.L.O. smoking the final cigarette in a now-discarded package. Cigarettes or no cigarettes, it seems plain that Choplick would have punished T.L.O. one way or another.

T.L.O.'s second step requires considering whether a search's scope is excessively intrusive given the nature of the infraction. Rather than focusing on Choplick's entry into the zippered compartment within T.L.O.'s purse, the Court might have weighed more carefully whether the alleged initial infraction could justify the examination of T.L.O.'s purse at all. Smoking is, of course, a serious health matter, one that continues to claim the lives of too many citizens—a large percentage of whom become addicted to nicotine during adolescence. But there is little reason to believe that smoking *in a lavatory*—rather than, say, the student lounge or some other designated area—constitutes a grave violation of school rules. When one considers that this relatively mild infraction of school regulations permitted Choplick to invade T.L.O.'s purse—a place where many students place some of their most intimate items—it seems quite plausible to believe that the initial search for cigarettes exceeded the bounds of reasonableness. If, as the Court stated in *T.L.O.*, the reasonable suspicion standard is designed to guarantee "the interests of students will be invaded *no more than is necessary* to achieve the legitimate end of preserving order in the schools," it is difficult to understand Choplick's rummage as satisfying that burden.[31]

This muscular application of the reasonable suspicion test—in contrast to *T.L.O.*'s anemic application—is hardly a professor's flight of legal fancy. Indeed, this analysis strongly resembles that of the New Jersey Supreme Court, which found below that the search of T.L.O.'s purse failed its reasonableness test.[32] Presciently, this lower court decision eyed with wariness the prospect of school administrators transforming themselves into junior varsity police detectives.

In the three decades since *T.L.O.*, initial fears about the elasticity of the reasonable suspicion standard have proven all too warranted. Where Fourth Amendment cases arise in schools, lower courts have consistently demonstrated tremendous flexibility to support reasonable suspicion even in reviewing highly dubious student searches. Most Fourth Amendment cases that find judicial resolution involve underlying facts where educators succeeded in unearthing some legally prohibited item. Given this context, it should hardly be surprising that judges have evinced great reluctance to find that educators conducted a fruitful search without satisfying reasonable suspicion. It is important to realize, however, that simply because most judicial cases involve students with contraband in no way means that most student searches yield contraband. Student searches making their way to court account for a tiny fraction of the overall number of searches that occur in the nation's thousands of public schools every year.[33] Few students and their parents possess the patience, resources, and temperament required to file a lawsuit opposing school authorities when an errant student search produces no adverse consequences—apart, of course, from the intrusion of privacy. This set of circumstances encourages school authorities to search pupils at the slightest provocation and to worry about articulating a basis for reasonable suspicion only in the event that doing so becomes necessary down the line.[34]

In recent years, some lower courts have resisted the nearly search-at-will mentality that has flourished in *T.L.O.*'s wake by invalidating student searches that exceed any credible connection to an asserted violation of school rules. Thus, for example, the Massachusetts Supreme Judicial Court in 2001 found that a student's truancy did not provide school officials with reasonable suspicion to search his clothing for drugs.[35] Three years later, a California state court determined that a student who disrupted class by leaving to use the restroom over the teacher's objection (a request that should have been granted due to the student's certified medical condition) did not justify searching the student's purse, which turned out to contain a knife.[36] While it is encouraging that courts have imposed at least some limitations on educators' virtual carte blanche authority to search, it is simultaneously disheartening that those constraining opinions are necessary and that they are so scarce.

Such judicial inventions are laudable, but their significance ought not be overestimated. For school officials who are truly determined to search a student, these judicial constraints pose minor obstacles in reaching that goal. An enterprising educator, perhaps aided by a school board's attorney after a lawsuit has been filed, must identify only some reasonable basis for believing that a student possesses an item on a school's (often lengthy) list of contraband, which includes even marker pens in some jurisdictions.* If this modest chore proves too burdensome, at least one federal appellate court has upheld a search based primarily on a teacher contending that a usually reserved student behaved in an outgoing manner as she entered class one morning.† The court's acceptance

---

* At oral argument in *Safford Unified County School District v. Redding*, 557 U.S. 364 (2009), Justice Antonin Scalia confessed that he was "astounded" to the lawyer defending the school district that his client forbade the possession of markers. Oral Argument Transcript, *Redding*, No. 08-479, 14 (April 21, 2009). When counsel explained that the markers were forbidden in order to prevent students from inhaling their fumes, this response seemed to eliminate Justice Scalia's befuddlement.

† See *Hedges v. Musco*, 204 F.3d 109, 117–19 (3d Cir. 2000). The—ultimately fruitless—search at issue here required a high school student, Tara Hedges, to submit to uri-

of that slender reed as a basis for reasonable suspicion accurately captures how courts—barring unusual circumstances—have seldom invalidated student searches.

Did the Supreme Court realize at the time of *T.L.O.* that its lax application of the reasonable suspicion standard would provide educators with something approaching free rein to conduct searches, or instead have lower courts enfeebled a legal test that the Court initially anticipated would provide students meaningful protections? Considerable evidence suggests that even in 1985 the Supreme Court understood lower courts would interpret *T.L.O.* as establishing meager constitutional safeguards within schools and that it intended this outcome. As Justice White's opinion for the Court in *T.L.O.* indicated, the majority of lower courts that contemplated the Fourth Amendment's meaning in schools had employed some version of the reasonable suspicion test.[37] Several academic surveys of this emerging body of reasonable suspicion law condemned the results, as judges typically failed both to scrutinize the facts motivating the search and to regulate the search's scope. As Professor William Buss commented in a law review article criticizing reasonable suspicion, "A slightly cynical but reasoned conclusion based on the results of the decided cases might indicate that a school principal can make whatever student searches he or she wishes, at least if some attempt is made to use 'common sense.'"[38] Briefs filed in *T.L.O.* brought Buss's evaluation—and other scholarship offering similarly dim appraisals of reasonable suspicion—to the Supreme Court's attention.[39]

Even if the justices were unaware of this academic research, however, additional evidence nonetheless suggests that the Court affirmatively wanted *T.L.O.* to establish a toothless framework for

---

nalysis and a blood test on suspicion of drug or alcohol use. Among the factors that provided Hedges's teacher with reasonable suspicion in this case, the U.S. Court of Appeals for the Third Circuit led with the following factor: "As [Hedges] entered the classroom, [the teacher] observed that she seemed uncharacteristically talkative and outgoing." Ibid., 112. In addition to her outgoing behavior, the teacher contended that some aspects of Hedges's physical appearance suggested intoxication (that is, a flushed face and glassy, irritated eyes). But the teacher also acknowledged that other physical factors cut in Hedges's favor (that is, she did not exhibit slurred speech, nor did she smell of alcohol or drugs). As emerged after her tests proved negative, Hedges's appearance was evidently owed to suffering from seasonal allergies. See Appellants' Brief, *Hedges v. Musco*, 204 F.3d 109 (3d Cir. 2000), 1999 WL 33613738, at 9. Intriguingly, then-Judge Alito joined the Third Circuit's panel opinion in *Hedges*.

evaluating school searches. As addressed earlier, one of the primary reasons that Justice White's opinion in *T.L.O.* applied reasonable suspicion, not probable cause, stemmed from a desire to spare educators the headache of internalizing the intricacies of Fourth Amendment law. At first glance, this explanation seems perfectly sound; teachers are not police officers, after all, and do not possess their knowledge. Upon closer inspection, however, this justification reveals that *T.L.O.*'s reasonable suspicion standard is more persuasively understood as being designed to dissolve students' Fourth Amendment protections than to demarcate an area providing slightly diminished protections. If *T.L.O.*'s reasonable suspicion standard were meant to represent a meaningful category of Fourth Amendment protections in schools, educators would eventually be forced to familiarize themselves with the myriad situations and cases that fall on either side of the line. In other words, enunciation of the reasonable suspicion standard should have eventually presented educators with a reconfigured set of administrative headaches, not eliminated them altogether. That Justice White did not view *T.L.O.*'s test as creating a significant set of borderline cases that may trouble school administrators indicates the Court conceived of the opinion as providing students with vanishingly thin constitutional protection. *T.L.O.*, viewed through this lens, can thus be understood as effectively instructing lower courts to uphold student searches in all but the most egregious circumstances, and lower court judges have, of course, overwhelmingly obliged.[40]

In *T.L.O.*, the Supreme Court envisioned a bifurcated world where schools, on the one hand, and police officers, on the other, occupied two distinct spheres. Yet it was clear even from the facts of *T.L.O.* itself that those worlds were already beginning to converge. After all, Choplick did not merely use the marijuana evidence for school disciplinary purposes; instead, he proceeded to turn the evidence over to the police for the purpose of having the student declared a juvenile delinquent. Yet even if the Court were committed to the reasonable suspicion standard for purposes of maintaining order in schools, it nevertheless could have required any evidence of wrongdoing that would be introduced for prosecutorial purposes to pass the higher probable cause threshold. This guiding framework would acknowledge that school disciplinary matters, while significant, are quite distinct from—and, indeed, typically pale in severity to—matters adjudicated by courts. Under this theory, as in *T.L.O.*, school officials would still not be required to learn precisely what satisfies probable cause, and they would continue to enjoy considerable latitude to conduct searches and impose school discipline as they deemed fit. Following the school's disciplinary actions, however, law enforcement officials would then need to assess independently whether the relevant search satisfied probable cause, if they wanted to pursue sanctions through the legal system. Judges would then also provide an additional check on law enforcement's probable cause determination. This context-sensitive inquiry that turns on the government's purpose—either school discipline or judicial sanction—would determine whether the fruits of a particular student search violated the Fourth Amendment in that specific setting.[41]

This contextualized model enjoys some support in judicial opinions. Before *T.L.O.*, several lower courts issued decisions upholding school searches based on mere reasonable suspicion in part because the state did not seek punishment beyond school discipline, and further held open the possibility that evidence for criminal purposes may require probable cause.[42] After *T.L.O.*, as will be detailed below, the Supreme Court twice upheld suspicion-less drug-testing policies for students in part because failed tests were used for internal school purposes only and were not provided to law enforcement officials.[43] Outside the student rights context, moreover, the Court has also recognized that the governmental purpose of a search can properly inform whether a search complies with the Fourth Amendment. In 2001, the Court found that a state hospital that conducted urinalysis testing on pregnant women to detect cocaine usage violated the Fourth Amendment because the plan was designed with a law enforcement purpose. The "special needs" of employees in a government-run hospital, the Court reasoned, did not extend to efforts intended to uncover patients' illegal actions.[44] By importing these insights into the *T.L.O.* context, then, the judiciary could upend the current model that imposes precisely the same reasonable suspicion standard in all contexts—irrespective of whether evidence is used by educators or by judges. A reexamination of this one-size-fits-all approach to student searches is long overdue.

T.L.O.'S STANDARD: BETTER THAN PLAUSIBLE ALTERNATIVES?

Given the broad criticisms of *T.L.O.* within legal academia—which have grown only more intense with the passage of time—it may seem as though only a crackpot or an ideologue would dare rise to defend the opinion. Not quite. Professor William Stuntz—widely saluted as the foremost criminal procedure scholar of his generation—mounted a sophisticated defense of *T.L.O.* in the *Stanford Law Review* in 1992.[45] In their rush to assail *T.L.O.*, Stuntz maintained, academic detractors failed to consider how school administrators would have responded had the Supreme Court ruled that the search of T.L.O.'s purse violated the Fourth Amendment. "[T]he relevant comparison is not between a search and nothing," Stuntz wrote, "but between a search and whatever else the principal would (legally) do instead, if the search were unavailable. From the student's point of view, the search may be the better option."[46] Overlooking the essential compared-with-what question, Stuntz can be understood as arguing, permitted *T.L.O.*'s critics to fixate on reasonable suspicion's vices without comprehending its considerable virtues.

Had the Court denied educators the ability to search students based on reasonable suspicion, Stuntz reasoned, school administrators could have plausibly adapted to that rule in two different ways. First, administrators might respond by adopting a more expansive approach to suspensions, issuing them when they had mere inklings, but nothing approaching proof, that students had committed infractions. Second, administrators might respond by tightening school regulations that made it more difficult to commit infractions in the first instance. Confronted with those two unattractive alternatives, Stuntz argued, most students—if given an option—would prefer the low barrier to searches that the Supreme Court actually implemented. In effect, *T.L.O.* blessed what Stuntz termed an "implicit bargain" that students and schools had struck, whereby students agreed to permit educators to search their belongings without probable cause in exchange for being free from hair-trigger suspensions and highly restrictive campus regulations. As Stuntz distilled his argument, offering a slightly stylized account of *T.L.O.*, "The risk of having one's purse opened may be worth bearing, if the alternative is a risk of unjustified suspension or substantial restrictions on movement around school grounds."[47]

Stuntz's argument is elegant, illuminating, and wrong. The argument merits commendation because, in a hallmark of Stuntz's scholarship, it identified important considerations that had somehow managed to escape analysis. Despite helpfully spotlighting relevant concerns that had been enshrouded in darkness, Stuntz's claim founders because it misapprehends the actual dynamics that govern public schools in the modern era. School administrators, contrary to Stuntz's highly theoretical world, do not enjoy broad searching authority *instead of* issuing suspensions in uncertain situations; rather, administrators search broadly *in addition to* suspending students widely. Negligible evidence indicates that educators regard suspensions as a scarce resource. Even in the 1990s, it had become apparent that schools employed their robust searching authority as a complement to, not as a substitute for, abundant imposition of student suspensions.[48]

Similarly, in an issue that is felt most acutely in the nation's inner-city schools, students often do not enjoy broad freedom to roam about school grounds as they deem fit, but instead have their daily movements extensively regulated. Consider one account offered by a teacher in an inner-city school that prohibited students from accessing restrooms during breaks between periods, and instead had teachers usher them en masse during class time. "Before classes began," this teacher further recalled, "students were not permitted to walk around in the school, go to the library, sit outside, or even sit at their desks. Rather, students were required to sit on the floor in the hallways or the gymnasium until the first bell rang when they would march to their first class."[49] While surely an extreme example, intensively regulated schools are hardly a new phenomenon.[50] Students attending these schools are—again, contra Stuntz—subjected to institutions that are both highly searched and highly regulated. Given that much of Professor Stuntz's scholarship demonstrates an admirable sensitivity to how criminal law disproportionately imposes burdens on marginalized groups, it is somewhat surprising that he disregarded how sharply varying conditions in actual schools might complicate his abstraction.[51]

A final reason that Stuntz's pro-*T.L.O.* position misaligns with modern reality stems from its incorrect conception of student searches as always being conducted by educators acting without involvement from police officers. *T.L.O.*'s permissive approach to student searches should not be especially feared, Stuntz claimed, because "one kind of harm suffered in police search cases is by definition absent: the trauma or indignity that comes from being singled out as a suspect by a uniformed police officer." Stuntz continued, "Principals can no doubt be intimidating, but the intimidation is surely less than when the police search and seize suspects."[52] In the modern era, however, police officers have become ubiquitous presences in schools throughout the nation, and evidence suggests that they frequently play a significant role in student searches. Accordingly, this justification for supporting *T.L.O.*'s rule again collides with contemporary conditions. It seems quite plausible, moreover, that police officers selecting a student to be searched at school—in front of one's classmates—may serve, if anything, to heighten the feelings of trauma and indignity that Stuntz identified as ordinarily accompanying unwanted police inspections. Admittedly, Stuntz's law review article appeared as the presence of police officers in schools began to skyrocket. Still, criticizing Stuntz on this point does not amount to blaming him for possessing a faulty crystal ball, as police officers regularly began playing roles in student searches well before the publication of his article. Indeed, *T.L.O.* expressly identified, but avoided resolving, what legal standard—reasonable suspicion or probable cause—should govern when police officers are involved in student searches, and cited a federal district court case from 1976 treating the issue.[53] The Supreme Court has still not resolved this pressing question. Its diffidence on this matter has become increasingly momentous with the ascent of a law enforcement figure called the school resource officer.

THE RISE AND RISE OF SCHOOL RESOURCE OFFICERS

The presence and significance of police officers in the nation's public schools have changed dramatically during the last several decades. Through the end of the 1950s, officers were seldom seen in school corridors. On the few occasions when police officers did appear, moreover, educators did not invariably welcome their expertise. As late as 1971, a prominent educational authority could write the following: "In the high school the police officer's role is similar to that of an American military advisor overseas. His presence may be unwelcome, his advice only grudgingly heard. When needed to respond to a serious fight, for example, he may insist on

resolving it in ways that are contrary to the principal's wishes."[54]
This strained educator-officer relationship arose from dueling professional impulses: where the educator might have inclined toward
lenience when dealing with wayward pupils, the police officer preferred overt intervention when responding to reported criminal
conduct.

These days, however, the educator's reflexive unease toward
a police officer's appearance in school has long since dissipated.
Police uniforms in school, once a rare sight, have now grown routine. By 2007, police had become a daily presence in more than
50 percent of public high schools across the nation, according to
the Department of Education. The nineteen thousand uniformed
police officers that are today assigned to patrol public schools on a
full-time basis are typically called "school resource officers," so designated in order to communicate the notion that their portfolios are
not confined to law enforcement matters, but include roles ranging from coach to counselor, from friend to role model. By allowing students to gain exposure to police officers in informal school
settings, the hope ran, students would be less likely to view police
officers antagonistically outside schools—a sort of Officer Friendly
program on a much grander scale. Although school resource officers began appearing many years ago, the dramatic expansion of
police in schools dates back to the Safe Schools Act of 1994, which
permitted schools to obtain federal funding for hiring officers. Not
surprisingly, this increased police presence has materially altered the
educator-officer relationship. If educators and officers found themselves at loggerheads in the 1970s, they now work together hand in
glove, as the educator's traditional inclination toward lenience has
yielded to the police officer's preference for enforcement.[55]

The rise of the school resource officer since the 1990s has witnessed a corresponding rise in the occurrence of student arrests. As
with suspensions, black students account for a disproportionately
large percentage of these arrests. The marked increase of arrested
students cannot be attributed, moreover, to a surge in serious criminal activity that has engulfed schools in recent years. No such surge
has occurred. Instead, the higher number of student arrests stems
overwhelmingly from trivial offenses—matters so minor that in a
prior era the infractions would have warranted no penalty more
severe than after-school detention. In one of the more egregious
instances of a minor infraction generating major punishment, a

school resource officer in Paris, Texas, arrested a fourteen-year-old student named Shaquanda Cotton in 2005 for shoving one of her high school's hall monitors. Although the monitor suffered no physical injuries, Cotton was nevertheless convicted of "felony assault on a public servant" and sentenced to prison for a term not to exceed seven years.[56]

The most notorious incident involving a school resource officer in the nation's history also witnessed a student arrest for misbehavior that would once have been deemed relatively mild and in no way a matter for police involvement. In October 2015, Ben Fields—a school resource officer assigned to Spring Valley High School in Columbia, South Carolina—confronted a black student as she sat at her desk, flipped her backward from the chair, and then heaved her body along the floor. Video footage of that incident, captured by students' cell phones, went viral on social media and received intense coverage from national media outlets. Viewers widely castigated Officer Fields's violent treatment of the student, and many observers—galvanized by the Black Lives Matter movement—also questioned whether a white student who disobeyed the teacher's instruction to exit the classroom for using her cell phone (the supposedly inciting event) would have been similarly handled. Shortly after the incident, Richland County's sheriff, Leon Lott, dismissed Officer Fields for breaching proper arrest technique, and the nation's attention quickly subsided.[57]

Generally lost amid the opprobrium directed toward Officer Fields's conduct was the South Carolina law that the arrested student was charged with violating: "disturbing schools." This statute renders it a criminal offense—punishable by a maximum of either one thousand dollars, or ninety days in jail—"to interfere with or to disturb in any way or in any place the students or teachers of any school . . . , to loiter about such school . . . premises or . . . to act in an obnoxious manner thereon."[58] Although this law lacks a striking visual image capable of demanding national attention like Fields's ferocious arrest, its existence may actually be more worthy of indignation because it has undoubtedly tarnished the lives of many more South Carolinians. In at least one recent year, the "disturbing schools" charge was the single most frequent justification for juvenile delinquency proceedings in the entire state of South Carolina. Conduct satisfying a "disturbing schools" charge may be sufficiently inconsequential that it would fail to satisfy any other offense on the books, as appears to have been the case at Spring Valley. Apart from the families of students who are charged with violating this statute, frustration with this law may be most severe among those who enforce it. "Unfortunately, our legislature passed a law that's called 'disturbing schools,'" Sheriff Lott commented after dismissing Fields. "If a student disturbs school—and that's a wide range of activities, 'disturbing schools'—they can be arrested."[59] (Underscoring Lott's concern about the breadth of conduct that the measure prohibits, contemplate for a moment how many teenagers could legitimately plead not guilty to a charge of behaving "obnoxious[ly]" in school.) While Sheriff Lott further suggested that Spring Valley educators should probably have handled the misbehaving student on their own without requesting a police officer, he also emphasized that educators need "to understand when they call us, we're going to take a law enforcement action."[60] Apart from South Carolina, at least fourteen states have enacted their own versions of statutes outlawing school disturbances.[61]*

In a positive development, some judicial and policy responses have begun to rein in the more flagrant abuses of school disturbance laws. On the judicial front, in a juvenile delinquency case involving a sixth-grade boy who had launched spitballs and sought to enter the girls' restroom, a state court invalidated Ohio's school disturbance statute because it failed to articulate the conduct it prohibited with sufficient specificity. "[T]here is no guidance as to

---

* In 2016, a school resource officer in Albuquerque, New Mexico, arrested a seventh-grade student under the state's disturbing school statute for repeatedly belching in physical education class. Although referring the student to the principal's office and (if necessary) informing his parents should have more than sufficed, the officer instead took a more aggressive approach: patting the middle-schooler down, handcuffing him, and transporting him in a police cruiser to a juvenile detention facility. Alarmingly, the U.S. Court of Appeals for the Tenth Circuit, in a 2–1 decision, found that the arrest did not violate clearly established law. See A.M. v. Holmes, 830 F.3d 1123 (10th Cir. 2016). Judge Neil Gorsuch, less than one year before his elevation to the Supreme Court, wrote a compelling, persuasive dissent that would have found the officer's actions impermissible. Gorsuch's dissent concluded,

> Often enough the law can be "a ass—a idiot," Charles Dickens, Oliver Twist 520 (1838)—and there is little we judges can do about it. . . . Indeed, a judge who likes every result he reaches is very likely a bad judge, reaching for results he prefers rather than those the law compels. So it is I admire my colleagues today, for no doubt they reach a result they dislike but believe the law demands. . . . It's only that, in this particular case, I don't believe the law happens to be quite as much of a ass as they do.

Ibid., 1170 (10th Cir. 2016) (Gorsuch, J., dissenting).

what constitutes a disruption, disturbance, or interference of school activity," the court reasoned. "As a result of this vague language, a charge may be filed for something as minor as throwing a spitball to something as serious as assaulting an employee of the school."[62] South Carolina's school disturbance statute—and perhaps many others besides—appears vulnerable to a challenge under this void-for-vagueness rationale.[63]

On the policy front, moreover, some districts have success-fully implemented alternatives to arresting students for minor infractions, at least as a measure of first resort. In Clayton County, Georgia, for instance, officials noticed in 2003 that student refer-rals to local police for misdemeanors—including for school distur-bance violations—had risen steeply since the introduction of school resource officers to its campuses. In 1996, the last year without police stationed in Clayton's schools, 46 students had been referred to police for misdemeanor infractions; in 2003, only seven years later, the number of such referrals had swelled to 1,147, a more than twenty-fold increase. That year, however, Clayton altered its rules so that students would receive two warnings before officially being referred for a misdemeanor charge. Ten years after the rule change, the number of such referrals had dramatically decreased to only 154.[64] Impressive as this reduction is, however, it must be observed that Clayton's number of post-reform referrals remained consid-erably higher than its figures before the introduction of school resource officers.

The Supreme Court ought to resolve definitively whether school resource officers who execute student searches are governed by the relaxed reasonable suspicion standard or the more demanding probable cause standard. In *T.L.O.*, the Court expressly noted that Choplick searched the student's purse acting on his own authority as a school administrator, and observed further that the reasonable suspicion standard might not govern when student searches occur "in conjunction with or at the behest of law enforcement agen-cies."[65] Somewhat surprisingly, though, when school resource offi-cers conduct student searches, lower courts have typically applied reasonable suspicion, not probable cause.[66] Judges who have taken this approach contend that resource officers act primarily in fur-therance of the school's mission of maintaining order during their workdays.

This feeble justification, however, fails to persuade. It blinks away the fundamental reality that, in the midst of being searched by police, students see not Officer Friendly but Officer Krupke. The search could result in juvenile delinquency charges or even being charged as an adult, and no sound basis justifies permitting police officers' ancillary responsibilities to overshadow their core law enforcement function. In addition, one primary basis for not applying probable cause to student searches in *T.L.O.* was to avoid burdening school administrators with legal minutiae. No substantial added burden exists, of course, for resource officers, whose training entails internalizing probable cause. Indeed, the presence of police officers in many schools complicates a key justification for conferring the reasonable suspicion standard on educators; in borderline cases that do not demand quick determinations, after all, educators might avail themselves of the police officer's expertise before determining whether to execute a search. But even if the existence of school resource officers is not understood to extinguish the reduced Fourth Amendment threshold for educators, it is exceedingly difficult to believe that sworn police officers should be authorized to employ it. Such a practice seems quite likely to give students who are searched by police officers on the basis of slim evidence a diminished, jaded attitude toward law enforcement officials—presuming, of course, that they did not already hold that view. That result would thereby affirmatively harm one overriding goal of stationing officers in schools in the first instance: improving student perceptions of the police.[67]

In recent times, legal scholars and lawyers who focus on educational reform have observed the role that school resource officers have played in forming "the school-to-prison pipeline." That haunting metaphor has gained some traction in our national discourse. Its effectiveness as a tool for achieving meaningful victories, however, risks being limited through overuse, as commentators now often invoke this metaphor to decry a vast array of social ills that, for many, the term will not readily conjure. To take only one of many available examples, the first page of a book from 2010, titled simply *The School-to-Prison Pipeline*, identified the following issues as helping to form that much-reviled structure: "[o]vercrowded classrooms," "racially and socioeconomically isolated environments," "a lack of effective teachers and school leaders," and "insufficient funding for 'extras' such as counselors."[68] A few pages later, the book even ascribed the pipeline's formation partly to "inadequate exposure to the arts."[69] People otherwise inclined to agree that our systems of education and law enforcement are excessively intertwined may be alienated from joining efforts to combat "the school-to-prison pipeline," if that term is understood to summon this dog's breakfast of issues—some major, others relatively minor—bearing at most a roundabout connection to the pipeline's core considerations. Accordingly, the "school-to-prison pipeline" terminology should be invoked less promiscuously, reserved for instances where the students' conduct in school leads directly to their involvement with courts. While education reformers should continue to address these other concerns, the school-to-prison pipeline, properly conceived, presents simply too pressing a matter to risk stalling the political and judicial energy necessary to alleviate this issue.

SUSPICIONLESS SEARCHES: DRUG TESTING FOR EXTRACURRICULAR ACTIVITIES

In 1999, a high school official in the tiny town of Tecumseh, Oklahoma—located forty miles away from Oklahoma City—interrupted Lindsay Earls's first class of the day and instructed her to report to the gymnasium's restroom for a drug test. Earls hardly matched the classic profile of a student drug user, as she not only received outstanding marks that allowed her to join the National Honor Society but also participated in a bevy of extracurricular activities, including Academic Team, Marching Band, and Show Choir. Earlier that school year, however, Tecumseh High School introduced a new policy requiring any student who joined an extracurricular club to submit to urinalysis drug testing, even without any basis for suspicion. Earls desperately wished to avoid partaking in this testing process, not because she used drugs, but because she found the prospect of producing a sample—with her teachers outside the stall listening for sounds of normal urination—to be disconcerting. Despite her apprehension, Earls felt that she had no choice other than to submit because refusal would mean ending her extracurricular commitments, severely damaging her hopes of gaining admission to an Ivy League college. The actual drug-testing experience might have been even worse than Earls anticipated, as she termed the event "horrible" and "really tense." Earls heard one of the monitoring teachers remark that the scene of numerous students, all producing their samples simultaneously, reminded her of a "potty training" exercise. After Earls produced her sample, moreover, she recalled that the teacher handled the vial to ensure it was an appropriate temperature, and then proceeded to hold the vessel up toward the light to examine her urine's color and clarity. Although Earls's drug test ultimately revealed no evidence of drug usage, she nevertheless filed a lawsuit contending that the school district's policy violated her Fourth Amendment right to be free from unreasonable searches.[70]

As the case wound its way through the lower courts, both supporters and opponents of Tecumseh's policy could locate powerful reasons to believe that the Supreme Court's closest precedent on point bolstered their preferred outcomes. Supporters could note that, in a 6–3 decision of quite recent vintage, the Court in *Vernonia School District v. Acton* validated a rule requiring student-athletes to submit to suspicionless drug testing in a program that was administered in a comparable fashion to Tecumseh's program. Admittedly, the Fourth Amendment traditionally disfavors suspicionless searches because of their non-targeted, dragnet quality, which broadly impinge on citizens' privacy without the expectation of uncovering wrongdoing in any particular circumstance. Such objections, however, were simply noted and rejected in *Acton*. In that case, moreover, Justice Antonin Scalia's opinion for the Court minimized the intrusiveness of urinalysis testing by asserting that students provided samples in conditions that did not deviate significantly from standard public restroom conditions. To the extent that sample collections differed at all, moreover, Tecumseh's policy demonstrated slightly more respect for student privacy because it—unlike the one at issue in *Acton*—afforded male students the option of producing a sample within a closed stall rather than at a urinal. After upholding *Acton*'s policy, why would the Court suddenly upend Tecumseh's policy—particularly given that its composition had not changed since the prior decision?

In response, however, opponents could note that the Court's justifications for upholding the drug-testing policy in *Acton* failed to support Tecumseh's policy. Justice Scalia's opinion in *Acton* provided three primary, related reasons for upholding suspicionless drug testing. First, the school system in *Acton* had recently experienced a major drug problem that adversely affected student discipline. Second, the program encompassed only participants in interscholastic athletics, activities where drug usage could cause students to suffer serious injury from delayed reaction times and insensitivity to pain. Third, student-athletes—in addition to being leaders of the local drug culture—possessed diminished expectations of privacy as a result of changing into their uniforms in locker room settings. "School sports are not for the bashful," Scalia quipped.[71]* Underscoring that *Acton* should not be taken to bless all urinalysis policies, he explained, "We caution against the assumption that suspicionless drug testing will readily pass muster in other contexts."[72] And it would be awfully difficult to envision a school context more "other" from *Acton* than the circumstances in Tecumseh. Earls's school system did not even purport to have a major issue with drugs. The policy, moreover, applied not only to athletes but to anyone who participated in any extracurricular activity whatsoever, including clubs that had neither a diminished expectation of privacy nor a heightened risk of injury. It hardly required extensive training in constitutional law to realize that the situations in *Acton* and Tecumseh contained glaring, seemingly irreconcilable differences. As Lindsay Earls herself observed on one of these points, "I know [*Acton*] talked about how athletes have a risk of physical harm. But we're not going to hurt ourselves in choir."[73]

At an astonishing oral argument session, however, hopes that the Supreme Court would view Tecumseh's program as constitutionally distinct from *Acton* suffered a major setback. Various reporters characterized the questions hurled at Lindsay Earls's lawyer as "fierce," "unusually antagonistic," "downright nasty," and even as containing "a stinging verbal attack . . . on a teenage girl."[74] Justice Scalia, the author of *Acton*, seemed to make his sympathies clear by expressing incredulity that Tecumseh's absence of school discipline issues should necessarily foreclose it from suspicionless drug test-

---

* Legal scholars immediately challenged Justice Scalia's emphasis on the fact that student-athletes change into uniforms as a basis for legitimating the testing. After all, athletes are not the only students who change into a uniform in front of their classmates. As Professor David Gottlieb contended, "Mandatory participation in physical education programs and the use of locker rooms is a part of the life of virtually all high school students." David J. Gottlieb, "Drug Testing, Collective Suspicion, and a Fourth Amendment out of Balance," 6 *Kansas Journal of Law and Public Policy* 28, 32–33 (1997). Law professors continue to ridicule the potentially far-reaching implications that would flow from taking this thread in *Acton* seriously. See Stephen J. Schulhofer, *More Essential than Ever: The Fourth Amendment in the Twenty-First Century* 110 (2012) ("It could hardly be said that adults who shower in the locker room of their sports club have waived their Fourth Amendment protection from government-mandated urinalysis tests").

ing. "So long as you have a bunch of druggies who are orderly in class, the school can take no action," Scalia remarked. "That's what you want us to rule?"[75] Justice Anthony Kennedy upped the ante by personalizing the matter, suggesting that Earls's lawsuit revealed that she would rather attend a school teeming with "druggies" than provide a urine sample. Kennedy—whose demeanor during oral argument typically ranges somewhere between composed and solemn—appeared flushed with emotion as he asserted to Earls's attorney, "No parent would send their child to a 'druggie' school, except perhaps your client."[76]

This disparagement aimed at the Earlses in Washington, D.C., bore some faint resemblance to the vitriol directed toward the family back home in Tecumseh, Oklahoma, where the lawsuit's filing prompted several undesirable events. Rumors circulated among the town's six thousand residents holding that Earls used drugs. Criticisms of her family's values ran on local airwaves and in local publications. Some critics even asserted that Earls was insufficiently committed to her Christian faith, an acrimonious charge in the overwhelmingly Protestant town.[77]

In a 5–4 decision, Justice Clarence Thomas wrote an opinion for the Court in *Board of Education v. Earls* in 2002, rejecting the claim that Tecumseh High School's policy violated the Fourth Amendment. Brushing aside the objection that Tecumseh's absence of a serious drug problem should doom the program, Justice Thomas in effect reframed the inquiry from the local level to the national level. "The drug abuse problem among our Nation's youth has hardly abated since [*Acton*] was decided in 1995," Thomas instructed. "In fact, evidence suggests that it has only grown worse. . . . The health and safety risks identified in [*Acton*] apply with equal force to Tecumseh's children. Indeed, the nationwide drug epidemic makes the war against drugs a pressing concern in every school."[78] It made no sense, Thomas contended, to require a particular school district to suffer from the scourge of drugs before empowering it to address the problem. For Justice Thomas, invalidating the policy in *Earls* would represent needless interference with the decisionmaking authority of local school boards. In addition, Thomas rejected the notion that *Acton* was in any way predicated upon the program involving athletes exclusively. But he nevertheless further noted that many extracurricular activities demanded off-campus travel and that they all involved regulations inapplicable to the general student body—factors that led him to conclude that students in Earls's position are entitled to only diminished expectations of privacy. Apparently subscribing to the theory that the best defense is a good offense, Justice Thomas depicted the drug policy's suspicionless basis as a virtue rather than a vice. If the policy required individualized suspicion, Thomas noted, the brunt of the policy's burden might fall on members of unpopular groups. Finally, Justice Thomas emphasized that, as in *Acton*, the results of positive drug tests in *Earls* were not turned over to law enforcement authorities. Rather, the only consequence of testing positive involved revocation of extracurricular activities.[79]

Justice Ruth Bader Ginsburg, who voted in *Acton* to uphold the drug policy, wrote the lead dissenting opinion in *Earls*. One important feature that distinguished the two cases for Ginsburg was that Tecumseh's policy governed not only athletics but extracurricular activities as a whole. Mocking the idea that these activities involved much in the way of danger, Ginsburg floated "nightmarish images" of "colliding tubas" amid the marching band, "livestock run amok" in the Future Farmers of America, and "out-of-control flatware" from the Future Homemakers of America.[80] On a more serious note, she criticized the Court's position by combining Justice Jackson's idea from *Barnette* that schools have a special responsibility to honor constitutional protections with Justice Louis Brandeis's view—expressed in a celebrated dissent from 1928—that the government acts as a teacher through its own treatment of citizens. "The government is nowhere more a teacher than when it runs a public school," Ginsburg reasoned. "[S]chools' tutelary obligations to their students require them to 'teach by example' by avoiding symbolic measures that diminish constitutional protections."[81]

Word of the decision bearing her name reached Lindsay Earls shortly after she completed her first year at Dartmouth College in Hanover, New Hampshire. According to *The Dartmouth*, the Ivy League's oldest newspaper, Earls declared it "a sad day for students' rights."[82] Earls's father added that the opinion marked a grim day for parents' rights. Endorsing a line of reasoning that the Supreme Court had embraced more than seven decades earlier in *Pierce v. Society of Sisters*, David Earls commented, "I am angry for parents and kids subjected to [drug testing]. As a parent, I had something taken away from me that I felt was a God-given right. I should be making the decision for my kids, not them."[83]

If at least some families received *Earls* with disillusionment, school officials in locations throughout the country welcomed the decision for providing some much-desired clarity post-*Acton*. As one California school superintendent explained, "Everyone's been confused these recent years, because no one's sure which part of the court's ruling [in *Acton*] was the important one. Was it that they were athletes, or that they were leaders of a drug culture? I got a 10-page opinion from our lawyer about the situation."[84]

Earls generated a wide range of responses in newspapers. Among *Earls*'s critics, the *Los Angeles Times* published a particularly acerbic assessment, suggesting that the Court's validation of the contested policy succeeded in creating a perverse incentive structure for students to abandon their extracurricular activities to "[f]ocus all [their] attention on drugs." As the piece noted, "[E]very child experimenting with drugs will now choose between making drugs their exclusive interest and going drug-free with the chess club."[85] Among *Earls*'s admirers, *The Washington Post* picked up on this same point but arrived at the conclusion that Tecumseh's policy did not go far enough in testing students. "Just as it makes no sense to distinguish between athletes and cheerleaders," the *Post* commented, "the logic of the court's opinion . . . raises the question of why a school should focus only on those engaged in extracurricular programs." Deciding to administer drug tests to all students, no students, or somewhere in between was, in the *Post*'s view, "best left to local officials, not the Supreme Court."[86]

From overseas, a columnist for the London *Observer* attributed *Earls* to "self-styled religious fundamentalist 'drug warriors' in the United States," and called the opinion "a startling example of the ideological shift in American politics since George W. Bush moved in the White House" eighteen months earlier.[87] Supporting this view, the Bush administration filed an amicus brief backing Tecumseh's policy, and in *Earls*'s wake the White House Office of National Drug Control Policy distributed a guide promoting drug testing in schools. "Testing has been shown to be extremely effective at reducing drug use in schools and businesses," the guide stated. "As a deterrent, few methods work better or deliver cleaner results."[88] President Bush himself, moreover, successfully advocated a sharp increase in the amount of federal funds available for schools to implement drug-testing policies, highlighting the issue in his 2004 State of the Union address: "The aim here is not to punish children, but to send them this message: We love you, and we do not want to lose you."[89]

Yet support for drug-testing measures in schools did not map quite so tidily onto the left–right political spectrum as the *Observer* columnist supposed. After all, when the Court decided *Acton* in 1995, President Bill Clinton welcomed the opinion as sending "exactly the right message to parents and students: Drug use will not be tolerated in our schools."[90] Clinton's antidrug czar similarly trumpeted *Acton* as "a major victory for kids."[91] Furthermore, whereas left-leaning politicians cheered *Acton*, at least some right-leaning figures disdained it. As the conservative newspaper columnist James J. Kilpatrick contended, "[*Acton*'s] policy teaches the wrong lesson. In the continuing conflict between the rights of an individual and the power of the state, a better lesson would teach the children that the power of the state is not unlimited. It stops where our constitutional liberties begin."[92]*

As Kilpatrick's comment suggests, suspicionless drug testing of students contains considerably larger drawbacks than the Court acknowledged in either *Acton* or *Earls*. Being required to produce a urine sample not for health reasons but for the purpose of detecting misconduct involves a serious intrusion into a domain that almost invariably remains private. Professor Charles Fried made this point in *The Yale Law Journal* back in 1968: "[I]n our culture the excretory functions are shielded by more or less absolute privacy."[93] That it is school officials who are responsible for monitoring, collecting, and inspecting students' bodily fluids makes the intrusion all the more severe. Indeed, the very act of handing over a vial of one's own urine to another human being renders it anything but the ordinary trip to the restroom that both *Acton* and *Earls* conjured. While the Court had previously validated suspicionless drug testing as applied to government railroad employees who were involved in train acci-

---

* With his opposition to drug testing, the conservative Kilpatrick found an improbable common cause with the self-described hippie Wayne Acton, father of the student who challenged the drug-testing policy for athletes. See Jan Crawford Greenburg, "Court to Weigh School Drug Tests," *Chicago Tribune*, March 27, 1995, 1 (noting that the Actons styled themselves as hippies and that they "learned the art of protest during [their] student days in California"). Wayne Acton's testimony in the trial court in 1992 nicely anticipated Kilpatrick's sentiments: "[Suspicionless testing] sends a message to children that are trying to be responsible citizens . . . that they have to prove that they're innocent . . . , and I think that kind of sets a bad tone for citizenship." *Vernonia School District v. Acton*, 515 U.S. 646, 682 (1995) (O'Connor, J., dissenting) (quoting trial testimony).

dents, it had never before considered—let alone upheld—a program that potentially applied to literally millions of people, in the form of public school students who play sports and participate in extracurricular programs.[94]

The Court's determination to uphold urinalysis policies, even in the face of serious objections, shines through perhaps most clearly in three different respects. First, in *Acton*, the Court sidestepped a problematic requirement holding that when students are tested, they must reveal their prescription medications, which would have the effect of disclosing students' private medical information that schools are not entitled to demand. But Justice Scalia's opinion—in an unorthodox judicial move designed to preserve testing—simply read into the policy an option for students to provide their prescription drug information directly to testing labs (which would preserve students' confidentiality) rather than to schools. Second, in *Acton*, the Court noted that parents overwhelmingly approved the school system's drug-testing policy. But that fact is best understood as presenting an argument in favor of either families requiring children to take drug tests or schools administering them on a purely voluntary basis. Instead, highlighting this fact seems to have constituted a submission of students' constitutional rights to a show of hands—a practice that *Barnette* purported to outlaw more than five decades earlier. Third, in *Earls*, the Court's effort to transform the policy's dragnet quality into a feature, rather than a bug, succeeds in proving too much. If intruding into the intimate affairs of many innocent people without even the slightest suspicion of wrongdoing is attractive in schools, that logic might well be imported into the broader Fourth Amendment context—a development that would have disastrous consequences for fundamental notions of privacy.[95]

For some consequentialist-minded observers, though, such skepticism about the legitimacy of suspicionless drug testing could be overcome if the implementation of those policies meaningfully reduced students' consumption of illicit substances. For these individuals, the essential question is, do the programs work? The most reliable evidence indicates that implementing testing programs does not reduce drug usage among students whatsoever. In 2003, one year after *Earls*, a comprehensive study conducted by the University of Michigan, funded by the federal government, found that students' drug usage rates were virtually identical in schools with random testing and schools without such testing. As one of the study's lead researchers informed *The New York Times*, "[The data] suggests that there really isn't an impact from drug testing as practiced. It's the kind of intervention that doesn't win the hearts and minds of children."[96] Several subsequent studies have reinforced this conclusion.

Despite this clear evidence, suspicionless drug testing in public schools has only expanded. Today, approximately one in seven public school districts randomly tests some portion of its student body, a dramatic increase compared with only twenty years ago. In addition to testing athletes and participants in extracurricular activities, some schools now require students who merely want to attend a school-related event outside the typical school day to submit to suspicionless drug testing. Going even further, slightly less than one-third of schools that conduct suspicionless drug tests impose the practice on all students.[97] In the near future, the Supreme Court ought to revisit this area to consider for the first time whether merely attending a public school provides a sufficient condition to force students into taking drug tests without any basis for suspicion. When it does so, it should avail itself of the opportunity to reexamine the entire suspicionless drug-testing regime in schools.[98]

What of suspicionless searches outside the urinalysis context? When lower courts have addressed this issue, they have often struck an appropriate balance between the needs for student privacy and student safety. Thus, for example, a federal appellate court invalidated a program in Little Rock, Arkansas, where school officials would unexpectedly appear in a classroom, instruct students to empty their pockets and place all of their belongings on their desks, and then search through those items for contraband as students waited outside in the hallway. During one of these searches, officials discovered marijuana in a student's purse, which they turned over to police, leading to her conviction of a misdemeanor. Although the case was decided after *Acton* and *Earls*, the federal appellate court nonetheless nullified the suspicionless search, citing both the intrusive nature of the dragnet and the school's practice of routinely passing the contraband it discovered to police for prosecution.[99] In addition, at least two federal appellate courts have invalidated suspicionless searches when schools have permitted drug-sniffing dogs to get in close proximity to students in an effort to uncover contraband on their persons. In the course of invalidating one Texas school system's program—where Doberman pinschers and German shep-

herds regularly brought their snouts into contact with the clothing and even the bodies of students—the court reasoned, "[T]he
intensive smelling of people, even if done by dogs, [is] indecent and
demeaning. Most persons in our society deliberately attempt not to
expose the odors emanating from their bodies to public smell."[100]*

Lower courts have also appropriately issued decisions upholding the suspicionless searches that occur when schools require students to pass through metal detectors as they enter the building.
The reflexive temptation here is to analogize a school to an airport, as both places are security-sensitive, and no one in the mainstream believes that requiring airline passengers to pass through
metal detectors violates the Constitution. Upon reflection, though,
that facile analogy falls apart, as airline passengers can avoid metal
detectors by simply selecting another form of travel. As Judge
Henry Friendly explained back in 1974, airport metal detectors are
reasonable "so long as the search is conducted in good faith for the
purpose of preventing hijacking or like damage and with reasonable scope and the passenger has been given advance notice of his
liability to such a search so that he can avoid it by choosing not to
travel by air."[101] Even today, in the era of the No Fly List, there is
not yet a Must Fly List. Public school students—as a result of compulsory education laws—are differently situated from airline passengers regarding the voluntariness of appearing in their respective
security-sensitive places. Despite this meaningful difference, however, courts should generally uphold schools using metal detectors,
given that the devices involve a minimal intrusion into student privacy and that the potential harm avoided through the discovery of
illegal weapons is vast. In order to provide students with notice and
to increase the deterrent effect of such devices, schools should—
consistent with the approach outlined by Judge Friendly above—

---

* In April 2017, police officers in Sylvester, Georgia, conducted a particularly outrageous dragnet search of virtually all nine hundred students at Worth County High
School. Dozens of officers arrived early one morning and informed students that the
high school was on "lockdown." Police then proceeded to pat down the student body
in an extremely invasive manner, as several female students complained that officers
inserted their fingers into their undergarments and several male students complained
that officers "squeezed" and "cupped" their genitals. Although the officers were evidently searching for illicit drugs, their search yielded none. See Jacey Fortin, "'How Far
Can They Go?' Police Search of Hundreds of Students Stokes Lawsuit and Constitutional Questions," *New York Times*, June 13, 2017.

inform students at the beginning of the school year that they may be required to pass through metal detectors.[102]

SAFFORD UNIFIED SCHOOL DISTRICT V. REDDING:
THE PROBLEM OF STRIP SEARCHES

On October 8, 2003, Savana Redding—an eighth-grade honors student in a small Arizona mining town—reported to the nurse's office at Safford Middle School and endured what she would subsequently label "the most humiliating experience" of her life.[103] Redding found herself in the nurse's office not due to illness but so that two female school employees could subject her to a strip search. Earlier that day, a student who was discovered with four prescription-strength ibuprofen tablets—in violation of the school's zero-tolerance policy—informed Assistant Principal Kerry Wilson that Redding had given her the pills. Wilson did not ask the student whether she believed Redding held more contraband, but he nevertheless removed Redding from mathematics class and searched her backpack. When that initial search yielded no contraband, Wilson instructed a secretary and the school nurse to search Redding in a more comprehensive fashion. In the nurse's office, the school employees instructed Redding to remove her butterfly-adorned black stretch pants and her pink T-shirt. Then, as Redding recalled, left standing only in her undergarments, "they asked me to pull out my bra and move it from side to side," revealing her breasts, and "[t]hey made me open my legs and pull out my underwear," exposing some of her pelvic area.[104]

Although school officials testified that the eighth grader appeared neither nervous nor embarrassed during the search, Redding explained that she held her face down so they would not see she was fighting back tears. When asked why she did not resist the order to disrobe, Redding responded, "I'm one of those kids who does what they're told."[105] The fruitless search lasted only a short while, but it devastated Redding's young life: she never returned to Safford Middle School after the ordeal, subsequently developed ulcers that she attributed to the search, and even years afterward continued to think about the event daily. Redding noted that the strip search might have been particularly traumatizing for her because she was overweight—an issue that caused her to feel so self-conscious about her physique that she never wore tank tops or shorts to school, despite living in the desert heat. Redding's wounds remained raw even six years later, when her case challenging the strip search made its way to the Supreme Court for oral argument. At that time, a reporter asked Redding what she would do if someone instructed her to strip-search a student, and it became clear from her emotional response that she found the very prospect revolting: "Why would I want to do that to a little girl and ruin her life like that?"[106]

Following oral argument in *Redding*, many seasoned Supreme Court watchers deemed it highly improbable that the justices would decide that Safford school officials violated the Constitution. *Slate's* Dahlia Lithwick went so far as to proclaim that "it's plain" *Redding* would lose.[107] The oral argument provided ample justification for doubting that Redding's claim held any genuine prospect of carrying the day. Many of the justices posed questions highlighting the difficulties school administrators face with keeping students safe, and minimizing the invasiveness of the search that Redding endured. In one moment of unintentional comedy that attracted widespread media attention, Justice Stephen Breyer misspoke in the course of analogizing Redding's search to a commonplace school activity: "In my experience when I was 8 or 10 or 12 years old, you know, we did take our clothes off once a day, we changed for gym, okay? And in my experience, too, people did sometimes stick things in my underwear."[108] With that indelible image in mind, Justice Thomas erupted in raucous laughter, and the rest of the courtroom followed suit. Breyer, evidently realizing the misstep, sought to correct the record: "Or not my underwear. Whatever. Whatever."[109] Although the blunder drew a chuckle from Justice Ginsburg, she regarded the case as anything but a laughing matter. Some courtroom observers noted that Ginsburg appeared on the verge of exasperation with her colleagues—eight males at the time of *Redding*—because their questioning, in her view, betrayed a failure to grasp the search's humiliating effect.[110]

Roughly two weeks after oral argument in *Redding*, Ginsburg's evident frustration seemed to boil over in a highly unusual interview that she gave to the veteran Supreme Court reporter Joan Biskupic. Ginsburg's comments to Biskupic were abnormal because she offered detailed, on-the-record statements about *Redding* while the case was still pending resolution. Typically, justices go to elaborate lengths to avoid making pointed public comments about cases in that posture. Ginsburg informed Biskupic that—since Justice Samuel Alito replaced Justice Sandra Day O'Connor in 2006—the Court's altered composition resulted in an institution less well equipped to handle cases involving gender, citing the *Redding* oral argument as a paradigmatic instance. "They have never been a 13-year-old girl," Ginsburg stated. "It's a very sensitive age for a girl. I didn't think that my colleagues, some of them, quite understood." In a remark that seemed designed to counter Breyer's reference to gym clothes, Ginsburg continued, "Maybe a 13-year-old boy in a locker room doesn't have that same feeling about his body. But a girl who's just at the age where she is developing, whether she has developed a lot . . . or . . . has not developed at all [might be] embarrassed about that."[111] Given that the justices had already met in Conference to discuss *Redding*'s resolution when Ginsburg spoke to Biskupic, these remarks had the appearance of someone who was either airing grievances publicly that tradition would have dictated remain private (at least for the moment) or attempting to use the media to reach her colleagues in the hopes of shaping a still-uncertain outcome.

Although the strip search of Savana Redding yielded no contraband in 2003, it did produce a landmark judicial opinion in 2009. To the surprise of many observers, the Supreme Court in *Safford Unified School District v. Redding* held that the school officials violated the Fourth Amendment by strip-searching the eighth-grade student, and did so in a lopsided fashion, 8–1. Justice David Souter's opinion for the Court determined that the search failed the reasonable suspicion test for two central reasons. First, Souter noted that the prescription-strength ibuprofen tablets prompting that search were not a notably dangerous substance, as one of the pills was equivalent to two Advils. Second, Souter observed school officials had no reason to believe that Redding had stowed any pills in her undergarments. The combination of these two factors rendered the strip search impermissible, according to Souter, because it contravened *T.L.O.*'s requirement that the scope of student searches not be excessively intrusive in light of the alleged violation of school rules. "[B]efore a search can reasonably make the quantum leap from outer clothes and backpacks to exposure of intimate parts," Justice Souter wrote, educators must have "reasonable suspicion of danger or of resort to underwear for hiding evidence of wrong-doing."[112] As *Redding* further explained, "[t]he meaning of [a strip] search, and the degradation its subject may reasonably feel," place such searches into a distinct conceptual category, "demanding its own specific suspicions" that Safford school officials lacked.[113]

Justice Thomas, *Redding*'s lone dissenter, renewed yet again his originalist call to restore the in loco parentis doctrine, meaning here that students would retain no constitutional rights whatsoever against unreasonable searches. "The perils of judicial policymaking inherent in applying Fourth Amendment protections to public schools counsel in favor of a return to the understanding that existed in this Nation's first public schools," Thomas wrote.[114] In Thomas's estimation, the judiciary simply had no business interfering with how educators saw fit to administer their institutions: "Judges are not qualified to second-guess the best manner for maintaining quiet and order in the school environment."[115] Finally, Thomas attacked *Redding* on consequentialist grounds, asserting that the Court's willingness to invalidate the strip search in question would encourage students to begin storing drugs, and perhaps other forbidden items, in their underwear. "Redding would not have been the first person to conceal pills in her undergarments," Thomas warned. "Nor will she be the last after today's decision, which announces the safest place to secrete contraband in schools."[116]

The media overwhelmingly praised *Redding* for finding that the strip search violated the Fourth Amendment. *The New York Times*, for example, contended the decision "sends an important message to schools about the need to respect their students' privacy when they conduct investigations."[117] *USA Today* proclaimed the opinion a "victory for common sense," and the *Chicago Tribune* termed it "a relief," before posing a simple rhetorical question about the conduct of Safford officials: "What were they thinking?"[118] In a testament to how well-turned phrases from Supreme Court opinions occasionally enter the nation's popular discourse, some commentators assessed *Redding* in roughly the same terminology that *Tinker* introduced forty years earlier. Thus, *The Denver Post* editorialized, "We were glad to see the court draw the line on student searches, protecting young people from unjustified invasions of their privacy. Students shouldn't have to check their rights at the schoolhouse door."[119] One newspaper columnist similarly observed that, while school administrators should possess discretion to protect student safety, "that doesn't mean students check their constitutional rights at the schoolhouse door."[120]

In response to losing *Redding*, Safford's attorney magnified Justice Thomas's fear that the decision may inspire students to deposit forbidden items into their intimate apparel: "We can only hope that this decision does not compound the problem further, by emboldening more students to smuggle such contraband into the nation's schools."[121] For her part, Savana Redding found the Supreme Court's vindication of her constitutional claim deeply satisfying. Although Redding admitted not exactly relishing the media's spotlight, she felt motivated to mount the six-year legal campaign with the aim of guaranteeing that other students would not be forced to withstand similarly haunting experiences: "I wanted to make sure that no other person would have to go through this, so I am pleased by the Court's decision. I'm glad to have helped make students feel safer in school."[122] Some education officials, however, thought *Redding* contained too much vagueness to signal anything approaching the end of schools conducting strip searches. One Connecticut official, for example, contended that the opinion's lack of clarity regarding the available options to educators portended more litigation on the issue: "What I would have hoped came out of [*Redding*] was something more definitive. . . . We feel strongly the waters are muddy."[123] In this instance, at least, the view from the front lines resembled the view from the ivory tower. As one law professor who evaluated *Redding*'s significance for a reporter commented, "The court seems to think it made things clearer, but I don't think they did. Officials now know they can't do exactly what was done in Safford," but little else.[124] A law review article appraising *Redding* arrived at the same conclusion: "While the Court made some clarifications in the law, it created more ambiguity than lucidity."[125]

Redding undeniably marked a crucial moment in this arena of student rights, as it represented the first—and to date the only—time that the Supreme Court has held that school officials violated the Fourth Amendment's prohibition on unreasonable searches. Educators have conducted strip searches in the nation's public schools with alarming frequency for many years—dating back even to before *T.L.O.*—and *Redding* established that the most egregious of these searches violate the Fourth Amendment. Thus, for example, *Redding* suggests educators will no longer be able to—consistent with the Constitution—subject students to strip searches whenever money goes missing from a classroom, a repugnant practice that has given rise to a stunning amount of litigation, including in recent years. *Redding*'s rejection of such abhorrent practices represents a welcome, if belated, development.[126]

Redding should also be applauded for refusing to crumble in the face of assertions that the opinion's existence would motivate more students to place contraband in their undergarments. When the Court decided *Redding*, several states (including California, Iowa, New Jersey, Oklahoma, Washington, and Wisconsin) and major metropolitan areas (including New York City) had already enacted measures that forbade school officials to conduct strip searches altogether. Even though those measures extend further than the rule articulated in *Redding*, none of those jurisdictions reported any significant issues attributable to those rules. It is difficult to understand how complying with *Redding*'s holding would meaningfully increase contraband-related problems in schools when a diverse array of jurisdictions, featuring far more sweeping prohibitions on strip searches than *Redding*, have not encountered such issues. Given the absence of alarming developments in jurisdictions that prohibit student strip searches, many observers may believe that the Court's rejection of the increased-contraband argument was a foregone conclusion. But it is all too easy to envision the Supreme Court, driven by fears about impeding efforts to wage the war on drugs in schools, issuing a decision validating the strip search.[127]

One of *Redding*'s underappreciated virtues stems from its potential for undercutting the drug-testing regimes that *Acton* and *Earls* condoned. In a crucial, typically overlooked passage, Justice Souter's opinion for the Court refuted the notion that Redding's strip search could helpfully be analogized to changing clothes before physical education class: "Changing for gym is getting ready for play; exposing for a search is responding to an accusation reserved for suspected wrongdoers and [can] fairly [be] understood as . . . degrading."[128] This analysis implicitly complicates an important analytical strand in both *Acton* and *Earls*, which minimized the intrusiveness of those searches because students provided their samples in circumstances that roughly approximated typical restroom conditions. Justice Souter's insight in *Redding*, however, persuasively observes that—even if the student's actions during a search resemble everyday school occurrences—the context of the search itself can transform otherwise innocuous events into constitutionally troublesome actions. Importing Justice Souter's insight from *Redding* to the circumstances in *Acton* and *Earls* could well demand different outcomes. On this view, urinating in a public restroom in the presence of strangers is a common occurrence; producing a specimen in a cup for drug-testing purposes with witnesses listening for the telltale sounds of urination can fairly be understood as demeaning. Admittedly, part of Souter's analysis here mentions that the search of Redding was predicated upon suspicion of wrongdoing, a dynamic not present in *Acton* and *Earls* because they reviewed suspicionless testing regimes. But this factor seems unlikely to have driven *Redding*'s analysis, as student strip searches lacking individualized suspicion—which have, alas, been implemented on occasion—seem *more* rather than *less* objectionable. *Redding*'s warning against blithely analogizing government-mandated searches to routine school activities for Fourth Amendment purposes could well succeed in unsettling the Court's ratification of randomized drug testing in schools.[129]

While *Redding* admirably defended students' Fourth Amendment rights in certain respects, it is nevertheless difficult to escape the conclusion that the opinion inadequately reined in school administrators. The dominant problem with *Redding* is that the opinion failed to prohibit strip searches of students in many instances where those searches should—even under *T.L.O.*'s reasonable suspicion standard—be deemed unconstitutional. In its controlling portion, *Redding* provides that educators may not engage in strip searches of students when they lack "reasonable suspicion of danger or of resort to underwear for hiding evidence of wrongdoing."[130] The single most important word in that quotation may all too readily elude detection: its usage of the disjunctive "or," instead of the conjunctive "and." *Redding*'s deployment of this disjunction cannot be dismissed as inadvertent; the opinion repeats this holding in slightly different formulations throughout, and each time the word "or" appears. This small word matters enormously because *Redding*'s rule, as so crafted, leaves open the disturbing possibilities that had school personnel been in search of a drug more potent than ibuprofen (marijuana? methamphetamine?), or if they reasonably believed that Redding had stowed ibuprofen in her underwear, then strip-searching her might well have been permissible.

The Court in *Redding, at an absolute minimum,* should have held that in order to strip-search students, school officials must possess reasonable suspicion both that the student is concealing an item of contraband that poses significant danger *and* that the item is contained in the student's undergarments. Supporting the adoption of such a rule cannot be dismissed as the product of wild-eyed liberalism. Indeed, the Rutherford Institute, the Goldwater Institute, and the Cato Institute jointly filed an amicus brief in *Redding* that advocated adopting a version of this rule—only the brief went further, requiring school officials to gather enough evidence to satisfy the more demanding probable cause standard along both the danger dimension and the location dimension.[131]*

EXAMINING JUSTICE GINSBURG'S COMMENTARY ON SEX AND STRIP SEARCHES

After the Court issued *Redding*, several astute commentators—including Linda Greenhouse and Dahlia Lithwick—credited Justice Ginsburg's comments to Biskupic with helping to transform the case's outcome.[132] Ginsburg's own post-*Redding* public statements have largely supported this intuition that she played a pivotal role, facilitating the Supreme Court's conclusion that the case involved a Fourth Amendment violation. Immediately on the decision's heels, when an interviewer asked Ginsburg whether the Court's deliberations in *Redding* benefited from having a woman present, she answered in the affirmative, largely reiterating what she had previously told Biskupic. "I think [the inclusion of a woman] makes people stop and think, Maybe a 13-year-old girl is different from a 13-year-old boy in terms of how humiliating it is to be seen undressed," Ginsburg said. "I think many of [the male justices] first thought of their own reaction. It came out in various questions. You change your clothes in the gym, what's the big deal?"[133] Speaking on

---

* *Redding* extended the educators qualified immunity—which shielded the school district from liability in this instance—because it found that the strip search did not violate clearly established law. See *Redding*, 557 U.S. 364, 366 (2009). This part of the decision was misguided because—as Justice Stevens and Justice Ginsburg noted—*Redding* is best understood as simply applying the rule established in *T.L.O.* twenty-five years earlier. That foundational opinion held, of course, that a student search cannot be "'excessively intrusive in light of . . . the nature of the infraction.'" Ibid., 380–81 (Stevens, J., concurring in part and dissenting in part) (quoting *New Jersey v. T.L.O.*, 469 U.S. 325, 342 [1984]); and ibid., 381–82 (Ginsburg, J., concurring in part and dissenting in part) (quoting *T.L.O.*, 469 U.S. at 342).

a panel a few years later, Justice Ginsburg revisited *Redding*, where she maintained—and even intensified—this notion that the case highlighted the importance of having women serve on the Supreme Court: "Every woman would understand what a mortifying experience that [search] was for a thirteen-year-old girl. Every man did not have that understanding. It was good to have people at the table who could explain the girl's extreme discomfort to others."[134] At least one newspaper columnist has viewed *Redding* through the prism established by Ginsburg: "Anyone who knows a 13-year-old girl or has been a 13-year-old girl herself would have known not to go there—to strip-search a middle school student at school to look for banned prescription pain pills."[135]

Justice Ginsburg's repeated references to Savana Redding's tender emotional state—which she construes as a dual product of age and sex—doubtlessly exert a formidable grip on the instincts and perhaps even the emotions of many readers. On this view, thirteen year-old boys—unlike their female counterparts—are simply not sensitive about their bodies, or much of anything else for that matter. Supporting this notion, Ginsburg's public comments can be understood as honoring *T.L.O.*'s instruction that a search's intrusiveness should be considered "in light of the age and sex of the student."[136] Even if Justice Souter's opinion for the Court in *Redding* did not focus on this precedential language—and in no way suggested Safford Middle School officials could have constitutionally strip-searched a thirteen-year-old boy in otherwise identical circumstances—many surely believe Ginsburg articulated simple, powerful truths to her colleagues regarding fundamental aspects of girlhood.

Upon reflection, though, Ginsburg's position invites analysis. Consider for a moment what work is done, precisely, by emphasizing that the strip search occurred when Redding was thirteen—an age that, as Justice Ginsburg correctly noted, often falls right around the onset of puberty. That age is surely a particularly awkward time for many adolescents, but does it materially alter the Fourth Amendment analysis in any way? Would Redding's strip search have been constitutional if it occurred five years earlier, at age eight, when most girls remain prepubescent? Lower courts have made that type of determination in the past, and the resulting opinions seem deeply misguided. For example, when two eight-year-old girls in Talladega, Alabama, were implicated in the theft of seven dollars, their second-grade teacher accompanied them to the lavatory and instructed them to pull down their underwear. A federal appellate court mentioned the girls' relative youth in the course of ruling that *T.L.O.* did not plainly prohibit this invasive search for that trivial sum of money.[137] Examining the age consideration from the opposite angle, would Redding's strip search have passed constitutional muster if it occurred five years later, at age eighteen, when the overwhelming majority of young women are postpubescent? Even more clearly than with younger students, the answer here seems likely a resounding no. Many readers may well hold that subjecting a young woman in her senior year of high school to a strip search evokes deeper-seated social anxieties than does strip-searching a "developing" adolescent, in Ginsburg's argot.[138] Admittedly, it seems highly implausible that Ginsburg would deem it permissible to strip-search an eight-year-old Redding, an eighteen-year-old Redding, or a Redding who fell anywhere in between for that matter. But if that assumption is accurate, it reduces Ginsburg's emphasis on Redding's age into sheer makeweight.

The second aspect of Justice Ginsburg's dual-pronged position—holding that strip searches are uniquely objectionable to female students—also demands scrutiny. Very few male students, it seems safe to posit, would be indifferent to the experience of school officials requiring them to disrobe in a search for contraband. Boys, perhaps now more than ever, are hardly impervious to feeling inadequate about their physiques.[139] More important, just about no one relishes the opportunity to stand around, clad scantily, as a school official inspects her or his exposed body. Even if female students may as a general proposition experience greater feelings of humiliation and vulnerability than male students during strip searches, the difference seems more readily understood as being one of degree rather than of kind. To the extent that the sexes experience strip searches in different manners, moreover, it seems important to acknowledge that a considerable portion of that difference stems from stereotypical gender roles that pervade society, treating females as delicate beings who fundamentally require their privacy and males as sturdy creatures who basically have nothing to hide. When Ginsburg was a pioneering attorney in the legal fight against sex discrimination during the 1970s, she admirably conceived of herself as combating laws that locked men and women into stereotyped positions—a philosophical commitment that a leading assessment of her litigating career has dubbed Ginsburg's "anti-stereotype principle."[140]* It seems at least somewhat lamentable that Justice Ginsburg's public commentary on *Redding* has perpetuated hoary gender stereotypes—accentuating girls' vulnerability and boys' resilience—that should be unnecessary to condemn the irrational strip search at issue in that case.†

Happily, lower courts weighing strip-search cases post-*Redding* have not interpreted the decision to apply in the more limited fashion that Justice Ginsburg's public commentary might be read as suggesting. Protecting male students from unnecessary strip searches seems desirable not least because some evidence indicates, predictably, that those searches can also have catastrophic consequences for boys. In February 2011, a public school in Georgia forced a seventh-grade student—called "D.H." by courts—to submit to an ultimately unavailing strip search for marijuana that occurred in front of three classmates. D.H. recalled feeling scared and powerless to resist the search: "I didn't know if I could say something while he was searching me. I didn't know if I had any rights."[141] Like Redding before him, D.H. never returned to the school where the strip search occurred, and experienced profound difficulties after the incident. According to the federal district court that eventually declared the school's actions unconstitutional, D.H. "suffered deep embarrassment" from the search.[142] In addition to

---

* Recently, Justice Ginsburg's commitment to combating sex-based stereotypes with the Equal Protection Clause appeared in her opinion for the Court in *Sessions v. Morales-Santana*, an immigration case that invalidated a citizenship measure for foreign-born children that treated mothers and fathers differently. *Sessions v. Morales-Santana*, 137 S. Ct. 1678, 1692 (2017) (condemning "the familiar stereotype" of "unwed citizen fathers" who "would care little about . . . their nonmarital children"); ibid., 1693n13 ("Even if stereotypes frozen into legislation have 'statistical support,' our decisions reject measures that classify unnecessarily and overbroadly by gender when more accurate and impartial lines can be drawn"). See also Linda Greenhouse, "Justice Ginsburg and the Price of Equality," *New York Times*, June 22, 2017 ("At the core of Ruth Ginsburg's lifelong project is the conviction that there should be no separate spheres for men and women in the eyes of the law, and that distinctions based on what 'most' men or women do, on the choices that 'most' of them make, is an obstacle to full legal equality").

† One might suspect that Justice Ginsburg trafficked in gender stereotypes here not because she believed them deep down but because she wanted to ensure that Redding's claim prevailed. On this account, Ginsburg used perhaps the only tool at her disposal to prevent an opinion legitimating the search. That justification cannot explain, however, why Ginsburg has continued to repeat, and indeed embellish upon, the stereotype-based account after *Redding* was safely on the books. Even if she understandably would not have wanted to disavow her earlier interpretation, she was under no obligation to perpetuate those ideas post-*Redding*. Yet that is the path she selected.

motivating him to discard the pair of boxers that he wore during the ordeal, the search led him to begin changing clothes for school athletics in a restroom stall and to distrust adults in authority positions. According to D.H.'s mother, moreover, the traumatic experience even damaged her son's approach to school itself: "This situation has broken the very foundation of my child's education because in order for him to learn, he has to believe that what schools are trying to teach him is right and now he questions them after they stripped him of his clothes and dignity."[143]

J.D.B. V. NORTH CAROLINA: THE FIFTH AMENDMENT'S RIGHT TO REMAIN SILENT

In late September 2005, a school resource officer in Chapel Hill, North Carolina, removed a seventh-grade student from his social studies class and informed him that an investigator from the local police department wished to speak with him. The officer then escorted the student—designated "J.D.B." by courts—to one of the school's conference rooms, where the investigator and two school officials awaited their arrival. After the conference room door was closed, J.D.B. answered somewhere between thirty and forty-five minutes of questions that were designed to establish that the young man had recently broken in to two homes and stolen assorted items. Eventually, on the heels of a school administrator advising J.D.B. to "do the right thing" because "the truth always comes out in the end," the thirteen-year-old student confessed to committing the crimes. North Carolina thereafter sought to introduce J.D.B.'s incriminating statements in proceedings to have him declared a juvenile delinquent. J.D.B.'s public defender, in response, sought to suppress the confession. As it turned out, one of the questions that J.D.B. never had an opportunity to answer during the schoolhouse questioning was whether he understood his right to remain silent.[144]

The failure to inform J.D.B. of his Fifth Amendment right against self-incrimination, as famously interpreted by the Supreme Court in *Miranda v. Arizona,* was almost certainly not an oversight but instead part of a concerted effort to circumvent the rule. Police officers can avoid issuing *Miranda* warnings to criminal suspects, and still take advantage of any adverse statement in legal proceedings, provided that the statement does not occur during an "in custody," or "custodial," interrogation. When are suspects considered in police custody, and therefore within *Miranda*'s ambit? The governing standard provides two inquiries: First, under what circumstances did the interrogation occur? And second, in light of those circumstances, would a reasonable person feel free to end the interrogation by leaving the scene? Thus, the fundamental issue raised by *J.D.B. v. North Carolina*, when it arrived at the Supreme Court, could have been condensed as follows: Would a seventh-grade student in J.D.B.'s shoes (having been plucked from class by a uniformed police officer) feel at liberty to terminate his exchange with two law enforcement officials and two school administrators by exiting the school conference room? If the Court answered that question yes, then police would not have been required to issue J.D.B. *Miranda* warnings, and his confession would almost certainly be admitted against him. But if the Court answered that question no, then J.D.B.'s statement would be deemed inadmissible.[145]

In *J.D.B. v. North Carolina*, the Supreme Court in 2011 issued an opinion announcing by a 5–4 margin that a suspect's youth informs the determination of whether an individual is in custody for *Miranda* purposes. Provided that a police officer either knew or should have known that a suspect is a minor, the Court concluded, the officer must incorporate that factor into the custodial calculus. As Justice Sonia Sotomayor's opinion for the Court in *J.D.B.* reasoned, this conclusion aligned with basic reality: "It is beyond dispute that children will often feel bound to submit to police questioning when an adult in the same circumstances would feel free to leave."[146] Sotomayor rejected claims that incorporating youth into the custodial determination would impose staggering burdens on the officials charged with implementing the standard. "[O]fficers and judges need no imaginative powers, knowledge of developmental psychology, training in cognitive science, or expertise in social and cultural anthropology to account for a child's age," Sotomayor contended. "They simply need the common sense to know that a 7-year-old is not a 13-year-old and neither is an adult."[147] Despite this forceful language, *J.D.B.* stopped well short of concluding that minors must always receive *Miranda* warnings during police questioning in order for their confessions to be deemed admissible. "This is not to say that a child's age will be a determinative, or even a significant, factor in every case," Sotomayor wrote. "It is, however, a reality that courts cannot simply ignore."[148] Indeed, the

Court even refused to resolve definitively whether J.D.B.'s questioning at school occurred while he was in custody for *Miranda* purposes, and sent the case back to North Carolina's courts to apply the newly articulated standard.

Justice Alito, writing on behalf of the four dissenters, criticized *J.D.B.* for taking what had previously presented police officers with an objective test and transforming it into a subjective one—forcing them to consider for the first time how one particular trait altered the questioning experience from the perspective of criminal suspects. "Today's decision shifts the *Miranda* custody determination from a one-size-fits-all reasonable-person test into an inquiry that must account for at least one individualized characteristic—age—that is thought to correlate with susceptibility to coercive pressures," Alito wrote.[149] *J.D.B.*'s transformation of this standard was unnecessary, Alito further contended, in part because the custodial inquiry had always incorporated the location of police questioning into the analysis, based on the insight that suspects feel less comfortable at stationhouses than, say, in their own living rooms. Accounting for police questioning that occurs within the schoolhouse setting, he maintained, would address many of the issues that *J.D.B.*'s consideration of age sought to remedy without the disadvantage of warping doctrine. Somewhat surprisingly, given this emphasis on setting, Alito's opinion did not take the small additional step of concluding that the police questioning of J.D.B. actually occurred in custody; instead, in terms of its bottom line, the dissent concerned itself exclusively with combating the Court's finding that youth properly informed the custodial assessment.

Newspaper editorial boards generally approved the Court's opinion in *J.D.B.* In the most enthusiastic appraisal, the *Los Angeles Times* asserted that "[a]ny other decision would have been unconscionable," especially because the increased police presence in schools makes students more vulnerable to arrests: "When the school functions as a police station, it's important that children be told their rights."[150] *The New York Times* offered a muted response, terming the outcome "sensibl[e]" and predicting police officers "will find that considering a suspect's age in delivering *Miranda* warnings a prudent safeguard for that individual's rights and also for their work."[151] *J.D.B.* generated considerably more consternation at *The Washington Post*, which waited until the end of August, more than two months after the decision, before publishing its decidedly lukewarm assessment. "Students will not be the only ones trying to make sense of new material as the school year begins," the *Post* warned, as school officials and police officers alike must confront "a new assignment" due to the Court's decision "chang[ing] the rules" of *Miranda*. Despite this wary tone, the *Post* drew some solace from the fact that *J.D.B.* did not evidently alter the applicable rules governing when educators, rather than police officers, question students.[152]

Law professors sharply diverged in their assessments of *J.D.B.*'s importance. Some legal academics deemed the decision momentous because police officers have traditionally evinced strong preferences for questioning juveniles at school—viewing it as in effect a *Miranda*-free zone—and *J.D.B.*'s animating logic suggested that this time-honored loophole would finally be closed. Other law professors, however, concluded *J.D.B.* would prove thoroughly inconsequential. According to this skeptical reading, *J.D.B.*'s existence would motivate police officers merely to issue *Miranda* warnings before they began questioning students at school. The recitation of these familiar warnings, skeptics hastened to add, would lead only to a trivial number of students actually ending police interrogations; instead, the overwhelming majority of students would simply waive their right to remain silent after receiving it. Skeptics of *J.D.B.*'s import could confidently predict that the recitation of *Miranda* warnings would not meaningfully diminish schoolhouse confessions, because even adults typically waive their Fifth Amendment rights and minors, predictably, comprehend the meaning of those warnings far less well than adults. On this jaundiced view, *J.D.B.* can be regarded as merely placing a speed bump on the police's path toward obtaining a juvenile confession.[153]

If issuing *Miranda* warnings to students does not actually pose much of an impediment to obtaining confessions, why did the police investigator not simply read J.D.B. his rights and then obtain the confession? The most persuasive explanation requires some additional knowledge of North Carolina's legislative backdrop and—to a lesser extent—the particular attitudes of J.D.B.'s primary caretakers. During custodial interrogations, North Carolina law provides juvenile criminal suspects with significant protections that extend well beyond anything federal law requires. Thus, in addition to the standard *Miranda* warnings, juveniles in North Carolina who are subjected to custodial interrogation must be warned of their right to have a parent, or parental figure, present during questioning.

Even more important for present purposes, though, North Carolina law at the time provided further that for children younger than fourteen any incriminating statement uttered during custodial interrogation would be inadmissible unless the statement was made in the presence of the child's parent, or parental figure.[154] Given that J.D.B. was only thirteen years old at the time of questioning, the Chapel Hill investigator who was assigned to the police department's juvenile division understood that issuing the student his *Miranda* rights would trigger these additional protections. Investigators have a strong incentive to avoid that scenario by questioning a young suspect in a setting that will be deemed "non-custodial," because locating a juvenile's parent to observe an interrogation presents a hassle and the parent's presence may decrease the likelihood of obtaining a confession.

The Chapel Hill police department had particular reason to believe, moreover, that J.D.B.'s family members were not inclined to watch passively as he confessed. On the day the break-ins were committed, an officer briefly detained and questioned J.D.B. for looking into a house and recorded the young man's name and address. When the officer subsequently visited J.D.B.'s home, his grandmother—who acted as his legal guardian—and aunt responded to the officer with what he characterized as "resistance," "hostility," and an accusation that the boy had been stopped for "racially motivated" reasons.[155]* This police officer subsequently conferred with the investigator who conducted J.D.B.'s examination, and it hardly seems fantastic to suppose that he would have relayed these familial impressions. J.D.B.'s circumstances, in sum, provided ample rea-

---

* At oral argument in *J.D.B.*, Justice Antonin Scalia posed a question to the juvenile's attorney (based on hypothetical facts) that contained ugly racial overtones: "When the policeman sees him, he's *dressed in baggy jeans, you know, down around his thighs*, and when the judge sees him he's wearing a Buster Brown jumper suit. You don't really think that it's going to be equivalent?" Oral Argument Transcript, *J.D.B. v. North Carolina*, No. 09-11121, 13 (March 23, 2011) (emphasis added). That a Supreme Court justice uttered this racially inflammatory remark at a relatively recent oral argument—held in 2011—is deeply dismaying. That Scalia's question failed to draw a rebuke from a fellow justice, or to elicit commentary from any major news organization, is more dismaying still. In response to Scalia's question, J.D.B.'s attorney confessed that she failed to appreciate its import. Setting aside for the moment the question's linking black youth to criminality, Justice Scalia's question was designed, I gather, to suggest that considering age for custodial interrogation purposes would be difficult to implement. That is, a criminal suspect's casual attire may make him look older than his age (to a police officer) and his court attire may make him look younger than his age (to the judge).

son for an investigator who wished to obtain a confession to avoid interviewing him with his guardian present. By circumventing the *Miranda* warnings, the investigator could also circumvent J.D.B.'s family members.

J.D.B. v. North Carolina is one of the most unusual Supreme Court decisions, taken from any field, within recent memory. As an initial matter, Justice Sotomayor's opinion in *J.D.B.* articulated an incredibly narrow legal holding, even as assessed by the slim standards in this hour of judicial minimalism.[156] While observing that a criminal suspect's age is relevant to *Miranda*'s custodial determination, it also noted that this factor may well not prove decisive (or even significant) in reaching that determination. The opinion's narrowness is perhaps best exemplified by its failure to announce that J.D.B.'s questioning in fact constituted custodial interrogation, despite overpowering evidence supporting that conclusion. Although the holding was surely preferable to one flatly declaring age irrelevant to custodial assessments, *J.D.B.* does not guarantee that juveniles will receive *Miranda* warnings even in similar circumstances going forward.*

The Court's fixation on age and relative disregard for the school setting, moreover, seem strange and regrettable. If an overriding aim of the custodial assessment seeks to ascertain whether a reasonable suspect would feel free to terminate a discussion with police officers, the general norms and rules that govern students within schoolhouses certainly contain relevance for that determina-

---

* Admittedly, some—perhaps even most—of the Court's unwillingness to declare that J.D.B.'s questioning involved custody likely stems from the difficulty of retaining the five votes necessary to form a majority. When the Court divides 5–4, the majority's opinion is only as strong as the tentative fifth vote permits it to be. Although it is impossible to know at this point which justice in the *J.D.B.* majority was most apprehensive about buttressing *Miranda*, it seems quite plausible that the critical vote belonged to Justice Anthony Kennedy. In addition to being the most conservative member of the majority, Justice Kennedy wrote a significant opinion undermining *Miranda* only one year before the Court decided *J.D.B.* See *Berghuis v. Thompkins*, 560 U.S. 370, 388–89 (2010) (holding that criminal suspects must expressly invoke their right to remain silent in order to bring interrogation to an end, even if they remain silent in the face of hours of questioning before ultimately confessing). Four justices (Alito, Roberts, Scalia, and Thomas) sided with the prosecution in *Thompkins* and *J.D.B.*, and three other justices (Breyer, Ginsburg, and Sotomayor) sided with the defense in both cases. Indeed, Justice Kennedy was the only member of the Court who voted with the prosecution in one *Miranda*-related case (*Thompkins*) and then shifted to vote for the defense in the other *Miranda*-related case (*J.D.B.*). (Between *Thompkins* and *J.D.B.*, Justice Kagan replaced Justice Stevens, but both justices voted with the defendant in their respective cases.)

tion. The typical public school setting is a restrictive environment, one that prizes obedience, cooperation, and deference to authority.[157] Students do not, moreover, usually control their own whereabouts during the school day, roaming wherever happens to strike their fancy; instead, they report to their assigned classrooms and request permission from teachers if they need to be excused for some reason. The student handbook at J.D.B.'s middle school offers some instruction in this regard, in that it commanded students to "[f]ollow directions of all teachers/adults the first time they are given," "[s]top moving when [addressed by] an adult," and "[w]alk away only after [being] dismissed."[158] These days, of course, a student's failure to follow instructions may lead not merely to detention but even to trouble with the law.[159] The restraint on freedom of movement that schools typically exercise over students becomes all the more pronounced when a police officer beckons for a word.

Oddly, however, Justice Sotomayor's opinion in *J.D.B.* resisted the contention that the school setting, independent of age, mattered for custodial determinations. She illustrated this point by suggesting that parents who volunteer at their child's school would feel quite differently about their own ability to terminate police questioning than would their child. "Without asking whether the person questioned in school is a minor," Sotomayor wrote, "the coercive effect of the schoolhouse setting is unknowable."[160] But this way of articulating the point may—perhaps unwittingly—permit lower courts seeking to curb even *J.D.B.*'s limited holding to find that students who have reached the age of eighteen would not even be entitled to the decision's hazy protections when investigators visit schoolhouses. Such an interpretation could have real consequences, as public school students often reach the age of majority; recall that Joseph Frederick was eighteen at the time he unfurled his controversial banner, and Dwight Lopez was nineteen when Columbus High suspended him. Yet surely the salience of one's status as a student is more significant than whether one has turned eighteen for purposes of assessing if one feels free to terminate an encounter with the police. Students are particularly pliant in the face of police questioning, regardless of whether they have reached the age of majority. Justice Alito's dissent seemed to recognize this point, but that recognition did not prompt him to conclude that J.D.B.'s *Miranda*-less interrogation was therefore improper. Instead, Alito—as if in full parliamentary debater mode—appeared content to score points on the abstract question of age's import for custody, and seemed uninterested in identifying a sensible solution to an important legal question. Conservatives' long-standing anathema toward *Miranda* seems as good an explanation as any for why Justice Alito's outcome in *J.D.B.* clashed with his reasoning.

In *J.D.B.*, the Court should have crafted a legal approach to recognize that the Fifth Amendment's right against self-incrimination affords particular protection to students in school. Such a ruling would have aligned with the Supreme Court's repeated recognition that the Constitution assumes distinct contours within the schoolhouse due to that institution's unique role in American society. When police officers question students in school, *J.D.B.* should have held, those sessions presumptively constitute custodial interrogations—a default rule that would encourage officers to issue *Miranda* warnings to students they question if they wish to use a resulting confession as evidence.[161]

This approach would be sensible because, as discussed earlier, the school setting—by its very nature—typically disables students from feeling free to terminate police questioning. In addition, this approach would have the virtue of eliminating any uncertainty that police officers may have about whether extended questioning of students in schools constitutes custodial interrogation. As matters currently stand, because of *J.D.B.*'s indeterminate holding, a police officer might credibly conclude that questioning an eleven-year-old in school amounts to a custodial interrogation but that questioning a seventeen-year-old does not. Extending the custodial presumption to all elementary and secondary students would eliminate that guesswork. Adopting the school-based approach would not, moreover, have prohibited the Supreme Court from simultaneously implementing the age-based test that it actually announced in *J.D.B.* But the age-based protection would have, under this view, served as an additional layer of protection for juvenile suspects in nonschool settings. Finally, the school-based presumption would also not prevent states—following North Carolina's lead—from enacting legislation that provides juveniles suspected of committing crimes with additional protections against self-incrimination that extend beyond the constitutionally established minimum. Such legislation is advisable, of course, because evidence indicates that young people are particularly susceptible to false confessions.[162]

Some students have filed lawsuits claiming their rights have been violated when, without receiving *Miranda* warnings, they make statements responding to questions posed by school officials, not police officers. Lower courts have overwhelmingly rejected these claims, typically reasoning that school officials require flexibility to ask students questions in an unencumbered fashion in order to manage schools effectively and safely; even if *Miranda* regulates police officers' questioning in schools, these courts contend, teachers need not concern themselves with running afoul of the Fifth Amendment.[163] Is that reasoning sound? The answer to that question should depend upon the type of adverse action that the student is challenging. When a student alleges a *Miranda* violation in an effort to withdraw a confession to school officials that has led merely to school-imposed sanctions, judges stand on solid ground in rejecting that claim. Thus, a federal appellate court has appropriately found that *Miranda* provided no comfort to a student who was transferred to a different school after she confessed to a school administrator that she activated a school fire alarm as a prank.[164]

In contrast, when a student cites a *Miranda* violation seeking to suppress a confession to a school official that yields criminal charges, courts ought not be so cavalier in dismissing such claims. As the Supreme Court of New Hampshire stated in 2001 in one of the very few cases that resulted in the suppression of an incriminating statement made to a school official,

> [W]hen school officials search for contraband in order to foster a safe and healthy educational environment, they are afforded greater flexibility than if a law enforcement officer performed the same search. If school officials agree to take on the mantle of criminal investigation and enforcement, however, they assume an understanding of constitutional criminal law equal to that of a law enforcement officer. In such circumstances, even if school officials claim their actions fall within the ambit of their administrative authority, they should be charged with abiding by the constitutional protections required in criminal investigations.[165]

Acknowledging the line separating police officers from school officials for Fifth Amendment purposes will minimize the possibility that educators are seeking to extract student confessions at the behest of police officers, a dynamic that has sometimes emerged. Some critics may object that if courts suppress incriminating statements to school officials in the criminal realm, that rule might result in more police officers in schools because administrators will be incentivized to turn over nascent criminal investigations to the police, in order to ensure that any resulting confession holds up in court. The response to this concern contains three related elements: first, police officers are already a pervasive presence in schools, hence that particular Rubicon has already been crossed; second, a strong case can be made that, if an interrogation is going to occur, police should conduct it; and third, recalling Professor Seavey's admonition, if criminal charges are foreseeably in the offing, students should at least enjoy the benefit of the relevant criminal procedural protections that are afforded to a common pickpocket.

AFTER COLUMBINE—AND BEFORE

At this point, some readers may object that the proposals for legal reform contained in this chapter are shockingly ill-suited to reflect the current mood toward school safety. That mood crystallized in April 1999 with the armed massacre of fourteen students (including the two perpetrators, who committed suicide) and one teacher at Columbine High School.[166] For many people who can recall first hearing of that horrific event, and who have its images etched in their minds, the Columbine massacre represented the dawn of an entirely new era of fear surrounding schools. The legal community has hardly proven immune to such fears. Indeed, judges have relentlessly observed in recent years that we now inhabit a "post-Columbine world."[167] In that world, the thinking runs, educators and school resource officers should have every conceivable tool at their disposal in order to prevent violence. This powerful intuition finds reinforcement with each new school shooting, particularly when there are large numbers of casualties, as occurred at Sandy Hook Elementary in Newtown, Connecticut, in December 2012, and at Marjory Stoneman Douglas High School in Parkland, Florida, in February 2018.[168]

It would be misguided, however, to permit fears of school shootings to establish the contours of constitutional criminal procedure within the nation's public schools. Precisely because reports of school shootings affect many people in a visceral fashion, Americans dramatically overestimate the likelihood that their lives will be intimately touched by a Columbine-style massacre.[169] In April 1999, immediately on the heels of Columbine, Gallup found in a nation-wide survey that 68 percent of adults believed that such an event was either very likely or somewhat likely to occur in their com-munities. The passage of time did not erode that belief; in fact, it became only more widespread. In March 2005, nearly six full years after Columbine, Gallup revisited this issue and found that 73 per-cent of adults deemed a student massacre very likely or somewhat likely to occur in their communities.[170] In actuality, though, school shootings of any dimension are unlikely in the extreme to occur in any particular community. Even in our post-Columbine world, it has been noted that students were more likely to die as a result of a lightning strike than a school homicide, one involving a gun or by any other means, for that matter.[171] In 2010, a comprehensive study indicated that student homicides occur with such infrequency that a randomly selected school should anticipate a student being killed on its premises roughly once every six thousand years.[172] As Secretary of Education Arne Duncan reported in 2012, "Schools are among the safest places for children and adolescents in our country."[173]

None of the foregoing should be mistaken to argue against enacting sensible firearm regulations designed to preserve school safety. Indeed, the Supreme Court's foundational Second Amend-ment opinion in 2008 expressly noted that its recognition of an individual's right to bear arms should not be viewed as casting doubt on "laws forbidding the carrying of firearms in sensitive places such as schools."[174] It is to argue, however, that judges, edu-cators, and legislators ought to appreciate the actual (rather than the misperceived) risk of school homicide, and that policies should not be implemented that wildly overreact to that risk. The judi-ciary should not, moreover, permit hysteria over school violence to excuse broadly invasive searches by school authorities, particularly when the school's actions do not even purport to ferret out danger-ous weapons, but instead are aimed at other forms of contraband.[175] In addition, it should be appreciated that when schools adopt poli-cies in a fruitless effort to eliminate *any* risk of school homicide or other types of violence, those policies themselves impose significant costs on American society. The most prominent cost, of course, is the heavy toll placed on developing notions of what it means to be an American citizen.

Some readers may believe that it has now become necessary

for schools to impose new, highly restrictive regulations in order to counteract the excesses of today's youth—a generation of adolescents that seems more reckless, more uncontrollable, and more criminally inclined than prior generations. The cover of *Newsweek* captured this sentiment, luridly proclaiming, "Let's Face It: Our Teen-Agers Are out of Hand." The accompanying article warned of "a national teenage problem," made by "[o]ur vicious young hoodlums," who accounted for "shocking," and "increas[ing]" percentages of various crimes, including "[m]urder, burglary, auto theft, stolen property, rape, . . . and assault."[176] These trends prompted one judge, quoted in *Newsweek*, to conclude, "We've got a different breed of young criminals—it's not just crime, it's sadistic crime."[177] Alarming as this report is, however, realizing that such concerns have been articulated intermittently since at least the end of World War II may help to dampen enthusiasm for the notion that the modern adolescent is truly a breed apart who requires tough innovations to tame.

To appreciate this point, contemplate that the disquieting *Newsweek* article cited above did not purport to chronicle today's youth, because it was not published in current times. Nor did this article appear as recently as the mid-1990s, when the media and public officials—under the influence of the political scientist John DiIulio Jr.—stoked fears of "super-predators" who were preparing to unleash havoc on the nation.[178] Nor did this article even emerge during the panic of the late 1970s, when *Time* magazine's cover warned of "the youth crime plague"—a trend that it partly traced to perceptions of declining authority in schools and increasing rights consciousness among adolescents.[179] Instead, the *Newsweek* article appeared more than six decades ago, back in 1954—a period that is not widely remembered today as being dominated by an unhinged criminal youth element. To the contrary, the 1950s are now generally recalled as a time that was characterized by relative tranquillity among youth; *Leave It to Beaver* casts a longer shadow over the national psyche than, say, *Blackboard Jungle*.[180] Ever harsher school policies should not be driven by rank nostalgia for yesteryear. In addition, realizing that the overstated fear of a new type of wild, crime-prone student forms a lengthy—if not exactly distinguished—aspect of our national heritage should encourage would-be educational reformers to exercise caution the next time that a youth dread again seizes the public imagination.

5

Equal Protection I:
Racial Segregation and the Enduring
Battle over *Brown v. Board of Education*

The Supreme Court's decision in *Brown v. Board of Education*, declaring that racially segregated schools violated the Fourteenth Amendment's Equal Protection Clause, stands alone as the most revered judicial opinion of the twentieth century. *Brown* receives near-universal veneration today in no small part because different readers ascribe radically different meanings to the decision. Thus, while every justice on the current Supreme Court doubtless pledges allegiance to *Brown*'s understanding of racial equality, they simultaneously turn to salute in competing directions. In 2007, these starkly divergent interpretations of *Brown* surfaced in *Parents Involved in Community Schools v. Seattle School District No. 1*, where the Court, by a 5–4 vote, invalidated school boards' student-assignment plans that are designed to enhance integrated educational opportunities—at least if those plans do so by racially classifying individual pupils. *Parents Involved* represented an unusually intense clash over *Brown*'s true meaning. But such battles over *Brown* are nothing new. Rather, they have shadowed the opinion at least since its inception.

Parents Involved can usefully be understood as the successful culmination of a conservative legal effort, extending back several decades, to mold and constrain *Brown*'s meaning. Although many white southerners initially contended that the Supreme Court erred in *Brown*, the most sophisticated segregationists quickly developed a backup strategy that sought to curtail the opinion's effects. Once it became apparent that the Court would not reverse *Brown*, the decision's opponents shifted their focus, aiming instead to minimize desegregation and to convert the opinion into a principle requiring constitutional colorblindness. These strategies eventually attained considerable success in large part because the Court, after deciding *Brown*, abandoned any effort to develop a meaningful desegregation jurisprudence for well over a decade. While some of the Court's preliminary hesitation about wading into these hotly contested waters might have been understandable, its extended absence from this domain destroyed the prospect that *Brown* would lead to robust racial integration in schools across the nation. In the early 1970s, the Court under Chief Justice Warren Burger's leadership issued a trilogy of busing-related decisions that—while upholding judicial efforts requiring states with Jim Crow schools to desegregate—made it extremely difficult to achieve desegregation in non–Jim Crow jurisdictions. In the 1990s, moreover, the Court led by Chief Justice William Rehnquist issued several opinions making unmistakably clear that the time for court-ordered desegregation directives had run its course. Consequently, the judiciary largely retreated from ordering desegregation not all that long before *Parents Involved*, under Chief Justice John Roberts's direction, went further by invalidating school boards' voluntarily undertaken desegregation plans. This legal landscape has left many progressives despondent. In recent years, the stubborn persistence of racial isolation in many underperforming urban schools across the country has motivated some sophisticated students of *Brown* even to question whether the twentieth century's most widely admired decision actually merits any admiration at all.

BROWN V. BOARD OF EDUCATION:
THE EQUAL PROTECTION CLAUSE CONFRONTS SEGREGATION

In September 1950, a railroad welder in Topeka, Kansas, named Oliver Brown accompanied his seven-year-old daughter, Linda, on what he knew was a doomed effort to enroll her in the local elementary school that stood a mere seven blocks from their house. After arriving at the Sumner School, Brown entered the principal's private office, leaving Linda outside in the waiting room, where she could nonetheless overhear adults using elevated voices to discuss her potential enrollment in a brief, but increasingly acrimonious, meeting. As predicted, the principal informed Brown that Sumner did not accept black students, relying upon statewide legislation that permitted Kansans to segregate or integrate schools in their communities as they deemed fit. That the outcome was predictable, however, evidently did little to cushion the blow for Brown, an intensely religious man who served as an assistant pastor in a local church. Even many years later, Linda could still recall the aggravation that consumed her typically subdued father when he retrieved her from the waiting room, took her by the hand, and walked briskly toward home. The rejection from Sumner meant that Linda would be forced to resume her studies at the all-black Monroe School, located much farther away than Sumner. In order to arrive on time at Monroe, Linda was forced to depart from home eighty minutes before classes began and to walk several blocks— part of which took her through a railroad-switching yard—in order to reach a bus that transported her the remaining distance. This unwelcome state of affairs motivated the Browns, with the assistance of the NAACP's Legal Defense and Educational Fund (LDF), to initiate a lawsuit challenging racial segregation in Topeka's public schools. On May 17, 1954, nearly four years after the Topeka dispute began, the Supreme Court resolved the matter along with four additional school segregation cases—originating in Wilmington, Delaware; Clarendon County, South Carolina; Prince Edward County, Virginia; and Washington, D.C.—that have collectively come to be known as simply *Brown v. Board of Education.*[1]

Chief Justice Earl Warren's opinion for a unanimous Court in *Brown* held that segregated public schools violated the Equal Protection Clause. In reaching that conclusion, Warren contended that inquiring what the Fourteenth Amendment's framers thought of racially segregated education in 1868, when the amendment was ratified, or even how the Court in *Plessy v. Ferguson* understood that issue in 1896, represented a futile endeavor because the nation's public schools had dramatically expanded since those times. Warren sidestepped *Cumming v. Richmond County Board of Education* and *Lum v. Rice* by observing that neither case directly challenged the constitutionality of school segregation, but instead involved more tangential claims. Whatever precedent indicated, moreover, Warren emphasized that segregated schooling had grown incompatible with the modern role of education, which the opinion called "the very foundation of good citizenship" and "perhaps the most important function of state and local governments." "Today [education] is a principal instrument in awakening the child to cultural values, in preparing him for later professional training, and in helping him to adjust normally to his environment," he continued. "In these days, it is doubtful that any child may reasonably be expected to succeed in life if he is denied the opportunity of an education. Such an opportunity . . . is a right which must be made available to all on equal terms."[2] Warren further noted that the Court had recently rejected *Plessy's* "separate, but equal" doctrine in the context of graduate schools, and contended that the logic of those decisions contained "added force . . . in grade and high schools. To separate [black children] from others of similar age and qualifications solely because of their race generates a feeling of inferiority as to their status in the community that may affect their hearts and minds in a way unlikely ever to be undone."[3]* After declaring segregated schools unconstitutional, Warren concluded by noting that the Court would revisit how to remedy the violation in the coming months.†

---

* Warren continued, "Whatever may have been the extent of psychological knowledge at the time of *Plessy v. Ferguson*, this finding is amply supported by modern authority." *Brown v. Board of Education*, 347 U.S. 483, 494 (1954). Warren appended to this sentence *Brown's* notorious footnote 11, which cited a variety of sociological and psychological materials, including Gunnar Myrdal's *American Dilemma: The Negro Problem and Modern Democracy* (1944) and studies involving race and doll preferences conducted by Kenneth Clark. Warren's citation of these materials, which struck many as decidedly nonlegal, generated a firestorm of criticism. Notably, some of the skepticism on this point originated from quarters that would have been expected to accord *Brown* a warm reception. See, for example, James Reston, "A Sociological Decision: Court Founded Its Segregation Ruling on Hearts and Minds Rather than Laws," *New York Times*, May 18, 1954, 14 ("The court's opinion read more like an expert paper on sociology than a Supreme Court opinion"); and Edmond Cahn, "Jurisprudence," 30 *NYU Law Review* 150 (1955). For recent scholarship exploring footnote 11, see Michael Heise, "*Brown v. Board of Education*, Footnote 11, and Multidisciplinarity," 90 *Cornell Law Review* 279 (2005); and Sanjay Mody, "*Brown* Footnote Eleven in Historical Context: Social Science and the Supreme Court's Quest for Legitimacy," 54 *Stanford Law Review* 793 (2002).

† The Supreme Court in *Bolling v. Sharpe* invalidated school segregation in Washington, D.C., but used a different rationale from the cases arising from the states. Rather than relying upon the Fourteenth Amendment—which applies to state, but not federal, entities—the Court relied upon the Fifth Amendment. While the Fifth Amendment does apply to the federal government (including Washington, D.C.), and contains a Due Process Clause, it lacks an Equal Protection Clause. Chief Justice Warren's opinion for the Court in *Bolling* reasoned that "the concepts of equal protection and due process, both stemming from our American ideal of fairness, are not mutually exclusive"

Many mainstream newspapers celebrated *Brown*, even as they sometimes offset their praise by noting that the opinion would prove difficult to implement. *The Washington Post*, foremost among mainstream celebrants, greeted *Brown* with unqualified admiration. "It is not too much to speak of the Court's decision as a new birth of freedom," the *Post* exalted.[4] Trailing not far behind the *Post's* appreciation, *The Cincinnati Enquirer* predicted *Brown* "will prove to be the most important judicial finding in the field of racial relations in our entire national history," and announced, "What the justices have done is simply to act as the conscience of the American nation."[5] *The New York Times* endorsed a strikingly similar position: "The highest court in the land, the guardian of our national conscience, has reaffirmed its faith—and the undying American faith—in the equality of all men and all children before the law." Yet the *Times* tempered its assessment by emphasizing that "[t]hese matters cannot be hurried" and asserting that "[n]o one can deny that the mingling of the races in [desegregated schools] will create problems" by upending "[t]he folkways in Southern communities."[6] The *New York Herald Tribune* matched its competitor's ambivalence toward *Brown*, as consecutive sentences adopted competing tenors: "In yesterday's historic decision the Supreme Court . . . squared the country's basic law with its conscience and deepest convictions. No one can deny that it will be difficult to abolish segregation for the public school system of the South."[7]

Among prominent non-southern editorial boards, *The Wall Street Journal* accorded *Brown* the most skeptical reception. Although it both called *Brown* "inevitable" and asserted that "[t]he justices have not so much made history as followed it," the *Journal* nevertheless registered a Burkean objection, contending the decision rashly toppled the South's time-honored cultural traditions:

> [I]t does not comport . . . with the equity of government to require the people of a large region to tear down overnight the whole social structure which, though we are apt to forget it today, is rooted in ancient social necessity. To many Southerners today the concern over ending segregation in the public school is not

---

and concluded that "it would be unthinkable" to invalidate segregated schools in the states but to preserve them in Washington, D.C. *Bolling v. Sharpe*, 347 U.S. 693, 693–95 (1954).

a matter of prejudice about race as such. Rather it is a concern over a conflict of cultures, and an honest conviction on the part of Southerners that their children will be injured in many areas by submergence in a culture that has not had time fully to mature.*

The *Journal* further declared that a judicial decree standing on its own could not successfully initiate such a foundational change to southern society: "[C]ourt rulings can avail little until the majority of a people who must live under them are able to accept them."[8]

While newspapers in the South almost invariably criticized *Brown*, they tended to use restraint in expressing their disapproval. *The Atlanta Constitution* produced perhaps the South's most conciliatory assessment. "[I]t is no time for hasty or ill-considered actions," the *Constitution* advised. "It is no time to indulge demagogues on either side or those who are always ready to incite violence and hatred. . . . It is a time for Georgia to think clearly. Our best minds must be put to work, not to destroy, but to arrive at constructive conclusions."[9] Relatedly, the New Orleans *Times-Picayune*'s reaction to *Brown* evinced more despondency than indignation: "The disappointment and frustration of the majority of Southerners at the revolutionary overturn of pra[c]tice and usage cannot immediately result in the improvement of race relations."[10] In Alabama, although *The Birmingham News* affirmed its continued belief in the "separate, but equal" view of the Equal Protection Clause, it did so with equanimity: "The *News* believes that the considerations of public interest and states' rights which underlay the superseded decision of [*Plessy*] still apply and would better serve progress in racial relations and education."[11] A glaring exception to the south-

---

* Although *National Review* did not debut until after the Court decided *Brown*, the publication also rejected the notion that opposing the decision should be viewed as tantamount to opposing racial equality. Instead, the magazine contended that opposing *Brown* could stem from distrust of an overreaching federal government: "[S]upport for the Southern position rests not at all on the question of whether Negro and White children should, in fact, study geography side by side; but on whether a central or a local authority should make that decision." "The South Girds Its Loins," *National Review*, Feb. 29, 1956, 5. To underscore this point, *National Review* added, "Segregated schooling, we repeat, is not the issue." Ibid., 6. *National Review*'s attempt to portray opposition to *Brown* as stemming from federalism concerns was not an isolated incident but part of a consistent strategy. To wit, "Whether considered juridically or morally, [school segregation] is a problem that should be solved not by the central government, but locally—in the states and their local subdivisions, and in the hearts of men." "Segregation and Democracy," *National Review*, Jan. 25, 1956, 5.

ern newspapers' trend of offering relatively mild criticisms of *Brown* arose in Jackson, Mississippi, where the *Daily News* denounced the opinion in the most incendiary terms available. "Human blood may stain Southern soil in many places because of this decision but the dark red stains of that blood will be on the marble steps of the United States Supreme Court building," the *Daily News* remonstrated. "White and Negro children in the same schools will lead to miscegenation. Miscegenation leads to mixed marriages and mixed marriages lead to mongrelization of the human race."[12]

In contrast, the black press saluted *Brown* as a major triumph in the quest for racial equality—a sentiment that the larger African American community shared. "Neither the atom bomb nor the hydrogen bomb will ever be as meaningful to our democracy as the unanimous declaration of the Supreme Court that racial segregation violates the spirit and letter of our Constitution," *The Chicago Defender* opined. "This means the beginning of the end of the dual society in American life and the . . . segregation which supported it."[13] Harlem's *Amsterdam News* concurred, calling *Brown* "the greatest victory for the Negro people since the Emancipation Proclamation."[14] Just outside Harlem, at Ralph Ellison's home, a radio bulletin trumpeting *Brown* caused the esteemed novelist to tremble with emotion as tears suddenly filled his eyes. "What a wonderful world of possibilities are unfolded for the children," Ellison rejoiced.[15] At least one black child affirmed Ellison's assessment of *Brown*—and selected similar words in so doing—as a young man in Natchitoches, Louisiana, said of the opinion, "I think it's the wonderfullest thing that's ever happened to America."[16] As Thurgood Marshall sat in the courtroom listening to Chief Justice Warren deliver *Brown*, the architect of the legal attack on school segregation was euphoric. "I was so happy, I was numb," Marshall recalled.[17] At a press conference following the decision, he predicted that it would take at most five years for school segregation to vanish from the nation. Back in Topeka, Linda Brown remembered her father arriving at home, receiving the welcome news, and—overwhelmed by its magnitude—embracing his family as he said solemnly, "Thanks be to God for this."[18]

While *Brown* has been a ubiquitous feature of the nation's constitutional conversation since 1954, both the opinion and its legacy remain unfamiliar in important respects. Returning to the text of

Brown itself helps to appreciate better why the opinion in some meaningful sense remains hidden in plain sight. *Brown*'s legacy, in turn, has become something of an awkward mishmash—as the opinion receives plaudits on the basis of some doubtful logic, and, conversely, revisionist scholars seek to demote *Brown*'s importance, also on the basis of questionable reasoning. By challenging claims that *Brown*'s unanimity accounts for a major part of its significance and, alternately, that the opinion emerged organically from a burgeoning national consensus supporting racial equality, we can attain a firmer grasp on what made *Brown* a distinct achievement and what did not.

At the outset, two insights about *Brown*'s text bear mentioning. First, in a framing choice that anticipated the future of education law, but that generally escapes detection in legal circles, *Brown* conceived of the constitutional deprivation at issue as belonging primarily to the students themselves, rather than—as some previous cases had—belonging more to their parents. In the most direct manifestation of this conceptual approach, Warren wrote, "In each of the cases, minors of the Negro race, through their legal representatives, seek the aid of the courts in obtaining admission to the public schools of their community on a nonsegregated basis."[19] Advancing the notion that pupils themselves hold constitutional rights that debuted in *Farrington v. Tokushige*, Warren's phrasing renders students the protagonists in this legal drama and consigns parents to a supporting role—a technique that would become commonplace within the Court's constitutional opinions involving education, and one that would contain significant implications. Spotlighting the students heightened the stakes involved—both by making clear that a constitutional deprivation here harms people in their most vulnerable, formative years and by stressing that the quality of their schooling would shape their entire lives. Americans have long imbued education with special meaning, and it is this exaltation of the schooling environment that made *Brown* the Supreme Court's most indispensable decision of the twentieth century. Had the Court undercut *Plessy* in a case arising from a different context—involving, say, transportation—that opinion would not have acquired the sanctified status that is accorded *Brown*. In addition, *Brown*'s construing students as constitutional stakeholders in their own right paved the path toward the watershed First Amendment decision in *Tinker*, where the Court extolled the importance of students expressing their independent ideas within schoolhouses fifteen years after *Brown*.[20]

Second, and of perhaps even greater moment, *Brown* left major questions unanswered regarding what the opinion actually prohibited. In the opinion's sentences that come closest to a summation, Warren wrote, "We conclude that in the field of public education the doctrine of 'separate but equal' has no place. Separate educational facilities are inherently unequal."[21] Did that statement indicate that *Brown* had condemned segregation in schools but left unaffected other forms of segregation, including in commuter travel and public parks? The Court soon clarified that this narrow, education-only reading of *Brown* was incorrect by issuing several terse decisions invalidating segregation in other walks of life. But other, gnawing questions lingered regarding what *Brown* required of educators. Did *Brown* merely eliminate state laws that either mandated or permitted school segregation? Or did it also require states to take affirmative steps to guarantee school integration? What applicability, if any, did *Brown* have on education in the North—where laws requiring school segregation had at least officially been abandoned before *Brown* but schools nonetheless remained racially identifiable?

It should have been no great surprise to the Supreme Court that *Brown* sparked a fierce contest to shape and control the opinion's meaning. Perceptive observers appreciated that this contest, involving such a combustible dispute, would occur—almost regardless of what the opinion actually held. Even before the Court issued *Brown*, a pair of law professors at the University of Arkansas wrote an article in the *Harvard Law Review* predicting with uncanny precision the dynamics that would soon engulf the Court's eagerly anticipated opinion:

> [N]obody will be really satisfied with the Court's decision. Each opposing group will at once start thinking about new litigation designed to press the Court forward—or backward, or sideways—to some more partisanly acceptable position. And legal issues in the new litigation will almost surely be presented not only in terms of what the Court actually says when it decides the pending cases but also in terms of what it might have said. . . . [S]killed lawyers will exploit the techniques of a system of law which from its beginnings has often made it easier to delay relief

than to give it, particularly when judges honestly sympathize with defendants' views.[22]

The authors also correctly predicted that segregationists would respond to an adverse decision in *Brown* by marshaling arguments that would endorse "voluntary" segregation, gerrymandered district lines to avoid integration, and other efforts to minimize the decision's effects.*

A central feature of *Brown*'s mythic status centers on its unanimity. The absence of dissenting opinions defending school segregation—particularly on a Supreme Court where justices had grown up under segregated conditions in Alabama (Justice Hugo Black), Kentucky (Justice Stanley Reed), and Texas (Justice Tom Clark)—arrived as a genuine surprise and earned immediate notice. As *The Washington Post*, to cite only one contemporaneous example, commented, "The unanimity of the decision . . . stand[s] as a tribute to the leadership of Chief Justice Earl Warren."[23] Stories eventually emerged from the Court's internal deliberations holding that Warren—who joined the Court only one year before *Brown*, after having served as governor of California—unleashed his formidable retail politicking skills on his fellow justices to pursue unanimity. On these accounts, Warren successfully cajoled his dubious and wavering colleagues, including some northerners, into joining *Brown*—until only Justice Reed retained his commitment to segregated schooling. Warren personally visited the final holdout to underscore yet again the importance of the Court being unanimous in order to avoid inflaming southern resistance. "Stan, you're all by yourself in this now," Warren said. "You've got to decide whether

---

* Within academia, scholars overwhelmingly defended *Brown*'s legitimacy. See, for example, Charles Fairman, "The Supreme Court, 1955 Term—Foreword: The Attack on the Segregation Cases," 70 *Harvard Law Review* 83, 83 (1956) (contending that in *Brown* the "Court [was] right, that it . . . acted with courage, and that it merits our confidence and support"). Five years after *Brown*, however, Professor Herbert Wechsler of Columbia aired doubts about the decision's theoretical underpinnings, even as he pledged his support for the cause of racial equality. See Herbert Wechsler, "Toward Neutral Principles of Constitutional Law," 73 *Harvard Law Review* 1 (1959). Wechsler's reservations about *Brown* received a swift, severe, and voluminous rebuke from his fellow scholars. See, for example, Charles L. Black Jr., "The Lawfulness of the Segregation Decisions," 69 *Yale Law Journal* 421 (1960); Arthur S. Miller and Ronald F. Howell, "The Myth of Neutrality in Constitutional Adjudication," 27 *University of Chicago Law Review* 661 (1960); and Louis H. Pollak, "Racial Discrimination and Judicial Integrity: A Reply to Professor Wechsler," 108 *University of Pennsylvania Law Review* 1 (1959).

[dissenting is] really the best thing for the country."[24] With this last push, Reed relented, and Warren had secured his much-prized unanimity. Insight into the significance that Warren attached to *Brown's* unanimity appears in the almost mystical fashion he discussed the matter in his posthumously published memoirs. Recounting his public delivery of the opinion, Warren wrote, "When the word 'unanimously' was spoken, a wave of emotions swept the room; no words or intentional movement, yet a distinct emotional manifestation that defies description."[25] One lawyer in attendance at the courtroom that day, Thurgood Marshall, said immediately afterward, "[T]he thing that is gratifying to me [about *Brown*] is that it was unanimous."[26] Apart from the case's central participants, moreover, some of legal academia's most insightful, sophisticated observers have periodically appeared to worship at the altar of *Brown's* unanimity. In 1979, Professor J. Harvie Wilkinson, not long before his elevation to the federal judiciary, asserted, "[I]t was . . . the unusualness of unanimity [on so divisive a question] that made [*Brown*] so effective."[27] In 2004, on the occasion of *Brown's* fiftieth anniversary, Professor Cass Sunstein wrote in *The New Yorker*, "[T]he fact that [*Brown*] was unanimous was little short of miraculous."[28]

Yet when one steps back to assess the implicit assumptions motivating such reverential attitudes toward *Brown's* unanimity, it becomes possible to appreciate that they proceed on highly dubious assumptions. The Court's unanimity was essential in *Brown*, Warren claimed, because a dissenting opinion would have encouraged southern opposition. As subsequent events would demonstrate, however, southerners proved more than capable of locating extrajudicial sources of encouragement for fomenting resistance to *Brown*. In 1956, for example, nineteen U.S. senators and approximately eighty congressmen joined forces to issue a document called the Southern Manifesto denouncing *Brown* as wrongly decided. And while it is theoretically true that the existence of a dissenting opinion would have further intensified anti-*Brown* sentiment in the South, that position seems strained because the actual opposition to racial equality manifested itself in a maximal form. To illustrate this point, consider that anti-*Brown* forces eventually coalesced around a rallying cry holding that they would accept racial integration exactly "never!" But this expression of resistance means that any additional boost provided by a dissenting opinion in *Brown* might have succeeded merely in shifting back their ideal timeline to never

and a day. What difference can that possibly make? The veneration of *Brown's* unanimity appears to rest on a severely exaggerated
understanding of the Supreme Court's ability to stifle opponents
by speaking with one voice, particularly on highly salient social
topics (as was true of racial segregation). Many, many outlets exist
for venting disagreement with a judicial opinion other than the
Supreme Court's official reporter.

Observers who continue to venerate *Brown's* unanimity mistakenly fail to contemplate what would have occurred had Justice Reed
opted to go it alone, filing a solitary dissent. Under this scenario,
a more attractive state of affairs might have ultimately emerged. It
seems eminently plausible to believe that Warren, without needing
to keep his least enthusiastic supporter on board, could have written
a more muscular opinion in *Brown*, adopting a harder line against
school segregation. Whatever extraordinarily small gain Warren
realized from *Brown's* unanimity in the form of squelched dissent, in
other words, could have been counterbalanced—and perhaps even
outweighed—by the attendant loss of watering down the opinion's
condemnation of Jim Crow. Finally, it would, of course, be inaccu-
rate to believe that the existence of a dissent—even a vehement one,
even on a highly combustible issue—necessarily means that foes of
a decision will become implacable. Two of the Court's experiences
protecting students' freedom of expression demonstrate this point:
it refused to require Jehovah's Witnesses to salute the American flag
during World War II, and it refused to allow educators to suppress
student opposition to the Vietnam War during the 1960s. While
few subjects possess greater capacity to stir passions than patriotism, those decisions did not encounter bitter-ender opposition—
even though they both were issued over the objection of apocalyptic
dissents. Thus, rather than continuing to champion Chief Justice
Warren's behind-the-scenes maneuvering in *Brown* uncritically, one
might more appropriately view those actions as well-intentioned
but ultimately misguided.[29]

In recent years, several prominent legal scholars have attempted
to diminish the significance of the Supreme Court's opinion
in *Brown* by contending that it grew from an emerging national
consensus on racial equality that only the South rejected. On this
account, school segregation laws are depicted as "outliers," as the
South is construed as a region whose racial backwardness stands
apart from the rest of a nation inclined toward racial egalitarian-

ism. Revisionists writing in this tradition frequently emphasize that post-*Brown* polling indicated that a narrow majority of Americans supported the opinion, and note further that only twenty-one states either required or permitted racial segregation in 1954, whereas twenty-seven states had no such laws. Instead of viewing *Brown* as an instance where the Court bravely protected a marginalized group in American society, revisionists insist that it is more accurate to view the decision as articulating the ascendant views of American society itself.[30]

This revisionist assessment of *Brown* misses the mark. As an initial matter, branding a phenomenon located in twenty-one states an "outlier" stretches that term beyond recognition. Jim Crow was no isolated practice, found in a handful of aberrational jurisdictions, but prevailed in much of the land.

In addition, the revisionist account falters because it mistakenly disregards the racial composition of the states as they existed during the 1950s. Revisionists thus attribute a sense of outrage about racial inequality to many northern whites who, to the extent they thought about black citizens at all, likely viewed America's racial dynamics more as an abstraction than as a reality. That claim is plausible because the overwhelming majority of black citizens lived in the twenty-one states that either required or permitted racially segregated schools. According to the 1950 census, thirteen states had populations greater than 10 percent black, and all thirteen of those states had racially segregated schools. Of the twenty-seven states where Jim Crow did not exist, moreover, fully nineteen had less than 3 percent black residents, and twelve had less than 1 percent black residents. If larger concentrations of black citizens existed throughout the country in 1954, it seems quite plausible that *Brown* would have garnered even less support than it did in fact. Shortly after the Court issued *Brown*, a white southerner who supported racial integration memorably pressed precisely this idea in an interview with Robert Penn Warren. "It is not a question of being Southern," he explained to Warren. "You put the same number of Yankee liberals in [a predominantly black] county and in a week they'd be behaving the same way [as southern segregationists]. Living with something and talking about it are two very different things, and living with something is always the slow way."[31]

This revisionist account also fails to persuade because it offers a much sunnier portrait of racially egalitarian attitudes in non-southern states than actually existed during the 1950s. Substantial polling data suggests that the nation's commitment to *Brown*, and by extension racial egalitarianism, was much weaker than revisionists typically allow. When Gallup conducted a nationwide poll asking whether the Constitution should be amended to overturn *Brown* in 1959, some five years after the Court's decision, a majority of respondents supported a constitutional amendment enabling states to determine for themselves whether schools were integrated or segregated. That same poll revealed, moreover, that 53 percent of respondents agreed *Brown* caused more trouble than it was worth, and only 37 percent of respondents disagreed. The results of a January 1956 poll revealed that, when asked whether most black citizens were being treated fairly or unfairly, 63 percent of respondents indicated that the treatment of blacks was fair, and just 32 percent stated that blacks were treated unfairly. A poll published in *Scientific American* in December 1956, which also asked whether most blacks were being treated fairly, revealed no dramatic regional disagreement on this question. Where the *Scientific American* poll found that 69 percent of the white public contended that most blacks were being treated fairly, 65 percent of white northerners agreed with the sentiment (in comparison with 79 percent of white southerners). Among northern whites thus the predominant reaction to black subordination seems more accurately characterized as apathy than enmity.

The decidedly limited commitment to racial equality on the part of white northerners after *Brown* can also be glimpsed by comparing their attitudes with white southerners' in subsequent years. In September 1956, when asked whether black students and white students should attend the same schools, 60 percent of white northerners indicated that they should attend the same schools. By comparison, in mid-1965, 55 percent of white southerners responded that students should attend integrated schools. Few people today, of course, would contend that the South had resolved its profound racial problems as early as mid-1965, a time that preceded even the Voting Rights Act's passage. Yet given the similarity in poll responses, it seems difficult to reconcile the vision of racially enlightened northern whites during the mid-1950s with the suggestion of racially backward southern whites during the mid-1960s.[32]

A SECOND LOOK AT *BROWN II*

Slightly more than a year after declaring segregated schools unconstitutional in *Brown*, the Supreme Court in May 1955 issued its follow-up decision, explicating how that decree would be implemented. This decision clarifying school segregation's remedy, which lawyers commonly call *Brown II*, occupies an ignominious place in the Court's history. Indeed, it risks only mild exaggeration to suggest that commentators love *Brown* and loathe *Brown II* in equal measures. *Brown II* is principally known for its enigmatic formulation, ordering desegregation to proceed "with all deliberate speed." Observers assert that this phrasing and the opinion generally represented the height of cowardice, betraying black schoolchildren by remanding the case to lower courts and refusing to grant immediate relief. As Professor Derrick Bell wrote in 2004, "Black people were disappointed . . . when the Court [issued *Brown II*]. Reflecting that disappointment, civil rights lawyer-historian Loren Miller wrote at the time, 'The harsh truth is that the first *Brown* decision was a great decision; the second *Brown* decision was a great mistake.'"[33] Professor Charles Black, who helped Thurgood Marshall's team draft the briefs challenging segregation, rendered a similarly negative verdict on *Brown II*: "I cannot acquit the Court of having made a terrible mistake in its . . . 'all deliberate speed' formula. There was just exactly no reason, in 1955, for thinking it would work better than an order to desegregate at once."[34]

Although these derisive assessments now capture the received wisdom toward *Brown II*, they make no genuine effort to contemplate the implementation issue from the vantage point of 1955. Situating *Brown II* in its actual historical moment, rather than one dimly perceived through the fog of memory, reveals that this derision directed toward the opinion surfaced only well after the event. Contrary to Professor Bell's characterization, Miller did not deliver his scathing assessment of *Brown II* until 1966—eleven long years after the decision. And Professor Black's excoriation of the decision would not appear until 1970. Proponents of racial equality did not immediately shower *Brown II* with condemnation, in large part because the opinion had not yet been distilled into the "all deliberate speed" axiom, which eventually became shorthand for the Court's desultory approach to desegregation. But it was not yet clear in 1955 that the Court would effectively retreat from this field for more than a decade. To the contrary, *Brown II* contained some countervailing language, now generally forgotten, suggesting that the Court would not countenance substantial delays in desegregation. The Court not only "require[d] . . . a prompt and reasonable start toward full compliance with [*Brown*]" but further stated that "it should go without saying that the vitality of these constitutional principles cannot be allowed to yield simply because of disagreement with them."[35] Ignoring such firm language in *Brown II* incorrectly suggests that an opinion's eventual reputation is always clear from the outset.

Appreciating how the public, the newspapers, and even the civil rights lawyers themselves received *Brown II* may temper at least some of the invective aimed at the Court for this decision. Following *Brown II*, when Gallup conducted a poll asking whether school integration should occur "gradually" or "in the near future," 74 percent of respondents in both the South and the non South preferred the gradual approach.[36] Major newspapers contended that the Court's implementation decree had struck an appropriate balance among the competing considerations in this thorny area. The *Los Angeles Times* contended that, while *Brown II* "will not suit the extremists, . . . we think most reasonable people will agree with it."[37] *The New York Times* echoed the notion that *Brown II* exhibited Solomonic judgment, as "[d]esegregation will move too slowly for some among us, perhaps too rapidly for others," and even commended the Court for avoiding "[t]he error of a static and ineffective edict."[38] *The Wall Street Journal* stated simply, "It was a fair decision and a wise one."[39]

While the lawyers pursuing desegregation had encouraged the Court to specify some particular date for compliance, any immediate disappointment with *Brown II*'s looser approach quickly subsided. On the heels of the decision, Thurgood Marshall and his associate Robert Carter co-authored an article in *The Journal of Negro Education* calling *Brown II* "a good [decision]"—one that should instill "an attitude of quiet confidence"—and suggested "the formula devised is about as effective as one could have expected."[40] Some may dismiss this document as seeking merely to feign a brave public face to mask what was in fact a grievous blow. But this interpretation collapses when one considers that Marshall's early private reaction to *Brown II* strongly resembled his public position. In a telephone conversation with an old friend following the decision, Marshall exclaimed, "I think it's a damned good decision!" In his folksy manner of speaking, Marshall added that any dissatisfaction with *Brown II* should be rejected as permitting the perfect to be the enemy of the good. "[S]ome people want most of the hog, other people insist on having the whole hog, and then there are some people who want the hog, the hair, and the rice on the hair. What the hell!"[41]*

Understanding the Court's high degree of uncertainty surrounding whether President Dwight Eisenhower would support a decision calling for immediate, widespread school desegregation in 1955 further complicates efforts to portray *Brown II* as an inexcusable error. One year earlier, President Eisenhower had squarely resisted several opportunities to embrace the Court's opinion in *Brown*. "I think it makes no difference whether or not I endorse it," he stated.[42]† Without the executive branch's backing, a judicial order calling for desegregation to occur overnight would run an incredibly high risk of being declared dead on arrival. Such a declaration might have severely impeded the quest for racial equality. The Court might have quite conceivably preferred an ambiguous order, producing at least some desegregation, over an aggressively phrased order that would wilt in the face of modest resistance.

Even before the Court officially issued its initial decision rejecting segregated schools, moreover, Chief Justice Warren had powerful reason to believe that Eisenhower supported Jim Crow. In the spring of 1954, Warren arrived at the White House for a small dinner party and was surprised to learn that one of his dining compan-

---

* By the late 1970s, Justice Marshall began asserting that *Brown II* deeply disappointed him immediately: "In 1954 . . . I thought I was the smartest lawyer in the entire world. In 1955 . . . I thought I was the dumbest Negro in the United States." Dennis J. Hutchinson, *"Brown in the Supreme Court,"* 6 *Journal of Appellate Practice and Process* 11, 16 (2004). Marshall's disappointment with *Brown II*, however, seemed to have grown exponentially over time, as he—like many of us—appeared to recast subsequent impressions of events as having materialized in the first instance.

† Several perceptive commentators have suggested that Ike's non-endorsement of *Brown* bears a large share of the responsibility for fomenting southern resistance. Constance Baker Motley—an esteemed civil rights attorney who eventually became a federal judge—assailed him in the strongest terms possible: "Eisenhower should never be forgiven for his failure to lead the nation into its new era at that critical time." Constance Baker Motley, *Equal Justice Under Law* 110 (1998). Chief Justice Warren similarly contended, "With his popularity, if Eisenhower had said that black children were still being discriminated against [and] that the Supreme Court of the land had now declared it unconstitutional to continue such cruel practices, . . . we would have been relieved . . . of many of the racial problems which have continued to plague us." Earl Warren, *The Memoirs of Earl Warren* 291 (1977).

ions was John W. Davis, who had represented the South Carolina school district at oral argument. Eisenhower—despite knowing that the Court had *Brown* under review—not only seated Warren close to Davis but also sang Davis's praises at length to Warren. Following dinner, as the guests retired to an adjacent room for coffee, Eisenhower took Warren by the arm and made a stunning statement that went to the heart of opposition to school desegregation. "These are not bad people," Eisenhower said, speaking of white southerners. "All they are concerned about is to see that their sweet little girls are not required to sit in school alongside some big black bucks."[43] Given Eisenhower's crude expression of sympathy for opponents of interracial intimacy, the marvel of the Court's pair of *Brown* decisions seems less that the second opinion adopted a circumspect approach to the pace of desegregation, and more that the first opinion prohibited the practice at all.

Eisenhower's language, while detestable, accurately identified the crux of white opposition to school desegregation: a crippling fear that integrated classrooms would lead to integrated bedrooms. While prominent segregationists frequently identified antimiscegenation as the foremost reason for opposing *Brown*, that reasoning no longer occupies a central place in the cultural imagination of school desegregation. Recovering this language, however, is essential both to apprehending what fundamentally animated the intense hostility to *Brown* and to understanding more fully why the Court would have been hesitant in *Brown II* to require immediate school integration. Neither a reflexive squeamishness about discussing sexual matters nor reluctance to address stereotypes of black male hypersexuality should be permitted to prevent grappling with this significant issue of the *Brown* era.

Examples abound where prominent southerners equated opposition to *Brown* with opposition to miscegenation. Shortly after *Brown*, the Alabama state senator Sam Engelhardt Jr. offered a particularly hysterical version of the antimiscegenation argument, fulminating, "[D]esegregating the schools will lead to rape! . . . The nigger is depraved! Give him the opportunity to be near a white woman, and he goes berserk! . . . The nigger isn't just a dark-skinned white man. He's a separate individual altogether."[44] But even more refined articulations of this view drew upon a common vocabulary of inflammatory rhetoric—warning of "amalgamation," "mongrelization," and racial destruction. The Mississippi judge

Tom P. Brady, a graduate of the Lawrenceville School and Yale University, quickly produced a slender volume condemning *Brown*, provocatively titled *Black Monday: Segregation or Amalgamation . . . America Has Its Choice*. For Brady, defending school segregation meant protecting "the inviolability of Southern Womanhood"—a vital mission because "[t]he loveliest and the purest of God's creatures . . . is a well-bred, cultured Southern white woman or her blue-eyed golden haired little girl."[45]* Fellow Mississippian and U.S. senator James Eastland stated, "Generations of Southerners yet unborn will cherish our memory because they will realize that the fight we now wage [against *Brown*] will have preserved for them their untainted racial heritage, their culture, and the institutions of the Anglo-Saxon race."[46] In *U.S. News and World Report*, South Carolina's governor Jimmy Byrnes—a former U.S. Supreme Court justice—forthrightly acknowledged that the "fundamental objection to integration" stemmed from whites' "fear of mongrelization." "Southerners fear that the purpose of those who lead the fight for integration in schools," Byrnes explained, "is to break down social barriers in childhood and the period of adolescence, and ultimately bring about intermarriage of the races. . . . To prevent this, the white people of the South are willing to make every sacrifice."[47] James J. Kilpatrick, an intellectual leader of the South's resistance to *Brown* based in Richmond, Virginia, shared Byrnes's dire assessment: "To integrate the schools of the Southern States . . . is to risk . . . a widespread racial amalgamation and a debasement of the society as a whole. This the Southern States are determined to resist. They will resist for a long, long time."[48]†

---

* Incredibly, in the mid-1960s, some Mississippians attacked Brady for being soft on segregation. After overturning an African American's criminal conviction because blacks had systematically been excluded from the jury, Brady received threatening late-night phone calls asserting he was a "nigger lover." See Neil R. McMillen, *The Citizens' Council: Organized Resistance to the Second Reconstruction, 1954–64* 265–66 (1994).

† White southerners' fears that desegregated schools would lead to interracial sex were so strong that many school districts in the 1960s and 1970s opted to integrate students along racial lines but simultaneously imposed segregation along gender lines. With that technique, black girls and white girls would attend schools together, and black boys and white boys would do the same, but the most dreaded sexual combination of white females and black males could safely be averted. Relying upon *Brown II*, many federal lower courts blessed this practice over many years. Indeed, federal courts preserved this arrangement until the astoundingly late date of 1977, more than two decades after *Brown II*, when an appellate court finally eliminated this rearguard technique. See *United States v. Hinds County School Board*, 560 F.2d 619 (5th Cir. 1977) (invalidating sex-

While such antimiscegenation rhetoric may further the widely held impression that white southerners universally greeted *Brown* with obstinacy and intransigence, it is essential to realize that some segregationists reacted to the decision with creativity and flexibility. In the wake of *Brown II*, no single individual better exemplified how tenacious support for Jim Crow could peacefully coexist alongside sophisticated legal efforts to forestall school desegregation than Senator Sam Ervin of North Carolina.

In April 1956, Ervin—a graduate of Harvard Law School and a former justice on the North Carolina Supreme Court—wrote a remarkable article in *Look* where he announced, "I believe in racial segregation as it exists in the South today," and condemned those "who seek immediate mixing of races in public schools."[49] Rather than only attacking *Brown*, however, Senator Ervin—in the beginning stages of a trajectory that many others would eventually follow—also began to hedge his bets. "While the Supreme Court decision is deplorable from the standpoint of constitutional law and ought to be reversed for that reason," Ervin stated, "it is not as drastic as many people think."[50] To support the notion that *Brown* should not be understood as mandating the dreaded day of integration, Ervin latched onto a recently decided lower court opinion that construed *Brown* very narrowly—finding it required only the ending of officially segregated schools, and therefore imposed no affirmative obligation on districts to create integrated schools. But after initially claiming that *Brown* was both "deplorable" and "not as drastic as many people think," Ervin eased away from the first part of that formulation, leaving only the second.

By August 1963, Ervin made a concerted effort to limit *Brown*'s reach during hearings about a civil rights bill. Rather than repudiating *Brown* in his questioning of Attorney General Robert Kennedy, Ervin criticized "educators who want racially balanced schools," and posed the following loaded question:

---

segregated public schools in Amite County, Mississippi). For an early article examining the constitutionality of such sex segregation, written by a law student who would eventually become an influential attorney and a power broker in the book publishing world, see Robert B. Barnett, Comment, "The Constitutionality of Sex Separation in School Desegregation Plans," 37 *University of Chicago Law Review* 296 (1970). For a thoughtful historical treatment of the topic, see Serena Mayeri, "The Strange Career of Jane Crow: Sex Segregation and the Treatment of Anti-discrimination Discourse," 18 *Yale Journal of Law and the Humanities* 187 (2006).

Do you not agree with me that denying a school child the right
to attend his neighborhood school and transferring him by bus
or otherwise to another community for the purpose of racially
mixing the school in that other community is a violation of the
Fourteenth Amendment as interpreted by the Supreme Court in
Brown versus Board of Education?[51]

Kennedy responded that he did not quite understand the question and, according to one reporter in attendance, "twisted a bit
in his chair," as Ervin repeated the precisely worded query. "You
could make an argument along those lines," Kennedy weakly and
noncommittally responded. "I don't see how you can disagree with
me," Ervin replied with a grin.[52] Five years later, Ervin announced
his conversion to the gospel of colorblind constitutionalism.

Finally, when his autobiography appeared in 1984, Ervin
acknowledged that he now fully accepted that *Brown* was correctly
decided in the first instance and that he was wrong to have ever
doubted its legitimacy. "The Constitution is . . . color-blind as
the first Justice John Marshall Harlan maintained in his dissent in
Plessy v. Ferguson," Ervin wrote, "and [*Brown*] requires the States to
ignore the race of school children in assigning them to their public
schools."[53] It is this same colorblind understanding of the Equal
Protection Clause that many modern legal conservatives espouse
today.

The foregoing effort to complicate the withering attacks on
Brown II should in no way be mistaken for commending the Court's
handling of desegregation as a general proposition. To the contrary,
I heartily endorse the criticism holding that the Warren Court
moved much too slowly in pursuing school desegregation, even as I
insist that its tentative approach in 1955, when placed in the broader
historical context, has received excessive scorn. The predominant
problem with the Court's approach to desegregation dates not to
1955 but to the late 1950s and extends through the 1960s. After
issuing *Brown II*, the Court—incomprehensibly—disengaged from
the field for the next thirteen years. When President Eisenhower in
1957 dispatched federal troops to Little Rock, Arkansas, to secure
the integration of Central High School, it should have been clear
to the Court that Ike's qualms about *Brown* were superseded by his
commitment to enforcing the rule of law. Although one year later

the Court issued an opinion emanating from the dispute, it seized the opportunity primarily to assert its own authority as the ultimate interpreter of the Constitution, rather than to establish the ultimate importance of school desegregation. Even allowing for some period of reluctance about returning to the race question following the Little Rock episode, however, cannot explain why the Warren Court watched idly during the whole of the John Kennedy administration and nearly the entirety of the Lyndon Johnson administration before its members began to flesh out the meaning of *Brown*.[54]

Not until May 1968, one month before Chief Justice Warren announced that he would resign, did the Supreme Court issue a desegregation decision of any real consequence in *Green v. County School Board of New Kent County*. The case arose from a small town in rural Virginia that had only two high schools. Prior to *Brown*, whites attended one school and blacks attended the other. Following passage of civil rights legislation in the 1960s, which threatened economic sanctions against the South's segregated school districts, New Kent County introduced a student choice mechanism. But precious little changed. Three years after the new system was adopted, no white child had ever elected to attend the (theoretically former) all-black school, and only 15 percent of the black pupils elected to attend the formerly all-white school. The Supreme Court in *Green* voted unanimously to invalidate this choice plan as violating the Fourteenth Amendment and stated it was incumbent upon the school board to take "whatever steps might be necessary" to eliminate segregation, "convert[ing] promptly to a system without a 'white' school and a 'Negro' school, but *just schools*."[55] Instead of permitting the passive approach to desegregation, *Green* imposed upon district officials "the affirmative duty to take whatever steps might be necessary to convert to a unitary system in which racial discrimination would be eliminated root and branch."[56] Making clear that the time for "all deliberate speed" had elapsed, *Green* required the school board "to come forward with a plan that promises realistically to work, and promises realistically to work *now*."[57]

After the justices filed into the courtroom to announce the decision in *Green*, Chief Justice Warren passed a celebratory note down to the opinion's author, his dear friend Justice William Brennan. "When this opinion is handed down, the traffic light will have changed from *Brown* to *Green*. Amen!"[58] As things turned out, however, Warren's metaphor would unwittingly prove all too accurate, for not long after his exclamation the traffic light of desegregation briefly flashed a cautionary yellow before turning solidly red.

DESEGREGATION AND BUSING IN CHARLOTTE, NORTH CAROLINA, DENVER, COLORADO, AND DETROIT, MICHIGAN

In the early 1970s, the Supreme Court in rapid succession issued three major opinions implicating the use of busing for desegregation. Although the first opinion—*Swann v. Charlotte-Mecklenburg Board of Education*—heartened desegregation's proponents by upholding an extensive busing plan ordered by a district court, the Supreme Court did so only in the course of further entrenching the troubling distinction between de facto and de jure segregation. While the second opinion—*Keyes v. School District No. 1, Denver, Colorado*—acknowledged that unconstitutionally segregated schools existed outside the South, the Court nevertheless imputed liability to non-southern jurisdictions only by identifying intentionally discriminatory acts, a technique that made it unduly difficult for civil rights plaintiffs to prevail on desegregation suits. In the final opinion of this trilogy, the Supreme Court in *Milliken v. Bradley* invalidated a district court order requiring cross-district busing in Detroit, Michigan, closing the door on any realistic hope of meaningful integration in many metropolitan areas during an era when many whites fled cities for suburbia. With the benefit of hindsight, it seems clear that Chief Justice Warren Burger's early maneuvering in *Swann*, to write the opinion in as minimalist a fashion as possible to uphold the Charlotte decree, proved critical in facilitating the diminishment of busing as a consequential tool of desegregation.

SWANN V. CHARLOTTE-MECKLENBURG BOARD OF EDUCATION

In 1964, a six-year-old black student in Charlotte, North Carolina, named James Swann was denied admission to his local elementary school, not far from his home on a college campus, where his father worked as a theology professor. Due to the family's relative insulation from economic reprisals that often visited challengers of the racial status quo, local civil rights lawyers identified the Swanns as ideal lead plaintiffs to challenge not merely James's exclusion from his local school but all vestiges of the discriminatory dual school system in Charlotte's Mecklenburg County. The mammoth school system encompassed the entire county, whose 550 square miles ran nearly twice the size of New York City; approximately 30 percent of its eighty-four thousand students traveled to school by bus—even before busing for the purpose of racial desegregation ever entered the picture. Extensive uses of school buses occurred so commonly throughout the state that North Carolina had once proudly branded itself "the schoolbusingest state in the Union." But that moniker was selected long before the iconic yellow school bus had become transformed into a divisive symbol of the search for desegregated educational opportunities. In the late 1960s, a federal district court, taking its cue from the Supreme Court's decision in *Green*, ordered Mecklenburg County to engage in a busing program designed to ensure that its black students, who were concentrated within Charlotte's city limits, did not continue attending racially isolated schools. In a fascinating twist, Senator Sam Ervin, a leader of the South's legal opposition to *Brown*, was responsible for placing the district court judge who issued *Swann* on the federal bench. "I am not infallible," Ervin stated, "and . . . conclusive evidence of that fact is to be found in my recommendation of Jim McMillan for the District Judgeship."[59]

Within many white homes in suburban Charlotte, Judge McMillan's busing mandate provoked anxiety, mobilization, and—finally—determination to overturn the decision. In a significant shift, however, opposition to the judicial order did not generally manifest itself in the overtly racist appeals that emerged in the wake of *Brown* fifteen years earlier. Instead, opponents of the busing order generally framed their opposition in nonracial terms, depicting themselves as concerned about neighborhood schools, quality education, and the disruptions that would flow from revising the existing school arrangements. As the case worked its way to the Supreme Court, *The New York Times*—in an article headlined "Parents in Charlotte, Even Those Who Favor Integration, Deeply Resent Racial Busing"—portrayed the order's opponents sympathetically. "When Mrs. Jane Love found that her young son would have to be bused this year to a school 12 miles from their neighborhood," the article opened, "she cried. . . . Silly or not, there is nothing unusual nowadays about Mrs. Love's instinctive, emotional reaction against the idea of moving children around in buses to achieve racial balance in the schools. Indeed, few things seem to stir American passions so deeply." The article also detailed a white family who relocated to North Carolina from Little Rock, Arkansas, where they claimed to entertain black guests regularly in their home, but who nonetheless rejected "the absurd idea that [their] child must sacrifice in the name of social reform."[60] Almost overnight, bumper stickers emblazoned with "No Forced Busing"—printed in red, white, and blue—became a ubiquitous sight in Mecklenburg County, and some white students protested the district court order by carrying placards that read, "Integration, Yes! Busing, No!"[61] The tenor of antibusing attitudes, even in the absence of explicitly racial appeals, often reached a frenzied pitch. At an antibusing rally held in a school auditorium, for example, a military veteran reported, "I served in Korea, I served in Vietnam, and I'll serve in Charlotte if I need to."[62]

Disdain for the busing order motivated an insurance executive named Thomas Harris, a graduate of Duke University who owned a home in suburban Charlotte, to start the Concerned Parents Association (CPA), the region's most prominent antibusing organization. Like many Charlotte citizens, Harris consistently maintained that CPA did not oppose integration, but instead opposed only the judicial order that he deemed an almost surreal instance of governmental overreach. "My first reaction [to the busing order] was one of disbelief," Harris observed. "I did not believe there was any possibility whatsoever that the government was going to dictate where my kids were going to public school. It was crazy; it was not going to happen."[63] One of Harris's fellow CPA leaders echoed this basic idea: "I couldn't believe such a thing could happen in America. So many of us made the biggest investment of our lives—our homes—primarily on the basis of their location with regard to schools. It seemed like an absurdity that anyone could tell us where to send our children."[64] In order to illustrate their purported lack of racial animus, CPA affirmatively sought to recruit black parents to join their fight. Those overtures, however, yielded little success. "Where were the cries of indignation when millions of blacks were bused daily . . . to lesser schools?" one black father wondered. "Where were the cries of 'unconstitutional'?"[65]

During the months preceding the Supreme Court's official consideration of *Swann v. Charlotte-Mecklenburg Board of Education*, two developments of national significance occurred that warrant addressing. First, in March 1970, President Richard Nixon issued an elaborate written statement indicating his administration's opposition to expanding efforts to achieve meaningfully integrated schools. President Nixon dutifully recited his support for *Brown* and efforts to challenge what he referred to as the "[d]eliberate racial segregation of pupils," but he also emphasized that neighborhood schools should serve as the default assignment for students and signaled his opposition to busing: "Transportation of pupils beyond normal geographic school zones for the purpose of achieving racial balance will not be required."[66] Nixon further instructed that racially imbalanced schools may be attributable to a mixture of de jure and de facto considerations. "In such a case, it is appropriate to insist on remedy for the de jure portion, which is unlawful, without insisting on a remedy for the lawful de facto portion," Nixon asserted. "De facto racial separation, resulting genuinely from housing patterns, exists in the South as well as in the North."[67] (This final claim motivated Jack Greenberg, Thurgood Marshall's successor at the NAACP's Legal Defense and Educational Fund, to sputter in response, "How can you have de facto segregation in Jackson, Mississippi?")[68] Nixon's statement used the bully pulpit in anticipation of *Swann* to influence public sentiment generally, but he might have also had in mind a more targeted audience; at that time, Nixon had already succeeded in tapping Warren Burger to replace Earl Warren as chief justice and would soon get Harry Blackmun confirmed to replace Abe Fortas as an associate justice, the first two of what would eventually become his four Supreme Court appointments.

The second noteworthy pre-*Swann* development, in some tension with the first, involved external expectations of how broadly the next Supreme Court opinion involving schools and race would sweep, as several commentators expected that the Court would no longer treat school segregation as a peculiarly southern phenomenon. As *Time* commented in September 1970, one month before oral argument in *Swann*, "The implications of the court's decision will be important to both the South and the North. Court support for integration would force the North to take action to eliminate the *de facto* segregation that prevails in such cities as Boston, New York, Chicago and Los Angeles."[69] Similarly, the *Chicago Tribune* projected the same month that *Swann* would amount to "a national landmark decision," upending student assignment plans in the Windy City and beyond, by requiring "busing and other techniques to achieve racial balance."[70] Even after oral argument, an op-ed piece published in *The Wall Street Journal*, while allowing that *Swann* originated in the South, still confidently predicted, "[T]he decision will affect every public school in the land."[71]

The Supreme Court defied these expectations in 1971, when Chief Justice Burger wrote a unanimous opinion in *Swann* upholding the district court's pro-desegregation order but making no effort to articulate a nationwide judicial standard that would also cover de facto segregated schools. In the course of validating the lower court order under review, however, Burger's opinion adopted an extremely tough legal line on locales that practiced de jure segregation. Most saliently, Burger's opinion emphatically refused to invalidate—let alone demonize—the practice of busing. To the contrary, Burger observed that the school bus was, in effect, as American as the Fourth of July—as he noted that nearly 40 percent of the nation's students rode buses to school, making it "a normal and accepted tool of educational policy."[72] Accordingly, Burger could see no reason why the judiciary should be prohibited from altering Mecklenburg County's bus routes to overcome segregation.

In addition, *Swann* endowed courts combating de jure segregation with great authority to use what it termed even "drastic . . . gerrymandering" of school attendance zones, as the order under review created "zones [that] are neither compact nor contiguous . . . [and] may be on opposite ends of the city."[73] In spelling out this authority, Burger noted that a school district with de jure segregation could not overcome its history simply by beginning to assign students to schools on a colorblind basis. "[A]ffirmative action in the form of remedial altering of attendance zones is proper to achieve truly nondiscriminatory assignments," Burger wrote. "[A]n assignment plan is not acceptable simply because it appears to be neutral."[74] *Swann* established that district courts, in formulating remedies for de jure segregation, were permitted to contemplate the school system's racial composition as a whole—a practice that advocates of colorblindness loathed because they claimed it would lead to "racial balancing."[75] Finally, in language that would become hotly disputed during the Court's most recent school desegregation decision in 2007, *Swann* expressly noted that *educators*—though not *judges*—retained discretion to consider the race of students to promote integration, even if they chose to do so in the context of de facto segregation:

> School authorities are traditionally charged with broad power to formulate and implement educational policy and might well conclude, for example, that in order to prepare students to live in a pluralistic society each school should have a prescribed ratio of Negro to white students reflecting the proportion for the district as a whole. To do this as an educational policy is within the broad discretionary powers of school authorities.[76]

Major newspapers from a range of ideological perspectives praised *Swann*, with a conspicuous strand of this commentary lauding Chief Justice Burger for refusing to enshrine President Nixon's political rhetoric into constitutional doctrine. As *The New York Times* editorialized, "Chief Justice Burger has served notice to those inside and outside the Administration who would ignore or obstruct earlier rulings identified with his predecessor that he does not intend to allow the Supreme Court to be undercut or influenced by political pressures in the area of civil rights."[77] *The Washington Post* added that *Swann* "shatter[ed] this Nixon doctrine [on busing], and reopen[ed] the desegregation issue that he had sought to foreclose in the cities of the South."[78] But a *Los Angeles Times* columnist expressed this point most memorably: "Burger has shown that he didn't come on the court to be President Nixon's judicial messenger boy."[79]* Although *The Wall Street Journal* did not frame its *Swann* editorial as a repudiation of President Nixon, it nonetheless viewed the opinion in favorable terms, however grudgingly. "[I]t's difficult to fault the Supreme Court's decision supporting busing to promote racial desegregation of the schools," the *Journal* noted. "Local officials actually had given the court little choice. . . . The fact is that school buses have been used increasingly for many years. In some Southern districts, where busing to achieve desegregation has

---

* In a sophisticated analysis, this column proceeded to contend that—while Chief Justice Burger's vote clashed with President Nixon's busing position—*Swann* may ultimately be viewed as redounding to Nixon's electoral benefit in his impending reelection campaign: "Actually—and here is the irony of it—by deciding contrary to Mr. Nixon's position (of minimal desegregation and the neighborhood 'walk-in' school) he may have helped Mr. Nixon politically. For the decision takes the constitutional props out from under Mr. Nixon's position and thus gives him an out with his Southern constituencies." Max Lerner, "Round Two on Integration," *Los Angeles Times*, April 25, 1971, G6.

been bitterly opposed, buses were used to preserve segregation."[80] Finally, the *Minneapolis Tribune* fused the anti-Nixon commentary with the *Journal*'s critique that the outcome in *Swann* had been dictated by educators' prior bad-faith considerations of race: "The Court directly rejected President Nixon's oft-stated case against compulsory busing to achieve racial balance, implicitly exposing the hypocrisy of northerners and southerners who have used busing to achieve racial separation."[81]

Swann also placed many white southerners in mind of hypocrisy. They tended to read the decision as imposing a demanding standard on their region and effectively sparing the North, with no compelling justification for the disparate treatment. Among southern editorial boards, for instance, the *Clarion-Ledger* in Jackson, Mississippi, emphasized this point with gallows humor, as it suggested *Swann*'s "supreme irony [means] many Southern families seeking segregated public schools for their children might find it necessary to emigrate North . . . where segregation survives unruffled by Supreme Court decisions."[82] Southern elected officials, who practiced widely varying racial politics, also bemoaned the Court's regional double standard. Governor Jimmy Carter of Georgia, who espoused relatively enlightened racial positions for the era, grumbled that *Swann* was "clearly a one-sided decision; the court is still talking about the South; the North is still going free."[83] Senator Eastland of Mississippi, who long embodied southerners' racial rear guard, made a similar point, claiming the decision "solidly reaffirms a policy of the Warren Court by singling out the South for punitive, vindictive and discriminatory treatment in the operation of the public schools."[84] The Burger Court's apparent continuity with its predecessor on segregation also galled ordinary white southerners, including one Charlotte resident who objected after *Swann*, "It's the same old Supreme Court. Nixon just changed the names but he didn't go fooling with the ideas. It's the same old court."[85]

Some of *Swann*'s most sophisticated southern white critics, however, contended that the opinion should in fact be understood as embodying discontinuity with the Warren Court and the colorblind ideal that critics claimed the Court had previously enunciated in school segregation cases. At the forefront of this effort stood the newspaper columnist James J. Kilpatrick—a staunch segregationist during the 1950s—who now branded *Swann* "a scheme of racist lunacy," as he sought to cloak himself securely in *Brown*'s mantle.

"The *Brown* decision of 1954 said, in effect, that pupils could not be assigned to schools by reason of their race; [*Swann*] lay[s] down precisely the opposite rule: Pupils must be assigned to schools by reason of their race," Kilpatrick wrote. "The teaching of *Brown* was that all children must be treated equally; the teachings of [*Swann*] are that some are more equal than others." Kilpatrick further contended that *Swann* represented a betrayal of its recent opinion in *Green v. County School Board of New Kent County:* "So it is back to racism. . . . We can forget about the court's statement a couple of years ago that it wants neither black schools nor white schools, but 'just schools.' It is not possible to maintain 'just schools' when the sole criterion underlying every decision is the criterion of race."[86]

Viewed in hindsight, perhaps the most remarkable aspect of *Swann* is not the opinion's failure to mandate busing throughout the country but instead that it mandated busing in any region of the country. When the Court decided *Swann*, the dominant sentiment throughout the nation opposed busing as a remedy for school segregation. *Time*'s issue recognizing its People of the Year for 1969 contended that the mother of the Middle American family "worried about her children being bused" and placed the issue on par with concerns about drugs and safety.[87] The accompanying article quoted Mildred Budion, a police officer's wife living in Brooklyn, New York, who feared "'the mixture' in public schools," before she hastened to add, "I'm not against all blacks."[88] In 1971, Irene McCabe—who spearheaded a fervent antibusing movement in Pontiac, Michigan—spoke at many rallies and invoked a curious inspiration for her antibusing activism. "Martin Luther King walked all over and he got a lot of things done," McCabe instructed. "This is our civil rights movement."[89] Back in 1967, Boston's foremost antibusing activist—an attorney named Louise Day Hicks—espoused a rather different tack: "I believe in the neighborhood school, and I'm opposed to busing. And if that's being anti-Negro, then I guess I'll have to live with it."[90]

Supporting such anecdotes, the available polling data illustrates the prevalence of antibusing sentiment when the Court issued *Swann*. A poll commissioned for a special issue of *Newsweek* in 1969, examining white Americans' attitudes, asked, "What should be done about Negro demands for better education?" A mere 2 percent of respondents favored busing, and only an additional 25 percent favored other government policies designed to spur school integration; more than two-thirds of respondents favored improving black schools, permitting blacks to run their own schools, or ignoring their demands because they were unjustified. Some of this anemic level of support for integrative measures must be attributable to the astounding fact that in 1969 more than 40 percent of whites asserted that blacks had "a better chance" of securing well-paying jobs and good educations for their children than whites, despite voluminous evidence pointing to precisely the opposite conclusion. At that time, whites constituted 90 percent of the country's total population, thus expanding the pool to include nonwhites would not have dramatically altered support for integration.[91] A nationwide Gallup poll taken in 1971, meanwhile, found that 76 percent of respondents opposed busing and that the quantum of opposition did not vary sharply according to region, as the East (71 percent), the West (72 percent), and the Midwest (77 percent) demonstrated almost as much opposition as the South (82 percent). Among only black respondents, moreover, slightly more opposed busing (47 percent) than supported the practice (45 percent).[92] *Swann* thus illustrates how the Supreme Court possesses the institutional capacity to issue opinions in the educational sphere that challenge the preferences of clear majorities.[93]

Swann's author privately expressed hopes that the Court's position on desegregation would not conflict with public sentiment for long. Chief Justice Burger articulated that view in a revealing private meeting with President Nixon held in the White House in June 1972, slightly more than one year after the decision. In comments captured by the Oval Office's secret recording system, Nixon said to Burger that the Supreme Court, as led by Earl Warren, had caused the forgotten Americans to "los[e] confidence. They see these, you know, they see these hippies, and frankly, the Negro problem[,] . . . and then there's busing. That just drives them up the damn wall." Burger responded, "That *Swann* case was thoroughly misrepresented by the press. . . . They wanted it to be just a busing decision. . . . It was the first time the Court could put limits on busing."[94] Where advocates of desegregation within legal academia and the civil rights community viewed *Swann* as merely the beginning, Burger instead viewed it as the beginning of the end.

For the last few decades, Burger has widely been dismissed as a pompous, ineffectual, and dull-witted leader of the Court, someone whose distinguished physical appearance allowed him to look the part—"the Chief Justice from central casting," as he was often labeled—but who was in reality an empty robe.[95] This depiction appeared in *The Brethren*, a behind-the-curtains view of the Court co-authored by Bob Woodward in 1979, and subsequent years have only hardened it.[96] Yet, if his actions in the school desegregation realm offer any indication, the received wisdom on Chief Justice Warren Burger invites revision. As Burger's comment to Nixon suggests, *Swann* might more accurately be understood not by the constraints it placed on segregating school districts but instead by the constraints it placed on the federal judiciary. Burger did not yet have the votes on the Court in *Swann* to impose President Nixon's antibusing views on the entire country, though that would have been his first-order preference. So instead he did the next best thing: he held the fort (by writing the opinion himself in as narrow a fashion as his pro-busing colleagues would permit) and waited for antibusing reinforcements to arrive.

Focus upon *Swann* once more, this time through Burger's alternate, negative prism: contemplating what the opinion withheld, rather than what it bestowed. Although its bottom-line conclusion certified the forceful desegregation approach undertaken in Mecklenburg County, Burger's opinion also contained some noteworthy language that established the foundation for cabining the judiciary's involvement in this arena. Most important, as mentioned above, *Swann* did not endeavor to craft guidance for lower court judges who considered lawsuits challenging segregated schools in de facto jurisdictions. Instead, Burger's opinion indicated that judges should refrain from taking it upon themselves to issue non-colorblind desegregation orders in communities where students had not intentionally been assigned to different schools. "Absent a constitutional violation there would be no basis for judicially ordering assignment of students on a racial basis," Burger wrote. "All things being equal, with no history of discrimination, it might well be desirable to assign pupils to schools nearest their homes."[97] But even where schools were segregated de jure, *Swann* emphasized that judicially ordered desegregation plans should not be expected to continue forever in time. "At some point," Burger instructed, "[Mecklenburg County's] school authorities and others like them should have achieved full compliance with this Court's decision in *Brown I*. The systems would then be 'unitary' in the sense required by our decisions."[98] Furthermore, *Swann* sought to lower the ambitions of legal reformers, as it cautioned district courts against attempting to tackle every racial discrimination problem under the sun through school desegregation decrees. "The target of the cases from *Brown I* to the present was the dual school system," Burger wrote. "The elimination of racial discrimination in public schools is a large task and one that should not be retarded by efforts to achieve broader purposes lying beyond the district of school authorities. One vehicle can carry only a limited amount of baggage."[99] Finally, Burger's opinion held that the existence of some single-race schools within a district did not necessarily render the school system unconstitutional.

This understanding of what Chief Justice Burger would call *Swann*'s "limit[ations]" appeared to exert an extremely powerful anchoring effect on the Supreme Court's next two major school desegregation decisions, as it contemplated lawsuits arising outside the South. Significantly, by the time the Court considered these non-southern instances of school segregation, President Nixon had succeeded in appointing two new members to the Supreme Court—Justice Lewis F. Powell Jr. and Justice William H. Rehnquist—both of whom would ultimately prove to be the antibusing reinforcements that Burger had hoped would join him.

KEYES V. SCHOOL DISTRICT NO. 1, DENVER, COLORADO

In *Keyes v. School District No. 1, Denver, Colorado*, the Supreme Court in 1973 resolved a lawsuit that black and Latino students filed contending that segregation plagued schools in the Mile-High City. Because neither Denver nor Colorado had ever enacted official laws requiring racially segregated schools, many observers predicted (yet again) before *Keyes* that the Court would seize the opportunity to devise a standard to regulate de facto segregation. *The New York Times*, for example, wrote in anticipation of the decision, "In all probability the *Keyes* decision will tell us whether the Court intends to launch a major attack on school segregation in the North."[100]

As it turned out, however, the Supreme Court (yet again) confounded such expectations. Rather than broadly requiring educators to remedy segregated school conditions—wherever they appeared, and whatever their origins—*Keyes* held Denver liable for its racially isolated schools by issuing a highly fact-sensitive decision finding fault with the school board itself. In a 7–1 decision, with Justice Byron White recused, Justice Brennan wrote an opinion for the Court emphasizing that the board had intentionally gerrymandered attendance zones near the city's predominantly black Park Hill community—and even built an atypically small school in the middle of that neighborhood—in efforts to maintain segregated education. Such actions were, according to *Keyes,* sufficient to render the entire school system's pupil-assignment method presumptively unconstitutional, as the board's actions evinced the *"purpose* or *intent* to segregate."[101]* That criterion would become the essential inquiry for determining whether racially isolated schools violated the Constitution in jurisdictions that lacked Jim Crow laws. In certain respects, however, President Nixon's two recent Court appointments—Powell and Rehnquist—wrote more noteworthy opinions in *Keyes* than the majority opinion.

Justice Powell's separate opinion endorsed the Court's conclusion in *Keyes* but would have reached that destination via a markedly different route. Knowledgeable observers eagerly awaited Powell's vote in *Keyes* because it represented the first time that he would weigh in on school desegregation—at least as a member of the Supreme Court. Powell's prior involvement with these issues pro-

---

* The Denver School Board argued that some of its schools should be regarded as integrated because African Americans and Mexican Americans attended the institutions together, even though they were joined by a trivial number of white students. *Keyes,* however, flatly rejected this argument, concluding in effect that schools that happen to be located where the barrio meets the ghetto do not adequately present the idea of racial integration that the Court envisioned. *Keyes* held that it was erroneous to "separat[e] Negroes and Hispanos for purposes of defining a 'segregated' school" because "much evidence [indicates] Hispanos and Negroes have a great many things in common." *Keyes v. School District No. 1, Denver, Colorado,* 413 U.S. 189, 197 (1973). The two racial groups' shared history of "discrimination in treatment when compared with the treatment afforded Anglo students" meant that legal challengers were "entitled to have schools with a combined predominance of Negroes and Hispanos included in the category of 'segregated' schools." Ibid., 198. This understanding of segregation complicates the argument advanced by some commentators who have asserted that the nation's increased racial diversity in recent decades, which has affected the composition of the nation's public schools, indicates that schools predominantly made up of students from two different minority groups should be viewed as evidence of a desegregating nation. See Nicholas O. Stephanopolous, "Civil Rights in a Desegregating America," 83 *University of Chicago Law Review* 1329, 1393–415 (2016); Edward Glaeser and Jacob Vigdor, *The End of the Segregated Century: Racial Separation in America's Neighborhoods, 1890–2010* (2012). *Keyes*'s logic may find at least some support in the underlying facts of *Lum v. Rice,* where a Chinese American girl in Mississippi during the 1920s challenged her assignment to the school for black students. Even if Lum and many other Chinese Americans attended the formerly all-black school, that development would not have rendered Mississippi's schools somehow desegregated.

vided advocates of robust approaches to desegregation with little, if any, reason for believing that he would champion their cause. As chairman of the Richmond School Board when the Court issued *Brown*, Powell oversaw a system that for six full years after the decision saw not a single black student attend school with white students. In 1959, when educators in Prince Edward County decided to close their schools rather than integrate them, Powell announced "public education will be continued in our city—although every proper effort will be made to minimize the extent of integration when it comes."[102] Assessed only by the racial composition of Richmond's schools, Powell proved to be a man of his word. When he departed the school board in the spring of 1961, only two of the city's more than twenty thousand black pupils attended school with whites. During his confirmation hearings, which yielded an 89–1 vote in his favor, Powell successfully avoided responsibility for this dismal desegregation record by noting that Virginia had removed pupil-assignment authority from local school boards and instead consigned that authority to a state agency. In the intervening years, however, Powell had not exactly acquired a reputation as a crusading proponent of desegregation. To the contrary, he filed an amicus brief in *Swann*, where he mounted a relentless attack against busing on consequentialist grounds. Busing would result in a perverse failure, Powell maintained, because its introduction would serve only to accelerate white flight, thus intensifying the very problem that it sought to alleviate. According to Powell, "[Busing] frustrates the aspirations of *Brown*, namely, the promotion of equal educational opportunity; it assures in time the resegregation of most of the blacks in many urban communities. This will result in deteriorating educational opportunities both for poorer blacks and whites who cannot afford to move."[103]

To the surprise of many onlookers, however, Powell's opinion in *Keyes* proposed nothing less than fundamentally reconceptualizing the judiciary's approach to the racial composition of schools by calling for the abandonment of the de jure/de facto distinction, and the implementation of "a uniform, constitutional approach to our national problem of school segregation."[104] Instead of examining a school board's motives in areas that lacked formal laws requiring segregated education, as the majority did in *Keyes*, Powell contended that courts throughout the nation should concentrate on correcting the existence of racially isolated schools—hardly an unknown phenomenon in northern jurisdictions: "[I]f our national concern is for those who attend [segregated] schools, . . . we must recognize that the evil of operating separate schools is no less in Denver than in Atlanta."[105] Extending upon the Court's decision in *Green*, which required a school district in rural Virginia to take affirmative steps to discontinue its dual school system, Powell promoted the adoption of a nationwide rule that would have *required*, under the Constitution, schools to pursue racial integration. Powell maintained that students should now be understood as possessing "the right, derived from the Equal Protection Clause, to expect that . . . local school boards will operate *integrated school systems* within their respective districts. This means that school authorities . . . must make and implement their customary decisions with a view toward enhancing integrated school opportunities."[106] Powell's new constitutional standard would have compelled school officials, among other measures, to establish attendance zones that would facilitate integration, open schools in locations to foster integration, and, if the district provided students with transportation to school, draw routes within reason to promote integration. This far-reaching opinion would have mandated schools in de facto segregated jurisdictions to pursue racial integration in a far more aggressive fashion than anything the Court had yet required, or has done so to date.

Cutting against this sweeping remedy, however, Powell did aim in *Keyes* to dial back the status quo in one major respect: he would not have obligated schools to bus students solely for the purpose of maximizing integration, even in areas of de jure segregation. Powell repeatedly expressed anxieties about students—particularly young students—being bused great distances away from their homes. This aversion to extensive busing programs, Powell noted, stemmed from concerns that such practices could devastate the sense of community engendered when youngsters living in the same neighborhood attended the same school. Powell espoused an early iteration of the federalism-inflected ideas that would become his mantra in the domain of education law:

> Neighborhood school systems . . . reflect the deeply felt desire of citizens for a sense of community in their public education. Public schools have been a traditional source of strength to our

Nation, and that strength may derive in part from the identification of many schools with the personal features of the surrounding neighborhood. Community support, interest, and dedication
to public schools may well run higher with a neighborhood attendance pattern: distance may encourage disinterest. Many citizens
sense today a decline in the intimacy of our institutions—home,
church, and school—which has caused a concomitant decline in
the unity and communal spirit of our people. I pass no judgment
on this viewpoint, but I do believe that this Court should be wary
of compelling in the name of constitutional law what may seem
to many a dissolution in the traditional, more personal fabric of
their public schools.[107]

Consistent with his overarching requirement for integration, however, Powell made clear that he used the term "neighborhood
school" in an elastic sense—meaning not necessarily the absolute
closest school to one's residence but instead indicating a preference
for assigning students to schools closer, rather than farther, from
their homes.[108]

Justice Rehnquist in *Keyes* became the first Supreme Court justice to file a written dissent in a case involving race and education
since before *Brown*. Rehnquist joined the Court only one year earlier, following a bruising confirmation battle that centered on ideas
he expressed about *Brown* in the 1950s, when he worked on the case
as a law clerk for Justice Robert Jackson. An intra-chambers memorandum Rehnquist wrote—titled "A Random Thought on the
Segregation Cases"—during this era stated in unequivocal terms,
"I realize that it is an unpopular and unhumanitarian position, for
which I have been excoriated by 'liberal' colleagues, but I think
Plessy v. Ferguson was right and should be re-affirmed."[109] By the
early 1970s, *Brown's* correctness as a matter of legal doctrine had
become an indispensable belief for all lawyers within the constitutional mainstream, and the memo's surfacing thus placed Rehnquist
in an awkward position. While Rehnquist conceded during his Senate confirmation hearings that he wrote the memo, he insisted it
conveyed not his thoughts on the case but those of Justice Jackson.
This explanation of the document's provenance severely strained
credulity, as the memo almost certainly captured Rehnquist's own
dubious assessment of court-ordered desegregation. Nevertheless,

it proved sufficient to secure his confirmation, albeit over the objections of more than two dozen senators.*

One might imagine that, after such a harrowing escape, Justice Rehnquist would have initially suppressed any urge to strike out on his own in the fraught area of school desegregation. But Rehnquist emerged in *Keyes* unbowed. The dissent marked the unveiling of his judicial project designed to minimize *Brown's* reach—a project he would command for more than three decades. Rehnquist avoided questioning the legitimacy of *Brown* itself, but he voiced grave skepticism of *Green's* instructing educators to take affirmative steps to eliminate de jure segregation—a decision he termed a "drastic extension of *Brown*" and one that in his view lacked legal justification. Rehnquist suggested that *Brown* should be understood as requiring assignment to neighborhood schools on a colorblind basis, and not one whit more. "To require that a genuinely 'dual' system be disestablished, in the sense that the assignment of a child to a particular school is not made to depend on his race is one thing," Rehnquist

---

* When he joined the Court in the early 1970s, Rehnquist's memorandum on *Brown* was far from the only action he had taken that provided a basis for doubting his commitment to racial equality. In the mid-1960s, for example, Rehnquist testified before the City Council of Phoenix, Arizona, to oppose the passage of a public accommodations measure that prohibited hotel and restaurant proprietors from refusing to serve black and brown customers. See William H. Rehnquist, "Public Accommodations Law Passage Is Called 'Mistake,'" *Arizona Republic*, June 4, 1964, reprinted in *Nominations of William H. Rehnquist and Lewis F. Powell Jr.: Hearings Before the Senate Committee on the Judiciary*, 92d Congress 307 (1971). This position placed Rehnquist to the right of Senator Barry Goldwater of Arizona, who notoriously opposed the public accommodations provision in the Civil Rights Act of 1964 because, he insisted, that measure exceeded Congress's authority. Yet even Goldwater supported Phoenix's public accommodations measure, as it did not, of course, require federal authority. See Rick Perlstein, *Before the Storm: Barry Goldwater and the Unmaking of the American Consensus* 363 (2001); Justin Driver, "Reactionary Rhetoric and Liberal Legal Academia," 123 *Yale Law Journal* 2616 (2014). Intriguingly, Rehnquist—along with Harry Jaffa—drafted a speech that Goldwater delivered during his 1964 presidential run that embraced constitutional colorblindness and attacked busing:

> To me it is wrong to take some children out of some of the schools they normally would attend and bus them to others just to get a mixture of ethnic and racial groups that somebody thinks is desirable. This forced integration is just as wrong as forced segregation. It has been well said that the Constitution is colorblind. And so it is just as wrong to compel children to attend certain schools for the sake of so-called integration as for the sake of segregation.

Matthew F. Delmont, *Why Busing Failed: Race, Media, and the National Resistance to School Desegregation* 94 (2016).

wrote. "To require that school boards affirmatively undertake to achieve racial mixing in schools where such mixing is not achieved in sufficient degree by neutrally drawn boundary lines is quite obviously something else."[110] Without affirming the legitimacy of such race-conscious measures in confronting de jure segregation in rural Virginia, Rehnquist contended that such an approach had no place whatsoever in Denver, amid its history of de facto segregation. Placing the entire Denver school system into what he termed "a federal receivership," Rehnquist maintained, exceeded the Court's constitutional authority: "[U]nless the Equal Protection Clause . . . now be held to embody a principle of 'taint,' found in some primitive legal systems but discarded centuries ago in ours, [Keyes] can only be described as the product of judicial fiat."[111]

Keyes marked a pivotal moment in the Court's desegregation jurisprudence because it—more acutely than any other single decision—shone a light on what could have been, and indeed what already should have been, in this area. In Keyes, the Court faced a clear opportunity to move away from the hunt for bad actors and toward considering whether school districts throughout the country in fact contained pockets of racially isolated schools. Wherever such pockets occurred, the Court should have made it incumbent upon educators to address that issue. Instead, Keyes clung to the de jure/de facto distinction, tweaking the mindset ever so slightly by finding that there were some evildoers in the North and the West who acted with an impermissible purpose by taking identifiable steps to isolate racial minorities and who in effect should be treated as operating de jure segregated school systems. In so doing, the Court wrongly perpetuated the fiction that many communities existed throughout the nation where racial minorities simply happened to cluster due to their own preferences, rather than being forced into racialized ghettos through a complex web of mutually reinforcing public and private exclusions.

The Court's emphasis on discriminatory intent seems particularly misguided in the educational sphere, moreover, because it obfuscates how segregated schools are invariably the product of some official governmental action, namely the assignment of students to attend designated schools. When educators' current pupil-assignment plans result in racially identifiable schools, they must make a decision either to perpetuate or to remediate that condition. Perpetuating de facto segregation in schools by retaining pupil-

assignment plans should not, however, be misunderstood as tantamount to making no decision at all. Embracing an effects-based test
for school segregation would have had the virtue of dramatically
lightening the evidentiary burden on litigants and civil rights organizations. Rather than being required to identify some particular
wayward step where the actions of school officials revealed impermissible racial considerations, parties seeking desegregation could
simply have identified schools with student bodies that were predominantly racial minorities. In other words, the Supreme Court
should have interpreted the Constitution to require school districts
to pursue racial integration throughout the nation regardless of
their recent history—taking a cue from Justice Powell's opinion in
Keyes, even if it declined to adopt his aversion to busing. That an
opinion written by Justice Powell—a man who steadfastly sought to
prop up Jim Crow's crumbling edifice, even as an adult member of
the bar—could in any meaningful sense be understood as seeking
to advance the Court's pursuit of school integration serves only to
underscore the disgraceful timidity with which the Court regulated
the racial composition of schools during the long post-*Brown* era.[112]

Had the Supreme Court in *Keyes* embraced a more results-
oriented approach to locating unconstitutional segregation in
schools, the adoption of such a standard could well have had profound implications for the judiciary's interpretation of the Equal
Protection Clause as a general proposition. The Court decided
Keyes three years before it decided *Washington v. Davis*, the single
most influential opinion in shaping the Fourteenth Amendment's
racial landscape issued during the last five decades. *Davis* involved a
lawsuit challenging the legitimacy of a standardized test for becoming a police officer that black applicants failed at a disproportionately high rate compared with white applicants. *Davis* interpreted
the Equal Protection Clause to mean measures that produce racially
discriminatory *effects*, but that were not adopted for racially discriminatory *purposes*, do not—absent highly unusual circumstances—
violate the Equal Protection Clause. *Davis*'s holding has succeeded
in making it extremely difficult for racial minorities to prevail on
claims under the Equal Protection Clause in the modern era. But
that outcome at least plausibly might have been different if *Keyes*
had adopted an effect-based segregation standard, and that standard
informed the Court's general view of the Equal Protection Clause
that it would subsequently devise in *Davis*. Viewed from the oppo-

site angle, *Keyes*'s purpose-based standard can be understood as laying the foundation for the Court's reasoning in *Davis*.[113]*

Criticizing *Keyes* for its failure to realize the prospect of momentous school integration throughout the nation should not be dismissed as the product of hindsight. To the contrary, a prominent theme of the media's contemporaneous coverage of *Keyes* emphasized the decision's refusal to articulate a sufficiently demanding desegregation standard for non-southern jurisdictions. Thus, the *Chicago Defender* noted that lawyers "believe that the Supreme Court missed a precious opportunity to end any legal distinction between de facto discrimination and de jure segregation."[114] The *Los Angeles Times* added, "By its decision, the court in effect has accepted a double standard in which the intent of school boards is irrelevant in the South and paramount in the North in determining judicial remedy to segregation."[115] In a similar vein, *The Washington Post*'s editorial board noted that—though "Denver was generally thought to be the first 'de facto' segregation case the Court would rule on"—*Keyes* in fact "made essentially a 'Southern' finding" by "deal[ing] with Denver on 'de jure' lines." The *Post* further lamented, "A genuine 'de facto' or 'racial balance' decision one way or the other still seems a long way off."[116]

By the time of *Swann*, no one could seriously doubt the prevalence of segregation in many non-southern communities. In 1971, according to data collected by the federal government, the percentage of black students who attended schools where the student body was greater than 80 percent black stood at staggeringly high levels in many northern and western jurisdictions, including 90 percent in St. Louis, Missouri; 91 percent in Cleveland, Ohio; 91 percent in Newark, New Jersey; 96 percent in Gary, Indiana; and 98 percent in Compton, California. In Chicago, nearly half of the city's elementary schools reported greater than 90 percent black student bodies, and more than one in four reported 100 percent black student bodies. By at least one measure, moreover, non-southern jurisdictions at this time featured starker rates of school segregation than southern jurisdictions: although 44 percent of black students in the South attended schools with a majority of white students, only

---

* For evidence of this last proposition, see *Washington v. Davis*, 426 U.S. 229, 240 (1976) (citing *Keyes*, 413 U.S. 189) ("The school desegregation cases have also adhered to the basic equal protection principle that the invidious quality of a law claimed to be racially discriminatory must ultimately be traced to a racially discriminatory purpose").

28 percent of their counterparts in the North and the West could say the same.[117]

It would be profoundly mistaken, though, to believe that the issue of de facto segregation only recently attracted attention when the Court essentially opted to evade this fundamental question in 1973 with *Keyes*. Long before that time, individuals occupying a wide array of positions in American society—ranging from judges to journalists, from professors to politicians, from ordinary citizens to extraordinary essayists—had all identified de facto segregation as a serious problem that demanded remediation. In the early 1960s, some federal judges issued opinions that deemed de facto segregation unconstitutional, even as other federal judges disagreed; the Supreme Court, moreover, during that decade repeatedly denied invitations to reverse conservative circuit court decisions on this question that arose in various cities, including Gary, Indiana; Kansas City, Kansas; and Cincinnati, Ohio. As *Brown* approached its tenth anniversary in 1964, Anthony Lewis surveyed the broad landscape of segregation in *The New York Times Magazine*. "[I]t should not be disturbing that all the country is now engaged in the race problem," Lewis wrote. "The pretense that the problem existed only in the South was just that, a pretense, and it is better to have the truth out, however painful it is."[118]* One year later, Professor Owen Fiss wrote a significant article in the *Harvard Law Review* contending that *Brown*, and its requirement for "equality of educational opportunity, may in some instances be violated by the maintenance of racially imbalanced schools," and insisting further that "[t]he refusal to recoil from the specter of such reform is rooted in Brecht's intellectual injunction, 'When a thing continually occurs / Not on that account find it natural.'"[119] A few months later, President Lyndon Johnson requested a report from the U.S. Commission on Civil Rights examining racial isolation in public schools, presumably with an eye toward attacking segregation in non-southern venues. As far back as the 1950s, a protester of school conditions in New York City

---

* Four years later, *The New York Times Magazine* revisited this issue when an attorney named Lewis Steel published a critique of the Supreme Court's record on racial equality titled "Nine Men in Black Who Think White." Steel criticized the Court's failure to correct the repeated circuit court opinions approving of "accidental segregation" in schools and further commented that *Green*'s recent tough stance on segregation in rural Virginia "will yield small dividends unless the Court also agrees to tackle the question of *de facto* segregation." Lewis M. Steel, "Nine Men in Black Who Think White," *New York Times Magazine*, Oct. 13, 1968, 56, 112.

sought to draw attention to northern-style segregation by carrying a placard that read, "Is Brooklyn, New York above the Mason Dixon Line?"[120] Finally, in 1965, James Baldwin similarly highlighted the absurdity of the de facto category by quipping, "De facto segregation means Negroes are segregated, but nobody did it."[121]

Thus, despite vociferous complaints about de facto segregation arising in many different corners of the national discourse, the Supreme Court simply turned a deaf ear to this issue for many years. Had it demonstrated any alacrity whatsoever in combating de facto segregation when those issues initially appeared in the federal courts, the liberal Warren Court would have resolved the question, virtually guaranteeing a progressive victory. When the Supreme Court, under Chief Justice Burger's leadership, finally agreed to resolve a case arising from a de facto jurisdiction with *Keyes*, moreover, its analytical approach foundered badly by blinking the issue away, shunting Denver into the de jure framework. Disappointing as *Keyes*'s reasoning might have been for advocates of a vigorous, nationwide approach, however, matters stood on the brink of growing far worse.

MILLIKEN V. BRADLEY

In 1974, one year after *Keyes*, the Supreme Court in *Milliken v. Bradley* again addressed de facto segregation, this time in the context of Detroit, Michigan. A few years earlier, Ronald Bradley—a student who attended a virtually all-black elementary school and dreamed someday of joining the police force—became the primary litigant in a lawsuit contesting the constitutionality of Detroit's racially isolated schools. Rather than only suing the Detroit Public Schools and its officials, however, Bradley's lawsuit attacked the issue at the state level, identifying Michigan's governor, William Milliken, among others, as a defendant. The litigation decision to target the state was driven by the metropolitan area's racial demographics, which featured a heavily black city (served by the Detroit Public Schools) surrounded by a ring of overwhelmingly white suburbs (each of which operated its own school system). Prevailing in a lawsuit confined to Detroit itself would have meant that the remedy too stopped at the city limits, making a meaningful desegregation plan extremely difficult to implement due to the paucity of white students within the urban area. In 1971, District Court Judge Stephen Roth accepted the state-based argument and issued a desegregation order requiring interdistrict busing to occur throughout metropolitan Detroit. Not surprisingly, Judge Roth's detractors deemed implicating suburbanites in the desegregation remedy a foolish move. "Amalgamation of urban and suburban school districts is the logical way to get your hands on the required number of white children—if you think it is logical to go to that extreme to force integration," George Will provocatively phrased this critique. On the ground in Michigan, of course, this aspect of the decision also generated great resentment. Opponents heaped vitriol on Judge Roth himself, as various antibusing bumper stickers sniped, "Roth Is a Four-Letter Word" and even "Judge Roth Is a Child Molester." Somewhat more high-mindedly, thousands of homemade, cardboard signs decorated windows in suburban homes that declared simply, "This Family Will Not Be Bused." One white mother in Pontiac memorably expounded upon this idea, making it clear precisely where placing her child on a school bus headed for Detroit rested on her list of priorities. "I'd go to jail first," she explained.* Despite the outcry, the U.S. Court of Appeals for the Sixth Circuit affirmed Judge Roth's interdistrict desegregation order, setting the stage for the Court's review.[122]

Bradley arrived in July 1974, two weeks before Richard Nixon would depart the presidency, when the scandal swirling around the Watergate break-in forced his resignation. The decision perhaps granted Nixon a fleeting moment of solace during an hour of misery; all four of the justices that he placed on the Court voted en masse—and were joined by Justice Potter Stewart—to strike down Detroit's interdistrict desegregation order. Writing the opinion for the Court divided by a 5–4 margin, Chief Justice Burger contended that, without evidence that the suburban school districts acted with untoward racial motive or purpose, upholding Judge Roth's order would be tantamount to punishing innocent victims. An interdis-

---

* During the 1970s, many white residents of Detroit's suburbs expressed strikingly similar versions of this idea that confinement presented a preferable alternative to having one's child bused. Thus, *The New York Times* reported one white mother near Detroit asserting, "No kid of mine is ever going to get on a bus. I'd go to jail first." William K. Stevens, "Many White Parents Now See Their Children as Safe," *New York Times*, July 27, 1974, 60. And the *Los Angeles Times* quoted another white woman reading from that same playbook: "I'll go to jail before I let any of my kids ride in a bus." Robert Shogan, "White Voters' Hostility Runs High in Detroit," *Los Angeles Times*, Oct. 20, 1974, H1.

trict approach to desegregation, Burger insisted, demonstrated disrespect for school districts' basic autonomy. "[T]he notion that school district lines may be casually ignored or treated as a mere administrative convenience is contrary to the history of public education in our country," Burger wrote. "No single tradition in public education is more deeply rooted than local control over the operation of schools; local autonomy has long been thought essential both to the maintenance of community concern and support for public schools and to quality of the educational process."[123] Burger further contended that validating Judge Roth's opinion would witness the federal judiciary become "the 'school superintendent' for the entire area," awarding it "a task which few, if any, judges are qualified to perform and one which would deprive the people of control of schools through their elected representatives."[124]

Although *Bradley* drew three separate, strongly worded dissenting opinions, Justice Thurgood Marshall undoubtedly voiced the most poignant opposition—and also the most personal. After prevailing as counsel in *Brown*, among his many other Supreme Court victories, Marshall became the first justice who did not have white skin when President Johnson nominated him to the Court in 1967. But almost immediately after he broke the Court's color barrier, the institution whose jurisprudential commitments Marshall once revered began changing into one whose jurisprudential commitments he would soon abhor.

The Court issued *Bradley* only a matter of days after *Brown*'s twentieth anniversary, and the occasion found him in no mood to celebrate. Indeed, Justice Marshall signaled his extreme disagreement with the majority by announcing his dissent aloud from the bench. Following two decades "of small, often difficult steps" toward fulfilling *Brown*, Marshall contended that the Court in *Bradley* "today takes a giant step backwards."[125] *Bradley*, Marshall insisted, retreated from *Brown* to recognize artificial borders, even though doing so would prevent children from realizing their full potential. "Those children who have been denied that right in the past deserve better than to see fences thrown up to deny them that right in the future," Marshall wrote. "Our nation . . . will be ill served by the Court's refusal to remedy separate and unequal education, for unless our children begin to learn together, there is little hope that our people will ever learn to live together."[126] In a highly unorthodox suggestion by the standards of judicial opinion writing, Marshall concluded his dissent by attributing the outcome in *Bradley* to extralegal forces. "Today's holding, I fear, is more a reflection of a perceived public mood that we have gone far enough in enforcing the Constitution's guarantee of equal justice than it is the product of neutral principles of law," Marshall stated. "In the short run, it may seem to be the easier course to allow our great metropolitan areas to be divided up each into two cities—one white, the other black—but it is a course, I predict, our people will ultimately regret. I dissent."[127]

Justice Marshall's intuition that public support for desegregation had flagged finds at least some support in the editorial coverage of *Bradley*. It hardly seems revelatory that *The Wall Street Journal* viewed *Bradley* as providing hope that the nation would "find our way back to the principle that the Constitution is color-blind," and that it attributed antibusing sentiment "not [to] racism" but to disagreement with "the notion that a federal judge or bureaucrat could reach into a community . . . and overturn its local school system."[128] Yet it does seem quite noteworthy that *The Washington Post*—a staunchly liberal publication on most legal questions—editorialized that *Bradley* "strikes us as sound policy and sound law."[129] While *The New York Times* did adopt the expected liberal line by criticizing *Bradley*, it did so in relatively mild terms, contending that the opinion "seems as wrong as a matter of law as it is unfortunate as a matter of social policy."[130] Thus even in publications that portrayed *Bradley* as a lamentable development, it seems that the decision generally failed to singe left-leaning sensibilities.

Bradley exposed a large, bitter chasm within the black community and its views of busing—a divide that had been growing for some time. On one side of this divide, the traditional civil rights organizations embraced busing as an essential step on the path toward racial equality, and thus depicted busing's opponents as heading in the opposite direction. In 1972, Julian Bond—who co-founded the Student Nonviolent Coordinating Committee, before winning election to Georgia's statehouse—vividly encapsulated this view when speaking at Ohio State University: "What people who oppose busing object to, is not the little yellow school buses, but rather to the little black bodies that are on the bus."[131] On some occasions, speaking before black audiences, Bond condensed this idea further still. "It's not the bus," he contended, "it's us."[132] The NAACP Legal Defense and Educational Fund delivered a slight variation on this theme by publishing a booklet bluntly titled *It's Not the Dis-*

tance, "It's the Niggers," where it avowed that proposals to eliminate busing "barely camouflage their racist motivation."[133] Predictably, the Court's decision in *Bradley* intensified such criticisms. Nathaniel Jones, the NAACP's general counsel, disparaged *Bradley* as "the sad but inevitable culmination of a national anti-black strategy."[134] Roy Wilkins, the NAACP's executive director, arguably raised the ante, suggesting, "A dark way of looking at [*Bradley*] is to say that the highest court in the nation has pointed the way to apartheid, the South African equivalent of strict racial separation."[135] Black newspapers almost without exception also reviled *Bradley*. The *New Pittsburgh Courier*, to select only one of many available examples, memorably likened *Bradley* to a blues number: "Well y'all, seems as though we can appropriately revitalize the old theme, 'The Thrill Is Gone.' For the first time in 20 years the U.S. Supreme Court has reversed its long trend of pro-school desegregation rulings and handed-down a decision that could ultimately mean, 'Jim Crow will fly again.' "[136]

On the other side of this divide, however, many black citizens harbored grave doubts about the wisdom of pursuing racial integration as a goal unto itself and reserved particular contempt for busing. As early as 1967, in a book titled *Black Power*, Stokely Carmichael and Charles Hamilton assailed racial integration as an "unrealistic" and "despicable" aim for the black community. "[Integration] is based on complete acceptance of the fact that in order to have a decent house or education, black people must move into a white neighborhood or send their children to a white school," the authors maintained. "This reinforces . . . the idea that 'white' is automatically superior and 'black' is by definition inferior. For this reason, 'integration' is a subterfuge for the maintenance of white supremacy."[137] In short order, such attitudes and language migrated from the black community's radical fringe into more mainstream circles. In 1972, the National Black Political Convention assembled in Gary, Indiana, where some eight thousand participants passed by acclamation a measure that declared busing an "obsolete and dangerous" practice and stated, "We condemn racial integration of schools as a bankrupt, suicidal method of desegregating schools, based on the false notion that black children are unable to learn unless they are in the same setting as white children."[138] Shortly before *Bradley*, *The New York Times* published an article headlined "To Some Blacks, the Bus Ride Isn't Worth It."[139] In a separate contemporaneous article, the

Times quoted Doris McCrary, a black mother in Detroit, expressing concern that busing could instill self-doubt in black students. "I've always been against busing," McCrary said. "I have built my kids where they have self-confidence in themselves. If you take them out to Grosse Pointe where they would be looked down on, that would do something to their self-image."[140] After the Court issued *Bradley*, Detroit's mayor, Coleman Young, held a press conference, where he endorsed McCrary's broad view of the issue: "I shed no big tears for cross-district busing."[141] Nor did *Bradley* appear to unsettle Professor Derrick Bell of Harvard Law School, who suggested—in language strongly reminiscent of *Black Power*—that busing courted ruin for African Americans: "The insistence on integrating every public school that is black perpetuates the racially demeaning and unproven assumption that blacks must have a majority white presence in order to either teach or learn effectively."[142]*

Such thinking has demonstrated remarkable staying power and has even appeared on the far right of the jurisprudential spectrum. Thus, Justice Clarence Thomas, seldom understood as a racial firebrand, seemed to channel his inner Stokely Carmichael in a Supreme Court decision arising from Kansas City, Missouri, in 1995, when he asserted,

> "Racial isolation" itself is not a harm; only state-enforced segregation is. After all, if separation itself is a harm, and if integration therefore is the only way that blacks can receive a proper education, then there must be something inferior about blacks. Under this theory, segregation injures blacks because blacks, when left on their own, cannot achieve. To my way of thinking, that conclusion is the result of a jurisprudence based upon a theory of black inferiority.[143]†

* Within legal academia, Professor Bell's relatively serene reaction to *Bradley* was uncommon, as most academics found the decision deeply unsound. Professor Charles Lawrence registered a far more representative response when he stated, "[*Bradley*] sentenced northern school desegregation to the death penalty before the baby had taken its first full breath." Charles R. Lawrence III, "Segregation 'Misunderstood': The *Milliken* Decision Revisited," 12 *University of San Francisco Law Review* 15, 15 (1977). Professor William Taylor also condemned the decision in strong terms, labeling *Bradley*'s theoretical underpinnings "seriously wrong." William L. Taylor, "The Supreme Court and Urban Reality: A Tactical Analysis of *Milliken v. Bradley*," 21 *Wayne Law Review* 751, 753 (1975).

† Justice Thomas's memoir, *My Grandfather's Son*, revealed that as an undergraduate at Holy Cross he identified with tenets of Black Power and Black Nationalism. Although

Predictably, *Bradley* elicited a much less divided response in suburban Detroit, where it stopped just short of causing dancing in the cul-de-sacs. The *New York Times* article surveying the jubilant scene opened, "In the suburbs of Detroit there were expressions of joy today, excited calling of friends to tell them that the Supreme Court had ruled that their school-children would not be bused into Detroit schools and a sense of relief among leaders who had spent several years battling a court-ordered busing proposal."[144] In two separate articles, the *Times* recounted suburbanites literally breaking out into applause upon learning of *Bradley*, with even one person exulting, "We won!"[145] When elaborating upon what their victory in *Bradley* represented, most suburbanites generally focused upon the safety of their children, but they sometimes invoked rather different language. In wealthy Grosse Pointe, one white mother expressed a theoretical commitment to racial equality but candidly conceded that busing would have imposed too high a toll on her family. "Intellectually, I'm for equality in education, and busing. But not in the Detroit area. . . . I do not want my child in the inner city and faced with the problems of the ghetto."[146] In more middle-class Roseville, another white mother explained her objection to busing in considerably coarser terms, as she explained fleeing Detroit's east side due to the sight of "those animals coming and going" and expressed fear that if black people moved into her area it could bring "that Aid to Dependent Children bunch."[147]

A CODA ON BUSING

It bears mentioning that the busing program engendered by *Swann* in Charlotte—after some initial turmoil—eventually garnered widespread acclaim. Following the Court's decision, many white families evaded the opinion's effects by removing their children from public schools and enrolling them instead in the more than

---

Thomas's memoir asserted he had long ago abandoned these ideological commitments, some legal academics have maintained that his jurisprudence continues to bear the imprint of those supposedly retired mindsets. See Mark Tushnet, "Clarence Thomas's Black Nationalism," 47 *Howard Law Journal* 323 (2004); Angela Onwuachi-Willig, "Just Another Brother on the SCT? What Justice Clarence Thomas Teaches Us About the Influence of Racial Identity," 90 *Iowa Law Review* 931 (2005); and Stephen F. Smith, "Clarence X? The Black Nationalist Behind Justice Thomas's Constitutionalism," 4 *NYU Journal of Law and Liberty* 583 (2009).

two dozen private schools—often called "segregation academies"—that blossomed around Mecklenburg County. These private institutions, at their height, educated fully one-sixth of the area's white students. For the students who remained in public schools, moreover, the early experiences of desegregated education were far from idyllic, as violence erupted with distressing frequency. "We were so segregated that many blacks had never encountered whites close up either," one Charlotte student recalled. "So there was a lot of tension. . . . A fight between two people, if one was white and the other black, became not just a personal thing, but the start of a race riot."[148] Yet it did not take long for this tense atmosphere to dissipate. Judge McMillan, with the assistance of the racially integrated Citizens Advisory Group, annually adjusted school populations both to minimize student travel time required by desegregation and to prevent schools from becoming more than 40 percent black—commonly understood as a "tipping point" that, if exceeded, would trigger mass white abandonment of public schools. By 1975, school conditions had so thoroughly stabilized that Judge McMillan announced, in an order subtitled "*Swann* Song," he would no longer personally oversee matters, provided only that the desegregation measures continued.[149] Prompted by McMillan's withdrawal, some national media outlets observed that Mecklenburg residents at that time generally "accepted" busing, and in 1983 *The New York Times* reported that a dominant majority of students "supported" the practice.[150]

While it may be enticing to attribute these rosy accounts to liberals' dreams masquerading as reported fact, they find support with contemporaneous evidence on the ground. In October 1984, President Ronald Reagan—less than one month away from his successful bid for reelection—delivered a speech in Charlotte, where he railed, "[B]using takes innocent children out of the neighborhood school and makes them pawns in a social experiment that nobody wants. . . . And we've found out that it failed."[151] Although Reagan anticipated the friendly audience would cheer this surefire applause line, the remark fell utterly flat and met only silence. After the speech, a Republican and Reagan supporter in the audience would call the remark "insensitive."[152] Residents of Mecklenburg County (even those who would attend a Reagan rally) viewed busing not as an unmitigated failure but as a rousing success. In this vein, *The Charlotte Observer*—in an editorial titled "You Were Wrong,

Mr. President"—firmly criticized Reagan for failing to appreciate that the area's "proudest achievement of the past 20 years is not the city's impressive new skyline or its strong, growing economy" but rather "its fully integrated public school system." The *Observer* rapped Reagan on the knuckles for stirring up "ugly emotions and unfounded fears that this community confronted and conquered" long ago: "Maybe we shouldn't expect you to know a great deal about Charlotte-Mecklenburg and its public schools. But, with all due respect, Mr. President, you flaunted your ignorance. . . . You sometimes speak of a 'shining city on a hill,' Mr. President. You visited one briefly [yesterday], but you didn't understand, or seem to care, what makes it shine."[153]

During the fifteen-year period after Reagan's miscalculated remarks, Mecklenburg County continued busing students, as the racial composition of the school system—and within individual schools—remained stable. Toward the end of the 1990s, however, a few disgruntled parents of students who were bused filed a lawsuit encouraging the school district in effect to declare victory for integration by contending that the former dual system had now become "unitary"—as Burger's opinion in *Swann* anticipated would eventually occur. Local legend held that the renewed opposition to busing was led not by members of the South's old guard but by northern transplants who had flocked to the area's booming financial sector. In 1999, a federal district court judge—whom Reagan placed on the bench at the behest of Senator Jesse Helms and who had actively opposed busing in the 1970s—accepted the parents' unitary status argument and invalidated the long-standing busing plan. In short order, Mecklenburg County's schools reassumed the skewed racial demographics of their surrounding neighborhoods, thus ending a remarkable run of meaningfully integrated schools in metropolitan Charlotte and making the region one small part of the broader phenomenon that has been labeled "the resegregation" of American education.[154]

The point here is not to suggest that busing always proved fruitful wherever it was undertaken. That claim cannot persuasively be made, as Boston's notorious busing experience all too vividly demonstrated—a series of disturbing images etched into national memory by J. Anthony Lukas's Pulitzer Prize–winning account, *Common Ground.* The point, rather, is to insist that Boston's disastrous encounter should no longer be permitted to act as synecdoche for the entirety of the nation's manifold busing experiences. Charlotte's involvement with busing establishes that such programs were not invariably fated to fail. And while Mecklenburg County's unusually large school district might have made it particularly fertile ground for a successful busing system, it would be severely mistaken to dismiss the area's positive experience as somehow sui generis. In 1981, in busing's heyday, a Harris poll surveying the parents of children who were bused to promote integration found that 87 percent of respondents deemed the experience either very satisfactory (54 percent) or partially satisfactory (33 percent), with only 11 percent of respondents deeming it not satisfactory. Harris concluded, "These latest findings are diametrically opposed to the general impression that such busing has been a disaster where it has been tried."[155] More than three decades later, these powerful figures have yet to dislodge the nation's overly jaded impression of busing.

PARENTS INVOLVED IN COMMUNITY SCHOOLS V. SEATTLE SCHOOL DISTRICT NO. 1: CHALLENGING VOLUNTARY INTEGRATION

In the fall of 1999, in a privileged enclave of Seattle, Washington, Kathleen Brose began helping her eighth-grade daughter, Elizabeth, explore the city's high school application process. The Seattle School District had recently introduced a novel procedure for pupil assignments in an effort to diminish the effects of segregated housing on education. Rather than automatically assigning students to their neighborhood schools, the district's new system permitted students to rank their preferences among its ten high schools from most desirable to least desirable. If more students sought admission to a particular high school than space existed, the district turned to a tiebreaker system that considered first whether the applicant had a sibling who attended the oversubscribed school and then—more controversially—how the applicant's race affected that school's racial composition in comparison with the entire district. Seattle aimed to ensure that each high school's student body did not deviate more than 10 percent from the district's overall racial composition, which it identified as 41 percent white and 59 percent nonwhite (a group that included African Americans, Asian Americans, and Latinos). As a practical matter, this integration goal meant that, when an oversubscribed school's composition fell outside the 10 percent safe harbor, the school admitted students who would help it broadly resemble the district's racial demographics.

After researching Seattle's public schooling options, Brose grew attached to the notion that Elizabeth would attend Ballard High School. Not only did Ballard's idyllic campus sit nearest their home, but it had also recently been rebuilt from the ground up, part of a thirty-five-million-dollar renovation that introduced state-of-the-art amenities, including a grand library, a television studio space, and even a genetics laboratory. When Elizabeth received her much-awaited school assignment notification in the spring of 2000, however, eager anticipation quickly yielded to bitter resentment. In addition to shattering the first-choice dream of Ballard, Seattle declined to grant Elizabeth's second and third selections, leaving her to attend Franklin High School, her fourth choice. Brose did not style herself an activist, but Elizabeth's school assignment experience spurred her to legal action. "Frankly, a lawsuit is a scary thing and many people just gave up," Brose explained. "Not me! I was too angry to let it go. Every fiber in my body told me to fight this injustice." Brose formed an organization called Parents Involved in Community Schools that filed a lawsuit contesting what she referred to as the district's "racist policy." Although when the case reached the Supreme Court a PBS reporter would refer to Franklin as "a heavily black school with lower test scores," Brose herself steered clear of such talk, strictly adhering to the language of constitutional colorblindness. "It is difficult enough being a teenager in our fast-paced world without being forced to go to a school you don't want to go to, just because you have the 'wrong' skin color," Brose contended. In a rhetorical question that conjured Senator Ervin's interrogation of Attorney General Robert Kennedy in the 1960s, Brose asserted, "Was not *Brown v. Board of Education* about making sure that children were not denied access to a school based solely on skin color? The U.S. Constitution is here for all of us, not some of us." Seattle's policy seeking to increase integration in its public schools represented not only a violation of the Constitution, according to Brose, but also a sacrifice of morality and national ideals: "It's wrong. It's illegal. To me, it's immoral. This is the United States. We do not discriminate." Upon agreeing to address the Brose-led lawsuit when it reached the Supreme Court in 2006, the Court consolidated it with one from Louisville, Kentucky, that raised the same fundamental question: Can school districts voluntarily initiate programs that classify students by race to advance integration, even in the absence of a court order requiring that action?[156]

When the dispute arrived at the Court, both detractors and supporters of these programs could locate reasons for optimism that the Court would resolve the issue in their favor. For detractors, the Supreme Court—under the leadership of Chief Justice Rehnquist, who inherited the post from Burger in 1986—issued a trio of decisions in the 1990s that quietly eroded lower courts' authority to order desegregation decrees, even in jurisdictions that featured de jure segregation. The overarching theme of these cases indicated that the time for court-ordered desegregation had ended, as that mechanism had simply run its course. First, in 1991, Rehnquist wrote an opinion for the Court holding that, even if vestiges of de jure segregation remained in a school system, desegregation orders must nevertheless be eliminated following "a reasonable period of time."[157] Then, one year later, Justice Anthony Kennedy wrote an opinion for the Court, similarly requiring courts to "[r]eturn[ ] schools to the control of local authorities at the earliest practicable date" and observing, "[W]ith the passage of time, the degree to which racial imbalances continue to represent vestiges of a constitutional violation may diminish."[158]* Finally, in 1995, Rehnquist wrote another opinion for the Court invalidating a judge-ordered magnet school program that was designed to attract white suburban pupils into a predominantly black school district. Before he struck down the desegregation program on the theory that the cross-district solution represented an inversion of the problem in *Bradley*, Rehnquist's opening sentence left no doubt that he felt this entire set of questions had grown stale. "As this school desegregation litigation enters its 18th year," Rehnquist began, "we are called upon again to review the decisions of the lower courts."[159] Following these decisions, many school districts successfully sued to have their formerly dual school districts be declared "unitary," and therefore no longer subject to judicial oversight on desegregation. In sum,

---

* Justice Antonin Scalia wrote a concurring opinion in this case, which arose from DeKalb County, Georgia, echoing this same temporal theme: "At some time, we must acknowledge that it has become absurd to assume . . . that violations of the Constitution dating from the days when Lyndon Johnson was President, or earlier, continue to have an appreciable effect upon current operation of schools." *Freeman v. Pitts*, 503 U.S. 467, 506 (1992) (Scalia, J., concurring).

Swann in 1971 had noted that desegregation decrees ought not be expected to last in perpetuity, and two decades later it seemed clear that time was up.

For supporters of race-conscious student assignments, the relevance of the Supreme Court's series of unkind decisions during the 1990s could be minimized, if not dismissed altogether, because each case involved desegregation remedies ordered by *judges*. In contrast, the plans at issue in Louisville and Seattle were voluntarily undertaken by *school boards*, and the Court previously indicated in *Swann* that educators enjoyed great discretion to pursue integration. In addition, supporters could take heart in a major, recent Supreme Court opinion upholding the University of Michigan Law School's affirmative action program. Although higher education could theoretically be distinguished from elementary and secondary school education, many observers—with a nod toward *Brown*—believed that the Court's vigorous defense of racial diversity at the University of Michigan Law School applied even more compellingly during students' most formative years of schooling. Supporters could also hope that Chief Justice John Roberts—whom President George W. Bush tapped to fill the Court's center seat following Rehnquist's death in 2005—would view race-conscious desegregation remedies more favorably than his predecessor. As a young lawyer, Roberts had served then-Justice Rehnquist as a law clerk in the early 1980s before taking various posts in the Reagan administration, positions that suggested he embraced constitutional colorblindness. Following his nomination to the Court, however, Roberts took pains to distance himself from the Federalist Society, clarifying that he was never a member of the organization, and legal liberals seized upon this action as signaling that his tenure may often eschew conservative constitutional dogma.[160]

In *Parents Involved in Community Schools v. Seattle School District No. 1*, Chief Justice Roberts in 2007 wrote an opinion—joined in full by three other justices (Alito, Scalia, and Thomas) and in its outcome by Justice Kennedy—invalidating the voluntary integration programs in Louisville and Seattle. Roberts summarily rejected the notion that the Court's recent precedent permitting affirmative action in higher education supported elementary and secondary schools in their pursuits of racial diversity. Roberts also sidestepped *Swann*'s language stating that districts could pursue integration of their own accord by labeling it obiter dicta, a legal term referring to portions of an opinion only incidental to its result. In the opinion's most momentous passages, Roberts squarely acknowledged that the case boiled down to a "debate" over "the heritage of *Brown*," and asserted that the storied opinion was best understood as vindicating Justice Harlan's defense of constitutional colorblindness in *Plessy*.[161] That notion prohibited schools from considering race in pupil assignments, according to Chief Justice Roberts, regardless of whether those considerations occurred in the name of Jim Crow segregation or modern-day integration. "Before *Brown*, schoolchildren were told where they could and could not go to school based on the color of their skin," Roberts wrote. "The school districts in these cases have not carried the heavy burden of demonstrating that we should allow this once again—even for very different reasons."[162] In an effort to secure his claim as *Brown*'s true inheritor, Roberts declared "history will be heard" and proceeded to quote a statement made by the NAACP LDF attorney Robert Carter during oral argument in *Brown*, appearing to articulate broad opposition to any racial classifications in school assignments: " 'We have one fundamental contention which we will seek to develop in the course of this argument, and that contention is that no State has any authority . . . to use race as a factor in affording educational opportunities among its citizens.' "[163] Finally, in the single most memorable line that Roberts has ever written, he concluded, "The way to stop discrimination on the basis of race is to stop discriminating on the basis of race."[164]*

---

* While Chief Justice Roberts credited no one with that line, Judge Carlos Bea—one of the circuit court judges in *Parents Involved* and a Federalist Society stalwart—used an uncannily similar construction in the case before it ever reached the Court. "The way to end racial discrimination is to stop discriminating by race," Judge Bea wrote. Ten years earlier, Theodore Olson—a Federalist Society mainstay who successfully argued *Bush v. Gore*—articulated an analogous formulation in expressing his opposition to affirmative action. The point here is not to suggest that Chief Justice Roberts—or Judge Bea, for that matter—plagiarized Olson, or anyone else; when a statement is repeated with sufficient frequency, its origins often become murky. The point instead is to observe the deep irony that Roberts—who assiduously resisted association with the Federalist Society prior to his confirmation—in authoring his most legendary sentence offered what appears to be merely a Federalist Society mantra. See *Parents Involved in Community Schools v. Seattle School District No. 1*, 426 F.3d 1162, 1222 (9th Cir. 2005) (Bea, J., dissenting); "Roberts Rules," *New Republic*, July 23, 2007, 1 (noting the similarity between Chief Justice Robert's phrasing and Judge Bea's, and linking it further back to Theodore Olson); and *Parents Involved in Community Schools v. Seattle School District No. 1*, 551 U.S. 701, 862 (2007) (Breyer, J., dissenting) (referring to Roberts's epigram as a "slogan" and quoting Judge Bea's statement).

At the opposite end of the spectrum, Justice Stephen Breyer—joined by three other justices—wrote a lengthy dissenting opinion that would have upheld the Louisville and Seattle integration plans in their entirety. Breyer read aloud portions of his dissent from the bench and spoke in a tone so intense, so impassioned that Linda Greenhouse—who had been covering the Court for *The New York Times* since the 1970s—noted she had never heard it from the typically cerebral Breyer. Consistent with this view, at a Harvard Law School symposium honoring Breyer for two decades of service as an associate justice held in 2014, more than seven full years after *Parents Involved*, he continued to identify this dissent as the single most important opinion of his entire judicial career. Retracting *Swann's* invitation to use racial classifications for purposes of integration constituted an enormously disruptive error, Breyer maintained, because school districts in areas around the country had relied upon that language to order their affairs. In addition, Breyer asserted that local school boards were far better positioned than federal judges to understand what desegregation solutions would work in their communities, and contended that the judiciary should defer to educators' greater expertise. "[J]udges are not well suited to act as school administrators," he contended.[165]*

Breyer took dead aim at Roberts's contention that *Brown* should be construed as a flat prohibition on racial classifications, and instead insisted that the landmark opinion be understood in a historically contextualized fashion. "[S]egregation policies did not simply tell schoolchildren 'where they could and could not go to school based on the color of their skin'; they perpetuated a caste system rooted in the institutions of slavery and 80 years of legalized subordination," Breyer wrote. "The lesson of history is not that efforts to continue racial segregation are constitutionally indistinguishable from efforts to achieve racial integration. Indeed, it is a cruel distortion of his-

---

* Astute readers will notice that Justice Breyer's position in *Parents Involved* afforded school authorities considerable deference—an argument that I have repeatedly contended ought not prevail in this constitutional domain. The more analytically persuasive pro-integration position in *Parents Involved* would have adopted and refined Justice Powell's concurrence in *Keyes*, that is, found that the Equal Protection Clause does not merely *permit* educators to pursue meaningfully integrated schools, but in fact *requires* them to do so. Yet by 2007, this position—one adopted by a quite racially conservative justice nearly thirty-five years earlier—had receded from prominence. Accordingly, it is difficult to fault Justice Breyer for not championing a position that very few were advancing.

tory to compare Topeka, Kansas, in the 1950's to Louisville and Seattle in the modern day."[166] After rejecting Roberts's opinion as an extended exercise in false equivalence, Breyer closed the dissent by staking his own claim to *Brown*'s mantle, reading the opinion to promote racial integration:

> [W]hat of the hope and promise of *Brown*? For much of this Nation's history, the races remained divided. It was not long ago that people of different races drank from separate fountains, rode on separate buses, and studied in separate schools. In this Court's finest hour, *Brown v. Board of Education* challenged this history and helped to change it. For *Brown* held out a promise. It was a promise embodied in three Amendments designed to make citizens of slaves. It was the promise of true racial equality—not as a matter of fine words on paper, but as a matter of everyday life in the Nation's cities and schools. . . . The last half century has witnessed great strides toward racial equality, but we have not yet realized the promise of *Brown*. To invalidate the plans under review is to threaten the promise of *Brown*. [Chief Justice Roberts's] position, I fear, would break that promise. This is a decision that the Court and the Nation will come to regret.[167]*

Splitting the distance between the polar views of Roberts and Breyer, Justice Kennedy wrote an opinion only for himself that, on the one hand, concluded the integration programs did not pass constitutional muster and, on the other hand, rejected the notion that educators must invariably ignore racial considerations. Kennedy's solo opinion merits examination for its jurisprudential innovation

---

* Writing only for himself, Justice John Paul Stevens also dissented in *Parents Involved*. In an unusually personal comment for a judicial opinion, Stevens suggested that the Court had grown almost unfathomably conservative on racial questions during his decades at the institution. "It is my firm conviction," Stevens wrote, "that no Member of the Court that I joined in 1975 would have agreed with today's decision." *Parents Involved*, 551 U.S. at 803 (Stevens, J., dissenting). While considerable evidence supports the broad proposition that the Court became more skeptical of race-conscious remedies during Stevens's tenure, it seems worth noting that Stevens himself traveled in the opposite direction, as he became markedly more liberal on those questions over time. In 1980, Justice Stevens likened an affirmative action program for minority business owners to Nazi Germany's treatment of Jews. See *Fullilove v. Klutznick*, 448 U.S. 448, 534n5 (1980) (Stevens, J., dissenting). For an article describing (and defending) Justice Stevens's leftward journey on the Court, see Justin Driver, "Judicial Inconsistency as Virtue: The Case of Justice Stevens," 99 *Georgetown Law Journal* 1263 (2011).

and because—given that four justices agreed with his conclusion, and a different four justices agreed with a portion of his reasoning—lower courts have accepted it as articulating *Parents Involved*'s governing standard. Along with the Roberts-led contingent, Kennedy shares a deep aversion to government programs that classify individual students according to race for student placement purposes. Kennedy's expression of this idea highlights notions of what might be termed "racial libertarianism." As Kennedy explained,

> When the government classifies an individual by race, it must first define what it means to be of a race. Who exactly is white and who is nonwhite? To be forced to live under a state-mandated racial label is inconsistent with the dignity of individuals in our society. . . . Under our Constitution the individual, child or adult, can find his own identity, can define her own persona, without state intervention that classifies on the basis of his race or the color of her skin.[168]

Kennedy parted company with the justices who voted to invalidate the programs, however, by creatively disentangling two concepts that had traditionally been lumped together, as he contended that opposing racial classifications did not necessarily entail embracing constitutional colorblindness. Indeed, Kennedy explicitly distanced his position from Harlan's elevation of the colorblind model in *Plessy*. "[A]s an aspiration," Kennedy wrote, "Justice Harlan's axiom must command our assent. In the real world, it is regrettable to say, it cannot be a universal constitutional principle."[169] Along with the Breyer-led contingent, moreover, Kennedy endorsed the notion that racial integration in schools constitutes a worthy, even a venerable goal. "This Nation has a moral and ethical obligation to fulfill its historic commitment to creating an integrated society that ensures equal opportunity for all of its children," Kennedy argued. "A compelling interest exists in avoiding racial isolation, an interest that a school district, in its discretion and expertise, may choose to pursue."[170]

How did Kennedy believe that educators could take account of race to achieve integrated schools while simultaneously believing they were prohibited from classifying students by race for pupil assignments? How, in other words, did Kennedy suggest school districts might go about threading this jurisprudential needle? In Kennedy's view, educators may attack the problem of racial isolation in schools by employing methods that "are race conscious but do not lead to different treatment based on a [racial] classification"—a category that he identified as including "strategic site selection of new schools; drawing attendance zones with general recognition of the demographics of neighborhoods; allocating resources for special programs; recruiting students and faculty in a targeted fashion; and tracking enrollments, performance, and other statistics by race."[171] Some readers will notice that the two leading items on Justice Kennedy's list of viable alternatives also appeared in Justice Powell's *Keyes* opinion—a debt that went unacknowledged by Kennedy, assuming that debt existed at all. The contexts of those two opinions, however, vary acutely; where Kennedy identified pro-integration site selections and attendance zones as two tactics that districts may pursue if they so elected, Powell identified those tactics as constitutionally *required*, at least in school systems plagued by racial isolation. That identical integration tactics went from being potentially compelled in the 1970s to—at most—merely being optional some three decades later vividly attests to the diminishing role that the Supreme Court assigned to school integration over time.

If *Parents Involved* can be reduced to a "debate" over *Brown's* meaning, as Roberts posited, the remaining lawyers who prevailed in the hallowed civil rights precedent wasted no time revealing their own scorecards, which awarded desperately few points to the chief justice's opinion. Only one day after the Court announced *Parents Involved, The New York Times* published various reactions from the *Brown* legal team admonishing Roberts's opinion—a high-profile reprimand that carried all the more sting because each of the quoted figures attained legendary status within the legal community. Robert Carter, who had become a distinguished federal judge in New York, announced that the chief justice's quotation from the *Brown* oral argument stripped it of the necessary historical context. "All that race was used for at that point in time was to deny equal opportunity to black people," Carter stated. "It's to stand that argument on its head to use race the way they use it now." Going further, Jack Greenberg—who became a professor at Columbia Law School after heading the NAACP LDF for nearly twenty-five years—called Roberts's interpretation "preposterous" because *Brown* challenged not racial classifications but "the marginalization and subjugation of black people." William Coleman—the first black law clerk at the Supreme Court back in the 1940s and an eventual member of President Gerald Ford's cabinet—labeled Roberts's opinion "100 percent wrong," adding, "It's dirty pool to say that the people *Brown* was supposed to protect are the people it's now not going to protect."[172]*

Media reactions to *Parents Involved* divided along the expected ideological lines, with liberals depicting the Court as dragging the nation backward to an earlier, repellent racial era. In an editorial titled "Resegregation Now," *The New York Times* commented, "There should be no mistaking just how radical this decision is. . . . The citizens of Louisville and Seattle, and the rest of the nation, can ponder the majority's kind words about *Brown* as they get to work today making their schools, and their cities, more segregated."[173] That tart assessment was mild, however, compared with the *San Francisco Chronicle*'s, which claimed *Parents Involved* marked "a shameful day in the long, elusive battle to instill equal opportunity in American schools" because its "twisted logic . . . echoes the Court's *Plessy vs. Ferguson* ruling of 1896."[174] *The Washington Post*'s Eugene Robinson, who noted that he benefited from attending integrated schools growing up in South Carolina, likened *Parents Involved* to the die-hard segregationist tactics of Alabama's governor George Wallace during the 1960s. "If we as a society . . . are going to work toward fairness, inclusion, equality and, yes, integration, we're going to have to do it by working around those dour men in black robes on Capitol Hill," Robinson wrote. "They have decided to stand in the schoolhouse door."[175]

In contrast, conservatives welcomed *Parents Involved* as a vindication of the colorblind vision of the Fourteenth Amendment, an idea that they attributed to *Brown*. "Starting now in Louisville and Seattle," *National Review* boasted, "students won't be blocked from certain schools simply because they lack the proper melanin

---

* Professor Pamela Karlan likened this stinging rebuke to the canonical scene in *Annie Hall*, where Woody Allen's character, stuck in a movie theater queue, overhears a pompous man blathering to his companion about Marshall McLuhan's views on media. Allen's character then interjects, "You don't know anything about Marshall McLuhan's work." When the bloviator objects and flashes some credentials, Allen settles the dispute by wandering out of the frame and producing McLuhan in the flesh, who verifies: "I heard, I heard what you were saying. You, you know nothing of my work." Pamela S. Karlan, "What Can *Brown®* Do for You? Neutral Principles and the Struggle over the Equal Protection Clause," 58 *Duke Law Journal* 1049, 1066 n90 (2009).

content."[176] *The Wall Street Journal* went further, construing *Parents Involved* as not only defending colorblindness but also striking down what it called "segregation," though, of course, the plans were in fact designed to combat segregation: "[T]he *Brown* precedent . . . said it is unconstitutional to deny students opportunities based on government-enforced racial segregation. The segregation here was concocted by the education bureaucrats themselves."[177]* George Will claimed that after *Brown* the Supreme Court for too long "instruct[ed] Americans to unlearn the lesson . . . that race must not be a source of government-conferred advantage or disadvantage." *Parents Involved* finally restored that fundamental lesson, Will contended, and rejected the mindset that "allows white majorities to feel noble while treating blacks and certain other minorities as seasoning, a sort of human oregano to be sprinkled across a student body to make the majority's educational experience more flavorful."[178]

Legal academia's assessment of *Parents Involved* also largely broke along the predicted ideological axis. From the left, Professor Goodwin Liu of Berkeley—who would soon take a seat on the California Supreme Court—compared Chief Justice Roberts's opinion to the Court's validation of separate railcars in *Plessy* because both opinions "fail[ed] to honestly confront the social meaning of segregation." Liu deemed the chief justice's failure to comprehend the message that segregation sent to society about racial equality "especially striking given [Roberts's] professed fidelity to *Brown*."[179] From the right, Judge J. Harvie Wilkinson III offered a far sunnier appraisal of *Parents Involved* in the pages of the *Harvard Law Review*. Wilkinson contended Breyer's dissent made the most persuasive case possible, as it commandeered arguments traditionally favored by legal conservatives—including deference to democracy, judicial restraint, and appreciation for local experimentation. Nevertheless, Wilkinson concluded, Breyer's strong argument could not overcome the basic righteousness of colorblindness. "[*Parents Involved*] took at least a small step toward establishing a principle that what unites us overshadows what divides us by race," Wilkinson wrote. "In doing so, it vindicated the ideals of the Declaration of Indepen-

---

* While Louisville and Seattle certainly engaged in racial *classifications* to battle racial isolation in schools, it is difficult to understand how their practices—which resulted in students attending more integrated schools than simple neighborhood assignment plans would permit—amount to segregation itself.

dence and the Fourteenth Amendment alike: that we are human beings in the sight of God and American citizens in the eyes of the law. No more, but no less. There is no other way."[180]

While Chief Justice Roberts's opinion in *Parents Involved* sits among the most analyzed Supreme Court opinions in recent years, perhaps its most troubling aspect has garnered insufficient attention. Many liberal legal academics have condemned Roberts's proclamation "[W]hen it comes to using race to assign children to schools, history will be heard."[181] These critics have contended that Roberts actually offered an ahistorical understanding of *Brown*, virtually ignoring the race-based caste system that the decision challenged. Viewed through this prism, such criticisms surely hit the mark.

In a deeper and even more disconcerting sense, though, Roberts can accurately claim that his opinion vindicated sentiments from the *Brown* era. Rather than embracing the views of those who initially proposed *Brown*, however, Roberts's opinion bears closer resemblance to the views of those who initially opposed it. The most ringing portions of Roberts's opinion sound as though they could have been ghostwritten by Senator Sam Ervin. In his autobiography, Ervin in 1984 expounded upon the ideas he began articulating in the 1950s and 1960s, as he assailed measures depriving "the States of the power to assign children to their schools on a non-racial basis," and "compel[ling] the States to make race the major consideration in assigning children to their schools."[182] At that time, of course, Ervin marshaled this colorblind rhetoric not against voluntary integration programs but against the Supreme Court's opinions buttressing *Brown* in *Green*, *Swann*, and *Keyes*. Ervin contended that these three opinions—which among them garnered a grand total of one dissenting vote—"repudiated [*Brown*] and the truth that the Constitution is color-blind" by "decree[ing] that the Constitution is color conscious."[183] While Roberts's opinion in *Parents Involved* identified different villains than Ervin did in 1984, the colorblind rhetoric remained exactly the same.

Although many commentators alternately hoped and feared that *Parents Involved* spelled the end of efforts to enhance racial integration in schools, those expectations have not yet materialized. Such plans are hardly pervasive, but neither are they unprecedented. The most reliable recent assessment indicates educators in approximately seventy school districts around the country continue to employ various methods of increasing racial integration in their schools. While these methods may not be as efficient at achieving meaningful integration as classifying students according to race, they do leave enterprising school districts with at least some room to maneuver. Typically, they do so by—consistent with Justice Kennedy's controlling opinion—establishing attendance zones with awareness of the racial demographics in various neighborhoods. Efforts to render that technique unconstitutional have thus far gone nowhere; all four of the federal appellate courts that have entertained racially inflected constitutional challenges to student assignment plans post–*Parents Involved* have rejected those challenges. In addition, some school districts—including in Cambridge, Massachusetts; Wake County, North Carolina; Dallas, Texas; and La Crosse, Wisconsin—have selected an indirect route to racial integration by integrating students according to their families' socioeconomic class. The Constitution does not prohibit schools from assigning students to schools on the basis of class, and educators are able to increase racial integration due to the strong correlation of low socioeconomic status with racial minority status.

It is certainly within the realm of possibility that, as some legal scholars have posited, *Parents Involved* and the threat of litigation have deterred school districts from voluntarily enacting integrationist plans when they would otherwise have done so. But that account seems a highly implausible explanation for the relative paucity of pro-integrationist school programs in existence today. Few school districts voluntarily pursued racial integration before the Court decided *Parents Involved,* and few do so afterward; the tepid appetite for genuine racial integration in education, at least as assessed by the enacted policies, represents a continuous theme in modern American education. The primary obstacle to realizing meaningfully integrated schools nowadays comes in the form of not an unbending judiciary but an inert body politic. In the event that a desire for meaningful racial integration in schools somehow gains traction, the current doctrine should not be misunderstood to foreclose attempts at advancing those interests.[184]

It seems important to note, however, that permitting school districts to manipulate attendance zones for the sake of promoting racial integration succeeds in undermining a central claim of many conservatives' visions of the Equal Protection Clause. Conservatives frequently assert that it is necessary to review all governmental considerations of race with deep skepticism, even if they occur in a program designed to help rather than hurt racial minorities. That skeptical approach is always warranted, many conservatives insist, because the government cannot distinguish beneficial considerations of race from invidious considerations of race. But that theoretical evenhandedness would not, taken seriously, permit an exception for establishing pro-integration school boundaries. There should be no doubt, of course, that if evidence demonstrated that a school district gerrymandered attendance zones for the purpose of augmenting racial segregation, rather than racial integration, the judiciary would invalidate that action under the Equal Protection Clause. Those very actions drew the Court's ire in *Keyes*, and—if a lawsuit that materialized today were supported by a similar fact pattern—the Court would no doubt reach the same conclusion. Permitting gerrymandered lines for the purpose of school integration, but not school segregation, demonstrates that legal conservatives do in fact believe that they can discern the difference between positive and negative considerations of race, at least when they are motivated to do so. While conservatives could, of course, seek to eliminate this jurisprudential inconsistency by beginning to invalidate pro-integration attendance zones, the more fruitful approach would address the issue moving in the opposite direction, by abandoning the simplistic pretense that holds the effects of race-conscious decisions are somehow consistently unfathomable.[185]

Proponents of race-conscious efforts to decrease racial isolation in public schools, the camp where my own loyalties lie, would do well to acknowledge more expansively than they usually do that the plans adopted by Louisville and Seattle contained objectionable features. When Louisville families sought to transfer their children from assigned schools to different schools with open spaces, the school board sometimes sent a letter home denying the request and explaining that permitting it would, given their child's race, harm that school's desired racial composition. Such missives have about as much to recommend them as would a university's affirmative action program that mandated notifying certain rejected white applicants that they would have received admission if they were black or Latino. While governmental transparency is a laudable goal in many contexts, such openness here seems likely to breed needless racial resentment and hostility. Seattle's plan, moreover, acknowledged only two broad racial categories, rendering all students either white or nonwhite. But that method lacks appropriate nuance and seems spectacularly ill suited for capturing the city's rich racial diversity—where Asian Americans made up roughly 14 percent of the population, Latinos 9 percent, African Americans 8 percent, and more than 5 percent identified as multiracial. On this last category—in an even more distressing aspect of Seattle's program—the board required parents to identify their children with one and only one racial group; if a parent checked more than a single racial box, Seattle instructed school officials to overrule that determination by selecting the lone applicable category. Seattle's excessively rigid racial policy thus not only erased biracial and multiracial identities (contravening the nation's growing recognition of those categories) but also recalled the vile Jim Crow tradition of government officials inspecting purportedly white students for the telltale signs of negritude.[186]*

Even if supporters of race-conscious pupil-assignment programs deem these blemishes of insufficient gravamen to require invalidation, the deficiencies should nonetheless be forthrightly recognized rather than studiously ignored. Attempting to paper over the flaws of the Louisville and Seattle programs may lead some observers to conclude, incorrectly, that such regrettable tactics will invariably arise whenever educators classify students by race. Conversely, acknowledging the shortcomings of these particular programs could help to dissuade other school districts from adopting similarly flawed policies, in the event that a future Supreme Court overturns *Parents Involved* by permitting racial classifications for pupil assignments.

In order to eliminate misunderstandings of these criticisms, I should emphasize that I do not believe educators in Louisville and Seattle acted with anything other than honorable intentions in their efforts to promote meaningfully integrated schools. Instead, the particular weaknesses of their plans are, in my view, most attributable to the fact that these school boards, and those around the

---

* In 1954, Sheriff Willis McCall of Mount Dora, Florida, asserted that a local man's five children were improperly attending the white school because, he believed, they actually had black ancestors. Over the principal's objections, McCall inspected the children, concluding that one boy's "features are Negro" and stating of a thirteen-year-old girl, "I don't like the shape of that one's nose." At a rally, McCall further contended, "[T]here must have been a smoked Irishman in the woodpile." "Look at Your Own Child," *Time*, Dec. 13, 1954, 83. For scholarly treatments of related controversies, see Ian Haney López, *White by Law: The Legal Construction of Race* (1996); and Ariela J. Gross, *What Blood Won't Tell: A History of Race on Trial in America* (2008).

country, have insufficient experience crafting and implementing pro-integration policies. Had the Court required school districts to adopt such programs on a widespread basis in the aftermath of *Brown*, along the broad contours Justice Powell suggested in *Keyes*, a set of best integrationist practices would have long ago emerged, and school districts in more recent years could have modified those practices, fine-tuning them as the times and their unique circumstances required.

ASSESSING *BROWN*'S LEGACY

Surveying the state of racial isolation in the country's public schools today, more than six decades after *Brown*, provides ample reason for pessimism about the rate of progress. Throughout the nation, more than one in three black students now attend schools whose student bodies are composed of at least 90 percent racial minorities; in the Northeast, more than one in two black students attend such schools. Perhaps even more distressingly, those figures have increased since the early 1990s, when the Supreme Court began its hasty retreat from this realm by allowing school districts to abandon their desegregation commitments. While the nation's schools have become more diverse in recent decades, largely due to the sharp increase of Latino students, Latinos are also concentrated in disproportionately minority schools. Some commentators in recent years have documented the rise of what they call "apartheid schools," where white students make up 1 percent or less of the student body; in 1988, there were fewer than three thousand such schools, but by 2011 there were nearly seven thousand, accounting for approximately 7 percent of the public schools in the entire nation. Relatedly, some major school districts—not schools, mind you, but entire districts—contain astonishingly tiny percentages of white pupils. In the school year that ended in 2013, for instance, a mere 5 percent of public school students in Dallas were white; that same figure was 9 percent in Los Angeles, 11 percent in Washington, D.C., and 12 percent in Boston. While public schools with very few nonwhite students have decreased in recent years, some scholars have suggested that this salutary development may have the regrettable effect of communicating a misleading impression to white families about the pace of progress with desegregation, obscuring the persistent racial isolation that continues to plague far too many schools.[187]

This bleak picture of school segregation had emerged with sufficient clarity in 2004, when *Brown* marked its fiftieth anniversary, that some observers loudly questioned whether the occasion deserved celebration at all. *Newsweek* called the event "bittersweet" and a time for tears to be shed, because *"Brown* . . . is something of a bust."[188] In an editorial called "Unhappy Anniversary," *National Review* added that "[i]t was impossible for anyone, whatever his political persuasion, not to be a bit melancholy" contemplating *Brown*'s legacy.[189] The pages of law reviews teemed with scholars debating whether *Brown* could legitimately be deemed successful, and a spate of books by prominent authors cast serious doubt on that proposition. In perhaps the most jaundiced assessment of all, Professor Derrick Bell suggested—presumably with apologies to Rehnquist's several decades' old law clerk memorandum—that it would have been better had the Supreme Court in *Brown* simply reaffirmed *Plessy v. Ferguson*. Had the Court required genuinely equal expenditures under "separate but equal," Bell reasoned, black students who continued to attend segregated schools would have at least obtained something of real value from the decision.[190]

Was *Brown* essentially all for naught? Such claims, however superficially appealing, founder upon close examination. Contentions that *Brown* should be understood as a failure stem more from disappointed expectations for comprehensive change than from a sober evaluation of what the opinion actually achieved. While it would be foolhardy to argue that *Brown* achieved everything, it would be reckless to maintain that *Brown* achieved nothing.

Brown's skeptics typically focus on the opinion's narrow effects on desegregation in education. If we examine the issue only through that lens for the moment, it is undeniably true that *Brown* can be construed as deficient along a few different dimensions. *Brown*'s skeptics emphasize, for example, that very few black students in the Deep South attended school with white students until the mid-1960s, when Congress enacted legislation supporting desegregation. *Brown*'s skeptics also stress, not surprisingly, that the Court refrained from addressing de facto segregation in a forthright manner, meaning that non-southern jurisdictions were generally left untouched. Such critiques have become so familiar in legal circles today that it has grown easy to lose sight of the fact that the opinion accomplished anything at all.

Brown's single most important contribution was, of course, its elimination of official regulations prohibiting students of color from attending public schools with white students. That core understanding of Brown's holding has not eroded or diminished at all over time. Even if one believes—as I do, and as Chief Justice Warren did, for that matter—that this understanding fails to honor that precedent fully, that belief should not be permitted to overshadow Brown's repudiation of Jim Crow.* Indeed, believing that the Court should have also deemed de facto school segregation unconstitutional hardly precludes recognizing that official policies enshrining racial subordination into law contained especially odious social messages, and that the elimination of those measures presented an urgent item on the racial egalitarian's agenda.

Even on the basic question of how many black students attended school with white students directly as a result of Brown and its progeny, the record here is more complex than the opinion's many detractors often suggest. Although now is not the occasion to recite the full litany of racial minorities across the country who attended meaningfully integrated schools as a result of judicial decisions, consider two underappreciated points. First, while desegregation proceeded at a leisurely pace post-Brown in the Deep South, the project moved at a perhaps surprisingly brisk pace in the border states. When the Court decided Brown II, only 11 percent of black students attended schools with whites in the border states, but one year later that figure skyrocketed to 40 percent, and it continued to increase steadily prior to federal legislation backing Brown. Second, despite the South's slow start to desegregation, it merits recalling that southern schools quickly attained lower levels of racial isolation for black students than did schools in any other part of the country. Even today, long after the peak of court-ordered integration, the

---

* Early in his memoir, Chief Justice Warren himself made clear that he viewed Brown as applying across the country—not only in the Jim Crow South. "Seventeen of our states, by their own laws, had racially segregated public schools [in 1954]," Warren wrote. "A number of others had de facto segregation because of the rapid growth of ghettos which concentrated minority groups in the larger cities. The Brown case, when it came before the Supreme Court, challenged such discrimination in public schools as being unconstitutional." Warren, Memoirs of Earl Warren, 2.

South continues to claim lower levels of racial isolation for racial minorities. The South's comparative success with desegregation stems from no deep mystery, as the South featured the highest concentration of successful school desegregation suits. The southern experience with court-ordered desegregation suggests that *Brown's* implementation might well have been even more effective if the Court's jurisprudence extending that precedent had made it easier to hold jurisdictions outside the South accountable for segregated schools. But there is an enormous difference between depicting *Brown* as failing to realize its full potential and portraying the opinion as an utter failure. Commentators who question whether *Brown* should be deemed a positive contribution to American society—let alone those who pine for the good old days of *Plessy*—elide that crucial distinction.[191]

Even if one concedes that *Brown* failed to achieve the paramount goal of integrating schools across the nation, that shortcoming should in no way be taken to demonstrate that the Supreme Court fundamentally lacks the ability to engender meaningful change. The effort to integrate schools involved many complex, moving parts and required compliance from a wide array of actors—including judges, educators, parents, and children—regarding some of the most fraught questions in American society. Judicial opinions typically have a much, much lower degree of difficulty than *Brown* and school integration. Racial discord constitutes this nation's deepest, most vexing issue, and—for that very reason—the issue provides an exceptionally weak basis for extrapolating a comprehensive view deeming the Supreme Court an impotent institution. Using *Brown* to derive conclusions about law's capacity for change, in other words, has only slightly less to recommend it than using cancer to derive conclusions about medicine's capacity for healing.

But assessing whether *Brown* "succeeded" primarily on the basis of how many black children attend school with white children offers an exceedingly constricted frame with which to appreciate the opinion's positive effects. More than any other case in education law, *Brown's* significance extends—and is, indeed, perhaps most apparent—outside its original context. Robert Carter expressed this point as elegantly as anyone in 1968 as he surveyed *Brown's* impact. While he expressed deep frustration with the decision's utility in the educational sphere, he also insisted that its import in other domains was nothing less than profound. "*Brown's* indirect consequences . . .

have been awesome," Carter wrote. "It has completely altered the style, the spirit, and the stance of race relations."[192] The opinion "fathered a social upheaval the extent and consequences of which cannot even now be measured with certainty," Carter maintained, as it "mark[ed] a divide in American life."[193] Carter contended that *Brown's* most salient transformation occurred within the minds of African Americans:

> [T]he psychological dimensions of America's race relations problem were completely recast. Blacks were no longer supplicants seeking, pleading, begging to be treated as full-fledged members of the human race.... They were entitled to equal treatment as a right under the law; when such treatment was denied, they were being deprived—in fact robbed—of what was legally theirs. As a result, the Negro was propelled into a stance of insistent militancy.[194]

Brown, properly understood, provided supporters of racial equality with a powerful rhetorical and moral weapon that helped to catalyze the nation toward the goal of racial equality. This understanding of *Brown's* import did not arise only in retrospect, but existed from the very beginning. Two months after *Brown,* Professor Arthur Sutherland of Harvard wrote, "One should never forget the immense moral pressure of such a great judgment as that just announced, and its capacity to persuade men of good will who have been doubting and hesitating."[195] Two years later, a similar version of this idea made its way south to New Haven, Connecticut, where Professor Alexander Bickel perceptively contended that desegregation's lethargic emergence from the starting blocks should not be mistaken for indicating *Brown* had no real influence on society. "[L]ike poetry, to call to mind a line of Auden's, declarations which do not invoke the power of the state to tell a specific party to do a specific thing make nothing happen," Bickel wrote. "[Y]et such declarations from the high priests of our secular religion, the Constitution, do affect our outlook and may even move some to action."[196]*

Such assessments of *Brown's* catalyzing effects were hardly con-

---

* Bickel alludes to Auden's famous—and famously protean—line that reads, "For poetry makes nothing happen: it survives." W. H. Auden, "In Memory of W. B. Yeats," in *Another Time* 93, 94 (1940).

fined to legal academia. Without *Brown*, it would have been impossible for the Reverend Martin Luther King Jr. in 1955 to proclaim as the head of the newly formed Montgomery Improvement Association, "If we are wrong, then the Supreme Court of this Nation is wrong. If we are wrong, the Constitution of the United States is wrong. If we are wrong, God Almighty is wrong."[197] Without *Brown*, it would have been impossible for President John F. Kennedy in 1963 to claim in a speech that established the foundation for what would become, following his assassination, the Civil Rights Act of 1964, "We are confronted primarily with a moral issue. It is as old as the Scriptures and is as clear as the American Constitution."[198] The Supreme Court's embrace of racial equality in *Brown* provided the moral vision and the constitutional clarity to a subject that had previously appeared bathed in myopia, and thus performed essential work guiding the nation's ensuing strides toward racial equality. Even if *Brown* did not single-handedly reach that destination, it is severely mistaken to deny that *Brown* represented a major milestone on that journey.

Modern appraisals of *Brown* too often overlook that the opinion continues to resonate constructively in the modern era. Quite apart from being used only to prohibit plans to achieve racial integration, the federal judiciary has also relied upon the landmark to check educators' racialized subordination of minority students. To offer one arresting example of *Brown*'s salutary effect from recent years, a federal judge in 2006 relied upon the iconic decision to invalidate a principal's method of assigning pupils to classrooms within an elementary school located in a wealthy North Dallas neighborhood. At Preston Hollow Elementary School, strong sworn evidence suggested that many Latino students were discriminatorily assigned to English as a second language (ESL) classrooms, despite being proficient in English. Stunningly, some Preston Hollow students were assigned to ESL classrooms despite speaking English at home, and a few had even been identified as "gifted and talented" students while being tested in English. The principal's motive for such specious classroom assignments stemmed from her apparent desire to create at least one classroom per grade where white students would predominate, forming in effect a school within a school to avert white flight.

Despite powerful evidence supporting the allegations of discriminatory assignments (including from teachers at the school),

Preston Hollow sought to defend the assignments by asserting—
among other contentions—that the ESL classrooms covered the
same material in the same sequence as the regular classes, and thus
the ESL-designated students could not successfully prove that they
had been denied equal educational opportunity. The district court
judge rejected this contention by quoting *Brown* for the proposition that "'[s]eparate educational facilities are inherently unequal'"
and concluded that the desire to retain white families in the school
system had unconstitutionally been permitted to supersede a basic
concern for educating all students.[199] While it is deeply regrettable
that even five decades after *Brown* the federal judiciary continued to
find occasions to use the opinion to block such ugly racial subjugation in schools, it would be far more regrettable if *Brown* did not
exist as a precedent to forestall this sort of malevolence.

6

Equal Protection II:
Funding Disparities, Sex Separations,
and Unauthorized Immigration

Beginning in the early 1970s, over the course of slightly less than a decade, the Supreme Court explored whether the Fourteenth Amendment's Equal Protection Clause constrained schools' operations—beyond the racial context—on three separate occasions. First, in *San Antonio Independent School District v. Rodriguez*, the Supreme Court in 1973 rejected the claim that the Constitution prohibited states from funding public schools in a manner that yielded massive disparities in per pupil expenditures between areas with high property values and areas with low property values. Next, in *Vorchheimer v. School District of Philadelphia*, the Supreme Court in 1977 declined to forbid localities from maintaining at least some public schools that limited admission to either male or female students. Third, in *Plyler v. Doe*, the Supreme Court in 1982 invalidated a Texas measure that authorized localities to exclude unauthorized immigrants from attending public schools altogether. Collectively, this trio of decisions can meaningfully be understood as fleshing out both the requirements and the limitations of the nation's constitutional commitment to school equality, most resoundingly articulated in *Brown v. Board of Education*.

Even taken on their own terms, however, these three cases touched on some of the most combustible issues in all of American society: fiscal inequality, sex separation, and unauthorized immigration. Perhaps predictably, then, all three of these divisive issues also elicited close divisions at the Supreme Court—as *Rodriguez* and *Plyler v. Doe* each produced 5–4 margins, and *Vorchheimer* left the Court deadlocked 4–4 (with one justice recused). These close divisions underscore the highly contingent nature of constitutional law, as a single changed vote in any of the cases would have altered the outcome and hence the legal framework governing public schools on a particularly volatile topic.

This equal protection trilogy merits renewed scrutiny now because each decision reveals a remarkable and underappreciated legacy of the Supreme Court's constitutional decisions involving schools. Following *Rodriguez*, school finance reformers directed their litigation efforts toward state supreme courts, which have on balance proven quite receptive to those claims. The aftermath of *Rodriguez* reveals thus that, even if federal courts prove initially hostile to rights claims under the federal Constitution, reformers can attain victories at least sometimes by invoking state constitutional provisions. Following *Vorchheimer*, although single-sex public schools dwindled in the late 1970s and the 1980s, the institutions witnessed a major resurgence beginning in the 1990s that has continued through the present. This revival of single-sex public schools demonstrates that the Supreme Court, even through its refusal to stamp out a practice that appears to be vanishing, shapes the educational landscape simply by leaving an issue on the table. Recently, the issue of sex classifications in schools obliquely returned to the Supreme Court's docket, when it agreed to hear—but did not ultimately resolve—a case addressing whether schools can exclude transgender students from accessing restrooms congruent with their gender identities. Following *Plyler v. Doe*, various jurisdictions around the nation have continued seeking to exclude unauthorized immigrants from public schools via both formal and informal mechanisms. Esteemed law professors in recent years have attempted to dismiss the opinion's significance because only Texas had enacted such legislation by 1982. But this criticism misconstrues *Plyler v. Doe* as—properly understood—it rests among the most egalitarian, momentous, and efficacious constitutional opinions that the Supreme Court has issued throughout its entire history.

SAN ANTONIO INDEPENDENT SCHOOL DISTRICT V. RODRIGUEZ:
CONTESTING FUNDING INEQUALITIES

In 1968, in a destitute neighborhood of San Antonio, Texas, called Edgewood, Demetrio Rodriguez grew dissatisfied with the education that his children were receiving at the local elementary school and devoted himself to the task of improving it. Rodriguez—a World War II veteran and third-generation Texan—had long ago received an object lesson in the importance of schooling. Although his parents were migrant farmworkers in the Rio Grande Valley, they sent six-year-old Demetrio more than two hundred miles north to live with an uncle in San Antonio, where they felt he would acquire a better education and the opportunity for a better job. The familial sacrifice paid off, as Rodriguez grew up to secure a steady position working in the sheet metal division at Kelly Air Force Base. Yet as Rodriguez now surveyed the school his own children attended, it was clear that Edgewood Elementary left much to be desired: the building itself had become severely dilapidated; classrooms lacked even basic supplies; and nearly half of the instructors relied upon emergency work permits because they lacked teaching certification.

The school's deficiencies, Rodriguez would subsequently conclude, stemmed from Edgewood Independent School District's comparatively low level of expenditures per pupil. Although Edgewood taxed property at the highest rate in the metropolitan area, the meager property values in the overwhelmingly Mexican American district yielded only $26 per pupil—a figure that contributions from the state and federal governments increased to $356 per pupil. Across town, in the predominantly white Alamo Heights Independent School District, the funding situation was dramatically different. Despite taxing property at a considerably lower rate than Edgewood, Alamo Heights's affluent property values produced $333 per pupil, which state and federal contributions raised to $594 per pupil. The upshot of this financing system meant that Edgewood expended on its students only 60 percent of the amount that Alamo Heights expended on its students. Accordingly, Rodriguez agreed to join a lawsuit contending that such school-funding discrepancies—which existed not only all over Texas but across the country—violated the Fourteenth Amendment's Equal Protection Clause. Rodriguez's decision to contest the state's financing method angered some of his fellow Texans, as a few co-workers hurled accusations that the lawsuit was motivated by communism and—far more distressingly—a few vandals hurled rocks through the windows of his family's home.[1]

In the years preceding the Supreme Court's resolution of *San Antonio Independent School District v. Rodriguez,* school finance reformers received several favorable signs regarding a legal challenge. In 1971, *Newsweek* noted that "many legal experts consider [it] likely" that the Court would invalidate Texas's method of school funding.[2] Notably, this understanding extended even to sophisticated analysts who dreaded this prospect, rather than dreamed of it. Writing in *The University of Chicago Law Review* in 1968, Professor Philip Kurland confidently—and woefully—predicted, "I should tell you . . . , with some assurance, that sooner or later the Supreme Court will affirm the proposition that a State is obligated by the equal protection clause to afford equal educational opportunity to all of its public school students."[3] This prediction was sound, Kurland maintained, because such a decision "is in keeping with the spirit of the times"—namely, the Warren Court's dual emphases on "egalitarianism" and the "expansion of judicial power."[4] Following Rodriguez's lower court victory, moreover, *The Wall Street Journal* thought that it spotted the same, unwelcome handwriting on the wall: "[T]here is every likelihood that the federal [judiciary] will seek to involve itself more deeply in the financing and administration of public schools, moving the locus of power still farther away from local communities. The homogenization of our society will thus have proceeded farther to the detriment of pluralism."[5] The emerging trend in lower courts offered reformers additional reason for optimism: apart from the invalidation of Texas's school-financing method, judicial bodies had already set aside the methods in no fewer than five other states prior to *Rodriguez.*[6]

Yet proponents of school-funding reform in the early 1970s also encountered many contrary signals, instilling doubt that the Court would actually validate their efforts. The enormous scale of the requested litigation reform stood prominent among the reasons for pessimism: if the Court rejected Texas's school-financing method, after all, that decision would have—setting aside the recent wave of lower court invalidations—upended the system in forty-eight additional states. While the Court might always be expected at least to hesitate when confronting a legal challenge to such a pervasive practice, the intricacies and uncertainties of school financing stood only to intensify the typical reservations. Even some firmly liberal voices expressed fears that invalidating school-financing schemes would both introduce novel, unknown harms and fail to improve substandard academic achievement in property-poor areas. On funding reform's potential unintended consequences, an article in *The New York Times* noted, "[T]he remedies that have been proposed so far seem to have led many people to question whether they should trade the present system for a new one that might create a whole new set of problems."[7] On the potential intractability of low academic achievement, a different *Times* article observed, "In the view of many, the true sources of educational deficiencies are rooted in the more basic inequalities among people, and no amount of reshuffling of tax dollars, however just, is going to change that."[8]

Relatedly, several observers contended before *Rodriguez* that reallocating school finances might yield nothing more than widespread academic mediocrity. *Newsweek* prominently struck this theme, as it commented, "[I]f equalization of school spending is uniformly enforced, it could well lead to uniformly mediocre education throughout the state."[9*] This fear of mediocrity found expositors in exclusive zip codes across the country—ranging from Beverly Hills, California, to Scarsdale, New York. The mayor of Beverly Hills—which spent twice as much money per pupil as neighboring communities, even though its tax rate reached only half as high— expressed this concern succinctly: "The way to lift the bottom isn't to drag down the top."[10] The president of Scarsdale's Board of Education adorned this anxiety somewhat, but the underlying message remained much the same: "There's a fundamental conflict between what's good for everyone and the natural desire of individuals to do the best they can for their own children. We feel a responsibility for others, but we do want to protect the kind of quality our people have come to expect."[11]

These conflicting stances on the desirability of school-financing

---

* *Newsweek*, evidently, was so enamored of this formulation that it repeated it nearly verbatim four months later, when it stated, "[M]any people fear that uniform educational spending could well lead to uniform educational mediocrity." "The Taxing Question," *Newsweek*, Jan. 31, 1972, 48.

reform that swirled within the larger American society can also be understood as appearing within the Nixon administration's attitude toward *Rodriguez*. As a formal matter, the administration watched *Rodriguez* unfold from the sidelines, as Nixon's solicitor general declined to file an amicus brief in the case. This formal silence on the case appears to have been driven not by studied equivocation but by portions of Nixon's political oratory that veered toward fiscal egalitarianism in the educational context. Thus, in the course of demanding a moratorium on busing for purposes of racial integration in 1972, Nixon intoned, "It is time for us to make a national commitment to see that the schools in central cities are upgraded so that the children who go there will have just as good a chance to get a quality education as do the children who go to school in the suburbs."[12] While Nixon's call for a busing moratorium sought primarily to ease suburban anxiety about the prospect of interdistrict racial integration, his attendant talk of increasing educational opportunity in the urban centers helped to prevent the position from appearing callous. Nixon did not thus sincerely intend to throw down the gauntlet for school-funding reform. But it would have been extremely delicate for his administration to file a brief rebuffing that cause only one year later, even if his sympathies did in fact align more with the status quo than with the reformers. This understanding of the Nixon administration's official noninvolvement with *Rodriguez* finds support in an additional public statement that the president made as the case wound its way to the Supreme Court in 1972. Nixon announced there was "one fundamental principle with which there can be no compromise: local school boards must have control over local schools." Astute contemporaneous observers linked Nixon's exaltation of local control to the swelling controversy over school financing.[13]

In 1973, the Supreme Court in *Rodriguez*, by a 5–4 margin, rejected the contention that Texas's system of school financing violated the Constitution. In a feature of the decision that garnered widespread notice, all four of President Nixon's appointees to the Court voted with the majority to uphold the funding method.*

---

* Justice Potter Stewart, whom President Eisenhower appointed, joined Nixon's four justices to form the majority. For a small sample of the commentary connecting *Rodriguez* to President Nixon's influence on the Court, see "Property-Tax Financing of Public Schools Upheld, 5–4, by Supreme Court, but Opponents Plan to Press Fight," *Wall Street Journal*, March 22, 1973, 3 ("The case divided the court along ideological lines,

Writing for the Court in *Rodriguez*, Justice Lewis F. Powell Jr. first rejected the contention that Texas's method of financing schools unconstitutionally discriminated against poor people. In addition to noting that the statute contained no language expressly grouping people on the basis of wealth, Powell entertained the possibility that some indigent citizens might in fact live in property-rich school districts and vice versa. Justice Powell also resisted the contention that the Constitution protects education as a fundamental right. The Constitution protected that right, Rodriguez had claimed, because it was integrally connected to exercising the freedom of speech and to participating in a constitutional republic. But Powell found this argument unavailing—at least in the context of Edgewood's students. "[W]e have never presumed to possess either the ability or the authority to guarantee to the citizenry the most *effective* speech or the most *informed* electoral choice," Powell opined. "That these may be desirable goals of a system of freedom of expression and of a representative form of government is not to be doubted [but] they are not values to be implemented by judicial intrusion into otherwise legitimate state activities."[14]

Despite this dismissal of Rodriguez's fundamental right claim, Powell's opinion did entertain the possibility that some extreme conditions may give rise to a constitutional violation. Whereas Edgewood's students contested merely relative differences in expenditure levels, Powell noted the Constitution could at least conceivably be violated either "if a State's financing system occasioned an absolute denial of educational opportunities to any of its children," or if a "charge fairly could be made that the system fails to provide each child with an opportunity to acquire the basic minimal skills necessary for the enjoyment" of speech and political participation.[15] Both of these conditions would loom large in subsequent education cases.

Perhaps of even greater significance than these doctrinal niceties, however, Powell's opinion in *Rodriguez* emphasized his predominant themes in cases involving constitutional law and public schools, as he asserted that federal judges possessed neither the

---

with all four Justices appointed by President Nixon voting with the conservative majority"); Warren Weaver Jr., "5 to 4 Against 'Upheaval,'" *New York Times*, March 25, 1973, 221 ("Voting to uphold the present system against claims of inequality were the four appointees of President Nixon"); and "School Tax Decision," *Chicago Defender*, March 31, 1973, 8 (noting that "[a]ll the Nixon appointees joined" *Rodriguez*).

competence nor the authority to review a decision that properly belonged to local officials. "[W]e stand on familiar ground when we continue to acknowledge that the Justices of this Court lack both the expertise and the familiarity with local problems so necessary to the making of wise decisions with respect to the raising and disposition of public revenues," Powell wrote.[16] Local control over school funding was paramount, Powell contended, because it meant providing an "opportunity [to participate] in the . . . process that determines how . . . local tax dollars will be spent," and that "[e]ach locality is free to tailor local programs to local needs."[17] Striking the pose of judicial humility, Powell observed that intervening in the school finance arena would be particularly unwise where the consequences of intervention would be massive and the proposed remedies were so novel. "We are unwilling to assume for ourselves a level of wisdom superior to that of legislators, scholars, and educational authorities in 50 States, especially where the alternatives proposed are only recently conceived and nowhere yet tested," Powell wrote.[18] In closing, Powell insisted that *Rodriguez* "not . . . be viewed as placing its judicial imprimatur on the status quo," but instead merely as indicating "the ultimate solutions must come from the lawmakers and from the democratic pressures of those who elect them."[19]

In dissent, Justice Thurgood Marshall denounced *Rodriguez* as a betrayal of *Brown v. Board of Education*'s robust understanding of the connection between education and the Equal Protection Clause. Although *Brown* arose in the context of racially segregated schools, the opinion also contained language that transcended racial inequality, including its observation that "where the state has undertaken to provide [education], it [ ] is a right which must be made available to all on equal terms."[20] Such statements enabled Marshall to contend that his colleagues in *Rodriguez* were unraveling his greatest achievement as an attorney: "[T]he majority's holding can only be seen as a retreat from our historic commitment [in *Brown*] to equality of educational opportunity and as unsupportable acquiescence in a system which deprives children in their earliest years of the chance to reach their full potential as citizens."[21] Developing this theme linking the responsibilities of citizenship to schooling, Marshall lambasted the Court for demonstrating an unduly cramped notion of fundamental rights. *Rodriguez* erred by not placing the right to education in this category, Marshall asserted, even though the Court had previously issued opinions acknowledging fundamental rights that the Constitution did not explicitly enunciate— including the right to procreate and the right to appeal a criminal conviction. In a nation predicated upon the ability of citizens to govern themselves effectively, Marshall at times seemed to wonder, what could possibly supersede education's importance? "Education serves the essential function of instilling in our young an understanding of and appreciation for the principles and operation of our governmental processes," Marshall wrote. "Education may instill the interest and provide the tools necessary for political discourse and debate. Indeed, it has frequently been suggested that education is the dominant factor affecting political consciousness and participation."[22]

Marshall further claimed that if the Court were actually committed to promoting local control over education, as Powell maintained, that consideration militated in favor of invalidating Texas's school-funding method. As Marshall explained, that financing method safeguarded local control only for those wealthy enough to purchase it:

> If Texas had a system truly dedicated to local fiscal control, one would expect the quality of the educational opportunity provided in each district to vary with the decision of the voters in that district as to the level of sacrifice they wish to make for public education. In fact, the Texas scheme produces precisely the opposite result. Local school districts cannot choose to have the best education in the State by imposing the highest tax rate. Instead, the quality of the educational opportunity offered by any particular district is largely determined by the amount of taxable property located in the district—a factor over which local voters can exercise no control.[23]

In a testament to the familiar adage holding that whenever God closes a door, He also opens a window, the one hundredth—and final—footnote of Marshall's opinion insisted that *Rodriguez* should not be mistaken to mean that all hope was lost for judicial intervention on school financing. "[N]othing in the Court's decision today should inhibit further review of state educational funding schemes

under state constitutional provisions," he wrote.[24] This parting suggestion to seek judicial remedies in state courts, rather than federal
courts, heralded the future of school finance reform.

Newspaper editorial boards across the ideological spectrum
commended *Rodriguez*. *The Wall Street Journal* asserted that a contrary decision in *Rodriguez* "would have cast great doubt over the
principle that local officials have . . . control over schools," potentially triggering unwelcome and "sweeping changes in the nation's
social and political structure" that would exceed the judiciary's
authority. "[T]he High Court cannot by edict dictate social justice,"
the *Journal* asserted. "It is such a subtle and elusive condition that it
can only be achieved by honest and forthright interactions among
individuals in their own communities."[25] In a particularly cynical
evaluation, the *Chicago Tribune* praised the Court for rejecting what
the newspaper dismissed as merely a ruse designed to raise teachers'
salaries.[26] Praise for *Rodriguez*, however guarded, also appeared in
more liberal publications. *The New York Times*, for example, commented that vindicating the school-financing claim in *Rodriguez*
"would raise questions about the future control . . . of public education," and asserted that the opinion's critics were "too simplistic" because they "ignore[d] the complexities of school support."[27]
The Washington Post added that the opinion "may be described as
a very cautious one, in an issue in which caution is essential," and
that it appropriately "drew back from the lower court's far too easy
assumptions." The *Post* contended that the appropriate venue for
pursuing school-funding reform was the statehouse, not the courthouse, and avowed further, "Neither the Court, nor anyone else,
has been able to devise a single nationwide rule of equality that
would not create new kinds of injustice, and threaten new restraints
on the improvement of American education."[28]

Back in Texas, *Rodriguez* caused many observers to exhale in
relief. "It's the best news I've heard in many a week," the superintendent of Dallas schools stated in reaction to the Court's decision. "Ain't it wonderful," another Dallas school official rejoiced.[29]
In Austin, Governor Dolph Briscoe, while demonstrating greater
equanimity, left no doubt that he endorsed the Court's refusal to
interfere with school funding. "I have said on many occasions that
I believe that every child should have the opportunity for a quality
education, regardless of where he lives," Briscoe noted. "But I also
believe in local control and participation."[30] In San Antonio, at least

one person seized upon *Rodriguez* as an occasion to heap ridicule upon the reproductive decisions of the case's lead plaintiff and those of other indigent citizens. In a breathtaking letter to the editor of the *San Antonio Express*, one Ruth Hill admonished,

> Instead of the 2.2 average which has been suggested for population control, many of the "poor" have 10 and 12 children to be educated by others. . . . Demetrio P. Rodriguez . . . has 5 children, 2.8 more than he should have produced for population control. Should the taxpayers be punished for his lack of restraint? After producing two offspring, parents should be taxed instead of being subsidized; then, no longer would it be "cheaper by the dozen"—for the other man to support.[31]

For his part, Demetrio Rodriguez pronounced himself "shocked and stunned" by the ruling and attributed the unforeseen, devastating loss to President Nixon's influence on the Court: "I cannot avoid at this moment feeling deep and bitter resentment against the supreme jurists and the persons who nominated them to that high position. The poor people have lost again."[32]

Examining *Rodriguez* today, more than four decades after it appeared, the opinion's most remarkable dimensions arise from temporal considerations. Had the question of school financing reached the Supreme Court a few years before *Rodriguez*—at the tail end of the Warren Court—it seems probable that a majority would have voted to invalidate the measure. In comments to the *San Antonio Express-News*, the attorney who represented Rodriguez embraced this conclusion on the decision's twenty-fifth anniversary: "I would never have dreamed of filing a case like that before a Supreme Court that existed when I argued before the court. When I filed the case in [district court in] 1968, the Court was not as conservative as the one that I argued before."[33] The reason that the funding reformers' chance of prevailing dimmed over that five-year lag is, of course, attributable to the personnel changes that occurred at the Court during that period. President Nixon's uncommonly good fortune of placing four justices on the Court—in just six years of office—seems to have been decisive in *Rodriguez*. If President Lyndon Johnson's nomination of Justice Abe Fortas to fill Earl Warren's seat as chief justice had succeeded in 1968—or even if Fortas had not been forced to resign from the Court due to a scandal in 1969—it seems virtually assured that school-funding methods around the nation would have been invalidated. *Rodriguez* thus casts into stark relief how the answer to significant constitutional questions can shift, even within relatively short periods of time, depending upon the Court's composition. Conscientious jurists who bring different perspectives to the position often reach divergent conclusions about what the Constitution permits and what it requires when interpreting the document's textually indeterminate provisions. Seldom have those competing constitutional visions been more vividly displayed than in *Rodriguez*.[34]

The passage of time, however, renders it less astonishing that Rodriguez lost his claim, and more astonishing that he managed to secure the votes of four Supreme Court justices in the first instance. Although the Court briefly contemplated serious engagement with issues of economic inequality during the 1960s, that moment now appears quite removed from the perspective of modern mainstream liberal constitutionalism. If the issue of school-funding discrepancies were to arrive at the current Supreme Court, it seems entirely plausible that challengers to those measures would find not a single justice who agreed that the Constitution prohibits arrangements resembling those contested in *Rodriguez*.

Consider the assessments of only two of the many prominent legal liberals who can be viewed as accepting—to varying extents—the bottom-line appraisal that the libertarian-inclined professor Richard Epstein recently offered: "The wisdom of [*Rodriguez*] seems beyond question."[35] In a radio interview from 2001, the then state senator (and University of Chicago Law School lecturer) Barack Obama described the Court in *Rodriguez* as "basically slap[ping] those kinds of [funding] claims down and say[ing], 'You know what—we as a court have no power to examine issues of redistribution and wealth inequalities with respect to schools. That's not a race issue, that's a wealth issue, and something we can't get into.'" Although that description may initially sound pejorative, Obama proceeded to make clear that he firmly endorsed *Rodriguez*'s rationale that issues of wealth inequality belonged in statehouses. "Maybe I am showing my bias here as a legislator as well as a law professor," Obama said, but "the [judiciary] just isn't structured that way."[36] In 2006, five years after Obama's statements, Professor Goodwin Liu published an article in *The Yale Law Journal* contending that public-school-funding disparities ought to be alleviated but charging

Congress—rather than the federal judiciary—with chief responsibility for undertaking that mission. Liu, who joined the California Supreme Court in 2011, contended that the enforcement power conferred on Congress by Section 5 of the Fourteenth Amendment obligated the legislative branch to enact a law "ensur[ing] a meaningful floor of educational opportunity throughout the nation."[37]

Some readers may object that both Obama and Liu staked out these positions when they had their sights trained on attaining higher offices. On this skeptical account, their statements should be discounted because they reflect not their genuine constitutional views but different sorts of political calculations. Even if we concede this account's accuracy, however, it is nevertheless revealing that both men—whose career prospects depended on remaining in good standing with the tenets of mainstream legal liberalism—took *Rodriguez* as granted, rather than as an affront.

Although *Rodriguez* succeeded in closing the federal courts to funding challenges for the next few decades, those suits eventually found a more receptive home in state supreme courts, where plaintiffs successfully invoked state constitutional provisions involving education to require more egalitarian school financing. In 1989, the Texas Supreme Court issued one of the nation's many such decisions in a case that originated in Edgewood. Demetrio Rodriguez found the long-awaited day declaring Texas's school-financing method invalid to be an emotional, even melancholy, experience. Speaking to a rally at an Edgewood high school, Rodriguez, who was by then a grandfather, stated, "I cried this morning because this is something that has been in my heart. . . . My children will not benefit from it. . . . Twenty-one years is a long time to wait."[38] In 1991, two years after Rodriguez's speech, Professor Mark Yudof offered the following witticism: "[S]chool finance reform is like a Russian novel: it's long, tedious, and everybody dies in the end."[39]

In truth, however, the battle over school finance reform in Texas's state courts had only just begun. The issue returned on what seemed to be a near-constant basis for decades thereafter because of the judicial approach adopted by the Texas Supreme Court. Rather than imposing any particular formula, the Texas Supreme Court—as was true in many of its sister institutions around the nation—simply invalidated the current financing scheme and required the legislature to devise a new approach.[40] In 2005, this dynamic prompted Demetrio Rodriguez to contend that the legal quest for school-financing reform was a job that "you never get finished with."[41] Ten years later, the Texas attorney general similarly called the saga "a never-ending cycle of perpetual litigation."[42] Over time, however, dissatisfaction with the school-financing system has shifted from property-poor areas to property-rich areas, whose residents frequently deride the Texas legislature's revised financing method as the "Robin Hood" plan.[43]

Some observers have questioned whether the legal victories school finance reformers achieved in state courts have translated into improved educational outcomes for students in previously underfunded schools. To be clear, those legal victories have frequently made a massive difference in per pupil expenditures in many states. In Texas, for example, beginning in the 1990s, the state's revised method of allocating money for public education succeeded in dramatically narrowing the gap between expenditures per pupil in Edgewood and in Alamo Heights; indeed, in 2008, Edgewood spent slightly more per pupil than Alamo Heights. Yet some observers emphasize that this altered financial landscape has not meaningfully improved the educational prospects for Edgewood's students. In this vein, Professor Richard Schragger recently contended, "[S]tudents who attend schools in Alamo Heights and Edgewood are in about the same place as they were in 1968. The chances of a high school student from Edgewood attending college is under ten percent; the chances of a high school student from Alamo Heights attending college is ninety-six percent."[44]

Other observers counter, however, that these sorts of comparisons place an inordinately high burden on school finance reformers to demonstrate success. A great number of factors shape students' academic performance, and increased funding alone should not be expected to cure—as if by magical elixir—all that ails students at low-achieving schools. Even if school-funding reform does not completely eliminate performance gaps between students at public schools that once had large financing disparities, these observers further insist, it would nevertheless be valuable if reform reduced the gap between these two groups, by lifting the academic performance of students at the formerly ill-funded schools. Consistent with this narrative, two of the most sophisticated studies of school financing recently found that increasing funding to previously underfunded schools yielded statistically significant academic benefits.[45]

Still other observers insist that long-standing debates about the efficacy of school finance reform are wholly irrelevant to the basic legal question. In this argument's strongest form, these observers assert that even if students at formerly underfunded schools demonstrate not one iota of improved academic performance as a result of a more equitable funding arrangement, that would in no way mean that these deserving students were less entitled to the increased expenditures. Proponents of this non-consequentialist position sometimes advocate for this view by posing a rhetorical question: Would the Supreme Court in *Brown v. Board of Education* have affirmed racially segregated schools if the leading sociologists and psychologists of the day suggested that Jim Crow schools did not actually harm black children? The question's force is meant to suggest that school finance reform—like racial segregation—should be evaluated squarely as a legal issue rather than being permitted to dissolve into a referendum on imperfect, hotly disputed social science.[46]

Although school-financing issues have predominantly appeared in state courts post-*Rodriguez*, the question of whether public schools can operate so poorly as to render them unconstitutional recently returned to federal court. In September 2016, a group of students who attend woefully performing public schools in Detroit, Michigan, sued Governor Rick Snyder in federal district court, contending that the Constitution protects a fundamental right to literacy. The students asserted that Michigan has deprived them of this fundamental right by sending them to public schools equipped with inadequate desks, textbooks, teachers, and even heat (among many other maladies), which combine to produce abysmal pupil outcomes. At one particularly grim Detroit elementary school, for instance, not a single sixth-grade student could read at a minimally proficient level. The lawsuit seeks to capitalize upon *Rodriguez*'s language allowing that schools may infringe upon a fundamental right if they fail to "provide each child with an opportunity to acquire the basic minimal skills necessary for" participation in democratic society.[47]* Michigan has shirked its responsibility for public educa-

---

* In 1986, the Supreme Court confirmed that it had not closed the door on the notion that the Constitution may protect some fundamental right to education: "As *Rodriguez* and *Plyler* indicate, this Court has not yet definitively settled the question[ ] whether a minimally adequate education is a fundamental right." *Papasan v. Allain*, 478 U.S. 265,

tion in Detroit's overwhelmingly black schools, the students contend, even though students in other, whiter parts of the state receive
first-rate educations. Although the district court has yet to resolve
the lawsuit, it has already garnered high-profile media attention,
and some eminent legal scholars—including Geoffrey Stone and
Laurence Tribe—have deemed the students' constitutional claim
persuasive. But whatever the district court judge determines, the
dispute seems almost certainly headed to the federal appellate court
and may even ultimately be taken up by the Supreme Court. And
if the Court acknowledged a fundamental constitutional right to
literacy, that decision could well have momentous consequences for
failing public schools, not only in Detroit, but around the country.[48]

VORCHHEIMER V. SCHOOL DISTRICT OF PHILADELPHIA AND THE
RETURN OF SINGLE-SEX PUBLIC SCHOOLS

In the spring of 1974, when Susan Vorchheimer completed the
ninth grade at a junior high school for gifted pupils in Philadelphia, Pennsylvania, she not only received the designation of "most
outstanding student" but also earned awards in a host of individual
subjects—including English, geometry, history, and science. After
she had amassed such a spectacular record, one might think that
Vorchheimer would have been guaranteed admission to Central
High School, the city's most elite public school. Vorchheimer dutifully toured Central as a ninth grader to ensure that the institution
felt like the right fit, and she emerged convinced that she would
thrive within its rigorous academic atmosphere. Central was, by
all accounts, an easy school to admire. Its legacy extended back to
1836; its exceptionally well-credentialed faculty would embarrass
those at even many private boarding schools; its science program
held particular renown, as Central became the first high school in
the country to feature its own planetarium; its graduates received
not mere diplomas but bachelor of arts degrees as symbols of their
academic achievement; and its alumni base included distinguished
artists, lawyers, economists, and industrialists. But this august insti-

285 (1986). For a recent article contending the Supreme Court should recognize a right
to education, see Barry Friedman and Sara Solow, "The Federal Right to an Adequate
Education," 81 *George Washington Law Review* 92 (2013).

tution rejected Vorchheimer's application for the simple reason that her sex rendered her ineligible to attend the all-male school. District officials observed that Vorchheimer could instead decide to attend the Philadelphia High School for Girls—the city's only school other than Central that received the "academic" designation. Vorchheimer's tour as a prospective student of the all-female alternative to Central, however, left her deeply apprehensive. "I just didn't like the impression [Girls High] gave me," Vorchheimer declared. "I didn't think I would be able to go there for three years and not be harmed in any way by it." Accordingly, Vorchheimer opted to attend a high school that, while it lacked the "academic" marker, did at least enroll members of both sexes. In addition, Vorchheimer elected to challenge the school district by filing a lawsuit contending Central's exclusion of female students violated the Equal Protection Clause.[49]

Publicity surrounding this litigation unleashed a tsunami of abuse upon the Vorchheimer home in the form of harassing phone calls and missives. Vorchheimer's father, for instance, fielded prank callers questioning the "real sex" of his child. One menacing postcard addressed to Vorchheimer, purporting to be sent by "Central High Alumni," stated, "Welcome to our school, and we hope you break your goddamn neck, you fresh, little trouble maker." Although this postcard's origins were uncertain, the actual alumni association did send Vorchheimer an unwelcoming (if far more restrained) message, as the nine-thousand-member organization formally opposed her admission, claiming it threatened Central's "proven ability" to provide "quality education . . . [to] young men, many of whom become prominent in our society." For his part, Central's principal, Howard Carlisle—who in the school's idiosyncratic parlance used the title "President"—justified his opposition to admitting Vorchheimer by contending the school's pedagogical approach required an all-male student body. "Our program is geared to a man-to-man relationship," Carlisle explained. "Our English students, for instance, read Chaucer in the unexpurgated edition, and I'm not sure that would or could be done with Susan in the class. We try to treat our boys as adults and in a coed class, there is certain language that just could not be used."[50]* Carlisle did not,

* During this era, Justice Brennan refused to hire women as law clerks in large part because he liked to use salty language. Brennan—who issued several progressive opin-

however, attempt to explain how Central's female instructors—who made up nearly one-fifth of the school's total faculty—went about establishing "a man-to-man relationship" with their students.

Although Vorchheimer prevailed in district court, a divided panel of the U.S. Court of Appeals for the Third Circuit reversed that decision in 1976 and upheld Central's all-male policy. Writing for the majority in *Vorchheimer v. School District of Philadelphia*, Judge Joseph Weis opened the opinion by framing the legal question presented in the most sweeping terms available. Rather than endeavoring to answer the comparatively narrow question of whether Philadelphia's most prestigious public high school could exclude qualified female applicants, Judge Weis opened, "Do the Constitution and laws of the United States require that every public school, in every public school system in the Nation, be coeducational?" The Third Circuit proceeded to answer that broad query in the negative and portrayed itself as defending the ability of school boards to offer a diverse set of schooling arrangements to students and their families. Granting Vorchheimer's desire to attend Central would expand her "freedom of choice," Weis allowed, but it would simultaneously contract the options available to students interested in selecting a single-sex learning environment. "If she were to prevail, then all public single-sex schools would have to be abolished," Weis maintained. "The absence of these schools would stifle the ability of the local school board to continue with a respected educational methodology. It follows too that those students and parents who prefer an education in a public, single-sex school would be denied their freedom of choice."[51] Weis depicted Central and Girls High as equivalent institutions, at least in broad strokes, though even he conceded that Central's science facilities were superior. Finally, Weis rejected any analogy between sex segregation and racial segregation in the educational context, because the former, unlike the latter, has "its basis in a theory of equal benefit and not discriminatory denial."[52]

In dissent, Judge John Gibbons wrote an impassioned opinion where he repeatedly likened the validation of Central's exclusionary admissions policy to the Supreme Court's validation of racially

---

ions advancing the cause of sex equality—nevertheless believed it would be inappropriate and ungentlemanly to swear before members of the opposite sex. See Seth Stern and Stephen Wermiel, *Justice Brennan: Liberal Champion* 388–401 (2010).

segregated railcars in *Plessy v. Ferguson*. Invoking *Brown v. Board of Education*'s repudiation of *Plessy* in 1954, Gibbons vented, "I was under the distinct impression . . . that 'separate but equal' analysis, especially in the field of public education, passed from the fourteenth amendment jurisprudential scene over twenty years ago."[53] Gibbons further contended that students who attended either Central or Girls High only on a "voluntary" basis should hardly be relied upon to preserve Philadelphia's arrangement. "Vorchheimer's choice of an academic high school was . . . 'voluntary,' but only in the same sense that Mr. Plessy voluntarily chose to ride the train in Louisiana," Gibbons wrote. "Philadelphia, like the state of Louisiana in 1896, offers the service but only if Vorchheimer is willing to submit to segregation. Her choice, like Plessy's, is to submit to that segregation or refrain from availing herself of the service."[54]

Although the Supreme Court accepted Vorchheimer's petition to address her exclusion from Central, the Court ultimately proved unable to do so. In April 1977, after hearing oral argument a few months earlier, the Court announced that it had deadlocked 4–4, with Justice William Rehnquist recused—apparently because he missed oral argument. As is customary when the Court divides equally, it produced no written opinions in Vorchheimer's case and simply issued an order leaving the decision below intact that created no binding precedent at the Supreme Court level. Prior to disclosing the Court's deadlock, Chief Justice Burger wrote a note to his colleagues urging them instead to schedule the matter for re-argument—when Justice Rehnquist's participation would presumably prevent another tie—because a nondecision here could be "valid[ly] critici[zed] as an institutional failure to meet our obligations."[55] Burger might have in fact pursued re-argument in *Vorchheimer* primarily because he believed that Rehnquist would join him in voting to uphold the validity of Central's policy, thus breaking the deadlock in a direction that suited him. But whatever his actual motivations, Burger's larger critique has accumulated potency over time. More than three decades later, this institutional obligation remains unfulfilled, as constitutional law scholars eagerly await the Court directly resolving the legitimacy of single-sex public schools.[56]

While the Court has yet to answer this question definitively, that inaction should not be misinterpreted as indicating that the landscape of single-sex public schools remains unchanged since the

1970s. In Philadelphia, for example, a state court decision in 1983 invalidated Central's male-only policy and threw open the school's doors to female students. On the basis of a more thoroughly developed factual record than existed in the earlier, federal case, the state court determined that Central's facilities and educational opportunities materially surpassed Girls High's along numerous dimensions—including library acquisitions, faculty qualifications, advanced course offerings, student test scores, and college acceptance rates. At Girls High, meanwhile, the situation has in recent years grown somewhat murkier. By 2010, Girls High discontinued its official policy limiting enrollment to females, and its website offered a nongendered mission statement of "graduating students who will treat others compassionately and live lives of personal integrity."[57] Yet no male has ever enrolled at Girls High, nor—evidently—has any student who enrolled as a female ever transitioned gender identity while attending the school.

Philadelphia's abandonment of Central as an all-male school and its preservation of Girls High as a de facto all-female school can be viewed as consistent with the Supreme Court's most recent guidance on single-sex education. In that case, which arose in the higher education context, the Supreme Court in an opinion by Justice Ruth Bader Ginsburg invalidated the all-male policy of the Virginia Military Institute (VMI) in 1996. Ginsburg predicated her opinion on the notion that VMI had a lengthy history of providing its cadets with an elite collegiate experience in highly austere circumstances, as she concluded that excluding interested women from this exceptional educational opportunity could not be squared with the Equal Protection Clause's requirement that sex-based classifications occur only if they stemmed from an "exceedingly persuasive justification."[58] While many women would be uninterested in enduring the arduous physical and psychological strain that formed a central part of VMI's student experience, Ginsburg noted, many men would also be uninterested in enduring that same strain. For Ginsburg, the essential point was that some women affirmatively sought out VMI's distinctive experience, and it was impermissible for the state to exclude women from educational opportunities based on sex stereotypes. Ginsburg further noted that the state's recent effort to establish an all-female military college—in the form of the Virginia Women's Institute for Leadership—did not come close to matching VMI in terms of its program, prestige, faculty, and alumni.

Based on this analysis, it seems virtually certain that—even had a Pennsylvania state court not invalidated Central's all-male policy in the 1980s—modern constitutional doctrine would require the high school to include female students in its first-rate educational environment. Indeed, Central's place at the summit of public secondary education in Philadelphia occupies an analogous position to VMI's elite status among students interested in pursuing higher education within a military atmosphere. Justice Ginsburg's public commentary following the judicial rejection of VMI's admissions policy underscored the connection between these two redoubtable institutions. Ginsburg, who as head of the ACLU's Women's Rights Project during the 1970s helped to draft the Supreme Court brief challenging Central, stated after authoring her triumphant judicial opinion that eliminated a bastion of all male privilege, "To me, it was winning the *Vorchheimer* case twenty years later."[59]

While the Court's opinion rejecting VMI's exclusion of women would thus seem to have required Central to open its doors to female students (had it not already done so), it was far less certain that the opinion should be interpreted as requiring Girls High to admit male students. In portions of the opinion that were not essential to the Court's conclusion, Ginsburg's reasoning suggested that it may not be necessary for all single-sex schools to become coeducational. "[D]iversity in educational opportunities is an altogether appropriate governmental pursuit and . . . single-sex schools can contribute importantly to such diversity," Ginsburg wrote in one footnote. "[I]t is the mission of some single-sex schools to dissipate, rather than perpetuate, traditional gender classifications. . . . We do not question the Commonwealth's prerogative evenhandedly to support diverse educational opportunities."[60] This passage can be understood in at least two ways regarding Girls High's exclusion of males. On the one hand, if the existence of Girls High were viewed as undercutting, instead of reinforcing, sex-based stereotypes, then its exclusion of male students may well be deemed constitutional. On the other hand, if Philadelphia's failure to offer an all-male "academic" high school were viewed as failing to comply with the requirements of evenhandedness, then Girls High's exclusion of males may well be deemed unconstitutional. The uncertainty surrounding what this language means likely accounts for Girls High's equivocal approach to its all-female student body.

Perhaps surprisingly, Justice Ginsburg's allowance in 1996 that single-sex public schools could even conceivably pass constitutional muster represents a departure from how she approached that issue in the wake of the Court's nondecision in *Vorchheimer*. During that era, she portrayed single-sex public schools as fundamentally incompatible with the Equal Protection Clause. As late as 1983, Ginsburg published an essay that construed *Vorchheimer* as challenging not only Central's admission policy but single-sex schooling as a general proposition—a stance that if successful would have required Girls High to admit males. Thus, in Ginsburg's telling, *Vorchheimer* "[p]resented . . . the question whether Philadelphia could maintain sex-segregated secondary schools for academically gifted boys and girls."[61] Even more starkly, Ginsburg at that time portrayed a hypothetical Supreme Court opinion upholding Philadelphia's schooling arrangements as a "ruling condoning 'separate but equal' public school education in the context of sex."[62]*

---

* While Ginsburg wanted the judiciary to stamp out all single-sex schools during the 1970s and 1980s, she did express some concerns in the wake of the Court's nondecision in *Vorchheimer* that the case might have reached the Court prematurely. When *Vorchheimer* arrived at the Court, Ginsburg noted, the institution had not yet begun to hollow out single-sex education, as had occurred with respect to racially segregated education by the time the Court confronted *Brown*. Ginsburg also identified a more promising context for the Court first to encounter single-sex education: the disputes arising from the South's introduction of public schools segregated by sex in the late 1960s and the 1970s. Those single-sex schools arose just as racial desegregation in the South was beginning in earnest to avoid the possibility of black males attending school with white females, a prospect that opponents of interracial intimacy greeted with horror. As one black school board member in Amite County, Mississippi, explained with irritation, "[Separating schools by sex] has always been a racial issue. The idea is to keep the black boys from having any contact with the white girls—pure and simple." Merrill Sheils, "Segregation by Sex," *Newsweek*, Sept. 19, 1977, 97. The white president of Amite County's school board did not reject this account of the board's motivation. When asked why Amite County did not introduce single-sex schools before 1969, the board president replied, "We didn't have integration then. We had one school for whites and one school for coloreds, that's why." Helen Dewar, "Blacks Boycott Sex-Segregated Schools," *Washington Post*, Sept. 4, 1977, A32. Presumably, Ginsburg preferred the Court first to encounter a dispute from this repellent milieu because, unlike in *Vorchheimer*, it would have been virtually impossible to imagine the justices in the 1970s crediting the notion that the southern school districts created single-sex education for any reason other than invidious discrimination. See Ruth Bader Ginsburg, "Gender and the Constitution," 44 *University of Cincinnati Law Review* 1 (1975); Ruth Bader Ginsburg, "The Burger Court's Grapplings with Sex Discrimination," 132, 144, in *The Burger Court: The Counter-revolution That Wasn't* (Vincent Blasi ed., 1983); Serena Mayeri, "The Strange Career of Jane Crow: Sex Segregation and the Transformation of Anti-discrimination

Which of Ginsburg's competing visions of single-sex public schools is more compelling: the earlier one that held the institutions as uniformly unconstitutional, or the more recent one holding that they may—at least in certain circumstances—pass constitutional muster? In my view, Ginsburg had it right the first time: critics of single-sex public schools make the more persuasive case that such schools violate the Equal Protection Clause, as they tend to promote stereotyped sex roles.

The case against permitting all-male public schools is rather straightforward. Admittedly, as the Third Circuit majority opinion emphasized in *Vorchheimer*, creating some all-male public schools within a larger coeducational school system increases the sorts of educational environments available to students. That enlarged set of educational options, however, cannot counteract the undesirable message that flows from maintaining all-male public schools in a society that is rife with sexism. As Christopher Jencks and David Riesman argued in the context of higher education in 1968,

> The pluralistic argument for preserving all-male [schools] is uncomfortably similar to the pluralistic argument for preserving all-white [schools]. . . . The all-male [school] would be relatively easy to defend if it emerged from a world in which women were established as fully equal to men. But it does not. It is therefore likely to be a witting or unwitting device for preserving tacit assumptions of male superiority—assumptions for which women must eventually pay.[63]

Educational endorsements of male superiority may be at their most pernicious when elite schools are reserved exclusively for males. But it would be mistaken to believe that those messages disappear altogether when even non-elite all-male public schools exist within our larger sex-stratified culture.

The closer constitutional question involves the legitimacy of all-female public schools. Proponents of such schools generally contend that they foster valuable social and academic atmospheres in which many young women thrive. Supporters often suggest

Discourse," 18 *Yale Journal of Law and the Humanities* 187, 262–64 (2006); and Jill Elaine Hasday, "The Principle and Practice of Women's 'Full Citizenship': A Case Study of Sex-Segregated Public Education," 101 *Michigan Law Review* 755, 789–90n142 (2002).

that females receive superior classroom instruction in single-sex schools, both because teaching strategies can be tailored to address how female students actually learn and because any pro-male attitudes that teachers harbor can find no outlet in the biased treatment of students based on sex. The absence of male students, advocates further maintain, guarantees that female students will assume leadership positions within the school. Relatedly, proponents contend that the absence of male students increases the likelihood that (heterosexual) female students will exert themselves to their full academic potential because they neither fixate on their physical appearances in an effort to attract male attention nor fear that exhibiting intellectual firepower will repel that attention. As Professor Susan Estrich—who graduated from Wellesley College before becoming the *Harvard Law Review*'s first woman president— memorably proclaimed in defending all-female academic environments, "Sometimes separate isn't equal; it's better."[64]

While some of these arguments undeniably contain appeal, the countervailing arguments even more compellingly suggest that all-female public schools cannot be squared with the demands of the Equal Protection Clause. The notion that females receive superior classroom instruction in single-sex schools is objectionable for at least two distinct reasons. First, separating students on the belief that females—as a sex—have a distinctive learning style from males masks variation within an individual sex and perpetuates the concept of inherent cognitive differences between the sexes. Wendy Kaminer, who graduated from Smith College, has forcefully asserted that single-sex schools "reinforce regressive notions of sex difference" and contended, "The sexism in girls' and women's schools is insidious. Whether manifested in feminine decor or in an approach to teaching that assumes a female penchant for cooperative, or 'connected,' learning, stereotypical notions of femininity often infect institutions for women and girls."[65] Second, even allowing that teachers' sexism harms coeducational classrooms, it is far from clear that sequestering female students in their own academic institutions provides the optimal solution to that problem. As Rebecca Bigler, a psychologist at the University of Texas, recently objected, "You say there's a problem with sexism, and instead of addressing the sexism, you just remove one sex."[66]

The alleged benefits that all-female schools confer upon their students due to the absence of males also collapse upon close

examination. Given that sex-based stereotypes continue to pervade society, achievements at all-female schools may well send the
regrettable, and false, message that female students cannot compete
effectively against their male counterparts—a signifier that dimin-
ishes and taints accomplishments, no matter how significant. Professor Gary Simson has suggested that though all-female schools
are often meant to "affirm[ ] girls' abilities and potential," the very
creation and maintenance of such institutions risks communicating "to both girls and boys that girls are in some sense inferior to
boys—whether that means more needy, less adaptable, more fragile, or some other disempowering comparative generalization."[67]*
In a similar vein, Professor Nancy Levit has contended, "[S]tate-
sponsored sex exclusivity is unlikely to vest segregation with new
meaning. Sex segregation with connotations of inequality is of too
recent vintage—indeed, it never left us. Equality of opportunity
requires boys and girls to live and to learn together, because life outside the classroom is coed."[68] Furthermore, supporting all-female
schools so that their students can focus on learning without wor-
rying about male students' perceptions incorrectly accommodates,
rather than challenges, the male gaze and—less loftily—propagates
the wrongheaded notion that intelligence and attractiveness cannot
coexist within the same female body. As Kaminer has suggested,
single-sex schools "encourage heterosexual women and girls to separate their social and intellectual lives, reinforcing the dissonance
bred into many achievement-oriented females."[69] By enabling "students to exercise the choice of being smart on weekdays and pretty
on weekends," Kaminer contended, single-sex schools provided
their students with a false choice: "The prospect of being intellectually assertive and [physically attractive] simultaneously, every day
of the week, was barely considered or, perhaps, even desired."[70]

Assessing the legitimacy of single-sex public schools today does
not involve a question solely of abstract significance, because, while
such schools verged on extinction during the mid-1990s, they have

* In 1992, Sharon Mollman elaborated upon the harmful social messages that all-female
schools may communicate. "The social cost of excluding boys is not their subsequent
feelings of inferiority, for their sense of power is too well entrenched," Mollman wrote.
"Instead, they perceive that girls are inferior because they will not compete with boys.
There is a danger too that girls might choose the single-gender school over the co-ed
one because they believe it must be less competitive, thus reinforcing their own sense
of personal and gender inferiority." Sharon K. Mollman, "The Gender Gap: Separating
the Sexes in Public Education," 68 *Indiana Law Journal* 149, 169 (1992).

become surprisingly commonplace in recent years. In 1995, only one year before the Court invalidated VMI's all-male policy, Philadelphia's Girls High was one of only three single-sex public schools in the entire country. Although Justice Scalia dissented from the majority opinion involving VMI, and decried the Court for leaving single-sex public education "functionally dead," those institutions—not long thereafter—came roaring back to life in elementary and secondary schools.[71] By 2005, thirty-four single-sex public schools existed—a more than tenfold increase from one decade earlier. But the truly spectacular growth occurred during the next decade, following the issuance of new federal guidelines by President George W. Bush's administration indicating single-sex public schools were valid, at least provided that students enrolled in them only on a voluntary basis.* The most recent Department of Education statistics, collected in 2014, revealed that some 850 public schools feature single-sex student bodies.[72] This rebirth of single-sex public education transpired even though polling data indicated that no groundswell of national support embraced the practice. In 2002, a Gallup poll found that 67 percent of respondents opposed making single-sex schools an option in their communities, and only 31 percent supported doing so. When Gallup isolated the responses of public school students' parents, moreover, the level of opposition surged to 74 percent.[73]

Legal scholars often suggest that the Supreme Court's decisions invalidating unusual measures contain little significance, because those practices would have either died out on their own or been repealed through democratic means. But the dramatic revival of single-sex public schools during the last decade undermines such tidy narratives. If an unusual measure gains sufficient popularity within particular pockets of society, the absence of a judicial opinion foreclosing that practice's adoption can have major consequences.[74]

Importantly, single-sex public schools are not evenly spread in various sorts of communities throughout the country. Instead, they appear overwhelmingly in inner-city neighborhoods, with

---

* In response to the new federal guidelines, Marcia Greenberger, of the National Women's Law Center, lamented, "It really is a serious green light from [George W. Bush's administration] to re-instituting official discrimination in schools around the country." Diana Jean Schemo, "Change in Federal Rules Backs Single-Sex Public Education," *New York Times*, Oct. 25, 2006, A1.

high poverty rates and high percentages of racial minorities. Beginning in the 1990s, frustration with the abysmal record of academic achievement and alarming rates of social dysfunction that plague many urban areas prompted reformers to introduce single-sex schools in a desperate effort to try something—anything—that might improve the situation. In perhaps the most prominent dispute over a single-sex public school, the ACLU's Women's Rights Project (the litigation outfit formerly headed by Ruth Bader Ginsburg) sought in 1996 to require the newly created Young Women's Leadership School in Harlem to accept male students so that they too might take advantage of the small class sizes and college preparatory programs that distinguished it from most other New York City public schools. Professor Derrick Bell—in a *New York Times* op-ed titled "Et Tu, A.C.L.U.?"—ridiculed the litigation effort as unwisely seeking to extinguish a valuable experiment in urban schooling: "We need to give innovative educational initiatives a chance before intervening with legal actions that—even when they succeed—do no more than maintain a woeful status quo."[75] Five years earlier, in 1991, a similarly heated—though lower-profile—controversy occurred when Detroit announced its intention to create three academies for black male students that would offer a special curriculum, featuring Afrocentric lessons and a "Rites of Passage" class. When a Detroit mother joined an ACLU-backed lawsuit attempting to gain access to one of the academies for her young daughter, the harassing phone calls and claims of community betrayal became so intense that she felt compelled to withdraw.[76]

Frustration with the wretched state of public schools in urban America is certainly understandable—indeed, I share that sentiment myself—but it is far from clear that the dire circumstances confronting those communities should suffice to render this new wave of single-sex education constitutionally permissible. While the public schools in many predominantly minority neighborhoods are broken, no persuasive evidence indicates that their coeducational status plays even an incidental role in their failure. Accordingly, it is difficult to understand how the state's creation of such single-sex schools, even if attendance at them is voluntary, can qualify as "an exceedingly persuasive justification," the Court's governing test for assessing gender classifications.[77]

Apart from lacking a sound evidentiary basis for their creation, moreover, single-sex educational environments in urban areas demonstrate a distressing propensity for disseminating precisely the sorts of gendered stereotypes that Justice Ginsburg once convincingly contended violate the Equal Protection Clause. Thus, for example, *The New York Times* recently reported that in one Florida school district, male students learn in classrooms lined with images of football players and race cars, whereas the decor for female students includes hot-pink desk caddies, walls bordered with cheetah and zebra prints, and a list of rules that instructs, "Act pretty at all times!"[78] Perhaps more disconcertingly, schools serving only black male students routinely offer patriarchal lessons of racial uplift—instructing that their community's well-being is predicated on their becoming the "*strong Black men*" needed to head both their families and the race.[79]

Even in the absence of promoting such retrograde messages, however, an independent reason remains for doubting their legitimacy. *Brown v. Board of Education* demonstrated awareness that schooling arrangements sometimes communicate objectionable messages to marginalized groups about their status within the community, and the heavily skewed demographics of single-sex public schools today could also well be understood to convey an untoward message about the status of indigent racial minorities. As Professor Verna Williams has explained,

> The fact that so much of the discourse surrounding single-sex education is about Black children in troubled urban school districts is cause for concern. Put another way, there generally is no concomitant rush to segregate public schoolchildren based on sex in predominately white Grosse Pointe, Michigan, a suburb of Detroit, . . . for example. If sex segregation were the silver bullet that its proponents suggest, one might expect more school districts across the board to jump on the bandwagon. But that is not the case. Sex segregation appears to be the remedy for what ails public schools peopled . . . by low-income students of color.[80]

Thus, the very prevalence of single-sex public schools found in areas serving poor, minority students can itself be viewed as suggesting that this population is so damaged that they require a highly abnormal form of schooling—one virtually unknown in modern American public schools that serve other populations.*

TRANSGENDER STUDENTS AND ACCESS TO RESTROOMS

Perhaps the single most polarizing education case that the Supreme Court has agreed to address in recent years involved whether schools can legally prohibit transgender students from accessing restrooms consistent with their gender identities. As the Court contemplated whether to hear a lawsuit posing that question in 2016, an article in *The New York Times* posited that "the most fiercely contested territory in America right now [may be] the bathroom."[81] Consistent with this claim, Texas's lieutenant governor, Dan Patrick—who opposed granting trans students access to requested restrooms—asserted the matter was "the biggest issue facing families and schools in America since prayer was taken out of public schools."[82] Supporters of permitting trans students such access agreed that the legal question was

---

* Sorting students by sex into entirely different schools presents an unusually intense form of separation, and therefore poses weightier constitutional questions than does separating students briefly during the school day (for, say, gym class) or afterward for extracurricular sports. Although the Supreme Court has never evaluated sex separations for school athletic events, which are generally justified on the basis of speed and strength differentials, lower courts have issued a wide variety of Equal Protection Clause decisions evaluating claims by students who wish to try out for a team that excludes members of their sex. Female students wishing to join male teams have—as a general proposition—experienced greater success making such claims than male students who seek to join female teams. Female students appear particularly likely to prevail in these legal pursuits, moreover, if the school fields a particular sports team for males but offers no comparable team to females (for example, football). See LynNell Hancock and Claudia Kalb, "A Room of Their Own," *Newsweek*, June 24, 1996, 76 ("As a general principle, federal law doesn't permit segregation by sex in the public schools. (Exceptions can be made for singing groups, contact sports and human-sexuality and remedial classes.)"); and Nancy Levit, "Separating Equals: Educational Research and the Long-Term Consequences of Sex Segregation," 67 *George Washington Law Review* 451, 524 (1999) ("[P]erhaps, in some contexts, for some limited purposes, single-sex classes are not inappropriate. Separating female and male middle school students for sex education classes (because of both our notions of modesty and the students' possible embarrassment) or gym classes (because of size and strength differences) may be useful."). For an incisive overview of the complicated terrain involving sex and sports, see Michael Imber et al., *Education Law* 233–34 (2014). See also *Force v. Pierce City R-VI School District*, 570 F. Supp. 1020 (W.D. Mo. 1983) (authorizing a female student to try out for the school football team); and *Williams v. School District of Bethlehem*, 998 F.2d 168 (3d Cir. 1993) (refusing to authorize a male student to join the girls' field hockey team).

momentous, even as they disdained Patrick's underlying position. For example, Chirlane McCray—spouse of New York City's mayor, Bill de Blasio—contended that granting the requested restroom access boiled down to a matter of basic human decency: "No child should face humiliation and embarrassment because of their gender identity, especially during such a private moment."[83]

The lawsuit that reached the Supreme Court grew out of events that began in 2014, when a rising tenth-grade student named Gavin Grimm informed school officials in Gloucester County, Virginia, that he wished to be referred to with masculine pronouns and addressed by his newly adopted legal name. The path leading to this request, however, started many years earlier. Ever since Grimm first appreciated the distinction between boys and girls, he felt that he was a transgender male—even if his vocabulary then lacked that terminology. At age six, Grimm began rejecting traditional feminine attire. When Grimm's parents required him to wear a dress on one occasion—to attend a family wedding—he found the experience so traumatizing that it rendered him "catatonic," because as he later explained, "It [was] like my self wasn't really living."[84] Years later, when Grimm came out as trans to his parents, they were initially stunned, as neither of them had ever previously encountered the transgender concept, let alone an actual person who so identified. But they educated themselves about the subject and soon resolved to assist with their child's transition. Grimm's parents, in addition to facilitating his name change, would help him secure hormonal treatments to lower his voice and to provide him with a more traditionally masculine appearance.[85]

Despite this affirming parental response, Grimm feared how school officials would react to news of his transition. In Gloucester County, a sparsely populated area within Virginia's tidewater region, many residents evinced deep religiosity and an almost instinctual aversion to anything that appeared to contravene local customs, according to Grimm. His trepidation, however, initially proved misplaced, as Gloucester High School's leadership not only accepted Grimm's request to recognize his male gender identity but even pledged its support. As Grimm recalled, "[The school] assured me that teachers and administrators would call me Gavin, and use male pronouns when referring to me, and if anyone gave me any kind of trouble, it would be resolved right away."[86] Roughly one month into the school year, Grimm sought and received permission from Gloucester's principal to begin using the boys' restroom, rather than the single-occupancy restroom located in the nurse's office that he had been using. Going to a separate part of the school—isolated from fellow students—to relieve himself caused Grimm to feel embarrassment and extreme discomfort. Due to the unusual arrangement, he explained, "I have this neon sign above my head that says I'm different from my peers."[87] After receiving school authorization, Grimm used the boys' restroom without incident for seven weeks. But this period of tranquillity would not last.

When adults in Gloucester County learned that Grimm was using the male bathroom, the school board held two separate meetings, where many community members attacked the arrangement. At the first meeting, several speakers emphatically used feminine terms, including "girl" and "young lady," to refer to Grimm. Yet that first meeting was positively decorous compared with the raucous second meeting. The nadir occurred when one speaker called Grimm "a freak" and likened him to a person who, believing he is actually a canine, attempts to urinate on fire hydrants.[88*] Grimm, who attended both meetings, pleaded with the school board, "All I want to do is to be a normal child and use the restroom in peace."[89] By a 6–1 vote, the board rejected Grimm's request, and enacted a policy requiring "students with gender identity issues" to use separate, private facilities from their classmates.[90] In response to this change, Grimm sought to avoid using the restroom at school altogether and consequently developed several urinary tract infections.[91] He also decided to mount a lawsuit contesting the school board's policy.

The U.S. Court of Appeals for the Fourth Circuit vindicated Grimm's claim in April 2016. In so doing, it yielded to the Obama administration's interpretation of regulations regarding Title IX of the Education Amendments Act of 1972. This statute prohibits discrimination "on the basis of sex" for educational entities that receive money from the federal government.[92] While Title IX con-

---

* Educators also sometimes suggest that trans students suffer from delusions and that their supposedly fantastical gender identities ought not be indulged. In explaining her opposition to permitting trans students to use restrooms congruent with their gender identities, one school official in Florida stated, "Every student that comes to school and says, 'I'm Cinderella'—should we give them a carriage to ride around in?" Jack Healy et al., "Solace and Fury as Schools React to Gender Policy," *New York Times*, May 14, 2016, A1.

tains regulations that permit sex-segregated bathrooms, the Obama administration instructed schools generally to treat trans students in accordance with their gender identities for purposes of those regulations, meaning that it would be impermissible to exclude Grimm from the boys' restroom. The Fourth Circuit found that the regulatory terms contained sufficient ambiguity that—in accordance with binding administrative law precedent—the executive branch's interpretation deserved deference. The Supreme Court then agreed to review the Fourth Circuit's opinion. Shortly before the Court was scheduled to hear oral argument in the case, however, the Trump administration rescinded the Obama administration's guidance. Several Trump administration officials defended the action by invoking the familiar justification that the federal government should not enter this sensitive schooling question that is better left to states and localities.* Following the withdrawal of the Obama administration's regulatory interpretation, the Supreme Court remanded the case to the lower courts for an assessment of whether Grimm should prevail even amid the transformed legal landscape. The choice to remand did not surprise close Court watchers, because the institution strongly prefers to avoid weighing in on legal questions that involve moving targets. Instead, the Court prefers to render a decision after it has the benefit of an appellate court opinion that has passed on the precise legal question, presented in the same basic posture, and briefing that parses the appellate opinion.†[93]

* The White House press secretary, Sean Spicer, defended the withdrawal by stating that President Donald J. Trump was a "firm believer in states' rights." "President Trump Breaks a Promise on L.G.B.T. Rights," *New York Times*, Feb. 24, 2017, A26. Although Secretary of Education Betsy DeVos internally contested the decision to withdraw the Obama administration's guidance, she nevertheless issued a statement asserting, "This is an issue best solved at the state and local level." Jeremy W. Peters et al., "Trump Rescinds Obama Directive on Bathroom Use," *New York Times*, Feb. 23, 2017, A1. Conservative media outlets also defended rescinding the guidance on federalism grounds. *The Wall Street Journal* averred, "[R]estroom policy should be determined by localities, not federal diktat." "Calling Off Obama's Restroom Cops," *Wall Street Journal*, Feb. 20, 2017. Similarly, *National Review* defended the move as "preserv[ing] federalism, [and demonstrating] respect [for] the principle of local control over local schools." "Returning Power to States and School Boards," *National Review*, Feb. 23, 2017. Chad Griffin, the president of Human Rights Campaign, memorably parried this federalism line of critique by contending, "This isn't a states' rights issue; it's a civil rights issue." Peters et al., "Trump Rescinds Obama Directive on Bathroom Use," A1.

† As of this writing, Grimm's case remains procedurally tied up in lower courts. Given that he graduated from high school in June 2017, the U.S. Court of Appeals for the

While Gavin Grimm graduated from high school before the Supreme Court ever definitively addressed his claim, it seems improbable that even if it does not hear Grimm's individual case, the institution will be able to avoid resolving his central legal question for long. One estimate suggests that there are somewhere between 165,000 and 555,000 transgender students attending various elementary and secondary schools in the United States, and many of them do so in jurisdictions where educational authorities treat them adversely. If the issue does soon return to the Court, moreover, it could quite plausibly pose a question not in the statutory and regulatory domain but in the constitutional domain.[94]

Only days after the Trump administration rescinded the previous administration's guidance, a district court judge in western Pennsylvania relied upon the Equal Protection Clause to reject a school board's efforts to prohibit three transgender students from accessing restrooms congruent with their gender identities. The Supreme Court's extensive jurisprudence interpreting the Equal Protection Clause to reject sex classifications, Judge Mark Hornak reasoned, provided protection to transgender students in this context: "[D]iscrimination based on transgender status in these circumstances is essentially the epitome of discrimination based on gender nonconformity, making differentiation based on transgender status akin to discrimination based on sex for these purposes."[95] With this foundation established, the school district's policy appeared tantamount to unconstitutional discrimination on the basis of transgender status. "The Plaintiffs are being distinguished by governmental action from those whose gender identities are congruent with their assigned sex," Judge Hornak wrote. "The Plaintiffs are the only students who are not allowed to use the common restrooms consistent with their gender identities."[96]

In Judge Hornak's view, the school district fell well shy of demonstrating that its restrictive restroom policy stemmed from an "exceedingly persuasive justification," as required by the Court's precedents involving sex discrimination.[97] As in Gavin Grimm's

---

Fourth Circuit remanded the lawsuit in August 2017 for the district court to determine whether the controversy had been rendered moot. Grimm insisted that the controversy remained active because he planned to return to his alma mater for alumni and community events and the bathroom question would therefore arise again. See Ann E. Marimow, "Case of Virginia Transgender Teen Gavin Grimm Put Off by Appeals Court," *Washington Post*, Aug. 2, 2017.

case, the Pennsylvania high school in question had initially permitted transgender students to use their requested bathrooms before the school board enacted a measure eliminating that access. Prior to the district's new policy, Judge Hornak noted, the school experienced neither bathroom disturbances nor intrusions upon student privacy. As to the latter point, Judge Hornak emphasized that the school's restrooms had locking bathroom stalls and that the urinals in the boys' restrooms were separated by partitions. Permitting transgender students to use only the various single-occupancy bathrooms located around the school did not, according to Hornak, satisfy transgender students' rights under the Fourteenth Amendment. This point might have been pressed further still by observing that if some students feel uncomfortable using a restroom in the presence of a trans student, those uneasy students could easily avail themselves of the single-occupancy facilities.[98]*

While it is predictable that many conservatives would disparage opinions vindicating transgender students' claims as ignoring and even eroding long-standing social distinctions between males and females, it may be surprising to learn that some commentators can be understood to denigrate such opinions from the left. For these critics, opinions such as Hornak's are mere half measures because they serve to bolster distinct bathrooms on the basis of sex, granting transgender people access to what effectively remain sex-segregated spaces. According to this radical critique, the notion that a human being can somehow use the "wrong" bathroom is itself profoundly wrong. Indeed, a few prominent legal scholars have in recent years contended that it has grown increasingly difficult to justify sex-segregated bathrooms, redolent as they are of heteronormative assumptions and stereotypes holding that dainty females must be isolated from boorish males when they execute the same bodily

---

* In May 2017, a federal appellate court—relying upon both Title IX and the Fourteenth Amendment's Equal Protection Clause—issued a preliminary injunction requiring Tremper High School in Kenosha, Wisconsin, to permit a transgender student to use the restroom congruent with his gender identity. In August 2017, the Kenosha Unified School District filed a certiorari petition seeking review of that decision with the Supreme Court. In January 2018, however, the school district agreed to pay the student $800,000 to settle the lawsuit, thereby preventing the Supreme Court from addressing the issue. See *Whitaker v. Kenosha Unified School District No. 1 Board of Education*, 858 F.3d 1034 (7th Cir. 2017); Annysa Johnson, "Kenosha Schools Ask U.S. Supreme Court to Take Up Transgender Bathroom Issue," *Milwaukee Journal Sentinel*, Aug. 25, 2017; Jacey Fortin, "Transgender Student's Discrimination Suit Is Settled for $800,000," *New York Times*, Jan. 10, 2018.

functions.[99] Grimm's attorney expressly disavowed such a goal, stating that his client "is not trying to dismantle sex-segregated restrooms. He's just trying to use them."[100]

Whatever Grimm's precise objectives, though, surely some trans people would regard abolishing sex-segregated bathrooms as an important victory, even if they also acknowledged it is one that seems unlikely to materialize in the current climate.* The trans community, like all communities, holds varied ideals and aspirations. As Jennifer Finney Boylan—author of a best-selling autobiography titled *She's Not There: A Life in Two Genders*—has memorably expressed this point, "If you've met one trans person, you've met . . . one trans person."[101] In one form or another, then, it seems possible the restroom will remain a contested social space in schools—and the larger society that contains them—for many years to come.

PLYLER V. DOE AND PERSISTENT EFFORTS TO EXCLUDE UNAUTHORIZED IMMIGRANTS FROM PUBLIC SCHOOLS

In 1974, Humberto Alvarez departed Mexico City and headed north in search of a better way of life for his spouse, Jackeline, and their four young children. After crossing the U.S. border without authorization, Alvarez ended up settling in Tyler, Texas, a small city located roughly one hundred miles southeast of Dallas that branded itself the "Rose City of America." Alvarez secured work at a local meatpacking plant and then sent for his family, who joined him in

---

* One reason that trans people may support eliminating sex-segregated bathrooms is that doing so would alleviate pressure to meet traditional notions of how males and females must appear before they can enter the restroom without inciting controversy or violence. There would be no need for courts, even those protecting transgender rights, to inspect photographs to assess whether transgender students convincingly look the part. See, for example, *Evancho v. Pine-Richland School District*, 237 F. Supp. 3d 267, 275 (W.D. Pa. 2017) ("Ms. Evancho's photo, which shows that her appearance is completely consistent only with the gender identity that she lives every day, is in the record"); and ibid. ("Plaintiff Ridenour's photo, which shows that her appearance is consistent only with the gender identity that she lives every day, is in the record"). In this vein, Professor Mary Anne Case has contended that eliminating sex-segregated bathrooms would mean that "[i]ndividuals will not be forced to conform to any standard of what it is appropriate for a man or a woman to look like in order safely to enter a public restroom. Other forms of gender nonconformity [would] be made easier as well." Mary Anne Case, "Why Not Abolish the Laws of Urinary Segregation?," in *Toilet: Public Restrooms and the Politics of Sharing* 211, 219 (Harvey Molotch and Laura Norén eds., 2010).

Tyler two years later. The Alvarez children enrolled in the local public schools and set about the business of learning English, along with the other cultural components of their new country. One year after the Alvarez children arrived, however, Tyler education officials declared that unauthorized immigrants had effectively been banished from the schools. Relying upon a statewide law that refused to allocate funds to localities for the education of noncitizens and even permitted their exclusion from public schools, Tyler announced that unauthorized immigrants would be required to pay one thousand dollars in tuition annually for each child who attended school. From Humberto Alvarez's perspective, the thousand-dollar tuition fee—which amounts to slightly more than four thousand dollars in today's figures—might as well have been a million dollars. Tyler's school superintendent, James Plyler, contended that the state's new policy imposed serious financial strain on the district and called the excluded students "a burden." But this explanation seems difficult to credit as, according to Plyler's own testimony, unauthorized immigrants accounted for only twenty-four of the sixteen thousand students in the district. After Alvarez witnessed his children stay home from school day after day after day at the beginning of the 1977 school year, he finally decided to join three other families in filing a lawsuit contesting the constitutionality of Texas's exclusionary law under the Equal Protection Clause. Alvarez's decision required genuine bravery because he felt that doing so substantially increased the risk of deportation for him and his family. The federal trial court in Tyler—in a decision written by Judge William Wayne Justice—rewarded Alvarez's risk by requiring the schools to readmit the excluded students.[102]*

---

* Judge Justice issued many important opinions during his decades as a federal judge. These opinions often vindicated liberal constitutional values, and conservative elements in Tyler, Texas, directed deep hostility toward both Judge Justice and members of his family. In 1998, Professor Lino Graglia asserted, "[Judge Justice] has wreaked more havoc and misery and injury to the people of Texas than any man in the last 25 years." Douglas Martin, "William Wayne Justice, Judge Who Remade Texas, Dies at 89," *New York Times*, Oct. 16, 2009, B11. Among his many significant opinions, one biographer noted, *Plyler v. Doe* occupied a special place in the heart of Judge Justice's spouse:

> Shortly after Justice issued [*Plyler v. Doe*], a little bouquet of flowers arrived at the Justice home. The card contained two X's and one illegible signature. Sue [Justice] called the florist who had prepared the bouquet. He told her that three Mexican laborers had put down two dollar bills and some change—

In 1982, the Supreme Court in *Plyler v. Doe* endorsed that assessment by deeming Texas's exclusionary measure unconstitutional in a 5–4 decision. Justice William Brennan's opinion for the Court rested on three primary, overlapping justifications. First, Brennan emphasized that the Texas law penalized minors not because of their own conduct but because of their parents' unlawful actions. *Plyler v. Doe* repeatedly referred to targeted students as "innocent children" and observed further that "legislation directing the onus of a parent's misconduct against his children does not comport with fundamental conceptions of justice."[103]

Second, Brennan contended that the measure's absolute exclusion of unauthorized immigrants from school imposed a severe burden on this vulnerable group. Although the Court as a formal matter did not disavow *Rodriguez*'s refusal to acknowledge education as a constitutionally protected fundamental right, *Plyler v. Doe* did acknowledge that it would be improper to treat education as "merely some governmental 'benefit.'"[104] The complete absence of even a basic education, Brennan observed, would "impose[ ] a lifetime hardship" on young unauthorized immigrants because "[t]he stigma of illiteracy will mark them for the rest of their lives"—irredeemably harming not only their own individual economic prospects but also their ability to contribute to the nation's civic life.[105]

Third, Brennan suggested that upholding Texas's law would also damage the United States as a whole. Upholding the Texas statute, Brennan maintained, threatened to intensify the isolation of a "shadow population" and also "raise[d] the specter of a permanent caste of undocumented resident aliens."[106] The measure brought those unappealing scenarios to the fore, Brennan advised, by imprudently curtailing access to American public schools—traditionally, an invaluable aid in sociocultural assimilation to the United States. "[E]ducation has a fundamental role in maintaining the fabric of society," he wrote. "We cannot ignore the significant costs borne by our Nation when select groups are denied the means

---

all the money they had—and asked that the flowers be sent to Mrs. Justice. "That very meager bouquet of flowers went a long way to make up for all the suffering I've experienced," she says.

Frank R. Kemerer, *William Wayne Justice: A Judicial Biography* 248–49 (1991).

to absorb the values and skills upon which our social order rests."[107] Brennan explained that the Texas law represented a betrayal of the nation's deepest constitutional commitments: "The existence of [a permanent unauthorized] underclass presents most difficult problems for a Nation that prides itself on adherence to principles of equality under law."[108] Elaborating upon this point, Brennan stated, "[D]enial of education to some isolated group of children poses an affront to one of the goals of the Equal Protection Clause: the abolition of governmental barriers presenting unreasonable obstacles to advancement on the basis of individual merit."[109]

Chief Justice Burger wrote a dissenting opinion, joined by three other justices, portraying the Texas statute as a valid (if misguided) exercise of constitutional authority, and disparaging the majority opinion as a paragon of "unwarranted judicial action," one that exemplified a troubling tendency "to become an omnipotent and omniscient problem solver."[110] Burger left no doubt that he found the law under review imprudent, at least from a policymaking standpoint. "Were it our business to set the Nation's social policy," he wrote, "I would agree without hesitation that it is senseless for an enlightened society to deprive any children—including illegal aliens—of an elementary education."[111] Nonetheless, Burger insisted that this measure violated no constitutional provision. "The Constitution does not provide a cure for every social ill, nor does it vest judges with a mandate to try to remedy every social problem," he contended. Echoing the position that Justice Felix Frankfurter espoused in the compulsory flag-salute cases of the 1940s, Burger construed the judiciary's intervention in *Plyler v. Doe* as sapping vitality from the democratic experiment itself. "[W]hen this Court rushes in to remedy what it perceives to be the failings of the political processes," Burger explained, "it deprives those processes of an opportunity to function. When the political institutions are not forced to exercise constitutionally allocated powers . . . , those powers, like muscles not used, tend to atrophy."[112] Burger did draw at least some measure of solace, however, from *Plyler v. Doe* because the opinion "rests on such a unique confluence of theories and rationales that it will likely stand for little beyond the" educational context.[113]

Plyler v. Doe elicited divergent assessments in prominent media outlets. In perhaps the sunniest appraisal, *The Boston Globe* suggested that excerpts of Justice Brennan's opinion should "be framed and hung in every American school house."[114] Likewise, *The New York Times* contended that the decision "struck a blow for minimal decency" and that "any other result would have been a national disgrace."[115] *The Washington Post*, however, viewed the opinion with skepticism, essentially endorsing Burger's dissenting position. While deeming Texas's exclusionary policy "unwise," the *Post* resisted concluding that its flaws rendered it unconstitutional: "In sorting out society's responsibilities for those who are in this country without permission and in violation of law, the courts would be wise to attach greater weight to the decisions of elected legislatures."[116] Going further, *The Wall Street Journal* panned the opinion, observing that "local communities are in a better position than the Supreme Court to judge how much they should discourage illegal immigration," and lamenting that the judiciary "has taken yet another decision out of local hands."[117]

When the Court decided *Plyler v. Doe*, no state in the country other than Texas had enacted legislation eliminating unauthorized immigrants' access to education. This legislative background has, in recent years, motivated some sophisticated constitutional scholars to dismiss *Plyler v. Doe* as an insignificant opinion that invalidated merely an "outlier" statute. On this account, the Court's decision is understood as eliminating a blatantly outrageous measure—one that would not have gained traction outside the Lone Star State, where an outlandish cowboy mentality prevails. Accordingly, scholars who subscribe to this mindset maintain, it would be sorely mistaken to understand *Plyler v. Doe* as providing a meaningful contribution to America's constitutional legacy of protecting minority rights, because the opinion simply ratified the prevailing view across the nation. When the justices issue outlier-suppressing opinions, this scholarly approach posits, they do not shape society's foundations; instead, they merely tweak society's edges.[118]

But such dismissive assessments of *Plyler v. Doe* are erroneous. Rather than some trivial event in the nation's constitutional history, it seems far more accurate to understand the opinion as preventing the Texas measure from spreading to other states, and thus forestalling what was an isolated measure from becoming the dominant approach. Although initially rejecting a policy located only in Texas, the decision has enjoyed broad applicability throughout the nation, and has served as a vital bulwark against widespread efforts to deprive unauthorized immigrants of access to education. Accordingly, *Plyler v. Doe* can persuasively be understood as providing a momentous contribution to the nation's constitutional legacy. Indeed, it is difficult to identify many opinions in the Supreme Court's entire history that have had more profound consequences, in more vital arenas, than *Plyler v. Doe*'s guaranteeing that the schoolhouse doors cannot be closed to one of modern society's most marginalized, most vilified groups. The opinion has single-handedly enabled innumerable children to use education to expand both their minds and their horizons.

Academic portrayals of *Plyler v. Doe* as an insignificant decision have flourished in part because legal scholars have expended too little effort placing the case in historical perspective. Examining the opinion in context, however, renders its major contributions to the American legal landscape unmistakable.

The Supreme Court itself in no way construed the Texas statute as a jarring legislative innovation that inexplicably found traction in a single state. Although the Court might have plausibly cast the statute as an idiosyncratic departure from long-standing practice, Justice Brennan's opinion instead expressly noted that unauthorized immigrants "now live within various States" and framed the decision as holding nationwide implications.[119] Similarly, in a concurring opinion, Justice Lewis F. Powell Jr. opened by emphasizing that Texas was far from alone in feeling the effects of unauthorized immigration and observed, "This is a problem of serious national proportions."[120] In addition, it seems worth recalling that four Supreme Court justices voted to uphold the Texas statute, hardly suggesting that Texas's statute was viewed as incomprehensible from a national perspective. During the Court's internal deliberations, moreover, Justice William Rehnquist referred to unauthorized immigrants as "wetbacks."[121] That a Supreme Court justice would use such inflammatory language in discussing a closely divided case with colleagues vividly attests to the unvarnished animus directed toward unauthorized immigrants—even on the national stage, even in the most rarefied environments. Perhaps even more tellingly, though, only one of Rehnquist's colleagues—Justice Marshall—appears to have voiced objection to the incendiary epithet.

Outside the Court, Texas's exclusionary measure was perceived as neither trivial nor eccentric in the early 1980s. In *The New York Times*, Linda Greenhouse's preview of the Court's upcoming term profiled *Plyler v. Doe* as the single most significant case for her readers. The civil rights community likewise viewed the case as momentous, not least because they feared that a decision upholding the Texas measure would provoke other states to entertain analogous statutes. Irma Herrera, an attorney for the Mexican American Legal Defense and Educational Fund, articulated this very concern after the Court vindicated her organization's position. "Had we lost," Herrera said, "many other states would have attempted to pass [similar] legislation."[122] It seems erroneous to dismiss Herrera's statement as merely an advocate's paranoia, as disinterested commentators both at the time and in more recent years have reached this same conclusion.[123] On the other end of the spectrum, a young lawyer working in the Reagan administration named John Roberts—who would, of course, go on to become chief justice of the United States in 2005—viewed the *Plyler v. Doe* decision as a missed opportunity. In his capacity as special assistant to Attorney General William French Smith, Roberts co-authored a memorandum in 1982 bemoaning the Department of Justice's failure to file an amicus brief in the case supporting Texas's position because he speculated doing so might have prompted the Court to uphold the measure.[124]

Although no public opinion polling data gauged the contemporaneous reaction to *Plyler v. Doe*, it hardly seems implausible to maintain that a national majority would have supported Texas's effort to exclude unauthorized immigrants from public schools. Two years after the opinion, a Gallup poll found that 55 percent of the public deemed unauthorized immigration a "very important" problem, and respondents in states bordering Mexico expressed that view only slightly more frequently than respondents in other states. In May 1995, when Gallup conducted the first nationwide poll asking respondents whether they favored or opposed "providing free public education, school lunches, and other benefits to the children of" unauthorized immigrants, 67 percent expressed opposition and only 28 percent expressed support.[125] If this question were asked today—more than twenty years later and amid the current wave of nationalist fervor—it seems eminently plausible that an even higher percentage of respondents would wish to exclude unauthorized immigrants from schools. Even though many Americans no doubt disagree with *Plyler v. Doe*—or, rather, precisely because of this broad disagreement—the opinion should be appreciated as making a vital contribution to closing the expansive gap that too often separates the nation's lofty rhetoric from its lowly realities.

Texas might have been the first state to adopt this legislation, moreover, but it was far from the last jurisdiction seeking to ban unauthorized immigrants from school. Voters in California during the 1990s and legislators in Alabama two decades later enacted their own versions of these initiatives, as supporters of both measures hoped to spark a reassessment of *Plyler v. Doe*. Predictably, in both instances, lower federal courts swiftly applied the precedent to invalidate those measures. In the absence of a Supreme Court precedent on the question, though, it seems virtually guaranteed that many additional states (and even local communities) would have enacted similar measures during the intervening years. Consistent with this theory, civil rights lawyers have utilized *Plyler v. Doe* in communities around the nation to prevent school districts from adopting measures that demand information from enrolling students that unauthorized immigrants cannot provide. Those enrollment practices are not confined to school districts located in either southern states or states that border Mexico. Instead, such practices have arisen in a wide variety of states—including Illinois, Indiana, Maryland, Michigan, Nebraska, New Jersey, and New York. In recent years, civil rights groups have motivated state education officials in all of those jurisdictions to warn school districts against requiring information from enrolling students that would force unauthorized immigrants to disclose their immigration status. The Department of Justice, under President Barack Obama, joined the chorus condemning these enrollment practices by invoking *Plyler v. Doe* to inform school administrators that the practices violated federal law.[126]

Fully examining *Plyler v. Doe* requires addressing the case's underlying racial dimensions. Given that the Texas legislature's measure sought to exclude unauthorized immigrants from school, and that the overwhelming percentage of students touched by the law would have hailed from Mexico, some readers today may understand the law as stemming purely from Anglos' animus toward their brown-skinned neighbors. During the 1980s, some commentators condemned the measure using racially inflected language. For example, Ruben Bonilla, leader of a prominent Latino civil rights organization, asserted in 1980 that the statute stemmed from "the Alamo mentality" and Texas's long-standing desire "to keep the Mexicans out."[127] In a similar vein, *Newsweek* depicted the Mexican American community in Texas as united in opposition to the law.

While it is impossible to ascertain with any degree of certainty how large a role such racialized sentiments figured in motivating the statute, the available evidence complicates the notion that Anglos were the only Texans who supported the measure. In fact, the state-wide exclusionary measure mimicked a local ordinance enacted by a small town on the U.S.-Mexico border, where Mexican Americans accounted for 95 percent of the population. After the statewide measure's adoption, moreover, some of its most vocal support originated in Brownsville, Texas, a city in the Rio Grande Valley where more than 90 percent of students traced their origins to Mexico. Brownsville's school superintendent, Raul Besteiro, adamantly supported the exclusionary measure and hardly sounded as though he ailed from "the Alamo mentality." Besteiro—who described himself as "Mexican-American and . . . proud of it"—reported harboring no "animosity" toward unauthorized immigrants and sympathetically allowed, "I know these kids need an education."[128] Besteiro further observed, "They're looking for a better life. You can't blame them for trying." Nevertheless, Besteiro surveyed Brownsville's severely overcrowded classrooms, even with the addition of forty portable classroom units per year, and reasoned that the 1,400 students from unauthorized immigrant families were "diluting" the quality of education for the other 28,100 students.[129] Besteiro contended that Brownsville's residents, who were overwhelmingly Mexican Americans of limited economic means, demonstrated no appetite for raising their taxes to assist unauthorized immigrants. To be clear, I do not mean to suggest that racism played no role in marshaling support for Texas's measure, as immigration-related laws and racial anxieties enjoy a lengthy, sordid history in the United States. I do mean to suggest, however, that support for Texas's law should not be dismissed as stemming *exclusively* from racial animus toward brown-skinned students.

Plyler v. Doe's protection of unauthorized immigrants' access to public schools has endured for more than thirty-five years. The opinion's durability is remarkable because it challenges an ascendant school of thought within legal academia, suggesting that the Supreme Court affords protection to particular groups only after a social movement has first succeeded in transforming cultural attitudes within the larger nation. That narrative undoubtedly encapsulates several important constitutional developments. But it is virtually impossible to construe the Court's decision in *Plyler v. Doe* as the culmination of a mass social movement that altered American attitudes toward unauthorized immigration. No such movement existed in the early 1980s. Scholars interested in exploring the capacity of courts to vindicate constitutional rights—even in the absence of widespread popular support—would be well advised to examine *Plyler v. Doe*'s successful effort to retain access to education for all minors, including unauthorized immigrants.[130]

It would be misguided, moreover, to construe *Plyler v. Doe* as a desirable decision exclusively from the perspective of the children it enabled to receive an education. Rather, the decision can, as Justice Brennan predicted, also be understood as benefiting the nation. In 1994, a reporter for the *Los Angeles Times* successfully tracked down thirteen of the original sixteen children who contested Texas's law. All thirteen of those individuals went on to become lawful permanent residents of the United States, and ten graduated from high school in Tyler. The group includes many productive members of society who pay taxes and work in a variety of positions, including auto mechanic, stock clerk, and assembly-line worker. The *Plyler* Court thus correctly anticipated that denying a basic education to a group of people who were likely to remain in the country would have inflicted catastrophic consequences on the polity. Laura Alvarez, one of Humberto's children, grew up to become a teacher's aide in Tyler—working for the very school system that had banished her seventeen years earlier when she was preparing to enter the third grade. "Without an education, I don't know where I'd be right now," Laura said in 1994, offering a sentiment that was roundly embraced by her erstwhile co-plaintiffs.[131] By 2007, on the opinion's twenty-fifth anniversary, even the Tyler school superintendent who initially decided to impose the tuition fee on unauthorized immigrants had come around to express approval of the Court's decision. "I'm glad we lost . . . so that those kids could get educated," Plyler stated.[132] Had his initial position prevailed, the retired superintendent supposed, "[i]t would have been one of the worst things to happen in education—they'd cost more not being educated."[133]

Despite Plyler's belated embrace of the outcome, the opinion that bears his name has not yet attained anything approaching universal approbation. To the contrary, prominent right-leaning commentators assail the opinion as a lawless aggrandizement of judicial authority. But *Plyler v. Doe*'s detractors often lodge their criticisms on the basis of fundamental misapprehensions. In 2014, for example, Professor Richard Epstein disparaged the Court's opinion for intruding into "a classic question of state management of public resources," and further faulted it for botching "[t]he clear textual argument . . . that the citizen/alien classification cannot be regarded as arbitrary when it is built into the very fabric of the Fourteenth Amendment."[134] Epstein's textual claim, however, falls flat. While Epstein is correct that the Fourteenth Amendment's second sentence uses the term "citizens of the United States," the framers confined its usage in that sentence to the Privileges or Immunities Clause. The Fourteenth Amendment's Equal Protection Clause—the provision at issue in *Plyler v. Doe*—more broadly applies "to any person within [a state's] jurisdiction." The framers' invocation of these two distinct terms thus indicates, contra Epstein, that all "person[s]," regardless of citizenship status, are entitled to invoke the Equal Protection Clause.

As Chief Justice Burger predicted (and presumably hoped) in his dissenting opinion, the Supreme Court has not expanded *Plyler v. Doe*'s holding to apply beyond the narrow circumstance where jurisdictions impede unauthorized immigrants' access to education. A pair of cases, both decided in the 1980s, illustrates the Court's steadfast refusal to import the precedent into other, novel contexts.

In 1983, only one year after *Plyler v. Doe*, the Court upheld a different provision of the Texas code in a case called *Martinez v. Bynum*. The contested measure prohibited minors who lived apart from their parents or guardians from attending a public school in their residential districts if their living arrangements were driven by a desire to receive an education in that district. The dispute arose when Roberto Morales—who was born in McAllen, Texas, but whose parents now resided in Mexico—returned to McAllen to live with his sister, Oralia Martinez, primarily for schooling purposes. Although Martinez served as her brother's custodian, she professed no desire to become his guardian. In an 8–1 opinion written by Justice Powell, the Court quickly rejected the legal challenge by noting that *Plyler v. Doe* itself disclaimed interfering with school districts' traditional right "'to apply . . . established criteria for determining residence.'"[135] *Martinez* garnered only one solitary dissent, perhaps in part because the provision could be circumvented with relative ease. Minors who wish to attend school in a particular district where they live apart from their parents could elude the measure—either by having their custodian assume the guardian role or even more readily by identifying some noneducational reason (for example, safety) as the chief motive behind the minor's residential selection. Consistent with this theory, school districts have seldom invoked this statutory provision in an effort to exclude students following *Martinez*.[136]

The second, more contentious Supreme Court opinion limiting the applicability of *Plyler v. Doe* appeared in 1988, when the Court upheld a North Dakota law permitting localities to charge students—even from indigent families—a fee for bus transportation in *Kadrmas v. Dickinson Public Schools*. Sarita Kadrmas lived with her family some sixteen miles away from her elementary school, in a remote corner of North Dakota even as assessed by the state's standards. Dickinson's school buses had previously transported students to and from school free of charge. But the newly instituted ninety-seven-dollar annual transportation fee proved prohibitive to Kadrmas's family, whose income hovered near the poverty level and who relied upon her father's sporadic work in the oil fields. In a 5–4 decision, Justice Sandra Day O'Connor wrote an opinion determining that Dickinson's barring Kadrmas from riding the school bus did not violate the Equal Protection Clause, and rejecting the notion that excluding students from the bus resembled Texas's exclusion of unauthorized immigrants from schools. "Unlike the children in [*Plyler*], Sarita Kadrmas has not been penalized by the government for illegal conduct by her parents," O'Connor reasoned. "On the contrary, Sarita was denied access to the school bus only because her parents would not agree to pay the same user fee charged to all other families that took advantage of the service."[137]

Critics of this reasoning would surely retort that if prohibiting children in poor families from riding the bus meant they would not attend school at all, then the two situations would seem closely analogous—as the children excluded from the bus could be viewed as being penalized with a denial of education on account of their parents' destitution. As if seeking to preempt this point, Justice O'Connor repeatedly observed that the Kadrmases did manage to transport Sarita to school every day on their own. Yet it was far from clear that this fact should play any decisive role in resolving the larger legal question, which O'Connor framed as whether "the busing fee unconstitutionally places a greater obstacle to education in the path of the poor than it does in the path of wealthier families."[138] In dissent, Justice Marshall construed *Kadrmas* as only the latest in a long series of regrettable decisions—including *Rodriguez*—that marked the Court's "retreat from the promise of equal educational opportunity."[139] Marshall elaborated: "For the poor, education is often the only route by which to become full participants in our society. In allowing a State to burden the access of poor persons to an education, the Court . . . discourages hope."[140]*

When the Court issued *Kadrmas*, some commentators portrayed the decision as insignificant because the North Dakota statute permitting districts to charge students for transportation to and from school was extremely unusual when viewed within the nationwide legislative context, and indeed very few localities even within North Dakota opted to impose fees. Since *Kadrmas*, however, this practice has increased exponentially. Today, school districts in at least thirteen states—including California, Massachusetts, and Texas—impose transportation fees on students, and not all of these districts offer waivers or discounts to students from indigent families. It is one thing to require all participating students (regardless of economic circumstances) to pay fees for transportation to extracurricular events and field trips. But it is quite another to impose those fees upon students from indigent families simply for attending school, which state laws throughout the land require of minors. If school districts refuse to grant waivers or deductions to students from families who, say, qualify for free or reduced lunches, they can expect to have those policies challenged in court. The post-*Kadrmas* expansion of student transportation fees powerfully illustrates how the Court's unwillingness to invalidate constitutionally dubious—though at the time isolated—school policies can yield major consequences down the road. Thus, just as the Court deserves credit in *Plyler v. Doe* for nipping in the bud schools' efforts to exclude unauthorized immigrants, it also must bear responsibility for permitting the contested policy in *Kadrmas* to bloom.[141]

---

* Justice Marshall's law clerk who worked with him on this dissent subsequently revealed that of all the cases decided during her term at the Court, the justice "cared [most] about" *Kadrmas*. After the law clerk—whom Marshall designated "Shorty" on account of her diminutive stature—drafted the dissent, she recalled that Marshall repeatedly returned the document to her "for failing to express in a properly pungent tone . . . his understanding of the case." "Shorty" would eventually follow in Marshall's professional footsteps—first by serving in the Department of Justice as solicitor general and then by becoming an associate justice on the Supreme Court. See Elena Kagan, "For Justice Marshall," 71 *Texas Law Review* 1125, 1125, 1129 (1993); and Carl Hulse, "Senate Confirms Kagan as Justice in Partisan Vote," *New York Times*, Aug. 6, 2010, A1, A14.

7

The Quiet Détente over Religion and Education

In no sphere has the Supreme Court's jurisprudence involving education generated more sustained acrimony than its regulation of religion in public schools. Beginning in the early 1960s, the Court held that the First Amendment's prohibition on establishing religion barred public school educators from leading their pupils in religious exercises. This Establishment Clause ban applied regardless of whether those exercises assumed the form of reciting a nondenominational prayer composed by the state, reading aloud passages from the Bible, or uttering the Lord's Prayer. Those decisions proved so widely reviled because they contravened longstanding, cherished practices that occurred throughout much of the nation on a daily basis. Despite their unpopularity, however, the Court has consistently refused to retreat from those early decisions in subsequent decades. Instead, the Court has moved in the opposite direction, extending its precedents to make clear that public schools cannot post copies of the Ten Commandments, and that the ban on communal prayer applies even on special occasions, including graduation ceremonies and football games. These opinions demonstrate awareness both that the public school setting potentially imposes acute coercive pressure on students' religious beliefs and that this religiously diverse nation must take special steps to forestall any notion that simply receiving an education subjects students to proselytization. The Establishment Clause thus presents a highly aberrational mode of constitutional interpretation within the schoolhouse gate. Typically, the public school setting affords students *diminished* constitutional protections as compared with other locales—a dynamic evident in the domains of free expression and criminal procedure. In contrast, however, the Supreme Court has interpreted those special characteristics to endow public school students with *enhanced* protections under the Establishment Clause. This inversion of the standard approach to constitutional meaning within public schools, accordingly, offers educators less deference over religion than they generally receive.[1]

Although many commentators have contended that these decisions demonstrate the Supreme Court's hostility toward religion, recent decades have witnessed the emergence of several legal phenomena that have combined to dispel that impression. Due to two prominent Supreme Court opinions, public schools today now routinely host moments of silence and extracurricular religious organizations without fearing that doing so violates the Constitution. Similarly, it has become clearer that public school teachers may discuss the role of religion in society without running afoul of the Establishment Clause—provided that they do so in the course of conveying academic material and not to indoctrinate or proselytize. In addition, the widespread expansion of homeschooling beginning in the 1990s has permitted many religious families to educate their children in settings that do not create tensions with their faith-centered value systems. While the federal judiciary has steadily rejected religious families' efforts to use the First Amendment's Free Exercise Clause to secure exemptions from public school assignments, moreover, the availability of homeschooling has nonetheless preserved the option of exiting the public schools. Finally, the Supreme Court's most recent high-profile Establishment Clause decision involving education upheld the constitutionality of government vouchers for students to attend private schools, regardless of whether those institutions were affiliated with a religion. Without many people seeming to notice, these various developments have introduced a period of détente—even if not absolute peace—into the "culture wars" arguments that have long predominated legal discussions involving religion and education.[2]

To be sure, conservative and liberal camps have both expressed disagreement with particular portions of the dominant legal framework that controls the intersection of religion and education. Right-leaning commentators generally maintain that the Court is unduly restrictive of prayer in public schools and at school-related functions. Conversely, left-leaning commentators have often condemned the Supreme Court's decision legitimating vouchers. Yet even though both camps dislike parts of the Court's jurisprudence, its opinions can—and, in my view, should—be accepted in both the prayer and the funding contexts as coherently vindicating the principle of religious neutrality. Indeed, this point merits amplification: although each of the preceding chapters has leveled major critiques of various aspects of prevailing constitutional doctrine, I believe that the judiciary has—as a general proposition—resolved the contentious questions about religion and education in a sensible fashion. As will soon become clear, I certainly do not agree with the resolution of *every* decision in this area. But its broad strokes are, in my estimation, eminently sound.[3]

TEACHER-LED PRAYERS, BIBLE READING, AND THE TEN COMMANDMENTS

Engel v. Vitale

In 1958, a school board on Long Island, New York, voted 4–1 to enact a measure requiring teachers to open each day of classes by leading their students in a prayer that the New York State Board of Regents had recently crafted. The Regents' Prayer amounted to a grand total of twenty-two words: "Almighty God, we acknowledge our dependence upon Thee, and we beg Thy blessings upon us, our parents, our teachers and our country." For Lawrence Roth, the owner of a small business and the father of two sons enrolled in the local public schools, that was twenty-two words too many. Along with his wife, Frances, Roth began recruiting their friends and neighbors in New Hyde Park to oppose teacher-led prayer. "We believe religious training is the prerogative of the parent, and not the duty of the government," Roth explained. When the Roths and their compatriots expressed such dissatisfaction to the school board president, William Vitale, he firmly informed the group, "[T]he board has voted on this. If we say it's in, it's in." In slightly more expansive terms, Vitale defended the Regents' Prayer as legitimate because, he puzzlingly claimed, it had nothing to do with religion. "This is not a religious issue," Vitale explained. "It's simply a matter of giving our children additional moral and spiritual help and recognition of God." In addition, Vitale derided opposition to the Regents' Prayer as "a premeditated act to undermine the American heritage." Roth, confronted with such reasoning, contacted the local branch of the American Civil Liberties Union seeking legal assistance contesting the prayer. Although the ACLU agreed to represent Roth, it also warned him that filing a lawsuit would mean being "hated and despised by most of your neighbors, and [that] your children will have to face the scorn of many of their classmates."[4]

The ACLU's warning proved all too accurate. Of the fifty families who initially agreed to join the litigation challenging the Regents' Prayer, the ensuing enmity reduced the number to only five when the trial commenced in January 1959. As the employer of one plaintiff told *Newsweek*, "It's foolish to get mixed up in an unpopular cause."[5] The pressure for conformity was sufficiently intense that even the courageous families who continued with the lawsuit for the duration declined to exercise the option of having their children removed from classrooms during the daily prayer recitations. "[W]e didn't want to make pariahs of them," one mother explained.[6] The stalwart litigants arose from a wide range of approaches to religion—including atheism, Ethical Culture, Judaism, and Unitarianism—and evinced highly varying levels of religious observance. Whereas Roth (while born into the Jewish faith) tended toward skepticism of all religious expression, his fellow plaintiff Steven Engel enthusiastically observed Reform Judaism. Thus, Engel objected to the policy precisely because he believed that such diluted forms of prayer harmed genuine religious worship. "[W]hen you rattle these things off and they have no meaning . . . at all," Engel explained, "you vitiate the value of religion."[7]

In June 1962, Justice Hugo Black announced the Supreme Court's determination in *Engel v. Vitale*, holding that the Establishment Clause required invalidation of the Regents' Prayer. As Black delivered *Engel* from the bench, he spoke in quiet, emotional tones before an unusually rapt audience. Justice Black reasoned that neither the nondenominational quality of the Regents' Prayer nor the stipulation that participation was ostensibly voluntary altered the basic, condemning facts: the State of New York composed an official prayer for its public school students to recite, and in the process placed religious dissidents in an untenable position. "When the power, prestige and financial support of the government is placed behind a particular religious belief," Black explained, "the indirect coercive pressure upon religious minorities to conform to the prevailing officially approved religion is plain."[8] According to Justice Black, the nation's esteemed history as a haven for those fleeing religious persecution in Europe meant that, even though the Regents' Prayer was both brief and broadly phrased, "it is proper to take alarm at the first experiment on our liberties."[9]

Black also aimed to defuse contentions that *Engel* should in any way be perceived as indicating hostility toward prayer or religion. "It is neither sacrilegious nor antireligious to say that each separate government in this country should stay out of the business of writing or sanctioning official prayers and leave that purely religious function to the people themselves and to those the people choose to look for religious guidance," Black wrote.[10] Extending this point further, Black suggested that *Engel*, properly understood, stemmed from profound respect for religious observance: "The Establishment Clause . . . stands as an expression of principle on the part of the Founders of our Constitution that religion is too personal, too sacred, too holy, to permit its unhallowed perversion by a civil magistrate."[11] Though Black's voice trembled reciting the words "too personal, too sacred, too holy," he steadied himself to add an extemporaneous distillation of the decision's import—one that appears nowhere in the written opinion.[12] "The prayer of each man from his soul must be his and his alone," Black improvised. "That is the genius of the First Amendment. If there is any one thing clear in the First Amendment, it is that the right of the people to pray in their own way is not to be controlled by the election returns."[13]

Justice Potter Stewart cast the sole dissenting vote in *Engel*.* Whereas the majority found that the Regents' Prayer contravened the Establishment Clause, Justice Stewart in sharp contrast claimed "the Court . . . misapplied a great constitutional principle," and even appeared to flirt with asserting that *Engel* itself ran afoul of the students' rights under the Free Exercise Clause. "I cannot see

* Neither Justice Felix Frankfurter nor Justice Byron White participated in the resolution of *Engel*, making the margin 6–1, not 8–1, as otherwise might be inferred.

how an 'official religion' is established by letting those who want to say a prayer say it," Stewart wrote. "On the contrary, I think that to deny the wish of these school children to join in reciting this prayer is to deny them the opportunity of sharing in the spiritual heritage of our Nation."[14] Stewart then dedicated the bulk of his dissent to identifying prominent traditions that *Engel*'s logic might be construed as undermining. If teachers could no longer lead New York schoolchildren in prayer, Stewart wondered, would the president of the United States upon taking the oath of office now be forbidden to request the help of God? Would the Treasury Department henceforth be prohibited from inscribing "IN GOD WE TRUST" on U.S. currency? Moving closer to home, Stewart reminded his colleagues that *Engel* conceivably even threatened the opening words of every public session held at the Supreme Court. "Since the days of John Marshall our Crier has said, 'God save the United States and this Honorable Court.'"[15] Must that tradition, too, now be eliminated?

When *Engel* appeared, reporters called the Roth residence and received an ecstatic reaction from the students' mother. "We're so excited, we can't think straight," Frances Roth exclaimed. "I'm very proud of our country, where a group of people can take a stand on an issue . . . and be backed by the highest court in the land."[16] That early excitement and pride would quickly yield to other, less pleasant sentiments. Opponents of *Engel* bombarded the Roth household with anonymous, menacing telephone calls at all hours—totaling eight thousand in the first week alone—as they variously threatened, "Watch out for your children. . . . We're going to blow up your car. . . . Don't leave your house, something is going to happen to it. . . . We'll get you."[17] During this period, the Roths also began receiving hate mail, with many notes employing virulently anti-Semitic language. "You Communist Kike . . . why don't you go back to Russia?" one letter read.[18] Echoing those same odious themes, another missive stated, "If you don't like our God, then go behind the Iron Curtain where you belong, Kike, Hebe, Filth!" Even some letters that eschewed naked epithets nevertheless trafficked in standard tropes of anti-Semitism: "This [decision] looks like Jews trying to grab America as Jews grab everything they want in any nation. America is a Christian nation."[19] Perhaps more disturbingly still, picketers patrolled outside the family's home, spewing insults and carrying signs that read, "Roth—Godless Atheist," "F.B.I. Please Investigate Mr. Roth," and "Impeach the pro-Red

Supreme Court."[20] On one particularly harrowing occasion, a gasoline-doused cross was set aflame in the Roths' driveway. Given this onslaught, it can hardly be surprising that only one week after the decision Frances Roth's initial delight had curdled into despair. "I have a feeling of sadness because these are so-called godly people," Frances Roth said, commenting on the harassers. "If their God teaches them to wish my kids get polio and my house be bombed, then I think he hasn't done a very good job with them."[21]

The vitriol directed at the Roths conveys in a microcosm the historically explosive public reaction that engulfed *Engel. Newsweek*, examining the antipathy aimed at the decision, contemporaneously reported that a "thunderclap of outrage and shock [has] cracked across the land."[22] If anything, though, this assessment errs by understating the actual reaction. Never before in its entire history had the Supreme Court issued a constitutional decision that generated more pervasive, more intense animosity than its invalidation of the Regents' Prayer. Letters attacking the decision flooded the Supreme Court, establishing a new record for correspondence in response to a judicial opinion. One month after the decision, moreover, a Gallup poll revealed that nearly four in five respondents approved of religious observance in public schools. In a stunningly wide variety of settings—ranging from the editorial boardroom to the well of the Senate, from the preacher's pulpit to the superintendent's office, from living rooms in ordinary homes to lecture rooms in prestigious law schools—*Engel* elicited widespread loathing. Surveying in some depth the overwhelmingly, though not universally, negative reactions to *Engel* is worthwhile not only for their intrinsic interest but also because they help to underscore the significance of the Court's steadfast refusal to abandon the opinion in the intervening years.[23]

Many different publications sharply criticized *Engel*. The *Chicago Tribune* termed *Engel* "saddening," as it explained, "In an age that is always troubled and sometimes seems abandoned, an official prayer that might produce more saints and fewer sinners is not without merit."[24] For its part, the *Los Angeles Times* derided the opinion as "alarm[ing]."[25] Many southern editorial boards took an even dimmer view of *Engel*, as the Raleigh *News and Observer* called it "ridiculous," and *The Tulsa Tribune* labeled it "plainly nutty."[26] Notably, some of the media's condemnation revealed a misapprehension of the opinion's scope, as *Engel* addressed only teacher-led prayer and in no way sought to prohibit students from praying on their own initiative. In this vein, Chief Justice Earl Warren recalled in his memoirs seeing one post-*Engel* headline that announced, "Court Outlaws God."[27] While Warren's recollection may now appear so absurd as to seem apocryphal, editorial coverage from that era advanced similarly warped understandings of *Engel*. Thus, *National Review*, in an editorial titled "Thou Shalt Not Pray," asserted that *Engel* made "ours . . . the only nation outside the Iron Curtain where it is unlawful to pray in the public schools."[28] And *The Dallas Morning News* expressed incredulity that the Court had "outlaw[ed] acknowledgement of belief in a Supreme Being from the schools."[29]*

Elected officials widely repudiated *Engel*. "For several days all the serious business of the Congress of the United States was put aside while members spent their time denouncing the Supreme Court," *The New York Times* reported.[30] Within three months of *Engel*, moreover, no fewer than forty-nine separate constitutional amendments had been proposed in Congress to overturn the decision. Senator Prescott Bush of Connecticut, not usually considered a firebrand, called *Engel* "divisive," "most unfortunate," and "quite unnecessary."[31] But Bush's remarks were a model of restraint compared with those of many of his colleagues on Capitol Hill. "Somebody is tampering with America's soul," objected Senator Robert Byrd of West Virginia in response to *Engel*.[32] Representative Frank Becker, whose district included parts of Long Island, called *Engel* "the most tragic decision in the history of the United States" and, in an echo of FDR's remarks following the Japanese attack on Pearl Harbor, further contended, "June 25, 1962, will go down as a black

* *Engel* was not, of course, universally reviled within the media, as at least two prominent liberal newspapers applauded the decision. *The Washington Post* praised the decision for emancipating students, public schools, and even religious observance itself: "The decision is an act of liberation. It frees school children from what was in effect a forced participation by rote in an act of worship. . . . It frees the public schools from an observance much more likely to be divisive than unifying. And most important of all, perhaps, it frees religion from an essentially mischievous and incalculably perilous sort of secular support." "In Behalf of Religion," *Washington Post*, June 26, 1962, A12. Relatedly, *The New York Times* commended *Engel* for "wisely" purging a practice that invited social discord: "[N]othing could be more divisive in this country than to mingle religion and government in the sensitive setting of the public schools, and under circumstances regarded by minorities as coercive." "Prayer Is Personal," *New York Times*, June 27, 1962, 34.

day in our history."[33] For Representative Frank Chelf of Kentucky, *Engel* was "ridiculous, blasphemous, [and] anti-Christian," and the justices who joined the opinion "ought to be ashamed and ought to resign."[34] Politicians from the Deep South frequently portrayed *Engel* as only the latest instance of staggering judicial overreach, occurring as it did a mere eight years after *Brown v. Board of Education* rejected racially segregated schools. Lingering resentment over *Brown* informed the critique of Representative L. Mendel Rivers of South Carolina, who asserted *Engel* revealed the Court's "disbelief in God Almighty" and accused the justices of "legislating—they never adjudicate—with one eye on the Kremlin and the other on the National Association for the Advancement of Colored People."[35] Advancing this same theme, Senator Sam Ervin of North Carolina, who helped launch the Southern Manifesto, took to the Senate floor to wonder whether in *Engel* "the Supreme Court has held that God is unconstitutional and for that reason the public schools must be segregated against Him."[36] And in perhaps the most widely circulated politician's rebuke of *Engel*, Representative George Andrews of Alabama complained that the justices "put the Negroes in the schools and now they've driven God out of them."[37]

On one view, such denunciations of *Engel* stem purely from crass opportunism, nothing more than a ploy for votes. Professor Robert McCloskey floated an early version of this idea shortly after *Engel*. "Congressmen feel that defending prayer is like defending motherhood: it wins them some votes and costs them almost none," he wrote.[38] Over the decades, many insightful legal scholars have endorsed McCloskey's notion. Yet it seems mistaken to construe politicians' widespread anti-*Engel* commentary as sheer political posturing, rather than the expression of deeply held convictions that it often was. This suggestion finds support in the fact that some prominent politicians repudiated *Engel*, even though they had no hope of ever running for election again. The former president Dwight Eisenhower griped, "I always thought that this nation was essentially a religious one."[39] Even more significantly, the former president Herbert Hoover—by this point well into his eighties and some three decades removed from the Oval Office—contended that *Engel*'s rejection of the Regents' Prayer marked "a disintegration of one of the most sacred [aspects] of American heritage," and called on Congress "at once [to] submit an amendment to the Constitution which establishes the right of religious devotion in all governmental agencies—national, state or local."[40]*

In religious circles, many Protestant and Catholic leaders also lambasted *Engel*. The Reverend Billy Graham criticized the Court for secularizing the United States and mangling the First Amendment. "The framers of our Constitution meant we were to have freedom of religion, not freedom from religion," he lamented.[41] "God pity our country," Graham further commented, "when we can no longer appeal to God for help."[42] Reinhold Niebuhr—the nation's most distinguished Protestant theologian—extolled the Regents' Prayer as "a model of accommodation to the pluralistic nature of our society." *Engel* wielded "a meat ax" for a task that actually "require[d] a scalpel," Niebuhr contended, as the opinion unwisely threatened "the suppression of religion and . . . the impression that government must be anti-religion."[43] One Methodist bishop in Georgia memorably portrayed *Engel* as an affront to patriotism: "It's like taking a star or stripe off the flag."[44] Cardinal James Francis McIntyre of Los Angeles also contended *Engel* weakened national ideals. "The decision is positively shocking and scandalizing to one of American blood and principles," McIntyre stated.[45] Cardinal Francis Spellman of New York City appeared to read from

---

* Although some politicians rose to support *Engel*, their declarations appeared more halfhearted than full throated. For instance, consider the defensive posture adopted by Representative Emanuel Celler of Brooklyn, New York, who remarked he did not see how the Court had "any other choice" than to invalidate the Regents' Prayer. Anthony Lewis, "Both Houses Get Bills to Lift Ban on School Prayer," *New York Times*, June 27, 1962, 1. President John F. Kennedy supplied not only the most prominent defense of *Engel* but also the deftest. In a press conference held on the heels of *Engel*, the very first questioner solicited Kennedy's views on the opinion. His elegant, carefully crafted response suggested that the query hardly took him by surprise. Kennedy began by noting that "a good many people obviously will disagree with" *Engel* but then quickly added that "[o]thers will agree with it." Whatever one's personal take, though, Kennedy continued, "I think that it is important for us if we are going to maintain our constitutional principle that we support the Supreme Court decisions even when we may not agree with them." Finally, in his masterstroke, Kennedy pivoted to suggest subtly that even those who disagreed with *Engel* should not overestimate its negative effects on the availability of prayer. In so doing, Kennedy displayed a much firmer grasp of *Engel*'s holding than many other contemporaneous observers possessed. "[W]e have in this case a very easy remedy, and that is to pray ourselves," Kennedy explained. "[A]nd I would think that it would be a welcome reminder to every American family that we can . . . attend our churches with a good deal more fidelity, and we can make the true meaning of prayer much more important. . . . That power is very much open to us." William Anderson, "President Urges More Prayers in Homes," *Chicago Tribune*, June 28, 1962, A1.

a similar playbook, as he proclaimed the decision "shock[ing] and frighten[ing]."[46] In an editorial published two months after *Engel*, the typically progressive Jesuit publication *America* noted that Jewish leaders had detected increased anti-Semitism following the decision, and it then proceeded to blame the victim. "It would be most unfortunate if the entire Jewish community were to be blamed for the unrelenting pressure tactics of a small but overly vocal segment within it," the editorial avowed. "What will have been accomplished if our Jewish friends win all the legal immunities they seek, but thereby paint themselves into a corner of social and cultural alienation? . . . When court victories produce only a harvest of fear and distrust, will it all have been worth-while?"[47]*

Public school officials also scorned *Engel*. In Tennessee, one educator went so far as to proclaim, "I am of the opinion that 99 percent of the people in the United States feel as I do about the Supreme Court's opinion—that it was an outrage. . . . The remaining 1 percent do not belong in the free world."[48] In many states, superintendents pledged simply to ignore the decision. "We will not pay any attention to the Supreme Court ruling," said a leader of Atlanta's public schools. On Long Island, the reaction was much the same, as several superintendents pledged defiance, with one explaining, "A school without a prayer is not a school."[49]

Engel stunned many ordinary citizens around the country. In Quincy, Massachusetts, for example, one resident told *The Boston Globe* that *Engel* was "terrible," because praying was "as much a part of school as reading and writing."[50] Collective incredulity with the Court's decision prompted some critics to employ gallows humor as they lamented the situation. "Sometimes a nation abolishes God, but

* Some religious leaders did celebrate *Engel*. Perhaps predictably, leadership of marginalized religious minorities—including Jews and Mormons—accorded *Engel* the most enthusiastic response. Thus, for example, the New York Board of Rabbis issued a statement praising *Engel*, as it contended "the teaching of prayer" in public schools violates "the spirit of the American concept of the separation of church and state." Alexander Burnham, "Edict Is Called a Setback by Christian Clerics—Rabbis Praise It," *New York Times*, June 26, 1962, 1. See "The Court Decision—and the School Prayer Furor," *Newsweek*, 45 (noting that the head of the Synagogue Council of America supported *Engel* and that Mormons also supported the decision). But a few high-profile Protestants also supported the opinion. Most notably, the Reverend Martin Luther King Jr.—during his campaign against racial subordination in Albany, Georgia—called *Engel* "sound and good" because it "reaffirm[ed] something that is basic in our Constitution, namely, separation of church and state." Jonathan Zimmerman, *Whose America? Culture Wars in the Public Schools* 160 (2002).

fortunately God is more tolerant," a western Pennsylvanian quipped in a letter to *Newsweek*.[51] An *Atlanta Journal* reader—anticipating a source of cultural anxiety that would only intensify in subsequent decades—inquired whether the traditional late-December greeting of "Merry Christmas" would soon be replaced with "Happy Winter Festival."[52] But one broadly circulated yarn from the 1960s provides perhaps the sharpest insight into how *Engel* penetrated the national consciousness. According to the joke, a public school teacher happens upon a cluster of students kneeling in the hallway. "Why are you on your knees?" the teacher asks. "Shooting craps," they reply in unison. "Thank God," the teacher cries, genuinely relieved. "I thought you were praying."[53]

Disapproval of *Engel* was so pervasive that even in the elite precincts of the nation's leading law schools many eminent figures viewed the decision as severely misguided or—at minimum—an unforced error. Dean Erwin Griswold of Harvard Law School offered a notably antagonistic response, as he contended that the Supreme Court's decision erroneously interfered with local education customs, upending what he regarded as the nation's Christian foundation:

> [T]here are some matters which are essentially local in nature, important matters, but none the less matters to be worked out by the people themselves in their own communities, when no basic rights of others are impaired. . . . Does our deep-seated tolerance of all religions—or, to the same extent, of no religion—require that we give up all religious observance in public activities? Why should it? . . . This . . . has been, and is, a Christian country in origin, history, tradition and culture.[54]

Non-Christians should certainly be permitted to observe their own religions however they deem fit, Griswold maintained, but they should refrain from using the nation's religious tolerance as a cudgel to attack its Christian heritage. "The [religious minority] who comes here may worship as he pleases, and may hold public office without discrimination," Griswold argued. "That is as it should be. But why should it follow that he can require others to give up their Christian tradition merely because he is a tolerated and welcomed member of the community?"[55] Professor Louis Pollak of Yale, while stopping well short of Griswold's overt hostility to *Engel*, nevertheless dismissed the Regents' Prayer as an inane banality and argued therefore that the Court erred by agreeing to resolve the trifling matter in the first instance. "New York's attempt to write a prayer had produced such a pathetically vacuous assertion of piety as hardly to rise to the dignity of a religious exercise," Pollak wrote. "The Court might very reasonably have decided to save its scarce ammunition for a prayer that soared, rather than squander it on New York's clay-footed pigeon."[56]* Adopting this same theme, Professor Arthur Sutherland argued in the *Harvard Law Review* that the Court in *Engel* unwisely expended a precious judicial resource: its own capital.[57]†

This overwhelmingly negative reaction to *Engel* has, within the corridors of legal academia, led the decision to be viewed as a quintessential example of the Supreme Court's penchant for protecting constitutional rights even when doing so requires it to swim against the tide of popular opinion. Thus, even for legal scholars who doubt that the Court possesses the institutional capacity to check majoritarian preferences, *Engel* has long stood out as the exception that proves the rule. Recently, however, Professor Corinna Barrett Lain

---

* Professor Pollak's advocacy that the Supreme Court in *Engel* should have denied the petition for certiorari, and thereby refused to hear the case, exemplifies an approach that his Yale colleague Alexander Bickel termed the judiciary's "passive virtues." Alexander M. Bickel, "The Supreme Court 1960 Term—Foreword: The Passive Virtues," 75 *Harvard Law Review* 40 (1961). Bickel himself would subsequently embrace the notion that the Court should have declined to resolve *Engel*: "The decision in the New York case was unfortunate and should have been avoided altogether, as it could have been by a simple denial by the Court of the petition to review." Alexander M. Bickel, *Politics and the Warren Court* 206 (1973).

† A few legal academics did, however, rise to contend that the Supreme Court correctly invalidated the Regents' Prayer. An article in the *Michigan Law Review*, for example, commended the Court for "maintain[ing] the dignity and religious significance of prayer by keeping it free from state compulsion and interference." Paul G. Kauper, "Prayer, Public Schools, and the Supreme Court," 61 *Michigan Law Review* 1031, 1065 (1963). Writing in *The Supreme Court Review*, Professor Philip Kurland of the University of Chicago contended that *Engel* sensibly vindicated the principle of religious neutrality, which forbids governmental entities to either advance religion or inhibit it. Although the opinion initially suffered a beating in the court of public opinion, Kurland expressed confidence that *Engel*'s opponents would eventually become its champions: "It is hard to believe that many who now find this [decision] unpalatable will not soon . . . be applauding it. . . . [W]hen time gives the opportunity for thoughtful evaluation rather than emotional reaction, [*Engel*] may come to be recognized as one of the bulwarks of America's freedom." Philip B. Kurland, "The Regents' Prayer Case: 'Full of Sound and Fury, Signifying . . .'," 1962 *Supreme Court Review* 1, 33.

has challenged that notion, asserting in the *Stanford Law Review* that *Engel* should not be viewed as an exception at all because the actual opinion was not "countermajoritarian."[58]* Lain's revisionist assessment of *Engel* hinges on two primary points. First, she contends that prior to *Engel* the justices did not realize that their invalidation of the Regents' Prayer would stoke enormous resentment. Given that they failed to anticipate the firestorm, Lain asserts, the justices' defense of minority rights should be viewed less as brave than as blundering. Second, she contends that the public's venomous reaction to *Engel* stemmed fundamentally from misperceptions about what the opinion actually held, due to media accounts suggesting, for example, that the decision outlawed God. The general public did not so much despise *Engel,* Lain insists, as they despised their distorted understandings of *Engel;* accordingly, the opinion's genuine, relatively narrow holding would have deviated far less from popular preferences.

While Professor Lain marshals extensive, impressive historical research, her underlying claim should not be accepted uncritically. As an initial matter, it is far from clear that whether the justices initially anticipated that invalidating the Regents' Prayer would trigger a public backlash should erase the fact that the decision itself clashed with majoritarian preferences. When one assesses whether an opinion defied popular opinion, the justices' collective state of mind is inconsequential compared with the actual public reaction that their decision elicits. Even if the justices acted unknowingly in the first instance, moreover, they quickly became aware that *Engel* provoked deep hostility. They needed only to glance at the outraged headlines and the swelling mounds of disapproving mail to appreciate that point. On Lain's rationale, one might anticipate that, after the Court perceived deep dissatisfaction with *Engel,* it would seek to identify an opportunity to retreat from the opinion's core commitment. Yet precisely the opposite occurred, even though the general public has expressed intense, persistent opposition to the view that *Engel* adopted. Well after the earliest post-*Engel* polling data indi-

* Professor Alexander Bickel coined the term "counter-majoritarian difficulty" to describe the issues that arise when, in a society that styles itself a democracy, a bare majority of unelected justices possess the authority to invalidate democratically enacted pieces of legislation. See Alexander M. Bickel, *The Least Dangerous Branch: The Supreme Court at the Bar of Politics* 16–23 (2d ed. 1986) (1962).

cated that roughly four in five respondents disagreed with the decision, the high level of opposition has remained incredibly durable. Indeed, more than two decades after *Engel*—long after the initial shock had subsided, and the media coverage faded in memory—a Gallup poll taken over many years consistently revealed that about three in four respondents favored a constitutional amendment overturning *Engel*. Since *Engel*, despite numerous opportunities to back down from the views on school prayer it expressed in 1962, the Court has instead on occasion after occasion doubled down. For the moment, contemplate only two of those steadfast decisions: its invalidation of widespread teacher-led prayer exercises on the heels of *Engel*, and its invalidation of state efforts to post the Ten Commandments in public school classrooms nearly two decades later.[59]

Abington School District v. Schempp

As a formal matter, the Supreme Court in *Engel* invalidated only the Regents' Prayer. In 1963, one year after *Engel*, the Court in *Abington School District v. Schempp* went much further, invalidating state laws that required—at the beginning of each school day— recitation of the Lord's Prayer and verses to be read aloud from the Holy Bible. Justice Tom Clark's opinion for the Court in *Schempp* firmly rejected the contention that striking down the teacher-led prayers at issue somehow itself constituted an Establishment Clause violation because it advanced the religion of secularism. *Schempp* neither promoted nor impeded religion of any type, Clark insisted, but instead simply fulfilled the Court's duty to assume a position of neutrality toward religious observance. Justice Clark also rejected the notion that invalidating teacher-led prayers impinged upon the free exercise rights of students who wished to participate in teacher-led religious observances. "While the Free Exercise Clause clearly prohibits the use of state action to deny the rights of free exercise to *anyone*," he wrote, "it has never meant that a majority could use the machinery of the State to practice its beliefs."[60] That notion, Clark contended, had effectively been answered by Justice Robert Jackson's opinion in *West Virginia Board of Education v. Barnette*, where he observed that the Bill of Rights was designed " 'to place [certain subjects] beyond the reach of majorities and officials and to establish them as legal principles to be applied by the courts. One's right to . . . freedom of worship . . . may not be submitted to vote; [it] depend[s] on the outcome of no elections.'"[61] Clark clarified that the Establishment Clause in no way barred public school teachers from, as part of their secular instructional responsibilities, addressing the role of religion in society; instead, it prohibited them simply from leading their pupils in religious exercises. As in *Engel*, Justice Stewart cast the lone dissenting vote in *Schempp*. Although Stewart conceded that the Establishment Clause prohibited schools from exerting "any kind of pressure" on students to participate in religious exercise, he did not believe it mandated that "children are kept scrupulously insulated from any awareness that some of their fellows may want to open the school day with prayer."[62]*

While the public's reaction to *Schempp* failed to reach the hysterical levels that followed *Engel*, that development seems largely attributable to two interrelated dynamics. First, the public might have already presumed that the Court's invalidation of the Regents' Prayer meant that the Lord's Prayer and Bible reading would fall next. In addition, the sense of angry bewilderment that *Engel* provoked might have subsided twelve months later, particularly when citizens realized that, despite the cries of Chicken Little, the sky had not in fact fallen. Whatever the precise explanation for the less vehement reaction to *Schempp*, it certainly should not be chalked up to agreement with the decision. A post-*Schempp* Gallup poll revealed that only 24 percent of respondents approved of the opinion. Consistent with this low approval rating, members of the public harassed the plaintiffs who initiated the lawsuit, and various elected officials pronounced the decision "silly," "offensive," and a "major triumph for the forces of secularism and atheism which are bent on throwing God completely out of our national life."[63]

---

* Professor Lain does make at least some effort to accommodate *Schempp* into her general theory by noting, for example, that the Court adopted a more conciliatory tone toward religion's importance than it had displayed the previous year in *Engel*. See Corinna Barrett Lain, "God, Civic Virtue, and the American Way: Reconstructing *Engel*," 67 *Stanford Law Review* 479, 533–34 (2015). Although this observation accurately conveys *Schempp*'s tonal shift, Lain overplays its significance. The Court's reasoning matters to the general public far less than its bottom-line outcome. Few ordinary citizens immerse themselves in judicial opinions at all, let alone to contemplate nuanced matters like judicial tone. More important, however, Lain makes no effort whatsoever to account for developments in the Court's post-*Schempp* jurisprudence. Given that legal scholars who doubt the Court's capacity to resist majoritarian preferences frequently emphasize the difficulty of doing so for an extended period, it is confounding that Lain artificially truncates her inquiry in 1963, right after the Court's saga in this area commenced in earnest.

Stone v. Graham

In November 1980, more than fifteen years after *Schempp*, the Supreme Court quietly but forcefully demonstrated its continued commitment to maintaining religious neutrality within public schools when it issued *Stone v. Graham*. That now largely forgotten decision involved a challenge to a Kentucky statute that would have required every public school classroom in the entire state to display a copy of the Ten Commandments. The legislature in Frankfort, Kentucky, aimed to inoculate the measure against potential Establishment Clause objections by taking two main precautions. First, the statute provided that the Ten Commandments posters would be displayed only if funding could be secured through private volunteers, rather than being supplied directly by the government. Second, attempting to preempt claims that the displays were designed to promote religion, the measure required that all posters contain the following proclamation: "The secular application of the Ten Commandments is clearly seen in its adoption as the fundamental legal code of Western Civilization and the Common Law of the United States."[64]

In *Stone*, however, five justices joined an opinion rejecting Kentucky's effort to safeguard the Ten Commandments posters as the sheerest artifice. "The pre-eminent purpose for posting the Ten Commandments on schoolroom walls is plainly religious in nature," *Stone* concluded.[65] Neither the private funding, nor the secular disclaimer, nor even the fact that teachers were not instructed to read the Commandments aloud could override this basic conclusion. As *Stone* observed, while some of the Ten Commandments address arguably secular subjects (for example, prohibitions on murder, adultery, theft), they hardly confine themselves to such material. Instead, the first few Commandments explicitly impose duties on the faithful: "worshipping the Lord God alone, avoiding idolatry, not using the Lord's name in vain, and observing the Sabbath Day."[66] In *Stone*'s most notable dissent, Justice William Rehnquist derided the majority's opinion as an ill-advised, futile effort to scrub the world of its manifold religious influences, in domains ranging from art to music to architecture: "The fact is that, for good or for ill, nearly everything in our culture worth transmitting, everything which gives meaning to life, is saturated with religious influences, derived from paganism, Judaism, Christianity—both Catholic and

Protestant—and other faiths accepted by a large part of the world's peoples."[67]

Stone can be viewed as speaking quietly because the opinion did not arrive through the Court's usual channels, with extensive briefing and oral argument, which help to raise the salience of legal disputes. Instead, *Stone* summarily reversed the decision below in a short, unsigned per curiam opinion, not long after the petition seeking review arrived at the Court. Along similar lines, at the time of *Stone*, Kentucky had the only active statute of its kind in the nation—a legislative peculiarity that further minimized the opinion's relatively modest cultural impact.

Yet *Stone* can also be viewed as speaking forcefully because the decision reaffirmed the Court's opposition to permitting states to indoctrinate students in public schools. As Professor Jesse Choper commented in 1980, *Stone* should be understood as the justices' refusal to back down in the face of the religious right's efforts to erode *Engel* and *Schempp*. "They're not going to let people chisel away at the perimeters," Choper remarked.[68] Although Kentucky's Ten Commandments measure stood alone in 1980, moreover, ample reason exists for supposing that such measures would have become commonplace had the Court not stopped this statutory development before it gathered steam. The idea of requiring schools to post the Ten Commandments contains appeal beyond the Bible Belt.* Thus, *Stone* can be viewed as powerfully shaping the nation's public school classrooms, by keeping the walls that surround students on a daily basis free from a fundamentally religious text. The decision seems even more potent when one considers that *Stone* appeared less than two weeks after the election of President Ronald Reagan, who throughout his successful 1980 campaign proposed a constitutional amendment that would have had the effect of overturning *Engel*.† Accordingly, *Stone* illustrates how the Supreme

* For example, North Dakota had previously enacted a statute requiring the Ten Commandments be displayed in public schools. Prior to *Stone*, however, a federal district court judge invalidated the measure. See Jim Mann, "Display of Ten Commandments in Public Schools Is Unconstitutional, Justices Rule," *Los Angeles Times*, Nov. 18, 1980, B5; and *Ring v. Grand Forks Public School District No. 1*, 483 F. Supp. 272 (D. N.D. 1980).

† Throughout his presidency, Ronald Reagan proposed a constitutional amendment that ran as follows: "Nothing in this Constitution shall be construed to prohibit individual or group prayer in public schools or other public institutions. No person shall be required by the United States or by any state to participate in prayer." "Reagan Proposes School Prayer Amendment," *New York Times*, May 17, 1982, A24. At various points,

Court can, even in the absence of vocal support from elected officials, successfully bring its constitutional vision to bear in public
schools throughout the nation.[69]

* * *

Before we turn to the Supreme Court's more recent decisions
assessing prayers at graduation ceremonies and sporting events, it is
necessary first to examine whether its earliest opinions on prayers
in public schools—*Engel* and *Schempp*—have helped to eliminate
the religious observance that marked the beginning of school days
around the country in the early 1960s. It is one thing for the Court
to issue a decision, and it is quite another for schools to heed that
decision. The Supreme Court, of course, possesses no magic wand
to implement its opinions. Moreover, judicial opinions that seek to
alter deeply ingrained practices across highly diffuse settings serve
only to increase the standard implementation challenges because
monitoring transgressions presents many procedural difficulties.
Religion possesses perhaps an unrivaled ability to stir passions, as
the educators' pledges of defiance discussed above richly attest.
Consistent with such comments, some contemporaneous studies
found widespread noncompliance with *Engel* and *Schempp* during
the 1960s—most prominently in the South, where a majority of
schools continued with teacher-led prayers and Bible-reading ses-

---

Reagan offered different formulations to support his proposed amendment. "I believe
that it would be beneficial for our children to have an opportunity to begin each school
day" with a prayer, Reagan explained, upon announcing the proposal in 1982. "Since
the law has been construed to prohibit this, I believe that the law should be changed."
Ibid. In January 1984, Reagan quipped, "[I]f we could get God and discipline back in our
schools, maybe we could get drugs and violence out." Lou Cannon, "Reagan Renews
Appeal for Anti-abortion Action," *Washington Post*, Jan. 31, 1984, A1. Later that same
year, he contended, "The pendulum has swung too far toward intolerance against genuine religious freedom. . . . Sometimes I can't help but feel the First Amendment is being
turned on its head." "President Renews Call for Prayer Amendment," *New York Times*,
Feb. 26, 1984, A28. In a weekly radio address from 1985, Reagan proclaimed, "[T]he
good Lord who has given our country so much should never have been expelled from
our nation's classrooms." Bruce J. Dierenfield, *The Battle over School Prayer: How Engel v.
Vitale Changed America* 196 (2007). Finally, in 1987, Reagan declared in his State of the
Union address, "Why is it that we can build a nation with our prayers, but we can't use
a schoolroom for voluntary prayer? The 100th Congress of the United States should be
remembered as the one that ended the expulsion of God from America's classrooms."
"Transcript of President's Message to Nation on State of Union," *New York Times*,
Jan. 28, 1987, A16.

sions. These findings have prompted some scholars to depict the Supreme Court as an essentially ineffectual institution.[70]

Yet it would be myopic to view southern noncompliance as indicating that the Supreme Court did not make an enormous difference by prohibiting teacher-led prayer and Bible reading in public schools. Even the studies that noted widespread southern resistance to the Court's prayer decisions during the early 1960s do not deny that they succeeded in eliminating teacher-led religious observance in millions of classrooms around the nation. Across the entire country—including the recalcitrant South—religious observance in public schools declined almost immediately by more than half, as teacher-led prayer decreased from occurring in 60 percent of public school classrooms to 28 percent and Bible reading dropped from existing in 48 percent of public school classrooms to 22 percent. The Court's transformation of school prayer practices becomes even clearer when one concentrates on its impact in particular regions. In the Mid-Atlantic states, for example, 80 percent of public school teachers led their students in prayer pre-*Engel* in 1962. But that figure plunged to only 7 percent three years later. After *Schempp*, that region witnessed a similarly stark decrease in Bible reading. While religious observances in public schools were not common in the West and the Rocky Mountain regions in the early 1960s, the Court's interventions nevertheless reduced the practice by more than half. It is also far from obvious that the inquiry over the Court's effect in this area should cease beginning in the mid-1960s; as early as 1973, the national compliance level with *Engel* and *Schempp* had soared to 90 percent. Recall that public schools overwhelmingly adhered to the requirements articulated in *Engel* and *Schempp*, even though polling has consistently indicated that clear majorities supported a constitutional amendment undoing those decisions, even decades after they first appeared. Thus, rather than viewing the Court's entrance into this domain as demonstrating its fecklessness, it seems more accurate to construe it as revealing its formidability.[71]

In the communities that actively resisted these decisions, moreover, the Supreme Court's intervention nevertheless provided families with powerful ammunition to end school prayer and Bible reading by either bringing the matter to school authorities directly or identifying a legal organization that could help to vindicate their constitutional rights. The existence of *Engel* and *Schempp* certainly offered no guarantee of success, but the absence of those decisions virtually guaranteed failure. Thus, although legal scholars sometimes intimate that the Supreme Court can suffer no greater injury than issuing decisions that go unheeded, it seems helpful to understand that noncompliance is not an entirely foreign feature of our constitutional order. *Engel* and *Schempp* suggest that it may be worse for the Court to avoid issuing decisions honoring constitutional rights that may not immediately be heeded everywhere if the alternative is to decline recognizing those rights in the first instance.[72]

LEE V. WEISMAN:
WEIGHING PRAYERS AT GRADUATION CEREMONIES

In the spring of 1989, Daniel Weisman, a professor of social work, relished the prospect of watching his daughter Deborah receive the award for best school spirit at her upcoming graduation from Nathan Bishop Middle School in Providence, Rhode Island. But he also viewed the event with some apprehension because of the highly sectarian prayer that preceded the graduation of Deborah's older sister from the same school three years earlier. On that occasion, a Baptist minister named Virgil Wood instructed the students and their families to rise and "thank Jesus Christ" for making "these kids what they are today." Even several years later, Weisman could still recall the feeling of "absolute[ ] humiliat[ion]" that impinged upon what should have been a joyous occasion. Weisman and his wife, Vivian, who worked at the Jewish Community Center of Rhode Island, telephoned the school the following day to complain that such prayers should be eliminated from future graduation exercises because they violated the Constitution. Three years later, when Weisman reminded school officials that he believed prayer should be omitted at Deborah's approaching graduation ceremony, the principal replied, "You don't have anything to worry about; we've gotten a rabbi this year." The Weismans' worry, however, very much remained, for they sought not their faith's representation in the graduation prayer but the prayer's elimination. Vivian Weisman contended that, while soliciting leaders of various religions to deliver prayers on an annually rotating basis might have been well-intentioned, this method nevertheless presented an inadequate solution for addressing graduation audiences, particularly so at a religiously diverse school like Nathan Bishop, whose student body included many pupils of the Buddhist, Christian, Jewish, and Muslim faiths. "We see prayer in public schools . . . as being very divisive," she argued. "It really cuts out the minorities for whom the public school system has been a gateway for full inclusion in our society. . . . No one should feel like they are outside of things at their own graduation."[73]

With this view in mind, the Weismans sought injunctive relief in federal district court that would have blocked the planned prayer at Deborah's graduation from taking place. The district court judge, however, denied the Weismans' request. Despite this setback, the family opted to attend Deborah's graduation ceremony as their case worked its way through the appellate legal system. At the ceremony, the Weismans heard Rabbi Leslie Gutterman deliver an opening prayer that might most accurately be described as consisting of equal portions greeting card mawkishness, Boy Scout Oath outtakes, and generic appeals to a higher power. "God of the Free, Hope of the Brave," Gutterman began, shortly before he intoned in one maudlin but representative passage, "For the destiny of America we thank You. May the graduates of Nathan Bishop Middle School so live that they might help to share it."[74] In Gutterman's defense, the milquetoast content of his prayer may be partly attributed to a pamphlet titled "Guidelines for Civic Occasions."[75] In preparation for the event, Nathan Bishop's principal gave a copy of this document to Gutterman to help him identify themes for nonsectarian prayers that would avoid giving offense.

Poignantly, as the constitutional dispute made its way to the Supreme Court, many Americans registered considerable offense, not at the prayer, but that the Weismans would dare to challenge it. The Weismans received so much hate mail that they decided to form an odd sort of family scrapbook, assembling the letters that teemed with vulgarities, death threats, anti-Semitic epithets, and assertions that they lacked patriotism. As Vivian Weisman suggested, deep incongruity surrounds the fact that these events unfolded in Rhode Island, of all states, long known as a land of religious tolerance—stretching back even before the Constitution to the days of Roger Williams. "[T]he greatest irony is that our family has been accused of being un-American because here we are fighting for the Bill of Rights . . . in the one state that would not sign onto the Constitution unless the Bill of Rights was included," Weisman noted.[76]

In June 1992, Justice Anthony Kennedy in *Lee v. Weisman* wrote an opinion on behalf of a 5–4 majority holding that Rabbi Gutterman's prayer violated the Establishment Clause. Kennedy viewed this outcome as practically required by *Engel*'s insistence that government had no business composing official prayers. While it is certainly accurate that school officials did not write the remarks Gutterman delivered, Kennedy emphasized, the principal's determination that a religious figure ought to lead the assembled group in prayer in the first instance rendered "this . . . choice attributable to the State, and from a constitutional perspective it is as if a state statute decreed that the prayers must occur."[77] *Weisman* rejected the notion that a Supreme Court precedent from the 1980s, which authorized a brief prayer at the beginning of a state legislature session, somehow required affirming the legitimacy of opening prayers at graduation exercises. Citing the major contextual differences separating schoolhouses from statehouses—relating not only to the age of their respective populations but also to disparate norms regarding freedom of movement—Kennedy observed that the potential for coercion within the nation's public schools demanded vigilance in monitoring the Establishment Clause:

> [T]here are heightened concerns with protecting freedom of conscience from subtle coercive pressure in the elementary and secondary public schools. . . . Our decisions in *Engel* [and *Schempp*], recognize . . . prayer exercises in public schools carry a particular risk of indirect coercion. The concern may not be limited to the context of schools, but it is most pronounced there. . . . What to most believers may seem nothing more than a reasonable request that the nonbeliever respect their religious practices, in a school context may appear to the nonbeliever or dissenter to be an attempt to employ the machinery of the State to enforce a religious orthodoxy.[78]

In addition, *Weisman* rejected the contention—urged by both school officials and President George H. W. Bush's Department of Justice—that the prayer should be deemed constitutionally permissible because attendance at the graduation ceremony was not formally required. "Law reaches past formalism," Kennedy instructed. "And to say a teenage student has a real choice not to attend her . . . graduation is formalistic in the extreme. True, Deborah could elect not to attend commencement without renouncing her diploma; but [e]veryone knows that in our society . . . graduation is one of life's most significant occasions."[79] Finally, *Weisman* noted that graduates had no viable options to signal their nonparticipation in the prayer, and that the Constitution was particularly designed to protect the religious scruples of minorities. "While in some societies the wishes of the majority might prevail," Kennedy wrote, "the Establishment Clause . . . is addressed to this contingency and rejects the balance urged upon us. The Constitution forbids the State to exact religious conformity from a student as the price of attending her own . . . graduation. This is the calculus the Constitution commands."[80]*

Justice Antonin Scalia—joined by Chief Justice William Rehnquist, Justice Clarence Thomas, and Justice Byron White—issued one of his signature dissents in *Weisman* that alternated between scornful and comedic approaches. Deriding the majority's reasoning variously as "incoherent," "ludicrous," and "beyond the absurd," Justice Scalia contended that the Court's reliance on the coercive potential of graduation prayers amounted to nothing more than uninformed, indeterminate psychobabble.[81] "[I]nterior decorating is a rock-hard science compared to psychology practiced by amateurs," Scalia warned. "A few citations of '[r]esearch in psychology' . . . cannot disguise the fact that the Court has gone beyond the realm where judges know what they are doing."[82] For Scalia, *Weisman*'s prohibition of Rabbi Gutterman's prayer extended well beyond anything required by *Engel* or *Schempp*. Unlike in those cases, Scalia contended that the prayer at issue in *Weisman* could be distinguished on no fewer than three distinct bases: first, it involved a one-time event, rather than a daily practice, and therefore such modest exposure to religion should not be viewed as overpowering; second, it arose outside the state's compulsory schooling require-

* The outcome in *Lee v. Weisman* was perhaps closer than the 5–4 tally initially suggests—if such a thing is even possible. When the justices met privately to discuss *Weisman* during Conference, Justice Kennedy tentatively voted to uphold the graduation prayer, meaning that the Court as a whole would have—by a 5–4 margin—upheld the prayer. After attempting to draft the opinion with that conclusion, however, Justice Kennedy ultimately changed his mind about the correct disposition in the case and instead wrote the opinion to invalidate the prayer. See Edward Lazarus, *Closed Chambers: The First Eyewitness Account of the Epic Struggles Inside the Supreme Court* 471 (1998). Kennedy's eleventh-hour change of heart may play some modest role in explaining the tone of Justice Antonin Scalia's dissenting opinion in *Weisman*, which is caustic even by his own acidic standards.

ments, which should diminish concerns about religious appeals directed toward a captive audience; and, third, it did not occur within the instructional classroom—a setting that might reasonably be viewed as raising particularly acute concerns about religious coercion. All three factors, in Justice Scalia's view, strongly militated against concluding that the prayer violated the Establishment Clause.

Apart from such factual distinctions, Scalia insisted that the majority erred by permitting the Weismans' preference for nonreligion to override the preferences of many devout citizens who feel that the collective aspect of public prayers represents an essential dimension of religious observance. Scalia pressed this point with an irreverent analogy:

> The reader has been told much in this case about the personal interest of Mr. Weisman and his daughter, and very little about the personal interests on the other side. They are not inconsequential. Church and state would not be such a difficult subject if religion were, as the Court apparently thinks it to be, some purely personal avocation that can be indulged entirely in secret, like pornography, in the privacy of one's room. For most believers it is *not* that, and has never been.[83]

Scalia concluded by asserting that *Weisman*'s recognition of an Establishment Clause violation, given the innocuous content of Gutterman's prayer, unwisely permitted hypersensitivity to all things religious to carry the day. The decision, he observed, would squelch invaluable opportunities for people of various backgrounds to join together and unite during momentous occasions: "To deprive our society of that important unifying mechanism [of prayer], in order to spare the nonbeliever what seems to me the minimal inconvenience of standing or even sitting in respectful nonparticipation, is as senseless in policy as it is unsupported in law."[84]*

---

* *Weisman* marked Justice Clarence Thomas's first major opinion involving the Establishment Clause. In 1985, before he became a federal judge, Thomas stated, "My mother says that when they took God out of the schools, the schools went to hell. She may be right." Nancy Gibbs, "America's Holy War," *Time*, Dec. 9, 1991, 60. *The Wall Street Journal* has offered a similar assessment of the supposedly deleterious effects of the Court's Establishment Clause jurisprudence on public schools: "[W]e are . . . a nation that in the wake of [*Engel*] spent . . . three decades actively expunging every vestige of the religious impulse from public life and discourse. It is hardly a coincidence that this

Following *Weisman*, most newspaper editorial boards endorsed the decision. Not surprisingly, the opinion generated the most enthusiastic responses along the northeast corridor. *The New York Times* called *Weisman* "as welcome as its narrow 5-to-4 margin is distressing," and chided Justice Scalia's dissent for "unrealistically" construing graduation exercises as truly voluntary.[85] *The Washington Post*, following the Court's framing, portrayed *Weisman* as a straightforward application of *Engel* and *Schempp*: "A graduation prayer, no matter how carefully nondenominational, is as constitutionally invalid as the long-banned morning ritual in the classroom. In neither case may the government put schoolchildren in a position in which they have to choose between participation and protest."[86] In a sea change since the days of *Engel*, the editorial pages of many southern newspapers also approved *Weisman*, even if they withheld the ringing endorsements offered by their northern counterparts. Thus, *The Atlanta Journal-Constitution* depicted its support for *Weisman* as simply embracing the lesser of two evils: "We would hate to live in a nation without religion; but, looking around the world at the examples that exist, like Iran, we would hate to live under a government that had one."[87] For its part, *The Dallas Morning News* avowed, "As controversial as the court's decision may be, it was the right one to make."[88]

Conservative media outlets, however, accorded *Weisman* a considerably cooler reception. The syndicated columnist James J. Kilpatrick issued a sarcastic "[c]ongratulations" to "Little Debbie" and "her daddy" for "making a travesty of the First Amendment."[89] *National Review* seized upon *Weisman* as an opportunity to lament anew that Justice Kennedy—author of the offending opinion—occupied the seat that it believed should have been filled by the rejected nominee Judge Robert Bork. In an editorial titled "The Borked Court," the leading conservative publication complained, "[Kennedy's] opinion, while perhaps forming the foundation for some future multicultural and humanist Constitution, draws little upon the [original meaning] of . . . our present Constitution. . . . As with . . . school prayer [losses] over the past three decades, the impact of the latest loss . . . will be felt everywhere around us."[90] This disparaging assessment of *Weisman* within conservative media

---

same period saw the rise of many social pathologies." "Church and State," *Wall Street Journal*, April 4, 1994, A12.

circles echoed the assessment offered by many right-leaning politicians. To provide only the foremost example, President George
H. W. Bush—roughly reenacting his father's take on *Engel*—stated
that *Weisman* left him "very disappointed" because it "unnecessarily cast away the venerable and proper American tradition of nonsectarian prayer at public celebrations."[91]

In *Weisman*'s wake, with clergy members effectively forbidden to deliver prayers at public schools, proponents of religion
placed greater emphasis on students as potential vehicles to deliver
prayers. Focusing on students, rather than on clerics, as religious
speakers enabled religiously motivated advocates to portray their
cause as a modern analogue to the Tinkers' protest of the Vietnam
War. Whereas the schools in Des Moines, Iowa, sought to suppress
political speech, they argued, schools nowadays seek to suppress
religious speech. In 1993, one year after *Weisman*, Jay Sekulow of
the American Center for Law and Justice began laying the ground-
work for this revised approach, invoking the free speech rights of
students. "In 1969, when the Vietnam War controversy was raging, the Supreme Court ruled that students' expression against the
war could not be squashed in public schools," Sekulow explained.
"America survived those protests, some of which posed very real
threats to life and property. Should not student prayers, which pose
no threat to the Establishment Clause and which the people want,
also be permitted?"[92] The Supreme Court, in relatively short order,
issued its first—and to date only—high-profile opinion weighing
the permissibility of students delivering public prayers at official
school events.

SANTA FE INDEPENDENT SCHOOL DISTRICT V. DOE: WEIGHING PRAYERS AT FOOTBALL GAMES

In 2000, the Supreme Court yet again refused to retreat from
its Establishment Clause principles when it contemplated a high
school's prayer policy in Santa Fe, Texas. That policy permitted
students to elect one of their classmates to deliver a prayer over
the stadium loudspeaker prior to the kickoff at each home game
during the football season. The homogeneity of Santa Fe—a community located near Galveston, in eastern Texas—would be difficult to overstate: its nearly ten thousand residents included a grand

total of nine black people and one Jewish family. Protestant zeal ran so high among some Santa Fe residents that the two parents who filed the lawsuit—one Catholic and the other Mormon—sought (and obtained) anonymity because they feared retribution. That fear was well founded, as some ministers implored their congregants to uncover the identities of those who objected. The district court judge felt compelled to issue an unusual document, ordering the entire community—including school officials, teachers, and parents—to cease attempting to "ferret out" the plaintiffs' identities "by means of bogus petitions, questionnaires, individual interrogation, or downright 'snooping.'" Violators, the judge warned, would "face the harshest possible contempt sanctions from this court, and may additionally face criminal liability." Local residents suggested to reporters that religious dissidents would not be coddled in Santa Fe. "If somebody gets offended by somebody praying, they just shouldn't listen," one Santa Fe barber reasoned. "The government is trying to take the Lord out of our hearts and minds, and it's going to be the downfall of this country. . . . The devil is getting too much say here." Perhaps the only item that rivaled Christianity as a subject of worship in Santa Fe was the spectacle of high school football, a subject indelibly captured by H. G. Bissinger's *Friday Night Lights*. The presiding federal judge emphasized that the football field's lights shone plenty bright in Santa Fe: "[H]igh school football . . . is the apex of their social function. It is a very big deal to the community. The entire community turns out for these [games]. And it really is a big part of these kids' lives." Comparing football's significance to the rite of passage at the center of *Weisman*, the federal judge concluded, "I think . . . football is probably a heck of a lot more important [to locals] than graduation."⁹³*

The Supreme Court in *Santa Fe Independent School District v.*

---

* Shortly before the Supreme Court resolved the dispute in Santa Fe, *Texas Monthly* published an ode to high school football in the Lone Star State:

> [Football is] a game, an extracurricular activity, a community bond, the state religion, the biggest show in town every Friday night in the fall, a character builder, a revered symbol, an inspirational rallying point that offers a rare moment [to] put aside their differences to get behind the home team, a traffic generator for the local Dairy Queen, and topic A in coffee shops from Roscoe . . . to Itasca.

Joe Nick Patoski et al., "Three Cheers for High School Football," *Texas Monthly*, Oct. 1999, 111.

Doe rejected the high school's prayer policy. Justice Stevens's opinion for the Court reasoned that the high school's elaborate involvement with the prayer transformed the pregame message into the government's religious expression (which the Establishment Clause prohibits), rather than an individual student's religious expression (which the Free Speech and Free Exercise Clause protect). As Justice Stevens explained the Court's rationale, in a highly fact-sensitive opinion, "The delivery of such a message—over the school's public address system, by a speaker representing the student body, under the supervision of school faculty, and pursuant to a school policy that explicitly and implicitly encourages public prayer—is not properly characterized as 'private' speech."[94] For Stevens, these factors combined to render the pregame prayers constitutionally indistinguishable from the graduation prayer invalidated by *Weisman*; in both instances, observers would construe the school as having placed its imprimatur on the messages, and those statements would reasonably be construed as coercive in the unique environment of public schools. Not only were some students effectively required to attend football games—including the players, the band, and the cheerleaders—but Justice Stevens concluded that, even if attendance were actually voluntary, the pregame prayers would illegitimately induce attendees to join an act of religious worship.

In contrast to the responses to several prior decisions involving religion and public schools, the reaction to the Court's invalidation of Santa Fe's prayer policy was surprisingly subdued in general—even among right-leaning audiences. Among conservatives, the relatively mild response began at the very top, as Chief Justice William Rehnquist's dissenting opinion registered misgivings more about the majority's tone (which he contended "bristle[d] with hostility" toward public religious expressions) than its outcome.[95] Indeed, Rehnquist's dissent did not even insist that Santa Fe's policy necessarily passed constitutional muster; instead, he advanced the far more modest claim that the policy *might* be implemented in such a way as to avoid offending the Establishment Clause. Similarly, Professor Douglas Kmiec—who served in President Reagan's Justice Department—found Stevens's rationale excessively sweeping, but he seemed to accept the Court's invalidation of the policy under review. "Given the peculiar facts of the case," Kmiec allowed, "the Supreme Court may have been right . . . to strike down a Texas school district's policy of allowing students to pray before football games."[96] Similarly, *The Wall Street Journal*'s editorial page conceded, "[T]he Santa Fe school district probably did smudge the line between a constitutionally appropriate prayer and the official encouragement not only of Christianity but of a particular brand of Christianity."[97]

In Santa Fe, Texas, not surprisingly, the Supreme Court's decision invalidating the local policy found few admirers—at least who were willing to praise the outcome publicly. Immediately after the decision, the *Los Angeles Times* reported that "a sampling of local opinion revealed little sympathy for the ruling," and quoted one local school board official as complaining, "Is the Supreme Court telling us if you're on public property you're not allowed to express religious speech? If so, I think our First Amendment rights are being trampled on."[98]

The most eagerly anticipated reaction in Santa Fe, however, would not occur until more than two months later, when the high school would host its first football game following the decision. Television cameras and newspaper reporters from all over the country descended on Santa Fe's football stadium on the first Friday in September 2000, hoping to capture a spectacle. By some measures, the town lived up to expectations. A local barbecue restaurant, the Cowboy, created a sign encouraging the football players that read, "Our Prayers Are with You," and another sign appeared alongside Farm Road 646, near the entrance to town, that rhymed, "We Still Pray in Santa Fe."[99] Even more notably, a few of the scenes that appeared at the stadium would not have been out of place had they occurred at an old-time religious revival. As one journalist recounted, "Two men bearing large pine crosses across their backs stood in silent protest at the stadium gates, while a dark-eyed teenager walked among the crowd singing hymns and weeping, his Bible held aloft, as if he were seeking divine intercession."[100]

By other measures, however, Santa Fe did not put on much of a show. The stands were much emptier than anticipated, as less than half of the predicted crowd of ten thousand spectators ultimately materialized. No one, moreover, defied the Supreme Court by delivering a prayer over the public-address system. While some fans sought to fill this perceived gap by quietly praying aloud prior to kickoff, estimates placed the number of participants at two hundred, or less than 5 percent of the total crowd. No serious legal scholar would contend that this display, which occurred utterly without the involvement of school officials, violated the Establishment Clause. Praying in the stands does not, in all events, appear to have become a new tradition in Santa Fe. Instead, as one law professor who attended a Santa Fe football game a few years after the decision noted, the public-address announcer instructed the crowd to pause for a moment of silence prior to kickoff. For some in attendance, though, that moment proved all too fleeting. "More like a second of silence," a fan grumbled.[101]

The most recent, and still unresolved, prominent controversy over the Establishment Clause's meaning in the public school context can be viewed as flowing from the Supreme Court's decision reining in Santa Fe. In September 2012, cheerleaders on the sidelines at a high school football game in Kountze, Texas—located roughly one hundred miles northeast of Santa Fe—began displaying banners featuring various biblical passages. The cheerleaders conceived of the idea themselves, with no guidance from their faculty adviser, and paid for the materials to make the religious banners out of their own funds. Should these messages be construed as student-initiated prayers that rest beyond the reach of the Establishment Clause, or should the speech be attributed to the school and therefore violative of the Establishment Clause? Although the Texas courts have yet to definitively resolve this question, many observers—including the Kountze Independent School District—have concluded that displaying the signs violates the Establishment Clause. As one wag contended, Kountze's cheerleaders "are supposed to represent school spirit [not] the spirit of Jesus."[102] In expounding upon this intuition, several commentators have suggested that Kountze's banners violate the Establishment Clause because cheerleading is a school activity, the cheerleaders wear school uniforms while displaying the religious messages, and the football game is a school event.

While I agree with the conclusion that the banners are unconstitutional, the conventional explanation leaves much to be desired. As the objection is articulated above, one might believe that the Establishment Clause also prohibits a star high school football player from saying during a halftime television interview, "The glory goes to my Lord and Savior, Jesus Christ." After all, the interviewed player—like the Kountze cheerleader—is participating in a school activity, makes a religious statement while in uniform, and does so at a school event. Yet the football player's hypothetical statement cannot reasonably be viewed as violating the Establishment Clause. Accordingly, efforts to explain why Kountze's banners are constitutionally impermissible should also highlight the expressive function of the cheerleading activity itself—something that does not apply to a football player's off-the-cuff comments. Spectators would be far more likely to attribute school approval to a statement that appears on a cheerleader's banner—or even a statement that the cheerleaders utter in unison—than to a football player's interview. And it is this central issue of government endorsement of religious speech that distinguishes the two situations for purposes of the Establishment Clause.[103]

In recent years, have public school officials typically refrained from promoting prayers at graduation ceremonies and sporting events? The honest answer is that the extent of compliance with the Supreme Court's two leading Establishment Clause cases during the modern era is unknown, as no study has examined these issues in a comprehensive fashion. Today, these compliance questions demand detailed exploration, and statistically inclined scholars should undertake those efforts. Yet even presuming *Weisman* and *Santa Fe Independent School District v. Doe* are sometimes—or even often—honored in the breach, their existence nevertheless matters greatly because they shape behavior of the many, many school officials who wish to avoid violating the Constitution. Simply tracing the trajectory of these cases in this area since 1990 reveals this statement's veracity. Few stronger signals of *Weisman*'s real-world influence can be glimpsed than the fact that the high school in homogeneous Santa Fe, Texas, did not select a religious figure in the 1990s to offer public prayer before football games, but instead sought to tap a student for the position. Similarly, few stronger signals of *Santa Fe Independent School District v. Doe*'s real-world influence can be witnessed than realizing that the school board in Kountze—another small town in eastern Texas—prohibited its cheerleaders from waving their banners with religious quotations. Each of these successive constitutional disputes reveals effort to find outlets for religious expression that, depending on one's perspective, either circumnavigate or circumvent extant Supreme Court precedent. Even if these episodes are most accurately understood as crossing the constitutional lines that judicial precedent has sketched, it should not escape notice that school officials seem to be aware of those lines and seek to avoid directly flouting them.[104]

THE UNDERAPPRECIATED TRANSFORMATION AT THE
INTERSECTION OF RELIGION AND EDUCATION

Although legal controversies regarding the appropriate place of prayers in various public school settings have occupied a tremendous amount of energy among law professors, it is important to understand that the last three decades have witnessed a trio of major legal developments involving religion and education that have combined to decrease the temperature dramatically at this long incendiary crossroads. First, the Supreme Court has clarified that students need not shed their religious identities at the schoolhouse gate—by both clearing the way for public schools to observe a moment of silence at the beginning of classes and affirming the legitimacy of extracurricular clubs with a religious focus. These decisions have helped assuage the anxiety of at least some parents who might have harbored doubt that their children could simultaneously retain their religious identities and attend public schools. Second, the meteoric rise of homeschooling—an option exercised largely by families for religious purposes—has siphoned off a significant source of legal disputes. Many devout families who in prior generations would have sent their children to public schools now select homeschooling, and that transformation has thus eliminated a host of potential constitutional claims contesting public schools' curricula under the Free Exercise Clause. Third, the Supreme Court validated the constitutionality of tuition vouchers for use at private schools, regardless of whether they are affiliated with a religious tradition. That opinion eliminated a primary source of frustration for a subset of conservative intellectuals who demonstrated a fierce commitment to introducing free-market principles into the educational domain.

It will not escape the notice of various readers that these three developments can readily be construed as victories for religiously minded citizens. While some readers will welcome these developments as overdue recognitions of religion's significance in society, others will bemoan them as evincing—or perhaps presaging—an inappropriate intermingling of the religious and the secular spheres. Before readers of the first variety get too high and readers of the second variety get too low, however, it merits noticing the basic constitutional backdrop against which these developments emerged: the Supreme Court's opinions have consistently protected public school students from involuntarily participating in religious observance. These developments do nothing to alter that basic reality. The trends have, however, had the salutary consequence of diminishing the erroneous notion that religion and education must remain wholly separate—unless families have sufficient funds to afford sectarian education at a private school. Quite apart from their practical benefit to the underappreciated détente over religion and education, moreover, these developments pass constitutional muster as each satisfies the overarching constitutional principle of religious neutrality.

PUBLIC SCHOOLS NEED NOT BE RELIGION-FREE ZONES

The first reason that public education has witnessed reduced legal hostility over religious matters is that it has become increasingly clear in recent years that the Supreme Court's doctrine does not seek to transform public schools into religion-free zones—places where praying, mentioning the Almighty, or acknowledging the role of faith in society is invariably prohibited. Although such concerns may sound either fanciful or paranoid, some actual educators have in fact mistakenly suggested the word "God" cannot appear in public schools.* In actuality, of course, the Court's decisions in this arena have involved the far narrower issues of teacher-led worship and prayers holding meaningful potential to coerce impressionable students. The growing appreciation that religion and public schools can, at least sometimes, mix without violating the Establishment Clause stems from developments in two main areas: observing "moments of silence" in many public schools; and permitting religious groups to enjoy the same terms of entry to public schools that nonreligious groups enjoy outside instructional time, due to a federal measure called the Equal Access Act. These twin developments have pleased religious students and their families who have sometimes feared that attending public schools requires abandoning their religious identities when within those corridors.

Discussions of formally introducing moments of silence into public schools began almost immediately after the Supreme Court's

* As *Time* magazine reported in 1991, "In Decatur, Ill., a primary-school teacher discovered the word God in a phonics textbook and ordered her class of seven-year-olds to strike it out, saying that it is against the law to mention God in a public school." Nancy Gibbs, "America's Holy War," *Time*, Dec. 9, 1991, 60.

decision in *Engel* invalidated teacher-led prayer in 1962.* Educators, parents, and the public generally seized upon moments of silence as a sensible alternative—one that might bring consolation to many religious citizens and irritation to virtually no one. The Supreme Court, however, did not weigh in on the practice for more than two decades, until 1985, when it addressed Alabama's moment-of-silence measure in *Wallace v. Jaffree*.

Significantly, the background of the Alabama statute at issue in *Jaffree* stood out as highly idiosyncratic. Whereas advocates of such statutes generally identified at least one secular purpose for initiating a moment of silence, the primary sponsor of Alabama's measure conceded that he had "no other purpose in mind" apart from returning prayer to schools.[105] In addition, the text of Alabama's statute expressly identified "prayer" as an animating purpose, whereas statutes in other states typically remained silent on that particular score—with the tacit understanding that many individuals would use the time for that purpose, and required no prompting.† Additionally, during the lower court proceedings in *Jaffree*,

---

* I use the term "formal[ ] . . . moments of silence" here because there can be no doubt that informal moments of silence have been a regular occurrence in schools since time immemorial. As Justice Thurgood Marshall humorously pressed this point during oral argument in *Wallace v. Jaffree*, "[D]oes the teacher have a right in the public schools . . . to tell the children to [']shut up for the next five minutes, and I don't want to hear a sound out of you,['] without a statute?" Oral Argument Transcript, *Wallace v. Jaffree*, 1984 U.S. Trans. LEXIS 60, at *17. See also Linda Greenhouse, "High Court Weighs Silence in School for Prayer or Meditation," *New York Times*, Dec. 5, 1984, A18.

† In 1981, Alabama revised its moment-of-silence measure so that it no longer explicitly provided time only "for meditation" but instead now provided time "for meditation *or voluntary prayer*." Ala. Code § 16-1-20.1 (emphasis added). While the addition of those last three words may initially seem innocuous, Professor Walter Dellinger has advanced an ingenious argument designed to demonstrate that they in fact pose Establishment Clause concerns. As Dellinger explained,

> Imagine a statute providing that a moment of silence be conducted at the beginning of each school day for "meditation or erotic fantasy." Could one plausibly say in that case that the statute is being wholly "neutral" with regard to "erotic fantasy," that the statute merely reflects the fact that students can (and some no doubt will) use any period of silence for that purpose? In my view, the seemingly trivial fact of the addition of the word "prayer" crosses the line of constitutionality precisely because it is utterly unnecessary to the goal of creating a formal opportunity for reflection in which students can, if they wish, choose to pray.

Walter Dellinger, "The Sound of Silence: An Epistle on Prayer and the Constitution," 95 *Yale Law Journal* 1631, 1636 (1986).

a district court judge in Mobile, Alabama—Brevard Hand—wrote an opinion flouting the Supreme Court's Establishment Clause jurisprudence in the course of upholding the questionable statute. This unusual confluence of circumstances prompted the Supreme Court—in a 6–3 opinion, written by Justice Stevens—to invalidate that particular version of Alabama's moment-of-silence measure. Justice Stevens wrote the opinion for the Court in a narrow fashion, avoiding any suggestion that moment-of-silence statutes must generally fall in light of *Jaffree*. Thus, while the Reverend Jerry Falwell of the Moral Majority apocalyptically asserted that *Jaffree* indicated that the Court did not "understand what freedom's all about," more knowledgeable Court watchers understood *Jaffree*'s tightly limited scope.[106] For example, the former solicitor general Rex Lee of the Reagan administration received *Jaffree* as a "victory in that moment-of-silence statutes in general will survive," and Linda Greenhouse's article distilling the opinion in *The New York Times* reached this same conclusion regarding the continued viability of such statutes.[107]

Despite the isolated setback suffered in *Jaffree*, moment-of-silence measures have flourished during the last three decades, as Lee and Greenhouse anticipated. Today, thirty-four states have statutes either permitting or requiring public schools to hold a moment of silence during each school day. (In the remaining sixteen states, moreover, public schools may independently opt to introduce a moment of silence, as no state currently prohibits the practice.) While the state measures have on a very few occasions been challenged under the Establishment Clause following *Jaffree*, lower courts have thus far appeared wholly uninterested in vindicating these challenges. Nor has the Supreme Court post-*Jaffree* demonstrated any appetite for policing moments of silence. That choice is completely defensible from a constitutional perspective, as moments of silence provide students who wish to pray with an opportunity to do so, but they cannot reasonably be viewed as coercing uninterested students into prayer. Non-praying students can instead meditate, review their schoolwork, or—perhaps most plausibly—allow their minds simply to wander. Provided that a state drafts its moment-of-silence statute in a manner that evinces neutrality toward religion, no real dangers threaten its validity. And that is exactly as it should be.[108]

WESTSIDE SCHOOL DISTRICT V. MERGENS:
UPHOLDING THE EQUAL ACCESS ACT

Perhaps of even greater significance, the Supreme Court power-fully communicated the message that religion could constitution-ally exist within public schools in 1990, when it upheld the Equal Access Act in *Westside School District v. Mergens*. Congress enacted the Equal Access Act principally to ensure that, when public schools permit extracurricular activities to occur on campus during nonin-structional time (for example, after school), they do not prohibit religiously themed clubs from organizing and meeting. The ani-mating idea behind the federal law held that schools should nei-ther advantage nor disadvantage "religious . . . content" and should instead treat those ideas with neutrality.[109] While the Equal Access Act conceded that teachers and other governmental employees could not, consistent with *Engel* and *Schempp*, lead students in religion-oriented extracurricular clubs, it provided that students themselves may initiate such groups—provided that student atten-dance is voluntary and the group does not disrupt the school envi-ronment. Despite this federal law, Westside High School, in Omaha, Nebraska, rejected the twelfth grader Bridget Mergens's petition to form a Christian Bible Study Club for interested students. Westside rejected Mergens's request because official recognition of extracur-ricular clubs formed an essential part of the high school's mission, and therefore complying with the act's dictates would force the high school to violate the Establishment Clause.

The Supreme Court, in an 8–1 decision, held that Westside's rejection of the proposed Bible Study Club contravened the Equal Access Act, and determined further that adhering to the act did not require infringing upon the Establishment Clause. Given the wide variety of extracurricular activities at high schools, Justice O'Connor's opinion for the Court reasoned that students would not reasonably confuse Westside's allowing a student-led religious club to form with its officially endorsing that club's religious mis-sion—or that of any other clubs' religious mission for that matter. In addition, Justice O'Connor suggested that honoring the Equal Access Act posed little risk of religious coercion because the act itself prohibited educator involvement; the activities would take place outside formal classroom activities; and no students were required to attend. In the most notable passage of *Mergens*, Justice O'Connor observed that public school students retain free exercise rights within schools and that implementing those rights should not be misconstrued as automatically raising Establishment Clause concerns: "[T]here is a crucial difference between government speech endorsing religion, which the Establishment Clause forbids, and private speech endorsing religion, which the Free Speech and Free Exercise Clauses protect."[110]* While Westside could have opted to end its extracurricular programs altogether without violating the Equal Access Act, it could not in effect single out religion as the only form of student-initiated extracurricular club that would go unrecognized.

Permitting such student-led, voluntary religious activity to occur on school grounds has no doubt assuaged the concerns of many students who wish both to attend public schools and to maintain their religious identities during the school week. Even if *Engel* in no way can be viewed as requiring the Equal Access Act, and its enactment infringes upon local authority by requiring a uniform rule, the lopsided margin at the Supreme Court suggests that the act's principles fall firmly within the constitutional mainstream.†

---

* This sentence drew only four votes in *Mergens*, technically making it on behalf of a plurality rather than on behalf of the Court. But in subsequent decisions, a majority of justices have embraced that critical sentence. See, for example, *Santa Fe Independent School District v. Doe*, 530 U.S. 290, 302 (2000).

† In addition to religious groups, the major extracurricular groups that have benefited from the Equal Access Act are those based on sexual orientation. Although school boards have routinely protested the creation of student groups dedicated to gay equality, the Equal Access Act has consistently protected them. See Regina M. Grattan, "It's Not Just for Religion Anymore: Expanding the Protections of the Equal Access Act to Gay, Lesbian, and Bisexual High School Students," 67 *George Washington Law Review* 577 (1999).

Justice Kennedy wrote a concurring opinion in *Mergens* that emphasized the Establishment Clause's anti-coercion principle more so than Justice O'Connor's majority opinion, which—inspired by *Lemon v. Kurtzman*, 403 U.S. 602 (1971)—relied more heavily on the anti-endorsement principle. See *Westside School District v. Mergens*, 496 U.S. 226, 258 (1990) (Kennedy, J., concurring in part and concurring in the judgment). As indicated by Justice Kennedy's opinion for the Court in *Lee v. Weisman*, 505 U.S. 577 (1992), the anti-coercion idea has ascended in significance since *Mergens* and the notorious three-part *Lemon* test has correspondingly descended. In *Mergens*, Justice Marshall also wrote a concurring opinion. See *Mergens*, 496 U.S. at 262 (Marshall, J., concurring in the judgment). Justice John Paul Stevens cast the lone dissenting vote in *Mergens*. See ibid., 270 (Stevens, J., dissenting).

THE ASCENT OF HOMESCHOOLING AND
ITS MISUNDERSTOOD RELATION TO *WISCONSIN V. YODER*

The second reason that public schools have seen diminished legal hostility over religion derives from a transformational development in American education: the explosion of homeschooling during the last twenty-five years. This ascent of homeschools has served as a sort of release valve for students and their families who may well otherwise file litigation asserting that public schools were excessively secular. With homeschooling, of course, parents elect to enroll their children in neither public nor private schools but instead decide to educate their children without the assistance of professional teachers. Homeschooling in the post–World War II era can be traced back to the theories of John Holt, a progressive educator who in the 1950s argued that children learn best outside the rigid strictures of formalized schooling—with their prefabricated programs of study and debilitating obsession with order. Rather than kindling students' capacity for learning, Holt maintained, formalized schooling too often extinguished it. Holt's theories existed for decades before they gained any appreciable traction within the United States. As recently as 1987, a major education scholar noted that the state courts that had addressed homeschooling at that time concluded "with virtual uniformity . . . that home instruction may be prohibited."[111] The judicial reasoning upholding such bans was simple; as a New Mexico court concluded in 1983, requiring minors to attend school outside the home guaranteed that—apart from their parents—students would encounter "at least one [additional] set of attitudes, values, morals, lifestyles, and intellectual abilities."[112] In the 1990s, many states continued to outlaw homeschooling, and even prosecuted parents who engaged in the practice.

Today, matters have changed dramatically, as homeschooling, by either law or custom, is permissible in all fifty states, and the practice has grown exponentially. Although only about 15,000 students were homeschooled in the early 1970s, that figure skyrocketed to 1.8 million children in 2012, according to data from the Department of Education. That figure means that 3.4 percent of all students in the nation are homeschooled. In order to appreciate the magnitude of the phenomenon, consider that the number of homeschooled students exceeds the number of students who attend all the public schools of Alaska, Delaware, Hawaii, Montana, New

Hampshire, North Dakota, Rhode Island, South Dakota, Vermont, and Wyoming combined. Although Holt's theories of homeschooling might have initially appealed to liberals disaffected with what they regarded as an excessively conservative educational establishment, moreover, that demographic now accounts for a modest slice of the homeschooling phenomenon.[113]

The rise of homeschooling in recent decades has been attributable overwhelmingly to its growth among conservative Christians, who have departed public schools en masse, disenchanted with what they regard as rigid secularity and even an anti-Christian ethos that pervades those institutions. Educating their children at home, these families conclude, offers the best way to shield them from the dangerous cultural influences that they will encounter from their peers, and even their teachers. While some families undoubtedly select homeschooling for nonreligious reasons, the best estimates suggest that roughly nine out of ten families who homeschool their children do so for reasons stemming from their religious scruples. These religion-oriented families typically comprise two parents, only one of whom generally works outside the home. The most influential organization within the homeschooling movement—the Home School Legal Defense Association (HSLDA)—reflects its roots in evangelical Christianity. Michael Farris, co-founder and guiding force of HSLDA, before he started Patrick Henry College, has proclaimed, "[P]arents have the constitutional right to obey the dictates of God concerning the education of their children."[114] HSLDA has played an indispensable role in organizing families who homeschool their children into a highly effective coalition of advocates; its organizational potency has been felt in activities ranging from successful efforts to demand that JCPenney cease selling an insulting T-shirt that read, "Home Skooled," to staving off immensely popular legislative efforts that would require homeschoolers to take the same standardized tests that public school students are required to take.[115]

Families who attempt to challenge public schools' curricula on the basis that assigned materials impede their rights under the Free Exercise Clause have consistently had those claims denied—a development that has surely accelerated the trend toward homeschooling in recent years. One of the earliest and most notorious religious-based lawsuits that sought exemption from assigned materials occurred in the mid-1980s in Hawkins County, Tennessee, where Robert Mozert objected to the Holt Basic textbook series that students used in the local schools. In particular, Mozert deemed objectionable a story for beginning readers—where Pat, a girl, and Jim, a boy, prepared a meal—that read in relevant part as follows: "Pat has a big book. Pat reads the big book. Jim reads the big book. Pat reads to Jim. Jim cooks." In Mozert's view, this seemingly innocuous tale unconstitutionally impeded his ability to guide his child's religious development because it communicated the idea "that there are no God-given roles for the different sexes."[116] Mozert encountered additional material he found abhorrent in the Holt series—including passages that addressed magic, a planetary society, and women who earned renown for nondomestic work. Other parents of schoolchildren in Hawkins County voiced similar religion-based complaints, as one mother found the Holt series suffused with anti-Christian references to the occult. Exercises that instructed students to use their imaginations—including a story titled "A Visit to Mars" and a passage titled "Seeing Beneath the Surface"—served as particular sources of anxiety because she felt they transgressed scriptural authority.[117]

In 1987, the U.S. Court of Appeals for the Sixth Circuit rejected these Free Exercise Clause claims, concluding that mere exposure to the Holt materials did not unconstitutionally burden the students' and parents' religious beliefs. If Mozert and like-minded parents found the Holt series truly intolerable, the Sixth Circuit reasoned, they should remove their children from Hawkins County's public schools and find a curriculum more to their liking. When the Supreme Court declined to review Mozert's case, HSLDA's co-founder Michael Farris responded, "It's time for every born-again Christian in America to take their children out of public schools."[118] Several of the plaintiffs in Hawkins County heeded Farris's call, with some turning to private religious schooling and others to homeschooling.

The Sixth Circuit's denial of the Mozert-led plaintiffs' claims accurately foretold how the federal courts would generally receive religion-based objections to various aspects of public school curricula. In subsequent years, federal courts have reliably turned back such lawsuits attempting to wield the Free Exercise Clause against, for example, an AIDS awareness program that emphasized safe sex rather than abstinence, and books geared toward elementary school students that portrayed same-sex couples. Permitting parents and students to opt out of assignments and materials, courts typically conclude, could threaten the ability of public schools to function. As one federal appellate court expressed this sentiment in 1995, "If all parents had a fundamental constitutional right to dictate individually what the schools teach their children, the schools would be forced to create a curriculum for each student whose parents had genuine moral disagreements with the school's choice of subject matter."[119] On one telling, such judicial thinking has become sufficiently familiar that religious families with children attending public schools have, over time, grasped that legally contesting school assignments under the Free Exercise Clause is futile. On another, perhaps more persuasive telling, the paucity of such lawsuits is more directly attributable to the rise of homeschooling, as families who thirty years ago would have contested an assignment in public schools on religious grounds now preemptively educate their children at home. Although compelling reasons may well exist for lamenting this widespread exodus from the public schools, it is important to understand that homeschooling's prevalence has doubtless served to diminish religion-based constitutional conflict occurring within the nation's public schools.*

Admittedly, some portion of the legal disputes that in prior decades might have been aimed toward public schools has simply relocated, as homeschooling families have sought to impose legal limitations on the state's authority to regulate and monitor their educational practices. HSLDA's Farris adopted a hard-line approach on these questions, vehemently opposing virtually any state effort to ensure that homeschooled students receive appropriate educations.

---

* Circuit courts have also consistently rejected students' efforts to challenge school assignments as placing unconstitutional constraints on their religious freedom. See *Settle v. Dickson County School Board*, 53 F.3d 152 (6th Cir. 1995); and *C.H. v. Oliva*, 226 F.3d 198 (3d Cir. 2000). Telling students that they may not, for example, prepare a book report in history class on Jesus Christ does not represent a form of unconstitutional viewpoint discrimination. If such claims were legally cognizable, federal courts would find themselves in the business of routinely invalidating assignments on that basis. Standard assignments that instruct a class to prepare a paper examining a hero of the civil rights movement or examining the temporal motif in Richard Wright's *Native Son* doubtless limit the viewpoints that may be expressed, but such assignments cannot plausibly be construed as violating students' freedom of expression. For a persuasive analysis of this issue, see Kent Greenawalt, *Does God Belong in Public Schools?* 164–66 (2005).

Relatedly, the rise of homeschooling may also help to explain why the Supreme Court has not needed to invalidate a state law in more than thirty years that seeks to promote creationism as a scientific theory. For earlier iterations of related issues, see *Epperson v. Arkansas*, 393 U.S. 97 (1968); and *Edwards v. Aguillard*, 482 U.S. 578 (1987).

"The right of parents to control the education of their children is so fundamental that it deserves the extraordinary level of protection as an absolute right," Farris declared.[120] States have imposed widely varying requirements for homeschoolers; whereas some states conduct on-site visits to observe the educational environment, others do not even require guardians to inform anyone that minors are being homeschooled. Families who challenge state homeschooling regulations frequently do so by asserting that ordinances that seem to exert even modest oversight are dangerous because they intrude into a private, even a sacred place—the familial home—and distort it into an outpost in a vast governmental bureaucracy. Presumably, in an effort to clear the necessary constitutional hurdles, some families have contended that the education of their children itself constitutes a form of religious practice, and that homeschooling regulations therefore interfere with rights protected by the Free Exercise Clause. Confronted with such complaints, lower courts have typically affirmed the legitimacy of homeschooling measures as valid exercises of state authority. Those courts have been correct to do so. When the Supreme Court in 1925 invalidated Oregon's referendum that sought to abolish private schooling, *Pierce v. Society of Sisters* explicitly recognized "the power of the state reasonably to regulate all schools, to inspect, supervise and examine them, their teachers and pupils."[121] While homeschooling had not yet become a phenomenon in 1925, the larger legal principle should nevertheless apply to this novel context; indeed, it stands to reason that the affirmative decision to turn one's home into a schooling environment subjects that environment, and its educational processes, to state oversight that homes not containing schools may avoid.

States should, as a general proposition, dedicate considerably greater resources than they currently do to ensuring that homeschooled children are actually being exposed to stimulating academic environments. Even assuming that the bulk of homeschooled students enjoy such exposure, it is difficult to exaggerate the negative consequences for even a relatively small percentage of students who are educationally neglected by their guardians—their sole scholastic instructors. Given that nearly two million students are homeschooled, it would be astounding if at least some fraction of those students were not in fact immersed in environments unsuitable for genuine learning. Consider, for example, the account of one fifteen-year-old homeschooled student in Naperville, Illinois, who left public school following the third grade and told *Time* magazine that she "make[s] pretty much all the decisions about what to study. . . . I wasn't interested in math or composition, so I didn't really do it. I liked to dance."[122] This homeschooler held out hope that if she and her mother concentrated on mathematics and learning to write for one year of intense study, she could remedy her academic deficits. But this aspiration—with its naive timeline—unwittingly served only to confirm the magnitude of those deficits.

Although some homeschooled students suffer from an absence of curricular focus, other homeschooled students suffer from curricular content itself that communicates highly retrograde concepts. A distressingly common strain of materials geared toward Christian homeschooling families asserts that females must subordinate themselves to males and contends further that women should occupy only the domestic sphere. It hardly seems extravagant to maintain that parents who explicitly communicate these noxious ideas to their daughters in the twenty-first century may well afford them lesser educations than they offer to their sons. Even if the state does not seek to counteract or even supplement this misogyny with other attitudes, it ought at a minimum to obtain at least a general sense of its prevalence. But unduly lax homeschooling regulations shed insufficient light on this matter. While the laissez-faire approach to monitoring homeschooled students that has prevailed in many states has long been a problem, the increased prevalence of homeschooling in recent years renders the need for meaningful oversight all the more apparent—and urgent.[123]

Many legal scholars have suggested that the Supreme Court's decision in *Wisconsin v. Yoder* in 1972 anticipated the dramatic expansion in homeschooling that subsequently transpired. In *Yoder,* the Court granted the Old Order Amish an exemption from Wisconsin's compulsory education law that required minors generally to attend school through age sixteen. Interpreting the Free Exercise Clause, the Court accepted the claim that ending the formal education of Amish children following the eighth grade was essential because otherwise the worldly influences they would encounter in high school would pose an existential threat to their faith. While linking *Yoder* to the surge in homeschooling may initially seem intuitive, the relationship between those two developments is in fact far more attenuated than is commonly supposed. If the dispute were to arise today, the generally accepted legality of homeschooling does not, as is sometimes asserted, necessarily render the Court's outcome in *Yoder* a foregone conclusion. To the contrary, *Yoder*— a constitutionally questionable decision, even at the time—seems more dubious today as a result of a transformation in the prototypical Amish workplace, a major shift in constitutional doctrine, and the emergence of an avowedly skeptical approach toward home-schooling within the Amish community. In order to appreciate how severely destabilized *Yoder* appears against the modern landscape, however, it is necessary first to appreciate more fully the opinion's logic, assumptions, and commitments.[124]

Chief Justice Warren Burger's opinion for the Court in *Yoder* justified granting the requested exemption from Wisconsin's compulsory schooling measure by, above all, invoking the lengthy and successful track record of the Old Order Amish as a stand-alone society. As if seeking to avoid elevating the hopes of hippies everywhere, Burger emphasized *Yoder* had in no sense granted an exemption to a newfangled "group claiming to have recently discovered some 'progressive' or more enlightened process for rearing children for modern life."[125] The Amish community, Burger seemed to contend, was the very antithesis of all things groovy. "The [Amish litigants] assert as an article of faith . . . that their [community's] religious beliefs and what we would today call 'life style' have not altered in fundamentals for centuries," Burger explained. "Their way of life in a church-oriented community, separated from the outside world and 'worldly' influences, their attachment to nature and the soil, is a way inherently simple and uncomplicated, albeit difficult to preserve against the pressure to conform."[126]

Requiring Amish minors to attend high school, Burger maintained, would impermissibly burden their faith by bringing them into contact with mindsets and attitudes that contradict central Amish values. "The high school tends to emphasize intellectual and scientific accomplishments, self-distinction, competitiveness, worldly success, and social life with other students," Burger noted. "Amish society emphasizes informal learning-through-doing; a life of 'goodness,' rather than a life of intellect; wisdom, rather than technical knowledge; community welfare, rather than competition; and separation from, rather than integration with, contemporary worldly society."[127] The Amish way of life, moreover, imposed no significant harms on the larger society, as the group committed virtually no crimes and rejected all forms of government welfare (including Social Security and Medicaid). With its focus on family-run farms, *Yoder* insisted that the Amish embodied "Jefferson's ideal of the 'sturdy yeoman'"—a group thought to form the backbone of a democratic society—and presented no cause for alarm. "There is no intimation that the Amish employment of their children on family farms is in any way deleterious to their health or that Amish parents exploit children at tender years," Burger explained. "Moreover, employment of Amish children on the family farm does not present the undesirable economic aspects of eliminating jobs that might otherwise be held by adults."[128]

Even during the early 1970s, *Yoder* struck many observers as troubling because it did not seriously entertain the possibility that the interests of parents and their children may well meaningfully diverge. Justice William O. Douglas dissented in part from the majority in *Yoder* because he insisted that the views of Amish children ought to be considered, rather than simply assuming that they perfectly aligned with those of their parents. "While the parents . . . normally speak for the entire family, the education of the child is a matter on which the child will often have decided views," Douglas wrote. "He may want to be a pianist or an astronaut or an oceanographer. To do so he will have to break from the Amish tradition. . . . If he is harnessed to the Amish way of life by those in authority over him . . . , his entire life may be stunted and deformed."[129] Douglas portrayed the consequences of granting these educational exemptions as irreparable, and he therefore insisted that Amish minors themselves should be consulted before their school days ended prematurely. One year before the Court decided *Yoder, The Washington Post*'s editorial page prefigured Douglas's position when it weighed in supporting Wisconsin's compulsory education measure, even as applied to the Amish. While acknowledging that the Amish lifestyle contained "great virtue" and "picturesqueness," the *Post* emphasized that "a narrowly limited education effectively circumscribes all options," and insisted that "individual choice can more fairly be made out of knowledge than out of ignorance."[130]*

---

* In 1973, Hillary Rodham, then of the Children's Defense Fund, praised Justice Douglas's opinion in *Yoder* as "ground-breaking," because he understood that the interests of parents and their children may diverge. Hillary Rodham, "Children Under the Law," 43 *Harvard Educational Review* 487, 504 (1973). Justice Douglas dissented only "in part" in *Yoder* because one of the Amish children suggested at trial that her own wishes accorded with Amish tradition, but the preferences of the other children in the lawsuit remained

To reach the outcome in *Yoder* required the Supreme Court to sidestep one of its precedents from the 1940s that refused to grant a requested free exercise exemption to a general law, where it expressly observed the potential divergence of interests between religious parents and their children. In declining to waive a Massachusetts child-labor regulation applied to a nine-year-old girl who sold religious literature alongside her guardian, the Supreme Court reasoned, "Parents may be free to become martyrs themselves. But it does not follow they are free . . . to make martyrs of their children before they have reached the age of full and legal discretion when they can make that choice for themselves."[131] *Yoder* unconvincingly sought to distinguish this precedent by observing that the Massachusetts regulation involved an activity that threatened to harm society. While *Yoder* was pending at the Court, the lead plaintiff from New Glarus, Wisconsin, made public comments strongly supporting the notion that at least some Amish parents viewed themselves as imposing a sort of involuntary martyrdom on their offspring. "We aren't doctors, we aren't lawyers, we aren't newspaper reporters," Jonas Yoder stated. "We're just plain dirt farmers. *We feel by keeping our children away from so much high education, we can keep 'em where we want to have them; they accept what we want them to do.*" Yoder further suggested that the urge to prevent Amish children from attending secondary school arose from considerations more economical than ecclesiastical. "We don't feel education is so important; I can easily make a living without it. It costs a lot of money to send 'em beyond the eighth grade," Yoder explained.[132] Given that Yoder's children attended tuition-free public schools, it seems plain that the "costs" he had in mind were the lost fruits from their labor.*

---

unknown (and thus required further inquiry). Professor Emily Buss has questioned whether Justice Douglas's proposed solution in *Yoder* was actually viable. "While Frieda [Yoder] may, in fact, have believed precisely what she said [affirming her desire to discontinue her schooling], and even believed it with fervent conviction, it is impossible to ascertain whether her words, in fact, reflect such true beliefs," Buss wrote. "Her words could have been offered, just as easily, as the response that she was required to make by her position in her family and her community." Emily Buss, "What Does Frieda Yoder Believe?," 2 *University of Pennsylvania Journal of Constitutional Law* 53, 68 (1999).

* Some insightful legal scholars have contended that the Amish tradition of *rumspringa*, a phenomenon that went unacknowledged in *Yoder,* may alleviate concern about the potential for Amish adolescents feeling compelled to remain members of the faith due to their abbreviated educations. These scholars note that *rumspringa* (from the German *herumspringen,* meaning "to jump around") permits older teenagers to leave the Amish community to sample the wider world before they may voluntarily return to the flock

The passage of time has only intensified doubts about *Yoder's* legitimacy. First, a central factual predicate that Chief Justice Burger relied upon to justify the outcome in *Yoder*—the Amish's agriculture-based livelihood—has shifted substantially in the intervening four decades. Whereas the overwhelming majority of Amish men were farmers during the early 1970s, roughly two-thirds of those families have now abandoned farming in favor of industries, including sawmills, woodworking, and metal manufacturing. That professional reorientation matters greatly because, unlike Burger's idyllic image of the Amish as latter-day Jeffersonian farmers, the federal government has identified those industries as "among the most hazardous occupations for adults, with a death rate that is five times the national average for all industries . . . and [featuring] an exceptionally high non-fatal injury rate."[133] Even apart from the increased danger accompanying Amish labor practices, though, the Amish community's resounding move toward industry more readily triggers concerns about the economic exploitation of minors than does toiling on the family farm.

Second, as a matter of constitutional doctrine, *Yoder* appears

---

to settle down for adult baptism, more securely for having experienced at least some aspects of the society outside that they are abdicating. On this rosy account, *rumspringa* represents a meaningful option to exit the Amish community by presenting adolescents with a tailor-made opportunity to join the larger world. Yet *rumspringa* also lends itself to darker, more jaundiced interpretations. Viewed through an alternate prism, *rumspringa* is designed to demonstrate to uneducated Amish adolescents that they have no genuine ability to gain an economic or cultural toehold in the outside world. On this gloomier account, *rumspringa* seems designed less to enable Amish youth to exercise meaningful choice, and more designed to establish that they have no real choice to exercise at all. Accordingly, an Amish adolescent on *rumspringa* is a little like a declawed cat whose owner has released him into the backyard to prove a point; the question is not *whether* he will aim to return to the safe, familiar environment but *when*. For sanguine accounts of *rumspringa*, see Buss, "What Does Frieda Yoder Believe?," 69n66; and Martha C. Nussbaum, *Liberty of Conscience: In Defense of America's Tradition of Religious Equality* 141–43 (2008). See also Ed Klimuska, "'It's Party Time!' An Evening with Amish Youth," *Lancaster New Era*, Aug. 6, 1998, A1 (describing *rumspringa*). For an earlier articulation of the skeptical conception of *rumspringa*, see Louise Weinberg, "The McReynolds Mystery Solved," 89 *Denver University Law Review* 133, 156–57 (2011). Consistent with this skeptical view of *rumspringa*, a few contemporaneous observers portrayed the Amish youth as being exploited. Thus, Wisconsin's assistant attorney general stated in oral argument in *Yoder*, "These Amish kids have no other options than to stay and join the order: it's hard for them to get into the mainstream without a high school education." Bryce Nelson, "Supreme Court Weighs Amish View on Schools," *Los Angeles Times*, Feb. 28, 1972, B6. A local businessman in Wisconsin went even further: "These kids are in a sense enslaved; guys without a high school education are no longer able to cope effectively." Ibid.

increasingly anomalous. In perhaps the most important decision involving religion in many years, the Supreme Court in 1990 held that as a broad proposition states do not violate the Free Exercise Clause by enacting neutral laws of general applicability without granting exemptions to religious objectors. Wisconsin's compulsory attendance measure presented a classic example of a neutral law that applied to the general population. Although the Supreme Court in 1990 expressly sought to preserve the validity of *Yoder*, legal commentators have roundly derided its specious rationale in advancing that claim. Accordingly, with *Yoder* hanging on by a thread, it would hardly be surprising if the Court overruled the precedent in an effort to enhance doctrinal clarity.[134]

Finally, although some scholars have suggested that Amish families today would—if pressed—simply assert that they were homeschooling their children, that speculation founders on the reality of Amish skepticism toward the homeschooling endeavor. Amish communities philosophically reject homeschooling because, they believe, the practice breeds isolation, independence, and self-sufficiency of individual households—traits that are disdained within a church-centered community that prioritizes unity. As one Amish leader articulated the community's opposition to homeschooling, "We all need the help of others in shaping our children's character. We all need the church and the community to enable our children to develop and to be able to function with others."[135] Nor is it at all clear that Amish families would feel comfortable dissembling to the state about their children's schooling activities, which continue today to conclude following the eighth grade. The upshot is that if the Supreme Court revisited—and reversed—*Yoder* in the modern era, it could well transform life for the thousands of Amish school-aged children within the United States.

ZELMAN V. SIMMONS-HARRIS AND THE LEGALIZATION OF SCHOOL VOUCHERS

A third reason that tensions arising at the intersection of religion and schools have receded in recent years stems from the Supreme Court's decision in *Zelman v. Simmons-Harris*. In 2002, that decision upheld the legitimacy of voucher programs for students who elect to attend private schools—including religious schools—thus eliminating a major source of aggravation for many right-leaning intellectuals. School vouchers had been a pet issue within certain academic circles since at least 1955, when the University of Chicago economist Milton Friedman first floated the idea, which essentially seeks to introduce marketplace concepts into the educational domain. But while many conservatives championed some version of Friedman's idea, a cloud of legal uncertainty surrounded whether students could in effect use public funds in the form of vouchers to pay portions of their tuition at sectarian schools without violating the Establishment Clause.

The program at the heart of *Simmons-Harris* arose in response to the Cleveland City School District's truly abysmal public education system. During the 1990s, the Cleveland District as a whole failed to satisfy even one of the eighteen state standards for measuring minimal proficiency, and approximately two-thirds of its students dropped out before graduating. Matters grew so dire that a federal district court eventually required the State of Ohio to take control of Cleveland's schools in an effort to bring the languishing performances of that city's students more into line with other Ohioans. In response to this crisis, Ohio created a voucher program that sought to provide Cleveland students from indigent families with a predetermined amount of money that could be used in public schools (where it would fund additional tutoring) or in private schools, including both parochial and non-parochial schools (where it would offset tuition). Of the fifty-six private schools that participated in the program, forty-six—or 82 percent—were religiously affiliated schools. Of the more than three thousand students who used the vouchers in private schools, moreover, 96 percent redeemed them at sectarian schools. Participating private schools could use the funding received from student vouchers in any way they deemed appropriate.

Doris Simmons-Harris, a hospital clerk with a son who attended Cleveland's public schools, agreed to join a lawsuit challenging the program's constitutionality filed against Ohio's superintendent Susan Zelman. "I've paid my tax money," Simmons-Harris said, "and I believe that money should go to the public schools." Simmons-Harris further allowed that she did not contemplate applying for a student voucher because she doubted that any nonpublic school would accept her son in light of his spotty behavioral record. Vouchers for private schools, she insisted, harmed the students who were left behind in the public schools: "We need to educate all our children, not just a few." But Roberta Kitchen, a mother of five children who at one point attended Cleveland's public schools, praised the transformational effects of participating in the voucher program. "My children will never go back to public schools," Kitchen pledged. "It's like sentencing them to death." Solicitor General Theodore Olson filed an amicus brief encouraging the Court to grant the petition for review in *Simmons-Harris*, even though the Court had not yet asked for his views and the United States was not a party to the case. This unusually aggressive approach indicated the premium that President George W. Bush and his administration placed on having the Court remove the legal uncertainty surrounding vouchers.[136]

In a 5–4 decision, Chief Justice William Rehnquist's opinion for the Court in *Simmons-Harris* held that the voucher program did not violate the Establishment Clause. Although 82 percent of private schools participating in Cleveland's voucher program were religious, Rehnquist contended that figure should not be damning because it was virtually identical to the 81 percent of private schools that were religious within the state of Ohio. Moreover, while 96 percent of voucher recipients who attended private schools redeemed them at sectarian institutions, Rehnquist further insisted no evidence indicated that parents were somehow "coerc[ed]" into subjecting their children to religious instruction.[137] For Rehnquist, vouchers enabled Cleveland parents simply to select from a wider range of schooling options for their children than were previously within their reach. Under this view, the program neither deprived them of a meaningful independent choice about education, nor distributed funding directly to religious schools, nor privileged sectarian schooling over nonsectarian schooling. To the contrary, Rehnquist contended that the program's defining feature was its religious neutrality, as it treated private nonreligious schools and private religious schools in identical fashions. As Rehnquist summed up the governing rule that emerged from *Simmons-Harris*, "[W]here a government aid program is neutral [regarding] religion and provides assistance directly to . . . citizens who, in turn, direct government aid to religion schools wholly as a result of their own genuine . . . private choice, the program is not readily subject to challenge under the Establishment Clause."[138]

The Court's four-justice liberal bloc—Justices Stephen Breyer,

Ruth Bader Ginsburg, David Souter, and John Paul Stevens—
produced three overlapping opinions in dissent. Viewed in concert, these opinions advanced three primary arguments to contend
Cleveland's voucher program violated the Establishment Clause.
But each of these arguments is unavailing. First, the dissents contended that the voucher program sowed the seeds of religious divisiveness, risking a nation united becoming fractured by religiously
balkanized educational subcommunities. Taken seriously, this contention presents an argument against not only vouchers but the
existence of religious education altogether. And that, of course, is
a position that the Supreme Court—correctly—rejected nearly a
century ago in *Pierce v. Society of Sisters*. If wealthier families can
choose to educate their children in religious schools, why should
indigent families necessarily be prohibited from doing so, provided
that sectarian schooling is one option of several offered on their
educational menus? As a factual matter, moreover, it may be worth
noting that Cleveland's program actually served to bring students
from different religious backgrounds together, as many students
from Protestant families ended up attending Catholic schools.[139]

Second, attempting to respond to the rhetorical question in the
preceding paragraph, the dissenters contended that taxpayers may
feel aggrieved because their money would be used to fund a religion
that they do not practice, which seems to raise core Establishment
Clause considerations. Yet upon reflection it becomes apparent
that this particular legal horse long ago left the barn. Backed with
governmental funding from the GI Bill and Pell Grants, college
students have for several decades elected to attend religious institutions of higher education, including Boston College, the University of Notre Dame, and Yeshiva University. No mainstream
scholar maintains that those arrangements violate the Establishment Clause, presumably in large part because religious institutions
receive funding due to an individual student's choice. Yet Cleveland's voucher program uses this same indirect mechanism. While
it is true that the voucher program serves younger and therefore
more impressionable students than, say, the GI Bill, that distinction
should not make a difference, because parents elect to send students
to the religious schools in the first instance. Thus, unlike teacher-
led religious observance that occurs in public schools, voucher
programs do not raise the same concerns about the unwelcome
religious indoctrination of young minds.[140]

Third, the dissenters contended that the voucher program breached "the wall of separation between church and state." This final objection may well be accurate, but—regrettably, from the perspective of voucher opponents—it does not necessarily constitute an Establishment Clause violation. While this striking metaphor originated with Thomas Jefferson, it appears nowhere in the Constitution. Today, moreover, the most esteemed scholars of the Constitution's religion clauses, from a wide variety of ideological perspectives, contend that the metaphor obscures more than it illuminates, and therefore ought to be discarded. The more useful Establishment Clause test turns not on strict separation but on neutrality, inquiring whether the state's conduct through its express terms either advances or inhibits religion and nonreligion. As *Simmons-Harris* determined, the availability of private nonsectarian schools and public schools under the voucher program sufficed to render it neutral regarding religion.[141]

Some opponents of vouchers also make policy arguments, rather than constitutional arguments, against the practice. These anti-voucher arguments include, as Doris Simmons-Harris herself intimated, that students who are left behind in public schools due to vouchers are ultimately harmed because the students who avail themselves of private schooling options often have engaged parents, who would in the absence of vouchers draw upon their resources to improve the public schools as a whole. In addition, some opponents maintain that the vouchers are typically too modest to make a difference. Shortly before *Simmons-Harris*, Jonathan Kozol offered a memorable version of this critique. "[Conservatives] are proposing a voucher of a couple thousand dollars which at best would allow a handful of poor children or children of color to go to a pedagogically marginal private school," Kozol contended. "The day the conservative voucher advocates in America tell me that they would like to give every inner-city black, Hispanic, or poor white kid a $25,000 voucher to go to Exeter, I will become a Republican."[142]

Such arguments may well have some merit, but they also seem vulnerable to powerful counterarguments. To Simmons-Harris's concern, for example, a voucher proponent might respond that it is unreasonable to hold motivated parents hostage to improve a malfunctioning system, particularly because many of their wealthier counterparts have already availed themselves of the exit option to attend private schools. To Kozol's concern, moreover, one might respond that his evaluation reveals a man who fails to appreciate half a loaf of bread; that is, the relevant question asks not whether Cleveland's students who use relatively modest vouchers would be better off if they could afford Exeter but whether they are better off than they were under the pre-voucher regime. In the end, I offer no firm judgment whether vouchers are an affirmatively desirable idea for school systems to pursue. I do maintain, though, that the Establishment Clause does not prohibit the endeavor.

The single most notable aspect of *Simmons-Harris* is how prominently racial considerations figured into the justices' analyses, even though as a formal matter the case did not turn on race. At times, one might be forgiven for believing that the case somehow involved the Equal Protection Clause rather than the Establishment Clause. Chief Justice Rehnquist's opening paragraph, for example, sets the scene by observing of the students enrolled in Cleveland's public schools, "The majority of these children are from low-income and minority families. Few of these families enjoy the means to send their children to any school other than an inner-city public school."[143] In a similar fashion, Justice Clarence Thomas began a concurring opinion in *Simmons-Harris* by quoting Frederick Douglass—the first of the opinion's two citations to the great abolitionist—for the proposition that " '[e]ducation . . . means emancipation' " and then hastened to add,

> Today many of our inner-city public schools deny emancipation to urban minority students. Despite this Court's observation nearly 50 years ago in *Brown v. Board of Education*, that "it is doubtful that any child may reasonably be expected to succeed in life if he is denied the opportunity of an education," urban children have been forced into a system that continually fails them.[144]

Later in the opinion, Thomas cited the economist Thomas Sowell to support the notion that black families particularly "just want the best education for their children" and have no time for "romanticized ideal[s]" when it comes to schooling.[145]

These racial invocations in *Simmons-Harris* are particularly striking because both Rehnquist and Thomas have been among the Court's most ardent champions of colorblind constitutionalism, which holds that governmental entities must almost invariably refrain from classifying citizens according to race, even if they do so with benign intent. Thus, Rehnquist and Thomas have repeat-edly insisted that the potential harms attending racial classifications require nullifying affirmative action in the employment and higher education contexts. That habitual stance does not, however, inhibit them from citing Cleveland's racial demographics in an effort to cast vouchers in a more sympathetic light.[146]

In many ways, these judicial efforts to frame *Simmons-Harris* as a case centering on racial equality are attributable to the efforts of Clint Bolick, then a lawyer with the libertarian Institute for Jus-tice.* Bolick defended the voucher program at the Supreme Court in large part by portraying the voucher movement as the modern legal heir to the civil rights movement. It can hardly have been happenstance that *Brown* became both the first case and the last case that Bolick's Supreme Court brief cited. Thus, Bolick opened the brief by extolling *Brown*'s "sacred promise of equal educational opportunities for all American school children," and closed it by observing that before *Brown* "children were forced to travel past good neighborhood schools to attend inferior schools because the children happened to be black; today, many poor children are forced to travel past good schools to attend inferior schools because the schools happen to be private."[147] One year after the Court's opinion, Bolick published a book recounting the path leading to *Simmons-Harris*, where he called the desegregation-voucher anal-ogy his "strategic overriding communications objective," both because it claimed the moral high ground and because he believed in its accuracy. "For the many families we have represented over the course of the past dozen years," Bolick wrote, "the promise of *Brown* . . . was illusory—until [*Simmons-Harris*]."[148] In addition, Bolick credited the analogy with "dissipat[ing] the largest single obstacle standing in the way of school choice."[149]

A stunningly large number of high-profile conservatives, in the course of touting *Simmons-Harris*, also embraced the desegregation-voucher comparison. Most prominently, President George W. Bush delivered an address in downtown Cleveland where he equated the historical significance of *Simmons-Harris* with *Brown*. "The Supreme Court in 1954 declared that our nation cannot have two education systems, and that was the right decision," Bush proclaimed. "Last week . . . the Court declared that our nation will not accept one

---

* In January 2016, Bolick became an associate justice on the Arizona Supreme Court.

education system for those who can afford to send their children to a school of their choice and [another] for those who can't, and that's just as historic."[150] Bush's secretary of education, Rod Paige, who attended Jim Crow schools in the South, endorsed similar reasoning. "With *Brown*, education became a civil rights issue, and the decision introduced a civil rights revolution that continues to this day," Paige commented. "*Zelman v. Simmons-Harris* . . . recasts the education debates in this country, encouraging a new civil rights revolution and ushering in a 'new birth of freedom' for parents and their children everywhere in America."[151] The columnist George Will contended that *Simmons-Harris* brought "socially disadvantaged children . . . their best day in court since *Brown* . . . in 1954."[152] In perhaps the most exuberant display of this analogy, *The Wall Street Journal*—under the headline "Vouchers Have Overcome"—claimed *Simmons-Harris* "struck the greatest blow for equal public education since *Brown*," and "stripped away the last Constitutional and moral figleaf from those who want to keep minority kids trapped in failing public schools."[153]*

Many African Americans disparaged this effort to analogize school desegregation to school vouchers. The NAACP Legal Defense and Educational Fund—in an amicus brief that opposed Cleveland's program—termed the analogy "manipulative and shal-

---

* *The Wall Street Journal* demonstrated something bordering on an obsession with comparing school desegregation to school vouchers. The *Journal*'s editorial praising *Simmons-Harris* also contended, "In 1954, Linda Brown's right to a decent education was threatened by a public education system that kept her out of a successful white school. Today, voucher supporters understand that . . . children just like Miss Brown are threatened by a system that is once again separate but unequal." "Vouchers Have Overcome," *Wall Street Journal*, June 28, 2002, A12. Several months earlier, in anticipation of the decision, the *Journal* invoked this same basic idea: "The critics cry that upholding the Cleveland program would spell the end of public education. But the evidence coming in from the cities tells us that for today's Linda Browns, public education died long ago. Vouchers may be the only way to revive it." "Our *Brown v. Board*," *Wall Street Journal*, Feb. 19, 2002, A26. A few months before that, the *Journal* encouraged the Court to hear the case by contending, "In a landmark decision . . . , the Supreme Court ruled that a child named Linda Brown could not be excluded from a decent school because of her skin color. What the Court now needs to decide is whether the Linda Browns of today must remain locked into failing schools." "Cleveland Rocks," *Wall Street Journal*, Sept. 26, 2001, A20. This genre's antecedents stretch back at least to 1990, when the *Journal* published an editorial, titled "Blocking the Schoolhouse Door," comparing Arkansas's governor Orval Faubus—who called out the National Guard to prohibit black students from entering Little Rock's Central High School in 1957—to a Wisconsin school superintendent who opposed the creation of a voucher program. See "Blocking the Schoolhouse Door," *Wall Street Journal*, June 27, 1990, A12.

low," before contending that it "insult[ed] the thousands of courageous African-American parents and students who made ... *Brown* ... become a reality."[154] Theodore Shaw, an LDF attorney, found the analogy to racial desegregation particularly galling because legal conservatives, as a general proposition, had long advanced constitutional colorblindness as a way to stymie affirmative action policies, but "all of a sudden race is all over this [voucher] issue."[155] Even some African American supporters of vouchers nevertheless found the *Brown* analogy profoundly misguided. To take only one example, Brent Staples of *The New York Times*, a staunch vouchers advocate, called analogizing *Simmons-Harris* to *Brown* "preposterous on its face." Staples allowed that "it anger[ed him] to hear people equate a small-bore voucher program with the epochal transformations set in motion by *Brown*," an opinion that he credited with opening the elite institutions of American society— including the august *New York Times*—to black members of his own generation.[156]

But other African Americans—particularly younger members of the black intelligentsia—adamantly insisted that the desegregationvoucher analogy held genuine appeal. Two years before the Court decided *Simmons-Harris*, Omar Wasow, a graduate of Stanford who eventually became a political science professor at Princeton, construed the voucher movement as the logical outgrowth of *Brown*. In Wasow's view, both movements at bottom sought access to stronger educational environments for racial minorities. "The black freedom struggle has fundamentally been about trying to produce a society where black individuals have as much freedom and agency as white Americans," Wasow asserted. "As long as black people are trapped in failing public schools, we will never achieve the kind of dignity and power that has been the central cause of the black freedom struggle for more than 200 years."[157] Cory Booker— a Rhodes Scholar and graduate of Yale Law School, who was then a member of the Newark City Council—concurred with Wasow's assessment, as he contended that inner-city education must be improved, with apologies to Malcolm X, by any means necessary. Identifying the absence of vouchers as "one of the last remaining major barriers to equality of opportunity in America," Booker commented, "I don't necessarily want to depend on the government to educate my children—they haven't done a good job in doing that.

Only if we return power to the parents can we find a way to fix the system."[158]

Irrespective of one's view of vouchers, it is important to understand that they occupy nothing more than a tiny niche within the nation's various educational systems and that this arrangement is likely to continue for some time. As of December 2016, more than fourteen years after *Simmons-Harris* made clear that neutrally designed vouchers do not violate the Establishment Clause, voucher programs existed in only fourteen states along with the District of Columbia. Even more notably, those programs collectively served a not-so-grand total of 250,000 students—or about one-tenth the number of students who are homeschooled and an infinitesimal fraction of the students who attend public schools. Admittedly, both President Donald Trump and his secretary of education, Betsy DeVos, have recently trumpeted school vouchers as an important tool of educational reform. That pair has touted a proposal urging Congress to authorize a twenty-billion-dollar-per-year federal subsidy that states would be expected to augment heavily from their own coffers, all so that children living beneath the poverty level could afford to attend nonpublic schools.[159]

Despite such high-profile advocacy, however, experts believe that very little reason exists for anticipating that vouchers are on the verge of expanding broadly, let alone becoming the new national norm. The political obstacles working to prevent Congress from adopting the Trump-DeVos proposal appear truly staggering. To begin, the current moment in the United States is, to put the point mildly, not primarily known for its frictionless political processes. Apart from the standard gridlock, though, the federal voucher proposal's prospects are particularly bleak because it claims opponents on both sides of the political aisle. Many Democrats—partly due to their association with teachers' unions—dislike vouchers, as do many Republicans, especially those living in highly rural states, where the notion of choosing another school presents a geographic impossibility. Given that the voucher program is expressly designed to benefit students from indigent families, moreover, it seems virtually impossible to believe the issue will soon rise atop the congressional agenda. Even setting aside the Trump-DeVos proposal, moreover, thirty-eight states have independent provisions in their state constitutions prohibiting the use of public funds to "aid" or "benefit" religious schools, and some (though not all) state courts have already relied upon those provisions to invalidate state voucher programs. When one considers that the educational budgets in many states remain severely strained as a result of the Great Recession, it seems more improbable still that vouchers will soon be poised for widespread adoption.[160]*

A CODA ON RELIGION

None of the foregoing should be mistaken for asserting that contentious disputes over the role of religion in public schools have vanished altogether and will never reappear on the Supreme Court's docket. Such a claim would be foolhardy. To offer only one example of a potential decision that would roil the nation, contemplate if the Supreme Court issued an opinion prohibiting students from reciting the Pledge of Allegiance because the inclusion of the words "one Nation *under God*" violated the Establishment Clause. In 2004, the Supreme Court seemed to be on the cusp of addressing that question after an atheist named Michael Newdow filed a lawsuit on behalf of himself and his daughter, who attended a public school near Sacramento, California. Newdow's challenge to the pledge prevailed in the U.S. Court of Appeals for the Ninth Circuit, which found that having classes recite those two controverted words transformed a patriotic exercise into an unconstitutional affirmation of faith— even if, in light of *Barnette*, no individual students were required to

* Secretary DeVos's confirmation hearings in 2017 revealed insufficient knowledge about important matters of educational policy, and I applaud those who opposed her narrow confirmation to a cabinet position. The secretary of education is a major position and deserves a more informed occupant. Yet I also believe that claims contending DeVos somehow "would single-handedly decimate our public education system if she were confirmed," as Senator Charles Schumer of New York maintained, were overstated. The simple reason is that public school policy within the United States is too diffuse for any single federal official to destroy. For an insightful argument along these lines, see Jonathan Chait, "Why Was Betsy DeVos the One Trump Nominee Who Provoked Opposition?," *New York*, Feb. 10, 2017. When Gallup has asked Americans whether they would like to reform public education or seek alternatives—including vouchers— roughly seven in ten respondents have consistently expressed preferences to improve the public school system. See William J. Reese, *America's Public Schools: From the Common School to "No Child Left Behind"* 323 (2011) (reporting Gallup polling responses from the late 1990s); and Lowell C. Rose and Alec M. Gallup, "The 38th Annual Phi Delta Kappa/Gallup Poll of the Public's Attitudes Toward the Public Schools," *Phi Delta Kappan*, Sept. 2006, 41, 43, 53–56.

participate. Ultimately, however, the Supreme Court in *Elk Grove Unified School District v. Newdow* wriggled free from resolving that question by finding that Newdow lacked the legal authority to file a valid lawsuit raising the issue. Newdow lacked "standing" to present this question, according to the Supreme Court, because he was a noncustodial parent and his ex-wife (who retained all custodial rights over their daughter) did not wish to challenge the pledge.[161]

Whatever the legitimacy of the Court's denial of standing, there can be no doubt that had the Supreme Court affirmed the Ninth Circuit, that decision would have provoked greater animosity than any constitutional decision in recent memory. A Gallup poll from 2004 revealed that more than 90 percent of respondents supported the pledge including the words "under God," and both houses of Congress voted by overwhelming margins to support a resolution affirming the pledge's legitimacy, with the measure passing 99–0 in the Senate and 416–3 in the House. Even in liberal precincts, where the Ninth Circuit's ruling might be expected to garner some support, however tepid, the notion that the Pledge of Allegiance violated the Constitution struck most observers as absurd. Following the Ninth Circuit's decision, *The Washington Post* chided, "If the court were writing a parody, rather than deciding an actual case, it could hardly have produced a more provocative holding than striking down the Pledge of Allegiance while this country is at war."[162] *The New York Times* added, "In the real pantheon of First Amendment concerns, this one is off the radar screen."[163] Left-leaning constitutional scholars, including Professors Cass Sunstein and Laurence Tribe, agreed that the case presented no serious Establishment Clause issues because the pledge constituted a patriotic ritual, not a religious one.[164]

Even if the fundamental issue presented in *Newdow*—or some other controversial question, for that matter—should emerge somewhere down the line, however, its appearance will not have erased the period of relative calm that has surrounded schooling and religion in recent years. Although religion occupied a central place in legal battles over education for decades, that issue has now largely retreated to the margins. Constitutional decisions—including several from the Supreme Court—have played a major role in generating this underappreciated measure of serenity, and they ought to be saluted. While some citizens undoubtedly disagree with particular aspects of the governing jurisprudence, those disagreements

THE SCHOOLHOUSE GATE

should not obscure the fact that the nation's collective temperature has never been lower in this arena since the dawn of widespread public schooling. This current state of affairs appears all the more improbable, considering that the Supreme Court's first meaningful foray into the question of school prayer in 1962 seemed initially to portend disaster.[165]

Conclusion

Surveying the legal landscape of the United States since the late nineteenth century, it is breathtaking to step back and observe how many of the Supreme Court's decisions that meaningfully advance the causes of constitutional liberty and constitutional equality have arisen from clashes in public schools. Contemplate only a sampling of the Court's numerous interventions in this domain that have vindicated core constitutional protections by rejecting illegitimate exercises of governmental authority and how those decisions have transformed public education. Without the Supreme Court, public schools today could still require students to salute the American flag or otherwise face expulsion, a practice that *West Virginia State Board of Education v. Barnette* invalidated in 1943. Without the Supreme Court, public schools today could still rely upon explicit state authority to prohibit all racial minorities from attending school with white students, a practice that *Brown v. Board of Education* invalidated in 1954. Without the Supreme Court, public schools today could still routinely permit teachers to lead students in prayers and Bible-reading exercises, practices that *Engel v. Vitale* and *Abington School District v. Schempp* invalidated in the early 1960s. Without the Supreme Court, public schools today could still preemptively prohibit students from displaying symbols to express controversial ideas to their classmates, a practice that *Tinker v. Des Moines Independent Community School District* invalidated in 1969. Without the Supreme Court, public schools today could still suspend or expel students without affording them even a brief hearing, a practice that *Goss v. Lopez* invalidated in 1975. Without the Supreme Court, public schools today could still display the Ten Commandments on classroom walls, a practice that *Stone v. Graham* invalidated in 1980. Without the Supreme Court, public schools today could still prohibit unauthorized immigrants from receiving a tuition-free education, a practice that *Plyler v. Doe* invalidated in 1982. Without the Supreme Court, public schools today could still openly embargo books from their library shelves because of the provocative ideas that they contain, a practice that *Island Trees School District v. Pico* cast grave doubt upon in 1982. The upshot of this procession of opinions indicates that had the Supreme Court continued to honor its initial refusal to enter the educational domain, the condition of both the nation's public schools and our constitutional order would be impoverished.[1]

These salutary contributions to understandings of students' constitutional rights merit highlighting because, taken together, they confound a prominent view within modern legal academia that depicts the Supreme Court as a fundamentally fragile, almost inert institution. These judicial decisions, when considered within their surrounding legal and historical contexts, establish that the Court has played an instrumental role in shaping constitutional realities within the school setting. In some of these instances, the Court prevented unconstitutional practices in public schools from becoming widespread, and thus molded public education in profound ways by eliminating what would have been an attractive option to school districts across the country. It seems safe to conclude, for example, that *Stone v. Graham* permitted millions of students to attend classes—in Kentucky and beyond—without depictions of the Ten Commandments looming over them, and that *Plyler v. Doe* permitted millions of unauthorized immigrants—in Texas and beyond— simply to attend classes at all, enabling a much-maligned group to receive an education who would otherwise have been banished from schools altogether. In other instances, the Court successfully altered already prevalent practices regarding the appropriate role of students in the United States. Thus, *Barnette*—by allowing students to remain quiet during the pledge—blocked students in forty-eight different states from being expelled for insubordination; conversely, *Tinker*—by affirming students' rights to speak up as an integral part of the educational process—challenged the prevailing view that students may not articulate their own controversial ideas about

American society in the school setting. In still other instances, the Court issued opinions espousing constitutional visions in relatively obscure cases, making it tempting to dismiss them as insignificant because they did not loudly demand a radical reconception of students' rights across the country. Yet while neither *Lopez*'s granting due process rights to students targeted for suspensions nor *Pico*'s rebuff of book banning might have required most school districts to change their standard operating procedures, those opinions nevertheless contained important statements about the nation's constitutional commitments. In yet other instances, the Court confronted deep-seated cultural practices, and while those opinions met with some important successes, they also encountered nontrivial resistance. *Brown*'s invalidation of measures permitting racially segregated schools can be understood as falling into this category, along with the rejection of teacher-led prayer and Bible reading in *Engel* and *Schempp*.

But one need not maintain that all of the Supreme Court's school decisions achieved universal, instantaneous success in order to acknowledge that its interventions have benefited both American education and American society. A clear-eyed view of these decisions demonstrates that the Supreme Court is neither a Leviathan striding the earth (as scholars of yore often maintained) nor a Lilliputian standing in place (as scholars now frequently suggest). Instead, upon close inspection, it seems most accurate to contend that the institution has taken several significant steps on the path toward fully recognizing students' constitutional rights.

* * *

Acknowledging the federal judiciary's meaningful contributions in this area, however, should hardly be mistaken for complacency with the constitutional status quo in schools. To the contrary, the Supreme Court has—in recent decades—often issued either erroneous or deficient opinions in this field, and these misguided decisions have imposed baleful consequences on our constitutional order. Given that students carry their early intuitions about constitutional authority with them long after their school days conclude, these persistent obstacles residing at the intersection of law and education demand national attention, lest we "strangle the free mind at its source and teach youth to discount important principles of our government as mere platitudes."² Consider only three of the most urgent areas that the Supreme Court has botched or neglected that belong high atop the reform agenda for students' rights.

First, although *Tinker* represented an important breakthrough for recognizing students' freedom of speech, the Supreme Court has consistently failed to build upon that landmark opinion. Instead, the Court has issued a series of dubious decisions permitting educators to suppress students' First Amendment rights—including its most recent installment that permitted viewpoint discrimination in *Morse v. Frederick.* The Supreme Court should make clear that students possess the First Amendment right to communicate contentious ideas on campus, that would-be student hecklers will not be permitted to silence legitimate student speech by issuing threats of violence, and that students enjoy expansive speech rights off campus. In the absence of such decisions, public schools risk being transformed into the very "enclaves of totalitarianism" that *Tinker* sought to repudiate.³

Second, the Supreme Court should revisit its decision in *Ingraham v. Wright* and establish that the Eighth Amendment, properly understood, prohibits educators in public schools from inflicting corporal punishment on students. Public school students are the last remaining group of Americans whom governmental employees may strike with impunity, even when they pose no threat whatsoever to anyone's safety. Whatever *Ingraham*'s constitutional legitimacy in 1977, the last four decades leave no doubt that wooden paddles have no business on the behinds of public school students. Although the overwhelming number of states permitted corporal punishment during the 1970s, that number has dwindled to fewer than twenty today, and even many jurisdictions within those states have jettisoned the practice. Little evidence suggests, however, that the remaining jurisdictions that have elected to retain this retrograde custom will soon decide to cease paddling students of their own volition. That public school educators continue striking students today—well into the twenty-first century—is nothing less than an abomination, and it must stop.⁴

Finally, the Supreme Court should revisit its severely deformed public school jurisprudence involving the Fourth Amendment's prohibition on unreasonable searches. The Supreme Court misfired badly when it first encountered this issue in 1985, when *New Jersey v. T.L.O.* authorized educators to search students' belongings to find evidence for violations of mere school rules. Although *T.L.O.*'s rationale evinced serious flaws from the outset, subsequent developments have made it only worse. Most notably, the ascent of school resource officers has undercut the notion that students should invariably receive only watered-down Fourth Amendment protections, as too many schoolhouses now bear a disturbing resemblance to stationhouses. In addition, the lax attitude that the Supreme Court has exhibited toward schools that administer suspicionless drug tests to students demands reexamination. Even the Court's recent decision that appropriately invalidated the strip search at issue in *Safford Unified School District v. Redding* in 2009 nonetheless erred by enunciating a legal standard that afforded educators excessive discretion to conduct those incredibly invasive procedures.[5]

Yet if the Supreme Court refuses to act on any of these three particularly pressing fronts—or upon any other lingering issue, for that matter—this judicial inaction would not necessarily mean that all hope for reform has vanished. The federal judiciary is responsible for demarcating boundaries that educators cannot transgress regarding students' rights without violating the Constitution. But the federal judiciary's role in no sense prohibits states and localities from building upon those interpretations to extend additional protections to students that exceed the constitutional minimum.

Three examples from the preceding chapters illustrate this phenomenon at work. First, while *San Antonio Independent School District v. Rodriguez* rejected the effort to require greater equity in school funding in 1973, many state courts have interpreted provisions of their state constitutions to grant that request. Second, after *Hazelwood School District v. Kuhlmeier* refused to require school newspapers to publish contested articles in 1988, several states enacted legislation granting student journalists certain protections. Third, even before *Redding* evaluated strip searches of pupils in 2009, a few states and localities adopted measures barring school personnel from conducting such searches under any circumstances.[6]

Thus, even in the absence of Supreme Court intervention, several potential avenues—including school boards, city councils, state legislatures, and state judiciaries—remain available to pursue educational reforms. Looking forward, while *Vorchheimer v. School District of Philadelphia* might have failed to resolve the constitutionality of single-sex public schools at the elementary and secondary levels in 1977, that nondecision does not prevent jurisdictions from prohibiting their resurgence in underprivileged, urban areas within the United States. Relatedly, while *Parents Involved in Community Schools v. Seattle School District No. 1* might have prohibited pupil assignments that racially classify particular students in 2007, that decision did not bar jurisdictions from affording students educational experiences that are integrated—racially and otherwise—through a variety of available mechanisms. Finally, while the Supreme Court has never entertained a case squarely addressing the legitimacy of homeschooling, its silence on this question, of course, in no way prevents jurisdictions from adopting sensible regulations to monitor the practice while ensuring not to intrude upon a family's right to educate their children responsibly.[7]

* * *

In a book that fundamentally appraises students' constitutional rights, it seems hard to envision addressing a legal dispute featuring a more improbable plaintiff than Morris H. Kramer—an unmarried, college-educated thirty-one-year-old stockbroker who fathered no children and lived with his parents in an affluent part of Long Island, New York. Yet Kramer's triumphant encounter with the Supreme Court provides a fitting place to conclude because it highlights an essential, underappreciated dimension of our nation's public school system. During the 1960s, a New York statute provided that, in order to vote for local school board elections, residents must own or lease property within the district or must have custody of children enrolled in the public schools. Kramer, who fit neither qualification, filed a lawsuit challenging the constitutionality of these voter eligibility requirements. In 1969, Chief Justice Earl Warren—in the course of writing a majority opinion that invalidated these voting restrictions—summarized Kramer's legal contention in resonant language that recognized the paramount significance of schools to the nation. "[Kramer] contends that he and others of his class are substantially interested in and significantly affected by the school [board's] decisions," Warren explained. "All members of the community have an interest in the quality and structure of public education, [Kramer] says, and he urges that the decisions taken by local boards . . . may have grave consequences to the entire population."[8]

Although Kramer might have made an unlikely messenger, his underlying message merits preserving: the constitutional condition of the nation's public schools carries great relevance for every member of our society. That statement holds regardless of whether the individual in question is a teacher in public school, a student who attends public school, the parent of a child who attends public school, and, yes, even an unmarried stockbroker who lives with his wealthy parents. As the foregoing chapters have demonstrated, however, recent decades have witnessed the Supreme Court too often turn its back on vindicating the constitutional rights of students. Indeed, the worst of these rulings risk signaling that the nation's public schools have been transformed into zones where core constitutional protections go unrecognized. This judicial retreat threatens to impose profoundly negative consequences on our constitutional republic. Students who have had their rights suppressed by the government in public schools seem ill-positioned to become the sorts of engaged, dynamic, and disputatious citizens upon whom our nation depends. At no time in recent memory has the United States more desperately needed such citizens. And no civic task is more essential than ensuring that the Constitution is viewed in public schools not as some abstract piece of parchment that a social studies teacher occasionally invokes in class but as a vital, meaningful document whose principles inform students' lives every time they step within the schoolhouse gate.

Acknowledgments

Given this book's long period of gestation, I have incurred an unusually large number of debts that I now have the pleasure of recognizing. At the beginning of my legal career, I had the great good fortune to work as a law clerk for three eminent jurists: Judge Merrick B. Garland, Justice Stephen Breyer, and Justice Sandra Day O'Connor. Each of them emphasized that judicial opinions involving constitutional law, though sometimes intensely theoretical, are anything but abstract, as they affect millions of Americans in their everyday lives. This common, vital lesson runs throughout this book. Most immediate to the book's subject, I worked with Justice Breyer during the 2006 term, when the Supreme Court issued some of its most high-profile decisions involving students' constitutional rights in recent decades—including *Morse v. Frederick* (also known as "BONG HiTS 4 JESUS") and *Parents Involved in Community Schools v. Seattle School District No. 1* (which wrestled with the legacy of *Brown v. Board of Education*). Justice Breyer invested enormous amounts of time and energy in both disputes, and in so doing demonstrated the importance of education law to our constitutional order.

I completed this book with the unstinting support of the University of Chicago Law School, my incomparable intellectual home. That support began with its leadership. When I expressed interest in teaching a new course titled "The Constitution Goes to School" to the former dean Michael Schill, he eagerly welcomed my proposal. His successor, Dean Thomas Miles, has also embraced this project, celebrating analytical breakthroughs along the way and ensuring that I had the time necessary to commit those breakthroughs to paper. Various colleagues have offered incisive criticisms of the manuscript, exhibiting the engagement with ideas that makes the University of Chicago a model academic community. I am particularly grateful for the feedback of Daniel Abebe, William Baude, Emily Buss, Daniel Hemel, Aziz Huq, Dennis Hutchinson, Alison LaCroix, Genevieve Lakier, Jonathan Masur, Richard McAdams, Martha Nussbaum, Corbin Page, John Rappaport, Gerald Rosenberg, Geoffrey Stone, Lior Strahilevitz, David Strauss, and Laura Weinrib. I also appreciate the students who have enrolled in "The Constitution Goes to School" over the years for grappling with the course materials and my ideas. An intrepid platoon of research assistants took time away from their own work as law students to help me with this work: Jennifer Beard, Claire Bonelli, Devin Carpenter, Madison Clark, Sarah David, Adam Davidson, Alison Frost, Samuel Fuller, Madeline Hall, Alyssa Howard, Saif Kazim, Christopher Keen, Kevin Kennedy, Jacob Rierson, Jeremy Rozansky, Kathryn Running, Lindsay Stone, Adam Weiner, and Joseph Wenner. Several of these research assistants taught in public schools prior to beginning law school, and I deeply benefited from hearing at an early stage their reactions to my proposals for reform. All of these research assistants improved the final version, not least by tracking down sources that allowed me to depict both the events underlying students' major constitutional claims and the contemporaneous responses to judicial opinions. Staff members of the law school's library also provided crucial assistance with this endeavor, including Constance Fleischer, Sheri Lewis, Greg Nimmo, and Margaret Schilt. I received support from the Herbert and Marjorie Fried Faculty Research Fund and the Roger Levin Faculty Fund.

Several professors at other institutions also provided illuminating feedback, notably Bruce Ackerman, Akhil Reed Amar, Kate Andrias, Jack Balkin, Richard Banks, Stephen Carter, Owen Fiss, James Forman Jr., Barry Friedman, Heather Gerken, Jacob Gersen, Julius Getman, Pratheepan Gulasekaram, Laura Kalman, Randall Kennedy, Randy Kozel, Douglas Laycock, Sanford Levinson, Lisa Marshall Manheim, John Manning, Tracey Meares, Ajay Mehrotra, Martha Minow, Nicholas Parrillo, Lucas Powe Jr., David Pozen, David Rabban, Christopher Schmidt, Louis Michael Seidman, Scott Shapiro, and Matthew Shaw. I look forward to the day when I can at least attempt to repay these generous interlocutors. James T. Patterson deserves a special salute not only for his insights into this project, but for hiring me as a research assistant when I was an undergraduate. That intellectual experience influenced every page of this book.

Several dear friends provided essential encouragement and guidance: William Edwards, Abelardo Fernández, Danielle Gray, Christopher Hsu, Jonathan Kravis, Brian Nelson, Daniel Oppenheimer, Adam Orlov, Nicola Orlov, James Powers, Noam Scheiber, Jake Sullivan, and Tali Farhadian Weinstein. These sustaining friendships have enriched this book and its author.

My literary agent, Melissa Flashman of Janklow & Nesbit Associates, consistently provided astute advice. At no point was her guidance more crucial than when she steered this project to my distinguished editor, Erroll McDonald of Pantheon, who deftly shepherded this book to publication. At Pantheon, I also had the pleasure of working with Altie Karper, Josefine Kals McGehee, Ingrid Sterner, and Nicholas Thomson, each of whom handled the project with grace and aplomb.

During the past few years, I have presented and refined my ideas about students' constitutional rights in a variety of settings, including workshops held at Brown University, Drake University Law School (where I also spoke as part of its Constitutional Law Center's Distinguished Lecture Series), Harvard Law School, Loyola University Chicago School of Law, the University of Chicago Law School, the University of Washington School of Law, and Yale Law School. I appreciate the insightful feedback that participants offered me on these occasions.

Although my scholarly writings to date have been aimed primarily toward constitutional law audiences rather than education law audiences, undertaking this project has enabled me to appreciate how frequently I have chosen to explore constitutional phenomena through cases involving students. Accordingly, in a few assorted places throughout this book, I draw on themes and formulations that originally appeared in some of my prior publications: "The Consensus Constitution," 89 *Texas Law Review* 755 (2011); "The Significance of the Frontier in American Constitutional Law," 2011 *Supreme Court Review* 345; "Recognizing Race," 112 *Columbia Law Review* 404 (2012); "Constitutional Outliers," 81 *University of Chicago Law Review* 929 (2014); "Supremacies and the Southern Manifesto," 92 *Texas Law Review* 1053 (2014); and "Reactionary Rhetoric and Liberal Legal Academia," 123 *Yale Law Journal* 2616 (2014). I am grateful to these journals for permitting me to reproduce selected portions of my work in this volume.

The biggest debt, however, is to my family. My brother, Adam Driver, has supported my interests since before I can remember, and provided shrewd counsel on this undertaking.

For the last sixteen years, Laura Ferry has placed the first pair of eyes (not lodged in my own head) on every word of every first draft that I have written that is intended for publication. Even in our first year as law school students, she possessed an uncanny knack for appreciating when I needed a pat on the back and when I needed a kick on the backside, and for knowing precisely how much force to apply in each case. I stand honored by her belief in this project, and in disbelief that she agreed to spend her life with me. By right and by reason, this book should be dedicated to her and the two darling children that we have the privilege of raising together, Claire Ellison Driver and Darcy Eleanor Driver.

Yet this book, my first, would not exist were it not for the stimulating home environment created by my parents: Terrell Glenn Driver and Rebecca Callen Driver. They both sacrificed enormously to allow me to obtain a first-rate education and made me feel as though it were their genuine pleasure to do so. To capitalize upon Washington, D.C.'s open-enrollment school practices, my father departed our house in the wee hours of one morning, drove across the city, and slept fitfully in his car to ensure that he would be among the first parents in the required queue for out-of-district students to enroll in Alice Deal Junior High School. He also ensured that I possessed the confidence and the curiosity necessary to succeed at Deal and beyond. When the time came to apply to college, my mother insisted that I attend whatever institution of higher learning I desired, regardless of tuition, and that somehow—through scholarships, financial aid, and part-time jobs—we would find a way to make it work. Long before that day arrived, she instilled the importance of lofty expectations, the necessity of hard work, and the joy of engaging conversation. My foremost regret about this volume is that she is not alive to hold a published copy in her hands. While I know very well that she would have disagreed with some arguments in this book, I also know that she would have cherished its existence.

Notes

INTRODUCTION

1. "Felix Frankfurter Is Dead," *New York Times*, Feb. 23, 1965, 1. See Penny Singer, "The Luxury Home Market Carries On," *New York Times*, July 31, 1994, N10 (noting that Seven Springs once included one thousand acres and the mansion's square footage, among other features); "The Residence of Eugene Meyer Jr., Esq.," *House and Garden*, Nov. 1918, 28–29; and Kristin Tablang, "12 Billionaire Vacation Homes," *Forbes*, March 3, 2016 (noting the property's various amenities). Donald J. Trump purchased Seven Springs in 1996, apparently intending to transform the property into a golf course, but instead he retained it as one of his residences. See ibid. See also "Father Gives Bride Away in Ceremony at the Family Home," *Washington Post*, June 6, 1940, 14; Katharine Graham, *Personal History* 121–22 (1997) (recounting her wedding day and the fateful luncheon); and Shawn Francis Peters, *Judging Jehovah's Witnesses: Religious Persecution and the Dawn of the Rights Revolution* 70 (2000) (same).

2. Graham, *Personal History*, 122.

3. Ibid. See Tracy Campbell, *Short of the Glory: The Fall and Redemption of Edward F. Prichard Jr.* 69 (1998) ("Frankfurter grew angry and stated that he would never again participate in a discussion about Court business"); C. David Heymann, *The Georgetown Ladies' Social Club: Power, Passion, and Politics in the Nation's Capital* 29 (2003) (describing Frankfurter's agitation).

4. Graham, *Personal History*, 122.

5. Peters, *Judging Jehovah's Witnesses*, 37. Early in the litigation process, the courts misspelled the litigants' surname "Gobitis," rather than the actual spelling, "Gobitas." See ibid., 38. In addition to Peters's book, my rendering of *Gobitis* draws upon several other fine works that examine the case and its backdrop in detail. See David R. Manwaring, *Render unto Caesar: The Flag-Salute Controversy* (1962); Noah Feldman, *Scorpions: The Battles and Triumphs of FDR's Great Supreme Court Justices* (2010); and Vincent Blasi and Seana Shiffrin, "The Story

of *West Virginia State Board of Education v. Barnette:* The Pledge of Allegiance and the Freedom of Thought," in *Constitutional Law Stories* 409 (Michael C. Dorf ed., 2d ed. 2009). Although David Halberstam suggested that the notorious row at the wedding day luncheon stemmed from a judicial opinion involving communism, this account seems difficult to credit. See David Halberstam, *The Powers That Be* 172–73 (1979). Not only did the timing of the wedding fall on the heels of *Gobitis,* at least two people who attended the luncheon—Katharine Graham and Joseph Rauh—both identified the flag-salute decision as the case that ignited the controversy. See Graham, *Personal History,* 122; and Campbell, *Short of the Glory,* 69, 291n23.

6. *Minersville School District v. Gobitis,* 310 U.S. 586, 595–96 (1940).
7. Ibid., 598.
8. Ibid., 597–98. Justice Harlan Fiske Stone wrote the sole dissenting opinion in *Gobitis,* as he criticized the majority's decision for "surrender[ing] the constitutional protection of the liberty of small minorities to the popular will." *Gobitis,* 310 U.S. at 606 (Stone, J., dissenting).
9. Peters, *Judging Jehovah's Witnesses,* 27–28.
10. Ibid., 70.
11. See Manwaring, *Render unto Caesar,* 187; Francis H. Heller, "A Turning Point for Religious Liberty," 29 *Virginia Law Review* 440, 449 (1943) (observing *Gobitis* "was followed by almost countrywide enactment of flag salute statutes and rules"); ibid., 447 (noting increased nationalist sentiment, evident in flag sales and polling data); ibid., 449 ("Statutes were enacted holding the parents liable (criminally in some instances) if their children refused to salute the flag"); and Victor W. Rotnem and F. G. Folsom Jr., "Recent Restrictions upon Religious Liberty," 36 *American Political Science Review* 1053, 1062 (1942) (noting prosecutions of Jehovah's Witness parents for failing to have their children enrolled in school following expulsions). One superior court in Michigan City, Indiana, for example, convicted a Jehovah's Witness mother of contributing to the delinquency of her two daughters following their expulsions and expressly noted that this outcome flowed from *Gobitis.* See "Sect Member Mother Guilty in Salute Case—Faces Jail If Children Fail to Honor Flag," *Chicago Daily Tribune,* Aug. 9, 1942, 19.
12. *Christian Science Monitor,* June 6, 1940 (quoted in Manwaring, *Render unto Caesar,* 159). See Alpheus Thomas Mason, *Harlan Fiske Stone: Pillar of the Law* 532 (1956).
13. "The Court Abdicates," The *Christian Century,* July 3, 1940, 845, 846. *The Christian Century* also noted, "Unpopular minorities are not always adequately protected by legislative bodies or appointed boards. The Constitution and the courts are their resource." Ibid.
14. Paul L. Blakely, S.J., "Omnipotent Schoolboards," *America,* June 22, 1940, 286, 287.
15. David Tyack, *Seeking Common Ground: Public Schools in a Diverse Society* 1 (2003). Claudia Goldin, among others, has explained how the expansion of secondary education in the United States during the first third of the twentieth century created the conditions for the U.S. economy to thrive. This widespread investment in education was a uniquely American phenomenon during this era, and—indeed—for several decades thereafter. See Claudia Goldin, "America's Graduation from High School: The Evolution and Spread of Sec-

ondary Schooling in the Twentieth Century," 58 *Journal of Economic History* 345 (1998).

16. Alexis de Tocqueville, *Democracy in America* 270 (George Lawrence trans., J. P. Mayer ed., 1969) (1835).

17. *West Virginia State Board of Education v. Barnette*, 319 U.S. 624, 637 (1943).

18. *Tinker v. Des Moines Independent Community School District*, 393 U.S. 503, 506 (1969).

19. See *Digest of Education Statistics* (2016) (noting millions of students and teachers in public schools); and Nicholas Lemann, in *School: The Story of American Public Education* v (Sarah Mondale and Sarah B. Patton eds., 2001) (noting the large fraction of the U.S. population within public school buildings on school days).

20. For an elegant articulation of the idea that constitutional cases involving education reflect larger cultural anxieties, with particular attention to opinions involving freedom of expression, see Allen Rostron, "Intellectual Seriousness and the First Amendment's Protection of Free Speech for Students," 81 *University of Missouri–Kansas City Law Review* 635, 636–39 (2013).

21. Walter Lippmann, *American Inquisitors* 22–23 (1928) (quoted in Jonathan Zimmerman, *Whose America? Culture Wars in the Public Schools* 1–2 [2002]). For an impressive treatment of these controversies, see Edward J. Larson, *Summer for the Gods: The Scopes Trial and America's Continuing Debate over Science and Religion* (1997).

22. Hillary Rodham, "Children Under the Law," 43 *Harvard Educational Review* 487, 498 (1973). Rodham would not marry Bill Clinton until 1975.

23. See David Tyack, "Introduction," in *School: The Story of American Public Education* 1, 2 ("When citizens deliberate about the education of the young, they are also debating the shape of the future for the whole nation").

24. *Barnette*, 319 U.S. at 637.

25. *Brown v. Board of Education*, 347 U.S. 483, 493–94 (1954).

26. *Shelton v. Tucker*, 364 U.S. 479, 487 (1960).

27. *New Jersey v. T.L.O.*, 469 U.S. 325, 385–86 (1985) (Stevens, J., concurring in part and dissenting in part).

28. Four scholars have produced works that most closely resemble this volume. See James E. Ryan, "The Supreme Court and Public Schools," 86 *Virginia Law Review* 1335 (2000); Betsy Levin, "Educating Youth for Citizenship: The Conflict Between Authority and Individual Rights in the Public School," 95 *Yale Law Journal* 1647 (1986); Anne Proffitt Dupre, "Should Students Have Constitutional Rights? Keeping Order in the Public Schools," 65 *George Washington Law Review* 49 (1996); and Tyll van Geel, *The Courts and American Education Law* (1987). While I have learned much from each of these writings, my project differs in substantial ways. First, as a matter of audience, these works all target judges, lawyers, and legislators. While my book certainly seeks readership among those audiences, I also aim to make my work accessible to the uninitiated, for I believe that these issues demand consideration by every segment of American society. Second, as a matter of approach, my work expends substantial energy both in placing these opinions in their historical context and in making vivid the litigants' backstories. Third, as a matter of normative commitments, the views I advance in this book depart meaningfully from previous efforts. The law review articles—characteristic of the genre—espouse the most readily discernible opinions. Professor Ryan aimed to marshal an analytically defen-

sible reading of the Court's existing decisions, drawing a distinction whereby the judiciary may regulate schools acting in their social capacities, but refuses to do so when schools act in their educational capacities. For her part, Professor Dupre asserted that the Supreme Court's opinions interfered far too much with school autonomy, and in the process undermined educators' authority. To place these positions on a crude political spectrum, both viewpoints sit well to the right of the positions that I advocate herein, as I frequently—though not invariably—contend that the Court's modern jurisprudence evinces an unduly parsimonious conception of students' constitutional rights. In contrast, Professor Levin's viewpoint sits well to the left of mine, because she contends that students' constitutional rights should assume precisely the same form beyond the schoolhouse gate that they assume within the schoolhouse gate. As will become clear during the course of this volume, I believe that Professor Levin's approach would be unsound. Finally, as a matter of simple timing, the Supreme Court's jurisprudence in this arena has evolved dramatically since 2000 (when Professor Ryan's article appeared), to say nothing of the 1980s (when Professor Levin's article and Professor van Geel's book appeared). Since the turn of the century, major cases adjudicating students' constitutional rights have occurred in the following realms: the First Amendment's Free Speech Clause, the First Amendment's Establishment Clause, the Fourth Amendment's prohibition on unreasonable searches, the Fifth Amendment's right to remain silent, and the Fourteenth Amendment's Equal Protection Clause. At a minimum, then, this book is necessary to account for the major constitutional developments that have transpired during the last eighteen years.

29. *Elk Grove Unified School District v. Newdow*, 542 U.S. 1, 15 (2004).
30. Alexander M. Bickel, "Ninety-Six Congressmen Versus the Nine Justices," *New Republic*, April 23, 1956, 11, 13. For an early claim that the Constitution does not touch education, see Ellwood P. Cubberley, *Public Education in the United States: A Study and Interpretation of American Educational History* 54 (1919) ("By the tenth amendment to the Constitution . . . the control of schools and education passed, as one of the unmentioned powers thus reserved, to the people of the different States to handle in any manner which they saw fit"). For a more recent claim, which elicited Bickel's response, see "Text of 96 Congressmen's Declaration on Integration," *New York Times*, March 12, 1956, 19 (known as "the Southern Manifesto") ("The original Constitution does not mention education. Neither does the Fourteenth Amendment nor any other Amendment.").
31. Joel Klein, *Lessons of Hope: How to Fix Our Schools* xv (2014). For judicial opinions that invoke the belief in local control over schools as a justification for nonengagement, see *United States v. Lopez*, 514 U.S. 549, 565–66 (1995); ibid., 580–81 (Kennedy, J., concurring); and *Milliken v. Bradley*, 418 U.S. 717, 741–42 (1974). For similar reasoning in the legal literature, see Anne Proffitt Dupre, *Speaking Up: The Unintended Costs of Free Speech in Public Schools* 31 (2009) ("After *Tinker*, the last word regarding student speech within this singularly local endeavor—the schoolhouse—resides in unelected federal judges, rather than elected school board members or their agents (school principals)"). For works chronicling the expanded federal role within the educational sphere, see Gareth Davies, *See Government Grow: Education Politics from Johnson to Reagan* (2007); Carl F. Kaestle and Marshall S. Smith, "The Federal Role in Ele-

mentary and Secondary Education, 1940–1980," 52 *Harvard Education Review* 384 (1982); and William J. Reese, *America's Public Schools: From the Common School to "No Child Left Behind"* (2005).

32. *Barnette*, 319 U.S. at 640. See J. Harvie Wilkinson III, "*Goss v. Lopez:* The Supreme Court as School Superintendent," 1975 *Supreme Court Review* 25, 63 (contending that in recent education decisions "the modern Court has demonstrated a faith that judicial competence knows few horizons"); and Lino A. Graglia, "Constitutional Law Without the Constitution: The Supreme Court's Remaking of America," in *"A Country I Do Not Recognize": The Legal Assault on American Values* 1, 29–30 (Robert H. Bork ed., 2005) (contending that the Court's education decisions demonstrate unwarranted faith in matters beyond its ken).

33. Joshua M. Dunn and Martin R. West, "The Supreme Court as School Board Revisited," in *From Schoolhouse to Courthouse: The Judiciary's Role in American Education* 3, 4 (Joshua M. Dunn and Martin R. West eds., 2009).

34. *Hobson v. Hansen*, 269 F. Supp. 401, 517 (D.D.C. 1967). See also Rodham, "Children Under the Law," 506 ("Legislation granting rights in either category probably is preferable to judicial opinions decreeing them, but both governmental branches should be pressed to reexamine and revise children's status under the law. Legal positions will contribute to a new social attitude toward children's rights.").

35. For prominent scholars who have portrayed the Supreme Court as a fragile institution, one that overwhelmingly reflects the consensus views of the American people, see, for example, Barry Friedman, *The Will of the People: How Public Opinion Has Influenced the Supreme Court and Shaped the Meaning of the Constitution* (2009); and Michael J. Klarman, *From Jim Crow to Civil Rights: The Supreme Court and the Struggle for Racial Equality* (2004). For a related idea, see Jack M. Balkin, "What *Brown* Teaches Us about Constitutional Theory," 90 *Virginia Law Review* 1537, 1546 (2004). For a foundational work that inspired much of the subsequent skepticism of the judiciary's role in American society, see Gerald N. Rosenberg, *The Hollow Hope: Can Courts Bring About Social Change?* (1991). For works that challenge these conceptions of an enfeebled Supreme Court, see Justin Driver, "Why Law Should Lead," *New Republic*, April 8, 2010, 28; Justin Driver, "The Consensus Constitution," 89 *Texas Law Review* 755 (2011); Justin Driver, "Constitutional Outliers," 81 *University of Chicago Law Review* 929 (2014); Justin Driver, "Reactionary Rhetoric and Liberal Legal Academia," 123 *Yale Law Journal* 2616 (2014); and Richard H. Pildes, "Is the Supreme Court a 'Majoritarian' Institution?," 2010 *Supreme Court Review* 103.

36. See Corinna Barrett Lain, "God, Civic Virtue, and the American Way: Reconstructing *Engel*," 67 *Stanford Law Review* 479 (2015).

37. *Barnette*, 319 U.S. at 637.

38. See, for example, *Pickering v. Board of Education*, 391 U.S. 563 (1968) (articulating a standard governing teachers' free speech rights); *Board of Education v. Rowley*, 458 U.S. 176 (1982) (interpreting the All Handicapped Children Act, a predecessor to the IDEA); *Regents of the University of California v. Bakke*, 438 U.S. 265 (1978) (upholding the permissibility of affirmative action in higher education); Rodney A. Smolla, *The Constitution Goes to College: Five Constitutional Ideas That Have Shaped the American University* (2011); Mark Kelman

and Gillian Lester, *Jumping the Queue: An Inquiry into the Legal Treatment of Students with Learning Disabilities* (1997); and David Rubin and Steven Greenhouse, *The Rights of Teachers: The Basic ACLU Guide to a Teacher's Constitutional Rights* (1983). For an insightful cultural history of disputes over teachers in the United States, see Dana Goldstein, *The Teacher Wars: A History of America's Most Embattled Profession* (2014).

1 EARLY ENCOUNTERS WITH RACE, CULTURE, RELIGION, AND PATRIOTISM

1. For helpful background on and analysis of *Cumming v. Richmond County Board of Education*, 175 U.S. 528 (1899), see J. Morgan Kousser, "Separate but *Not* Equal: The Supreme Court's First Decision on Racial Discrimination in Schools," 46 *Journal of Southern History* 17, 28 (1980); C. Ellen Connally, "Justice Harlan's 'Great Betrayal'? A Reconsideration of *Cumming v. Richmond County Board of Education*," 25 *Journal of Supreme Court History* 72 (2000); Leroy Davis, *A Clashing of the Soul: John Hope and the Dilemma of African American Leadership and Black Higher Education in the Early Twentieth Century* 33–34 (1988); Michael J. Klarman, *From Jim Crow to Civil Rights: The Supreme Court and the Struggle for Racial Equality* 45–52, 57–60 (2004); Richard Kluger, *Simple Justice: The History of* Brown v. Board of Education *and Black America's Struggle for Equality* 82 (2004 ed.) (1975); and Linda Przybyszewski, *The Republic According to John Marshall Harlan* 99–102 (1999).
2. "The Ware High School," *Augusta Chronicle*, Dec. 24, 1897, 4.
3. "The Ware High School," *Augusta Chronicle*, March 25, 1898, 4.
4. *Cumming*, 175 U.S. at 544.
5. Ibid., 545.
6. Editorial, *Cleveland Gazette*, Dec. 30, 1899, 2. See also "The Ware High School Case," *Augusta Chronicle*, Dec. 19, 1899, 1; "No Negro High School," *Macon Telegraph*, Dec. 19, 1899, 2; "Fourteenth Amendment Decision," *Washington Post*, Dec. 19, 1899, 5; Comment, "Schools," 9 *Yale Law Journal* 227, 229 (1899); and Note, "Constitutional Law," 6 *Virginia Law Register* 57, 57 (1900).
7. See Kousser, "Separate but *Not* Equal," 43–44; James D. Anderson, *The Education of Blacks in the South, 1860–1935* 192–93 (1988). For a probing examination of whether passing should be regarded as an act of racial disloyalty, see Randall Kennedy, *Sellout: The Politics of Racial Betrayal* 144–85 (2008).
8. Diane Ravitch, *Left Back: A Century of Battles over School Reform* 367–68 (2000); Klarman, *From Jim Crow to Civil Rights*, 46–47.
9. Klarman, *From Jim Crow to Civil Rights*, 43, 45–47. For a related formulation, see Erwin Chemerinsky, "Separate and Unequal: American Public Education Today," 52 *American University Law Review* 1461 (2003). See also *Plessy v. Ferguson*, 163 U.S. 537, 544–45, 551 (1896) (identifying Congress's decision to impose racial segregation on Washington, D.C.'s public schools as a sort of bedrock form of segregation that did not violate the Fourteenth Amendment).
10. *Plessy*, 163 U.S. at 540 (quoting Separate Car Act, 1890 La. Acts. No. 111, 152 [1890]).
11. Ibid., 550.
12. See Klarman, *From Jim Crow to Civil Rights*, 45–47; and Justin Driver, "The

Significance of the Frontier in American Constitutional Law," 2011 *Supreme Court Review* 345, 363–69.

13. G. Edward White, *The American Judicial Tradition: Profiles of Leading American Judges* 109 (3d ed. 2007).

14. See Kousser, "Separate but *Not* Equal," 40–42 (recounting various explanations for Harlan's vote in *Cumming*); Connally, "Justice Harlan's 'Great Betrayal'?," 86 (advancing a sympathetic assessment of Harlan's vote in *Cumming*); and Benno C. Schmidt Jr., "Principle and Prejudice: The Supreme Court and Race in the Progressive Era," 82 *Columbia Law Review* 444, 470 (1982) (contending "more has been made of *Cumming* . . . than is justified, since the case was mishandled by counsel").

15. *Plessy*, 163 U.S. at 559 (Harlan, J. dissenting).

16. Ibid., 561.

17. Ibid., 559. For a prominent article criticizing the most famous portion of Harlan's dissent in *Plessy*, see Neil Gotanda, "A Critique of 'Our Constitution Is Color-Blind,'" 44 *Stanford Law Review* 1 (1991).

18. See Mark V. Tushnet, "The Politics of Equality in Constitutional Law: The Equal Protection Clause, Dr. Du Bois, and Charles Hamilton Houston," 74 *Journal of American History* 884, 886 (1987).

19. My appraisal of Justice Harlan's position on segregated schools tracks the assessments articulated by some previous scholars. See Kousser, "Separate but *Not* Equal," 42 (contending Harlan "simply desired the result in *Cumming*"); and Przybyszewski, *Republic According to John Marshall Harlan*, 100–101 (contending that, in Harlan's view, public schools involved social rights but that travel accommodations involved civil rights).

20. For helpful factual background and analysis of *Lum v. Rice*, see Jeannie Rhee, "In Black and White: Chinese in the Mississippi Delta," 19 *Journal of Supreme Court History* 117, 122–25 (1994); G. Edward White, "The Lost Episode of Gong Lum v. Rice," 18 *Green Bag* 2d 191 (2015); Klarman, *From Jim Crow to Civil Rights*, 146–48; Kluger, *Simple Justice*, 120–21; Taunya Lovell Banks, "Both Edges of the Margin: Blacks and Asians in Mississippi Masala, Barriers to Coalition Building," 5 *Asian Law Journal* 7, 13–18 (1998); and James W. Loewen, *The Mississippi Chinese: Between Black and White* 27, 66–68, 74–83 (2d ed. 1988).

21. Brief for Plaintiff, *Lum*, 275 U.S. 78, at *9–*10 (1927).

22. Ibid., 13–14.

23. Ibid., 10. In a similar vein, the brief stated, "[H]as not the Chinese citizen the same right to protection that the Caucasian citizen has? Are they not all equal before the law? . . . Can we arrogate to ourselves the superior right to so organize the public school system as to protect our racial integrity without regard to the interests or welfare of citizens of other races?" Ibid., 14.

24. Brief for the Defendants, *Lum*, 275 U.S. 78, *36 (1927).

25. *Lum v. Rice*, 275 U.S. 78, 85 (1927).

26. Ibid., 87.

27. Ibid., 86–87.

28. Arthur E. Sutherland, "Book Review," 79 *Harvard Law Review* 222, 226 (1965) (reviewing Alpheus Thomas Mason, *William Howard Taft: Chief Justice* [1964]). See "A. Sutherland, Legal Scholar, Is Dead at 71," *Harvard Crimson*, March 10, 1973. Professor Michael Klarman's view of *Lum v. Rice* sits almost dia-

metrically opposite from Professor Sutherland's portrayal. In Klarman's view, "For the Court to have invalidated school segregation in 1927 seems almost inconceivable." Klarman, *From Jim Crow to Civil Rights,* 147.

29. "Race Segregation," *Los Angeles Times,* Nov. 23, 1927, A4. See "Upholds Segregation of Chinese in Schools: Supreme Court Validates Mississippi Action on Girl Barred from White Classes," *New York Times,* Nov. 22, 1927, 14; "Rules Chinese Girl Must Go to Negro School," *Chicago Tribune,* Nov. 22, 1927, 38; and "Supreme Court Upholds Segregation in Schools," *Washington Post,* Nov. 22, 1927, 14.

30. "Constitutional Law," 37 *Yale Law Journal* 518, 519 (1928); and "Recent Important Decisions," 2 *Mississippi Law Journal* 251, 258 (1929). See also William Gorin, "Constitutional Law," 8 *Boston University Law Review* 127, 134 (1928) (straightforwardly recounting *Lum*); and Hoke F. Henderson, "Separation of Races in Schools," 32 *Law Notes* 141, 150 (1928) (observing that race prejudice "is not created by law and probably cannot be changed by law").

31. "True to Form," *Chicago Defender,* Oct. 22, 1927, A2. For a recent book chronicling the significance of *The Chicago Defender* to the nation, see Ethan Michaeli, *The Defender: How the Legendary Black Newspaper Changed America* (2016).

32. "Constitutional Law," 16 *California Law Review* 346, 347 (1928); and Comment, "Racial Segregation in Public Education: *Gong Lum v. Rice,*" 2 *St. John's Law Review* 215, 216 (1928).

33. For insightful background on and analysis of *Meyer v. Nebraska,* see William G. Ross, *Forging New Freedom: Nativism, Education, and the Constitution, 1917–1927* 2–5 (1994); Barbara Bennett Woodhouse, "'Who Owns the Child?' *Meyer* and *Pierce* and the Child as Property," 33 *William and Mary Law Review* 995, 1077 (1992); and Arthur F. Mullen, *Western Democrat* 214–20 (1940).

34. "Cleaning the Language," *New York Times,* July 7, 1918, 38.

35. Ibid.; Louise Weinberg, "The McReynolds Mystery Solved," 89 *Denver University Law Review* 133, 136 (2011).

36. "A Help to Americanization," *Washington Post,* Dec. 28, 1919, 4. See also John Walker Harrington, "German Becoming Dead Tongue Here," *New York Times,* July 14, 1918, 34.

37. "Nebraska Germans Remain Unchanged," *Boston Globe,* Sept. 21, 1919, E5. See "Making English Constitutional," *New York Tribune,* Feb. 26, 1923, 8 ("It is astounding that any one can question the right and the necessity of making English the fundamental language in all schools in America").

38. "Urges Unity of Language," *New York Times,* Nov. 10, 1918, 19.

39. "Forbid New German Classes in Schools," *New York Times,* May 25, 1918, 14.

40. Sheila Curran Bernard and Sarah Mondale, "'You Are an American,'" in *School: The Story of American Public Education* 95 (Sarah Mondale and Sarah B. Patton eds., 2001).

41. Ellwood P. Cubberley, *Public Education in the United States* 341 (1919). For information on Cubberley's background, see Ravitch, *Left Back,* 95–98; and Bernard and Mondale, "'You Are an American,'" 97–98.

42. Ellwood P. Cubberley, *Changing Conceptions of Education* 15 (1909); and Cubberley, *Public Education in the United States,* 342. In 1909, Cubberley identified schools as having a large role to play in achieving nativist ends by dissolving immigrant enclaves. "Everywhere these people tend to settle in groups or settlements, and to set up here their national manners, customs, and obser-

vances," Cubberley instructed. "Our task is to break up these groups or settlements, to assimilate and amalgamate these people as a part of our American
race, and to implant in their children, so far as can be done, the Anglo-Saxon
conception of righteousness, law and order, and popular government." Cubberley, *Changing Conceptions of Education*, 15.

43. Various authorities arrive at slightly different conclusions regarding precisely
how many states enacted language prohibitions during this era. See Ross, *Forging New Freedoms*, 61 (contending thirty-seven states enacted foreign-language
prohibitions); Rosemary C. Salomone, *True American: Language, Identity, and
the Education of Immigrant Children* 35 (2010) (contending that thirty-four
states enacted foreign-language prohibitions); and David Tyack, *Seeking Common Ground: Public Schools in a Diverse Society* 77 (2003) (contending that thirty-
five states enacted foreign-language prohibitions).

44. *Meyer v. Nebraska*, 262 U.S. 390, 400 (1923).

45. Ibid., 401.

46. Ibid., 402.

47. Ibid., 399.

48. Ibid., 400.

49. *Bartels v. Iowa*, 262 U.S. 404, 412 (1923) (Holmes, J., dissenting) (emphasis
added).

50. "The Right to Learn Foreign Tongues," *New York Times*, June 6, 1923, 20.

51. "Foreign Language Decision," *Washington Post*, June 6, 1923, 6. *The Washington Post* also commented, "In other lands and at other times discrimination
against certain languages has been made the engine of oppression all the more
cruel because it was of the intellectual kind. The interpretation given by the
Supreme Court, in [*Meyer*,] . . . will effectually prevent any such sinister practice in the United States." Ibid.

52. "Back to Freedom," *Boston Globe*, June 6, 1923, 16. For additional newspaper
commentary praising *Meyer*, see "The Decision in the Language Cases," *Chicago Tribune*, June 26, 1923, 8 (contending the opinion should elicit "satisfac-
tion not alone among foreign born persons, but also among the greater part of
native born Americans").

53. Ellwood P. Cubberley, "The American School Program from the Standpoint
of the Nation," 61 *National Education Association: Addresses and Proceedings of the
Sixty-First Annual Meeting* 180, 181 (1923).

54. I. N. Edwards, "State Educational Policy and the Supreme Court of the United
States," 26 *Elementary School Journal* 22, 25, 29 (1925). At various times in his
article, Professor Edwards attempted to assume a pose of neutrality toward
Meyer. But the article—when read as a whole—leaves no doubt that its author
construes the opinion as representing improper judicial encroachment into the
educational arena. See ibid., 29 ("[S]tate educational policy is, as a rule, not a
matter of law").

55. R. T. W. Duke Jr. and Beirne Stedman, "The Fourteenth Amendment: Aliens
Protected by It, but the English Language Not," 9 *Virginia Law Register* 371,
378 (1923).

56. Ibid., 379.

57. Charles E. Hughes, "Liberty and Law," 11 *American Bar Association Journal*
563, 566 (1925).

58. See Ross, *Forging New Freedoms*, 206.

59. For illuminating background, context, and analysis of *Pierce v. Society of Sisters*, see Paula Abrams, *Cross Purposes:* Pierce v. Society of Sisters *and the Struggle over Compulsory Education* (2009); Tyll van Geel, *The Courts and American Education Law* 21–22 (1987); Ross, *Forging New Freedoms*, 148–73; David Tyack, Thomas James, and Aaron Benavot, *Law and the Shaping of Public Education, 1785–1954* 177–90 (1987); John Higham, *Strangers in the Land: Patterns of American Nativism, 1860–1925* 288–91, 296–99 (2d ed. 1965); David B. Tyack, "The Perils of Pluralism: The Background of the *Pierce* Case," 74 *American Historical Review* 74, 74–77 (1968); Kenneth B. O'Brien Jr., "Education, Americanization, and the Supreme Court: The 1920's," 13 *American Quarterly* 161 (1961); "He That Soweth Sparingly," *Portland Telegram*, Oct. 26, 1922, 1; "Klan Candidate Carries Oregon," *New York Times*, Nov. 8, 1922, 3; and "What the Klan Did in Oregon Elections," *New York Times*, Dec. 3, 1922, 1.

60. See Abrams, *Cross Purposes*, 125–26; WPA Adult Education Project, *History of Education in Portland* 101–5 (Howard McKinley Corning and Alfred Powers eds., 1937); and Sisters of the Holy Names of Jesus and Mary, *Gleanings of Fifty Years: The Sisters of Holy Names of Jesus and Mary in the Northwest, 1859–1909* 123–27 (1909). In addition to the Society of Sisters, a private school called Hill Military Academy challenged the Oregon referendum.

61. *Pierce v. Society of Sisters*, 268 U.S. 510, 534 (1925).

62. Ibid., 534–35.

63. Ibid., 535.

64. "Intolerance Rebuked," *Los Angeles Times*, June 10, 1925, A4.

65. "A Bad Law Voided," *New York Times*, June 2, 1925, 22.

66. "Child Is Not the Mere Creature of the State," *Boston Globe*, June 2, 1925, A6.

67. "The Oregon School Law," *Chicago Tribune*, June 3, 1925, 8.

68. See "The Blight of Standardization," *Washington Post*, June 7, 1925, E1 (contending the Oregon measure had "practically . . . taken the child away from parental control and made it the ward or the chattel of the State"); "The Supreme Court Speaks," *America*, June 13, 1925, 208 (calling the opinion "a victory over the forces which would make every American the abject creature of an omnipotent state"); and "Oregon School Law Invalid," *Journal of Education*, June 4, 1925, 652 (touting the Court for its rejection of the notion that "the individual is a chattel of the ruling authorities").

69. "The Law and the Schools," 11 *Virginia Law Register* 230, 231 (1925). For a more sanguine assessment of *Society of Sisters*—one that is representative of the approving contemporaneous commentary—see Clarence E. Martin, "The American Judiciary and Religious Liberty," 13 *Virginia Law Register* 641, 656–57 (1928).

70. Felix Frankfurter, "Can the Supreme Court Guarantee Toleration?," *New Republic*, June 17, 1925, 85 (reprinted in *Felix Frankfurter on the Supreme Court* 174, 175 [Philip Kurland ed., 1970]).

71. Ibid., 86.

72. Ibid. See Plato, "The Apology of Socrates," in *The Trials of Socrates: Six Classic Texts* 26, 26n1 (C. D. C. Reeve ed., 2002) (editor's note).

73. Frankfurter, "Can the Supreme Court Guarantee Toleration?," 86.

74. Ibid., 87.

75. "Private Schools in Oregon," *Los Angeles Times*, Nov. 12, 1922, 4. See generally "Oregon's Outlawing of Church Schools," *Literary Digest*, Jan. 6, 1923,

34. For a leading constitutional authority who has portrayed *Society of Sisters* as a case of modest significance because it involved the judicial invalidation of a legislative "outlier," see Klarman, *From Jim Crow to Civil Rights*, 453–54. For an analytical critique of this influential concept within constitutional law, see Justin Driver, "Constitutional Outliers," 81 *University of Chicago Law Review* 929 (2014). In the terminology that I offer in that article, *Society of Sisters* can be regarded as an "upstart" variant of outlier.

76. "The Oregon School Law in Court," *Literary Digest*, April 18, 1925, 32. See also Tyack, James, and Benavot, *Law and the Shaping of Public Education*, 179 (noting that plans had been hatched in a dozen additional states to abolish non-public schools); "The Oregon School Law," *New York Times*, Aug. 5, 1923, E4 (recounting plots to abolish nonpublic schools in California and Washington); Ernest Harvier, "What the Klan Did in Oregon Elections," *New York Times*, Dec. 3, 1922, 40 ("The 'school question' has always been a live wire in American politics. . . . The experiment of Oregon . . . will be of interest elsewhere.").

77. "A Bad Law Voided," *New York Times*, June 2, 1925, 22.

78. "The Oregon and Nebraska Acts," *Chicago Tribune*, Oct. 19, 1924, 8.

79. Laurence H. Tribe, *American Constitutional Law* 902–4 (1978).

80. See Robert H. Bork, *The Tempting of America: The Political Seduction of the Law* 49 (1990) ("[B]oth of those decisions could have been laid under the guarantee of freedom of speech in the first amendment, and the application of Oregon's statute to the Society of Sisters might have been invalidated as well under that amendment's guarantee of the free exercise of religion"); *Griswold v. Connecticut*, 381 U.S. 479, 482 (1965) (opinion of Douglas, J.) (identifying *Pierce* and *Meyer* as First Amendment opinions); *Troxel v. Granville*, 530 U.S. 57, 95 (2000) (Kennedy, J., dissenting) ("*Pierce* and *Meyer*, had they been decided in recent times, may well have been grounded upon First Amendment principles protecting freedom of speech, belief, and religion"). It is not altogether clear, though, that relying upon the Free Exercise Clause, taken in isolation, would suffice to invalidate Oregon's statute as applied to all entities. Even accepting its invalidation as applied to the Society of Sisters and other parochial schools, one of the challengers to the referendum was the Hill Military Academy—a private institution that was evidently unaffiliated with any church. It might well be argued that the Oregon statute should be permitted to abolish such private entities.

81. *Obergefell v. Hodges*, 135 S. Ct. 2584, 2600 (2015). Chief Justice Roberts, Justice Alito, Justice Scalia, and Justice Thomas all cast dissenting votes in the same-sex marriage case.

82. Henry Butler Schwartz, "The Foreign Language Schools of Hawaii," *School and Society*, Jan. 23, 1926, 98, 99, 101. For helpful background and analysis on *Farrington v. Tokushige*, see *Farrington v. Tokushige*, 273 U.S. 284, 290–98 (1927); Ross, *Forging New Freedoms*, 174–84; "The Cross Words at the Crossroads," *Literary Digest*, March 26, 1927, 10; O'Brien, "Education, Americanization, and the Supreme Court," 170–71; and Mark G. Yudof et al., *Educational Policy and the Law* 53–55 (5th ed. 2012).

83. *Tokushige*, 273 U.S. at 298.

84. Ibid., 299.

85. Ibid., 298.

86. Ibid., 298–99 (emphasis added).

87. "Hawaii's School Problem," *New York Times*, Feb. 23, 1927, 22.

88. "Hawaii, Oriental or Occidental?," *New York Times*, July 24, 1927, E8.

89. Ross, *Forging New Freedoms*, 183.

90. "Cross Words at the Crossroads," 10.

91. See Schwartz, "Foreign Language Schools of Hawaii," 102–3.

92. Michael J. Klarman, "Social Reform Litigation and Its Challenges: An Essay in Honor of Justice Ruth Bader Ginsburg," 32 *Harvard Journal of Law and Gender* 251, 267 (2009). See also David E. Bernstein and Ilya Somin, "Judicial Power and Civil Rights Reconsidered," 114 *Yale Law Journal* 591, 641 (2004) (describing McReynolds as "notoriously racist and anti-Semitic"). For an insightful overview of Justice McReynolds, see *The Forgotten Memoir of John Knox: A Year in the Life of a Supreme Court Clerk in FDR's Washington* vii–xxii (Dennis J. Hutchinson and David J. Garrow eds., 2002).

93. Weinberg, "McReynolds Mystery Solved," 142.

94. See ibid., 159.

95. My appraisal of Justice McReynolds was influenced by Professor Ross's incisive book. See Ross, *Forging New Freedoms*, 186–88.

96. For illuminating scholarship on *West Virginia State Board of Education v. Barnette*, 319 U.S. 624 (1943), including its background, see David R. Manwaring, *Render unto Caesar: The Flag-Salute Controversy* (1962); Shawn Francis Peters, *Judging Jehovah's Witnesses: Religious Persecution and the Dawn of the Rights Revolution* 244–59 (2000); Vincent Blasi and Seana V. Shiffrin, "The Pledge of Allegiance and the Freedom of Thought," in *Constitutional Law Stories* 433–75 (Michael C. Dorf ed., 2004); Betsy Levin, "Educating Youth for Citizenship: The Conflict Between Authority and Individual Rights in the Public School," 95 *Yale Law Journal* 1647 (1986); Noah Feldman, *Scorpions: The Battles and Triumphs of FDR's Great Supreme Court Justices* 226–34 (2010); Catherine J. Ross, *Lessons in Censorship: How Schools and Courts Subvert Students' First Amendment Rights* 16–21 (2015); Anne Proffitt Dupre, *Speaking Up: The Unintended Costs of Free Speech in Public Schools* 149–57 (2009); Douglas E. Abrams, "Justice Jackson and the Second Flag-Salute Case: Reason and Passion in Opinion-Writing," 36 *Journal of Supreme Court History* 30, 32–33 (2011); Leonard A. Stevens, *Salute! The Case of the Bible vs. the Flag* 125–38 (1973); and Gregory L. Peterson et al., "Recollections of *West Virginia State Board of Education v. Barnette*," 81 *St. John's Law Review* 755, 758–65 (2007).

97. "A Terrible Decision," *St. Louis Post-Dispatch*, July 24, 1940, 2C.

98. Fred Rodell, "Felix Frankfurter, Conservative," *Harper's*, Oct. 1, 1941, 449, 457. See also Laura Kalman, *Legal Realism at Yale, 1927–1960* (1986) (chronicling Rodell's disdain for Frankfurter's jurisprudence); and John Raeburn Green, "Liberty Under the Fourteenth Amendment: 1942–1943," 28 *Washington University Law Quarterly* 251, 263 (1943) ("Seldom has any decision of the Court been so generally and so sharply criticized"). See also Francis H. Heller, "A Turning Point for Religious Liberty," 29 *Virginia Law Review* 440, 450–52 (1943) ("Law Review comments were virtually unanimous in rejecting the majority view"); and Henry Steele Commager, *Majority Rule and Minority Rights* 3 (1943) ("Liberals . . . almost to a man denounced the opinion as illiberal").

99. Edward S. Corwin, *Constitutional Revolution Ltd.* 112 (1941). See also William F. Andersen, "Constitutional Law," 39 *Michigan Law Review* 149, 152 (1940)

("If individual liberties are something more than the by-product of a democratic process, if in fact they have an intrinsic value worthy of protection, it is difficult to justify a decision which subordinates a fundamental liberty to a legislative program of questionable worth"). For a broad sampling of the substantial academic criticisms of *Gobitis*, see Heller, "Turning Point for Religious Liberty," 451–52.

100. Beulah Amidon, "Can We Afford Martyrs?," *Survey Graphic*, Sept. 1940, 457. See Victor W. Rotnem and F. G. Folsom Jr., "Recent Restrictions upon Religious Liberty," 36 *American Political Science Review* 1053, 1061–63 (1942). After a violent outbreak occurred in New England post-*Gobitis*, the *New York Herald Tribune* editorialized in 1940, "We have the 'liberal' members of the Supreme Court to thank—at least in part—for the religious riots which have been breaking out in Maine. . . . [T]he Supreme Court's recent decision that the Jehovah's Witnesses must salute the flag seems to have convinced several hundred Maine rustics that it is their personal responsibility to see this decree carried out." Peters, *Judging Jehovah's Witnesses*, 82. Similarly, another observer stated, "It is no accident, that this long and violent succession of outrages against the Witnesses in recent weeks was coincident with the unfortunate decision of the Supreme Court refusing to interfere with the action of authorities in demanding the salute." Ibid.

101. *Jones v. Opelika*, 316 U.S. 584, 624 (1942) (dissent of Black, J., Douglas, J., and Murphy, J.). See Robert H. Jackson, *The Struggle for Judicial Supremacy: A Study of a Crisis in American Power Politics* 284, 284n48 (1941).

102. Richard A. Posner, *The Problems of Jurisprudence* 147 (1990).

103. *Barnette*, 319 U.S. at 641–42. For *Barnette's* language subtly reframing the case as involving free speech, see ibid., 635–36 ("The question which underlies the flag salute controversy is whether such a ceremony so touching matters of opinion and political attitude may be imposed upon the individual by official authority under powers committed to any political organization under our Constitution"); ibid., 641 ("Those who begin coercive elimination of dissent soon find themselves exterminating dissenters. Compulsory unification of opinion achieves only the unanimity of the graveyard. It seems trite but necessary to say that the First Amendment to our Constitution was designed to avoid these ends by avoiding these beginnings.").

104. Ibid., 642. My reading of *Barnette* is influenced by the work of Professor Christopher Eisgruber, who is now president of Princeton University. As Eisgruber has argued, "Jackson and his audience . . . have one peculiarly American set of stars in mind throughout the opinion: the stars on the flag. Throughout [*Barnette*], but especially by his reference to the 'constitutional constellation,' Jackson identifies America's flag with America's constitutional principles. The closing passage is a form of flag-waving." Christopher L. Eisgruber, "Is the Supreme Court an Educative Institution?," 67 *NYU Law Review* 961, 979 (1992).

105. *Barnette*, 319 U.S. at 640.

106. Ibid., 637–38.

107. *Minersville School District v. Gobitis*, 310 U.S. 586, 600 (1940).

108. *Barnette*, 319 U.S. at 637.

109. Ibid., 646–47 (Frankfurter, J., dissenting). Justices Roberts and Reed also dissented in *Barnette*, but neither wrote an opinion nor joined Justice Frankfurt-

er's dissent. See ibid., 642–43. See Feldman, *Scorpions*, 229–31 (noting that a few of Frankfurter's colleagues pleaded with him to remove the allusion to his religious identity); Dupre, *Speaking Up*, 156 (analyzing Frankfurter's reference to his Jewish identity in *Barnette*); and H. N. Hirsch, *The Enigma of Felix Frankfurter* 135–38 (2d ed. 2014) (1981) (analyzing Frankfurter's reference to his Jewish identity in *Barnette*).

110. *Barnette*, 319 U.S. at 666–67 (Frankfurter, J., dissenting).

111. Ibid., 670–71 (emphasis added).

112. Archibald MacLeish and E. F. Prichard Jr., *Law and Politics: Occasional Papers of Felix Frankfurter, 1913–1938* 195–97 (1939) (reprinting "Can the Supreme Court Guarantee Toleration?").

113. "Blot Removed," *Time*, June 21, 1943, 16.

114. "Goodbye to Gobitis," *America*, June 26, 1943, 324.

115. "Score for Freedom No. 2," *Saturday Evening Post*, July 10, 1943, 104. See "Victory for Freedom," *Washington Post*, May 5, 1943, 14 ("Both the tenets and the evangelical practices of the Witnesses are distinctly unpopular with many Americans. . . . The question, however, is not whether the Witnesses have invited persecution but whether religious liberty can be said to exist where the suppression of any sect, however fanatical, is given a legal sanction."). The *New York Times* editorial board also stated post-*Barnette*, "The very fact that the conduct and manners of a good many [Jehovah's Witnesses] strike some of us as outrageous makes the test more searching." "The Court on the Flag Salute," *New York Times*, June 19, 1943, 12.

116. "A Decision That Decides," *Wall Street Journal*, June 16, 1943, 6.

117. W. H. Lawrence, "Civil Liberties Gain by the Flag Decision," *New York Times*, June 20, 1943, E10.

118. Thomas Reed Powell, "The Flag-Salute Case," *New Republic*, July 5, 1943, 16, 18. See Manwaring, *Render unto Caesar*, 236–37 (recounting contemporaneous reactions to *Barnette* in law reviews).

119. Madaline Kinter Remmlein, "Editorial Notes," 12 *George Washington Law Review* 55, 80 (1943).

120. Ibid., 78.

121. As Manwaring has noted, "On the whole . . . state and local compliance with the *Barnette* ruling was immediate and substantial." Manwaring, *Render unto Caesar*, 242. Furthermore, Manwaring has stated, "The *Barnette* decision settled the flag-salute controversy, apparently permanently; the issue has not arisen again since 1946. In this aspect, . . . *Barnette* was applied willingly and to the full extent of its logic by the state courts." Ibid., 243.

122. Ross, *Lessons in Censorship*, 21 (citing Letter, Robert H. Jackson to Armistead Brown, July 13, 1943, box 127, folder 11, Robert Jackson Papers, Library of Congress).

2   FREEDOM OF EXPRESSION

FROM BLACK ARMBANDS TO BONG HITS 4 JESUS

1. For insightful background on *Tinker v. Des Moines Independent Community School District*, see John W. Johnson, "Behind the Scenes in Iowa's Great Case: What Is Not in the Official Record of *Tinker v. Des Moines Independent Com-*

munity School District," 48 *Drake Law Review* 473 (2000); and John W. Johnson, *The Struggle for Student Rights:* Tinker v. Des Moines *and the 1960s* 1–15, 29–66 (1997). See also *Tinker v. Des Moines Independent Community School District,* 393 U.S. 503, 504–5, 509n3 (1969); Joint Appendix, *Tinker v. Des Moines Independent Community School District,* at *15–*18, *22–*23, *26–*29, *30–*32, *45, *49–*51 (1968); Donald Janson, "Des Moines Stirs Liberties Protest," *New York Times,* Dec. 22, 1965, 3; Jack Magarrell, "Extend Ban on Arm Bands; D.M. School Board Split on Issue, 4–3," *Des Moines Register,* Dec. 22, 1965, 1; Stephen Seplow, "Dispute over High School Chant of 'Beat Viet Cong,'" *Des Moines Register,* Dec. 20, 1965, 1; and Jamin B. Raskin, "No Enclaves of Totalitarianism: The Triumph and Unrealized Promise of the *Tinker* Decision," 58 *American University Law Review* 1193 (2009).

2. *Tinker,* 393 U.S. at 506.
3. Ibid., 511. See ibid., 510–11 (criticizing Des Moines schools for selecting one "particular symbol—black armbands worn to exhibit opposition to this Nation's involvement in Vietnam—[and] singl[ing it] out for prohibition").
4. Ibid., 512 (quoting *Keyishian v. Board of Regents,* 385 U.S. 589, 603 [1967]) (internal quotation marks omitted, alteration in original).
5. Ibid.
6. Ibid., 507–8.
7. Ibid., 514.
8. Ibid., 512–13 (quoting *Burnside v. Byars,* 363 F.2d 744, 749 [5th Cir. 1966]).
9. Ibid., 509.
10. Ibid., 508–9 (internal citation omitted). Both Justice Stewart and Justice White authored brief concurring opinions. See ibid., 514–15 (Stewart, J., concurring); and ibid., 515 (White, J., concurring).
11. Fred P. Graham, "High Court Upholds a Student Protest," *New York Times,* Feb. 25, 1969, 1, 25.
12. *Tinker,* 393 U.S. at 522 (Black, J., dissenting).
13. Ibid., 515, 518. See ibid., 525–26 ("I, for one, am not fully persuaded that school pupils are wise enough, even with this Court's expert help from Washington, to run the 23,390 public school systems in our 50 States").
14. Ibid., 525.
15. Ibid., 524–25.
16. Ibid., 518, 525. Justice Harlan also wrote a short dissenting opinion, which would have accorded broader deference to school authorities than *Tinker* allowed. See ibid., 526 (Harlan, J., dissenting).
17. "The Armband Case," *Des Moines Register,* Feb. 27, 1969, 8.
18. "Rights for Students," *Boston Globe,* Feb. 27, 1969, 14.
19. "Armbands Yes, Miniskirts No," *New York Times,* Feb. 26, 1969, 46.
20. Fred P. Graham, "Freedom of Speech, but Not License," *New York Times,* March 2, 1969, E11.
21. Charles Alan Wright, "The Constitution on Campus," 22 *Vanderbilt Law Review* 1027, 1053, 1086 (1969). See also Theodore F. Denno, "Mary Beth Tinker Takes the Constitution to School," 38 *Fordham Law Review* 35 (1969).
22. "Freedom of Expression in the Schools," *Washington Post,* Feb. 26, 1969, A22. *The New York Times* called Black's dissent in *Tinker* "peppery." "Armbands Yes, Miniskirts No," 46.
23. "Armband Case," 8.

24. "Rights for Students," 14.

25. "Revolt Invited in the Romper Set," *Chicago Tribune*, Feb. 26, 1969, 20.

26. Johnson, "Behind the Scenes in Iowa's Great Case," 486, 488.

27. Roger K. Newman, *Hugo Black: A Biography* 592 (2d ed. 1997) (1994).

28. See, for example, Catherine J. Ross, *Lessons in Censorship: How Schools and Courts Subvert Students' First Amendment Rights* 32 (2015).

29. Newman, *Hugo Black*, 592.

30. For one case where Justice Black refused to recognize the free speech rights of civil rights protesters, see *Adderley v. Florida*, 385 U.S. 39 (1966). See Lyle Denniston, "High Court Studies Classroom Protests," *Washington Evening Star*, Nov. 13, 1968, D16 (noting Black's cutting questions at oral argument); Oral Argument Transcript 19–23, *Tinker*, 393 U.S. 503; and Johnson, *Struggle for Student Rights*, 161. The oral argument in *Tinker* can be heard on the Oyez website.

31. Newman, *Hugo Black*, 591. Justice Black did not send the letter to his daughter-in-law indicating that he was sorry to learn the news of his grandson's suspension until December 13, 1968, more than one month after oral argument in *Tinker*. Ibid., 592, 707n4. The leading biography of Justice Black—written by Roger Newman—notes that his grandson was suspended from school "[a]fter" oral argument in *Tinker* but does not reveal precisely when the suspension occurred or when Black learned of it. Ibid., 592. In the unlikely situation that both of these events occurred in the tiny interval between oral argument and the Court's Conference on *Tinker*, Newman would have been incentivized to have revealed this fact, because it would have bolstered his suggestion that the suspension loomed large in Black's mind as he drafted his dissent. See ibid., 593 ("Whether or not he was trying to chasten [his son] for [contemplating a lawsuit], Black wrote his [*Tinker* dissent] with [his son's] children directly in mind"). Newman enjoyed extensive access to the parents of Black's suspended grandson—interviewing both the mother and the father, even quoting from the latter's diary about interactions with the justice.

32. Laura Kalman, *Abe Fortas: A Biography* 287 (1990).

33. Ibid.

34. "Man and Woman of the Year: The Middle Americans," *Time*, Jan. 5, 1970, 10. For a useful overview of *Tinker*'s historical backdrop, see Allen Rostron, "Intellectual Seriousness and the First Amendment's Protection of Free Speech for Students," 81 *UMKC Law Review* 635, 638 (2013). For insightful examinations of President Nixon's 1968 campaign and its legal implications, see Kevin J. McMahon, *Nixon's Court: His Challenge to Judicial Liberalism and Its Political Consequences* 17–36 (2011); Michael J. Graetz and Linda Greenhouse, *The Burger Court and the Rise of the Judicial Right* (2016); and Rick Perlstein, *Nixonland: The Rise of a President and the Fracturing of America* (2008). For penetrating analysis of this *Time* issue and its implications for schooling debates, see James E. Ryan, *Five Miles Away, a World Apart: One City, Two Schools, and the Story of Educational Opportunity in Modern America* 63–64 (2010).

35. "Man and Woman of the Year: The Middle Americans," 13. A different resident of Pittsfield, Massachusetts, stated, "I don't think that [protesters] have the right to encroach upon the schools, the rules and regulations. . . . There is a movement in this country to discredit our nation." Ibid., 12.

36. *Tinker*, 393 U.S. at 509n3.
37. Daniel J. Boorstin, *The Decline of Radicalism: Reflections on America Today* 97 (1969). See ibid., xiv ("The old radicalisms were themselves rooted in a sense of sharing. But nowadays those who pass for 'radicals' are in fact desperate egolitarians. They lack the sense of community and in them we witness the decline of radicalism.").
38. The precise question asked, "Do you feel that students have the right to make their protests or not?" Hazel Erskine, "The Polls: Freedom of Speech," 34 *Public Opinion Quarterly* 483, 493 (1970).
39. *A Decade of Gallup Polls of Attitudes Toward Education, 1969–1978* 20 (Stanley M. Elam ed., 1978) ("[T]he biggest problem at the present time for the schools is the matter of discipline. This is the greatest criticism the public makes of the schools and the school officials.").
40. Seplow, "Dispute over High School Chant of 'Beat Viet Cong,'" 1. For insight into how citizens' attitudes toward the Vietnam War shifted between 1965 and 1969, and how the U.S. military's depth of engagement in Vietnam materially shifted during that time, see Scott A. Moss, "The Story of *Tinker v. Des Moines* to *Morse v. Frederick:* Similar Stories of Different Student Speech with Different Results," in *First Amendment Stories* 402–5 (Richard W. Garnett and Andrew Koppelman eds., 2012). See Joseph Carroll, "The Iraq-Vietnam Comparison," *Gallup News*, June 15, 2004, in *The Gallup Poll: Public Opinion 2004* 240–42 (Alec M. Gallup and Frank Newport eds., 2006) (observing that, in December 1965, 56 percent of respondents supported President Johnson's handling of the Vietnam War and only 26 percent of respondents did not support his handling of the war).
41. Seplow, "Dispute over High School Chant of 'Beat Viet Cong,'" 1.
42. Janson, "Des Moines Stirs Liberties Protest," 3.
43. Magarrell, "Extend Ban on Arm Bands," 1.
44. Johnson, "Behind the Scenes in Iowa's Great Case," 477.
45. Johnson, *Struggle for Student Rights*, 57–58.
46. Raskin, "No Enclaves of Totalitarianism," 1198.
47. Brief for Respondent, *Tinker*, 393 U.S. 503, 1968 WL 112603, at *6.
48. Ibid., *7; ibid., Appendix, 22–23; *Tinker*, 393 U.S. at 510.
49. Harry Kalven Jr., *The Negro and the First Amendment* 140 (1965).
50. See *Brown v. Louisiana*, 383 U.S. 131, 131n1 (1966).
51. See, for example, Richard L. Berkman, "Students in Court: Free Speech and the Functions of Schooling in America," 40 *Harvard Education Review* 567, 591 (1970) (contending *Tinker* presented an "invitation to the courts to apply . . . the 'Heckler's Veto,'" which it described as "involv[ing] a speaker whose words, while not inciting to the impartial observer, irritates to the point of violence an especially sensitive or already hostile crowd").
52. *Burnside v. Byars*, 363 F.2d 744, 746–47 (5th Cir. 1966).
53. For a captivating excavation and analysis of *Burnside* and *Blackwell*, see generally Kristi L. Bowman, "The Civil Rights Roots of *Tinker*'s Disruption Tests," 58 *American University Law Review* 1129 (2009). For first-rate historical treatments of the murders in Philadelphia, Mississippi, and assessments of the larger quest for racial equality within that state, see John Dittmer, *Local People: The Struggle for Civil Rights in Mississippi* 242–71 (1994); and Charles M. Payne,

I've Got the Light of Freedom: The Organizing Tradition and the Mississippi Freedom Struggle (1995).

54. *Burnside*, 363 F.2d at 747n4 (emphasis added).

55. Ibid., 748.

56. *Blackwell v. Issaquena County Board of Education*, 363 F.2d 749, 754 (5th Cir. 1966).

57. Ibid., 753.

58. My interpretation of *Burnside* as endorsing an actual disruption test may depart somewhat from Professor Bowman's analysis. At one point, Bowman seems to contend that *Burnside* required the actual disruption to occur because of the speakers, rather than the audience. As Bowman argues, "[I]t was the presence of disruptive *conduct* by the speakers themselves in *Blackwell* but not *Burnside* that led the Fifth Circuit to different conclusions in these two cases—not the message itself or the responsive speech or conduct of others." Bowman, "Civil Rights Roots," 1145. Admittedly, portions of *Blackwell* sound as though the opinion hinges on the fact that the students wearing the buttons created the commotion. See *Blackwell*, 363 F.2d at 752–54. But *Burnside* itself—by acknowledging the possibility that "the *presence* of 'freedom buttons'" could create a sufficient disruption to enable the principal to ban them—seems more accurately viewed as entertaining the notion that hostile audience reactions, not only boisterous speakers, may allow schools to eliminate student speech. *Burnside*, 363 F.2d at 748 (emphasis added).

59. Critiquing *Blackwell*, Professor Charles Alan Wright "wonder[ed] . . . why the school did not discipline the small number of button-wearers who created noise and disturbance rather than striking at the wearing of buttons itself." Charles Alan Wright, "The Constitution on Campus," 22 *Vanderbilt Law Review* 1027, 1053 (1969). See also *Ferrell v. Dallas Independent School District*, 392 F.2d 697, 705n1 (5th Cir. 1968) (Tuttle, J., dissenting).

60. See Erwin Chemerinsky, "The Deconstitutionalization of Education," 36 *Loyola University Chicago Law Journal* 111, 124 (2004) (calling *Tinker* "the high watermark of the Supreme Court protecting the constitutional rights of students"); and James E. Ryan, "The Supreme Court and Public Schools," 86 *Virginia Law Review* 1335, 1348 (2000) (noting that *Tinker* is "conventionally thought to represent the high-water mark of judicial protection of student speech").

61. For helpful background on *Fraser*, including a copy of his contested speech, see *Bethel School District v. Fraser*, 478 U.S. 675, 677–80 (1986); Brief for Respondent, *Fraser*, 478 U.S. 675, 1986 WL 720451, at *1–*5; Brief for Petitioner, *Fraser*, 478 U.S. 675, 1985 WL 667975, at *2–*6; *Fraser v. Bethel School District No. 403*, 755 F.2d 1356, 1357 (9th Cir. 1985); Ruth Marcus, "Student Suspended After Speech," *Washington Post*, March 2, 1986, A12; and many additional newspaper articles cited below.

62. Ronald W. Powell and Eric Pryne, "Supreme Court Hears High-School Speech Issue," *Seattle Times*, March 3, 1986, A3; Philip Hager, "School Challenges Ruling Upsetting Suspension over Sexual Remarks," *Los Angeles Times*, March 2, 1986, A4; and Edward Iwata, "UC Student's Free Speech Suit Going Before U.S. High Court," *San Francisco Chronicle*, Nov. 30, 1985, 4.

63. Matthew Neil Fraser, "Squelching Student Speech," *Seattle Times*, July 19, 1986, A15.

64. Hager, "School Challenges Ruling Upsetting Suspension over Sexual Remarks," A4.

65. In addition to its First Amendment analysis, the district court overturned the school's effort to bar Fraser from speaking at graduation under the Fourteenth Amendment's Due Process Clause because the school's disruptive conduct policy did not mention that penalty as a potential sanction. Both a federal appellate court and the U.S. Supreme Court determined that the question of removing Fraser's name from the ballot was moot because he had already delivered the speech. See *Fraser*, 755 F.2d at 1366; and *Fraser*, 478 U.S. at 686n*.

66. *Fraser*, 478 U.S. at 683–84.

67. Ibid., 683.

68. Ibid., 681 (internal quotation marks and citations omitted). For *Fraser*'s explicit citation to Justice Black's dissent in *Tinker*, see ibid., 686.

69. Ibid., 681.

70. Ibid., 683. See also ibid. ("Consciously or otherwise, teachers . . . demonstrate the appropriate form of civil discourse and political expression by their conduct and deportment in and out of class. Inescapably, like parents, they are role models.") In *Fraser*, Justice William Brennan wrote a brief opinion. Brennan disputed the Court's characterization of Fraser's speech, which he found "no more 'obscene,' 'lewd,' or 'sexually explicit' than the bulk of programs currently appearing on prime time television or in the local cinema." Ibid., 689n2 (Brennan, J., concurring in the judgment). Nevertheless, Brennan reasoned, "[I]t was not unconstitutional for school officials to conclude, *under the circumstances of this case*, that respondent's remarks exceeded permissible limits." Ibid., 687–88 (emphasis added). Had Fraser delivered the address not at a school assembly but instead, say, to his seatmates in the cafeteria, Brennan intimated that in his view the speech might have been constitutionally protected.

71. Ibid., 685–86.

72. Ibid., 692 (Stevens, J. dissenting). See also "Students and Speech," *Washington Post*, July 9, 1986, A24 ("Chief Justice Burger referred to him as a 'troubled boy,' while Justice Stevens called him 'an outstanding young man' ").

73. *Fraser*, 478 U.S. at 694–95 (Stevens, J. dissenting).

74. Ibid., 690 (Marshall, J., dissenting).

75. "Students and Speech," A24. For an even more exaggerated version of this view, see Raymond Coffey, "A Smart-Aleck Kid Gets His Due—Hooray!," *Chicago Tribune*, July 11, 1986, 16 ("At least one smart-aleck kid got put in his place this week, for which we can all give praise").

76. "Setting an Example; Speech in School," *New York Times*, July 15, 1986, A28.

77. "Students and Speech," A24 (noting *Fraser* would not have been punished for speech "essentially political in character"); "Setting an Example; Speech in School," A28 ("[I]n political debate, the most robust exchanges should be encouraged").

78. "A Little Lesson in the Limits of Law," *Chicago Tribune*, July 10, 1986, 18.

79. Diana Trilling, letter to the editor, *New York Times*, Aug. 12, 1986, A24.

80. Alan Dershowitz, "Free Speech at Bethel High," *Seattle Times*, March 21, 1986, A9.

81. See, for example, Nat Stern, "The Burger Court and the Diminishing Constitutional Rights of Minors: A Brief Overview," 1985 *Arizona State Law Journal* 865, 900. For a contrary view, see Anne Proffitt Dupre, *Speaking Up: The Unin-*

tended Costs of Free Speech in Public Schools 10 (2009); and Anne Proffitt Dupre, "Should Students Have Constitutional Rights? Keeping Order in the Public Schools," 65 *George Washington Law Review* 49, 98–99 (1996).

82. Jack Broom, "Spanaway School Wins Speech Case," *Seattle Times*, July 7, 1986, A1. See also Iwata, "UC Student's Free Speech Suit Going Before U.S. High Court," 4 ("At UC Berkeley, he and his debate partner have led their powerful team to a No. 2 national ranking").

83. Fred M. Hechinger, "About Education; Political Shift on 'Vulgar' Speech," *New York Times*, July 15, 1986, C1.

84. Ronald Reagan, "Remarks at the National Forum on Excellence in Education," *Public Papers of President Ronald W. Reagan*, Dec. 8, 1983.

85. See Dupre, *Speaking Up*, 50–51 (identifying the connection between the solicitor general's quotation of the U.S. history textbook and Burger's opinion in *Fraser*). The textbook in question was Charles Beard and Mary Beard, *New Basic History of the United States* 228 (rev. ed. 1968). It is ironic that the work of Charles Beard would be cited in a Supreme Court decision interpreting the Constitution, because his most prominent scholarly work, *An Economic Interpretation of the Constitution of the United States* (1913), criticized the document as being designed to protect the interests of its elite framers. For a recent work that builds upon and refines Beard's analysis, see Michael J. Klarman, *The Framers' Coup: The Making of the United States Constitution* (2016).

86. "Supreme Court Roundup; Court Backs School on Student's 'Vulgar' Speech," *New York Times*, July 8, 1986, A18. Gary Bauer, undersecretary of the Department of Education, contended, "We think [*Fraser*] is very positive. It is a reaffirmation of the role of education in transmitting values and the need for an atmosphere in the schools that is conducive to learning." Rita Ciolli, "Ruling Limits Student Speech Right," *Newsday*, July 8, 1986, 5.

87. Wendell L. Willkie, "A School Must Have Moral Authority," *Washington Post*, Sept. 13, 1986, A21.

88. For earlier articulation of some of these criticisms, see, for example, Mark G. Yudof, "*Tinker* Tailored: Good Faith, Civility, and Student Expression," 69 *St. John's Law Review* 365, 372–73 (1995) ("The holding in *Fraser* is difficult to understand when viewed in light of *Tinker*. If a nominating speech for political office is not political speech, then what constitutes political speech?").

89. Ryan, "Supreme Court and Public Schools," 1355, 1356.

90. *Morse v. Frederick*, 551 U.S. 393, 404 (2007).

91. My formulation touting "more speech" pays homage to Justice Brandeis's famous articulation of free speech in *Whitney v. California*. See *Whitney v. California*, 274 U.S. 357, 377 (1927) (Brandeis, J., dissenting) ("If there be time to expose through discussion the falsehood and fallacies, to avert the evil by the process of education, the remedy to be applied is more speech, not enforced silence").

92. See Hechinger, "Political Shift on 'Vulgar' Speech," C8 ("The Chief Justice may have been motivated by old-fashioned chivalry; but in the contemporary context, he has a sexist ring. Should high-school girls be sent out of the room when Shakespeare's 'lewd' ways of dealing with male sexuality and his frequent sexual metaphors and innuendo appear in literature classes?").

93. See "Court Backs School on Student's 'Vulgar' Speech," A18 (noting that Fraser stated Kuhlman was " 'a man who takes his point and pounds it in' " and was

"'a man who will go to the very end—even to the climax, for each and every one of you'"); Marcus, "Student Suspended After Speech," A12; Iwata, "UC Student's Free Speech Suit Going Before U.S. High Court," 4; and Powell and Pryne, "Supreme Court Hears High-School Speech Issue," A3 (reprinting the speech in full and noting publication of Fraser's speech by Bethel's school newspaper).

94. Brief for Respondent at *4, *Fraser,* 1986 WL 720451.

95. James Madison, "Report on the Virginia Resolutions, Jan. 1800," in 5 *The Founders' Constitution* 141, 143 (Philip Kurland and Ralph Lerner eds., 2000).

96. For extremely helpful background on *Hazelwood School District v. Kuhlmeier* that informs my analysis throughout, see Anne Proffitt Dupre, "The Story of *Hazelwood v. Kuhlmeier*: Student Press and the School Censor," in *Education Law Stories* 221–58 (Michael A. Olivas and Ronna Greff Schneider eds., 2008); Steve Visser, "A Civics Lesson at Hazelwood East," *Nation,* Oct. 24, 1987, 441–42; *Hazelwood School District v. Kuhlmeier,* 484 U.S. 260, 262–66 (1988); Brief for Petitioners, *Kuhlmeier,* 484 U.S. 260, 1987 WL 864172, at *3–*11; Brief for Respondents, *Kuhlmeier,* 484 U.S. 260, 1987 WL 864173, at *1–*3; Derek W. Black, *Education Law: Equality, Fairness, and Reform* 669–71 (2013) (reproducing *Spectrum*'s two controverted articles); "Too Hot for Hazelwood," *St. Louis Globe-Democrat: Globe Weekend,* Feb. 9, 1985, 5–11 (reprinting all of the deleted articles).

97. Mark Walsh, "Landmark Student-Press Ruling Resonates from 1988," *Education Week,* Jan. 9, 2013, 1.

98. Michael D. Sorkin and Tom Uhlenbrock, "Educators Elated; Not So Students," *St. Louis Post-Dispatch,* Jan. 14, 1988, A1; Brief for Respondents at *3, *Kuhlmeier,* 1987 WL 864173 (noting divorce story contained a quotation from Kuhlmeier).

99. *Kuhlmeier,* 484 U.S. at 271.

100. Ibid., 273.

101. Ibid., 274–75.

102. Ibid., 277 (Brennan, J., dissenting).

103. Ibid., 289–90.

104. Ibid., 290.

105. Ibid., 291.

106. Joseph R. Tybor, "1st Amendment Rights End at Door to School," *Chicago Tribune,* Jan. 17, 1988, 1.

107. Theodore R. Mitchell, "The High Court and *Hazelwood*: Chipping Away at Rights," *Christian Science Monitor,* Jan. 25, 1988. For additional commentators criticizing *Kuhlmeier,* see, for example, Fred M. Hechinger, "Students as Journalists," *New York Times,* March 3, 1987, C6; Nat Hentoff, "Student Free Speech Is in Trouble," *Washington Post,* Aug. 30, 1986, A23; and Clarence Page, "Press Freedom Isn't Always Free," *Chicago Tribune,* Jan. 17, 1988, C3.

108. "Censorship as a Lesson," *Los Angeles Times,* Jan. 16, 1988, A8. For other editorials criticizing *Kuhlmeier,* see, for example, "What Hath Hazelwood Wrought?," *St. Louis Post-Dispatch,* March 4, 1988, F2; and "First Amendment Lessons," *New York Times,* Jan. 15, 1988, A30.

109. Stuart Taylor Jr., "Court, 5–3 Widens Power of Schools to Act as Censors," *New York Times,* Jan. 14, 1988, C1 (contending that *Kuhlmeier* "continued a recent trend in which the Court has taken a narrower view of the constitutional

rights of public school students than that suggested by its earlier rulings"); and Al Kamen, "Schools' Power to Censor Student Publications Widened," *Washington Post*, Jan. 14, 1988, A1 (noting decision redefined *Tinker*).

110. David G. Savage, "Justices OK Censorship by Schools," *Los Angeles Times*, Jan. 14, 1988, B1.

111. Bari Sue Kenyon, "Drawing the Line on Student Rights," *New York Times*, Feb. 21, 1988, 18.

112. Kim Jenkins, "First Amendment: Is It Just for Adults?," *New York Times*, Jan. 31, 1988, A26. An article in *Time* on *Kuhlmeier* made this same point: "The Bill of Rights isn't stamped 'for adults only.'" Richard Lacayo, "Stop the Student Presses," *Time*, Jan. 25, 1988, 54.

113. "Vindication, Fearfulness on Decision," *New York Times*, Jan. 14, 1988, A26.

114. George Landau, "Key Players Discuss Hazelwood Court Case," *St. Louis Post-Dispatch*, Feb. 22, 1988, A4.

115. Savage, "Justices OK Censorship by Schools," B1. See ibid. (noting that education officials and counsel for Los Angeles Unified School District contended *Kuhlmeier* ratified the status quo); and Kamen, "Schools' Power to Censor Student Publications Widened," A1 (observing that counsel for the National School Boards Association noted most school officials felt they exercised wide authority over school newspapers before *Kuhlmeier*).

116. James J. Kilpatrick, "Just Like Letting Animals Run the Zoo," *Orlando Sentinel*, Feb. 12, 1987, A19.

117. Judy Mann, "Principal as Publisher," *Washington Post*, Jan. 15, 1988, C3. For one of the few newspaper editorial pages that agreed with the Court's outcome in *Kuhlmeier*, see "Journalism School," *Orange County Register*, Jan. 14, 1988, B10 (contending that Principal Reynolds's actions demonstrated "[p]oor judgment, perhaps, but that is not an unconstitutional sin").

118. Black, *Education Law*, 670.

119. Ibid., 671. Some of the critiques contained in this paragraph were also advanced by Justice Brennan's dissenting opinion in *Kuhlmeier*. See *Kuhlmeier*, 484 U.S. at 277 (Brennan, J., dissenting).

120. Mark G. Yudof, "Principal as Publisher, Not Censor," *Wall Street Journal*, Jan. 20, 1988, 28. Professor Yudof offers another evocative example of the potential absurdities that could flow from permitting Kuhlmeier to prevail: "[C]onsider that President Reagan may be [censoring] his speech writers." Ibid. For an inchoate articulation of government speech, see *Wooley v. Maynard*, 430 U.S. 705, 713–17 (1977). For the formal debut of the government speech doctrine, see *Rust v. Sullivan*, 500 U.S. 173, 199–200 (1991). For a recent, controversial application of government speech, see *Walker v. Sons of Confederate Veterans*, 135 S. Ct. 2239 (2015). See also Mark G. Yudof, *When Government Speaks: Politics, Law, and Government Expression in America* (1983); and Yudof, "*Tinker* Tailored," 374.

121. *Frederick*, 551 U.S. at 423 (Alito, J., dissenting).

122. See, for example, *Near v. Minnesota*, 283 U.S. 697 (1931); and *New York Times Co. v. United States*, 403 U.S. 713 (1971).

123. See "Too Hot for Hazelwood," 5–11; Ross, *Lessons in Censorship*, 108 (detailing *Chicago Tribune*'s publication of a story that originated at Naperville North High School).

124. For a helpful overview of state legislation that has offered greater protection

to student journalists than that provided by the Supreme Court, see Tyler J. Buller, "The State Response to *Hazelwood v. Kuhlmeier*," 66 *Maine Law Review* 89 (2013). For a recent article highlighting the importance that these measures can have on the ground, see Christopher Mele, "High School Journalists Land a Scoop, and the Principal Resigns," *New York Times*, April 5, 2017. These measures are sometimes designated "anti-*Hazelwood* statutes." For claims that lower court judges have severely and detrimentally expanded upon *Kuhlmeier*, see Ross, *Lessons in Censorship*, 96–125; and Emily Gold Waldman, "Returning to *Hazelwood*'s Core: A New Approach to Restrictions on School-Sponsored Speech," 60 *Florida Law Review* 63 (2008). For thoughtful analysis of *Kuhlmeier*, see Susannah Barton Tobin, "Divining *Hazelwood:* The Need for a Viewpoint Neutrality Requirement in School Speech Cases," 39 *Harvard Civil Rights–Civil Liberties Law Review* 217 (2004).

125. *Hazelwood School District v. Kuhlmeier*, 484 U.S. 260, 287 (1988) (Brennan, J., dissenting) (internal quotation marks and citations omitted, alterations in original).

126. For background on *Pico* and book banning generally, see *Board of Education, Island Trees Union Free School District No. 26 v. Pico*, 457 U.S. 853, 856–61, 872n24 (1982) (Brennan, J., plurality opinion), Gail Paulus Sorenson, "Removal of Books from School Libraries, 1972–1982: *Board of Education v. Pico* and Its Antecedents," 12 *Journal of Law and Education* 417 (1983); Mark Yudof, "Book Selection and the Public Schools," 59 *Indiana Law Journal* 527 (1984); Charles R. Babcock, "Book Banning Spreads: But a Court Test Could Stem the Tide," *Washington Post*, May 10, 1982, A1; Joseph Nocera, "The Big Book-Banning Brawl," *New Republic*, Sept. 13, 1982, 20; "The Growing Battle of the Books," *Time*, Jan. 19, 1981, 85; Dena Kleiman, "Parents' Groups Purging Schools of 'Humanist' Books and Classes," *New York Times*, May, 17 1981, A1; and Linda Greenhouse, "High Court Limits Banning of Books," *New York Times*, June 26, 1982, 1. For a cogent philosophical treatment of book banning, see Amy Gutmann, *Democratic Education* 97–101 (1987).

127. Stephen Arons, *Compelling Belief: The Culture of American Schooling* 63 (1983).

128. "L.I. Students File Suit to Overturn School Book Ban," *New York Times*, Jan. 5, 1977, 23. For accounts of Steven Pico's assessment of his fellow Levittowners, see Colin Campbell, "Book Banning in America," *New York Times*, Dec. 20, 1981, BR1; and Kay Bartlett, "Book-Banning Row Splits N.Y. Community," *Los Angeles Times*, Feb. 20, 1977, 2.

129. "L.I. Students File Suit to Overturn School Book Ban," 23. For remarks upon Levittown's homogeneity in the context of *Pico*, see "The Book Banning Controversy," *Wall Street Journal*, Jan. 18, 1982, 22; and Bartlett, "Book-Banning Row Splits N.Y. Community," 2. For an overview of Levittown and its history, see Herbert J. Gans, *The Levittowners: Ways of Life and Politics in a New Suburban Community* (1967). See also Carol Kopf, "Living in Levittown," *Newsday*, May 3, 1986, 5. The reason for my note of skepticism on whether Levittown's homogeneity actually played a causal role in generating the book-banning plan stems primarily from the fact that such practices were found in many different types of communities across the country. It is also important to realize that, while the plan originated with Levittown's school board, some Levittowners also disdained the proposal.

130. *Pico*, 457 U.S. at 872 (Brennan, J., plurality opinion) (citation omitted). See

also ibid., 875 (Blackmun, J., concurring in part and concurring in the judgment); and ibid., 883 (White, J., concurring in the judgment). Three justices wrote dissenting opinions in *Pico*. Justice Lewis Powell wrote perhaps the most noteworthy among them, because he emphasized the importance of local control: "School boards are uniquely local and democratic institutions. . . . Judges rarely are as competent as school authorities to make this decision; nor are judges responsive to the parents and people of the school district." Ibid., 894 (Powell, J., dissenting). For a bold argument building on *Pico* to suggest that school textbooks be scrutinized as sources of patriotic indoctrination, see Stephen E. Gottlieb, "In the Name of Patriotism: The Constitutionality of 'Bending' History in Public Secondary School," 62 *NYU Law Review* 497 (1987).

131. For useful sources that provide the background of *Morse v. Frederick*, see *Morse v. Frederick*, 551 U.S. 393, 396–99 (2007); Brief for Respondent's Brief at *1–*4, *Frederick*, 551 U.S. 393, 2007 WL 579230; Brief for Petitioner at *2–*7, *Frederick*, 551 U.S. 393, 2007 WL 118979; Moss, "Story of *Tinker v. Des Moines* to *Morse v. Frederick*," 416–21; Mark Walsh, "Rights at Stake in Free-Speech Case," *Education Week*, March 9, 2007, 1, 28–29; Robert Barnes, "Justices to Hear Landmark Free-Speech Case," *Washington Post*, March 13, 2007, A3; Linda Greenhouse, "Free-Speech Case Divides Bush and Religious Right," *New York Times*, March 18, 2007, A22; and Andrew Krueger, "Banner Canned," *Juneau Empire*, Jan. 29, 2002. Frederick also commented about the banner, "I wasn't trying to spread any idea. I was just trying to assert my [First Amendment] right." Deposition of Joseph Frederick, Aug. 21, 2002, Joint Appendix at *68, *Morse v. Frederick*, 2007 WL 119039 (U.S.).

132. *Frederick*, 551 U.S. at 397.

133. Ibid., 407.

134. Ibid., 421 (Thomas, J., concurring).

135. Ibid., 411–12.

136. Ibid., 421.

137. Ibid., 445n8, 448 (Stevens, J., dissenting).

138. Ibid., 448.

139. Ibid., 447–48.

140. "Three Bad Rulings," *New York Times*, June 26, 2007, A20. The *Los Angeles Times* shared this assessment; it contended *Frederick* "drained the life out of" *Tinker*. "Student Speech: No," *Los Angeles Times*, June 26, 2007, A22. For predecision commentary that advocated the Court adopting a strong First Amendment line in *Frederick*, see "Students' Right to Free Speech," *New York Times*, March 20, 2007, A18 ("The court should . . . rule that Mr. Frederick's rights were infringed"); ibid. ("[I]f schools can limit speech on any subject deemed to be important, students could soon be punished for talking about the war on terror or the war in Iraq because the government also considers those subjects important"); and "Precedent 4 Student Speech," *Washington Post*, March 21, 2007, A14 ("What is a bong hit 4 Jesus? We're not sure, and we doubt anyone really knows what the phrase means—which is one reason the Supreme Court ought not to regard it as prohibited speech.").

141. "A Less-than-Banner Ruling," *Washington Post*, June 27, 2007, A18.

142. Frederick Schauer, "Abandoning the Guidance Function: *Morse v. Frederick*," 2007 *Supreme Court Review* 205, 209–11. Professor Schauer may well believe that the Court in *Frederick* was justified in articulating a free speech rule that

applied within only that institutional setting. For thinking along these lines, see Frederick Schauer, "Towards an Institutional First Amendment," 89 *Minnesota Law Review* 1256 (2005). For an insightful, nuanced position on the First Amendment obligations of public schools as one variety of public institution, see Paul Horwitz, *First Amendment Institutions* 144–73 (2012). See also Ronald Dworkin, *The Supreme Court Phalanx: The Court's New Right-Wing Bloc* 63 (2008) ("It is hard to resist the suspicion that, for Roberts, anti-abortion groups have constitutional rights that students who joke about drugs and Jesus do not"); Martha C. Nussbaum, "The Supreme Court, 2006 Term—Foreword: Constitutions and Capabilities: 'Perception' Against Lofty Formalism," 121 *Harvard Law Review* 4, 93n419 (2007) (suggesting that both *Fraser* and *Frederick* "show a certain failure of imagination, in the sense that someone who lives (sympathetically) around adolescents or can imagine what it is like to be one would probably not be as shocked by the utterances in question as some of the Justices appear to be"); and Laurence Tribe and Joshua Matz, *Uncertain Justice: The Roberts Court and the Constitution* 137 (2014) (noting that *Frederick* "had all the makings of a one-off case—and yet it . . . dramatically limited student speech rights").

143. David French, "A Bong Hit to Free Speech," *National Review*, June 25, 2007. See also Ed Whelan, "A Small Step to the Right . . . and to the Center," *National Review Online*, July 3, 2007 (noting in *Frederick*'s wake that "many conservative public-interest groups have been at the forefront of defending disfavored student speech—which is hardly surprising given who runs the public schools").

144. Hans Bader, "Bong Hits 4 Jesus: The First Amendment Takes a Hit," 2007 *Cato Supreme Court Review* 133, 133.

145. Kenneth W. Starr, "From *Fraser* to *Frederick*: Bong Hits and the Decline of Civic Culture," 42 *UC Davis Law Review* 661, 676–77 (2009). For Starr's more expansive proposed legal rule governing student speech, see Brief for Petitioners, *Frederick*, 551 U.S. 393, 2007 WL 118979, at *21. The Solicitor General's Office advanced this same proposed rule. See Brief for United States as Amicus Curiae, *Frederick*, 551 U.S. 393, 2007 WL 118978, at *6. See also Kenneth W. Starr, "Our Libertarian Court: *Bong Hits* and the Enduring Hamiltonian-Jeffersonian Colloquy," 12 *Lewis and Clark Law Review* 1 (2008).

146. Robert Bork, " 'Thanks a Lot': Free Speech in High Schools," *National Review*, April 16, 2007, 24. For a similar view to Bork's, see George F. Will, "Quandaries 4 Justices," *Washington Post*, July 1, 2007, B7 ("Endless distinctions can—and actually, must—be drawn once a subject becomes a matter of constitutional litigation").

147. Some of the criticisms contained in this paragraph can also be found in Justice Breyer's opinion in *Frederick*. See *Frederick*, 551 U.S. at 425 (Breyer, J., concurring in the judgment in part and dissenting in part).

148. Lawrence M. Friedman, "Limited Monarchy: The Rise and Fall of Student Rights," in *School Days, Rule Days: The Legalization and Regulation of Education* 238, 251 (David L. Kirp and Donald N. Jensen eds., 1986) (emphasis added). See also *Scoville v. Board of Education of Joliet Township High School*, 425 F.2d 10, 15 (7th Cir. 1970); and Edward A. Wynne, "What Are the Courts Doing to Our Children?," *Public Interest* 3, 7–8 (Spring 1981).

149. *Nuxoll v. Indian Prairie School District*, 523 F.3d 668, 674 (7th Cir. 2008).

150. Ibid. (emphasis added). For cases expanding *Frederick* to apply to violent speech, see *Ponce v. Socorro Independent School District*, 508 F.3d 765 (5th Cir. 2007); *Boim v. Fulton County School District*, 494 F.3d 978 (11th Cir. 2007); and *B.C. v. Valley Central School District*, 677 F.3d 109 (2d Cir. 2012). For an incisive article that quickly identified the lower courts' expansion of *Frederick*, see Clay Calvert, "Misuse and Abuse of *Morse v. Frederick* by Lower Courts: Stretching the High Court's Ruling Too Far to Censor Student Expression," 32 *Seattle University Law Review* 1, 12–24 (2008). If *Tinker* offers an inadequate basis to address frightening, violent speech directed toward students and educators, it may be advisable for judges to view schools as enjoying a lower threshold for what constitutes a "true threat" compared with nonschool environments. If speech is viewed as constituting a "true threat," it enjoys no protection under the First Amendment. See *Watts v. United States*, 394 U.S. 705 (1969).

151. *Karr v. Schmidt*, 460 F.2d 609, 614 (5th Cir. 1972).

152. *Broussard v. School Board of the City of Norfolk*, 801 F. Supp. 1526, 1534 (E.D. Va. 1992).

153. Erwin Chemerinsky, "Students Do Leave Their First Amendment Rights at the Schoolhouse Gates: What's Left of *Tinker*?," 48 *Drake Law Review* 527, 529, 541 (2000).

154. Perry A. Zirkel, "The Rocket's Red Glare: The Largely Errant and Deflected Flight of *Tinker*," 38 *Journal of Law and Education* 593, 597 (2009); and Piotr Banasiak, "*Morse v. Frederick*: Why Content-Based Exceptions, Deference, and Confusion Are Swallowing *Tinker*," 39 *Seton Hall Law Review* 1059, 1099 (2009).

155. J. Marc Abrams and S. Mark Goodman, "End of an Era? The Decline of Student Press Rights in the Wake of *Hazelwood School District v. Kuhlmeier*," 1988 *Duke Law Journal* 706, 707; and Thomas J. Flygare, "Is *Tinker* Dead?," 68 *Phi Delta Kappan* 165, 165 (1986). See ibid. ("The apparent demise of *Tinker* is especially poignant for many of us because *Tinker* marked the emergence of school law as a discipline.")

156. Paul G. Haskell, "Student Expression in the Public Schools: *Tinker* Distinguished," 59 *Georgetown Law Journal* 37, 39 (1970).

157. See Scott A. Moss, "The Overhyped Path from *Tinker* to *Morse*: How the Student Speech Cases Show the Limits of Supreme Court Decisions—for the Law and for the Litigants," 63 *Florida Law Review* 1407 (2011).

158. *Barber v. Dearborn Public Schools*, 286 F. Supp. 2d 847 (E.D. Mich. 2003) ("International Terrorist"); *Gillman v. School Board for Holmes County*, 567 F. Supp. 2d 1359 (N.D. Fla. 2008) ("Pro-Gay Marriage"); and *Hawk v. Easton Area School District*, 725 F.3d 293 (3d Cir. 2013) ("I ♥ boobies!").

159. *Holloman v. Harland*, 370 F.3d 1252, 1275–76 (11th Cir. 2004). Lower courts have frequently vindicated the desire of students to sit during the Pledge of Allegiance. See *Banks v. Board of Public Instruction of Dade County*, 314 F. Supp. 285 (S.D. Fla. 1970) (validating a student's request to sit during the pledge as a "simple protest against black repression in the United States"); and *Lipp v. Morris*, 579 F.2d 834, 835 (3d Cir. 1978) (validating a student's request to sit during the pledge because, in her estimation, "the words of the pledge were not true").

160. *Fricke v. Lynch*, 491 F. Supp. 381, 387 (D. R.I. 1980). Fricke informed Judge Pettine at a hearing in his case, "I feel I have a right to attend [the prom]. I feel

I want to go for the same reason any other student would want to go. I'm fighting for my rights. It would be a statement for equal rights and human rights." "Ban on Homosexual's Prom Date Leads to Day in Court," *New York Times*, May 21, 1980, B4. Elsewhere, Fricke stated, "I think it would be dishonest to my sexual identity to go with a girl." Douglas S. Crocket, "Court to Hear Closing Testimony in Gay Prom Date Issue," *Boston Globe*, May 21, 1980, 26. The logistics of a same-sex prom couple appeared to flummox the school district's attorney, who asked Fricke during the hearing, "Would either you or [your date] wear a corsage?" Ibid.

161. *Doe v. Yunits*, 2000 WL 33162199 (Mass. Super. Oct. 11, 2000). See ibid., *5 ("Defendants vaguely cite instances when the principal became aware of threats by students to beat up the 'boy who dressed like a girl' to support the notion that plaintiff's dress alone is disruptive. To rule in defendants' favor in this regard, however, would grant those contentious students a 'heckler's veto.'") (citation omitted).

162. Tamar Lewin, "High School Tells Student to Remove Antiwar Shirt," *New York Times*, Feb. 26, 2003, A12 (reporting retreat on Palestinian flag); John Carlson, "Anti-abortion Message Meets Zero Tolerance," *Des Moines Register*, May 4, 2005, A13; and Veronica Rocha, "High School Teams Can Wear 'I Can't Breathe' T-Shirts After All," *Los Angeles Times*, Dec. 30, 2014.

163. See *Madrid v. Anthony*, 510 F. Supp. 2d. 425 (S.D. Tex. 2007); *Dariano v. Morgan Hill Unified School District*, 767 F.3d 764 (9th Cir. 2014); *Harper v. Poway Unified School District*, 445 F.3d 1166 (9th Cir. 2006); and *Defoe v. Spiva*, 625 F.3d 324 (6th Cir. 2010). Judge Reinhardt's opinion for the Ninth Circuit in *Harper* elevated a dormant passage in *Tinker* to sidestep the traditional requirement that educators reasonably forecast a substantial disruption before limiting speech. "We conclude that Harper's wearing of his T-shirt 'colli[des]' with the rights of other students' in the most fundamental way." *Harper*, 445 F.3d at 1178 (quoting *Tinker*, 393 U.S. at 508). The controlling opinion in *Defoe* upheld the Confederate flag prohibition—in the absence of anything that satisfied *Tinker*'s traditional test—by expanding the Court's reasoning in *Frederick* to apply to student speech that can reasonably be understood as promoting racial division. "If we substitute 'racial conflict' or 'racial hostility' for 'drug abuse,' the analysis in [*Frederick*] is practically on all fours with this case," Judge Rogers's controlling opinion stated. "The inescapable conclusion is that a school may restrict racially hostile or contemptuous speech in school, when school administrators reasonably view the speech as racially hostile or promoting racial conflict." *Defoe*, 625 F.3d at 339 (opinion of Rogers, J.). Although Judge Clay wrote an opinion trying to fit *Defoe* into *Tinker*'s framework, I agree with the other two judges on the panel that the evidence he cites is too attenuated to satisfy *Tinker*'s usual test.

164. Judge Posner has advocated importing a version of the fighting-words doctrine into the school context. See *Nuxoll*, 523 F.3d at 670–71. The Court first recognized the fighting-words doctrine in *Chaplinsky v. New Hampshire*, 315 U.S. 568, 572–73 (1942). Although the Court in *R.A.V. v. City of St. Paul* invalidated a fighting-words statute that mentioned specific identity-based characteristics, schools can enact policies that localities as a whole cannot. See *R.A.V. v. City of St. Paul*, 505 U.S. 377, 386 (1992). For a recent statement indicating that the fighting-words doctrine retains vitality, see *Elonis v. United States*, 135 S. Ct.

2001, 2027–28 (2015) (Thomas, J., dissenting). For criticism of the fighting-words doctrine, see Randall Kennedy, *Nigger: The Strange Career of a Trouble-some Word* 54–55 (2002).

165. *Boroff v. Van Wert City Board of Education*, 220 F.3d 465, 469 (6th Cir. 2000).

166. Ibid., 470. See also ibid., 474 (Gilman, J., dissenting).

167. *Blau v. Fort Thomas Public School District*, 401 F.3d 381, 385–86 (6th Cir. 2005).

168. "Armbands Yes, Miniskirts No," 46.

169. See Alison Mitchell, "Clinton Will Advise Schools on Uniforms," *New York Times*, Feb. 25, 1996, 24. Left-leaning politicians are not the only progressive voices who have supported school uniforms. See Charles Lane, "School Uniforms—the Answer to Free Speech Issues at High Schools," *Washington Post*, Sept. 24, 2015. For additional opinions upholding school dress codes, see *Palmer v. Waxahachie Independent School District*, 579 F.3d 502 (5th Cir. 2009); and *Jacobs v. Clark County School District*, 526 F.3d 419 (9th Cir. 2008).

170. *Doninger v. Niehoff*, 642 F.3d 334, 351 (2d Cir. 2011).

171. *J.S. v. Blue Mountain*, 650 F.3d 915, 921 (3d Cir. 2011).

172. Ibid., 920.

173. Ibid., 930.

174. *Layshock v. Hermitage School District*, 650 F.3d 205, 216 (3d Cir. 2011).

175. Edward Wyatt, "It Turns Out You Can Say That on Television, Over and Over," *New York Times*, Nov. 14, 2009, A1 (chronicling the increased use of "douche" on network television in recent years). For evidence suggesting that the federal court viewed the school's decision to prohibit Doninger from running for senior class secretary as a light punishment, see *Doninger*, 642 F.3d at 350 ("Doninger's discipline extended *only* to her role as a student government representative: she was not suspended from classes or punished in any other way") (emphasis added).

176. My thinking about the question of off-campus speech that criticizes other students was influenced by the following sources: Emily Bazelon, *Sticks and Stones: Defeating the Culture of Bullying and Rediscovering the Power of Character and Empathy* 271–79 (2014); Mary-Rose Papandrea, "Student Speech Rights in the Digital Age," 60 *Florida Law Review* 1027, 1102 (2008); and Ross, *Lessons in Censorship*, 207–44. See also Nirvi Shaw, Inside School Research, "Researchers: Cyberbullying Not as Widespread, Common as Believed," *Education Week*, Aug. 4, 2012; and Danielle Keats Citron, *Hate Crimes in Cyberspace* 248–50 (2014). For some of the opinions that broadly permit students to be punished for speech uttered off campus that is critical of students, see *Kowalski v. Berkeley County Schools*, 652 F.3d 565 (4th Cir. 2011); and *D.J.M. v. Hannibal Public School District*, 647 F.3d 754 (8th Cir. 2011).

177. *Nuxoll*, 523 F.3d at 671.

178. Ibid., 677–78 (Rovner, J., concurring in the judgment) (internal citations omitted).

3 SUSPENSIONS, CORPORAL PUNISHMENT,
AND INTOLERABLE "ZERO TOLERANCE" POLICIES

1. See, for example, Kerrin C. Wolf and Aaron Kupchik, "School Suspensions and Adverse Experiences in Adulthood," 34 *Justice Quarterly* 407 (2017); Tony

Fabelo et al., *Breaking Schools' Rules: A Statewide Study of How School Discipline Relates to Students' Success and Juvenile Justice Involvement,* Council of State Governments Justice Center and Public Policy Research Institute (2011); Russell J. Skiba et al., "More than a Metaphor: The Contribution of Exclusionary Discipline to a School-to-Prison Pipeline," 47 *Equity and Excellence in Education* 546 (2014); and Bruce Western, *Punishment and Inequality in America* (2006).

2. Frank R. Kemerer and Kenneth L. Deutsch, *Constitutional Rights and Student Life: Value Conflict in Law and Education* 463 (1979).

3. For helpful background on the underlying facts of *Goss v. Lopez,* see ibid., 409–99; Franklin E. Zimring and Rayman L. Solomon, "*Goss v. Lopez:* The Principle of the Thing," in *In the Interest of Children: Advocacy, Law Reform, and Public Policy* 450–508 (Robert H. Mnookin ed., 1985); "Racial Strife Hits Schools," *Columbus Evening Dispatch,* Feb. 20, 1971, 1; and Graydon Hambrick, "Central High Suspensions Follow Row," *Columbus Evening Dispatch,* Feb. 27, 1971, 1.

4. Warren A. Seavey, "Dismissal of Students: 'Due Process,'" 70 *Harvard Law Review* 1406, 1407 (1957).

5. *Dixon v. Alabama State Board of Education,* 294 F.2d 150, 158 (5th Cir. 1961).

6. See Mark G. Yudof, "Legalization of Dispute Resolution, Distrust of Authority, and Organizational Theory: Implementing Due Process for Students in the Public Schools," 1981 *Wisconsin Law Review* 891, 900–901; and William G. Buss, "Procedural Due Process for School Discipline: Probing the Constitutional Outline," 119 *University of Pennsylvania Law Review* 545, 552–53 (1971).

7. Charles Alan Wright, "The Constitution on Campus," 22 *Vanderbilt Law Review* 1027, 1032 (1969).

8. Fourteenth Amendment, U.S. Constitution. The Supreme Court's foundational due process precedents relied upon in *Lopez* include *Goldberg v. Kelly,* 397 U.S. 254 (1970) (requiring hearings to be conducted before the state could deprive individuals of their property interest in welfare benefits); and *Wisconsin v. Constantineau,* 400 U.S. 433 (1971) (requiring evidentiary hearings to be conducted before the state could deprive individuals of their liberty interest in reputation).

9. *Goss v. Lopez,* 419 U.S. 565, 581 (1975).

10. Ibid., 584. See also ibid., 580n9.

11. Ibid., 581, 583.

12. See J. Harvie Wilkinson III, "*Goss v. Lopez:* The Supreme Court as School Superintendent," 1975 *Supreme Court Review* 25, 45–46 (speculating that Powell's experiences on the Richmond School Board and Virginia State Board of Education influenced his dissent in *Lopez*). For an insightful biography of Powell, one that addresses the close relationships connecting the Powells and the Wilkinsons, see John C. Jeffries, *Justice Lewis F. Powell Jr.: A Biography* (1994). For Wilkinson's own account of his relationship with Powell, focusing on his clerkship, see J. Harvie Wilkinson III, *Serving Justice: A Supreme Court Clerk's View* (1974).

13. *Lopez,* 419 U.S. at 591 (Powell, J., dissenting).

14. Ibid., 585.

15. Ibid., 594n12.

16. Ibid., 594.

17. Ibid., 593.

18. Ibid., 598n19 (emphasis in original).
19. Yudof, "Legalization of Dispute Resolution, Distrust of Authority, and Organizational Theory," 902 (internal quotation marks omitted). See also Linda Mathews, "Suspensions Hearings for Pupils Upheld," *Los Angeles Times*, Jan. 23, 1975, A1 (noting that even before *Lopez* Los Angeles schools provided hearings to students prior to suspending them).
20. Robert Reinhold, "The Supreme Court and Rights of Pupils," *New York Times*, Jan. 27, 1975, 17 ("In New York City, officials say students already enjoy much due process under both state law and local rules, which require a written notification for parents and a hearing within five days of any exclusion. Decisions may be appealed.").
21. Dolores Barclay, "Ruling on Suspended Pupils' Rights Hit," *Los Angeles Times*, April 16, 1975, C10.
22. Gene I. Maeroff, "An End of Student Suspensions Is Urged," *New York Times*, Sept. 17, 1975, 36.
23. Fred M. Hechinger, "Unruly Students Deserve Due Process, Too," *Los Angeles Times*, April 13, 1975, L3 ("romantic notion"); and Leon Letwin, "After *Goss v. Lopez*: Student Status as Suspect Classification?," 29 *Stanford Law Review* 627, 646 (1977) ("euphoric view"). See also Robert A. Burt, "The Constitution of the Family," 1979 *Supreme Court Review* 329, 342 (observing that *Ingraham* appears animated by "[a]n idealized image of conflict-free interpersonal relations").
24. Nathan Glazer, "Towards an Imperial Judiciary?," 41 *Public Interest* 104, 107 (1975).
25. George F. Will, "Schools Beset by Lawyers and Shrinks," *Washington Post*, June 15, 2000, A33.
26. Richard Arum, "Sparing Rods, Spoiling Children," *National Review*, Oct. 11, 2004, 43, 43–44. For other writing where Arum suggests *Lopez* required elaborate due process procedures, see Richard Arum, *Judging School Discipline: The Crisis of Moral Authority* 204 (2003).
27. Philip K. Howard, *The Death of Common Sense: How Law Is Suffocating America* 128 (1994).
28. Henry S. Lufler Jr., "Courts and School Discipline Policies," 197, 207, in *Student Discipline Strategies: Research and Practice* (Oliver C. Moles ed., 1990).
29. Perry A. Zirkel and Mark N. Covelle, "State Laws for Student Suspension Procedures: The Other Progeny of *Goss v. Lopez*," 46 *San Diego Law Review* 343, 349–50 (2009).
30. In 1975, Professor Wilkinson provided a particularly sharp version of the claim that *Lopez* violated local control. "The rejection of such informal correctives by the Court is, in the end, nothing less than a rejection of the workings of the democratic process," Wilkinson wrote. "And introducing the Constitution to do what the disciplinary process so often accomplishes on its own makes all the good sense of traveling from New York to Washington by way of San Francisco." Wilkinson, "*Goss v. Lopez*: The Supreme Court as School Superintendent," 70. More than two decades later, Judge Wilkinson could be heard whistling the same tune: "When we take the important step of constitutionalizing a problem such as student discipline, we do two things. First, we remove it from the hands of the democratic process and place it in the lap of the federal courts. . . . [Second, we] indicate a preference for centralized rules and solu-

tions over disparate state and local prescriptions." J. Harvie Wilkinson III, "Constitutionalization of School Discipline: An Unnecessary and Counterproductive Solution," 1 *Michigan Law and Policy Review* 309, 312 (1996).

31. In 1996, Judge Patricia Wald of the D.C. Circuit contended that critics of *Lopez* would be better served by redirecting their anger toward local officials. See Patricia Wald, *"Goss v. Lopez:* Not the Devil, nor the Panacea," 1 *Michigan Law and Policy Review* 331, 334–35 (1996). My argument here builds upon Wald's insights.

32. Arum, *Judging School Discipline*, 4. For an early articulation of the ideas that Arum would explore in greater depth, see Edward A. Wynne, "What Are the Courts Doing to Our Children?," 64 *Public Interest* 3 (Summer 1981). Wynne argued, "American courts have undercut the parental role of the schools and have replaced the subtle and complex relations between pupil, teacher, and administrator . . . with discussions of children's 'rights.' . . . In response, educators, stripped of their authority and their aura of infallibility, have abdicated their parental duties and have become mere custodians. For children, then, the 'victory' won in their name for rights to protect them against the authority of school officials has been a pyrrhic one." Ibid., 3–4. For similar claims that the schools suffered from the burdens of honoring due process, see Gerald Grant, *The World We Created at Hamilton High* 50–51 (1988).

33. Anne Proffitt Dupre, *Speaking Up: The Unintended Costs of Free Speech in Public Schools* 34 (2009).

34. Lino A. Graglia, "Constitutional Law Without the Constitution: The Supreme Court's Remaking of America," in *A Country I Do Not Recognize: The Legal Assault on American Values* 29–30 (Robert H. Bork ed., 2005).

35. Robert H. Bork, *Slouching Towards Gomorrah: Modern Liberalism and American Decline* 96 (1996).

36. Ibid., 104.

37. Anne M. Glenzer, "Supreme Court Justice Says Religion Is Vital to Virtuous America," *Blue and Gray*, Oct. 30–Nov. 13, 2006, 1, 6 (observing that Scalia's comments attributed the decline of school discipline in part to the "application of due process to school affairs").

38. Heather Mac Donald, "Unsafe at Any Grade," *Wall Street Journal*, March 25, 2004, D6.

39. Philip K. Howard, *Life Without Lawyers* 105 (2009). Howard offered adumbrations of his anti-*Lopez* critique as early as 1994. Until *Lopez*, Howard insisted, "no one ever thought that due process had anything to do with running an elementary school or deciding to suspend an unruly eleventh grader. Principals and teachers had the authority to make decisions. Students, and their parents, did not think of their 'rights.' They had none. If you misbehaved, you were suspended or put on probation." Howard, *Death of Common Sense*, 158. See also Howard, *Life Without Lawyers* 113 (calling *Lopez* "debilitating" and asserting that its requirements were written in "migraine-inducing language"). For related arguments, see Grant, *World We Created at Hamilton High*, 50–57.

40. See Arum, *Judging School Discipline*, 208.

41. Martha Minow, "Interpreting Rights: An Essay for Robert Cover," 96 *Yale Law Journal* 1860, 1869–77 (1987). Minow's insights have influenced my view of *Lopez*.

42. See Lufler, "Courts and School Discipline Policies," 207.

43. See Derek W. Black, "The Constitutional Limit of Zero Tolerance in Schools," 99 *Minnesota Law Review* 823, 825 (2015).

44. See Julius Menacker and Ernest Pascarella, "How Aware Are Educators of Supreme Court Decisions That Affect Them?," 64 *Phi Delta Kappan* 424, 426 (1983).

45. *Lopez*, 419 U.S. at 582.

46. David L. Kirp, "Proceduralism and Bureaucracy: Due Process in the School Setting," 28 *Stanford Law Review* 841, 842 (1976).

47. Wilkinson, "*Goss v. Lopez:* The Supreme Court as School Superintendent," 72. Wilkinson also describes *Lopez*'s suspension procedures as "skeletal" and "threadbare." Ibid., 40, 42. For influential criticism of the Supreme Court's due process jurisprudence as a whole, and an article whose skeptical title is drawn from a stray phrase in *Lopez*, see Henry J. Friendly, " 'Some Kind of Hearing,' " 123 *University of Pennsylvania Law Review* 1267 (1975). Judge Friendly claimed *Lopez* forces considering "whether government can do anything to a citizen without affording him 'some kind of hearing.' " Ibid., 1275.

48. Letwin, "After *Goss v. Lopez*," 637.

49. Laurence H. Tribe, "Structural Due Process," 10 *Harvard Civil Rights–Civil Liberties Law Review* 269, 313n128 (1975). Well before the Court decided *Goss*, Professor Tribe made an observation that contains relevance for suspended students and their procedural rights: "[I]t is at least arguable that . . . the *process*, and *not the result in any particular case*, is all-important." Laurence H. Tribe, "Trial by Mathematics: Precision and Ritual in Legal Process," 84 *Harvard Law Review* 1329, 1381 (1971).

50. Buss, "Procedural Due Process for School Discipline," 547, 549.

51. "Fair Play at the Schoolhouse," *Chicago Tribune*, Jan. 31, 1975, A2.

52. See generally *The Burger Court: The Counter-revolution That Wasn't* (Vincent Blasi ed., 1983) (arguing that the Burger Court as a general proposition refused to extend the liberal Warren Court's jurisprudence, even if did not engage in the sharp rollback that many legal liberals feared). For a revisionist account suggesting that the Burger Court was more conservative than the conventional account suggests, see Michael J. Graetz and Linda Greenhouse, *The Burger Court and the Rise of the Judicial Right* (2016).

53. See Warren Weaver Jr., "Supreme Court, 5–4, Backs Rights of Suspended Pupils," *New York Times*, Jan. 23, 1975, 1 ("Voting in the [*Lopez*] minority were all four of former President Richard M. Nixon's appointees to the bench"). See also Charlotte Moulton, "Minorities Get Setbacks During Last Court Term," *Los Angeles Sentinel*, July 17, 1975, A8.

54. *Tinker v. Des Moines Independent Community School District*, 393 U.S. 503, 506 (1969) (emphasis added).

55. Professor Leon Letwin's astute article offered an early version of this idea. See Letwin, "After *Goss v. Lopez*," 638. My view of historical contingency within the Supreme Court's school discipline jurisprudence is indebted to Professor Letwin, who made the argument in real time, underscoring the doctrinal uncertainty that observers felt during the *Lopez* era.

56. "Seventh Annual Gallup Poll of Public Attitudes Toward Education," 57 *Phi Delta Kappan* 227, 236 (1975); *A Decade of Gallup Polls of Attitudes Toward Education, 1969–1978* 219 (S. Elam ed., 1978).

57. *Attitudes Toward Education, 1969–1978*, 2. See also Gordon F. Sander, "Schools Still Uncertain About Punishing Unruly," *New York Times*, Aug. 28, 1977, 150.

58. See, for example, Barry Friedman, *The Will of the People: How Public Opinion Has Influenced the Supreme Court and Shaped the Meaning of the Constitution* (2009). For a critique of this idea, see Justin Driver, "The Consensus Constitution," 89 *Texas Law Review* 755 (2011).

59. *Lopez*, 419 U.S. at 569.

60. See Brief of the National Association for the Advancement of Colored People et al., *Lopez*, 419 U.S. 565, 1974 WL 185916, at *10–*16 (1975); and Brief for the Children's Defense Fund of the Washington Research Project Inc. et al., *Lopez*, 419 U.S. 565, 1974 WL 185919, at *21.

61. Weaver, "Supreme Court, 5–4, Backs Rights of Suspended Pupils," 1. For contemporaneous commentary linking suspensions to race, see Vernon E. Jordan Jr., "Kids Get Pushed out of School," *Los Angeles Sentinel*, July 10, 1975, A7 ("Hundreds of thousands of children are expelled each year for disciplinary reasons, and black children form a disproportionately large percentage of them"); Maeroff, "End of Student Suspensions Is Urged," 36 (noting that the Children's Defense Fund "contends that minority school children suffer from the greatest abuses in the application of suspensions" because "[b]lack youngsters are suspended at a rate twice that of whites"); Mark G. Yudof, "Suspension and Expulsion of Black Students from the Public Schools: Academic Capital Punishment and the Constitution," 39 *Law and Contemporary Problems* 374, 378 (1975) ("The fact is that in many desegregated school systems blacks are excluded from the schools far more often than whites"); and NAACP Legal Defense Fund, Division of Legal Information and Community Service, *Report on Black Student "Pushouts"—a National Phenomenon* (1972). Before *Lopez*, one federal judge attributed the higher rates of suspensions that black students receive to "institutional racism." *Hawkins v. Coleman*, 376 F. Supp. 1330, 1337 (N.D. Tex. 1974). For a recent exploration of this phenomenon, see Monique W. Morris, *Pushout: The Criminalization of Black Girls in Schools* (2016).

62. Wilkinson, "*Goss v. Lopez*: The Supreme Court as School Superintendent," 30–31.

63. "Notable & Quotable," *Wall Street Journal*, Nov. 22, 1999, A22.

64. See Gun-Free Schools Act of 1994, 20 U.S.C. § 7151 et seq. (1994); and Michael Imber et al., *Education Law* 192 (5th ed. 2014).

65. For perceptive overviews of the rise of zero-tolerance policies, see Russell J. Skiba, Suzanne E. Eckes, and Kevin Brown, "African American Disproportionality in School Discipline: The Divide Between Best Evidence and Legal Remedy," 54 *New York Law School Law Review* 1071, 1083–84 (2009); Russell J. Skiba, "The Failure of Zero Tolerance," 22 *Reclaiming Children and Youth* 27 (2014); Black, "Constitutional Limit of Zero Tolerance in Schools"; and Eric Blumenson and Eva S. Nilsen, "One Strike and You're Out? Constitutional Constraints on Zero Tolerance in Public Education," 81 *Washington University Law Quarterly* 65, 84–85 (2003).

66. Blumenson and Nilsen, "One Strike and You're Out?," 66. For an important article exploring the difficulties endemic to reforming excesses in the criminal law arena that can be understood to contain implications for reforming

excesses in school discipline, see William J. Stuntz, "The Pathological Politics of Criminal Law," 100 *Michigan Law Review* 505 (2001).

67. As Professor Randall Kennedy has argued, "Thurgood Marshall carefully screened potential clients before agreeing to represent them [and] withheld his services . . . where he doubted that a person would be willing and able to present a good face to the public." Randall Kennedy, "Lifting as We Climb," *Harper's*, Oct. 2015, 24, 29.

68. Dirk Johnson, "7 Students Charged in a Brawl That Divides Decatur, Ill.," *New York Times*, Nov. 10, 1999, A19.

69. "Jesse Jackson's Wrong Target," *Economist*, Nov. 27, 1999, 29.

70. Johnson, "7 Students Charged in a Brawl That Divides Decatur, Ill.," A19.

71. Ethan Bronner, "Student Rights Losing Ground: Does Recent Supreme Court Ruling Reflect a Growing Generational Alienation?," *Boston Globe*, Feb. 7, 1988, A22. See ibid. (reporting that Clark "has become, in his way, an American hero"); and Sara Rimer, "Paterson Principal: A Man of Extremes," *New York Times*, Jan. 14, 1988, B1 (reporting that Secretary of Education William Bennett called Clark "a national folk hero").

72. Ezra Bowen, "Getting Tough," *Time*, Feb. 1, 1988, 52, 53.

73. See *Time*, Feb. 1, 1988; and *Lean on Me* (Warner Brothers Pictures 1989).

74. See Joe Clark (with Joe Picard), *Laying Down the Law: Joe Clark's Strategy for Saving Our Schools* 42 (1989).

75. I borrow the phrase "education law and order" from Sander, "Schools Still Uncertain About Punishing Unruly," 150.

76. Marc Fisher, "Drop That Spork! 'Zero Tolerance' Goes to Richmond," *Washington Post*, Feb. 7, 2002, B1; and Ian Urbina, "It's a Fork, It's a Spoon, It's a . . . Weapon? School Suspends Boy, 6," *New York Times*, Oct. 12, 2009, A1. For other critical coverage of zero tolerance, see, for example, Dirk Johnson, "Schools' New Watchword: Zero Tolerance," *New York Times*, Dec. 1, 1999, A1; Debra Nussbaum, "Becoming Fed Up with Zero Tolerance," *New York Times*, Sept. 3, 2000, NJ1; and Jessica Portner, "Zero-Tolerance Laws Getting a Second Look," *Education Week*, March 26, 1997, 14.

77. See, for example, Arum, *Judging School Discipline*, 195 ("Zero tolerance practices have likely been generally ineffective or counterproductive because they have failed to address the central problem of a decline in moral authority and legitimacy of school discipline"); Philip K. Howard, *The Rule of Nobody: Saving America from Dead Laws and Broken Government* 35 (2014) ("[A] seventh-grade girl in Indiana . . . gave back a pill (for attention deficit disorder) that a friend had put in her hand. The principal said he had no choice [but to apply zero tolerance], since she technically had 'possession' for a few seconds."); and George F. Will, "'Zero Tolerance' Policies Are Getting out of Hand," *Boston Globe*, Dec. 25, 2000, A23.

78. *Safford Unified School District No. 1 v. Redding*, 557 U.S. 364, 400 (Thomas, J., dissenting) (quoting Maureen Downey, "Zero Tolerance Doesn't Always Add Up," *Atlanta Journal-Constitution*, April 6, 2009, A11).

79. For his part, Justice Thomas has contended, "[T]he task of implementing and amending public school policies is beyond this Court's function. Parents, teachers, school administrators, local politicians, and state officials are all better suited than judges to determine the appropriate limits on searches conducted by school officials. Preservation of order, discipline, and safety in public

schools is simply not the domain of the Constitution. And, common sense is not a judicial monopoly or a Constitutional imperative." *Redding,* 557 U.S. at 402 (Thomas, J., dissenting).

80. Ibid., 401–2 (Thomas, J., dissenting) (quoting Valerie Richardson, "Tolerance Waning for Zero-Tolerance Rules," *Washington Times,* April 21, 2009, A3).

81. For an astute overview and analysis of Benjamin Ratner's case, which influenced my own views, see Black, "Constitutional Limit of Zero Tolerance in Schools," 860–62.

82. *Ratner v. Loudoun County Public Schools,* 2001 WL 855606, at *2 (4th Cir. 2001), *cert. denied,* 534 U.S. 1114 (2002).

83. Ibid., *3 (Hamilton, J., concurring).

84. *Lopez,* 419 U.S. at 586 (Powell, J., dissenting).

85. Julie Underwood, "The 30th Anniversary of *Goss v. Lopez,*" 198 *Education Law Reporter* 795, 803 (2005).

86. *Lopez,* 419 U.S. at 576 (internal quotation marks and citation omitted).

87. Ibid., 579, 583.

88. Even if it might be argued that Ratner has no claim under *procedural* due process (because, that is, he received the required process), he may still be able to prevail on *substantive* due process. See *Wood v. Strickland,* 420 U.S. 308, 326 (1975) ("Public . . . school students do have substantive and procedural rights while at school").

89. *Seal v. Morgan,* 229 F.3d 567, 581 (6th Cir. 2000).

90. See Mark G. Yudof et al., *Educational Policy and the Law* 383 (5th ed. 2012) (providing the spiked punch hypothetical). For a case that actually involved a school dance with punch that had been spiked so mildly (with Right Time Malt Liquor, no less) that no one detected the taste of alcohol, see *Strickland,* 420 U.S. 308.

91. See *Bundick v. Bary City Independent School District,* 140 F. Supp. 2d 735 (S.D. Tex. 2001) (repudiating *Seal v. Morgan's* holding that school officials must inquire into mindset and knowledge). For another instance of a court turning a blind eye to an egregious suspension, see *S.G. v. Sayreville Board of Education,* 333 F.3d 417, 424–25 (3d Cir. 2003) (upholding the suspension of a kindergartner who stated, while playing a game of cops and robbers at recess, "I'm going to shoot you"). For one of the relatively few cases that accords with the Sixth Circuit's approach in *Seal v. Morgan,* see *Colvin v. Lowndes County School District,* 114 F. Supp. 2d 504, 512 (N.D. Miss. 1999) ("Individualized punishment by reference to all relevant facts and circumstances regarding the offense and the offender is a hallmark of our criminal justice system") (internal quotation marks and citation omitted). For scholars casting serious doubt on the effectiveness of zero-tolerance policies, see, for example, Troy Adam, "The Status of School Discipline and Violence," 567 *Annals of the American Academy of Political and Social Science* 140, 148 (2000); and Russ Skiba and Reese Peterson, "The Dark Side of Zero Tolerance: Can Punishment Lead to Safe Schools?," 80 *Phi Delta Kappan* 372, 376 (1999).

92. For the relevant background on Ingraham's injuries and Charles Drew Junior High School, see *Ingraham v. Wright,* 498 F.2d 248, 256–59 (5th Cir. 1974); *Ingraham v. Wright,* 430 U.S. 651, 655–59 (1977); Brief for Petitioners, *Ingraham,* 430 U.S. 651, 1976 WL 194478, at *6–*17.

93. See Proverbs 13:24 and 22:15. For four additional verses from Proverbs that

trumpet corporal punishment, see Proverbs 19:18, 23:13, 23:14, and 29:15. For a compilation of these verses, see James Keith Franklin, *Corporal Punishment in the Public Schools* 12 (1963).

94. See Herbert Arnold Falk, *Corporal Punishment: A Social Interpretation of Its Theory and Practice in the Schools of the United States* 19 (1941) (quoting Dorchester Town Records, Jan. 4, 1645).

95. See Ellwood P. Cubberley, *Public Education in the United States* 57 (rev. ed. 1934).

96. "Stop That Rod," *New York Times*, May 30, 1976, 120.

97. Patricia Anstett, "Spanking in School—the Debate," *Boston Globe*, Oct. 5, 1976, 22.

98. Buss, "Procedural Due Process for School Discipline," 560.

99. "Bottoms Up in Big D," *Newsweek*, May 17, 1971, 99.

100. Marvin Pave and Ray Richard, "Paddling Is Out in Mass. Schools, Despite US Court," *Boston Globe*, Oct. 21, 1975, 1 (internal quotation marks omitted, quoting Donald H. Russell, director of the Massachusetts Courts Clinics).

101. Eighth Amendment, U.S. Constitution.

102. *Trop v. Dulles*, 356 U.S. 86, 101 (1958) (Warren, C.J., plurality opinion). See also *Kennedy v. Louisiana*, 554 U.S. 407, 419–21 (2008).

103. *Thompson v. Oklahoma*, 487 U.S. 815, 830 (1988).

104. Brief for Respondents, *Ingraham*, 430 U.S. 651, 1976 WL 194479, at *9.

105. See Irene Merker Rosenberg, "*Ingraham v. Wright*: The Supreme Court's Whipping Boy," 78 *Columbia Law Review* 75, 105n167 (1978) ("According to the statistics for 1971, Drew Junior High School had 1,217 students, all of whom were black. As of 1977, the student population has been reduced to 873 students, but the racial composition remains precisely the same."). Although one cannot know for certain, it seems probable that the justices realized that Ingraham and his classmates who were contesting corporal punishment were black. As a preliminary matter, the brief filed in the Supreme Court opposing corporal punishment quoted Ingraham and several of his fellow students testifying in the black English vernacular. See Brief for Petitioners, *Ingraham*, 1976 WL 194478, at *9–*17; the joint appendix also reproduced extensive student testimony spoken in black English vernacular. On the phenomenon of black English vernacular more broadly, see Herbert L. Foster, *Ribbin', Jivin', and Playin' the Dozens* (1974). Even if the brief did not racially identify the students, however, that does not mean that the justices were unaware of the students' race. That knowledge might have existed because Charles R. Drew Junior High School was named for a celebrated black scientist, and—by the racial conventions of that time—that fact alone strongly indicated that Drew's student body must have been largely black. Justice Thurgood Marshall once asked a question at oral argument demonstrating the racial connection between schools named for black figures and their student bodies when he inquired whether a certain "Washington High School" was "a George," or a "Booker T." Marshall dissented in *Ingraham* and certainly almost could have been counted on to alert his colleagues to the racial identity of Drew's students. See Sandra Day O'Connor, "Thurgood Marshall: The Influence of a Raconteur," 44 *Stanford Law Review* 1217, 1220 (1992) (disclosing that Justice Marshall often informed his colleagues of racial realities that they did not otherwise know).

106. *Ingraham*, 430 U.S. at 670 (1977). Prior to *Ingraham*, some lower federal courts

also disposed of Eighth Amendment challenges to corporal punishment without deeply engaging the question. See, for example, *Ware v. Estes*, 328 F. Supp. 657, 660 (N.D. Tex. 1971), *aff'd per curiam*, 458 F.2d 1360 (5th Cir. 1972), *cert. denied*, 409 U.S. 1027 (1972); and *Glaser v. Marietta*, 351 F. Supp. 555, 557–58 (W.D. Pa. 1972) ("A method of parental control originating in the mists of prehistoric times, commended in Biblical references, sanctioned by Blackstone's *Commentaries* and defended by many of today's child psychologists, is not lightly to be declared unconstitutional").

107. *Ingraham*, 430 U.S. at 681.
108. Ibid., 670n39.
109. Ibid., 684n1 (White, J., dissenting).
110. Ibid., 692.
111. See ibid., 688n4, 691 (citing *Estelle v. Gamble*, 429 U.S. 97 [1976]). For academic criticism of *Ingraham*'s notion that the Eighth Amendment's Cruel and Unusual Punishment Clause does not apply to noncriminal settings, see Rosenberg, "*Ingraham v. Wright*," 84; and Lawrence A. Alexander and Paul Horton, "*Ingraham v. Wright*: A Primer for Cruel and Unusual Jurisprudence," 52 *Southern California Law Review* 1305, 1340–48 (1979).
112. *Ingraham*, 430 U.S. at 695 (White, J., dissenting).
113. My formulation is inspired by James E. Ryan, "The Supreme Court and Public Schools," 86 *Virginia Law Review* 1335, 1367 (2000) ("Just as a bell cannot be unrung, a paddling cannot be undone").
114. Laurence H. Tribe, *American Constitutional Law* 916 (1978).
115. Rosenberg, "*Ingraham v. Wright*," 95–96.
116. J. Patrick Mahon, "*Ingraham v. Wright*: The Continuing Debate over Corporal Punishment," 6 *Journal of Law and Education* 473, 477 (1977).
117. "Teachers Don't Need Paddles," *Chicago Tribune*, April 24, 1977, A4.
118. "Supreme Court: Wrong on Spanking," *Los Angeles Times*, April 24, 1977, F4.
119. "Paddling Justice," *New York Times*, April 21, 1977, 24. For still more editorial criticism of *Ingraham*, see "Sparing the Child," *Boston Globe*, April 21, 1977, 28; and "A Remarkable Decision," 22 *Social Work* 4, July 1977, 258.
120. Merrill Sheils and Frederick V. Boyd, "Ruling on the Rod," *Newsweek*, May 2, 1977, 65.
121. Sander, "Schools Still Uncertain About Punishing Unruly," 150.
122. See "Don't Spare the Rod," *Time*, May 2, 1977, 58. Not surprisingly, the difficulty grasping that some schools continue to inflict corporal punishment on students has proven a persistent phenomenon. Some sophisticated observers even suggest that the Supreme Court has prohibited the practice. See Bork, *Slouching Towards Gomorrah*, 104–5 (linking the Supreme Court to a decline in student discipline and suggesting the Court outlawed "the paddle for students who disrupt study hall").
123. Robert H. Friedman and Irwin A. Hyman, "Corporal Punishment in the Schools: A Descriptive Survey of State Regulations," in *Corporal Punishment in American Education: Readings in History, Practice, and Alternatives* 157, 157 (Irwin A. Hyman and James H. Wise eds., 1979) (quoting *Martinsburg Journal*, April 22, 1977).
124. James J. Kilpatrick, "But It's Hearts That Bleed," *Los Angeles Times*, May 13, 1977, D7.
125. Gene I. Maeroff, "Spanking Rule Found an Aid to Discipline," *New York Times*,

April 25, 1977, 24. Some leaders within the education world disagreed with this assessment and professed to find *Ingraham* deeply confounding. Robert Chanin, the National Education Association's general counsel, stated, "This decision makes no sense to us." Sheils and Boyd, "Ruling on the Rod," 65.

126. "Spare the Rod?," *Newsweek*, Nov. 15, 1976, 105. Intriguingly, some evidence suggests that—despite Justice Powell's valorization of local control—many Dade County residents (perhaps even the majority) opposed corporal punishment. According to *Newsweek*, "[T]he Dade County school board has been holding public hearings, hoping to set guidelines. The board itself is unanimously opposed to corporal punishment—and parents have testified about 5 to 1 against it. But teach[ers] are overwhelmingly in favor, and they are demanding the right to set their own policies." Ibid. These cleavages on corporal punishment within Dade County make clear that "local control" is a term that admits of multiple meanings. For related criticism of *Ingraham*'s invocation of local control, see Note, "Due Process, Due Politics, and Due Respect: Three Models of Legitimate School Governance," 94 *Harvard Law Review* 1106, 1112–16, 1124 (1981) ("The record indicated that the Dade County School System was the sixth largest in the country; student enrollment was estimated to be over 240,000. The Court noted that abuses of corporal punishment were not epidemic but confined to one school. To the extent that the problem concerned parents in one neighborhood, the likelihood that the school board would experience significant political pressure was small.").

127. Sheils and Boyd, "Ruling on the Rod," 65, 66. For another article disclosing Ingraham's incarceration, see "Don't Spare the Rod," *Time*, 58.

128. Rosenberg, "*Ingraham v. Wright*," 89.

129. David B. Tyack, *The One Best System: A History of American Urban Education* 75 (1974).

130. Ellen Jane Hollingsworth, Henry S. Lufler Jr., and William H. Clune III, *School Discipline: Order and Autonomy* 111 (1984).

131. Eduardo Cue, "School Spanking Ruling Not Seen as Affecting Area," *Washington Post*, April, 22, 1977, C1.

132. See, for example, Deana Pollard Sacks, "State Actors Beating Children: A Call for Judicial Relief," 42 *UC Davis Law Review* 1165, 1175 (2009); James F. Gregory, "The Crime of Punishment: Racial and Gender Disparities in the Use of Corporal Punishment in U.S. Public Schools," 64 *Journal of Negro Education* 454, 457 (1995); Timothy John Nolen, "Smacking Lesson: How the Council of Europe's Ban on Corporal Punishment Could Serve as a Model for the United States," 16 *Cardozo Journal of Law and Gender* 519, 524 (2010); and Heddy Muransky and Linda J. Fresneda, "What Do Prisoners and Zoo Animals Have in Common? They Have More Protection from Physical Violence than School Children in Nineteen States," 5 *University of Miami Race and Social Justice Law Review* 73, 84 (2015).

133. Office for Civil Rights, U.S. Department of Education, Civil Rights Data Collection 2011–2012, Projected Values for the Nation (2012).

134. "Bottoms Up in Big D," 99.

135. Godfrey Anderson, "Dallas Called Capital of School Punishment," *Boston Globe*, Oct. 24, 1972, 21. As the title of this newspaper article attests, Dallas had an exceptionally high rate of corporal punishment in the early 1970s. The Dallas school superintendent Nolan Estes viewed the practice as a necessary

evil: "We don't think we ought to paddle, but until there is a utopian society we will use it as a method of discipline. It is a last resort." Despite this somewhat ambivalent attitude toward corporal punishment, Estes disclosed that he would sooner resign than lead a school system that prohibited paddling. See ibid.

136. Office for Civil Rights, U.S. Department of Education, Civil Rights Data Collection 2011–2012, Projected Values for the Nation (2012).

137. According to the U.S. Department of Education's Office of Civil Rights, male students received 78.3 percent of corporal punishment. Ibid.

138. Adah Maurer, "It Does Happen Here," in *Corporal Punishment in American Education* 219, 226. See also "Mother Warns Teachers Who Spanked Her Child," *San Antonio Star*, Oct. 2, 1977, 8.

139. Maurer, "It Does Happen Here," 226.

140. Ibid., 226–27.

141. See *Serafin v. School of Excellence in Education*, 252 F. App'x 684, 2007 WL 3226296, at *1 (5th Cir. Oct. 30, 2007) (unpublished opinion), *cert. denied*, 128 S. Ct. 2962 (2008). For a compelling critique of corporal punishment in schools and a vivid description of Serafin's case, see Sacks, "State Actors Beating Children," 1165, 1165–68, 1167n1. See also Deana A. Pollard, "Banning Corporal Punishment: A Constitutional Analysis," 52 *American University Law Review* 447 (2002). In the absence of a Supreme Court decision revisiting *Ingraham*, some lower federal courts have granted relief to students who received particularly outrageous forms of corporal punishment from educators by finding that the treatment violates substantive due process. The U.S. Court of Appeals for the Fourth Circuit's decision in *Hall v. Tawney*, the leading case in this area, announced that excessive corporal punishment violates students' substantive due process rights if "the force applied caused injury so severe, was so disproportionate to the need presented, and was so inspired by malice or sadism rather than a merely careless or unwise excess of zeal that it amounted to a brutal and inhumane abuse of official power literally shocking to the conscience." *Hall v. Tawney*, 621 F.2d 607, 613 (4th Cir. 1987). See also *Garcia by Garcia v. Miera*, 817 F.2d 650, 654 (10th Cir. 1987) ("Although *Ingraham* makes clear that ordinary corporal punishment violates no substantive due process rights of school children . . . we believe that opinion clearly signaled that, at some degree of excessiveness or cruelty, the meting out such punishment violates the substantive due process rights of the pupil"). Perhaps the most egregious set of facts that motivated a federal appellate court to find that an educator violated a student's substantive due process rights arose in the Eleventh Circuit's opinion in *Neal v. Fulton County Board of Education*. There, a school official struck a student who had been fighting with another student with a metal weight lock in his left eye—a blow so forceful that it knocked the student's eye completely out of its socket, leaving it wholly unusable. See 229 F.3d 1069 (11th Cir. 2000). For other instances where educators have corporally punished students in a way that did not involve paddling, see, for example, *London v. Directors of Dewitt Public Schools*, 194 F.3d 873, 875 (8th Cir. 1999) (educator dragged student across room and then banged his head against metal pole); *Metzger v. Osbeck*, 841 F.2d 518, 519–20 (3d Cir. 1988) (educator placed student in a chokehold that caused the student to lose consciousness and, upon falling to the pavement, to break his nose and fracture his teeth); and *Gaither v.*

Barron, 924 F. Supp. 134, 135–36 (M.D. Ala. 1996) (teacher head-butted student). That lower federal courts have in some particularly alarming instances found a way to work around the Supreme Court's inaction on corporal punishment in no way indicates that the Court should not also eliminate more workaday instances.

142. See Adrian Vermeule, "The Judiciary Is a They, Not an It: Interpretive Theory and the Fallacy of Division," 14 *Journal of Contemporary Legal Issues* 549, 550 (2005).

143. Ryan, "Supreme Court and Public Schools," 1368. For two well-known articles that wrestle with the tension between the Court's opinions in *Lopez* and *Ingraham*, see Anne Proffitt Dupre, "Should Students Have Constitutional Rights? Keeping Order in the Public Schools," 65 *George Washington Law Review* 49, 59–68 (1996); and Emily Buss, "Constitutional Fidelity Through Children's Rights," 2004 *Supreme Court Review* 355, 378.

144. See, for example, Rosenberg, *"Ingraham v. Wright,"* 88 ("[T]he Court's decision on the eighth amendment issue is perhaps most accurately seen as a response to increasing violence within the nation's public schools").

145. Ibid., 88n77 (citing "Challenge for the Third Century: Education in a Safe Environment—Final Report on the Nature and Prevention of School Violence and Vandalism," Subcommittee to Investigate Juvenile Delinquency of the Senate Committee on the Judiciary, 95th Cong., 1st Sess. 7–19 [Comm. print 1977]). For newspaper coverage of school violence post-*Lopez*, see Enid Nemy, "Violence in Schools Now Seen as Norm Across the Nation," *New York Times*, June 14, 1975, 1; Bart Barnes et al., "Violence Proliferates in Area Schools," *Washington Post*, May 18, 1975, 1; and Bart Barnes, "Violence Soars in U.S. Schools," *Washington Post*, April 10, 1975, 1.

146. "Public Schools," *Time*, Nov. 14, 1969, 49.

147. See Buss, "Procedural Due Process for School Discipline," 549, 549n12.

148. See Glazer, "Towards an Imperial Judiciary?"; Thomas Ehrlich, "Legal Pollution: Increasingly Often, There Ought Not to Be a Law," *New York Times Magazine*, Feb. 8, 1976, SM5; and Jerrold K. Footlick, "Too Much Law?," *Newsweek*, Jan. 10, 1977, 42.

149. Footlick, "Too Much Law?," 42–43.

150. Philip Hager, "School Paddlings—Is It Constitutional?," *Los Angeles Times*, Nov. 4, 1976, 4.

151. *Ingraham*, 430 U.S. at 670n39.

152. *Lopez*, 419 U.S. at 597–99 (Powell, J., dissenting). Justice Powell's parade of horribles has not materialized. Indeed, the Supreme Court itself quickly made clear that due process typically had no applicability to academic assessments. See *Board of Curators of University of Missouri v. Horowitz*, 435 U.S. 78, 85–91 (1978) (distinguishing *Lopez*).

153. See Alan Reitman, "The Law and Corporal Punishment: Recent Legal Decisions on Corporal Punishment in Schools," paper presented at the Annual Convention of the American Psychological Association, Sept. 1, 1975, 34–35 (noting that a 1970 Gallup poll found 62 percent of respondents supported corporal punishment in lower grades). For additional polling data on corporal punishment during the 1970s, see the sources cited in Justice Powell's opinion for the Court in *Ingraham*, 430 U.S. at 661n17. For a more recent survey gaug-

ing attitudes toward corporal punishment, see "Disciplining a Child," *Survey USA* (2005) (revealing that only 23 percent of respondents supported corporal punishment in schools, ranging from a high of 53 percent in both Arkansas and Mississippi to a low of 8 percent in New Hampshire); and "Ipsos Poll Conducted for Reuters: Corporal Punishment Topline," Ipsos, Oct. 6, 2014 (finding 35 percent of U.S. correspondents agreed that "corporal punishment should be allowed at school, as long as it isn't excessive").

154. *Trop*, 356 U.S. at 100–101.
155. Office for Civil Rights, U.S. Department of Education, Civil Rights Data Collection 2011–2012, Projected Values for the Nation (2012).
156. See *Graham v. Florida*, 560 U.S. 48 (2010).
157. "Corporal Punishment Policies Around the World," CNN, Nov. 9, 2011.
158. See, for example, *Thompson*, 487 U.S. at 830; and *Roper v. Simmons*, 543 U.S. 551, 576–78 (2005).
159. The Department of Education's Office of Civil Rights collected these figures in 2006 and 2012. See Office for Civil Rights, U.S. Department of Education, Civil Rights Data Collection 2006, Projected Values for the Nation (2006); and Office for Civil Rights, U.S. Department of Education, Civil Rights Data Collection 2011–2012, Projected Values for the Nation (2012).
160. *Cooper v. McJunkin*, 4 Ind. 290, 292 (1853) (Stuart, J.).

4 POLICING STUDENT INVESTIGATIONS

1. My account is derived from *New Jersey v. T.L.O.*, 469 U.S. 325, 327–33n1 (1985); Brief for Petitioner, *T.L.O.*, 469 U.S. 325, 1984 WL 565537, at *3–*5; Brief for Respondent, *T.L.O.*, 469 U.S. 325, 1984 WL 565542, at *2–*6; and Joint Appendix, *T.L.O.*, 1983 S. Ct. Briefs LEXIS 1209. The notion that Assistant Vice Principal Choplick might have searched T.L.O.'s purse on something of a fishing expedition receives some support from his own testimony. After discovering rolling papers in T.L.O.'s purse, Choplick stated, "[F]rom then on I went to see what else was in there because from my experiences that seems to be a sign that someone is smoking marijuana." Brief for Respondent, *T.L.O.*, *3. In *New Jersey v. T.L.O.*, the U.S. Supreme Court initially agreed to consider whether the exclusionary rule (which generally bars evidence found in violation of the Fourth Amendment from being used against criminal defendants) applies to public schools. See *New Jersey v. T.L.O.*, 464 U.S. 991 (1983) (granting petition for writ of certiorari). After hearing oral argument, the Court requested briefing on the antecedent question of whether Choplick's search violated the Fourth Amendment at all. The Supreme Court has yet to resolve whether the exclusionary rule applies to Fourth Amendment violations that occur on school grounds, but most courts that have addressed the issue have held that it does apply.
2. Robert Pear, "Reagan Expected to Present Plan to Fight Crime in Public Schools," *New York Times*, Jan. 1, 1984, 1.
3. Associated Press, "U.S. Asks Court to Give Schools Right to Search," *Los Angeles Times*, July 31, 1984, 2 (reporting on Reagan's radio address from January). Dating back to December 1983, President Reagan delivered a speech

to educators in Indianapolis urging that schools "need to restore good old-fashioned discipline." See Pear, "Reagan Expected to Present Plan to Fight Crime in Public Schools," 1.

4. Brief for the United States as Amicus Curiae, *T.L.O.*, 464 U.S. 991, 1984 WL 565546, at *23 (1984) ("The sad truth is that many classrooms across the country are not temples of learning teaching the lessons of good will, civility, and wisdom that are central to the fabric of American life").

5. Ibid., *2, *23.

6. See Leslie Maitland Werner, "U.S. Asks Court to Back School in a Search Case," *New York Times*, Aug. 1, 1984, A8; Caroline Rand Herron and Michael Wright, "More Power to the Schools?," *New York Times*, Aug. 5, 1984, 2E; and Ronald J. Ostrow, "U.S. Asks Court to Let Schools Search Students," *Los Angeles Times*, Aug. 1, 1984, 10. See also Ted Galen Carpenter, "The New Antiyouth Movement," *Nation*, Jan. 19, 1985, 39 ("In [*T.L.O.*], the Justice Department has filed a brief that advocates giving local school districts wide latitude to search students for weapons or illicit drugs. A victory for the government in the case would virtually negate the Fourth Amendment's guarantees against unreasonable searches and seizures as they pertain to teen-age students.").

7. *T.L.O.*, 469 U.S. at 343.

8. Ibid., 342.

9. Ibid., 349 (Powell, J., concurring).

10. Ibid., 349–50.

11. Ibid., 352 (Blackmun, J., concurring in the judgment).

12. Ibid., 351. In one passage, where Justice Blackmun articulates the necessity of the special needs doctrine, he writes, "The elementary and secondary school setting presents a special need for flexibility justifying a departure from the balance struck by the Framers." Ibid., 352. After the rise of originalism, it seems unlikely that this formulation—openly indicating that the judicial approach betrays, rather than advances, the framers' vision—would appear in a Supreme Court opinion. On these general themes, see William Baude, "Is Originalism Our Law?," 115 *Columbia Law Review* 2349 (2015). For an article examining and defending the special needs doctrine as a general proposition, see William J. Stuntz, "Implicit Bargains, Government Power, and the Fourth Amendment," 44 *Stanford Law Review* 553, 563 (1992).

13. See *T.L.O.*, 469 U.S. at 353, 354, 364, 368–69 (Brennan, J., concurring in part and dissenting in part) (citing Wayne LaFave, 3 *Search and Seizure* § 10.11, 459–60 [1978]).

14. *T.L.O.*, 469 U.S. at 377 (Stevens, J., concurring in part and dissenting in part).

15. Ibid., 385.

16. Ibid., 373.

17. Ibid., 385–86. In addition to Justice Jackson's opinion in *Barnette*, Justice Stevens's opinion identifies a precursor in one of Justice Louis Brandeis's foundational dissenting opinions from a criminal case assessing the constitutionality of warrantless wiretaps: "Our government is the potent, the omnipresent teacher. For good or for ill, it teaches the whole people by its example." *Olmstead v. United States*, 277 U.S. 438, 485 (1928) (Brandeis, J., dissenting). For illuminating analysis of Brandeis's dissent, see Carol S. Steiker, "Brandeis in *Olmstead*: 'Our Government Is the Potent, the Omnipresent Teacher,'" 79 *Mississippi Law Journal* 149 (2009).

18. *T.L.O.*, 469 U.S. at 354 (Brennan, J., concurring in part and dissenting in part). Although Justice Brennan's opinion appears before Justice Stevens's in *T.L.O.* because Brennan had been on the Court for a longer period, Brennan graciously credits Stevens with the citizenship insight. See ibid. For an early academic articulation of this view, see William G. Buss, "The Fourth Amendment and Searches of Students in Public Schools," 59 *Iowa Law Review* 739, 792 (1974) ("There is a very good chance that an erosion of privacy and the destruction of human values that go with privacy is a greater long-range danger than the behavior that would be detected and deterred by student searches. It would be highly desirable if the citizens of the United States who are now in school learn to value privacy, learn by the school's example that the society respects it, and learn that the courts will protect it from invasion by governmental searches that violate fourth amendment principles."). For a more recent academic articulation of related ideas, see Irene Merker Rosenberg, "The Supreme Court, the Fourth Amendment, and the Public Schools: An Ominous Mixture," *Criminal Law Bulletin*, Sept.–Oct. 2000, 360, 372 ("It is important that our public schools not be turned into fortresses that are so preoccupied with student misbehavior that they are willing to abandon individualized suspicion and opt for random searches of innocent children, who, we must remember, are in the overwhelming majority"). For empirical evidence suggesting that when citizens are stopped and questioned by police, the experience contributes to increased distrust of government, see Vesla M. Weaver and Amy E. Lerman, "Political Consequences of the Carceral State," 104 *American Political Science Review* 817 (2010). It would hardly be surprising if this dynamic applied to police contact with students in schools.

19. Ezra Bowen, "Search Rules," *Time*, Jan. 28, 1985, 77; and Alfonso A. Narvaez, "Principal Extols Searches Decision," *New York Times*, Jan. 16, 1985, A17.

20. Bowen, "Search Rules," 77.

21. Stephen Wermiel, "Students May Be Searched If School Has 'Reasonable Grounds,' High Court Rules," *Wall Street Journal*, Jan. 16, 1985, 5.

22. "Ruling on School Searches Greeted with Praise, Caution," *Seattle Times*, Jan. 17, 1985, A3; and "Freer Hand to Search Students," *New York Times*, Jan. 20, 1985, E1.

23. Nat Hentoff, "Students of the 'Real World,'" *Washington Post*, Feb. 21, 1985, A19. Within the ACLU, Mary Heen of the organization's New Jersey chapter stood out from her colleagues by expressing disappointment with *T.L.O.*: "I think it will probably mean that students are going to be subjected to more intrusive searches in deprivation of their constitutional rights." Paul Houston and Scott Harris, "High Court Search Ruling Praised by School Officials," *Los Angeles Times*, Jan. 16, 1985, SD1.

24. "A Need for Prudence," *Los Angeles Times*, Jan. 17, 1985, C4.

25. "Searching Students," *New York Times*, Jan. 18, 1985, A26.

26. "Treating Children as Children," *Chicago Tribune*, Jan. 17, 1985, 26.

27. "Searches in the Schools," *Boston Globe*, Jan. 17, 1985, 18. For other editorials that criticized *T.L.O.*, see "Administrators Must Protect Student Rights," *Seattle Times*, Jan. 16, 1985, A14; and "School Search Decision Is a Blow to Basic Rights," *Fort Lauderdale Sun Sentinel*, Jan. 23, 1985, A14.

28. David Margolick, "Students and Privacy," *New York Times*, Jan. 21, 1985, B4.

29. Austin Sarat, "Leaving the Constitution at the Schoolhouse Door," *New York Times*, Jan. 30, 1985, A22.
30. Geoffrey R. Stone, "Diluting the 4th Amendment," *Chicago Tribune*, Feb. 14, 1985, 27. For a contemporaneous law review article that criticized *T.L.O.*, see Nat Stern, "The Burger Court and the Diminishing Constitutional Rights of Minors: A Brief Overview," 1985 *Arizona State Law Journal* 865, 889–90, 900–902 (arguing that *T.L.O.* improperly infringed upon minors' rights). For a recent effort by a legal academic contending that the Fourth Amendment should function within schools in precisely the same way as it does outside schools, see Barry C. Feld, "*T.L.O.* and *Redding*'s Unanswered (Misanswered) Fourth Amendment Questions: Few Rights and Fewer Remedies," 80 *Mississippi Law Journal* 847, 952 (2011) ("*T.L.O.* created a school search exception to the Fourth Amendment where none was necessary"). For legal scholarship linking *T.L.O.* to citizenship, see Betsy Levin, "Educating Youth for Citizenship: The Conflict Between Authority and Individual Rights in the Public School," 95 *Yale Law Journal* 1647, 1671 (1986) ("The Supreme Court in *T.L.O.* has, once again, left unresolved society's ambivalence between a concern for order and safety and the desire to inculcate in students an understanding of the constitutional rights of individuals"); and Donald L. Beci, "School Violence: Protecting Our Children and the Fourth Amendment," 41 *Catholic University Law Review* 817, 833 (1992) ("Undoubtedly, the approaches tomorrow's leaders will take toward the amendment will be shaped by the lessons they learn as today's school children. Students learn about the liberty, privacy and security guaranteed by the Fourth Amendment more through actions than words."). Professor Edward Wynne offered one of the few positive contemporaneous assessments of *T.L.O.* within academic circles. In Wynne's view, *T.L.O.* compensated for some of the excesses of the Court's decisions in *Tinker* and *Lopez*. "The schools adjusted to a moderate level of disorder that would have been intolerable in the past," Wynne contended after those decisions, but *T.L.O.* "will send a signal to school people that they can operate in a common-sense fashion." Lawrence Feinberg, "'Search' Ruling Hailed: School Officials Welcome Court's Support," *Washington Post*, Jan. 21, 1985, B1.
31. *T.L.O.*, 469 U.S. at 343 (emphasis added).
32. See *State ex rel. T.L.O.*, 463 A.2d 934, 942 (N.J. 1983).
33. See Jason P. Nance, "Random, Suspicionless Searches of Public School Students' Belongings: A Legal, Empirical, and Normative Analysis," 84 *University of Colorado Law Review* 367, 409 (2013).
34. See Eric Blumenson and Eva S. Nilsen, "One Strike and You're Out? Constitutional Constraints on Zero Tolerance in Public Education," 81 *Washington University Law Quarterly* 65, 73 (2003); Feld, "*T.L.O.* and *Redding*'s Unanswered (Misanswered) Fourth Amendment Questions," 901; and Nance, "Random, Suspicionless Searches of Public School Students' Belongings," 428–29. The phenomenon described here appears outside the school context as well. See generally William J. Stuntz, "Warrants and Fourth Amendment Remedies," 77 *Virginia Law Review* 881 (1991).
35. See *Commonwealth v. Damian D.*, 752 N.E.2d 679, 682–83 (Mass. 2001). For a recent case that adhered to *Damian D.*'s reasoning to invalidate a student search in similar circumstances, see *In re Anthony F.*, 37 A.3d 429, 432–33 (N.H. 2012).

36. *In re Lisa G.*, 23 Cal. Rptr. 3d 163, 166 (Ct. App. 2004) ("A correlation between the wrongful behavior of the student and the intended findings of the search is essential for a valid search of the student under the Fourth Amendment"). For a similar opinion, where the court invalidated a search of a student who was in the hallway without a hall pass, see *State v. Pablo R.*, 137 P.3d 1198, 1202 (N.M. Ct. App. 2006) ("[T]here must be a nexus or a connection between the item searched for and the suspected violation").

37. See *T.L.O.*, 469 U.S. at 332n2.

38. Buss, "Fourth Amendment and Searches of Students in Public Schools," 789. As Professor Buss explained, "There is little indication . . . that 'reasonable suspicion' has entailed a close examination and assessment of the facts that arguably establish the occasion for the search or the appropriate scope of the resulting search." Ibid., 788.

39. See, for example, Brief of the ACLU et al. as Amici Curiae, *T.L.O.*, 469 U.S. 325, 1984 WL 565550, at *17, *33, *35 (citing Buss, "Fourth Amendment and Searches of Students in Public Schools," 739). See also ibid., *35n17 ("The use of a standard lower than probable cause for the search of a juvenile in school has been severely criticized by commentators"); William Tucker Cotton and Lisa Anne Haage, Comment, "Students and the Fourth Amendment: 'The Torturable Class,' " 16 *UC Davis Law Review* 709, 723–27 (1983); and Martin Schiff, "The Emergence of Student Rights to Privacy Under the Fourth Amendment," 34 *Baylor Law Review* 209, 214–17 (1982).

40. *T.L.O.*'s asserted desire to save educators from learning the intricacies of the Fourth Amendment's probable cause standard may also exaggerate how demanding probable cause was for police officers to learn. Indeed, the Court's landmark probable cause opinion—decided less than two years before *T.L.O.*—announced a totality-of-the-circumstances test that was not all that different from the reasonable suspicion test, even if the probable cause threshold level of certainty is more demanding. See *Illinois v. Gates*, 462 U.S. 213, 241–46 (1983).

41. For an intriguing, related argument, see Michael Pinard, "From the Classroom to the Courtroom: Reassessing Fourth Amendment Standards in Public School Searches Involving Law Enforcement Authorities," 45 *Arizona Law Review* 1067, 1123 (2003). Professor Pinard's proposal would apply probable cause to searches by police officers and also to searches conducted by teachers in search of criminal activity. If teachers conducted a student search for violating a school rule that does not impose independent criminal liability, however, Pinard's proposal would permit the fruits of that evidence to be turned over to police for arrest and prosecutorial purposes—even if the search was justified only by reasonable suspicion. In my view, this approach leaves too large a loophole that school administrators could manipulate.

42. See *Bahr v. Jenkins*, 539 F. Supp. 483, 485–86 (E.D. Ky. 1982); *Stern v. New Haven Community Schools*, 529 F. Supp. 31, 35–36 (E.D. Mich. 1981); and *Doe v. Renfrow*, 475 F. Supp. 1012, 1024 (N.D. Ind. 1979), *affirmed in relevant part*, *Doe v. Renfrow*, 631 F.2d 91, 92 (7th Cir. 1980). For scholarship noting the idea of imposing a probable cause standard for evidence to be used in court against students, see Feld, "*T.L.O.* and *Redding*'s Unanswered (Misanswered) Fourth Amendment Questions," 859n65; and Erica Tina Helfer, "Search and Seizure in Public Schools: Are Our Children's Rights Going to the Dogs?," 24 *St. Louis University Law Journal* 119, 127–30 (1979).

43. See *Vernonia School District 47J v. Acton*, 515 U.S. 646 (1995); *Board of Education of Independent School District No. 92 of Pottawatomie County v. Earls*, 536 U.S. 822 (2002).

44. See *Ferguson v. City of Charleston*, 532 U.S. 67 (2001). For insightful commentary establishing a connection between *Ferguson* and the Court's Fourth Amendment jurisprudence of schools, see Catherine Y. Kim et al., *The School-to-Prison Pipeline: Structuring Legal Reform* 121–22 (2010); Note, "Policing Students," 128 *Harvard Law Review* 1747, 1761–64 (2015); and Pinard, "From the Classroom to the Courtroom," 1099–1104.

45. See Stuntz, "Implicit Bargains, Government Power, and the Fourth Amendment," 555 (defending the Supreme Court's special needs doctrine, of which *T.L.O.* is a leading example, against its many critics and maintaining that the doctrine gets matters "about right"). At the time of Professor Stuntz's death in 2011, Dean Martha Minow of Harvard Law School stated, "He leapt to the top of the field in the early days of his entering the law professor world." Justice Elena Kagan also praised Stuntz in effusive terms: "What was fascinating about him was that everybody read him and listened to him and took seriously what he said." See Douglas Martin, "W. J. Stuntz, Who Stimulated Legal Minds, Dies at 52," *New York Times*, March 20, 2011, A23. Harvard University Press posthumously published a book that tied together and elaborated upon Professor Stuntz's impressive body of scholarly articles. See William J. Stuntz, *The Collapse of American Criminal Justice* (2011). For a probing, skeptical evaluation of Stuntz's book, see Stephen J. Schulhofer, "Criminal Justice, Local Democracy, and Constitutional Rights," 111 *Michigan Law Review* 1045 (2013). For a more celebratory assessment of Stuntz's volume by a leading jurist, see Richard A. Posner, "Incarceration Blues," *New Republic*, Nov. 17, 2011, 36–39.

46. Stuntz, "Implicit Bargains, Government Power, and the Fourth Amendment," 564.

47. Ibid. I label Professor Stuntz's account of *T.L.O.* "slightly stylized" because, in his scenario, a teacher enters a restroom and discovers two girls not smoking cigarettes (as actually happened) but instead two girls and cigarette smoke merely "hanging in the air," creating uncertainty as to whether the girls had been smoking. Ibid., 562. Stuntz correctly acknowledges that guilty students would not prefer the rule articulated in *T.L.O.* He contends, however, that the situation should be approached with a view toward maximizing student welfare rather than protecting guilty parties. See ibid., 565–66. For a powerful critique of Stuntz's defense of the special needs doctrine, see Richard H. McAdams, Dhammika Dharmapala, and Nuno Garoupa, "The Law of Police," 82 *University of Chicago Law Review* 135, 151–58 (2015).

48. See Linda M. Raffaele Mendez et al., "Who Gets Suspended from School and Why: A Demographic Analysis of Disciplinary Infractions in a Large School District," 26 *Education and Treatment of Children* 30, 31 (2003).

49. Jason P. Nance, "School Surveillance and the Fourth Amendment," 2014 *Wisconsin Law Review* 79, 81.

50. See Joe Clark (with Joe Picard), *Laying Down the Law: Joe Clark's Strategy for Saving Our Schools* (1989). I vividly recall from my own experience in Washington, D.C.'s public schools that students at Alice Deal Junior High School were prohibited from being in the halls during classes without a "hall pass,"

typically a wooden block with those two words scrawled across it in black felt-tip marker.

51. See Stuntz, *Collapse of the American Criminal Justice System*, 1–5.

52. Stuntz, "Implicit Bargains, Government Power, and the Fourth Amendment," 574.

53. See *T.L.O.*, 469 U.S. at 341n7 (citing *Picha v. Wieglos*, 410 F. Supp. 1214, 1219–21 [N.D. Ill. 1976]) (applying probable cause to student searches involving police officers). See also *Martens v. District No. 220*, 620 F. Supp. 29 (N.D. Ill. 1985); and *Cason v. Cook*, 810 F.2d 188 (8th Cir. 1987). For evidence that some districts began bringing police officers into schools during the 1960s and 1970s, see Heather Ann Thompson, "Why Mass Incarceration Still Matters," 97 *Journal of American History* 703, 710–11 (2010).

54. Robert J. Rubel, "Cooperative School System and Police Responses to High-Risk and Disruptive Youth," in *Student Discipline Strategies: Research and Practice* 213, 220 (Oliver C. Moles ed., 1990) (quoting S. D. Vestermark, *Responses to Collective Violence in Threat or Act, National Technical Information Service, Collective Violence in Educational Institutions* 12 [1971]).

55. Gun-Free Schools Act of 1994, 20 U.S.C. § 7151 et seq. (1994). In 1998, the Omnibus Crime Control and Safe Streets Act of 1968 was amended to spur schools to implement resource officers. An Act to Amend Part Q of the Omnibus Crime Control and Safe Streets Act, Pub. L. No. 105-302, § 1112 Stat. 2841 (1998). For helpful background on the rise of school resource officers that informs my understanding, see Gary Fields and John R. Emshwiller, "For More Teens, Arrests by Police Replace School Discipline," *Wall Street Journal*, Oct. 20, 2014; Sarah Jane Forman, "Countering Criminalization: Toward a Youth Development Approach to School Searches," 14 *Scholar* 301, 325–37 (2011); Rachel Dinkes et al., National Center for Education Statistics, U.S. Department of Education, *Indicators of School Crime and Safety: 2007* 61; Lisa H. Thurau and Johanna Wald, "Controlling Partners: When Law Enforcement Meets Discipline in Public Schools," 54 *New York Law School Law Review* 977, 978–81 (2010); and Mark G. Yudof et al., *Educational Policy and the Law* 344 (5th ed. 2012). For insightful work that chronicles and analyzes how police officers have become a presence in schools in a way that was unfathomable at the time of *T.L.O.*, and contends that the Fourth Amendment doctrine in schools should change accordingly, see Pinard, "From the Classroom to the Courtroom," 1075–76; and Josh Kagan, "Reappraising *T.L.O.*'s 'Special Needs' Doctrine in an Era of School–Law Enforcement Entanglement," 33 *Journal of Law and Education* 291, 295 (2004).

56. See Richard Pérez-Peña et al., "Rough Student Arrest Puts Spotlight on Officers in Schools," *New York Times*, Oct. 28, 2015, A15; Bob Herbert, "6-Year-Olds Under Arrest," *New York Times*, April 9, 2007, A17; Howard Witt, "To Some in Paris, Sinister Past Is Back," *Chicago Tribune*, March 12, 2007, 1; Matthew T. Theriot, "School Resource Officers and the Criminalization of Student Behavior," 37 *Journal of Criminal Justice* 280 (2009); and Charles Richards, "Student Sent to TYC for Shoving Aide," *Paris (Tex.) News*, March 12, 2006, 1A. For other examples of students being arrested by school resource officers on flimsy grounds, see Ann M. Simmons, "High School Scuffle Exposes a Racial Rift," *Los Angeles Times*, Oct. 11, 2007, B1 (chronicling

a school resource officer's arrest of a sixteen-year-old girl in an incident that was sparked by the student's failure to clean up completely a piece of birthday cake that she dropped); and Sharif Durhams, "Tosa East Student Arrested, Fined After Repeated Texting," *Milwaukee Journal Sentinel*, Feb. 18, 2009, B8 (chronicling a school resource officer's arrest of a fourteen-year-old girl in an incident sparked by text messaging during class).

57. See Richard Fausset and Ashley Southall, "Videos Show Officer Flipping and Dragging Student, Bringing Inquiry," *New York Times*, Oct. 27, 2015, A14; Pérez-Peña et al., "Rough Student Arrest Puts Spotlight on Officers in Schools," A15; Holly Yan, "South Carolina School Officer Fired, but More Fallout Possible," CNN, Oct. 29, 2015.

58. S.C. Code § 16-17-420 (2012).

59. Yan, "South Carolina School Officer Fired, but More Fallout Possible."

60. Pérez-Peña et al., "Rough Student Arrest Puts Spotlight on Officers in Schools," A15.

61. See Kim et al., *School-to-Prison Pipeline*, 128 (noting the "disturbing schools" offense accounted for the largest number of juvenile court referrals in South Carolina during 2007–2008); and Catherine Y. Kim, "Policing School Discipline," 77 *Brooklyn Law Review* 861, 886 (2012). For state statutes that addressed disturbing schools, see Ariz. Rev. Stat. Ann. § 13-2911 (2002); Ala. Educ. Code § 32210 (West 2002); Ga. Code Ann. § 20-2-1181 (2004); Iowa Code § 718.3 (2003); Mass. Gen. Laws Ch. 272, § 40 (2009); Md. Code Ann., Educ. § 26-101 (2002); Mont. Code Ann. § 20-1-206 (1971); Nev. Rev. Stat. § 392.910 (2003); N.C. Gen. Stat. § 14-288.4 (2007); N.D. Cent. Code § 15.1-06-16 (1999); R.I. Gen. Laws § 11-11-1 (2007); S.D. Codified Laws § 13-32-6 (1982); Tex. Educ. Code Ann. § 37.123 (2006); Utah Code Ann. § 76-9-103 (1973).

62. *In re Williams*, 2000 WL 222033, at *2 (Ohio Ct. App. 2000).

63. See *Papachristou v. City of Jacksonville*, 405 U.S. 156, 162 (1972) (invalidating a vagrancy statute because it was unconstitutionally vague). For an illuminating assessment of *Papachristou*, including its connection to unconstitutional vagueness, see Risa Goluboff, *Vagrant Nation: Police Power, Constitutional Change, and the Making of the 1960s* 298–344 (2016). For foundational scholarship on the concept of vagueness generally, see Anthony G. Amsterdam, Note, "The Void-for-Vagueness Doctrine in the Supreme Court," 109 *University of Pennsylvania Law Review* 67 (1960); and John C. Jeffries Jr., "Legality, Vagueness, and the Construction of Penal Statutes," 71 *Virginia Law Review* 189 (1985).

64. See Fields and Emshwiller, "For More Teens, Arrests by Police Replace School Discipline."

65. *T.L.O.*, 469 U.S. at 341n7.

66. Although a few lower court decisions have held school resource officers to the usual probable cause standard, this view is clearly in the minority. Most lower courts require mere reasonable suspicion, even when officers initiate searches or conduct them alone. For one of the few lower court opinions that has adopted the appropriate probable cause standard to assess searches conducted by school resource officers, see *State v. Scott*, 630 S.E.2d 563, 566 (Ga. Ct. App. 2006). For the most influential opinion employing a reasonable suspicion standard to evaluate school resource officers, see *People v. Dilworth*, 661 N.E. 2d 310, 317 (Ill. 1996). See also *In re William V.*, 4 Cal. Rptr. 3d 695, 698 (Ct. App. 2003); *Russell v. State*, 74 S.W. 3d 887, 891–92 (Tex. App.

2002) (quoting *Dilworth* and concluding that school resource officers acting on their own initiative are subject to the relaxed *T.L.O.* standard); and *Commonwealth v. J.B.*, 719 A.2d 1058, 1066 (Pa. Super. Ct. 1998). The focus here is on school resource officers because courts overwhelmingly apply probable cause to searches conducted by police officers who are unaffiliated with the relevant school.

67. See Forman, "Countering Criminalization," 326–27.

68. See Kim et al., *School-to-Prison Pipeline*, 1.

69. Ibid., 9. For additional sources that offer capacious understandings of the school-to-prison pipeline, see Johanna Wald and Daniel J. Losen, "Defining and Redirecting a School-to-Prison Pipeline," 99 *New Directions for Youth Development* 9, 9 (2003) ("The public school system in the United States, like the country as a whole, is plagued by vast inequalities—that all too frequently are defined along lines of race and class. Students in high-poverty, high-minority schools are routinely provided fewer resources, fewer qualified teachers, and fewer advanced-level courses than their more affluent white peers."). See NAACP Legal Defense and Educational Fund Inc., *Dismantling the School-to-Prison Pipeline* 4 (2005) ("Addressing the School-to-Prison Pipeline requires focusing on where it begins: a neglected and under-resourced public education system").

70. For helpful background on *Board of Education of Independent School District No. 92 of Pottawatomie County v. Earls*, see 536 U.S. at 826–28; Joint Appendix, *Earls*, 536 U.S. 822, 2001 WL 34093961, at *16, *17, *97–*98, *150–*51; Robert M. Bloom, "The Story of *Pottawatomie County v. Lindsay Earls*: Drug Testing in the Public Schools," in *Education Law Stories* 337–40 (Michael A. Olivas and Ronna Greff Schneider eds., 2008); Anne Gearan, "Supreme Court to Hear School Drug-Testing Case," *Milwaukee Journal Sentinel*, Nov. 9, 2001, 3A; Tamar Lewin, "Schools Across U.S. Await Ruling on Drug Tests," *New York Times*, March 20, 2002, A26; and Robert S. Greenberger, "Supreme Court to Hear Arguments in Case Pitting Policy Against Privacy," *Wall Street Journal*, March 15, 2002, B5.

71. *Acton*, 515 U.S. at 657.

72. Ibid., 655.

73. Lewin, "Schools Across U.S. Await Ruling on Drug Tests," A26.

74. Joan Biskupic, "Drug-Testing Case Generates Sparks," *USA Today*, March 20, 2002, A2 ("fierce," "unusually antagonistic"); Linda Greenhouse, "Supreme Court Seems Ready to Extend School Drug Tests," *New York Times*, March 20, 2002, A1 ("downright nasty"); and Lyle Denniston, "Justice Kennedy Attacks Student's Views," *Boston Globe*, March 20, 2002, A2 ("a stinging verbal attack . . . on a teenage girl").

75. Greenhouse, "Supreme Court Seems Ready to Extend School Drug Tests," A1, A26.

76. Denniston, "Justice Kennedy Attacks Student's Views," A2. Later, Kennedy's voice oozed sarcasm as he chided, "It is hardly a revelation that the government is concerned about drugs among our youth. This is not exactly rocket science." Ibid.

77. Bloom, "Story of *Pottawatomie County v. Lindsay Earls*," 340.

78. *Earls*, 536 U.S. at 834.

79. Ibid., 833–36. Justice Breyer wrote a short concurring opinion in *Earls*, where

he stated, "I cannot know whether the school's drug testing program will work. But, in my view, the Constitution does not prohibit the effort." Ibid., 842 (Breyer, J., concurring).

80. Ibid., 852 (Ginsburg, J., dissenting).

81. Ibid., 855. See also *West Virginia Board of Education v. Barnette*, 319 U.S. 624, 637 (1943) ("That [schools] are educating the young for citizenship is reason for scrupulous protection of Constitutional freedoms of the individual, if we are not to strangle the free mind at its source and teach youth to discount important principles of our government as mere platitudes"); and *Olmstead v. United States*, 277 U.S. 438, 485 (1928) (Brandeis, J., dissenting) ("Our government is the potent, the omnipresent teacher. For good or for ill, it teaches the whole people by its example.").

82. Robinson Hall, "Court Ruling in Earls Case Disappoints," *Dartmouth*, July 2, 2002.

83. Bloom, "Story of *Pottawatomie County v. Lindsay Earls*," 361.

84. Lewin, "Schools Across U.S. Await Ruling on Drug Tests," A26 (noting that school officials in Mathews County, Virginia, and Conway, Arkansas, delayed implementing drug-testing programs to await the *Earls* outcome).

85. Jonathan Turley, "Court's Message to Students: Just Say No to the Chess Club," *Los Angeles Times*, June 28, 2002, B15.

86. "Drug Tests in School," *Washington Post*, July 1, 2002, A16.

87. Lawrence Donegan, "U.S. Pupils Face Random Drug Testing," *London Observer*, June 2, 2002, 20.

88. Tamar Lewin, "With Court Nod, Parents Debate School Drug Tests," *New York Times*, Sept. 29, 2002, 1.

89. President George W. Bush, "Text of President Bush's 2004 State of the Union Address," *Washington Post*, Jan. 20, 2004. See Bloom, "Story of *Pottawatomie County v. Lindsay Earls*," 361 (chronicling increased federal funding for drug testing).

90. Tony Mauro, "Student Drug Tests Upheld," *USA Today*, June 27, 1995, 1A.

91. Paul M. Barrett, "Court Says Schools Can Do Random Drug Tests," *Wall Street Journal*, June 27, 1995, B1.

92. James J. Kilpatrick, "Court to Rule on Drug Tests for Teen-Agers," *Buffalo News*, Jan. 2, 1995, B3.

93. Charles Fried, "Privacy," 77 *Yale Law Journal* 475, 487 (1968).

94. See *Skinner v. Railway Labor Executives' Association*, 489 U.S. 602 (1989).

95. For the relevant passages revealing the Supreme Court's desperation, see *Acton*, 515 U.S. at 659; ibid., 665; and *Earls*, 536 U.S. at 832–38. For adumbrations of Justice Thomas's effort to extol the virtue of suspicionless drug testing, see Anne Proffitt Dupre, "Should Students Have Constitutional Rights? Keeping Order in the Public Schools," 65 *George Washington Law Review* 49, 100 (1996) ("Testing only on individual suspicion would transform the procedure into an accusatory process, with all the shame that goes with it, together with lawsuits claiming incorrect accusations or too little process"). A few noted criminal procedure scholars have supported randomized searches—exemplified by sobriety checkpoints—because they diminish police discretion and thus also reduce objectionable forms of discrimination (including racial discrimination). See, for example, Bernard E. Harcourt and Tracey L. Meares, "Randomization and the Fourth Amendment," 78 *University of Chicago Law Review* 809

(2011). The sweep of these arguments ought not be overstated. Harcourt and Meares do not, for example, support suspicionless searches, but instead support randomization provided that a base level of suspicion has been satisfied. See ibid., 817. It is not at all clear that these scholars would support searches of the variety disputed in *Earls*. That is true not least because one of the primary virtues of randomized searches may not materialize in that arena. Advocates of randomized searching emphasize that the approach distributes the burdens of searches throughout many different communities, generating greater democratic accountability and perhaps even pushback on excessively intrusive policing methods. In the context of stop-and-frisk policies, for instance, the rationale would hold that such measures would never be permitted if wealthy white people—rather than indigent black and brown people—were routinely subjected to them. Yet given the homogeneous composition of many schools—and even many school districts—it seems likely that the burdens of suspicionless searches would remain concentrated in particular communities rather than diffused throughout all segments of society. If blanket drug testing were eliminated, moreover, it seems probable that educators would not target particular students and instead would simply cease urinalysis testing altogether. Finally, even if these scholars would support suspicionless searches in schools, the mass interference on student privacy flowing from such measures nevertheless counsels against their usage.

96. Greg Winter, "Study Finds No Sign That Testing Deters Students' Drug Use," *New York Times*, May 17, 2003, A1.

97. According to a comprehensive study published in May 2008, one in seven public schools conducted suspicionless drug tests. Chris Ringwalt et al., "Random Drug Testing in US Public School Districts," 98 *American Journal of Public Health*, May 2008, 826. See Winter, "Study Finds No Sign That Testing Deters Students' Drug Use," A1 (reporting on the University of Michigan's study); and Ryoko Yamaguchi et al., "Relationship Between Student Illicit Drug Use and School Drug-Testing Policies," 73 *Journal of School Health*, April 2003, 159. For some of the subsequent studies that have corroborated the University of Michigan's findings, see Linn Goldberg et al., "Outcomes of a Prospective Trial of Student-Athlete Drug Testing: The Student Athlete Testing Using Random Notification (SATURN) Study," 41 *Journal of Adolescent Health* 421 (2007); Sharon R. Sznitman and Daniel Romer, "Student Drug Testing and Positive School Climates: Testing the Relation Between Two School Characteristics and Drug Use Behavior in a Longitudinal Study," 75 *Journal of Studies on Alcohol and Drugs* 65 (2014); and Kevin B. Zeese, *Drug Testing Legal Manual*, § 8.4 Drug Testing Programs in Schools (2d ed. 2014).

98. Prior to *Acton*, the National School Boards Association's general counsel stated, "Drug-testing programs in schools are relatively rare, but if the Supreme Court approves this one, it'll spread." Aaron Epstein, "Supreme Court to Decide on School Drug Testing," *Denver Post*, Nov. 29, 1994, A3. See also Linda Greenhouse, "High Court Upholds Drug Tests for Some Public School Athletes," *New York Times*, June 27, 1995, A1 (observing that before *Acton* "school board lawyers ... regarded [suspicionless drug testing] as constitutionally dubious and an invitation to lawsuits"). The prediction of drug testing's expansion post-*Acton* has been borne out. By 2002, at the time of *Earls*, roughly 5 percent of schools conducted drug tests for student athletes, and approximately 2 percent

did so for students involved in extracurricular activities. See Lewin, "Schools Across U.S. Await Ruling on Drug Tests," A26. And testing practices have spread only further after *Earls*.

99. See *Doe ex rel. Doe v. Little Rock School District*, 380 F.3d 349, 354–55 (8th Cir. 2004).

100. *Horton v. Goose Creek Independent School District*, 690 F.2d 470, 478 (5th Cir. 1982) (internal citation and quotation marks omitted). For an opinion adopting the same logic on facts where canines did not sniff students quite so closely as in *Horton*, see *B.C. v. Plumas Unified School District*, 192 F.3d 1260, 1265–68 (9th Cir. 1999). For a countervailing view, validating suspicionless drug-sniffing dogs of students, see *Renfrow*, 631 F.2d at 92–93. The Supreme Court's denial of certiorari on the Seventh Circuit's validation of this practice drew a vigorous dissent from Justice Brennan. See *Doe v. Renfrow*, 451 U.S. 1022, 1027–28 (1981) (Brennan, J., dissenting from denial of certiorari) ("We do not know what class petitioner was attending when the police and dogs burst in, but the lesson the school authorities taught her that day will undoubtedly make a greater impression than the one her teacher had hoped to convey. . . . Schools cannot expect their students to learn the lessons of good citizenship when the school authorities themselves disregard the fundamental principles underpinning our constitutional freedoms.").

All three of these federal appellate courts have determined, consistent with the closest Supreme Court opinion on the question, that the smelling of lockers—as distinct from student's persons themselves—does not violate the Fourth Amendment. See *United States v. Place*, 462 U.S. 696, 707 (1983) (holding that a canine's sniffing unattended luggage does not constitute a search). To the extent that readers believe that canines' sniffing inanimate objects ought to be impermissible, their objection lies less with how the Constitution has been interpreted in schools and more with Fourth Amendment doctrine broadly conceived. For an indication that the Supreme Court may be beginning to reconceive the relationship between drug-sniffing dogs and the Fourth Amendment, see *Florida v. Jardines*, 569 U.S. 1 (2013) (invalidating a drug-sniffing canine's search of a private home's front porch).

101. *United States v. Edwards*, 498 F.2d 496, 500 (2d Cir. 1974) (Friendly, J.) (internal quotation marks and citation omitted).

102. For lower court decisions upholding the legitimacy of metal detectors, see, for example, *In the Interest of F.B.*, 658 A.2d 1378 (Pa. Super. 1995); *People v. Pruitt*, 662 N.E.2d 540 (Ill. App. 1 Dist. 1996); and *People v. Dukes*, 580 N.Y.S.2d 850 (City Crim. Ct. 1992). For an argument that suspicionless searches should be unconstitutional, see Martin R. Gardner, "Student Privacy in the Wake of *T.L.O.*: An Appeal for an Individualized Suspicion Requirement for Valid Searches and Seizures in the Schools," 22 *Georgia Law Review* 897 (1988). For empirical research offering some reason to believe that metal detectors lower the percentage of students with weapons, see Abigail Hankin et al., "Impacts of Metal Detector Use in Schools: Insights from 15 Years of Research," 81 *Journal of School Health* 100, 100 (2011). For an article that criticizes the "surprise" use of metal detectors in schools, see Udi Ofer, "Criminalizing the Classroom: The Rise of Aggressive Policing and Zero Tolerance Policies in New York City Public Schools," 56 *New York Law School Law Review* 1373, 1385 (2011–2012).

103. "Unreasonable Search," *New York Times*, April 20, 2009, A26; and Marjorie

Cortez, "Strip-Search Is Case Lesson for School Officials," *Salt Lake Deseret News*, June 30, 2009, A15. Additional background material on Redding's strip search, which informs my views, can be found in the following sources: *Safford Unified School District No. 1 v. Redding*, 557 U.S. 364, 368–70 (2009); Brief for Respondents, *Redding*, 557 U.S. 364, 2009 WL 852123, at *1–*8; Joan Biskupic, "Strip Searches at School: Discipline Gone Too Far?," *USA Today*, April 16, 2009, A1; Robert Barnes, "Strip-Search Case Could Redefine Student Privacy," *Washington Post*, April 11, 2009, A1; David G. Savage, "High Court to Consider Limits on Strip-Searches at Schools," *Los Angeles Times*, April 19, 2009, A6; Adam Liptak, "Strip-Search of Young Girl Tests Limit of School Policy," *New York Times*, March 24, 2009, A1; and Arthur H. Rotstein, "Top Court to Hear Teen's Strip-Search Case," *Salt Lake Deseret News*, April 20, 2009, A12.

104. Liptak, "Strip-Search of Young Girl Tests Limit of School Policy," A1; and *Redding*, 557 U.S. at 369.
105. Rotstein, "Top Court to Hear Teen's Strip-Search Case," A12.
106. Liptak, "Strip-Search of Young Girl Tests Limit of School Policy," A1.
107. Dahlia Lithwick, "Search Me: The Supreme Court Is Neither Hot nor Bothered by Strip Searches," *Slate*, April 21, 2009. In similar—if more measured—tones, David Savage's article recapping oral argument in *Redding* began with the following: "The Supreme Court gave a skeptical hearing yesterday to lawyers who were urging a rule against strip searching students at school." David G. Savage, "High Court Hears Strip-Search Case," *Los Angeles Times*, April 22, 2009, A11.
108. Oral Argument Transcript, *Safford County School District v. Redding*, No. 08-479, 58 (April 21, 2009). For some of the media coverage that noted Justice Breyer's misspoken question and the ensuing hilarity, see Robert Barnes, "Justices' Takes on Strip Search Vary," *Washington Post*, April 22, 2009, A3 ("As his seatmate Clarence Thomas guffawed and the rest of the court joined in, Breyer added, 'not my underwear'"); Adam Liptak, "Court Debates Strip Search of Student," *New York Times*, April 22, 2009, A13 ("The courtroom rocked with laughter, and the justice grew a little flustered at having apparently misspoken"); Savage, "High Court Hears Strip-Search Case," A11 (noting Breyer's line); and Joan Biskupic and Greg Toppo, "Girl's Strip Search Argued in Court," *USA Today*, April 22, 2009, A3 (noting Breyer's line).
109. Oral Argument Transcript, *Redding*, No. 08-479, 58 (April 21, 2009).
110. See, for example, Barnes, "Justices' Takes on Strip Search Vary," A3.
111. Joan Biskupic, "Ginsburg: The Court Needs Another Woman: Panel's Lack of Diversity Wears on Female Justice," *USA Today*, May 6, 2009, A1.
112. *Redding*, 557 U.S. at 377. Justice Souter's opinion in *Redding* also attempted to provide further definition to the standard of "reasonable suspicion." Where prior case law provided that probable cause requires at least a "fair probability" or a "substantial chance" that a search will reveal evidence of criminal activity, Justice Souter explained that reasonable suspicion required "a moderate chance of finding evidence of wrongdoing." Ibid., 371 (internal quotation marks and citations omitted). Although Souter's effort to provide clarity here is admirable, it seems doubtful that the undertaking proved successful.
113. Ibid., 377.
114. Ibid., 399 (Thomas, J., concurring in the judgment in part and dissenting in

part). It merits noting, at least in passing, that Justice Antonin Scalia, the Court's only other avowed originalist, declined to join Justice Thomas's originalism-inflected opinion in *Redding*. That the two justices parted company in this case suggests that originalism contains a good deal more discretion, uncertainty, and flexibility than popular understandings generally allow. One explanation for their divergence in *Redding* is owed to the fact that Justice Scalia's variant of originalism contained greater respect for precedent than Justice Thomas's variant. For a powerful, elegant critique of originalism, see David A. Strauss, *The Living Constitution* 7–31 (2010). For an argument that originalism and living constitutionalism are intimately related, see Jack M. Balkin, *Living Originalism* (2011).

115. *Redding*, 557 U.S. at 393 (Thomas, J., concurring in the judgment in part and dissenting in part).

116. Ibid., 390 (citations omitted).

117. "An Unreasonable Search," *New York Times*, June 26, 2009, A24. For additional commentary praising *Redding*, see "Strip Searches and the Law," *Washington Post*, June 26, 2009, A24; and James Taranto, "Underwear Inspector, Zero Tolerance Goes to the Supreme Court," *Wall Street Journal*, June 26, 2009. Editorial boards did arrive at different conclusions regarding whether the Court should have extended qualified immunity to school officials. Where *The New York Times* contended that granting qualified immunity was mistaken, *The Washington Post* termed it "[a] smart compromise."

118. "Strip-Search Case Ends in Victory for Common Sense," *USA Today*, June 26, 2009, A12; and "School Strip-Searches," *Chicago Tribune*, July 3, 2009, 24.

119. "Drawing the Line on Searches of Students," *Denver Post*, June 28, 2009, D3.

120. Cortez, "Strip-Search Is Lesson for School Officials," A15. Professor Mark Tushnet has helpfully identified how memorable phrases from Supreme Court opinions enter the national discourse through newspaper coverage. Mark Tushnet, "Style and the Supreme Court's Educational Role in Government," 11 *Constitutional Commentary* 215, 219–20 (1994).

121. Adam Liptak, "Strip Search of Girl by School Officials Seeking Drugs Was Illegal, Justices Rule," *New York Times*, June 26, 2009, A16.

122. "U.S. Supreme Court Declares Strip Search of 13-Year-Old Student Unconstitutional," U.S. Newswire, June 25, 2009. For additional reactions from Savana Redding, see Robert Barnes, "Student Strip Search Illegal; School Violated Teen Girl's Rights, Supreme Court Rules," *Washington Post*, June 26, 2009, A1; and Liptak, "Strip Search of Girl by School Officials Seeking Drugs Was Illegal, Justices Rule," A16.

123. Lauren Garrison, "Area Schools Weigh Impact of Ruling in Ariz. Strip Search," *New Haven Register*, July 2, 2009, 1.

124. Associated Press, "Strip Search of Ariz. Teenager Illegal, Court Says," *Gainesville Sun*, June 25, 2009.

125. Diana R. Donahoe, "Strip Searches of Students: Addressing the Undressing of Children in Schools and Redressing the Fourth Amendment Violations," 75 *Missouri Law Review* 1123, 1126 (2010).

126. For only one of the many pre-*T.L.O.* strip-search cases, see *Renfrow*, 631 F.2d at 92–93 ("It does not require a constitutional scholar to conclude that a nude search of a thirteen-year-old child is an invasion of constitutional rights of some magnitude"). For some of the many strip-search cases involving miss-

ing money, where there was no reason to believe that the individuals had "crotched" the evidence, see *Jenkins v. Talladega County City Board of Education,* 115 F.3d 821, 822 (11th Cir. 1997); *Carlson ex rel. Stuczynski v. Bremen High School,* 423 F. Supp. 2d 823, 825–26 (N.D. Ill. 2006); *Oliver v. McClung,* 919 F. Supp. 1206, 1210–11 (N.D. Ind. 1995); and *State ex rel. Galford v. Mark Anthony B.,* 433 S.E.2d 41, 42–43 (W. Va. 1993).

127. For collections of statutes prohibiting strip searches, see Yudof et al., *Educational Policy and the Law,* 336; and Feld, "*T.L.O.* and *Redding*'s Unanswered (Misanswered) Fourth Amendment Questions," 870n128.

128. *Redding,* 557 U.S. at 375.

129. For three strip searches lacking individualized suspicion, all of which involved missing sums of money, see *Bellnier v. Lund,* 438 F. Supp. 47, 53–54 (N.D.N.Y. 1977) (declaring unconstitutional a school's decision to strip-search an entire fifth-grade class to locate three missing dollars); *Konop v. Northwestern School District,* 26 F. Supp. 2d 1189, 1206–7 (D. S.D. 1998) (declaring unconstitutional a school's decision to strip-search eight students to locate two hundred missing dollars); and *Thomas ex rel. Thomas v. Roberts,* 261 F.3d 1160, 1166–67 (11th Cir. 2001) (declaring unconstitutional a school's decision to strip-search an entire fifth-grade class to locate twenty-six missing dollars), *vacated on other grounds by Thomas v. Roberts,* 536 U.S. 953 (2002).

130. *Redding,* 557 U.S. at 377. In the opinion's introduction, Justice Souter similarly explained that Redding's strip search violates the Fourth Amendment "because there were no reasons to suspect the drugs presented a danger *or* were concealed in her underwear." Ibid., 368 (emphasis added). As the opinion makes clear, *Redding*'s rule pertains to strip searches for contraband generally, not just those involving drugs.

131. See Brief for the Rutherford Institute et al. as Amici Curiae, *Redding,* 557 U.S. 364, 2009 WL 931833, at *3 (advocating that strip searches of students should be permitted only when "highly credible evidence showing (1) the student is in possession of objects posing a significant danger to the school and (2) that the student has secreted the objects in a place only a strip search will uncover"). I take it that "highly credible evidence" at least equates, and likely even exceeds, the probable cause standard. For scholarly critiques of *Redding,* see Donahoe, "Strip Searches of Students"; and Lewis R. Katz and Carl J. Mazzone, "*Safford Unified School District No. 1 v. Redding* and the Future of School Strip Searches," 60 *Case Western Reserve Law Review* 363 (2010).

132. See Linda Greenhouse, "Keynote Speech at the Spring 2012 Pipeline to Power Symposium," 2012 *Michigan State Law Review* 1433, 1434–35 ("[Ginsburg's] words were understated, but the fact that a Justice would comment publicly on an undecided case spoke volumes"); and Dahlia Lithwick, "The Female Factor," *Newsweek,* June 6, 2010, 19 ("A court that appeared very sympathetic toward the school district after oral argument ended up voting 8–1 that the search was unconstitutional. . . . Nobody credits the Constitution with changing in those short weeks. What changed was that Ginsburg spoke out. . . . It was as close as most court watchers came to hearing Ginsburg speak fighting words.").

133. Emily Bazelon, "The Place of Women on the Court," *New York Times Magazine,* July 12, 2009, 26.

134. "*Reed v. Reed* at 40: Equal Protection and Women's Rights," 20 *American Uni-*

versity Journal of Gender, Social Policy, and the Law 315, 343 (2012) (transcript of panel discussion).

135. Cortez, "Strip-Search Is Lesson for School Officials," A15.

136. *T.L.O.*, 469 U.S. at 342.

137. See *Jenkins by Hall v. Talladega County Board of Education*, 115 F.3d 821, 822, 825 (11th Cir. 1997) (en banc). Judge Kravitch wrote a powerful dissenting opinion in this case.

138. For a case invalidating a strip search of a young woman in her senior year of high school that was predicated on flimsy evidence, see *Phaneuf v. Fraikin*, 448 F.3d 591 (2d Cir. 2006). For an argument contending that Justice Souter's opinion in *Redding* should have expressly made clear that age and sex were not significant factors for the Fourth Amendment in the context of strip searches, see Donahoe, "Strip Searches of Students."

139. See Douglas Quenqua, "Muscular Body Image Lures Boys into Gym, and Obsession," *New York Times*, Nov. 19, 2012, A1 ("It is not just girls these days who are consumed by an unattainable body image").

140. See Cary Franklin, "The Anti-stereotyping Principle in Constitutional Sex Discrimination Law," 85 *NYU Law Review* 83 (2010). Professor Franklin's excavation of Ginsburg's early legal career—including its surprising connection to Sweden—represents an exemplary work of scholarship. While Professor Franklin does analyze some modern Supreme Court opinions involving sex, she does not examine how Ginsburg's commentary in *Redding* can be reconciled with her larger legal project. This omission is perfectly understandable. In addition to the fact that the Court decided *Redding* only one year before Franklin's article appeared, the article focuses on the Fourteenth Amendment's Equal Protection Clause, not criminal procedure.

141. Rhonda Cook, "Clayton School District Sued over Strip-Search," *Atlanta Journal-Constitution*, Feb. 16, 2012, B1.

142. *D.H. ex rel. Dawson v. Clayton County School District*, 52 F. Supp. 3d 1261, 1273 (N.D. Ga. 2014). For one pre-*Redding* case that demonstrates at least some sensitivity to young men being forced to strip for searches, see *Cornfield by Lewis v. Consolidated High School District 230*, 991 F.2d 1316, 1323 (7th Cir. 1993) (noting that age sixteen is "an age at which children are extremely self-conscious about their bodies").

143. Greg Bluestein, "Student Sues Ga. School over Alleged Strip Search," *Charleston Daily Mail*, Feb. 16, 2012, D6.

144. The facts in this paragraph are drawn from *J.D.B. v. North Carolina*, 564 U.S. 261, 265–68 (2011); *In re J.D.B.*, 686 S.E.2d 135, 136–38 (N.C. 2009); and Brief for Petitioner, *J.D.B.*, 564 U.S. 261, 2010 WL 5168873, at *1–*8.

145. See *Miranda v. Arizona*, 384 U.S. 436, 478–79 (1966). For a prominent articulation of the governing standard for determining whether interrogations occur "in custody," see *Thompson v. Keohane*, 516 U.S. 99, 112 (1995). The rhetorical question that I pose in this paragraph as a way of framing the core issue in *J.D.B. v. North Carolina* owes a debt to the rhetorical question that Justice Sonia Sotomayor's opinion for the Court posed in an effort to ridicule the dissenting opinion. See *J.D.B.*, 564 U.S. at 275–76.

146. *J.D.B.*, 564 U.S. at 264–65.

147. Ibid., 279–80.

148. Ibid., 277.
149. Ibid., 283 (Alito, J., dissenting).
150. "*Miranda* Rights for Minors," *Los Angeles Times*, June 18, 2011, A16.
151. "*Miranda* Rights for Middle Schoolers," *New York Times*, June 17, 2011, A34.
152. "*Miranda* Rights for Children?," *Washington Post*, Aug. 29, 2011, A14. Some portion of *The Washington Post*'s disenchantment with *J.D.B.* may stem from its evident misapprehension regarding the precise scope of the opinion's holding. The *Post* editorial stated, "The court concluded that although there was no arrest and interrogation took place in a school and not a police station, the boy was essentially in custody since it was likely he did not believe he could leave or refuse to answer the officer's questions." In fact, though, the Court expressly refrained from determining whether *J.D.B.* was in custody for purposes of *Miranda*—even if the opinion tends toward that reading. Of course, the *Post*'s slight misreading of *J.D.B.* can realistically be understood to account for only a small fraction of its discontent.
153. For work suggesting that criminal suspects typically waive their *Miranda* rights, see Paul G. Cassell and Brett S. Hayman, "Police Interrogation in the 1990s: An Empirical Study of the Effects of *Miranda*," 43 *UCLA Law Review* 839 (1996). For helpful scholarship exploring how youth do not actually understand the rights *Miranda* confers, and showing that youth are particularly vulnerable to false confessions, see Kristin Henning, "Criminalizing Normal Adolescent Behavior in Communities of Color: The Role of Prosecutors in Juvenile Justice Reform," 98 *Cornell Law Review* 383, 441 (2013); and Barry C. Feld, "Behind Closed Doors: What Really Happens When Cops Question Kids," 23 *Cornell Journal of Law and Public Policy* 395, 454 (2013).
   Among *J.D.B.*'s celebrants, Professors Martin Guggenheim and Randy Hertz have identified the opinion's "game chang[ing]" possibilities. Martin Guggenheim and Randy Hertz, "*J.D.B.* and the Maturing of Juvenile Confession Suppression Law," 38 *Washington University Journal of Law and Policy* 109, 110 (2012). Similarly, Professor Steven Drizin called *J.D.B.* "huge," citing the opinion's ability to close the *Miranda* loophole that has applied in schools. Nina Totenberg, "High Court: Age Must Be Considered in Interrogation," NPR, June 16, 2011.
   Among *J.D.B.*'s skeptics, conversely, Professor Tamar Birckhead's commentary is notable for contending that the opinion will ultimately prove insignificant. "The irony is that many children don't understand the language or meaning of the warnings," Birckhead commented. "In most cases, when *Miranda* warnings are given, juveniles talk anyway." Donna St. George, "Miranda-Rights Debate Unfolds at Fairfax School," *Washington Post*, July 18, 2011, A1. See also Tamar R. Birckhead, "Good Guys, Bad Guys—and Miranda," *Los Angeles Times*, May 2, 2011, A19 (casting doubt on the notion that *J.D.B.* would provide meaningful help to juvenile criminal suspects). Professor Stephen A. Saltzburg likewise contended that after *J.D.B.* "it's doubtful . . . there will be many fewer confessions because of this opinion." Totenberg, "High Court: Age Must Be Considered in Interrogation."
154. N.C. Gen. Stat. § 7B-2101(b) (2011). The statute was amended in 2015 to raise the threshold age from fourteen to sixteen. 2015 North Carolina Laws S.L. 2015-58 (H.B. 879). The statute also indicates that a juvenile's in-custody

statement is admissible if, in lieu of a parent or parental figure, an attorney is present. But no attorney, of even meager competence, would permit a client to confess to an investigator in those circumstances.

155. Joint Appendix, *J.D.B. v. North Carolina*, 564 U.S. 261, 2010 WL 5178047, *117a (2010).

156. For important articulations of judicial minimalism, see Cass R. Sunstein, *One Case at a Time: Judicial Minimalism on the Supreme Court* (1999); and Associated Press, "Chief Justice Says His Goal Is More Consensus on Court," *New York Times*, May 22, 2006, A16 ("If it is not necessary to decide more to a case, then in my view it is necessary not to decide more to a case").

157. For a helpful exploration of the power dynamics surrounding police interrogations in school, see Paul Holland, "Schooling *Miranda:* Policing Interrogation in the Twenty-First Century Schoolhouse," 52 *Loyola Law Review* 39 (2006).

158. The information from the Smith Middle School Student Handbook is quoted in the dissenting opinion that Justice Brady wrote in *J.D.B.* when the case was at the North Carolina Supreme Court. See *In re J.D.B.*, 686 S.E.2d at 143 (Brady, J., dissenting).

159. Justice Hudson, of the North Carolina Supreme Court, pressed this point as well: "[I]n the school environment, where juveniles are faced with a variety of negative consequences—including potential criminal charges—for refusing to comply with the requests or commands of authority figures, the circumstances are inherently more coercive and require more, not less, careful protection of the rights of the juvenile." Ibid., 147 (Hudson, J., dissenting).

160. *J.D.B.*, 564 U.S. at 276 (citations and internal quotation marks omitted). At least one prominent legal scholar has applauded Sotomayor's opinion in *J.D.B.* for being firmly grounded in the real world of criminal law. See Rachel E. Barkow, "Justice Sotomayor and Criminal Justice in the Real World," 123 *Yale Law Journal Forum* 409, 414 (2014) ("*J.D.B.* . . . demonstrates Justice Sotomayor's attention to the actual circumstances of police interactions with suspects and her rejection of formal rules that do not reflect that reality"). This analysis has much to commend it. Yet Sotomayor's elevation of age over the school setting seems more redolent of an insufficiently fact-sensitive approach to law, one that would yield artificial applications in at least some real-world settings.

161. Professor Sally Terry Green introduced the thoughtful proposal that I now join her in supporting here. See Sally Terry Green, "A Presumptive In-Custody Analysis to Police-Conducted School Interrogations," 40 *American Journal of Criminal Law* 145 (2013). This custodial presumption would not, of course, prevent police officers from questioning students in the absence of *Miranda* warnings if any of the various exceptions to *Miranda* that the Supreme Court has articulated over the years apply, including the public-safety exception. See *New York v. Quarles*, 467 U.S. 649 (1984). For an article examining how *Quarles* should figure into the custodial interrogation context, see Holland, "Schooling *Miranda*," 111–12. For school interrogation cases that stopped short of adopting a custodial presumption, but that nevertheless suppressed incriminating statements from students to police officers who did not issue *Miranda* warnings, see *In re Interest of C.H.*, 763 N.W.2d 708, 715–16 (Neb. 2009); and *M.H. v. Florida*, 851 So. 2d 233 (Fla. Ct. App. 2003). There are no compelling reasons to exempt school resource officers from the need to Mirandize students.

For a case adopting this general approach, see *In re R.H.*, 791 A.2d 331, 334 (Pa. 2002).

162. See John Schwartz, "Confessing to Crime, but Innocent," *New York Times*, Sept. 14, 2010, A14 (noting that the young, along with the mentally ill and the cognitively impaired, are particularly likely to confess to crimes that they did not commit). For a valuable academic exploration of false confessions, see Brandon L. Garrett, "The Substance of False Confessions," 62 *Stanford Law Review* 1051 (2010).

163. See, for example, *Boynton v. Casey*, 543 F. Supp. 995, 997 (D. Me. 1982); *Salazar v. Luty*, 761 F. Supp. 45, 47 (S.D. Tex. 1991); *Pollnow v. Glennon*, 594 F. Supp. 220, 224 (S.D.N.Y. 1984); and *Jarmon v. Batory*, 1994 WL 313063, at *11 (E.D. Pa. 1994).

164. See *Betts v. Board of Education of City of Chicago*, 466 F.2d 629, 631n1 (1972).

165. *State v. Heirtzler*, 147 N.H. 344, 350–51 (2001) (internal citations omitted) (suppressing a student statement because the school official collected it as an agent of the police officer). For an opinion refusing to suppress a statement to a school official involving marijuana, see *People v. Pankhurst*, 848 N.E.2d 628 (Ill. App. Ct. 2006) (distinguishing *Heirtzler*).

166. For early-Columbine news coverage that overstated the number of casualties, see James Brooke, "2 Students in Colorado School Said to Gun Down as Many as 23 and Kill Themselves in a Siege," *New York Times*, April 21, 1999, A1. For subsequent coverage that accurately reported the number of casualties, see Jodi Wilgoren, "Society of Outcasts Began with a $99 Black Coat," *New York Times*, April 25, 1999, 30.

167. For a sampling of judicial opinions that use the phrase "post-Columbine world" or something akin, see *Prevatte v. French*, 459 F. Supp. 2d 1305, 1383n42 (N.D. Ga. 2006) (referring to "our post-Columbine world"); *In re Antrobus*, 519 F.3d 1123, 1126 (10th Cir. 2008) (Tymkovich, J., concurring) ("We live in a post-Columbine High School world"); *Williams v. Cambridge Board of Education*, 370 F.3d 630, 641 (6th Cir. 2004) (Moore, J., concurring in part and dissenting in part) (referring to "post-Columbine" conditions); *Strawn v. Holohan*, 2008 WL 65586, at *4 (referring to "post-Columbine" setting); *Gary Community School Corporation v. Boyd*, 890 N.E.2d 794, 799n1 (Ind. Ct. App. 2008) ("In the post-Columbine world in which we live, . . ."); *D.L. v. State*, 877 N.E.2d 500, 501 (Ind. Ct. App. 2007) (using the term "this post-Columbine world" in its first sentence); *Bolden v. Chartiers Valley School District*, 869 A.2d 1134, 1140 (Pa. Commw. Ct. 2005) (referring to "a post-Columbine world"); *Theodore v. Delaware Valley School District*, 836 A.2d 76, 92 (Pa. 2003) (invoking "this post-Columbine High School era"); and *In re T.J.*, 2016 WL 2754107, at *4 (Cal. Ct. App. 2016) (referring to "this post-Columbine era"). Many more judicial opinions, of course, refer to the Columbine massacre without attaching the prefix "post-."

168. See James Barron, "Gunman Massacres 20 Children at School in Connecticut," *New York Times*, Dec. 15, 2012, A1; and Julie Turkewitz et al., "Suspect Confessed to Police That He Began Shooting Students 'in the Hallways,'" *New York Times*, Feb. 15, 2018.

169. People generally misjudge the risk associated with a particular activity when they can quickly access intense memories of the activity's danger materializing. Amos Tversky and Daniel Kahneman have labeled this type of cognitive bias

the "availability heuristic." See Amos Tversky and Daniel Kahneman, "Availability: A Heuristic for Judging Frequency and Probability," 5 *Cognitive Psychology* 207 (1973). For thoughtful scholarship analyzing how this insight applies to legal issues, see, for example, Cass R. Sunstein and Richard Zeckhauser, "Overreaction to Fearsome Risks," 48 *Environmental and Resource Economics* 435 (2011). For a compelling popular treatment of Tversky and Kahneman's scholarship, see Michael Lewis, *The Undoing Project: A Friendship That Changed Our Minds* (2016).

170. See Heather Mason Kiefer, "Public: Society Powerless to Stop School Shootings," Gallup, April 5, 2005 (detailing the April 1999 results and the March 2005 results). Gallup has not collected data on this question since 2005.

171. See James Forman Jr., "Overkill on Schools: Zero-Tolerance and Our Exaggerated Images of Violence," *Washington Post*, April 23, 2001, A15; Associated Press, "Mass Shootings Are Not Growing in Frequency, Experts Say," *New York Daily News*, Dec. 15, 2012.

172. Randy Borum et al., "What Can Be Done About School Shootings? A Review of the Evidence," 39 *Educational Researcher* 27, 27 (2010). For a helpful work making the case that schools are in fact extremely safe, see Jason P. Nance, "Students, Security, and Race," 63 *Emory Law Journal* 1, 16 (2013).

173. Arne Duncan, "Resources for Schools to Prepare for and Recover from Crisis," *Homeroom: The Official Blog of the U.S. Department of Education*, Dec. 17, 2012.

174. *District of Columbia v. Heller*, 554 U.S. 570, 626 (2008).

175. *D.L.*, 877 N.E.2d at 501 (upholding as reasonable police officer's pat-down search for student identification, despite the student's admission that he did not have the identification on his person).

176. "Our Vicious Young Hoodlums: Is There Any Hope?," *Newsweek*, Sept. 6, 1954, 43. For an insightful overview of attitudes toward youth in the United States over time, see Steven Mintz, *Huck's Raft: A History of American Childhood* (2004).

177. "Our Vicious Young Hoodlums," 44.

178. See John J. DiIulio Jr., "The Coming of the Super-predators," *Weekly Standard*, Nov. 27, 1995, 23 (identifying super-predators as "severely morally impoverished juvenile [offenders]" who "fear neither the stigma of arrest nor the pain of imprisonment"); ibid. ("[Super-predators] live by the meanest code of the meanest streets, a code that reinforces rather than restrains their violent, hair-trigger mentality. . . . [T]hey will do what comes 'naturally': murder, rape, rob, assault, burglarize, deal deadly drugs, and get high."); and Richard Zoglin, "Now for the Bad News: A Teenage Time Bomb," *Time*, Jan. 15, 1996, 52 (noting that Professor DiIulio has "warn[ed] about a new generation of 'superpredators,' youngsters who are coming of age in actual and 'moral poverty,' without 'the benefit of parents, coaches and clergy to teach them right or wrong and show them unconditional love'"). During her presidential campaign in 2016, Hillary Clinton received criticism for using the term "super-predator" in a speech twenty years earlier, when she was First Lady. See Charles Blow, "I'm Not a Super Predator," *New York Times*, Feb. 29, 2016, A25 (noting criticisms of Clinton for using the racially inflammatory term and that she recently expressed regret for its usage).

179. "The Youth Crime Plague," *Time*, July 11, 1977, 18, 25. For a magisterial work that uses the lens of rights consciousness to examine post–World War II history in America, see James T. Patterson, *Grand Expectations: The United States, 1945–1974* (1996).

180. *Leave It to Beaver* (CBS Television 1957–1958; ABC Television 1958–1963); *Blackboard Jungle* (Metro-Goldwyn-Mayer Pictures 1955). *Newsweek* itself ran another cover article in 1970 titled "What's Wrong with the High Schools?" and noted inside, "Students now smoke marijuana as casually as a businessman drinks a second Martini at lunch." "What's Wrong with the High Schools?," *Newsweek*, Feb. 16, 1970, 65, 66.

5   EQUAL PROTECTION I

1. For vital background information on and analysis of *Brown*, see Richard Kluger, *Simple Justice: The History of* Brown v. Board of Education *and Black America's Struggle for Equality* (2004 ed.) (1975); James T. Patterson, Brown v. Board of Education: *A Civil Rights Milestone and Its Troubled Legacy* (2001); J. Harvie Wilkinson III, *From* Brown *to* Bakke: *The Supreme Court and School Integration, 1954–1978* (1979); and Bradley D. Hayes, "Linda Brown and the Fight for Educational Equality," in *Black, White, and* Brown: *The Landmark School Desegregation Case in Retrospect* 153 (Melvin Urofsky and Clare Cushman eds., 2004). For foundational work on civil rights lawyers before the decision to file *Brown*, see Mark V. Tushnet, *The NAACP's Legal Strategy Against Segregated Education, 1925–1950* (1987).

2. *Brown v. Board of Education of Topeka*, 347 U.S. 483, 493 (1954).

3. Ibid., 494.

4. "Equal Education for All," *Washington Post*, May 19, 1954, 14.

5. "Conscience of the Nation," *Cincinnati Enquirer*, reprinted in *New York Times*, May 18, 1954, 19. For additional enthusiastic appraisals of *Brown*, see "No Other Ruling Possible," *Cleveland Plain Dealer*, reprinted at ibid. ("We believe that the Supreme Court could not have ruled otherwise than it did on the basic issue. . . . We believe that Negroes have earned the right to be treated as first-rate citizens, and earned it the hard way."); and "Ruling Termed 'Inevitable,'" *Pittsburgh Post-Gazette*, reprinted at ibid. ("Every fair-minded American will, we believe, applaud the Supreme Court's unanimous decision against racial segregation in the public schools. . . . This ruling could hardly have come as a surprise to even the most determined advocate of segregation.").

6. "All God's Chillun," *New York Times*, May 18, 1954, 28. In the months following *Brown*, the *New York Times* editorial board repeatedly contended that the school segregation issue could not be settled overnight. In July 1954, the board asserted, "The change, when it comes, will demand patience and wisdom on all sides. . . . It is one thing to lay down general principles and it is quite another to work them out in real buildings with real human beings." "The Teachers Speak Out," *New York Times*, July 4, 1954, E6. In October 1954, the board noted, "What is asked of [southern states] is not easy." "Segregation: What Next?," *New York Times*, Oct. 3, 1954, E8. In May 1955, on *Brown*'s first anniversary, the board commented, "[T]he court's approach is evolutionary,

marked with the sense of moderation and understanding that must on all sides characterize desegregation if it is to go accomplish its great purpose." "Desegregation: 1954–55," *New York Times*, May 17, 1955, 28.

7. "To the Heart of America," *New York Herald Tribune*, reprinted in *New York Times*, May 18, 1954, 19.

8. "Society and the Law," *Wall Street Journal*, May 20, 1954, 10.

9. "No Time for Hasty Action," *Atlanta Constitution*, reprinted in *New York Times*, May 18, 1954, 19.

10. "Turmoil Is in Prospect," *New Orleans Times-Picayune*, reprinted in *New York Times*, May 18, 1954, 19.

11. "Decision Is Regretted," *Birmingham News*, reprinted in *New York Times*, May 18, 1954, 19.

12. "Bloodstains on White Marble Steps," *Jackson (Miss.) Daily News*, May 18, 1954, reprinted in *New York Times*, May 18, 1954, 19.

13. "End of Dual Society," *Chicago Defender*, reprinted in *New York Times*, May 18, 1954, 19.

14. "A Great Victory," *Amsterdam News*, reprinted in *New York Times*, May 18, 1954, 19.

15. Arnold Rampersad, *Ralph Ellison: A Biography* 298 (2007). Notably, Ellison also expressed optimism that *Brown* would soon be implemented. While Ellison anticipated some "resistance to desegregation," he nevertheless contended, "[T]he South is turning away from the mad task of trying to hold back the wheels of time which has drained away so much of its creative energy." Ibid., 299. As subsequent events would unmistakably demonstrate, however, Ellison's appraisal of the southern mindset proved unduly optimistic.

16. James D. Anderson, "Introduction," in *School: The Story of American Public Education* 123, 130 (Sarah Mondale and Sarah B. Patton eds., 2001).

17. Kluger, *Simple Justice*, 717. For an account of Marshall's post-*Brown* press conference, see Gerald N. Rosenberg, *The Hollow Hope: Can Courts Bring About Social Change?* 43 (1991).

18. Hayes, "Linda Brown and the Fight for Educational Equality," 153.

19. *Brown*, 347 U.S. at 487.

20. For works that informed my thinking on these questions, see Martha Minow, *In Brown's Wake: Legacies of America's Educational Landmark* (2010); and Patricia Albjerg Graham, *Schooling America: How the Public Schools Meet the Nation's Changing Needs* (2005).

21. *Brown*, 347 U.S. at 495.

22. Robert A. Leflar and Wylie H. Davis, "Segregation in the Public Schools—1953," 67 *Harvard Law Review* 377, 380, 404 (1954).

23. "Emancipation," *Washington Post*, May 18, 1954, 14.

24. Bernard Schwartz, *Super Chief: Earl Warren and His Supreme Court* 94 (1983). For an excavation of the Court's decade of unanimity on racial desegregation, see Dennis J. Hutchinson, "Unanimity and Desegregation: Decisionmaking in the Supreme Court, 1948–1958," 68 *Georgetown Law Journal* 1 (1979).

25. Earl Warren, *The Memoirs of Earl Warren* 3 (1977).

26. Juan Williams, *Thurgood Marshall: American Revolutionary* 227 (1998). Years later, Marshall remained extremely proud of *Brown*'s unanimity. See ibid., 229.

27. Wilkinson, *From Brown to Bakke*, 30.

28. Cass R. Sunstein, "Did *Brown* Matter?," *New Yorker*, May 3, 2004, 102. To

his credit, Professor Sunstein has exhibited greater willingness to question the significance of *Brown*'s unanimity in recent years. See Cass R. Sunstein, "Unanimity and Disagreement on the Supreme Court," 100 *Cornell Law Review* 769, 805 (2015) ("*Brown* was ... unanimous, but its unanimity did not come close to quelling public opposition. Perhaps the opposition would have been even worse if the Court had been divided—but perhaps not.").

29. See Sunstein, "Did *Brown* Matter?," 102; John Bartlow Martin, *The Deep South Says "Never"* (1957); and Randall Kennedy, "Schoolings in Equality," *New Republic*, July 5 and 12, 2004, 29, 32–33 (noting the "costs" associated with *Brown*'s unanimity). For an argument that Warren's opinion in *Brown* did not go nearly as far as some of its modern admirers assert, see Randall L. Kennedy, "Ackerman's *Brown*," 123 *Yale Law Journal* 3064, 3068 (2014) (reviewing Bruce Ackerman's *We the People: The Civil Rights Revolution* [2014]) ("Missing from the most honored race relations decision in American constitutional law is any express reckoning with racism"). See ibid., 3069 ("Warren's opinion is deficient in important respects").

30. For scholarship that identifies and critiques these revisionists' claims at length, see Justin Driver, "The Consensus Constitution," 89 *Texas Law Review* 755 (2011); and Justin Driver, "Constitutional Outliers," 81 *University of Chicago Law Review* 929 (2014). For additional scholarship that attends to legislative realities that exist on the ground, see Akhil Reed Amar, *America's Unwritten Constitution: The Precedents and Principles We Live By* 132 (2012) ("Honoring America's lived Constitution requires careful counting: We must assess the daily reality of rights.").

31. See "Mixed Schools. How Northern Parents Feel," *U.S. News and World Report*, March 23, 1959, 12; Bureau of the Census, U.S. Department of Commerce, "Statistical Abstract of the United States, Population, by Race, States: 1930–1950," 30 table 27; Stewart Alsop and Oliver Quayle, "What Northerners Really Think of Negroes," *Saturday Evening Post*, Sept. 7, 1963, 17, 20 (where a 1963 study among only northern whites found that 51 percent thought American blacks were treated about right, 38 percent thought they were treated insufficiently well, and an astounding 11 percent thought that blacks were treated excessively well); Driver, "Consensus Constitution," 806–7, 811–13; and Robert Penn Warren, *Segregation: The Inner Conflict in the South* 26–27 (1956).

32. See Hazel Gaudet Erskine, "The Polls: Race Relations," 26 *Public Opinion Quarterly* 137, 139 (1962); Herbert H. Hyman and Paul B. Sheatsley, "Attitudes Toward Desegregation," *Scientific American*, Dec. 1956, 35, 39; Paul B. Sheatsley, "White Attitudes Toward the Negro," 95 *Daedalus* 217, 219 chart 1 (1966); Joseph Carroll, "Race and Education 50 Years After *Brown v. Board of Education*," Gallup News Service, May 14, 2004; Driver, "Consensus Constitution," 804–6 (discussing polling data); and Justin Driver, "Supremacies and the Southern Manifesto," 92 *Texas Law Review* 1053, 1096 (2014) (discussing polling data).

33. Derrick Bell, *Silent Covenants:* Brown v. Board of Education *and the Unfulfilled Hopes for Racial Reform* 18 (2004) (citing Loren Miller, *The Petitioners: The Story of the Supreme Court and the Negro* 351 [1966]).

34. Charles L. Black Jr., "The Unfinished Business of the Warren Court," 46 *Washington Law Review* 3, 22 (1970).

35. *Brown v. Board of Education of Topeka*, 349 U.S. 294, 300 (1955).
36. Michael Murakami, "Desegregation," 18, 26–27, in *Public Opinion and Constitutional Controversy* (Nathaniel Persily et al. eds., 2008).
37. "Time Granted for Desegregation," *Los Angeles Times*, June 1, 1955, A4.
38. "Prompt and Reasonable," *New York Times*, June 2, 1955, 28.
39. "The Segregation Decision," *Wall Street Journal*, June 2, 1955, 10.
40. Robert Carter and Thurgood Marshall, "The Meaning and Significance of the Supreme Court Decree," 24 *Journal of Negro Education* 397 (Summer 1955), reprinted in *Thurgood Marshall: His Speeches, Writings, Arguments, Opinions, and Reminiscences* 157, 163 (Mark V. Tushnet ed., 2001). For analysis of Carter and Marshall, among other leading civil rights attorneys, see Kenneth W. Mack, *Representing the Race: The Creation of the Civil Rights Lawyer* (2012).
41. Kluger, *Simple Justice*, 750.
42. Ibid., 755.
43. Schwartz, *Super Chief*, 112–13. While this anecdote hardly portrays Eisenhower in a flattering light, Warren evidently felt compelled to sanitize the language in his memoirs. Rather than "big black bucks," Warren indicates that Eisenhower spoke of "big overgrown Negroes." Warren, *Memoirs of Earl Warren*, 291–92. In September 1957, Eisenhower expressed a similar view at a press conference, where he stated, "There are very strong emotions on the [southern] side, people that see a picture of mongrelization of the race, they call it." J. W. Peltason, *Fifty-Eight Lonely Men: Southern Judges and School Desegregation* 46 (1961). In 1960, four years after Eisenhower's statement, a district court judge in Dallas, Texas, invoked the archetype of the "overgrown Negro" in a school desegregation case. In *Borders v. Rippey*, Judge Thomas Whitfield Davidson explained that in the course of desegregation it could periodically prove wise to send certain children to schools that were not closest to their homes: "Without purposely and intentionally discriminating between the races you may for any good cause or reason assign pupils to schools other than that nearest to them." Judge Davidson illustrated this theory with a vivid example: "[I]f an overgrown Negro boy in an integrated school should be by premature growth inclined to sex and should write verses on the blackboard of an obscene character designedly for the white girls to read or should make improper approaches to them so as to provoke trouble in the school, he should be assigned to a school where the situation is different." *Borders v. Rippey*, 184 F. Supp. 402, 420 (N.D. Tex. 1960).
44. Peltason, *Fifty-Eight Lonely Men*, 38.
45. See Tom P. Brady, *Black Monday* 45 (1955). Ibid., 64 ("Very few negroes have true respect and reverence for their race. They sense their racial limitations. If there is a short cut they want it. . . . [T]hey desire a much shorter detour, via the political tunnel, to get on the intermarriage turnpikes. These Northern negroes are determined to mongrelize America!").
46. Dan Wakefield, "Respectable Racism," *Nation*, Oct. 22, 1955, 339.
47. James F. Byrnes, "The Supreme Court Must Be Curbed," *U.S. News and World Report*, May 18, 1956, 50, 56.
48. James J. Kilpatrick, *The Sovereign States: Notes of a Citizen of Virginia* 281 (1957). Consider only a few additional examples of antimiscegenation sentiment arising in the context of opposition to school desegregation. Senator John Stennis of Mississippi explained, "[P]lacing the children side by side over the years,

in primary, grammar and high-school grades, is certain to eventually destroy each race. . . . And we all believe that the bloodstream—the racial integrity of each group—is worth saving." "The Race Issue: South's Plans, How Negroes Will Meet Them," *U.S. News and World Report*, Nov. 18, 1955, 86, 89. Herbert Ravenel Sass stated that southerners' aversion to miscegenation lies "at the heart of our race problem, and until it is realized that this is the South's basic and compelling motive, there can be no understanding of the South's attitude." Herbert Ravenel Sass, "Mixed Schools and Mixed Blood," *Atlantic Monthly*, Nov. 1956, reprinted in Jane Dailey, *The Age of Jim Crow* 271, 273 (2009). Sass wrote further, "[T]he underlying and compelling reason for the South's refusal to operate mixed schools—its belief that mixed schools will result in ultimate racial amalgamation—has been held virtually taboo." Ibid., 276. In a similar vein, Austin Earle Burges stated, "Social equality leads to intermarriage as surely as night follows day, and unrestricted marriage between the two races would be a calamity for the white race because . . . the Negro race is inherently inferior to the white race." Austin Earle Burges, *What Price Integration?* 86 (1956). The Reverend Louis E. Dailey of North Carolina argued that black males were naturally so libidinous that they could not control themselves around white females: "White people of the South know that a large number of Negro teenage boys are nearly sex maniacs. . . . Only under the protection of a school heavily guarded by police officers would they have any peace of mind for the safety of their daughters from the attacks of such Negro boys." Louis E. Dailey, *The Sin or Evils of Integration* 38 (1962).

49. Sam J. Ervin Jr., "The Case for Segregation," *Look*, April 3, 1956, 32.

50. Margaret Kernodle, "'Lawful Means' Pledged to Reverse Court Decision," *New Orleans Times-Picayune*, March 12, 1956, 22. In a carefully crafted opinion, Judge John Parker contended *Brown* did not mean

> states must mix persons of different races in the public schools. . . .
> What it had decided, and all that it has decided, is that a state may
> not deny any person on account of race the right to attend any
> school that it maintains. . . . The Constitution, in other words,
> does not require integration. . . . It does not forbid such segrega-
> tion as occurs as the result of voluntary action. It merely forbids
> the use of government power to enforce segregation.

Briggs v. Elliott, 132 F. Supp. 776, 777 (E.D. S.C. 1955).

51. James E. Clayton, "Sam and Bob Show Enters Fourth Week," *Washington Post*, Aug. 9, 1963, A4.

52. Ibid.

53. Sam J. Ervin Jr., *Preserving the Constitution* 146 (1984). For perceptive treatments of the conservative effort to shape *Brown* in the judicial and political arenas that influenced my own account, see Reva B. Siegel, "Equality Talk: Antisubordination and Anticlassification Values in Constitutional Struggles over *Brown*," 117 *Harvard Law Review* 1470 (2004); and David A. Strauss, "Discriminatory Intent and the Taming of *Brown*," 56 *University of Chicago Law Review* 935 (1989). For a more recent article exploring adjacent concepts, see Christopher W. Schmidt, "Beyond Backlash: Conservatism and the Civil Rights Movement," 56 *American Journal of Legal History* 179 (2016). For an incisive biography of Ervin, see Karl E. Campbell, *Senator Sam Ervin: Last of the Founding Fathers* (2007).

54. See *Cooper v. Aaron*, 358 U.S. 1 (1958) (embracing the Court's supremacy over the Constitution).

55. *Green v. County School Board of New Kent County, Virginia*, 391 U.S. 430, 438, 442 (1968) (emphasis added). For relatively inconsequential school desegregation cases, decided between *Brown II* and *Green*, see *Goss v. Board of Education*, 373 U.S. 683 (1963); *McNeese v. Board of Education for Community Unit School District 187*, 373 U.S. 668 (1963); *Griffin v. County School Board*, 377 U.S. 218 (1964).

56. *Green*, 391 U.S. at 437–38.

57. Ibid., 439.

58. Patterson, *Brown v. Board of Education*, 146.

59. For probing treatments of *Swann*, see Bernard Schwartz, Swann's *Way* 3 (1986); Matthew D. Lassiter, *The Silent Majority: Suburban Politics in the Sunbelt South* (2006); Wilkinson, *From* Brown *to* Bakke, 134–40; Brief for Petitioners, *Swann*, 402 U.S. 1, 1970 WL 122649.

60. James T. Wooten, "Parents in Charlotte, Even Those Who Favor Integration, Deeply Resent Racial Busing," *New York Times*, Oct. 7, 1970, 34.

61. Schwartz, Swann's *Way*, 21; Lassiter, *Silent Majority*, 164.

62. Schwartz, Swann's *Way*, 21.

63. Lassiter, *Silent Majority*, 2.

64. Ibid., 1–2.

65. Ibid., 154.

66. Richard M. Nixon, *Public Papers of the Presidents of the United States* 315 (1970) (statement of March 24, 1970). See also John Herbers, "President Draws the Line on Integration," *New York Times*, March 29, 1970, E2.

67. Herbers, "President Draws the Line on Integration," E2.

68. Ibid.

69. "Desegregation: The South's Tense Truce," *Time*, Sept. 14, 1970, 41.

70. William Kling, "High Court School Ruling May Reach Far," *Chicago Tribune*, Sept. 6, 1970, A7.

71. Edward F. Cummerford, "Mere Creatures of the State?," *Wall Street Journal*, Nov. 16, 1970, 14.

72. *Swann v. Charlotte-Mecklenburg County School Board*, 402 U.S. 1, 29 (1971).

73. Ibid., 27.

74. Ibid., 28.

75. Ibid., 20–21. For criticism of "racial balancing," see Nathan Glazer, "Is Busing Necessary?," *Commentary*, March 1, 1972, 39.

76. *Swann*, 402 U.S. at 16.

77. "Justice Burger's Warning," *New York Times*, April 22, 1971, 40. *The New York Times* struck this theme again a few days later: "It was almost as if the Burger Court had stood the Nixon administration's desegregation policy on its head—the policy that desegregation should not override children's rights to attend neighborhood schools, and that the law of school integration should be the same in North and South." Fred P. Graham, "The Court to the South: Bus You Must," *New York Times*, April 25, 1971, E2.

78. Peter Milius, "Nixon's Approach Rejected," *Washington Post*, April 21, 1971, A1.

79. Max Lerner, "Round Two on Integration," *Los Angeles Times*, April 25, 1971, G6.

80. "The Purpose of Schools," *Wall Street Journal*, April 22, 1971, 16.
81. Kevin J. McMahon, *Nixon's Court: His Challenge to Judicial Liberalism and Its Political Consequences* 103 (2011).
82. Lassiter, *Silent Majority*, 248.
83. "A Supreme Court Yes to Busing," *Time*, May 3, 1971, 19.
84. Ronald J. Ostrow, "High Court Upholds Cross-City Bussing," *Los Angeles Times*, April 21, 1971, 1.
85. Jon Nordheimer, "Success Is Savored by Black Lawyer in Charlotte Busing Case: Some Whites, Too, Back High Court's Ruling," *New York Times*, April 22, 1971, 25.
86. James J. Kilpatrick, "School Decision Is Nonsense," *Los Angeles Times*, May 13, 1971, B7.
87. "Man and Woman of the Year: The Middle Americans," *Time*, Jan. 5, 1970, 10.
88. Ibid., 13.
89. Matthew F. Delmont, *Why Busing Failed: Race, Media, and the National Resistance to School Desegregation* 11–12 (2016).
90. Ibid., 77.
91. "The Troubled American: A Special Report on the White Majority," *Newsweek*, Oct. 6, 1969, 29, 34, 45.
92. Glazer, "Is Busing Necessary?," 41; and "The Gallup Poll #838," Gallup, Oct. 8–11, 1971. For additional polling data indicating widespread opposition to *Swann*, see Murakami, "Desegregation," 36 (reporting that in a Gallup poll taken in March 1970, only 14 percent of adults favored busing and 81 percent were opposed); and George Gallup, "3 to 1 Rap Fast School Integration," *Los Angeles Times*, March 12, 1970, B5 (reporting that many more people contended integration was proceeding too quickly compared with those who contended integration was moving too slowly).
93. For an article making this argument at length, and critiquing prominent scholars who have maintained otherwise, see Driver, "Consensus Constitution."
94. David S. Tatel, "Judicial Methodology, Southern School Desegregation, and the Rule of Law," 79 *NYU Law Review* 1071, 1100–101 (2004).
95. Justin Driver, "Challenging Conventional Perspective on Burger Court," *Washington Post*, June 19, 2016, B6. See Michael O'Donnell, "Justice Served," *Washington Monthly*, Nov.–Dec. 2011 ("Burger has been widely portrayed as a vainglorious boob: pompous, ineffectual in leadership, and incompetent in assigning and drafting opinions"). After *Swann*, Jack Greenberg of the NAACP Legal Defense and Educational Fund expressed hope that the opinion indicated neighborhood schools would no longer be deemed "sacrosanct." C. Gerald Fraser, "Desegregation Course Charted by Legal Unit After Bus Ruling," *New York Times*, April 23, 1971, 21. Similarly, the NAACP's executive director, Roy Wilkins, stated, "The neighborhood school is toppled from its perch as the determinant of desegregation policy." O'Neil Kendrick, "South Unhappy with Burger," *Chicago Defender*, April 22, 1971, 4. Professor Owen Fiss contended *Swann* signaled "the adoption of a general approach to school segregation which, by focusing on the segregated patterns themselves, is more responsive to the school segregation of the North." Owen M. Fiss, "The *Charlotte-Mecklenburg* Case—Its Significance for Northern School Desegregation," 38 *University of Chicago Law Review* 697, 704–5 (1971).
96. Bob Woodward and Scott Armstrong, *The Brethren: Inside the Supreme Court*

122–50 (1979). My evaluation of Warren Burger's ability to realize his own jurisprudential agenda on the Supreme Court is indebted to a recent revisionist account of the Burger Court. See Michael J. Graetz and Linda Greenhouse, *The Burger Court and the Rise of the Judicial Right* (2016). Where Graetz and Greenhouse generally focus on the Burger Court as an institution, I emphasize that Burger himself merits reconsideration.

97. *Swann,* 402 U.S. at 28.

98. Ibid., 31.

99. Ibid., 22.

100. Christopher Jencks, "Busing: The Supreme Court Goes North," *New York Times,* Nov. 19, 1972, SM40.

101. *Keyes v. School District No. 1, Denver, Colorado,* 413 U.S. 189, 208 (1973) (emphasis added). See ibid., 206 ("[T]he Board, through its actions over a period of years, intentionally created and maintained the segregated character of the core city schools").

102. James E. Ryan, *Five Miles Away, a World Apart: One City, Two Schools, and the Story of Educational Opportunity in Modern America* 47 (2010). For a thoughtful evaluation of Ryan's book, see Wendy Parker, "The Failings of Education Reform and the Promise of Integration," 90 *Texas Law Review* 395 (2011).

103. John C. Jeffries, *Justice Lewis F. Powell Jr.: A Biography* 286 (1994). In the fall of 1960, two black teenage girls began attending what had been an entirely white junior high school. See ibid., 141.

104. *Keyes,* 413 U.S. at 223 (1973) (Powell, J., concurring in part and dissenting in part).

105. Ibid., 219.

106. Ibid., 225–26. See ibid., 226 ("Where school authorities decide to undertake the transportation of students, this also must be with integrative opportunities in mind").

107. Ibid., 246. See ibid., 242 ("The Equal Protection Clause does, indeed, command that racial discrimination not be tolerated in the decisions of public school authorities. But it does not require that school authorities undertake widespread student transportation solely for the sake of maximizing integration.").

108. See ibid., 245n25 ("In the school context, 'neighborhood' refers to relative proximity, to a preference for a school near to, rather than more distant from, home").

109. Kluger, *Simple Justice,* 608–9. For a systematic effort to dismantle Rehnquist's explanation for his memorandum, see ibid., 609*–15.

110. *Keyes,* 413 U.S. at 258 (Rehnquist, J., dissenting).

111. Ibid., 257.

112. For works that influenced the ideas contained in the preceding two paragraphs, see David L. Kirp, *Just Schools: The Ideal of Racial Equality in American Education* 285 (1982); Cass R. Sunstein, *The Partial Constitution* (1993); Richard Rothstein, *The Color of Law: A Forgotten History of How Our Government Segregated America* (2017); and Ta-Nehisi Coates, "The Case for Reparations," *Atlantic,* June 2014, 54. For the proposition that blacks have not typically desired high levels of racial separation, see Lee Anne Fennell, "Searching for Fair Housing," 97 *Boston University Law Review* 349 (2017).

113. *Washington v. Davis*, 426 U.S. 229, 240 (1976). For an important critique of *Washington v. Davis*, see Charles Lawrence III, "The Id, the Ego, and Equal Protection: Reckoning with Unconscious Racism," 39 *Stanford Law Review* 317 (1987).

114. "As the Court Sees It," *Chicago Defender*, June 26, 1973, 13.

115. "The Court's Double Standard," *Los Angeles Times*, June 22, 1973, C6.

116. "Denver: A 'Southern' Finding in the West," *Washington Post*, June 22, 1973, A22.

117. See 118 Congressional Record 563–66 (Jan. 20, 1972); and Austin Scott, "20 Years After School Ruling Institutions Still Segregated," *Washington Post*, May 18, 1974, A2.

118. Wilkinson, *From Brown to Bakke*, 53 (quoting Anthony Lewis, "Since the Supreme Court Spoke," *New York Times Magazine*, May 10, 1964, 9, 93). See *Taylor v. Board of Education of New Rochelle*, 191 F. Supp. 181 (S.D.N.Y. 1961); *Bell v. School City of Gary, Indiana*, 213 F. Supp. 819 (N.D. Ind. 1963); *Bell v. School City of Gary, Indiana*, 324 F.2d 209 (7th Cir. 1963), *cert. denied*, 377 U.S. 924 (1964); *Deal v. Cincinnati Board of Education*, 369 F.2d 55 (6th Cir. 1966), *cert. denied*, 389 U.S. 847 (1967); *Downs v. Board of Education*, 336 F.2d 988 (10th Cir. 1964), *cert. denied*, 380 U.S. 914 (1965); and *Kelly v. Guinn*, 456 F.2d 100 (9th Cir. 1972), *cert. denied*, 413 U.S. 100 (1973). See also Diane Ravitch, *The Troubled Crusade: American Education, 1945–1980* 171 (1983).

119. Owen M. Fiss, "Racial Imbalance in the Public Schools: The Constitutional Concepts," 78 *Harvard Law Review* 564, 617 (1965). See Robert L. Carter, "The Warren Court and Desegregation," 67 *Michigan Law Review* 237, 241–42 (1968) ("The Court has not expanded or extended *Brown*. It has not dealt with the question of *de facto* school segregation—an issue which is as potentially explosive today as was formal segregation in 1954. Therefore, we do not know what equal education means in the context of Northern-style school segregation."); and Frank I. Goodman, "*De Facto* School Segregation: A Constitutional and Empirical Analysis," 60 *California Law Review* 275 (1972).

120. Delmont, *Why Busing Failed*, 37. See also U.S. Commission on Civil Rights, *Racial Isolation in the Public Schools* (1967); and Ravitch, *Troubled Crusade*, 171. Speaking from the floor of the U.S. Senate in 1972, Senator Abraham Ribicoff of Connecticut decried northern hypocrisy on segregation. "Our motto seems to have been 'Do to southerners what you do not want to do to yourself,'" Ribicoff contended. "Somehow residential segregation in the North was accidental or *de facto* and that made it better than the . . . *de jure* segregation of the South. It was a hard distinction for black children in totally segregated schools in the North to understand, but it allowed us to avoid the problem." 118 Congressional Record 5455 (1972).

121. Delmont, *Why Busing Failed*, 6.

122. George F. Will, "Busing Between Urban and Suburban Schools," *Washington Post*, June 4, 1974, A23; Joyce A. Baugh, *The Detroit School Busing Case: Milliken v. Bradley and the Controversy over Desegregation* 118 (2011); Robert L. Pisor, "Detroit Awaits Decision on City-Suburb School Busing," *Washington Post*, June 9, 1974, A12; William Grant, "Boy Plays Key Role in Busing Fight," *Detroit Free Press*, June 18, 1972, 3; and William E. Farrell, "School Integration Resisted in Cities of North," *New York Times*, May 13, 1974, 24. Although

the Sixth Circuit did not technically affirm Judge Roth's holding regarding residential segregation, it left the desegregation order substantively in place. See *Bradley v. Milliken*, 484 F.2d 215, 258 (6th Cir. 1973).

123. *Milliken v. Bradley*, 418 U.S. 717, 741–42 (1974).

124. Ibid., 744.

125. Ibid., 782 (Marshall, J., dissenting). See Oyez Project, *Milliken v. Bradley* (Opinion Announcement, July 25, 1974, Marshall, J., at 24:39–33:47); Patterson, Brown v. Board of Education, 180–81. Justice Douglas and Justice White also authored dissenting opinions in *Bradley*.

126. *Milliken*, 418 U.S. at 783 (Marshall, J., dissenting).

127. Ibid., 814–15.

128. "Slowing the School Bus," *Wall Street Journal*, July 31, 1974, 10.

129. "The Detroit Ruling," *Washington Post*, July 29, 1974, A26. Earlier, *The Washington Post*'s masthead criticized Judge Roth's district court opinion in *Bradley* as "highly questionable . . . not least on the grounds that it probably won't work." Ryan, *Five Miles Away, a World Apart*, 97.

130. "Wrong Without Remedy," *New York Times*, July 28, 1974, 172.

131. Delmont, *Why Busing Failed*, 168.

132. Thomas J. Sugrue, *Sweet Land of Liberty: The Forgotten Struggle for Civil Rights in the North* 483 (2008).

133. NAACP Legal Defense and Educational Fund, *It's Not the Distance, "It's the Niggers": Comments on the Controversy over School Busing* 2 (1972).

134. Jeffries, *Justice Lewis F. Powell Jr.*, 314.

135. Roy Wilkins, "Apartheid in America?," *Los Angeles Times*, Aug. 21, 1974, C7.

136. "The Thrill Is Gone: U.S. Court Back-Steps," *New Pittsburgh Courier*, Aug. 3, 1974, 7. For additional coverage from black newspapers that criticized *Bradley*, see "Giant Step Backwards," *Baltimore Afro-American*, Aug. 3, 1974, 4 ("It is not clear immediately how far back toward the separate but equal theory of the infamous [*Plessy*] Decision the reconstructed Supreme Court has taken the nation with its ruling in the Detroit school merger case. It definitely was a painful setback."); Woodrow L. Taylor, "High Court Edict Blow to Blacks," *New Pittsburgh Courier*, Aug. 3, 1974, 1 ("The Nixon Administration's apparent determination to go back to the old 'separate but equal' policy regarding education of children on a racial basis got a shot in the arm last week when the U.S. Supreme Court issued a verdict limiting busing pupils between city and suburban lines for the purpose of integration"); and Frank L. Stanley, "Not Enough Whites to Go Around," *Chicago Defender*, Sept. 7, 1974, 6.

137. Kwame Ture and Charles V. Hamilton, *Black Power: The Politics of Black Liberation in America* 54 (Vintage ed. 1992) (1967). Stokely Carmichael ultimately changed his name to Kwame Ture. For an important work exploring cleavages within the black community during the civil rights era, see Tomiko Brown-Nagin, *Courage to Dissent: Atlanta and the Long History of the Civil Rights Movement* (2011).

138. Delmont, *Why Busing Failed*, 181.

139. Robert Reinhold, "To Some Blacks, the Bus Ride Isn't Worth It," *New York Times*, July 14, 1974, E7.

140. William E. Farrell, "School Integration Resisted in Cities of North," *New York Times*, May 13, 1974, 24.

141. Agis Salpukas, "Joy Is Expressed in the Suburbs," *New York Times*, July 26, 1974, 17.

142. Robert Reinhold, "Impact of the Ruling," *New York Times*, July 26, 1974, 16. A few weeks earlier, Professor Bell similarly contended integration "casts blacks in the role of subordinates in every aspect of the public school process, enabling school systems to boast that they have complied with *Brown*, while effectively relegating black children to a status that all too frequently is 'integrated and unequal.'" Reinhold, "To Some Blacks, the Bus Ride Isn't Worth It," 175. William Raspberry also voiced contemporaneous opposition to busing: "A lot of us are wondering whether the busing game is worth the prize. Some of us aren't even sure just what the prize is supposed to be. . . . Nor is there much more enthusiasm among black parents for large-scale busing for the primary purpose of racial integration." "The Busing Dilemma," *Time*, Sept. 22, 1975, 7, 14.

143. *Missouri v. Jenkins*, 515 U.S. 70, 122 (1995) (Thomas, J., concurring).

144. Salpukas, "Joy Is Expressed in the Suburbs," 17.

145. Ibid.; and William K. Stevens, "Many White Parents Now See Their Children as Safe," *New York Times*, July 27, 1974, 60.

146. "Most Pleased with Busing Veto," *Detroit Free Press*, July 26, 1974, A3.

147. Stevens, "Many White Parents Now See Their Children as Safe," 60.

148. Lee A. Daniels, "In Defense of Busing," *New York Times Magazine*, April 17, 1983, 34. My coda on busing owes a significant debt to James Ryan's book *Five Miles Away, a World Apart*—as does my view of this topic generally.

149. B. Drummond Ayres Jr., "Cross-Town Busing, Begun in '71, Is Working Well in Charlotte," *New York Times*, July 17, 1975, 14.

150. "Busing Dilemma," 7, 11; and Ayres, "Cross-Town Busing, Begun in '71, Is Working Well in Charlotte," 14; Daniels, "In Defense of Busing," 37.

151. Tom Wicker, "Reagan and the Court," *New York Times*, Nov. 11, 1984, E21.

152. Frye Gaillard, "President's Busing Remarks Anger Schools Superintendent," *Charlotte Observer*, Oct. 9, 1984, 4A.

153. "You Were Wrong, Mr. President," *Charlotte Observer*, Oct. 9, 1984, 10A. Lincoln Caplan's estimable book on the Solicitor General's Office helped to highlight Reagan's antibusing comments in Charlotte and *The Charlotte Observer*'s vociferous response. See Lincoln Caplan, *The Tenth Justice: The Solicitor General and the Rule of Law* 82–83 (1987).

154. See *Capacchione v. Charlotte-Mecklenburg Schools*, 57 F. Supp. 2d 228 (W.D. N.C. 1999). The Fourth Circuit ultimately vindicated Judge Potter's determination. See *Belk v. Charlotte-Mecklenburg Board of Education*, 269 F.3d 305 (4th Cir. 2001) (en banc). For perceptive work depicting Mecklenburg's public schools after *Swann*, see Dana Goldstein, *The Teacher Wars: A History of America's Most Embattled Profession* 180–81 (2014); Lassiter, *Silent Majority*, 212–21; Ryan, *Five Miles Away, a World Apart*, 113–14; and Emily Yellin and David Firestone, "By Court Order, Busing Ends Where It Began," *New York Times*, Sept. 11, 1999, A1. See also "Resegregation Now," *New York Times*, June 29, 2007, A28.

155. Daniels, "In Defense of Busing," 36 (reporting on Harris poll findings). For the underlying poll itself, see "Busing for School Desegregation: The Debate on Selected Issues," Congressional Research Service, April 30, 1981, CRS 15. See J. Anthony Lukas, *Common Ground: A Turbulent Decade in the Lives of Three*

American Families (1985). For claims that Charlotte might have been particularly well positioned to have a fruitful busing experience and that it is mistaken to believe that busing was generally destined to fail, see Lassiter, *Silent Majority*; and Ryan, *Five Miles Away, a World Apart.*

156. For a helpful paper written by a law student that compiles the history of the Seattle lawsuit that culminated in the 2007 Supreme Court opinion, see Cara Sandberg, "The Story of *Parents Involved in Community Schools*," Educational Law Stories—Student Papers, University of California, Berkeley Law, 2011. For other helpful background information, see Kathleen Brose, "Seattle's School Parents Vindicated," *Seattle Times*, July 12, 2007; "Supreme Court Revisits Race in Public Schools," *PBS NewsHour*, Dec. 4, 2006; "An Imperfect Revolution: Voices from the Desegregation Era," American RadioWorks, APM; and Julie Peterson, "Modernizing Program Raises Hope—New Ballard High School Will Showcase Latest in Technology," *Seattle Times*, Oct. 8, 1998.

157. *Board of Education of Oklahoma City Public Schools, Independent District No. 89 v. Dowell,* 498 U.S. 237, 248 (1991).

158. *Freeman v. Pitts,* 503 U.S. 467, 490–92 (1992).

159. *Jenkins,* 515 U.S. at 73. Later, Rehnquist returned to this temporal theme: "This case has been before the same United States District Court Judge since 1977." Ibid., 74. For helpful distillations of the Court's trio of desegregation cases from the 1990s that sharpened my own understanding, see Michael J. Klarman, *Unfinished Business: Racial Equality in American History* 192 (2007); and Delmont, *Why Busing Failed,* 210.

160. See *Grutter v. Bollinger,* 539 U.S. 306, 378 (2003) (upholding the University of Michigan Law School's affirmative action program). For a perceptive analysis of this case, see Wendy Parker, "The Story of *Grutter v. Bollinger:* Affirmative Action Wins," *Education Law Stories* 83–110 (Michael A. Olivas and Ronna Greff Schneider eds., 2008). Not long after Roberts's nomination to the Court, Professor Sanford V. Levinson stated, "I would be shocked if he turned out to be a strict constitutionalist like Scalia or Thomas. This is a guy who went out of his way to say he was never a member of the Federalist Society. It's possible that he has waited until this moment to shake up the world, but I would be very surprised." Lynette Clemetson, "Meese's Influence Looms in Today's Judicial Wars," *New York Times*, Aug. 17, 2005, A1, A16. While Justice Samuel Alito also replaced Justice Sandra Day O'Connor in 2006, few observers would have predicted that he would vote to preserve race-conscious student assignment plans. Alito's involvement with the Concerned Alumni of Princeton, a group mainly known for opposing affirmative action, made his rejection of the actions undertaken by Louisville and Seattle a virtual lock. See Mark Tushnet, *In the Balance: Law and the Roberts Court* 69 (2013). In 2000, some seven years before the Court decided *Parents Involved*, Professor James Ryan impressively predicted that the days of school districts being permitted to voluntarily undertake integration programs were limited. See James E. Ryan, "The Supreme Court and Public Schools," 86 *Virginia Law Review* 1335, 1377 (2000) ("There is strong reason . . . to doubt that the Court today would so casually conclude that school authorities have the power to take steps to achieve integration as a matter of educational policy").

161. *Parents Involved in Community Schools v. Seattle School District No. 1,* 551 U.S. 701, 730n14, 747 (2007) (Roberts, C.J., plurality opinion). Justice Thomas's

concurring opinion in *Parents Involved* embraced Harlan's dissent in *Plessy* even more fervently than did Chief Justice Roberts's plurality opinion. Indeed, Thomas cited Harlan on no fewer than four separate occasions. To offer only one example, Thomas wrote, "I am quite comfortable in the company I keep. My view of the Constitution is Justice Harlan's view in *Plessy:* 'Our Constitution is color-blind, and neither knows nor tolerates classes among citizens.'" Ibid., 772 (Thomas, J., concurring).

162. Ibid., 747 (Roberts, C.J., plurality opinion).

163. Ibid., 746–47 (citing Oral Argument Transcript, *Brown v. Board of Education,* 347 U.S. 483, 7 [Dec. 9, 1952]).

164. Ibid., 748.

165. Ibid., 848–49 (Breyer, J., dissenting). Breyer contended the Constitution "grants local school districts a significant degree of leeway" and emphasized the need for deference to "democratic local decisionmaking by States and school boards." Ibid., 866.

166. Ibid., 867.

167. Ibid., 867–68. See Mark Tushnet, "*Parents Involved* and the Struggle for Historical Memory," 91 *Indiana Law Journal* 493, 493 (2016) (relaying Breyer's oral remarks at Harvard Law School's celebration of his twentieth year on the Supreme Court); and Linda Greenhouse, "Justices, 5–4, Limit Use of Race for School Integration Plans," *New York Times,* June 29, 2007, A1, A24 ("Speaking from the bench for more than 20 minutes, Justice Breyer made his points to a courtroom audience that had never seen the coolly analytical justice express himself with such emotion").

168. *Parents Involved,* 551 U.S. at 797 (Kennedy, J., concurring in part and concurring in the judgment). Lower courts have accepted Kennedy's opinion as providing the governing standard in *Parents Involved* in an apparent application of the *Marks* Rule. See *Marks v. United States,* 430 U.S. 188, 193 (1977) ("When a fragmented Court decides a case and no single rationale explaining the result enjoys the assent of five Justices, the holding of the Court may be viewed as that position taken by those Members who concurred in the judgments on the narrowest grounds"). The *Marks* Rule, admittedly, is notoriously nettlesome, resembling much more closely an art than a science. What matters most in this area is determining which opinion the legal community, as a general construct, deems authoritative. Kennedy's opinion, more than any other in *Parents Involved,* has attained that status.

169. *Parents Involved,* 551 U.S. at 788 (Kennedy, J., concurring in part and concurring in the judgment). For an article exploring at greater length how Justice Kennedy's *Parents Involved* opinion managed to express ideas that simultaneously opposed racial classification and racial colorblindness, see Justin Driver, "Recognizing Race," 112 *Columbia Law Review* 404, 450–56 (2012).

170. *Parents Involved,* 551 U.S. at 797 (Kennedy, J., concurring in part and concurring in the judgment).

171. Ibid., 789. For a helpful examination of Justice Kennedy's equal protection jurisprudence, see Heather K. Gerken, "Justice Kennedy and the Domains of Equal Protection," 121 *Harvard Law Review* 104 (2007). With a decade of hindsight, it now seems clear that Professor Gerken presciently identified *Parents Involved* as offering an important inflection point in Kennedy's evolving views on race—an evolution that has in recent years witnessed him become

far more comfortable with race-conscious government actions than he seemed to have been earlier in his tenure. See *Texas Department of Housing and Community Affairs v. Inclusive Communities Project Inc.*, 135 S. Ct. 2507, 2525–26 (2015) (concluding, in an opinion by Justice Kennedy, that the Fair Housing Act of 1968 permits actions challenging disparate impact in addition to overt discrimination); *Fisher v. University of Texas at Austin*, 136 S. Ct. 2198 (2016) (upholding, in an opinion by Justice Kennedy, an affirmative action program for college admissions). For an insightful treatment of *Fisher*, see David A. Strauss, "*Fisher v. University of Texas* and the Conservative Case for Affirmative Action," 2016 *Supreme Court Review* 1.

172. Adam Liptak, "The Same Words, but Differing Views," *New York Times*, June 29, 2007, A24.

173. "Resegregation Now," A28.

174. "A Setback to Equality," *San Francisco Chronicle*, June 29, 2007, B10.

175. Eugene Robinson, "Standing in the Schoolhouse Door," *Washington Post*, June 29, 2007, A21. For other newspaper editorials criticizing *Parents Involved*, see "Still Unequal," *Boston Globe*, June 29, 2007, A16 (contending Roberts's witticism "is a pithy slogan, but a gross oversimplification that ignores social reality" and that the opinion "revealed once again the court's conservative tilt"); "Seattle Schools: Court's Wrong Turn," *Seattle Post-Intelligencer*, June 29, 2007 (asserting that the opinion elevated "conservative ideology over reality" and relied "heavily on legalistic formulations"); "A Blow to Brown," *Washington Post*, June 29, 2007, A20 ("It's a strange view of the Constitution that requires a desegregation plan one day and prohibits it the next"); and "Roberts Rules," *New Republic*, July 2, 2007, 1.

176. "Diversity Without Decrees," *National Review*, June 28, 2007.

177. "Race and the Roberts Court," *Wall Street Journal*, June 29, 2007, A14.

178. George Will, "The Court Returns to Brown," *Washington Post*, July 5, 2007, A17.

179. Goodwin Liu, " 'History Will Be Heard': An Appraisal of the *Seattle/Louisville* Decision," 2 *Harvard Law and Policy Review* 53, 61 (2008). For Liu's extended analysis of *Parents Involved*'s stakes shortly before the Court issued the opinion, see Goodwin Liu, "*Seattle* and *Louisville*," 95 *California Law Review* 277 (2007). For other critical assessments of *Parents Involved* from a liberal vantage point, see Pamela S. Karlan, "What Can *Brown*® Do for You? Neutral Principles and the Struggle over the Equal Protection Clause," 58 *Duke Law Journal* 1049 (2009); Kimberly Jenkins Robinson, "Resurrecting the Promise of *Brown*: Understanding and Remedying How the Supreme Court Reconstitutionalized Segregated Schools," 88 *North Carolina Law Review* 787 (2010).

180. J. Harvie Wilkinson III, "The Seattle and Louisville School Cases: There Is No Other Way," 121 *Harvard Law Review* 158, 183 (2007).

181. *Parents Involved*, 551 U.S. at 705 (Roberts, C.J., plurality opinion).

182. Ervin, *Preserving the Constitution*, 179.

183. Ibid., 146–47.

184. See *Doe ex rel. Doe v. Lower Merion School District*, 665 F.3d 524 (3d Cir. 2011); *Spurlock v. Fox*, 716 F.3d 383 (6th Cir. 2013); *Lewis v. Ascension Parish School Board*, 806 F.3d 344 (5th Cir. 2015); and *Stevenson v. Blytheville School District #5*, 800 F.3d 955 (8th Cir. 2015). See also U.S. Department of Justice and U.S. Department of Education, Guidance on the Voluntary Use of Race to

Achieve Diversity and Avoid Racial Isolation in Elementary and Secondary Schools, Dec. 2, 2011; Richard D. Kahlenberg, "Rescuing Brown v. Board of Education: Profiles of Twelve School Districts Pursuing Socioeconomic Integration," Century Foundation (2007) (detailing, and promoting, class-based solutions as work-arounds to *Parents Involved*); Erica Frankenberg, "Assessing the Status of School Desegregation Sixty Years After Brown," 2014 *Michigan State Law Review* 677, 697–98 (indicating sixty-nine school districts continue to pursue integration post–*Parents Involved*); and Dana Goldstein, "In Dallas, Opening Up Long-Divided Schools," *New York Times*, June 20, 2017, A1. For an argument suggesting that *Parents Involved* placed school districts in an extremely uncertain litigating situation, see Kimberly Jenkins Robinson, "The Constitutional Future of Race-Neutral Efforts to Achieve Diversity and Avoid Racial Isolation in Elementary and Secondary Schools," 50 *Boston College Law Review* 277, 282 (2009). See also James E. Ryan, "The Supreme Court and Voluntary Integration," 121 *Harvard Law Review* 131 (2007) (suggesting that *Parents Involved* may dampen enthusiasm for pro-integration policies, even while acknowledging that few school districts had plans pursuing integration).

185. For an argument that conservatives should adopt an equal protection jurisprudence that would also require invalidating pro-integration districting decisions, see Brian T. Fitzpatrick, "The Hidden Question in *Fisher*," 10 *NYU Journal of Law and Liberty* 168 (2016).

186. See *Parents Involved*, 551 U.S. at 759 (Thomas, J., concurring) ("The petitioner in the Louisville case received a letter from the school board informing her that her *kindergartner* would not be allowed to attend the school of petitioner's choosing because of the child's race. Doubtless, hundreds of letters like this went out . . . every year."); ibid., 784–86 (Kennedy, J., concurring in part and concurring in the judgment) (noting Seattle's usage of white and nonwhite categories); U.S. Census Bureau, Seattle, Washington (2010); *Parents Involved*, 551 U.S. at 723n11 ("[Seattle's] parents are required to identify their child as a member of a particular racial group. If a parent identifies more than one race on the form, '[t]he application will not be accepted and, if necessary, the enrollment service person taking the application will indicate one box.' ").

187. See Gary Orfield et al., Brown *at 60: Great Progress, a Long Retreat, and an Uncertain Future*, Civil Rights Project, May 15, 2014, 18 (table 8), 24 (table 11) (reporting percentages of black students who attend schools with overwhelmingly racial minorities); Erwin Chemerinsky, *The Case Against the Supreme Court* 138 (2014) (noting low percentages of white students in some urban school districts); Gary Orfield et al., "*Brown* at 62: School Segregation by Race, Poverty, and State," Civil Rights Project 3 (May 2016) (noting that changes in school composition mean that "whites can perceive an increase in interracial contact even as African American and Latino students are increasingly isolated, often severely so"); James E. Ryan, "The Real Lessons of School Desegregation," in *From Schoolhouse to Courthouse: The Judiciary's Role in American Education* 73, 87 (Joshua M. Dunn and Martin R. West eds., 2009) (emphasizing that entire school districts, not only schools, exist in racial isolation); and Nikole Hannah-Jones, "Segregation Now . . . ," *Atlantic*, May 2014, 70–71 (documenting the ascent of "apartheid schools").

188. Ellis Cose, "A Dream Deferred," *Newsweek*, May 17, 2004, 53.

189. "Unhappy Anniversary," *National Review*, June 14, 2004, 17.
190. See Bell, *Silent Covenants*, 20–28. See also Charles Ogletree, *All Deliberate Speed: Reflections on the First Half Century of* Brown v. Board of Education (2004); and Erwin Chemerinsky, "Separate and Unequal: American Public Education Today," 52 *American University Law Review* 1461 (2003) (proposing a series of radical legal reforms to prevent *Brown* from becoming a nullity). For insightful appraisals of *Brown* that appeared during the fiftieth anniversary that shaped my own understandings of the landmark, see Sunstein, "Did *Brown* Matter?," 102; Kennedy, "Schoolings in Equality," 29; and David J. Garrow, "Why *Brown* Still Matters," *Nation*, May 3, 2004, 45.
191. See Rosenberg, *Hollow Hope*, 52 ("[S]tatistics from the Southern states are truly amazing. For ten years, 1954–1964, virtually *nothing happened*. Ten years after *Brown* only 1.2 percent of black schoolchildren in the South attended school with whites."); Ryan, "Real Lessons of School Desegregation," 77 (contending that school desegregation was never fully attempted in most parts of the country); Matthew E. K. Hall, *The Nature of Supreme Court Power* 211 (2011) (providing border-state desegregation figures following *Brown II*); Gary Orfield et al., Brown *at 60*, 17 (demonstrating the South achieved higher levels of success at avoiding racial isolation than other regions); Sarah J. Reber, "Court-Ordered Desegregation: Successes and Failures Integrating American Schools Since *Brown Versus Board of Education*," 40 *Journal of Human Resources* 559, 580 (2005) (indicating that school integration increased dramatically in places that were subject to court orders); Sunstein, "Did *Brown* Matter?," 102 (arguing *Brown*'s fiftieth anniversary presented a reason to celebrate what it did accomplish); and Kennedy, "Schoolings in Equality," 31–32 (focusing on *Brown*'s deficits). For an early and insightful effort to refute the growing chorus of *Brown*'s skeptics, see David J. Garrow, "Hopelessly Hollow History: Revisionist Devaluing of *Brown v. Board of Education*," 80 *Virginia Law Review* 151, 152–58 (1994) (contending *Brown* helped to spur the civil rights movement). See also Ackerman, *We the People*, 229–56 (portraying *Brown*'s contribution to civil rights in positive terms).
192. Robert L. Carter, "The Warren Court and Desegregation," 67 *Michigan Law Review* 237, 247 (1968).
193. Ibid., 246.
194. Ibid., 247.
195. Arthur E. Sutherland, "Segregation and the Supreme Court," *Atlantic*, July 1954.
196. Alexander M. Bickel, "Integration: The Second Year in Perspective," *New Republic*, Oct. 8, 1956, 12.
197. Martin Luther King Jr., "Speech at Holt Street Baptist Church, Montgomery, Alabama," Dec. 5, 1955, reprinted in *Eyes on the Prize: America's Civil Rights Years—a Reader and Guide* 44, 45 (C. Carson et al. eds., 1987). For an illuminating examination of King's significance for constitutional thought more broadly, see Randall Kennedy, "Martin Luther King's Constitution: A Legal History of the Montgomery Bus Boycott," 98 *Yale Law Journal* 999 (1989).
198. Anthony Lewis, "Washington: Kennedy Commits Administration to Determined Effort to Improve Conditions," *New York Times*, June 16, 1963, E3.
199. *Santamaria v. Dallas Independent School District*, 2006 WL 3350194, at *31 (N.D. Tex. 2006). For thoughtful work on *Santamaria*, see Kristi L. Bowman,

"Pursuing Educational Opportunities for Latino/a Students," 88 *North Carolina Law Review* 911, 951–53 (2010).

6 EQUAL PROTECTION II

1. For crucial background information on *San Antonio Independent School District v. Rodriguez,* see 411 U.S. 1, 4–17 (1973); Richard Schragger, "*San Antonio v. Rodriguez* and the Legal Geography of School Finance Reform," in *Civil Rights Stories* 85–109 (Myriam E. Gilles and Risa L. Goluboff eds., 2008); Michael Heise, "The Story of *San Antonio Independent School District v. Rodriguez:* School Finance, Local Control, and Constitutional Limits," in *Education Law Stories* 51–82 (Michael Olivas and Ronna Greff Schneider eds., 2008); James E. Ryan, *Five Miles Away, a World Apart: One City, Two Schools, and the Story of Educational Opportunity in America* (2010); Peter Irons, *The Courage of Their Convictions* 281–303 (1988); Jonathan Kozol, *Savage Inequalities: Children in America's Schools* 206–33 (1991); and William Celis III, "One Man's Legal Odyssey," *New York Times,* April 10, 1994, C31.
2. "Exit the Property Tax?," *Newsweek,* Sept. 13, 1971, 61.
3. Philip B. Kurland, "Equal Educational Opportunity: The Limits of Constitutional Jurisprudence Undefined," 35 *University of Chicago Law Review* 583, 583 (1968).
4. Ibid., 588.
5. "Homogeneous Education," *Wall Street Journal,* Dec. 30, 1971, 6.
6. See Andrew Barnes, "Arizona School Financing Held Unconstitutional," *Washington Post,* June 3, 1972, A2 ("Arizona is the fifth state in which financing of schools by the property tax has been declared unconstitutional, starting with California last August. Texas, Minnesota, and New Jersey have had similar rulings."); and *Rodriguez,* 411 U.S. 1, 70–71n1 (Marshall, J., dissenting) (identifying opinions invalidating various states' school-financing methods—including Wyoming's).
7. Linda Greenhouse, "Property Tax Reform Enthusiasm Lags," *New York Times,* Dec. 19, 1972, 1. See also John P. MacKenzie, "Court to Review Property Tax as Base for School Funding," *Washington Post,* June 8, 1972, A1 (noting that only Hawaii would be unaffected if the Supreme Court invalidated Texas's school-funding system).
8. Robert Reinhold, "Texas Ruling," *New York Times,* Dec. 25, 1971, 15.
9. "Exit the Property Tax?," 61.
10. Ibid.
11. Greenhouse, "Property Tax Reform Enthusiasm Lags," 36.
12. Ryan, *Five Miles Away, a World Apart,* 5. My understanding of the fine line that President Nixon sought to walk with respect to *Rodriguez* was influenced by Professor Ryan's interpretation. See also Kevin J. McMahon, *Nixon's Court: His Challenge to Judicial Liberalism and Its Political Consequences* 187 (2011).
13. "The Taxing Question," *Newsweek,* Jan. 31, 1972, 48.
14. *Rodriguez,* 411 U.S. at 36.
15. Ibid., 37.
16. Ibid., 41.
17. Ibid., 49–50. Relatedly, Justice Powell observed, "In an era that has witnessed

a consistent trend toward centralization of the functions of government, local sharing of responsibility for public education has survived." Ibid., 49.

18. Ibid., 55.

19. Ibid., 58–59. Justice Stewart also filed a concurring opinion. See *Rodriguez*, 411 U.S. at 59–62 (Stewart, J., concurring).

20. *Brown v. Board of Education*, 347 U.S. 483, 493 (1954).

21. *Rodriguez*, 411 U.S. at 70–71 (Marshall, J., dissenting).

22. Ibid., 113.

23. Ibid., 127–28.

24. Ibid., 133n100. In addition to Justice Marshall's dissent, which Justice Douglas joined, Justices Brennan and White wrote their own dissenting opinions in *Rodriguez*. See *Rodriguez*, 411 U.S. at 62 (Brennan, J., dissenting); *Rodriguez*, 411 U.S. at 63 (White, J., dissenting).

25. "What the Courts Can't Do," *Wall Street Journal*, March 23, 1973, 10.

26. "How to Pay for Schools?," *Chicago Tribune*, March 26, 1973, 16.

27. "Last Chance for Fairness," *New York Times*, March 26, 1973, 38.

28. "The Schools and Equality," *Washington Post*, March 22, 1973, A26. Even before the Court decided *Rodriguez*, *The Washington Post* expressed deep hostility to judicial interventions in the realm of school financing: "The Texas decision has a certain superficial attraction because it offers one simple thou-shalt-not. But it is a dangerous simplicity." "Schools, Money, and the Texas Case," *Washington Post*, May 31, 1972, A16.

29. Lea Donosky and Terry Kliewer, "Best News in Weeks, Estes, Officials Pleased with *Rodriguez*," *Dallas Morning News*, March 22, 1973, 39A.

30. "School Ruling Greeted with Relief at Capitol," *Austin American*, March 22, 1973, A62.

31. Ruth E. Hill, "Fewer People Needed," San Antonio *Express and News Weekender*, March 31, 1973, 6C.

32. "The Future: Appeals to Legislature, Governor Next, an Embittered Demetrio Rodriguez Says," *San Antonio Express*, March 22, 1973, 3-A; and Warren Weaver Jr., "Court, 5–4, Backs Schools in Texas on Property Tax," *New York Times*, March 22, 1973, 32.

33. Analisa Nazareno, "*SASD vs. Rodriguez* Ruling on Funding 25 Years Old Today," *San Antonio Express-News*, March 21, 1998 1A, 12A.

34. For analysis of Justice Fortas's rejected nomination to become chief justice and subsequent resignation from the Court, see Laura Kalman, *Abe Fortas: A Biography* 319–79 (1990). For a claim that *Rodriguez* arrived at the Court belatedly from the perspective of school finance reformers that also entertains the countervailing idea that it arrived prematurely at the Court for their purposes, see Ryan, *Five Miles Away, a World Apart*, 142.

35. Richard A. Epstein, *The Classical Liberal Constitution: The Uncertain Quest for Limited Government* 551 (2014).

36. Jeffrey Toobin, *The Oath: The Obama White House and the Supreme Court* 32 (2012).

37. Goodwin Liu, "Education, Equality, and National Citizenship," 116 *Yale Law Journal* 330, 334–41 (2006).

38. Joe Ball, "Efficient and Suitable Provision for the Texas Public School Finance System: An Impossible Dream?," 46 *Southern Methodist University Law Review* 763, 763n2 (1992). For the first decision in the series of school-financing deci-

sions from the Texas Supreme Court, see *Edgewood Independent School District v. Kirby*, 777 S.W.2d 391 (Tex. 1989).

39. Mark Yudof, "School Finance Reform in Texas: The *Edgewood* Saga," 28 *Harvard Journal on Legislation* 499, 499 (1991). See also Schragger, "*San Antonio v. Rodriguez* and the Legal Geography of School Finance Reform," 105; Ryan, *Five Miles Away, a World Apart*, 145.

40. See Schragger, "*San Antonio v. Rodriguez* and the Legal Geography of School Finance Reform," 105.

41. Heise, "Story of *San Antonio Independent School District v. Rodriguez*," 72–73.

42. Kiah Collier, "Paxton Blasts 'Never-Ending' School Finance Laws," *Texas Tribune*, Oct. 31, 2015.

43. Albert H. Kauffman, "The Texas School Finance Litigation Saga: Great Progress, then Near Death by a Thousand Cuts," 40 *St. Mary's Law Journal* 511, 537–38 (2008). For the most recent decision in the Texas school-financing saga, see *Morath v. Texas Taxpayer and Student Fairness Coalition*, 490 S.W.3d 826 (Tex. 2016) (unanimously upholding the state's financing method against a challenge on behalf of school districts in property-rich areas).

   Connecticut's method of school financing has also been subjected to extensive litigation asserting its illegitimacy under the state constitutional requirement. See, for example, *Sheff v. O'Neill*, 678 A.2d 1267 (Conn. 1996). For a helpful overview of this litigation, see James E. Ryan, "*Sheff*, Segregation, and School Finance Litigation," 74 *NYU Law Review* 529 (1999). For a recent high-profile judicial decision, calling for a major overhaul of the state's public education system, see *Connecticut Coalition for Justice in Education Inc. v. Rell*, 2016 WL 4922730 (Conn. Super. Ct., Sept. 7, 2016). See also Kate Zernike, "Crux of Grim Ruling: Schools Are Broken," *New York Times*, Sept. 9, 2016, A1; and Lincoln Caplan, "Two Connecticut School Systems, for the Rich and Poor," *New Yorker*, Sept. 14, 2016.

   For scholarship analyzing post-*Rodriguez* developments with school-funding litigation in state courts, see Jeffrey S. Sutton, "*San Antonio Independent School District v. Rodriguez* and Its Aftermath," 94 *Virginia Law Review* 1963 (2008); and Emily Zackin, *Looking for Rights in All the Wrong Places: Why State Constitutions Contain America's Positive Rights* 67–105 (2013). For a trenchant and skeptical assessment of these developments, see Kimberly Jenkins Robinson, "The High Cost of Education Federalism," 48 *Wake Forest Law Review* 287, 307–22 (2013).

44. Schragger, "*San Antonio v. Rodriguez* and the Legal Geography of School Finance Reform," 109.

45. See Julien Lafortune et al., "School Finance Reform and the Distribution of Student Achievement" (National Bureau of Economic Research, Working Paper No. 22011, 2016); C. Kirabo Jackson et al., "The Effects of School Spending on Educational and Economic Outcomes: Evidence from School Finance Reforms," 131 *Quarterly Journal of Economics* 157 (2016); and Kevin Carey and Elizabeth A. Harris, "It Turns Out Spending More Probably Does Improve Education," *New York Times*, Dec. 12, 2016.

46. See John E. Coons et al., *Private Wealth and Public Education* 30 (1970) ("Whatever . . . money may be thought to contribute to the education of children, that commodity is something highly prized by those who [have the most]. If money is inadequate to improve education, the residents of poor districts should . . .

have an equal opportunity to be disappointed by its failure."). As a doctoral candidate at the University of Chicago, Arthur Wise was the first person to argue in print that the Constitution prohibited school-financing disparities. See Arthur E. Wise, "Is Denial of Equal Educational Opportunity Constitutional?," 13 *Administrator's Notebook* 1, 1–4 (1965); and Arthur E. Wise, *Rich Schools, Poor Schools: The Promise of Equal Educational Opportunity* (1968).

47. See *Rodriguez*, 411 U.S. at 37.

48. See Class Action Complaint, *Gary B. et al. v. Snyder et al.*, 16-CV-13292 (filed in E.D. Mich., Sept. 13, 2016); Geoffrey R. Stone, "Are Terrible Schools Unconstitutional?," *New York Times*, Oct. 21, 2016, A27; and Laurence Tribe, "Classrooms with Rats Instead of Teachers," *Los Angeles Times*, Sept. 22, 2016.

49. For helpful background information and insight into *Vorchheimer v. School District of Philadelphia*, see Martha Minow, "Single-Sex Public Schools: The Story of *Vorchheimer v. School District of Philadelphia*," in *Women and the Law Stories* 93–132 (Elizabeth Schneider and Stephanie Wildman eds., 2011); Philip Hager, "Justices Cautious: Sex Discrimination Suits Inundate Supreme Court," *Los Angeles Times*, Aug. 22, 1976, A1; Carol H. Falk, "Top Court to Review Sex-Segregation Suit Filed by Philadelphia High School Girl," *Wall Street Journal*, Oct. 19, 1976, 4; "Justices Deadlock on Sex Segregation," *New York Times*, April 20, 1977, 26; "Boys' School Wins a Delay on Girl," *New York Times*, Sept. 5, 1976, 10; *Vorchheimer v. School District of Philadelphia*, 532 F.2d 880, 881–83 (3d Cir. 1976); and Brief for the Petitioners, *Vorchheimer*, 430 U.S. 703, 1976 WL 181263, at *4–*9, *14–*23.

50. "Boys' School Wins a Delay on Girl," 10.

51. *Vorchheimer*, 532 F.2d at 881, 888. For a sophisticated normative exploration of the government's ability to provide assorted configurations in the name of diversity in a variety of legal contexts, see Heather K. Gerken, "Second-Order Diversity," 118 *Harvard Law Review* 1099 (2005).

52. *Vorchheimer*, 532 F.2d at 882, 887.

53. Ibid., 888 (Gibbons, J., dissenting).

54. Ibid., 889.

55. Serena Mayeri, "The Strange Career of Jane Crow: Sex Segregation and the Transformation of Anti-discrimination Discourse," 18 *Yale Journal of Law and the Humanities* 187, 262 (2006). See *Vorchheimer v. School District of Philadelphia*, 430 U.S. 703 (1977).

56. See Mark V. Tushnet, *Making Constitutional Law: Thurgood Marshall and the Supreme Court, 1961–1991* 41 (1997) ("Burger tried to persuade his colleagues to have the case reargued after Rehnquist recovered, saying that the Court should not 'evade[ ]' the constitutional question and certainly anticipating that Rehnquist would vote to allow the 'separate but equal' schools"). See also Erin Miller, "Ask the Author: Interview with Martha Minow, Part II," *SCOTUSblog*, Aug. 3, 2010 (predicting that a case involving same-sex marriage would soon appear on the Court's docket).

57. Minow, "Single-Sex Public Schools," 109; and *Newberg v. Board of Public Education*, 26 Pa. D. & C.3d, 682 (C.P. Phila. 1983) (invalidating Central's all-male policy). My conclusion that Girls High has yet to have a student transition gender identity while enrolled at the school is due to the absence of media coverage of such an event. Consistent with this theory, the Philadelphia media

has reported on some disputes arising from transgender students attending single-sex public schools in the metropolitan area.

58. *United States v. Virginia*, 518 U.S. 515, 534 (1996).

59. Rosemary C. Salomone, *Same, Different, Equal: Rethinking Single-Sex Schooling* 165 (2003); Minow, "Single-Sex Public Schools," 115. See Jeffrey Toobin, "Heavyweight: How Ruth Bader Ginsburg Has Moved the Supreme Court," *New Yorker*, March 11, 2013, 38 (calling her opinion in *United States v. Virginia* "the most important majority opinion of her career"). For an excellent overview of how opposition to stereotypes animated Ginsburg's legal thought as an attorney, see Cary Franklin, "The Anti-stereotyping Principle in Constitutional Sex Discrimination Law," 85 *NYU Law Review* 83 (2010).

60. *United States v. Virginia*, 518 U.S. at 534n7 (internal quotation marks omitted).

61. Ruth Bader Ginsburg, "The Burger Court's Grapplings with Sex Discrimination," in *The Burger Court: The Counter-revolution That Wasn't* 132, 144 (Vincent Blasi ed., 1983).

62. Ibid., 152. Michael Heise, "Are Single-Sex Schools Inherently Unequal?," 102 *Michigan Law Review* 1219, 1229 (2004) ("Unlike her position two decades earlier in *Vorchheimer*, in *VMI* Justice Ginsburg appears intellectually open to the possibility that a public single-sex school can pass constitutional muster"). For a perceptive article identifying how Justice Ginsburg's opinion in *United States v. Virginia* rested in considerable tension with earlier positions on gender equality, see Jeffrey Rosen, "Single-Sex Schools and Double Standards," *New York Times*, July 3, 1996, A23.

63. Christopher Jencks and David Riesman, *The Academic Revolution* 297–98 (1968).

64. Susan Estrich, "For Girls' Schools and Women's Colleges, Separate Is Better," *New York Times Magazine*, May 22, 1994, 38, 39. For scholarship defending all-female schools, see Salomone, *Same, Different, Equal*; and Rosemary Salomone, "Rights and Wrongs in the Debate over Single-Sex Schooling," 93 *Boston University Law Review* 971 (2013). Leonard Sax, a former physician, became an evangelist for single-sex public schools and justified his belief in the practice based on the supposed neurological differences between boys and girls. See Leonard Sax, *Why Gender Matters: What Parents and Teachers Need to Know About the Emerging Science of Sex Differences* (2005). For scholarship that attacks the traditional justifications for all-female education, see Cynthia Fuchs Epstein, "Multiple Myths and Outcomes of Sex Segregation," 14 *New York Law School Journal of Human Rights* 185 (1998); and Cynthia Fuchs Epstein, "The Myths and Justifications of Sex Segregation in Higher Education: VMI and the Citadel," 4 *Duke Journal of Gender Law and Policy* 101 (1997).

65. Wendy Kaminer, "The Trouble with Single-Sex Schools," *Atlantic Monthly*, April 1998, 22, 34; and Nancy Levit, "Separating Equals: Educational Research and the Long-Term Consequences of Sex Segregation," 67 *George Washington Law Review* 451, 517 (1999) ("State-sponsored separation promotes the idea of inherent differences between the sexes").

66. Motoko Rich, "Old Tactic Gets New Use: Public Schools Separate Girls and Boys," *New York Times*, Dec. 1, 2014, A16.

67. Gary J. Simson, "Separate but Equal and Single-Sex Schools," 90 *Cornell Law Review* 443, 456 (2005).

68. Levit, "Separating Equals," 526. For a foundational work exploring the concept of "the male gaze," see Laura Mulvey, "Visual Pleasure and Narrative Cinema," 16 *Screen* 6, 6–18 (1975).

69. Kaminer, "Trouble with Single-Sex Schools," 34.

70. Ibid., 36.

71. *Virginia*, 518 U.S. at 596 (Scalia, J., dissenting). See Kimberly J. Jenkins, "Constitutional Lessons for the Next Generation of Public Single-Sex Elementary and Secondary Schools," 47 *William and Mary Law Review* 1953, 1956–57 (2006).

72. See Rich, "Old Tactic Gets New Use," A16; and Diana Jean Schemo, "Change in Federal Rules Backs Single-Sex Public Education," *New York Times*, Oct. 25, 2006, A1, A16.

73. Jennifer Robison, "Learning About Single-Sex Education," Gallup, Oct. 1, 2002.

74. For an argument countering the claim that the Supreme Court's invalidation of uncommon measures matters little, see Justin Driver, "Constitutional Outliers," 81 *University of Chicago Law Review* 929 (2014).

75. Derrick Bell, "Et Tu, A.C.L.U.? A Misguided War Against a Girls' School in Harlem," *New York Times*, July 18, 1996, A23. See Rich, "Old Tactic Gets New Use," A16 (observing prevalence of single-sex public schools found in high-poverty neighborhoods dominated by racial minorities).

76. See *Garrett v. Board of Education of School District of City of Detroit*, 775 F. Supp. 1004, 1006 (E.D. Mich. 1991) (recounting features of the academies designed for black male students); and Verna L. Williams, "Reform or Retrenchment? Single-Sex Education and the Construction of Race and Gender," 2004 *Wisconsin Law Review* 15, 16–18.

77. *Virginia*, 518 U.S. at 531; *Sessions v. Morales-Santana*, 137 S. Ct. 1678, 1690 (2017). See Rich, "Old Tactic Gets New Use," A16 (observing the paucity of evidence suggesting that single-sex public schools improve academic performance and summarizing a meta-study). For an argument that courts should relax the "exceedingly persuasive justification" standard, at least as applied to single-sex public schools with voluntary enrollment, see Jenkins, "Constitutional Lessons for the Next Generation of Public Single-Sex Elementary and Secondary Schools," 2022–35.

78. Rich, "Old Tactic Gets New Use," A16. See also Kaminer, "Trouble with Single-Sex Schools," 34 (noting the prevalence of walls painted pink at the Young Women's Leadership School, informally known as the East Harlem Girls' School). See also *Garrett*, 775 F. Supp. at 1007 ("Although co-educational programs have failed, there is no showing that it is the co-educational factor that results in failure"); and Kaminer, "Trouble with Single-Sex Schools," 36 (noting the paucity of evidence supporting the efficacy of single-sex schooling).

79. See Devon W. Carbado, "Men in Black," 3 *Journal of Gender, Race, and Justice* 427, 434 (2000); Williams, "Reform or Retrenchment?," 76–77; and *Garrett*, 775 F. Supp. at 1007 (noting that Detroit's school district suggested "a false dichotomy between the roles and responsibilities of boys and girls").

80. Williams, "Reform or Retrenchment?," 19–20.

81. Judith Shulevitz, "Is It Time to Desegregate the Sexes?," *New York Times*, Oct. 15, 2016, SR1.

82. Jack Healy et al., "Solace and Fury as Schools React to Gender Policy," *New York Times*, May 14, 2016, A1.
83. Ibid.
84. Moriah Balingit, "Gavin Grimm Just Wanted to Use the Bathroom," *Washington Post*, Aug. 30, 2016.
85. For illuminating background on Grimm's case, see Gavin Grimm, "The Fight for Transgender Rights Is Bigger than Me," *New York Times*, March 7, 2017; Balingit, "Gavin Grimm Just Wanted to Use the Bathroom"; Sheryl Gay Stolberg, "Teenage Voice Leads the Fight on Restrooms," *New York Times*, Feb. 24, 2017, A1; Samantha Allen, "This Mom's Supreme Court Battle Is for All Transgender Kids," *Daily Beast*, Feb. 14, 2017; Larry O'Dell, "Transgender Student's Battle over Restroom Divides Rural Virginia Town," Associated Press, Sept. 17, 2015; Katie Couric, "Gavin Grimm's Story (Extended)," *Gender Revolution: A Journey with Katie Couric*, Feb. 6, 2017; and *G.G. ex rel. Grimm v. Gloucester County School Board*, 822 F.3d 709, 714–17 (4th Cir. 2016), *cert. granted*, 137 S. Ct. 369 (2016), *vacated and remanded*, 137 S. Ct. 1239 (2017).
86. Grimm, "Fight for Transgender Rights Is Bigger than Me."
87. Stolberg, "Teenage Voice Leads the Fight on Restrooms," A1.
88. *Grimm*, 822 F.3d at 716.
89. Ria Tabacco Mar, "Transgender Students Will Win," *New York Times*, Feb. 24, 2017, A27.
90. *Grimm*, 822 F.3d at 716.
91. See ibid., 717.
92. 20 U.S.C. § 1681(a).
93. See 34 C.F.R. § 106.33; Healy et al., "Solace and Fury as Schools React to Gender Policy," A1; Robert Barnes and Moriah Balingit, "Supreme Court Takes Up School Bathroom Rules for Transgender Students," *Washington Post*, Oct. 28, 2016; Jeremy W. Peters et al., "Trump Rescinds Obama Directive on Bathroom Use," *New York Times*, Feb. 23, 2017, A1; and Robert Barnes, "Supreme Court Sends Virginia Transgender Case Back to Lower Court," *Washington Post*, March 6, 2017. The Fourth Circuit demonstrated *Auer* deference to the Obama administration's interpretation of Title IX regulations. See *Auer v. Robbins*, 519 U.S. 452 (1997). *Auer* deference—which can be traced back to *Bowles v. Seminole Rock & Sand Co.*, 325 U.S. 410 (1945)—is a cousin to *Chevron* deference. See *Chevron U.S.A. Inc. v. Natural Resources Defense Council Inc.*, 467 U.S. 837 (1984). *Auer* deference has been subjected to withering criticism in recent years. See, for example, *Perez v. Mortgage Bankers Association*, 135 S. Ct. 1199, 1213–25 (2015) (Thomas, J., concurring in the judgment). For an academic treatment that provided the foundation for criticizing *Auer*, see John F. Manning, "Constitutional Structure and Judicial Deference to Agency Interpretations of Agency Rules," 96 *Columbia Law Review* 612 (1996). For a defense of the practice, see Cass R. Sunstein and Adrian Vermeule, "The Unbearable Rightness of *Auer*," 84 *University of Chicago Law Review* 297 (2017).
94. See Healy et al., "Solace and Fury as Schools React to Gender Policy," A1 (citing estimate provided by the Williams Institute of the UCLA School of Law); and Jeannie Suk Gersen, "A New Phase of Chaos on Transgender Rights," *New Yorker*, March 13, 2017 (contending that "as the Title IX arguments grow weaker without the federal government's supporting interpretation, constitu-

tional arguments may well rise up to accomplish the same protection for trans-gender people").

95. *Evancho*, 237 F. Supp. 3d at 285–86 (citing inter alia *Glenn v. Brumby*, 663 F.3d 1312, 1316–17 [11th Cir. 2011]); and Elizabeth Behrman, "Legal Experts Say Pine-Richland Transgender Ruling Will Impact National Cases," *Pittsburgh Post-Gazette*, March 13, 2017.

96. *Evancho*, 237 F. Supp. 3d at 285.

97. Ibid., 287–89 (citing *United States v. Virginia*, 518 U.S. 515, 531 [1996]).

98. Ibid., 293. In the *Grimm* case, Judge Andre Davis pressed precisely this idea that any burdens resulting from trans students using gender-congruent bathrooms should be shouldered by uneasy students, who could use single-occupancy restrooms. Judge Davis contended that uneasy students using single-occupancy restrooms "[would] carr[y] no stigma whatsoever, whereas for [Grimm], using those same restrooms is tantamount to humiliation and a continuing mark of difference among his fellow students." *Grimm*, 822 F.3d 709, 729 (Davis, J., concurring). Judge Davis's account may underestimate the stigma that could attach to uneasy students using single-occupancy restrooms. It seems at least possible that such students could be accused of doing so because they are transphobic.

99. See Mary Anne Case, "Why Not Abolish the Laws of Urinary Segregation?," in *Toilet: Public Restrooms and the Politics of Sharing* 211 (Harvey Molotch and Laura Norén eds., 2010); Jeannie Suk Gersen, "Who's Afraid of Gender-Neutral Bathrooms," *New Yorker*, Jan. 25, 2016. For a prominent example of a legal conservative condemning the extension of protections to transgender students, see Ed Whelan, "Enforced Gender Conformity," *National Review*, Oct. 31, 2016.

100. Barnes and Balingit, "Supreme Court Takes Up School Bathroom Rules for Transgender Students."

101. Jennifer Finney Boylan, "The Best Draft of the Self," *New York Times*, June 18, 2017, BR19 (ellipsis in original). See also Jennifer Finney Boylan, *She's Not There: A Life in Two Genders* (2003).

102. For illuminating background on and analysis of *Plyler v. Doe*, see Paul Feldman, "Texas Case Looms over Prop. 187's Legal Future," *Los Angeles Times*, Oct. 23, 1994, 1; Barbara Belejack, "A Lesson in Equal Protection: The Texas Cases That Opened the Schoolhouse Door to Undocumented Immigrant Children," *Texas Observer*, July 13, 2007; Katherine Leal Unmuth, "25 Years Ago, Tyler Case Opened Schools to Illegal Immigrants," *Dallas Morning News*, June 11, 2007, 1A; Linda Greenhouse, "What Would Justice Powell Do? The 'Alien Children' Case and the Meaning of Equal Protection," 25 *Constitutional Commentary* 29 (2008); Frank R. Kemerer, *William Wayne Justice: A Judicial Biography* 237–49 (1991); Michael A. Olivas, *No Undocumented Child Left Behind: Plyler v. Doe and the Education of Undocumented Schoolchildren* (2012); and *Plyler v. Doe*, 457 U.S. 202, 205–10 (1982).

103. *Plyler*, 457 U.S. at 220, 224, 230.

104. Ibid., 221.

105. Ibid., 223. See also ibid., 222 ("Illiteracy is an enduring disability. The inability to read and write will handicap the individual deprived of a basic education each and every day of his life."); and ibid., 221 ("[E]ducation provides the basic tools by which individuals might lead economically productive lives").

106. Ibid., 218–19.
107. Ibid., 221.
108. Ibid., 219.
109. Ibid., 221–22. Justice Powell wrote a brief concurring opinion, largely echoing the broad themes of Justice Brennan's majority opinion. See ibid., 236–41 (Powell, J., concurring).
110. Ibid., 243, 253 (Burger, C.J., dissenting). Justices O'Connor, Rehnquist, and White joined Chief Justice Burger's dissent.
111. Ibid., 242. See ibid., 252 ("Denying a free education to illegal alien children is not a choice I would make were I a legislator").
112. Ibid., 253.
113. Ibid., 243. Legal scholars, including left-leaning ones, agreed with Chief Justice Burger that *Plyler v. Doe* would have limited significance beyond its specific context. See, for example, Dennis J. Hutchinson, "More Substantive Equal Protection? A Note on *Plyler v. Doe*," 1982 *Supreme Court Review* 167, 192–94.
114. "Educating Citizen or Stranger," *Boston Globe*, June 17, 1982.
115. "Teaching Alien Children Is a Duty," *New York Times*, June 16, 1982, A30.
116. "The Rights of Illegal Aliens," *Washington Post*, June 18, 1982, A30.
117. "'Illegals' and Local Government," *Wall Street Journal*, July 1, 1982, 18.
118. Professor Michael Klarman's influential scholarship has often invoked the notion of "outliers" to undercut the presumed significance of judicial opinions, including with respect to *Plyler v. Doe*. See Michael J. Klarman, "Antifidelity," 70 *Southern California Law Review* 381, 414 (1997) (construing *Plyler v. Doe* as suppressing an outlier); Michael J. Klarman, "Rethinking the History of American Freedom," 42 *William and Mary Law Review* 265, 279 (2000) ("Invoking the Constitution to invalidate extreme outlier practices hardly represents a momentous contribution to the story of American freedom"); Michael J. Klarman, "What's So Great About Constitutionalism?," 93 *Northwestern University Law Review* 145, 172 (1998) (contending that outlier-suppressing opinions "are consonant with dominant national norms and thus are best described as reflecting rather than producing national unity"); and Michael J. Klarman, *From Jim Crow to Civil Rights* 453 (2004) ("More constitutional law than is commonly supposed reflects this tendency to constitutionalize consensus and suppress outliers"). For examination and refinement of the "outlier" terminology within legal discourse, see Driver, "Constitutional Outliers."
119. *Plyler,* 547 U.S. at 205.
120. Ibid., 237 (Powell, J., concurring).
121. Seth Stern and Stephen Wermiel, *Justice Brennan: Liberal Champion* 475 (2010).
122. Fred Barbash and Charles R. Babcock, "Court Bars Denying Free Schooling to Aliens," *Washington Post*, June 16, 1982, A1, A10. See Linda Greenhouse, "Aliens' Rights and Curbs on Federal Power Among Cases Facing High Court," *New York Times*, Oct. 4, 1981, 34.
123. See, for example, "Texas Bar to Aliens in Public Schools Voided by U.S. Judge," *New York Times*, July 22, 1980, A1 ("Texas is the only state to enact such prohibitions so far. But today's decision was regarded as potentially important to other states . . . , since such laws could be enacted elsewhere."); Linda Greenhouse, "Breathing While Undocumented," *New York Times*, April 27, 2010, A23 ("I have no doubt that but for that ruling, public school systems all over the country would be checking papers and tossing away their undocumented

students like so much playground litter"); and Jennifer Radcliffe, "1982 Ruling a Catalyst in Immigration Debate," *Houston Chronicle*, May 21, 2006.

124. See Greenhouse, "What Would Justice Powell Do?," 30–31 (detailing Roberts's memorandum, co-authored with Carolyn B. Kuhl, on *Plyler v. Doe*).

125. Stanley M. Elam and Lowell C. Rose, "Phi Delta Kappa/Gallup Poll of the Public's Attitudes Toward the Public Schools," 77 *Phi Delta Kappan* 41, 52 (1995). See also Tom Morganthau et al., "Closing the Door?," *Newsweek*, June 25, 1984, 18, 20 (reporting that "residents of states along the Mexican border are only slightly more likely . . . to call the problem 'very important'" than citizens nationally).

126. See Nina Bernstein, "Despite Ruling, Many School Districts Ask for Immigration Papers," *New York Times*, July 23, 2010, A16, A20; Driver, "Constitutional Outliers," 977; *Hispanic Interest Coalition of Alabama v. Governor of Alabama*, 691 F.3d 1236 (11th Cir. 2012); and *League of United Latin American Citizens v. Wilson*, 908 F. Supp. 755 (C.D. Cal. 1995).

127. Warren Brown, "Texas Plans to Appeal Court Ruling Voiding State Law on Alien Schooling," *Washington Post*, July 23, 1980, C4.

128. Stuart Taylor Jr., "Conflict over Rights of Aliens Lies at Supreme Court's Door," *New York Times*, Sept. 28, 1981, A1, A17; and Eileen Ogintz, "Court Ponders Class Struggle While Aliens Seek Education," *Chicago Tribune*, Nov. 1, 1981, B8. See also "Costly Break for Illegal Aliens," *Newsweek*, Aug. 4, 1980, 60 (contending "Mexican-Americans . . . were predictably pleased with the [lower court] decision" invalidating the measure).

129. Taylor, "Conflict over Rights of Aliens," A17. See also Nick King, "A Small Boy, a Big Issue: Aliens' Rights," *Boston Globe*, Jan. 15, 1982, 1, 6 (providing breakdown of Brownsville's students).

130. Legal scholarship promoting the "social movement" understanding of constitutional law is voluminous. For only a few of the many important works in this tradition, see David Cole, *Engines of Liberty: The Power of Citizen Activists to Make Constitutional Law* (2016); Scott L. Cummings, "Rethinking the Foundational Critiques of Lawyers in Social Movements," 85 *Fordham Law Review* 1987 (2017); William N. Eskridge Jr., "Channeling: Identity-Based Social Movements and Public Law," 150 *University of Pennsylvania Law Review* 419 (2001); Douglas NeJaime, "Constitutional Change, Courts, and Social Movements," 111 *Michigan Law Review* 877 (2013); and Robert Post and Reva Siegel, "*Roe* Rage: Democratic Constitutionalism and Backlash," 42 *Harvard Civil Rights–Civil Liberties Law Review* 373 (2007).

131. Feldman, "Texas Case Looms over Prop. 187's Legal Future."

132. Mary Ann Zehr, "Case Touched Many Parts of Community," *Education Week*, June 6, 2007.

133. Unmuth, "25 Years Ago, Tyler Case Opened Schools to Illegal Migrants," 1A.

134. Epstein, *Classical Liberal Constitution*, 549.

135. *Martinez v. Bynum*, 461 U.S. 321, 345 (1983) (quoting *Plyler v. Doe*, 457 U.S. at 227n22). See also *Plyler v. Doe*, 457 U.S. at 240n4 (Powell, J., concurring) ("Of course a school district may require that illegal alien children, like any other children, actually reside in the school district before admitting them to the schools").

136. See Michael A. Olivas, "From a 'Legal Organization of Militants' into a 'Law

Firm for the Latino Community': MALDEF and the Purposive Cases of *Keyes*,
Rodriguez, and *Plyler*," 90 *Denver University Law Review* 1151, 1185 (2013).

137. *Kadrmas v. Dickinson Public Schools*, 487 U.S. 450, 452–56, 459 (1988).

138. Ibid., 458.

139. Ibid., 466 (Marshall, J., dissenting). Justice Brennan joined Justice Marshall's
dissenting opinion. In addition, Justice Stevens issued a dissent that Justice
Blackmun joined. See ibid., 472–73 (Stevens, J., dissenting).

140. Ibid., 471 (Marshall, J., dissenting).

141. See, for example, David G. Savage, "Court OKs Fees to Ride School Bus,"
Los Angeles Times, June 25, 1988, Q1 (calling *Kadrmas* "a case of minor significance"); and Florida Legislature Office of Program Policy Analysis and
Government Accountability, Report No. 11-24, "Some States Allow School
Districts to Charge Parents for School Bus Transportation or to Advertise
in or on School Buses to Raise Additional Revenue," Dec. 2011, 2, exhibit
1 (noting that thirteen states affirmatively permit school districts to charge
student transportation fees). See also Katheleen Conti, "Most School Districts
Can't Put Brakes on Bus Fees," *Boston Globe*, Aug. 20, 2015; and Jenni Bergal,
"School Districts Are Billing Parents for Bus Rides," PEW Charitable Trusts,
June 16, 2015.

7   THE QUIET DÉTENTE OVER RELIGION AND EDUCATION

1. For a cogent distillation of the Court's Jurisprudence involving the Constitution's religion clauses, see James E. Ryan, "The Supreme Court and Public
Schools," 86 *Virginia Law Review* 1335, 1380–90 (2000). Professor Laurence
Tribe has noted that "the special place of public schools in American life" is
indicated by society's refusal to permit schoolhouses—"the facilities through
which basic norms are transmitted to our young"—to be used "as a forum
for . . . religion." Laurence H. Tribe, *American Constitutional Law* 825 (1978).
See also William P. Marshall, " 'We Know It When We See It': The Supreme
Court and Establishment," 59 *Southern California Law Review* 495, 541 (1986)
("The Court has been its most consistent and forceful in the context of the
public schools").

2. See generally James Davison Hunter, *Culture Wars: The Struggle to Define
America* (1991).

3. See Douglas Laycock, "Substantive Neutrality Revisited," 110 *West Virginia
Law Review* 51 (2007) (demonstrating how the Supreme Court's seemingly disparate Establishment Clause jurisprudence can be reconciled). Professor Laycock's views on the Establishment Clause have influenced my own thinking
about religion in schools more deeply than any other single scholar's views on
any other schooling issue.

4. For vital background on and analysis of *Engel v. Vitale*, see Bruce J. Dieren-
field, *The Battle over School Prayer: How* Engel v. Vitale *Changed America* (2007);
Thomas C. Berg, "The Story of the School Prayer Decisions: Civil Religion
Under Assault," in *First Amendment Stories* 195–228 (Richard W. Garnett and
Andrew Koppelman eds., 2012); Martha C. Nussbaum, *Liberty of Conscience: In
Defense of America's Tradition of Religious Equality* 236–39 (2008); "The Offen-

sive Prayer," *Time*, March 9, 1959, 56; "The Court Decision—and the School Prayer Furor," *Newsweek*, July 9, 1962, 43; Roy R. Silver, "5 L.I. Parents Who Started Suit Hail Decision," *New York Times*, June 26, 1962, 17; Roy R. Silver, "L.I. Test Slated on School Prayer," *New York Times*, Jan. 27, 1959, 35; George E. Sokolsky, "Resistance to Prayer," *Washington Post*, Feb. 24, 1959, A17; Brief of the Petitioners, *Engel*, 370 U.S. 421, 1962 WL 115797, at *3–*7; Corinna Barrett Lain, "God, Civic Virtue, and the American Way: Reconstructing *Engel*," 67 *Stanford Law Review* 479 (2015); and Barry Friedman, *The Will of the People: How Public Opinion Has Influenced the Supreme Court and Shaped the Meaning of the Constitution* (2009). Prior to its decision in *Engel*, the Supreme Court decided two cases involving school programs that released students from classes for the purpose of religious observance. See *McCollum v. Board of Education*, 333 U.S. 203 (1948); and *Zorach v. Clauson*, 343 U.S. 306 (1952). These opinions, however, were of modest consequence compared with *Engel*.

5. "School Prayer Furor," 43.
6. Silver, "5 L.I. Parents Who Started Suit Hail Decision," 17.
7. Berg, "Story of the School Prayer Decisions," 201.
8. *Engel v. Vitale*, 370 U.S. 421, 431 (1962). "No Prayers in Schools, Supreme Court Orders," *Dallas Morning News*, June 26, 1962, 1 (noting Justice Black used "quiet tones [speaking] to a more-than-usually hushed audience jammed with tourists"); Roger K. Newman, *Hugo Black: A Biography* 522 (2d ed. 1997) (1994) ("When delivering the opinion, he leaned forward, resting his arms on the bench, and read with considerable emotion").
9. *Engel*, 370 U.S. at 436 (internal quotation marks and citation omitted).
10. Ibid., 435.
11. Ibid., 431–32 (internal quotation marks omitted).
12. Berg, "Story of the School Prayer Decisions," 210.
13. Anthony Lewis, "Supreme Court Outlaws Official School Prayers in Regents Case Decision," *New York Times*, June 26, 1962, 1. Justice William O. Douglas wrote a brief concurring opinion. See *Engel*, 370 U.S. at 437 (Douglas, J., concurring).
14. *Engel*, 370 U.S. at 444 (Stewart, J., dissenting).
15. Ibid., 448.
16. Dierenfield, *Battle over School Prayer*, 137.
17. Ibid., 139; "School Prayer Furor," 43; "Family Threatened for Prayer Lawsuit," *Boston Globe*, June 28, 1962, 17.
18. "Family Threatened for Prayer Lawsuit," 17.
19. Dierenfield, *Battle over School Prayer*, 139.
20. Ibid., 141; and "Leader of Prayer Fight Picketed," *Los Angeles Times*, July 8, 1962, A14.
21. "School Prayer Furor," 44; and Berg, "Story of the School Prayer Decisions," 214 (recounting the burning cross episode).
22. "School Prayer Furor," 43.
23. Berg, "Story of the School Prayer Decisions," 212–13 (recounting record-setting number of anti-*Engel* letters); and Linda Lyons, "The Gallup Brain: Prayer in Public Schools," Gallup, Dec. 10, 2002.
24. "Prayer in School," *Chicago Tribune*, June 27, 1962, 12.
25. "A Very Upsetting Little Prayer," *Los Angeles Times*, June 28, 1962, A4.
26. "Opinion of the Week: Prayers in School," *New York Times*, July 1, 1962, E9

(excerpting the *Raleigh News and Observer's* editorial); and "Papers Comment on Decision," *Dallas Morning News*, June 29, 1962, 4.2 (excerpting *The Tulsa Tribune's* editorial).

27. Earl Warren, *The Memoirs of Earl Warren* 315–16 (1977).

28. "Thou Shalt Not Pray," *National Review*, July 31, 1962, 51, 52.

29. "Thou Shalt Not Pray," *Dallas Morning News*, June 29, 1962, 4.2.

30. Anthony Lewis, "Court Again Under Fire," *New York Times*, July 1, 1962, E10. See also Jonathan Zimmerman, *Whose America? Culture Wars in the Public Schools* 174 (2002) (totaling the constitutional amendments proposed post-*Engel*).

31. Anthony Lewis, "Both Houses Get Bills to Lift Ban on School Prayer," *New York Times*, June 27, 1962, 1.

32. "Opinion of the Week: Prayers in School," E9.

33. Dierenfield, *Battle over School Prayer*, 147.

34. "Top Court Ban on School Prayer Stirs Congress' Ire," *Chicago Tribune*, June 26, 1962, 2.

35. Lewis, "Both Houses Get Bills to Lift Ban on School Prayer," 1.

36. Lewis, "Court Again Under Fire," E10.

37. "Top Court Ban on School Prayer Stirs Congress' Ire," 2.

38. Robert G. McCloskey, "Principles, Powers, and Values: The Establishment Clause and the Supreme Court," 2 *Religion and the Public Order: An Annual Review of Church and State* 3, 28 (1964). See also Lucas A. Powe Jr., *The Warren Court and American Politics* 362 (2000); and Friedman, *Will of the People*, 266.

39. Lewis, "Both Houses Get Bills to Lift Ban on School Prayer," 1, 20.

40. "Eisenhower, Hoover Rap Prayers Ruling," *Los Angeles Times*, June 27, 1962, 21.

41. "Prayers in School," E9.

42. Joan DelFattore, *The Fourth R: Conflicts over Religion in America's Public Schools* 102 (2004).

43. Reinhold Niebuhr, "The Regents' Prayer Decision," 22 *Christianity and Crisis* 125, 125 (1962); and Berg, "Story of the School Prayer Decisions," 213 (noting Niebuhr's concern that the ruling might "work so consistently in the direction of a secularization of the school system as to amount to the suppression of religion").

44. "School Prayer Furor," 43.

45. Alexander Burnham, "Edict Is Called a Setback by Christian Clerics—Rabbis Praise It," *New York Times*, June 26, 1962, 1.

46. "Top Court Ban on School Prayer Stirs Congress' Ire," 2.

47. "To Our Jewish Friends," *America*, Sept. 1, 1962, 665–66.

48. Richard Polenberg, *One Nation Divisible: Class, Race, and Ethnicity in the United States Since 1938* 172 (1980).

49. "School Prayer Furor," 45.

50. "The Citizens Dissent," *Boston Globe*, June 27, 1962, 29.

51. Nancy E. Musala, letter to the editor, *Newsweek*, July 23, 1962, 2.

52. "School Prayer Furor," 44.

53. This joke is a slightly altered version of the one recounted in Zimmerman, *Whose America?*, 179–80.

54. Erwin N. Griswold, "Griswold on Church-State," *America*, March 16, 1963, 374, 374–75.

55. Ibid., 375.
56. Louis H. Pollak, "The Supreme Court 1962 Term—Foreword: Public Prayers in Public Schools," 77 *Harvard Law Review* 62, 63 (1963).
57. Arthur E. Sutherland Jr., "Establishment According to *Engel*," 76 *Harvard Law Review* 25, 50 (1962) (casting doubt on whether in *Engel* "the game was worth the candle").
58. Lain, "God, Civic Virtue, and the American Way," 484. For skeptics of the Court's counter-majoritarian capacities who nevertheless have suggested that *Engel* belies the usual pattern, see Michael J. Klarman, "Rethinking the History of American Freedom," 42 *William and Mary Law Review* 265, 281–82 (2000); and Friedman, *Will of the People*, 263–66.
59. Lauren Maisel Goldsmith and James R. Dillon, "The Hallowed Hope: The School Prayer Cases and Social Change," 59 *St. Louis University Law Journal* 409, 438–46 (2015). Between 1983 and 2005, a Gallup poll indicated that approximately three in four respondents favored a constitutional amendment overturning *Engel*, vacillating between a high of 81 percent in 1983 and a low of 73 percent in 1994. See ibid., 430 (citing David W. Moore, "Public Favors Voluntary Prayer for Public Schools," Gallup, Aug. 26, 2005). See also Alison Gash and Angelo Gonzales, "School Prayer," in *Public Opinion and Constitutional Controversy* 62, 77 (Nathaniel Persily et al. eds., 2008) ("In the aggregate, public opinion has remained solidly against the Court's landmark decisions declaring school prayer unconstitutional. The public has been and continues to be highly supportive of a constitutional amendment overturning these decisions.").
60. *School District of Abington Township v. Schempp*, 374 U.S. 203, 226 (1963).
61. Ibid. (quoting *West Virginia Board of Education v. Barnette*, 319 U.S. 624, 628 [1943]). I have slightly altered Justice Clark's quotation of Justice Jackson's *Barnette* opinion.
62. *Schempp*, 374 U.S. at 316–17 (Stewart, J., dissenting). In *Schempp*, Justices Douglas, Brennan, and Goldberg all wrote concurring opinions. See ibid., 227 (Douglas, J., concurring); ibid., 230 (Brennan, J., concurring); ibid., 305 (Goldberg, J., concurring). For excellent scholarship explicating and analyzing *Schempp*, see Stephen D. Solomon, *Ellery's Protest: How One Young Man Defied Tradition and Sparked the Battle over School Prayer* (2007); and Douglas Laycock, "Edward Schempp and His Family," 38 *Journal of Supreme Court History* 63 (2013).
63. Laurence Stern, "Most Religious Leaders Support High Court Rule on School Prayer," *Washington Post*, June 18, 1963, A6 (quoting Senator Allen Ellender of Louisiana calling *Schempp* "silly"); "School Prayer Held Illegal," *Atlanta Journal*, June 17, 1963, 1 (quoting Senator Herman Talmadge of Georgia calling *Schempp* "offensive"); and Joseph Hearst, "High Court Nullifies Bible, Prayer Laws," *Chicago Tribune*, June 18, 1963, 1 (quoting Senator Strom Thurmond of South Carolina calling the decision a "major triumph for the forces of secularism and atheism which are bent on throwing God completely out of our national life"). See also George Gallup, "Rating of High Court Splits America Evenly," *Washington Post*, Aug. 30, 1963, A2 (reporting Gallup poll results); "Atheist Started School Prayer Case After Son Challenged Her Conviction," *Washington Post*, June 18, 1963, A6 (chronicling some of the unpleasantness

visited upon plaintiffs following the decision); and Berg, "Story of the School Prayer Decisions," 217–18 (same).

64. *Stone v. Graham*, 449 U.S. 39, 41 (1980) (internal quotation marks omitted). I suggest that *Stone* has been "largely forgotten" because prominent scholars have produced major surveys of the Supreme Court's jurisprudence on religion that omit the decision entirely. See, for example, Nussbaum, *Liberty of Conscience*; and Noah Feldman, *Divided by God: America's Church-State Problem—and What We Should Do About It* (2005). *Stone* has not, of course, become completely forgotten. For an insightful treatment of *Stone*, see Andrew Koppelman, *Defending American Religious Neutrality* 101–2 (2013).

65. *Stone*, 449 U.S. at 41.

66. Ibid., 42 (citing Exodus 20:1–11 and Deuteronomy 5:6–15).

67. Ibid., 43 (Rehnquist, J., dissenting). Justice Potter Stewart dissented in *Stone* with a single sentence, contending, "[T]he courts of Kentucky, . . . so far as appears, applied wholly correct constitutional criteria in reaching their decisions." Ibid. (Stewart, J., dissenting). Chief Justice Warren Burger and Justice Harry Blackmun dissented in *Stone* because they contended that the Court should have granted certiorari and decided the case after full briefing, rather than disposing of it in per curiam fashion. Ibid. (Burger, C.J., and Blackmun, J., dissenting).

68. "Church-State Commandments," *Time*, Dec. 1, 1980, 74. See Jim Mann, "Display of Ten Commandments in Public Schools Is Unconstitutional, Justices Rule," *Los Angeles Times*, Nov. 18, 1980, B5 (observing that *Stone* contains "symbolic significance because it is an extension of" *Engel* and that the Reverend Jerry Falwell's Moral Majority had the line of decisions in its crosshairs). See also William Baude, "Foreword: The Supreme Court's Shadow Docket," 9 *NYU Journal of Law and Liberty* 1 (2015) (noting and lamenting the rise of the Supreme Court's dissolution of cases through summary reversals in unsigned per curiam opinions).

69. See Lou Cannon, "Hill Gets Reagan's Prayer Amendment," *Washington Post*, May 18, 1982, A10 ("[Reagan's] advocacy of the amendment was a gesture to conservative evangelicals to whom Reagan had promised during the 1980 presidential campaign support for school prayer amendment"). Recently, legal scholars have shrewdly observed that the Supreme Court's Establishment Clause jurisprudence in public schools has unfolded "without substantial assistance from the other branches of the federal government in enforcing [its decisions] . . . in an area in which it must rely on non-judicial actors, including teachers, principals, school superintendents, and other education professionals, for direct implementation of its decisions." Goldsmith and Dillon, "Hallowed Hope," 440. This point complicates the view of many scholarly skeptics of judicial authority, who contend that the Supreme Court lacks the capacity to create social change because it is a fundamentally fragile institution. For an early, influential articulation of this idea, see Gerald N. Rosenberg, *The Hollow Hope: Can Courts Bring About Social Change?* (1991).

70. See "Senator Vows Fight," *Boston Globe*, June 19, 1963, 6 (reporting that Senator Olin Johnston of South Carolina urged teachers to defy the Court's prayer decisions); H. Frank Way Jr., "Survey Research on Judicial Decisions: The Prayer and Bible Reading Cases," 21 *Western Political Quarterly* 189 (1968); and

Rosenberg, *Hollow Hope,* 15–22 (espousing the view that the Supreme Court's ability to create change is severely constrained).

71. See Way, "Survey Research on Judicial Decisions," 189; Goldsmith and Dillon, "Hallowed Hope," 440–46 (discussing various implementation studies); Kenneth D. Wald and Allison Calhoun-Brown, *Religion and Politics in the United States* 99–100 (6th ed. 2011) (discussing studies); Matthew E. K. Hall, *The Nature of Supreme Court Power* 131–35 (2011) (discussing studies); Berg, "Story of School Prayer Decisions," 223–24 (discussing studies); and Jesse H. Choper, "Consequences of Supreme Court Decisions Upholding Individual Constitutional Rights," 83 *Michigan Law Review* 1, 78–79n527 (1984) (citing Diane Henry, "Prayer: An Issue Without an Amen," *New York Times,* April 20, 1980, E3) (observing the degree of compliance with *Engel* and *Schempp* in 1973).

72. See Hall, *Nature of Supreme Court Power,* 131–36 (observing varying levels of compliance within particular regions).

73. For helpful treatments of *Lee v. Weisman*'s factual background, see *Lee v. Weisman,* 505 U.S. 577, 580–86 (1992); Nussbaum, *Liberty of Conscience,* 248–52 (2008); DelFattore, *Fourth R,* 255–66; Dierenfield, *Battle over School Prayer,* 201–5; "To the Plaintiffs, a Prayer's a Prayer," *New York Times,* March 19, 1991, A16; and Kevin Cullen, "Prayer Challenge: High Court to Hear Church-State Lawsuit," *Boston Globe,* Nov. 6, 1991, 29.

74. *Weisman,* 505 U.S. at 581–82.

75. Ibid., 588.

76. Cullen, "Prayer Challenge," 29.

77. *Weisman,* 505 U.S. at 587.

78. Ibid., 592. While Justice Kennedy's opinion emphasized governmental coercion as the essential inquiry in Establishment Clause cases, two justices who joined Kennedy's opinion wrote separately to note that, in their view, coercion was not in fact a prerequisite for finding an Establishment Clause violation. See ibid., 604 (Blackmun, J., concurring); and ibid., 609 (Souter, J., concurring). For the Court's opinion validating the practice of legislative prayers, at least under certain circumstances, see *Marsh v. Chambers,* 463 U.S. 783 (1983). For a recent case exploring a related issue, see *Town of Greece v. Galloway,* 134 S. Ct. 1811 (2014).

79. *Weisman,* 505 U.S. at 595.

80. Ibid., 596. For an important scholarly article that established the foundation for Justice Kennedy's emphasis on coercion, see Michael W. McConnell, "Coercion: The Lost Element of Establishment," 27 *William and Mary Law Review* 933 (1986). Justice Harry Blackmun wrote a concurring opinion that was joined by Justices John Paul Stevens and Sandra Day O'Connor. See *Weisman,* 505 U.S. at 599 (Blackmun, J., concurring). In addition, Justice David Souter wrote an opinion that was joined by Justices Stevens and O'Connor. See ibid., 609 (Souter, J., concurring).

81. *Weisman,* 505 U.S. at 636, 637, 638 (1992) (Scalia, J., dissenting).

82. Ibid., 636. See ibid., 632 (contending "the Court invents a boundless, and boundlessly manipulable, test of psychological coercion").

83. Ibid., 645.

84. Ibid., 646.

85. "Religion Remains Free, 5–4," *New York Times*, June 25, 1992, A30.

86. "Graduation Prayers," *Washington Post*, June 25, 1992, A22.

87. "School Prayer Ruling Right," *Atlanta Journal-Constitution*, June 26, 1992, A10.

88. "School Prayer: Supreme Court Upholds Important Legal Precedent," *Dallas Morning News*, June 26, 1992, 22A.

89. James J. Kilpatrick, "Debbie and Her Daddy Must Be Happy Now," *Atlanta Journal-Constitution*, July 1, 1992, A13.

90. "The Borked Court," *National Review*, July 20, 1992, 12.

91. Ruth Marcus, "High Court Bans Graduation Prayer at Public Schools," *Washington Post*, June 25, 1992, A1.

92. Jay Alan Sekulow, "The Debate over School Prayer," *Atlanta Journal-Constitution*, May 20, 1993, A11. See Jay Alan Sekulow, "Voluntary School Prayer Does Not 'Establish Religion,'" *Washington Post*, May 27, 1993, A24 ("Our position is not a 'loophole' but an accurate analysis of the law. On Feb. 24, 1969, the Supreme Court ruled in *Tinker v. Des Moines School District* that student expression against the Vietnam War could not be quashed in public schools. . . . It is now 1993, and once again there are those who seek to limit student speech."). For a helpful distillation of Sekulow's intellectual contributions to the conservative legal movement, see Jeffrey Toobin, *The Nine: Inside the Secret World of the Supreme Court* 88–94, 125–27 (2007).

93. For extremely insightful background on and analysis of *Santa Fe Independent School District v. Doe*, see Paul Horwitz, "Of Football, 'Footnote One,' and the Counter-jurisdictional Establishment Clause: The Story of *Santa Fe Independent School District v. Doe*," in *First Amendment Stories* 481–512 (Richard W. Garnett and Andrew Koppelman eds., 2012); Erwin Chemerinsky, "The Story of *Santa Fe Independent School District v. Doe*: God and Football in Texas," in *Education Law Stories* 319–36 (Michael A. Olivas and Ronna Greff Schneider eds., 2007); Douglas Laycock, "Voting with Your Feet Is No Substitute for Constitutional Rights," 32 *Harvard Journal of Law and Public Policy* 29, 37–41 (2009); Mark Tushnet, *A Court Divided: The Rehnquist Court and the Future of Constitutional Law* 180–82 (2005); Peter Irons, *God on Trial: Dispatches from America's Religious Battlefields* 136–59 (2007); Dan Egan, "Jesus at the Football Game," *Salt Lake Tribune*, June 3, 2000, A1, C1; *Santa Fe Independent School District v. Doe*, 530 U.S. 290, 294n1 (2000) (capitalization altered); and Brief for Respondents, *Santa Fe Independent School District v. Doe*, 530 U.S. 290, 2000 WL 140928, at *6 (quoting Trial Transcript, Aug. 4, 1995, 23); H. G. Bissinger, *Friday Night Lights: A Town, a Team, and a Dream* (1990).

94. *Doe*, 530 U.S. at 310. I borrow the formulation distilling what the Establishment Clause forbids (government-backed religious speech) and what the Free Exercise Clause protects (religious speech uttered by individuals) from a Supreme Court opinion. See *Westside Community Schools v. Mergens*, 496 U.S. 226, 250 (1990) (O'Connor, J., plurality opinion).

95. *Doe*, 530 U.S. at 318 (Rehnquist, C.J., dissenting). Justices Antonin Scalia and Clarence Thomas joined Rehnquist's dissent.

96. Douglas W. Kmiec, "A Hail Mary for a Secular State," *Wall Street Journal*, June 20, 2000, A26.

97. "Let Us Pray," *Wall Street Journal*, June 21, 2000, A26. Not surprisingly, liberal newspapers praised the Court's decision invalidating Santa Fe's prayer policy.

See, for example, "No Games on School Prayer," *Washington Post*, June 20, 2000, A22 (concluding the Court reached "absolutely the right position"); and "Sound Ruling on School Prayer," *New York Times*, June 20, 2000, A24.

98. "Little Town in Texas Shows Little Sympathy for Ruling," *Los Angeles Times*, June 20, 2000, 20.

99. Dirk Johnson, "Prayer Comes First, but Football Game Is the Main Event," *New York Times*, Sept. 2, 2000, A12.

100. Pamela Colloff, "They Haven't Got a Prayer," *Texas Monthly*, Nov. 2000, 118.

101. Horwitz, "Of Football, 'Footnote One,' and the Counter-jurisdictional Establishment Clause," 511; and Jay Wexler, *Holy Hullabaloos: A Road Trip to the Battlegrounds of the Church/State Wars* 194–95 (2009). Santa Fe High School's principal noted prior to the first home game of the 2000 football season, "The crowd is much, much, much smaller than we had feared it would be." Johnson, "Prayer Comes First, but Football Game Is Main Event," A12. See also Associated Press, "Few Pray in Protest at Texas Prep Game," *Chicago Tribune*, Sept. 3, 2000, 6.

102. Erin Mulvaney, "Judge Sides with Cheerleaders in Bible Banner Lawsuit," *Houston Chronicle*, Oct. 18, 2012. For background on the Kountze dispute, see Clay Morton, "Mix of Bible Verses, Football Stirs Controversy in Southeast Texas Town," *Dallas Morning News*, Sept. 20, 2012; Erin Mulvaney, "Judge Rules Cheerleaders' Christian Banners Are OK for Now," *Houston Chronicle*, Sept. 20, 2012; and Emma Green, "Cheerleaders for Christ," *Atlantic*, April 5, 2016 (observing that the case has been bouncing around the Texas court system on procedural issues since 2012).

103. For a sampling of statements that appear to express under-theorized objections to the Kountze banners, see Ann Zimmerman, "Bible Verses on Banners Kick Off Texas Conflict," *Wall Street Journal*, Oct. 2, 2012, A3 (reporting Professor Douglas Laycock as stating, "I do not think there is much doubt that it is unconstitutional. . . . This was very specifically Christian and clearly sponsored by the school. Cheerleaders are a school activity and the game is a school activity. This is not a random group acting on their own."); Molly Hennessy-Fiske, "A Banner Day for Scripture," *Los Angeles Times*, Oct. 5, 2012, A1 (reporting that the Kountze school district's attorney stated, "The cheerleaders represent the school"); Mulvaney, "Judge Sides with Cheerleaders in Bible Banner Lawsuit" (reporting that an opponent of the banners stated, "These cheerleaders represent the school district, and government speech may not endorse religion"); "Sis Boom Bad Ruling," *Los Angeles Times*, Oct. 24, 2012, A16 (noting that "the cheerleaders wear school uniforms and perform at official school functions representing their school"); and "Redefining Team Spirit," *Washington Post*, Oct. 24, 2012, A20 (noting that "the cheerleading squad is a campus organization, with faculty oversight, and it represents the school, wears its uniform and occupies a privileged space on the playing field"). For a claim by a liberal commentator contending that the cheerleaders' religious signs ought to be permitted, see Jonathan Zimmerman, "Why Kountze Cheerleaders Deserve Liberals' Support," *Dallas Morning News*, Oct. 24, 2012.

104. In 2004—nearly fifteen years ago—Kevin McGuire conducted the only study examining public school compliance with *Lee v. Weisman* and *Santa Fe Independent School District v. Doe*. Yet the limitations of McGuire's study were profound, as his extraordinarily small sample of respondents drew exclusively

upon undergraduates who attended the University of North Carolina at Chapel Hill. Predictably, an overwhelming majority of McGuire's respondents—79 percent—attended public schools in North Carolina. For whatever it is worth, McGuire found that less than one in ten respondents who attended non-southern public schools did so at schools that disregarded the Court's directive on prayers at sporting events, and less than one in four respondents who attended non-southern public schools did so at schools that disregarded the Court's directive on prayers at graduation exercises. In McGuire's sample, southern public schools featured considerably higher degrees of noncompliance. That disparity is not surprising, as the South is disproportionately rural, less educated, and populated by conservative Christians, features that are all positively correlated with noncompliance. See Kevin T. McGuire, "Public Schools, Religious Establishments, and the U.S. Supreme Court: An Examination of Policy Compliance," 37 *American Politics Research* 50, 58–59 (2009). See also Goldsmith and Dillon, "Hallowed Hope," 454 (observing that scholars too often overlook "the autonomous normativity of law *qua* law—that is, the tendency of legal norms, simply by virtue of their status as *legal* norms, to motivate compliance independently of the subject's personal views of the wisdom or morality of particular legal rules").

105. *Wallace v. Jaffree,* 472 U.S. 38, 43 (1985) (internal quotation marks omitted). See "A Moment of Silence," *Washington Post,* June 28, 1962, A22 (contending that a moment of silence "[s]urely ... could give no offense to anyone and it might give solace to the many").

106. Al Kamen, "Prayer Ban in Schools Reaffirmed," *Washington Post,* June 5, 1985, A1, A14.

107. Ibid. See Linda Greenhouse, "High Court Upsets Moment's Silence for Pupil Prayer," *New York Times,* June 5, 1985, A1 ("[Stevens's] opinion strongly suggested that the Court would uphold a statute with a less one-sided history and with the broader purpose of enabling students to choose, without any pressure from the state, how to use their moment of silence"). See also Turner Rose, "The 'Moment of Silence' Is Not Dead," *Washington Post,* April 8, 1987, A21.

108. See Douglas Laycock, "Equal Access and Moments of Silence: The Equal Status of Religious Speech by Private Speakers," 81 *Northwestern University Law Review* 1, 8–9 (1986) (defending the legitimacy of moment-of-silence statutes because they are neutral). Even if a state law explicitly raises the possibility of "prayer," modern courts will not necessarily invalidate it. See, for example, *Brown v. Gilmore,* 258 F.3d 265, 281 (4th Cir. 2001), *cert. denied,* 534 U.S. 996 (2001) (upholding Virginia's moment of silence law, even though it mandated a time for "meditation, prayer or reflection"). See also Charles C. Haynes, "Fighting over a Moment of Silence," Gannett News Service, Nov. 26, 2007, 1 (observing that "the possibility that [moment-of-silence] laws will be found unconstitutional is remote," not least because post-*Jaffree* states generally craft the statutes so as to avoid the hurdle it encountered).

109. Equal Access Act, 98 Stat. 1302, 20 U.S.C. §§ 4071–74. For perceptive analysis of this statute, see Laycock, "Equal Access and Moments of Silence," 4–5.

110. *Mergens,* 496 U.S. at 250 (O'Connor, J., plurality opinion) (emphasis removed). The Supreme Court can be viewed as expanding upon the logic of *Mergens* in *Good News Club v. Milford Central School,* 533 U.S. 98 (2001), where Justice Clarence Thomas wrote a majority opinion affirming the notion that pub-

lic schools cannot discriminate on speakers' viewpoints—including religious speech—when they create a public forum.

111. Tyll van Geel, *The Courts and American Education Law* 22 (1987). For helpful distillations of the background of homeschooling, see Kimberly A. Yuracko, "Education off the Grid: Constitutional Constraints on Homeschooling," 96 *California Law Review* 123, 126 (2008); Patricia M. Lines, "Homeschooling Comes of Age," 140 *Public Interest* 74, 75–76 (Summer 2000); and Mark G. Yudof et al., *Educational Policy and the Law* 39–42 (5th ed. 2012).

112. *State v. Edgington,* 663 P.2d 374, 378 (N.M. Ct. App. 1983). See Michael Imber et al., *Education Law* 35 (5th ed. 2014). For related academic critiques of homeschooling, see Rob Reich, "Civic Perils of Homeschooling," 59 *Educational Leadership* 56 (2002); and Emily Buss, "The Adolescent's Stake in the Allocation of Educational Control Between Parent and State," 67 *University of Chicago Law Review* 1233, 1245–46, 1286 (2000).

113. See Hunter, *Culture Wars,* 208 (noting that 15,000 minors were homeschooled during the 1970s); Department of Education, National Center for Education Statistics (May 2015) (observing that 1.8 million minors were homeschooled in 2012); and Yuracko, "Education off the Grid," 124–25 (noting that even by conservative estimates the number of homeschooled students exceeds the public school population of the ten states with the lowest number of students).

114. Yuracko, "Education off the Grid," 127. See also Catherine J. Ross, "Fundamentalist Challenges to Core Democratic Values: Exit and Homeschooling," 18 *William and Mary Bill of Rights Journal* 991, 997–98 (2010) (observing that, in 2007, 83 percent of homeschoolers indicated making that educational selection to "provide religious or moral instruction," but then scrutinizing the data to conclude that the actual percentage of religion-oriented homeschoolers was higher); and "Kitchen-Classroom Conservatives," *Economist,* Aug. 8, 2009, 36–37 (observing prevalence of Christian conservatives among homeschoolers, calling "religion . . . the main force"). For a perceptive, lively examination of Patrick Henry College, which envisions itself as a Christian institution of higher education of the Ivy League's caliber, see Hanna Rosin, *God's Harvard: A Christian College on a Mission to Save America* (2007).

115. See John Cloud and Jodie Morse, "Home Sweet School," *Time,* Aug. 27, 2001, 47 (reporting on JCPenney discontinuing its "Home Skooled" T-shirt); and Daniel Golden, "Social Studies: Home Schoolers Learn How to Gain Clout Inside the Beltway," *Wall Street Journal,* April 24, 2000, A1 (noting that a Gallup poll revealed that 92 percent of Americans believe homeschoolers should take standardized exams).

116. "See Jim and Pat Cook. Jim Cooks First," *New York Times,* March 13, 1986, A26.

117. *Mozert v. Hawkins County Board of Education,* 827 F.2d 1058, 1062 (6th Cir. 1987).

118. James Forman Jr., "The Rise and Fall of School Vouchers: A Story of Religion, Race, and Politics," 54 *UCLA Law Review* 547, 560 (2007). My thinking about homeschooling is indebted to Professor Forman's work. For a claim that the Sixth Circuit's decision in *Mozert,* while defensible, gave short shrift to the parents' religious objections, see Kent Greenawalt, *Does God Belong in Public Schools?* 185 (2005).

119. *Brown v. Hot, Sexy & Safer Productions Inc.,* 68 F.3d 525, 534 (1st Cir. 1995)

(rejecting a Free Exercise Clause claim objecting to a program on sex education). See also *Parker v. Hurley*, 514 F.3d 87 (1st Cir. 2008) (rejecting a Free
Exercise Clause claim against a public school in Lexington, Massachusetts,
where young students were exposed to materials involving same-sex couples).
For an insightful historical treatment of sex education, see Jonathan Zimmerman, *Too Hot to Handle: A Global History of Sex Education* (2015). See also
Richard S. Myers, "Same-Sex Marriage, Education, and Parental Rights,"
2011 *BYU Education and Law Journal* 303, 321 (noting that those who object to
school curricula on religious grounds typically fare better pursuing paths "outside the courts," like state legislative changes); and Nomi Maya Stolzenberg,
" 'He Drew a Circle That Shut Me Out': Assimilation, Indoctrination, and the
Paradox of a Liberal Education," 106 *Harvard Law Review* 581 (1993) (analyzing cases involving families who seek religious exemptions from curricula).

120. Yuracko, "Education off the Grid," 127.
121. *Pierce v. Society of Sisters*, 268 U.S. 510, 534 (1925). See "George Bush's Secret
     Army," *Economist*, Feb. 28, 2004, 52–53 (observing the wide array of state vari-
     ations in approaches to regulating homeschooling); and "Michigan Asks Little
     of Teaching Parents," *Detroit Free Press*, Feb. 19, 2002, A1. See also *Combs v.
     Homer-Center School District*, 540 F.3d 231, 234 (3d Cir. 2008) (rejecting a chal-
     lenge to various homeschooling regulations, where a family contended that the
     "education of their children, not merely the religious education, is religion");
     Battles v. Anne Arundel County Board of Education, 904 F. Supp. 471, 474–76 (D.
     Md. 1995) (upholding an instructional observation requirement); *Blackwelder
     v. Safnauer*, 689 F. Supp. 106, 129–30 (N.D.N.Y. 1988) (upholding on-site visi-
     tation requirement for homeschooling families); and *State v. McDonough*, 460
     A.2d 977, 979–80 (Me. 1983) (validating requirement that homeschooling par-
     ents receive prior state authorization). But see *Brunelle v. Lynn Public Schools*,
     702 N.E.2d 1182, 1184 (Mass. 1998) (invalidating home visitations to monitor
     schooling).
122. Cloud and Morse, "Home Sweet School," 52.
123. My understanding of the sexism that pervades homeschooling materials is
     drawn from Professor Kimberly Yuracko's scholarship. See Yuracko, "Educa-
     tion off the Grid," 156–57.
124. See *Wisconsin v. Yoder*, 406 U.S. 205, 218 (1972). Notably, Professor Derek
     Black has advanced the notion that *Yoder* should be construed as anticipat-
     ing the homeschooling explosion. "*Yoder*'s immediate result . . . is of limited
     relevance [because] today homeschooling is allowed in all 50 states," Black
     contended. "While there is considerable variation, much regulation of home-
     schooling tends to be permissive, and today the Amish or communities with
     similar concerns would likely take advantage of the homeschooling option."
     Derek W. Black, *Education Law: Equality, Fairness, and Reform* 825–26 (2013).
     For related reasoning, see Martha Minow, *In Brown's Wake: Legacies of Amer-
     ica's Educational Landmark* 111 (2010) (" 'Homeschooling' received a major
     boost after the Supreme Court permitted Amish families to bypass the high
     school attendance requirement of Wisconsin's compulsory schooling statute
     in 1972"); and Patricia M. Lines, "An Overview of Home Instruction," 68 *Phi
     Delta Kappan* 510, 514 (1987) (observing that "*Yoder* . . . is, in many ways, a
     homeschooling case").
125. *Yoder*, 406 U.S. at 235.

126. Ibid., 217.

127. Ibid., 211.

128. Ibid., 229.

129. Ibid., 244–46 (Douglas, J., dissenting). Justice Byron White wrote a concurring opinion in *Yoder* that struck similar themes to Douglas's and sounded at times much like a dissent. "It is possible that most Amish children will wish to continue living the rural life of their parents, in which case their training at home will adequately equip them for their future role," White commented. "Others, however, may wish to become nuclear physicists, ballet dancers, computer programmers, or historians, and for these occupations, formal training will be necessary." Ibid., 239–40 (White, J., concurring).

130. "Religious Scruples and Education," *Washington Post*, June 8, 1971, A18. Not all newspaper editorials condemned *Yoder*. See, for example, "The Right to Be Different," *Boston Globe*, May 21, 1972, A4.

131. *Prince v. Massachusetts*, 321 U.S. 158, 170 (1944).

132. Bryce Nelson, "Supreme Court Weighs Amish View on Schools," *Los Angeles Times*, Feb. 28, 1972, B6 (emphasis added).

133. Lisa Biedrzycki, " 'Conformed to This World': A Challenge to the Continued Justification of the *Wisconsin v. Yoder* Education Exception in a Changed Old Order Amish Society," 79 *Temple Law Review* 249, 255 (2006).

134. See *Employment Division of Oregon v. Smith*, 494 U.S. 872, 882 (1990) (suggesting that *Yoder* retained vitality because it presented an instance of a "hybrid" claim under the Free Exercise Clause). For an example of the scorn heaped on this "hybrid" rights idea, see Rex E. Lee, "The Religious Freedom Restoration Act: Legislative Choice and Judicial Review," 1993 *BYU Law Review* 75, 87 ("This so-called hamburger-helper theory of constitutional laws is not an accurate description of those cases"). See also John E. Nowak and Ronald D. Rotunda, *Constitutional Law* § 17.6, 1749 (7th ed. 2004) ("*Yoder* stands out as the one instance in which the Court required the government to grant to persons who could not comply with the law due to their religious beliefs an exemption from a law regulating the conduct of all persons").

135. Donald B. Kraybill et al., *The Amish* 267 (2013).

136. For insightful overviews of the school voucher issue, see James E. Ryan, *Five Miles Away, a World Apart: One City, Two Schools, and the Story of Educational Opportunity in Modern America* 202–4 (2010); Nussbaum, *Liberty of Conscience*, 298–305; James Forman Jr., "The Secret History of School Choice: How Progressives Got There First," 93 *Georgetown Law Journal* 1287 (2005); Forman, "Rise and Fall of School Vouchers"; Douglas Laycock, "Why the Supreme Court Changed Its Mind About Government Aid to Religious Institutions: It's a Lot More than Just Republican Appointments," 2008 *BYU Law Review* 275; Mark Walsh, "High Court High Noon," *Education Week*, Feb. 13, 2002, 1; Mary Lord, "A Battle for Children's Futures," *U.S. News and World Report*, Feb. 25, 2002, 35; and Linda Greenhouse, "White House Asks Court for Voucher Ruling," *New York Times*, July 8, 2001, 19.

137. *Zelman v. Simmons-Harris*, 536 U.S. 639, 655 (2002).

138. Ibid., 652.

139. See, for example, ibid., 716–17 (Souter, J., dissenting) (raising concerns about religious "divisiveness"). Echoing a similar theme, *The New York Times* commented after *Simmons-Harris*, "In the religious schools that Cleveland taxpay-

ers are being forced to sponsor, Catholics are free to teach that their way is best, and Jews, Muslims and those of other faiths can teach their co-religionists that they have truth on their side." "The Wrong Ruling on Vouchers," *New York Times*, June 28, 2002, A26.

140. See *Simmons-Harris*, 536 U.S. at 728 (Breyer, J., dissenting) ("Parental choice cannot help the taxpayer who does not want to finance the religious education of children"). See Clint Bolick, *Voucher Wars: Waging the Legal Battle over School Choice* 194–95 (2003); Deroy Murdock, "Liking Some Vouchers," *National Review*, Feb. 21, 2002.

141. See *Simmons-Harris*, 536 U.S. at 686 (Stevens, J., dissenting) ("Whenever we remove a brick from the wall that was designed to separate religion and government, we increase the risk of religious strife and weaken the foundation of our democracy"). In this same spirit, *The New York Times* contended, "It is hard to think of a starker assault on the doctrine of separation of church and state than taking taxpayer dollars and using them to inculcate specific religious beliefs in young people." "Wrong Ruling on Vouchers," A26. See also Nussbaum, *Liberty of Conscience*, 283–85 (critiquing wall of separation idea); Christopher L. Eisgruber and Lawrence G. Sager, *Religious Freedom and the Constitution* 213 (2007); Douglas Laycock, *Religious Liberty, Volume 2: The Free Exercise Clause* 321–22 (2011); and Michael W. McConnell, "Religion and Its Relation to Limited Government," 33 *Harvard Journal of Law and Public Policy* 943, 948–50 (2010).

142. Sarah Mondale and Sarah B. Patton, eds., *School: The Story of American Public Education* 193–94 (2001). See "Wrong Ruling on Vouchers," A26 ("The problem with the Cleveland program begins with the size of the stipends").

143. *Simmons-Harris*, 536 U.S. at 644.

144. Ibid., 676 (Thomas, J., concurring) (internal citation omitted).

145. Ibid., 682. See also ibid., 684 ("As Frederick Douglass poignantly noted, 'no greater benefit can be bestowed upon a long benighted people, than giving to them, as we are here earnestly this day endeavoring to do, the means of an education'") (internal citation omitted); and ibid., 682 ("As Thomas Sowell noted 30 years ago: 'Most black people have faced too many grim, concrete problems to be romantics. They want and need certain tangible results, which can be achieved only by developing certain specific abilities.' The same is true today.") (internal citation omitted).

146. See, for example, *Grutter v. Bollinger*, 539 U.S. 306, 378 (2003) (Rehnquist, J., dissenting); and ibid., 349 (Thomas, J., concurring in part and dissenting in part).

147. Brief for Petitioner, *Simmons-Harris*, 536 U.S. 639, 2001 WL 1663809, at *4–*5, *49; Forman, "Rise and Fall of School Vouchers," 576 (observing that Bolick's brief in *Simmons-Harris* is book-ended with citations to *Brown*). For background on Bolick, see Steven A. Holmes, "Political Right's Point Man on Race," *New York Times*, Nov. 16, 1997, 24.

148. Bolick, *Voucher Wars*, 173.

149. Ibid., 198. For insightful analysis of how the analogy connecting *Brown* to *Simmons-Harris* gathered steam due to Bolick's efforts, see Linda Greenhouse, "Win the Debate, Not Just the Case," *New York Times*, July 14, 2002, C4. As Greenhouse suggests, however, Bolick can be understood as popularizing a strategy developed by Professor Joseph P. Viteritti, who initially advanced the

desegregation-voucher analogy in a book titled *Choosing Equality: School Choice, the Constitution, and Civil Society* (1999).

150. "Bush Promises to Push School Voucher Programs," *Chicago Tribune*, July 2, 2002, 12; and Forman, "Secret History of School Choice," 1314–15.

151. Rod Paige, "A Win for America's Children," *Washington Post*, June 28, 2002, A29.

152. George F. Will, "Implacable Enemies of Choice," *Washington Post*, June 28, 2002, A29.

153. "Vouchers Have Overcome," *Wall Street Journal*, June 28, 2002, A12.

154. Brief of the NAACP Legal Defense and Educational Fund Inc. et al. as Amici Curiae in Support of Respondents, *Simmons-Harris*, 536 U.S. 639, 2001 WL 1638648, at *6–*7.

155. Greenhouse, "Win the Debate, Not Just the Case," C4.

156. Brent Staples, "School Vouchers: A Small Tool for a Very Big Problem," *New York Times*, Aug. 5, 2002, A14. For a gripping memoir that chronicles one man's journey through America during the post–World War II era, see Brent Staples, *Parallel Time: Growing Up in Black and White* (1994). Staples's rendering of his years as a University of Chicago graduate student—particularly when he described his pastime, "scattering the pigeons"—made an indelible impression on me more than two decades ago, long before I had any connection with the institution.

157. Jodi Wilgoren, "Young Blacks Turn to School Vouchers as Civil Rights Issue," *New York Times*, Oct. 9, 2000, A1.

158. Ibid. See also Michael Leo Owens, "Why Blacks Support Vouchers," *New York Times*, Feb. 26, 2002, A25.

159. Cory Turner, "School Vouchers 101: What They Are, How They Work—and Do They Work?," NPR, Dec. 7, 2016; Stephanie Simon, "Taxpayers Fund Teaching Creationism," *Politico*, March 24, 2014; and Jonathan Chait, "Why Was Betsy DeVos the One Trump Nominee Who Provoked Opposition?," *New York*, Feb. 10, 2017.

160. See Turner, "School Vouchers 101." For an incisive overview of school vouchers, including the "Baby Blaine" amendments—that is, the state constitutional measures that some, though not all, state courts have used to block the implementation of voucher programs—see Ryan, *Five Miles Away, a World Apart*, 232–38. For a recent decision interpreting the Free Exercise Clause in a way that limits Missouri's Baby Blaine Amendment, see *Trinity Lutheran Church of Columbia Inc. v. Comer*, 137 S. Ct. 2012 (2017). As of this writing, it remains highly uncertain how widely this opinion's logic will sweep.

161. *Elk Grove Unified School District v. Newdow*, 542 U.S. 1, 15 (2004).

162. "One Nation Under Blank," *Washington Post*, June 27, 2002, A30. Charles Lane, "Justices Keep 'Under God' in Pledge; Atheist Father Lacked Standing to Sue on Behalf of Daughter, Court Rules," *Washington Post*, June 15, 2004, A1 (reporting Gallup polling results); and Warren Richey, "'One Nation'—but Under What?," *Christian Science Monitor*, March 24, 2004, 1 (reporting on congressional resolutions).

163. "One Nation Under God," *New York Times*, June 27, 2002, A28.

164. See Cass Cliatt, "Pledge Ruling Won't Affect Illinois," *Chicago Daily Herald*, June 17, 2002, 1 (reporting Sunstein's view); Maura Dolan, "Pledge of Allegiance Violates Constitution, Court Declares," *Los Angeles Times*, June 27,

2002, A1 (reporting Tribe's assessment). For overviews and analyses of *New-dow*, see David A. Toy, "The Pledge: The Constitutionality of an American Icon," 34 *Journal of Law and Education* 25, 26 (2005); and Douglas Laycock, "Theology Scholarships, the Pledge of Allegiance, and Religious Liberty: Avoiding the Extremes but Missing the Liberty," 118 *Harvard Law Review* 162, 218–40 (2004).

165. Charles Haynes has stated, "There has never been this much agreement in the history of public education on how to deal with religion and values. . . . That's pretty stunning after 150 years of public shouting." Edward Felsenthal, "End of a Culture War? How Religion Found Its Way Back to School," *Wall Street Journal*, March 23, 1998, A1. See ibid. (noting the emergence of new agreement on religion in public schools "that allows for extensive teaching about religions and their value systems, but no preaching"). For useful distillations of the Court's Establishment Clause jurisprudence, see Charles C. Haynes and Oliver Thomas, *Finding Common Ground: A First Amendment Guide to Religion and Public Schools* (2007); and Charles C. Haynes, *A Teacher's Guide to Religion in the Public Schools* (2008).

CONCLUSION

1. My approach in this opening paragraph is indebted to Louis Fisher, "When Courts Play School Board: Judicial Activism in Education," 51 *Education Law Reporter* 693, 693 (1989). See *West Virginia State Board of Education v. Barnette*, 319 U.S. 624 (1943); *Brown v. Board of Education*, 347 U.S. 483 (1954); *Engel v. Vitale*, 370 U.S. 421 (1962); *Abington School District v. Schempp*, 374 U.S. 203 (1963); *Tinker v. Des Moines Independent Community School District*, 393 U.S. 503 (1969); *Goss v. Lopez*, 419 U.S. 565 (1975); *Stone v. Graham*, 449 U.S. 39 (1980); *Plyler v. Doe*, 457 U.S. 202 (1982); and *Board of Education, Island Trees Union Free School District No. 26 v. Pico*, 457 U.S. 853 (1982).

2. *Barnette*, 319 U.S. at 637.

3. *Tinker*, 393 U.S. at 511. See *Morse v. Frederick*, 551 U.S. 393 (2007).

4. See *Ingraham v. Wright*, 430 U.S. 651, 664 (1977).

5. See *New Jersey v. T.L.O.*, 469 U.S. 325 (1985); *Vernonia School District 47J v. Acton*, 515 U.S. 646 (1995); *Board of Education of Independent School District No. 92 of Pottawatomie County v. Earls*, 536 U.S. 822 (2002); and *Safford Unified School District No. 1 v. Redding*, 557 U.S. 364 (2009).

6. See *San Antonio Independent School District v. Rodriguez*, 411 U.S. 1 (1973); *Hazelwood School District v. Kuhlmeier*, 484 U.S. 260 (1988); and *Redding*, 557 U.S. 364 (2009).

7. See *Vorchheimer v. School District of Philadelphia*, 430 U.S. 703 (1977); and *Parents Involved in Community Schools v. Seattle School District No. 1*, 551 U.S. 701 (2007).

8. *Kramer v. Union Free School District No. 15*, 395 U.S. 621, 630 (1969) (internal quotation marks omitted). For an assessment of *Kramer*'s significance for the Supreme Court's equal protection jurisprudence, see Rex E. Lee, "Mr. Herbert Spencer and the Bachelor Stockbroker: *Kramer v. Union Free School District No. 15*," 15 *Arizona Law Review* 457 (1973).

Index

A NOTE ABOUT THE AUTHOR

Justin Driver is the Harry N. Wyatt Professor of Law at the University of Chicago Law School. A graduate of Brown, Oxford (where he was a Marshall Scholar), and Harvard Law School (where he was an editor of the *Harvard Law Review*), Driver clerked for Supreme Court Justices Stephen Breyer and Sandra Day O'Connor. A recipient of the American Society for Legal History's William Nelson Cromwell Article Prize, Driver has a distinguished publication record in the nation's leading law reviews. He has also written extensively for lay audiences, including pieces in *Slate*, *The Atlantic*, *The Washington Post*, and *The New Republic*, where he was a contributing editor. A member of the American Law Institute and of the American Constitution Society's Academic Advisory Board, Driver is also an editor of *The Supreme Court Review*. Before attending law school, Driver received a master's degree in education from Duke and taught civics and American history to high school students.

A NOTE ON THE TYPE

This book was set in Janson, a typeface long thought to have been made by the Dutchman Anton Janson, who was a practicing typefounder in Leipzig during the years 1668–1687. However, it has been conclusively demonstrated that these types are actually the work of Nicholas Kis (1650–1702), a Hungarian, who most probably learned his trade from the master Dutch typefounder Dirk Voskens. The type is an excellent example of the influential and sturdy Dutch types that prevailed in England up to the time William Caslon (1692–1766) developed his own incomparable designs from them.

Composed by North Market Street Graphics,
Lancaster, Pennsylvania

Printed and bound by Berryville Graphics,
Berryville, Virginia

Designed by Soonyoung Kwon